Glenn Leggett

Former President, Grinnell College

C. David Mead

Michigan State University

William Charvat

Late of Ohio State University

With the editorial supervision of

Richard S. Beal

PRENTICE-HALL
HANDBOOK
FOR WRITERS

EIGHTH EDITION

PRENTICE-HALL, INC.,
Englewood Cliffs, N.J.
07632

Library of Congress Cataloging in Publication Data
Main entry under title:

Prentice-Hall handbook for writers.

Eighth ed.: Prentice-Hall handbook for writers/
GLENN LEGGETT, C. DAVID MEAD, WILLIAM CHARVAT.
Includes index.
1. English language—Rhetoric   2. English
language—Grammar—1950-   I. Leggett,
Glenn H., (date).
PE1408.P75 1982   808'.042   81-13973
ISBN 0-13-695734-X   AACR2

PRENTICE-HALL HANDBOOK FOR WRITERS
EIGHTH EDITION
LEGGETT, MEAD, CHARVAT, and BEAL

10   9   8   7   6   5   4   3   2   1

Development editor: Joyce Perkins
Editorial/production supervision by Virginia Rubens
Interior design by Walter Behnke
Cover design by Wanda Lubelska Design
Manufacturing buyer: Ray Keating

ISBN 0-13-695734-X

PRENTICE-HALL INTERNATIONAL, INC., *London*
PRENTICE-HALL OF AUSTRALIA PTY. LIMITED, *Sydney*
PRENTICE-HALL OF CANADA, LTD., *Toronto*
PRENTICE-HALL OF INDIA PRIVATE LIMITED, *New Delhi*
PRENTICE-HALL OF JAPAN, INC., *Tokyo*
PRENTICE-HALL OF SOUTHEAST ASIA PTE. LTD., *Singapore*
WHITEHALL BOOKS LIMITED, WELLINGTON, *New Zealand*

CONTENTS

SECTIONS 6-14

BASIC SENTENCE FAULTS **SEN FLT** 59

MANUSCRIPT MECHANICS **MS** 105

PUNCTUATION **P** 117

CONTENTS

THE LIBRARY AND THE RESEARCH PAPER 411

CONTENTS

PREFACE

The *Prentice-Hall Handbook* is both a reference for the writer and a text for class use. As a summary of grammar, usage, and elementary rhetoric, it provides essential information. Its format is designed to serve two purposes: (1) to provide the student with a convenient reference for both preparing and reviewing written work; and (2) to assist the instructor in reading papers, allowing him or her to direct attention readily to specific essentials. Ample examples and exercises provide ready help in study, review, or class discussion.

This edition has been revised to retain the full coverage of former editions, to expand several sections, and to add some new material. All changes have been in the interest of ensuring clear, straightforward, and adequate guidance for students.

Though the organization of the book remains essentially the same as that of previous editions, revised and new material appears in various ways. We have made three important changes. Section 1 on sentence sense has been reworked for greater clarity. Sections 4 and 5 have been extensively revised to provide two full sections on the central and often troublesome problems of verbs; Section 4 now addresses verb forms and their problems; Section 5, tense, mood, and voice. Finally, the entire description of internal punctuation has been revised to provide individual sections on each major mark of punctuation and on the punctuation of quoted material. Users of previous editions will want to note the necessary renumbering of Sections 3–5 and Sections 20–26.

In the material on larger elements (Sections 31–33) we have considerably revised Section 31, "The Whole Composition," to emphasize the importance of prewriting and revising and to allow the student to follow a single paper from its conception to its final corrected version with instructor comments. In Section 32, "Effective Paragraphs," the proportion of student paragraphs has been increased. And a new Section 33, "Writing Persuasively," incorporates information from Section 37 of earlier editions and places it more clearly in the context of persuasive writing. Both the revised Sections 31 and 33 display entirely new student papers for study and analysis.

The unit on effective sentences (formerly Sections 33–36, now Sections 34–37) has been extensively reworked. The revised sequence emphasizes the writer's need to generate stronger and more effective sentences rather than merely to avoid weak ones. New material includes information on using coordination as well as subordination as a successful strategy for relating ideas, on using various subordinating words to express different relationships among ideas, and on using appositives, participial phrases, and absolutes as well as subordinate clauses to generate effective sentences. Throughout the sequence, we have tried to stress the value of revising and to offer exercises that will invite students to explore various ways of expressing their ideas.

Throughout the remaining sections of the *Handbook* we have made a number of less basic but we believe nonetheless helpful revisions. In Sections 38–44, "Words," we have continued to emphasize exactness, directness, and appropriateness as the three principles of word choice, but we have tried to sharpen some of the explanations and to compress somewhat the information on dictionaries. In Section 46, "The Research Paper," we have updated all the conventions of research writing to conform to those of the *MLA Handbook* (1977) and have added additional note and bibliographical forms, information on forms commonly used in scientific writing, and new material on handling quotations in research papers. In the final sections of the text, we have revised and somewhat expanded Section 49, now entitled "Writing on the Job: Business Correspondence," to correspond wholly with current practice and to include a brief explanation of memorandum form. In both the usage glossary (Section 43) and the concluding glossary of grammatical terms (Section 50), we have added and revised items, many in accord with suggestions from users of the seventh edition.

Throughout the revision our purpose has been to make material more accessible to students and easier for instructors both to teach from and to refer to. To this end, we have expanded explanations whenever they seemed insufficient, briefly redefined terms when they recur in order to minimize the student's need to consult other sections of the text, and provided ample examples. We have updated and revised exercises through most of the sections of the book. While retaining the very plentiful exercises of previous editions, we have tried to redistribute them to ensure that all important subsections are followed by a set of exercises. Sections addressing the most critical problems, such as those of sentence fragments, pronoun forms and reference, and the like, have additional exercises where possible.

As we indicated earlier, the *Handbook* is consistently designed to be a useful and easy reference guide in preparing, correcting, and revising papers. It classifies the standards and conventions of writing and provides reference to them in three ways: (1) through a full index, (2) through a detailed table of contents, and (3) through the charts on the endpapers of the book. Each major rule is given a number and a symbol, and each subrule is designated by the number of the major rule plus a letter (5a, 16b, 22c, and so on). Thus in writing a paper the student may check readily any convention about which he or she is doubtful. The instructor, in reading papers, may conveniently call attention to a specific convention or a general principle by using either numbers or symbols, so that the student may easily locate the appropriate section in the *Handbook*. For an illustration of these possibilities, see the sample paragraphs on p. 109 and the final corrected draft of the student paper on pp. 220–221.

ACKNOWLEDGMENTS

We continue to be indebted to the many colleagues who over the years have suggested ways to improve each new edition of the *Prentice-Hall Handbook*. In preparing this edition, we have benefited from many perceptive criticisms of the seventh edition and of various sections of the manuscript for this new edition. For their extensive comments on the seventh edition, we are especially grateful to Art Albanese, San Diego State University; James Childs, Middlesex Community College, Connecticut; Robert Cosgrove, Saddleback College; Frank Garratt, Tacoma Community College; Robert Gregory, Carnegie-Mellon University; John Hanes, Duquesne University; Leonard Held, Chemeketa Community College; Thomas N. Huckin, University of Michigan; Gary Keedy, Catonsville Community College; Georgia A. Newman, Polk Community College; Lea Newman, North Adams State College; Robert Newsom, University of California, Irvine; John Reiss, Western Kentucky University; Charles Scarborough, Northern Virginia Community College; Richard Scorza, Broward Community College; Paul Suter, Chemeketa Community College; Mary Waldrop, Tyler Junior College, Texas; Samuel D. Watson, Jr., University of North Carolina at Charlotte; Dennis L. Williams, Central Texas College; and Laura M. Zaidman, South Georgia College. For their thoughtful comments on various parts of the manuscript for this edition, we are grateful to David S. Betts, State University of New York, Oneonta; Pamela Clements, University of Illinois; Macy Creek, Central Piedmont Community College; Ann Fields, Western Kentucky University; Thomas Kelly, State University of New York, College at Cortland; and Gretchen B. Niva, Western Kentucky University.

Special credit goes to two contributing authors who have joined us in this edition. To William Connelly, Middle State Tennessee University, we are indebted for his extensive revision of Sections 31 and 32, "The Whole Composition," and "Paragraphs." To Melinda Kramer, Purdue University, we are indebted for the new Section 33, "Writing Persuasively," which incorporates material from the logic section of earlier editions; and for the full revision of Section 49, "Writing on

ACKNOWLEDGMENTS

the Job: Business Correspondence." To both these contributing authors we also express our appreciation for their copious suggestions for improving the seventh edition and the manuscript for this edition.

Special thanks go also to Pamela Clements, University of Illinois, for preparing the text of the *Instructor's Manual* for this edition, and to Mamie Atkins, Purdue University, for preparing the handbook exercise answers incorporated in the *Instructor's Manual*.

Among the many at Prentice-Hall who have helped make this book possible, we want particularly to thank William H. Oliver, our editor, who has always been ready with advice and warm encouragement through this and earlier editions; Virginia Rubens, our production editor, who ensured that a manuscript became a book; and Joyce Perkins, our manuscript editor, who not only made our prose straight when crooked, clear when cluttered, and simple when complicated, but also always did so with grace and tact. Finally, our thanks to Caren Mattice, who through this and two earlier editions has faithfully typed and retyped manuscript and attended to permissions correspondence.

Throughout the *Handbook* we have quoted from copyrighted material and we are grateful to the copyright holders acknowledged below for their permission.

Maya Angelou, *I Know Why the Caged Bird Sings,* New York: Random House, Inc., 1969. By permission of Random House, Inc.

W. H. Auden, *Tales of Grimm and Andersen.* Copyright © 1952 by Random House, Inc.

Toni Cade Bambera, *Tales and Stories for Black Folks,* New York: Doubleday and Company, Inc., 1971. By permission of the author.

Jacques Barzun, *Teacher in America.* By permission of Little, Brown and Company, in association with the Atlantic Monthly Press.

Monroe Beardsley, *Practical Logic.* Copyright © 1950 by Prentice-Hall, Inc.

Isaiah Berlin, *Mr. Churchill in 1940.* By permission of the author and John Murray (Publishers) Ltd.

Pierre Berton, *The Klondike Fever* (Alfred A. Knopf, Inc., 1958).

Newman and Genevieve Birk, *Understanding and Using English.* By permission of the Odyssey Press, Inc.

Daniel J. Boorstin, *The Image.* Atheneum. Copyright © 1971 by Daniel J. Boorstin.

Claude Brown, *Manchild in the Promised Land* (The Macmillan Company, 1965).

Rachel Carson, *Silent Spring* (Houghton Mifflin Company, 1962).

Winston Churchill, *Blood, Sweat and Tears.* By permission of G. P. Putnam's Sons and Cassel and Company Ltd.

John Ciardi, "Confessions of a Crackpot," *Saturday Review,* Feb. 24, 1962.

Walter Van Tilburg Clark, *Track of the Cat.* By permission of Random House, Inc.

R. P. T. Coffin and Alexander Witherspoon, *Seventeenth Century Prose.* By permission of Harcourt, Brace and Company, Inc.

E. E. Cummings, "a man who had fallen among thieves." Copyright 1926 by Horace Liveright; published by Harcourt, Brace and Company, Inc.; used by permission of Brandt and Brandt.

Joan Didion, "On Keeping a Notebook," in *Slouching Toward Bethlehem,* New York: Farrar, Straus & Giroux, 1968. By permission of Farrar, Straus & Giroux.

Annie Dillard, *Pilgrim at Tinker Creek.* Copyright © 1974 by Annie Dillard. By permission of Harper & Row, Publishers, and Blanche C. Gregory, Inc.

Peter Drucker, "How to Be an Employee," *Fortune,* May 1952. Copyright © 1952 by Time, Inc.

Kent Durden, *Flight to Freedom.* Reprinted by permission of Simon & Schuster, Inc.

Loren Eiseley, "Little Men and Flying Saucers," copyright © 1953 by Loren C. Eiseley. Reprinted from *The Immense Journey* by permission of Random House, Inc.

T. S. Eliot, *Collected Poems.* By permission of Harcourt, Brace and Company, Inc.

The Foxfire Book, edited with an Introduction by Eliot Wigginton, Anchor Books, Doubleday & Company, Inc., 1972. By permission of Doubleday & Company, Inc.

William H. Gass, *In the Heart of the Heart of the Country.* Copyright © 1967 by William H. Gass. Reprinted by permission of International Creative Management.

Walker Gibson, *Tough, Sweet, and Stuffy.* Copyright © 1970. Indiana University Press.

From *Language in Thought and Action,*Third Edition, by S. I. Hayakawa, copyright © 1972 by Harcourt Brace Jovanovich, Inc. and reprinted with their permission and the permission of George Allen & Unwin Ltd.

From the book, *How Children Fail* by John Holt. Copyright © 1964 by Pitman Publishing Corporation. Reprinted by permission of Fearon-Pitman Publishers, Inc.

Jane Howard, *Families.* Copyright 1978 by Jane Howard. By permission of Simon and Schuster, a Divison of Gulf & Western Corporation. Reprinted by permission of A. D. Peters & Co. Ltd.

W. H. Ittelson and F. P. Kilpatrick, "Experiments in Perception," *Scientific American,* August 1951.

Jane Jacobs, "How City Planners Hurt Cities," *Saturday Evening Post,* Oct. 14, 1961.

Okakura Kakuzo, *The Book of Tea.* By permission of Charles E. Tuttle Company.

Elaine Kendall, "An Open Letter to the Corner Grocer," *Harper's* Magazine, December 1960. Reprinted by permission.

Jerzy Kosinski, NBC's *Comment.* By permission of Jerzy Kosinski.

Susanne K. Langer, "The Lord of Creation," *Fortune,* January 1944. Copyright © 1944 by Time, Inc.

George Laycock, "Games Otters Play," from *Audubon,* January, 1981. By permission of the National Audubon Society.

Henry S. Leonard, *Principles of Right Reason.* Published by Holt, Rinehart and Winston, Inc.

From p. 16 in *Guests: or How to Survive Hospitality* by Russell Lynes. Copyright 1951 by Harper & Row, Publishers, Inc. By permission of Harper & Row, Publishers, Inc.

William H. MacLeish, "The Year of the Coast," from *Smithsonian,* Sept. 1980.

Margaret Mead, "What Women Want," *Fortune* Magazine, December 1964. Reprinted by permission of the publisher.

H. L. Mencken, "Bryan," from *Selected Prejudices;* and *In Defense of Women.* By permission of Alfred A. Knopf, Inc.

Edmund S. Morgan, "What Every Yale Freshman Should Know," *Saturday Review,* Jan. 23, 1960.

Beth Neman, *Teaching Students to Write,* Columbus, Ohio: Charles E. Merrill Publishing Company, 1980. By permission of Charles E. Merrill Publishing Company.

ACKNOWLEDGMENTS

Russell Nye, *The Unencumbered Muse,* New York: Dial Press, 1970. By permission of Dial Press.

Bernard Pares, *Russia: Its Past and Present.* Copyright 1943, 1949 by The New American Library of World Literature, Inc.

S. J. Perelman, *Keep It Crisp.* By permission of Random House, Inc.

John Radar Platt, *Style in Science.* Reprinted from *Harper's* Magazine, October 1956.

Herbert Read, *The Eye of Memory.* Copyright 1947 by Herbert Read. By permission of Harold Ober Associates, Inc.

James Harvey Robinson, *The Mind in the Making.* By permission of Harper & Brothers.

Lionel Ruby, *The Art of Making Sense.* Copyright © 1968. Reprinted by permission of the publisher, J. B. Lippincott Company.

Herbert H. Sanders, *How To Make Pottery.* Copyright © 1974 by Watson Guptill Publications. Reprinted by permission.

May Sarton, *Plant Dreaming Deep,* New York: W. W. Norton & Co., Inc., 1968. By permission of W. W. Norton & Co., Inc.

Ben Shahn, *The Shape of Content.* By permission of Harvard University Press.

Mina P. Shaughnessy, *Errors and Expectations: A Guide to the Teaching of Basic Writing,* New York: Oxford University Press, 1977. Copyright © 1977 by Mina P. Shaughnessy. By permission of Oxford University Press.

Susan Sontag, *On Photography,* New York: Farrar, Straus, & Giroux, 1973, 1974, 1977. By permission of Farrar, Straus, and Giroux and Penguin Books Ltd.

George Summey, Jr., *American Punctuation.* Copyright 1949 The Ronald Press Company, New York.

Deems Taylor, *Of Men and Music.* By permission of Simon & Schuster, Inc.

James Thurber, *The Years with Ross.* Copyright © 1959 by James Thurber. Published by Atlantic-Little Brown. Originally printed in *The New Yorker.*

Barbara Tuchman, *A Distant Mirror,* New York: Alfred H. Knopf, 1978. By permission of Alfred H. Knopf.

John Updike, from "The Dogwood Tree," in *Five Boyhoods,* edited by Martin Levin (Doubleday). Copyright © 1962 Martin Levin. Reprinted by permission of Martin Levin.

Andrew Ward, "Yumbo." Copyright © 1978 by Andrew Ward. First published in the *Atlantic Monthly,* May, 1977. Excerpted by permission.

Eudora Welty, "Death of a Travelling Salesman," from *A Curtain of Green and Other Stories,* New York: Harcourt Brace Jovanovich 1941. By permission of Harcourt Brace Jovanovich. Reprinted by permission of Russell & Volkening as agents for the author.

E. B. White, *One Man's Meat.* By permission of Harper & Brothers.

A. N. Whitehead, *Science and the Modern World,* copyright 1925. By permission of The Macmillan Company.

William K. Zinsser, *On Writing Well,* New York: Harper & Row Publishers, Inc., 1980. By permission of Harper & Row Publishers, Inc.

INTRODUCTION

All life therefore comes back to the question of our speech, the medium through which we communicate with each other; for all life comes back to the question of our relations with one another.

HENRY JAMES, *The Question of Our Speech*

The growth of English

Like all languages, English changes constantly. Changes in vocabulary are the most rapid and obvious. *Butcher* once meant "a man who slaughters goats"; *neutron* and *proton,* key terms in physics today, were unrecorded fifty years ago; *biofeedback* appeared in dictionaries only in the 1970's. But language changes in more complex ways too. Today educated speakers avoid the multiple negatives of *She won't never do nothing.* But William Shakespeare's *nor this is not my nose neither* was good Elizabethan English. Even the sounds of language change. For Shakespeare, four hundred years ago, *deserts* rhymed with *departs,* and *reason* sounded much like our *raisin;* two hundred years ago, Alexander Pope properly rhymed *join* with *line* and *seas* with *surveys.*

The changes we see if we look back at the history of our language are far more dramatic. English is a Germanic language, descended from the language of the Germanic tribes (Angles, Saxons, and Jutes) who invaded the British Isles in the fifth and sixth centuries. In the centuries following, their language was subjected to a variety of influences. Its structure was loosened by the effects of the Danish invasions in the ninth and tenth centuries and by the Norman Conquest in 1066. To its vocabulary were added thousands of Latin, Scandinavian, and, particularly, French words. Spelling and pronunciation changed. Word meanings were modified or extended.

Perhaps the most important changes were gradual changes in **syntax,** the ways of showing relationships among the words in a sentence. The English of the sixth, seventh, and eighth centuries—Old English—was a highly **inflected** language. That is, it depended largely upon changes in the forms, and particularly the endings, of words to show their relationships to one another. Gradually, **word order** for the most part replaced such endings as the main way to convey sentence syntax. At the same time, **function words**—words like *the, yet, because,* and *with* (articles, conjunctions, and prepositions)—grew in number and importance. Thus, one of the great differences between Old English and English as we know it is this: in Old English, syntax depended heavily upon inflection, whereas syntax in Modern English depends mainly upon word order. Understanding this difference is important to using language well.

Look at the following brief passages to see something of the great changes that occurred between the time of King Alfred in the late ninth century and that of Shakespeare in the late sixteenth century.

Ða   gemette   hie   Æpelwulf aldorman on Englafelda, ond
Then   met   them Aethelwulf alderman in   Englefield, and
him þær   wiþ gefeaht ond sige   nam.
them there against fought and victory won.

KING ALFRED, *Anglo-Saxon Chronicle*, c. 880

But now, if so be that dignytees and poweris be yyven to gode men, the whiche thyng is full selde, what aggreable thynges is there in tho dignytees or power but oonly the goodnesse of folk that usen them?

GEOFFREY CHAUCER, from the translation of *Boethius*, c. 1380

Hit befel in the dayes of Uther Pendragon, when he was kynge of all Englond, and so regned, that there was a myghty duke in Cornewaill that helde warre ageynst hym long tyme, and the duke was called the duke of Tyntagil.   SIR THOMAS MALORY, *Morte d'Arthur*, c. 1470

A Proude Man contemneth the companye of hys olde friendes, and disdayneth the sight of hys former famyliars, and turneth hys face from his wonted acquayntaunce.

HENRY KERTON, *The Mirror of Man's Lyfe*, 1576

To us, these passages illustrate a steady development toward the English we know. But to people living then, the changes often seemed not growth but chaos. English, it appeared, would not hold still long enough to have any value as a means of communication. Some, like Sir Thomas More and Francis Bacon, preferred to write their greatest works in Latin. But others, like Chaucer and Malory, wrote in their native language. By doing so, they gave English a somewhat stabilizing prestige. The development of English printing and the growth of a national spirit helped even more to dignify and standardize the language. By the end of the sixteenth century, English had become a national language, as indicated by the great English translation of the Bible in 1611. Printing, together with the great increase in the number of people who could read and write, tended to slow change in the language, particularly in its written form. But though less rapid, change remains continuous as the language adapts to the changing needs of those who use it.

As always, change is most easily seen in vocabulary. In its very early history, the coming of Christianity brought into the language such Latin words as *angel, candle, priest,* and *school.* From the Danish came such basic words as the pronouns *they, their,* and *them,* and *skull, skin, anger, root,* and *ill.* After the Norman Conquest in 1066, French words poured into the language for nearly three hundred years, touching nearly every corner of life with words that are part of our everyday vocabulary: *dance, tax, mayor, justice, faith, battle, paper, poet, surgeon, gentle, flower, sun*—the list extends to thousands. In the seventeenth century, when Latin became greatly respected and avidly studied, thousands upon thousands of Latin words flooded into English. They included not only the words we think of as learned, but also many that are common such as *industry, educate, insane, exist, illustrate, multiply, benefit, paragraph, dedicate,* and the like. And as English reached into other parts of the world, it continued its habit of borrowing. It has played no favorites, drawing on Arabic *(alcohol, assassin),* Hebrew *(cherub, kosher),* East Indian *(jungle, yoga),* Japanese *(jujitsu, tycoon),* Spanish *(adobe, canyon),* and many others.

The borrowing process continues today. But in the past hundred years two other developments have had major consequences for English. The first is the rapid development of mass education and the resulting rise in literacy. The second is advancement in science and technology. Both of these developments have had complex effects upon the language and will doubtless continue to be strong influences. Though the effect of the first is difficult to measure, it is clear that a language that can reach many of its users in print and an even greater number through radio and television will develop differently from a language in which writing is addressed to a special minority or in which speech occurs largely in face-to-face exchange. The effect of the technological revolution and rapid specialization is clearer. It has given us a burgeoning vocabulary of technical terms ranging from the names of drugs to the specialized words in everything from do-it-yourself kits to space engineering.

Changes in grammar since the sixteenth century, though minor compared with the loss of inflections and the accompanying fixing of word order that came earlier, have continued in Modern English. Since the sixteenth century, reliance upon word order and function words has become even greater. Questions in the form of *Consents she?* and negations in the form of *I say not, I run not* have disappeared, to be replaced by the use of the auxiliary verb *do,* as in *Does she consent?, I do not say, I do not run.* Verb forms with *be* in the pattern of *He was speaking, We are going, It is being built* have multiplied greatly. Other changes include an increase in the number of verbs made from verbs combined with adverbs or with prepositions, as in *He looked up the word, He looked over Bill's new house, The fireplace was smoking up the room.* Similarly, nouns used as modifiers of other nouns, as in *college student, radio station, mathematics course, ice-cream stand,* have become more common. Such changes make it clear that the evolution of the language continues.

The following passages, though less strikingly dissimilar than those we saw earlier, demonstrate some of the changes in the language between 1600 and 1900. Many of the differences among these selections are differences of idiom or style rather than of grammar.

I had often before this said, that if the Indians should come, I should chuse rather to be killed by them than taken alive but when it came to the tryal my mind changed; their glittering weapons so daunted my spirit, that I chose rather to go along with those (as I may say) ravenous Bears, then that moment to end my dayes; and that I may better declare what happened to me during that grievous Captivity, I shall particularly speak of the severall Removes we had up and down the Wilderness.

MARY ROWLANDSON, *The Narrative of the Captivity*, c. 1682

About the twelfth year of my age, my Father being abroad, my Mother reproved me for some misconduct, to which I made an Undutifull reply & the next first-day, as I was with my Father returning from Meeting, He told me he understood I had behaved amis to my Mother, and Advised me to be more careful in future.

JOHN WOOLMAN, *The Journal*, 1756

I had stopped in Boston at the Tremont House, which was still one of the first hostelries of the country, and I must have inquired my way to Cambridge there; but I was sceptical of the direction the Cambridge horsecar took when I found it, and I hinted to the driver my anxieties as to why he should be starting east when I had been told that Cambridge was west of Boston.

WILLIAM DEAN HOWELLS, *Literary Friends and Acquaintances*, 1894

Variety and standards

Language not only changes with time, it also varies widely at any given time. It varies from one geographical area to another and from one occupational and social group to another. Further, the language each of us uses varies from situation to situation. The language of conversation differs from that in a public address, and that in turn differs from written language. Even carefully written and edited English varies according to the writer's audience and purpose.

One important variation of language is that between standard and nonstandard English. The term **standard English** is applied to the written language of business, journalism, education, law, public documents, and literature. It is also used to describe speech—the speech of people in the practice of the professions (medicine, teaching, theology, and so on), the speech of courtrooms, the speech of many public functions. In many occupations, competence in its use is necessary.

Nonstandard English describes language that varies in grammar and usage from the standard. Nonstandard commonly differs from standard English in verb and pronoun forms and in the use of double negatives, which are rare in standard. Such forms include *he give, growed, have saw; him and me is, hern, youse; can't never.* Nonstandard is also characterized by a relatively narrow range of vocabulary and a heavy dependence upon a small variety of sentence structures.

Distinctions between standard and nonstandard English are not distinctions between good and bad or right and wrong. The function of language is to communicate, and any language that makes for clear and accurate communication is good language. The reasons nonstandard forms are not used in business and the professions nor, ordinarily, in publications are social and historical rather than because they do not communicate. Nonetheless, standard English is the widely used and understood public language, and competence in its use is almost indispensable to taking part in the public functions in which it is used.

The following passages illustrate standard and one form of nonstandard English. Since nonstandard is primarily spoken, the illustration can only approximate it.

STANDARD

Today, as never before, the sky is menacing. Things seen indifferently last century by the wandering lamplighter now trouble a generation that has grown up to the wail of air-raid sirens and the ominous expectation that the roof may fall at any moment. Even in daytime, reflected light on a floating dandelion seed, or a spider riding a wisp of gossamer in the sun's eye, can bring excited questions from the novice unused to estimating the distance or nature of aerial objects.

LOREN EISELEY, "Little Men and Flying Saucers"

The voice we hear in an ad is not the official voice of the corporation that pays the bill. The voice in the ad is a highly fictitious created person, speaking as an individual in a particular situation. In a bathtub, for instance. No corporation official could ever say, officially, "I never, never bathe without Sardo." The official voice of the corporation appears, I suppose, in its periodic reports to its stockholders, or in its communications with government agencies.

WALKER GIBSON, *Tough, Sweet, & Stuffy*

NONSTANDARD

"I can't tell ya' [how to heal] because it's handed down from th' beginnin'. It's in th' Bible. If y'tell somebody, y'lose yer power—in other words, like a man doin' somethin' t'destroy his rights, y'know.

"In that now, I could learn two women, or three I think it is, and then one of 'em that I'd learnt could learn a man person. So about th' biggest point I get in that is t'add a little mystery t'th' party that don't believe, maybe we'll say, in fire drawin' [laughing].

"I learnt two, an' I studied about it after that. Never asked 'em yet if they've ever tried it t'see if it works. But I think th' one that learnt me said learn somebody not no kin to ya'. Well, these parties wasn't, but they'uz my brother's wives, see? But I've never asked them if they've tried it."

ELIOT WIGGINTON, ed., *The Foxfire Book*

Standard English varies too, according to its use or function. Such varieties are sometimes called **functional varieties.** The most general variation is that between informal and formal. **Informal** describes the English of everyday speaking and writing, casual conversation between friends and associates, personal letters, and writing close to general speech. **Formal** describes the language of scholarly books and articles, the reports of business, industry, and science, most legal writing, and literary prose.

Informal and formal cannot be clearly differentiated, for there are wide ranges of degree in each. In general, as language moves toward casual speech, it becomes more informal. At the extreme of informality is casual speech of educated people in familiar situations and the writing that tries to catch the flavor of such speech. Free use of contractions, loose sentence structures, and the use of informal words and expressions (such as *shape up* and *get going*) characterize informal language.

At the extreme of formality is careful scientific, scholarly, and legal writing, which needs to be exact. Note the elaborate sentence structure, the Latinate vocabulary, and the serious tone in the formal examples below. In the informal examples, the sentences become increasingly relaxed, the vocabulary is everyday, and the tone conversational. But if you catch yourself thinking that one is better than the other, remember that the purpose, subject matter, audience, temperament, and hence style of each author are quite different.

FORMAL

An antibiotic is a chemical substance, produced by microorganisms, which has the capacity to inhibit the growth of and even destroy bacteria and other microorganisms. The action of an antibiotic against microorganisms is selective in nature, some organisms being affected and others not at all or only to a limited degree; each antibiotic is thus characterized by a specific antimicrobial spectrum. The selective action of an antibiotic is also manifested against microbial vs. host cells. Antibiotics vary greatly in their physical and chemical properties and in their toxicity to animals. Because of these characteristics, some antibiotics have remarkable chemotherapeutic potentialities and can be used for the control of various microbial infections in man and in animals.

Quoted in SELMAN A. WAKSMAN, *The Actinomycetes and Their Antibiotics*

Dean Donne in the pulpit of old Paul's, holding his audience spellbound still as he reversed his glass of sands after an hour of exposition and application of texts by the light of the church fathers, of mortification for edification, of exhortation that brought tears to the eyes of himself and his hearers, and of analogies born of the study, but sounding of wings—there was a man who should have had wisdom, surely. For if experience can bring it, this was the man.

R. P. T. COFFIN and A. M. WITHERSPOON, "John Donne," in *Seventeenth Century Prose*

INFORMAL

All scientists are not alike. Look at any laboratory or university science department. Professor Able is the kind of man who seizes an idea as a dog seizes a stick, all at once. As he talks you can see him stop short, with the chalk in his fingers, and then almost jump with excitement as the insight grips him. His colleague, Baker, on the other hand, is a man who comes to understand an idea as a worm might understand the same stick, digesting it a little at a time, drawing his conclusions cautiously, and tunneling slowly through it from end to end and back again.   JOHN RADAR PLATT, "Style in Science"

Of all the common farm operations none is more ticklish than tending a brooder stove. All brooder stoves are whimsical, and some of them are holy terrors. Mine burns coal, and has only a fair record. With its check draft that opens and closes, this stove occupies my dreams from midnight, when I go to bed, until five o'clock, when I get up, pull a shirt and a pair of pants on over my pajamas, and stagger out into the dawn to read the thermometer under the hover and see that my 254 little innocents are properly disposed in a neat circle round their big iron mama.   E. B. WHITE, One Man's Meat

The colossal success of the supermarkets is based upon the fact that nobody, but nobody, can sell you something as well as you can by yourself. As a result, supermarkets now stock clothing, appliances, plastic swimming pools, and small trees. The theory is that if you succumb to an avocado today, tomorrow you may fall for an electronic range or a young poplar.

ELAINE KENDALL, "An Open Letter to the Corner Grocer"

The terms *colloquial* and *edited* are often used in discussing varieties of English. **Colloquial** means "spoken." The word is used to describe the everyday speech of educated people and the kind of writing that uses the easy vocabulary, loose constructions, contractions, and other characteristics of that speech. The informal style of E. B. White and Elaine Kendall illustrated above is colloquial. **Edited English** is the written language of many books, magazines, and newspapers. It may be more or less formal or informal, but it is always marked by its observation of conventional spelling, punctuation, grammar, and sentence structure.

The fact that English has such variety means that there can be no unvarying and absolute standard of correctness. But it does not mean that we can do entirely without standards or that what is appropriate for familiar conversation is appropriate for all kinds of communication. If people were to write as naturally as they talk, they might rid their writing of some affectation. But for much of its force, conversational English depends upon the physical presence of the speaker. Personality, gesture, and intonation all contribute to the success of spoken communication. Written English, on the other hand, uses structure, rather than the physical presence of the writer, to achieve clarity. Written English communicates through the precision of its diction, the orderliness of its sentence and paragraph structure, and the relative fullness of its detail. If it is to be taken seriously by a general audience, it must observe the conventions of spelling, punctuation, and grammar. In short, writers do conform to certain standards to get their meaning across.

A handbook somewhat arbitrarily classifies such standards into rules or conventions that cannot always be defended on logical grounds. Rather, they reflect the practices—some old, some new—of English and American writers. Most of these conventions are quite flexible. The rules for punctuation, for instance, permit many variations, and so do the standards for diction, sentence structure, and paragraphing. The truth is that the rules of writing represent "typical" or "normal" practices. Skillful writers interpret them very loosely and occasionally ignore those that seem too restrictive for their purposes. For most writers, however, the rules are a discipline and a security. Observing them does not make writers great, but it does help to make writing clear and orderly. And clarity and order are the marks of good writing.

BASIC GRAMMAR
GR

SENTENCE SENSE **SS** **1**

CASE **CA** **2**

ADJECTIVES AND ADVERBS **AD** **3**

VERB FORMS **VB** **4**

VERBS: TENSE, MOOD, AND VOICE **T** **5**

Good grammar is not merely grammar which is free from unconventionalities, or even from the immoralities. It is the triumph of the communication process, the use of words which create in the reader's mind the thing as the writer conceived it; it is a creative act. . . .

JANET AIKEN, *Commonsense Grammar*

The term *grammar* is used in two ways. In one sense, grammar is the system by which a language works. In this sense, learning to speak a language *is* learning its grammar. If you grew up speaking English, as soon as you learned the difference between such pairs as *toy* and *toys*, *home run* and *run home*, or *tiger tails* and *tiger's tail*, you had learned a good deal of English grammar. And by the time you could put together sentences such as *Howard's father gave him some new toys*, or *See the monkeys jumping around in the cages*, you had learned very complicated things about English grammar.

In another sense, grammar is a description of language. In this sense, grammar is in the same class as physics. Physics describes how light, sound, electricity, and other kinds of energy and matter work. Grammar describes the way a language works. It describes the kinds of words in a language (nouns, verbs, prepositions, and so on) and how users of the language put single words together into meaningful groups.

In the following pages, you will find many of the details of English grammar. One basic concept about language may help you to keep these details in perspective. Any language is composed of individual words and **grammatical devices** for putting them together meaningfully. A series of words such as *age, buggy, the, and, horse* is just a series of isolated English words. Each word makes sense by itself, but they aren't obviously related to one another. But *the horse-and-buggy age* makes a quite different kind of sense; the words have been put together into a meaningful combination. English has several devices for putting words into such combinations. The three most important are word order, function words, and inflections.

In English, grammatical meaning is largely determined by **word order.** *Blue sky* and *sky blue* mean different things: in the first, *blue* describes *sky;* in the second, *sky* describes *blue.* Here is the principle in action:

The thief called the lawyer a liar.
The lawyer called the thief a liar.
The liar called the lawyer a thief.

Our new neighbors bought an old house.
Our old neighbors bought a new house.

See how important word order can be in such a sentence as *The man in the black shoes with the sandy hair knocked on the door.* Word order has *with the sandy hair* describing *shoes,* but common sense tells us that shoes do not have sandy hair.

Function words, sometimes called **grammatical words,** are words such as *the, and, but, in, to, because, while, ought,* and *must.* The main use of function words is to express relationships among other words. Compare the following:

I am lonely *at* dark.   The cook prepared *a* rich feast.
I am lonely *in the* dark.   The cook prepared *the* rich *a* feast.

Inflections, less important in Modern English than they were in earlier stages of the language, are changes in the form of words that indicate differences in grammatical relationship. Inflections account for the differences in the following:

The boy*s* walk slowly.   Stop bother*ing* me.
The boy walk*s* slowly.   Stop*s* bother me.

Being able to control these grammatical devices—word order, function words, and inflections—is essential to writing clearly.

A distinction is sometimes made between grammar and *usage.* Grammar is concerned with generally applicable principles about a language. **Usage,** in contrast, is concerned with choices, particularly with differences between standard and nonstandard English and between formal and informal English. The differences between *tile floor* and *floor tile, he walks* and *he walked, he was biting the dog* and *the dog was biting him* are grammatical differences. The differences between *I saw* and *I seen, he doesn't* and *he don't,* and *let me do it* and *leave me do it* are differences in usage. They may identify the persons who use them, as speakers of standard or nonstandard dialects, but they do not mean different things. Since this book is concerned with providing guidelines for writing standard English, it is concerned with both grammar and usage. And since many questions of grammar and usage overlap, the two are not set apart sharply.

1   SENTENCE SENSE **SS**

Grammar describes the kinds of words in a language and the ways these words are fitted together into meaningful groups. Grammarians describe the words in a language by assigning them to different classes or groups according to their functions. The major kinds of words in English and the functions they usually perform are as follows:

Function	Kinds of Words
Naming	Nouns and pronouns
Predicating (stating or asserting)	Verbs
Modifying	Adjectives and adverbs
Connecting	Prepositions and conjunctions

Of these, nouns and verbs, the naming and stating words, are the basic elements. They are the bones of the sentence, the most important unit of writing. They work together to make our simplest sentences; other kinds of words and word groups expand and refine those simple sentences.

1a   Recognizing sentences and their basic words

A **sentence** is a group of words that contains a subject and a predicate and that is not introduced by a connecting word such as *although, because, when,* or *where* that makes it dependent upon another group of words to complete its meaning. *She is studying* and *What is she studying* are sentences. But *although she is studying* is not a sentence because the word *although* makes the whole word group depend upon something else for completion, as in the statement *Although she is studying, she will be finished soon.*

Subjects and predicates. All complete sentences have two main parts, a subject and a predicate. The **subject** names the person, thing, or concept that the sentence is about. The **predicate** makes a statement or asks a question about the subject.

Verbs. The predicate of a sentence *always* contains a **verb,** a word that makes some sort of assertion about the subject. A sentence cannot exist without a verb. Verbs indicate some kind of action, the occurrence of something, or the presence of some condition. Examples of verbs are *ask, eat, give, describe, criticize, seem, appear, become.*

In the simplest English sentences, a verb may stand alone as the predicate: *Lions hunt.* Or it may be followed by a word called its **object,** which indicates who or what receives the action of the verb: *Lions hunt prey.*

Verbs have the following characteristics of form:

1   When verbs indicate present time, they always add *-s* or *-es* to the form listed in the dictionary when their subjects are *he, she,* or *it* or a word for which *he, she,* or *it* can be substituted: *the boys run,* but *the boy* [he] *runs; the logs burn,* but *the log* [it] *burns.*

2   Almost all verbs have a separate form to indicate past tense. Most add *-d* or *-ed* to the form listed in the dictionary: *save, saved;*

walk, walked; repeat, repeated. A few indicate past time in irregular ways: *eat, ate; go, went; run, ran; sleep, slept.* A few verbs do not have a separate form: *cut, put, hit, hurt.*

3   The dictionary form of verbs can always be preceded by any one of the following words: *can, could; may, might; will, would; shall, should;* and *must,* as in *can talk, may go, would leave, should pay,* or *will read.* These words are called **auxiliaries** or **helping verbs** and are used with verbs to convey special shades of meaning. Other forms of the verb can combine with other auxiliaries to form verb phrases, such as *have been eating, will be finished, could have been working,* that express various time relationships as well as other shades of meaning. (For a full discussion of auxiliaries, see Section **4**.)

4   Many verbs have typical endings, called **suffixes,** such as *-ate, -en, -fy,* and *-ize,* as in *implicate, operate, widen, hasten, liquefy, simplify, recognize, modernize.*

Nouns. The subject of a sentence is usually a noun or a pronoun. **Nouns** name or classify things, places, activities, and concepts: *studio, committee, Carl, Detroit, athletics, courage, wealth.* Nouns have the following characteristics:

1   Nouns naming things that can be counted add *-s* or *-es* to make the plural form which indicates more than one: *chair, chairs; car, cars; church, churches; bush, bushes.* A few nouns have irregular plurals: *woman, women; foot, feet; sheep, sheep.* Nouns that name particular people or places *(Dorothy, Omaha)* and nouns that name things not usually counted *(gravel, milk, sugar, courage, honesty)* do not ordinarily have plural forms.

2   Nouns typically serve as the subjects *(The wind blew; Sally arrived; Honesty pays)* and the objects of verbs and prepositions *(Send John to the store).*

3   Many nouns have characteristic endings such as *-ance, -ence, -ism, -ity, -ment, -ness, -tion,* and *-ship: relevance, excellence, realism, activity, argument, darkness, adoption, seamanship.*

Pronouns. Pronouns are words that can substitute for nouns. Thus, pronouns can be subjects or objects of verbs or prepositions. The noun for which a pronoun substitutes is called its **antecedent.** In the sentence *Clara Barton is the woman who founded the American Red Cross,* the pronoun *who* refers to its antecedent, *woman.* In the sentence *Whichever he chooses will be acceptable,* it is impossible to know what *whichever* means. (Only if you saw this sentence in a larger context could you tell what *whichever* refers to.) In such sentences as *He who hesitates is lost,* the meaning of *he* is implied by the context itself; that is, *he* refers to any person who hesitates to take action. **Indefinite**

pronouns, words like *anybody, everybody,* and *somebody,* act as nouns and require no antecedent.

The **personal pronouns** *I, we, he, she,* and *they,* and the pronoun *who,* which is used either to relate one group of words to another or to ask a question, change form in the subjective, possessive, and objective cases; *you* and *it* change form as possessives only. (See Section **2.**)

Basic sentence patterns. All English sentences are built on a limited number of patterns, to which all sentences, no matter how long or complex, can be reduced. The five most basic patterns are described below. In all the patterns the subject remains a simple noun or pronoun. Differences among the patterns lie in the predicate part of the sentence—the verb and what follows it.

The simplest of all English sentence patterns consists of a subject and its verb. Sentences as simple as these are relatively rare in mature writing, yet simple sentences (subject-verb) are the core of all sentences.

PATTERN 1

Subject	Verb
Red	fades.
The woman	arrived.
The snow	fell.

The verbs in the second pattern are always action words that can pass their action on to another word called an object, or more exactly, a **direct object.** The direct object is always a noun, a pronoun, or a group of words serving as a noun that answers the question "what" or "whom" after the verb. Verbs that can take objects are called **transitive** verbs.

PATTERN 2

Subject	Verb	Direct Object
Dogs	eat	bones.
The carpenter	repaired	the roof.
John	prefers	the movies.
Someone	insulted	her.

With a few verbs, such as *appoint, believe, consider, judge, made,* and *name,* the direct object may be followed by another noun or a modifying word that renames or describes the direct object. These are called **object complements,** and they distinguish the third sentence pattern.

PATTERN 3

Subject	Verb	Direct Object	Object Complement
Henry	called	him	a traitor.
They	appointed	Shirley	chairperson.
We	made	the clerk	angry.
People	judged	her	innocent.

The fourth pattern introduces the **indirect object.** After such action verbs as *ask, give, send, tell,* and *teach,* the direct object is often preceded by an **indirect object** that names the receiver of the message, gift, or whatever, and always comes before the direct object.

PATTERN 4

Subject	Verb	Indirect Object	Direct Object
His father	gave	Sam	a car.
The college	found	me	work.
Wellington	brought	England	victory.
John	sold	her	a book.

The same meaning can usually be expressed by a phrase that begins with *to* or *for* and is positioned after the direct object: *Wellington brought victory to England; The college found work for me.*

The fifth pattern occurs only with a special kind of verb, called a **linking verb.** The most common linking verb is *be* in its various forms: *is, are, was, were, has been, might be,* etc. Other common linking verbs include *appear, become, seem* and in some contexts such verbs as *feel, grow, act, look, taste, smell,* and *sound.* Linking verbs are followed by a **complement,** which may be either a **predicate noun** or a **predicate adjective.** A complement following a linking verb, in contrast to an object after a transitive verb, is related to the subject of the sentence. Predicate nouns rename the subject; predicate adjectives modify the subject.

PATTERN 5

Subject	Linking Verb	Complement	
		Predicate Noun	Predicate Adjective
Napoleon	was	a Frenchman.	
My brother	remains	an artist.	
Natalie	may become	president.	
The book	seemed		obscene.
Work	was		scarce.
The fruit	tasted		bitter.

Other sentence patterns. The preceding five sentence patterns are the basis of all English sentence structure. Other kinds of sentences may be thought of either as additional patterns or as changes, called *transformation* by some grammarians, in these basic patterns. Thus, we create questions by inverting the subject and verb, as in *Will he run,* or by using a function word before the basic pattern, as in *Does he run.* We create commands by omitting the subject, as in *Open the can, Know thyself, Keep calm.*

Two kinds of patterns are especially important because they involve changes either in the usual actor-action relation of subject and verb or in the usual order of subject and verb.

The first of these is the **passive sentence.** The passive sentence is made from one of the basic patterns that have a direct object. In its most common form, the original object of the verb becomes the subject, and the original subject may be either omitted or expressed in a phrase beginning with *by.* In the passive sentence the subject no longer names the performer of the action described by the verb, as it does in active patterns. Rather, it names the receiver of the action. This characteristic makes the passive sentence especially useful when we do not know who performs an action. Thus we normally say *He was killed in action* rather than *Someone killed him in action.* (See "Voice," in Section **5.**)

The verb in passive sentences consists of some form of the auxiliary, or helping, verb *be* and the past participle.

ACTIVE

The carpenter *repaired* the roof.
Someone *insulted* her.
Henry *called* him a traitor.
Wellington *brought* England victory.

PASSIVE

Subject	Passive Verb	(Original Subject)
The roof	was repaired	(by the carpenter).
She	was insulted	(by someone).
He	was called a traitor	(by Henry).
Victory	was brought to England	(by Wellington).

Notice that in all passive sentences the original subject can be expressed by a prepositional phrase, but the sentence is complete without that prepositional phrase.

The second important kind of sentence that involves change in the word order allows us to postpone the subject of the sentence until after the verb by beginning with the **expletive** *there* or *it.*

Expletive	Verb	Complement	Subject
It	is	doubtful	that they will arrive.
There	is		no reply.
There	are		seven students.
There	will be		an opportunity.

EXERCISE 1a Identify the subjects, verbs, direct objects, indirect objects, and complements in the following sentences.

1 Poverty often deprives children of opportunity.
2 Alcoholism is a disease.
3 Television brings us many good movies.
4 The quarterback threw a long pass for a touchdown.
5 Sally bought her brother a new radio.
6 Some foods may cause cancer.
7 Local citizens sent the police many complaints about burglaries in the neighborhood.
8 Our football team was beaten only twice last year.
9 Dictionaries are useful for many kinds of information.
10 There were only seven people at the meeting.

1b   Recognizing modifiers, connecting words, and verbals

1b

If all sentences in English were limited to the basic patterns, our writing would be bare and monotonous indeed. Clearly, the variety and complexity of our sentences are not created by variety and complexity in these basic patterns. Rather, they are created by the addition of modifying words and by the use of several different kinds of word groups that can themselves serve as nouns and modifiers.

1   Modifying words: adjectives and adverbs. Modifiers are words or word groups that limit, qualify, make more exact the other words or word groups to which they are attached. Adjectives and adverbs are the principal single-word modifiers in English.

Adjectives modify nouns or pronouns. Typical adjectives are the underlined words in the following: *brown dog, Victorian dignity, yellow hair, one football, reasonable price, sleek boat.* Adjectives have distinctive forms in the **comparative** and **superlative:** *happy, happier, happiest; beautiful, more beautiful, most beautiful; good, better, best.*

Adverbs modify verbs, adjectives, or other adverbs, although they may modify whole sentences. Typical adverbs are the underlined words in the following: *stayed outside, walked slowly, horribly angry, fortunately the accident was not fatal.*

For a discussion of the special forms by which adjectives and adverbs show comparison, and of certain distinctions between the two, see Section **3.**

2 Connecting words: prepositions and conjunctions. Connecting words enable us to link one word or word group with another and to combine them in ways that allow us not only to express our ideas more concisely, but also to express the relationships between those ideas more clearly. We don't need to say *We had coffee. We had toast.* Rather, we can say *We had coffee and toast* or *We had coffee with toast.* We don't need to say *We talked. We played cards. We went home.* Rather, we can say *After we talked and played cards, we went home* or *After talking and playing cards, we went home.* The kinds of words that enable us to make these connections and combinations are prepositions and conjunctions.

A **preposition** links a noun or pronoun (called its **object**) with some other word in the sentence and shows the relationship between the object and the other word. The preposition, together with its object, almost always modifies the other word to which it is linked.

> The dog walks *on* water. [*On* links *water* to the verb *walks; on water* modifies *walks.*]
>
> The distance *between* us is short. [*Between* links *us* to the noun *distance; between us* modifies *distance.*]

Although a preposition usually comes before its object, in a few constructions it can follow its object.

> *In what town* do you live?
> *What town* do you live *in?*

The most common prepositions are listed below:

about	below	into	through
above	beside	near	to
across	by	next	toward
after	down	of	under
among	during	off	until
around	except	on	up
as	for	out	upon
at	from	over	with
before	in	past	within
behind	inside	since	without

Many simple prepositions combine with other words to form phrasal prepositions, such as *at the point of, by means of, down from, from above, in addition to, without regard to.*

Note that some words, such as *below, down, in, out,* and *up,* occur both as prepositions and as adverbs. Used as adverbs, they never have objects. Compare *He went below* with *He went below the deck.*

Note too that *after, as, before, since,* and *until* also function as subordinating conjunctions. (See below.)

A **conjunction** joins words, phrases, or clauses. Conjunctions show the relationship between the sentence elements that they connect.

Coordinating conjunctions *(and, but, or, nor, for, so, yet)* join words, phrases, or clauses of equal grammatical rank. (See **1d,** "Recognizing Clauses.")

WORDS JOINED	We ate ham *and* eggs.
PHRASES JOINED	Look in the closet *or* under the bed.
CLAUSES JOINED	We wanted to go, *but* we were too busy.

Correlative conjunctions are coordinating words that work in pairs to join words, phrases, clauses, or whole sentences. The most common correlative pairs are *both . . . and, either . . . or, neither . . . nor, not . . . but,* and *not only . . . but also.*

both courageous *and* loyal
either before you go *or* after you get back
neither circuses *nor* sideshows
not only as a child *but also* as an adult

Subordinating conjunctions join clauses that are not equal in rank. A clause introduced by a subordinating conjunction is called a *dependent* or *subordinate* clause (see **1d**) and cannot stand by itself as a sentence; it must be joined to a main, or independent, clause.

We left the party early *because we were tired.*
If the roads are icy, we will have to drive carefully.
Whether we like it or not, oil grows more expensive.

The following are the most common subordinating conjunctions:

after	even though	than	where
although	even if	that	wherever
as	if	though	whether
as if	in order that	unless	while
as though	since	until	
because	rather than	when	
before	so that	whenever	

3   Verbals. Verbals are special verb forms that have some of the characteristics and abilities of verbs but cannot function as predicates by themselves. Verbs make an assertion. Verbals do not; they function as nouns and modifiers. There are three kinds of verbals: infinitives, participles, and gerunds.

Infinitives are usually marked by a *to* before the actual verb *(to eat, to describe).* They are used as nouns, adjectives, or adverbs.

> *To see* is *to believe.* [Both used as nouns]
> It was time *to leave.* [Used as adjective]
> I was ready *to go.* [Used as adverb]

Participles may be either present or past. The present form ends in *-ing (eating, running, describing).* The past form usually ends in *-ed (described).* But note that some end in *-en (eaten),* and a few make an internal change *(begun, flown).* Participles are always used as adjectives.

> *Screaming,* I jumped out of bed. [Present participle]
> *Delighted,* we accepted his invitation. [Past participle]

Gerunds have the same *-ing* form as the present participle. The distinctive name *gerund* is given to *-ing* forms only when they function as nouns.

> *Writing* requires effort. [Subject of *requires*]
> You should try *swimming.* [Object of *try*]

Although verbals can never function by themselves as predicates, they can, like verbs, take objects and complements, and like verbs, they are characteristically modified by adverbs. Note the following:

> I prefer *to believe him.* [*Him* is the object of *to believe.*]
> It was time *to leave the house.* [*House* is the object of *to leave.*]
> *Screaming loudly,* I jumped out of bed. [The adverb *loudly* modifies the participle *screaming.*]
> Swimming *in the Atlantic* is refreshing. [The adverb phrase *in the Atlantic* modifies the gerund *swimming.*]

EXERCISE 1b   In the following sentences, identify the adjectives, adverbs, prepositions, coordinating conjunctions, subordinating conjunctions, and verbals.

1 Books are powerful weapons against ignorance.
2 Sally soon recovered from her severe injuries.
3 Misreading directions is a common mistake in taking examinations.
4 With the wind blowing furiously from the northeast, the storm raged for two days.
5 A man should never wear his best suit when he goes out to fight for freedom and truth.
6 Because scientists have warned about its dangers, great efforts have been made to control pollution.

7 Some resorts are strangely desolate in winter.
8 Marie would like to go to medical school, but she is concerned about the cost.
9 Nothing disturbs Joe when he is sleeping.
10 Peering into the fog, she could barely see the car in front of her.

1c   Recognizing phrases

A **phrase** is a group of related words that has no subject or predicate and is used as a single part of speech. Typical phrases are a preposition and its object *(I fell on the sidewalk)*, or a verbal and its object *(I wanted to see the parade)*.

Phrases are usually classified as prepositional, infinitive, participial, or gerund phrases.

Prepositional phrases. Prepositional phrases consist of a preposition, its object, and any modifiers of the object *(under the ground, without thinking, in the blue Ford)*. Prepositional phrases function as adjectives or adverbs and occasionally as nouns.

> He is a man *of action*. [Adjective modifying *man*]
> The plane arrived *on time*. [Adverb modifying *arrived*]
> We were ready *at the airport*. [Adverb modifying *ready*]
> She came early *in the morning*. [Adverb modifying *early*]
> *Before breakfast* is too early. [Noun, subject of *is*]

Infinitive phrases. Infinitive phrases consist of an infinitive, its modifiers, and/or its object *(to see the world, to answer briefly, to earn money quickly)*. Infinitive phrases function as nouns, adjectives, or adverbs.

> I wanted *to buy the house*. [Noun, object of verb]
> It is time *to go to bed*. [Adjective modifying *time*]
> We were impatient *to start the game*. [Adverb modifying *impatient*]

Participial phrases. Participial phrases consist of a present or past participle, its modifiers, and/or its object *(lying on the beach, found in the street, eating a large dinner)*. Participial phrases always function as adjectives.

> The dog *running in the yard* belongs to my mother.
> The man *walking his dog* is my father.
> *Covered with ice,* the road was dangerous.
> *Beaten twice by Susan,* Jim fought to win the last game.

1c

Gerund phrases. Gerund phrases consist of a gerund, its modifiers, and/or its object *(telling the truth, knowing the rules, acting bravely)*. Gerund phrases always function as nouns.

Collecting stamps is my hobby. [Subject]
She earned more by *working overtime.* [Object of preposition]
He hated *living alone.* [Object of verb]
Making a profit is their only purpose. [Subject]

Note that since both the gerund and the present participle end in *-ing,* they can be distinguished only by their separate functions as nouns or adjectives.

Absolute phrases. Absolute phrases are made up of a noun or pronoun and a participle. Unlike participial phrases, absolute phrases do not modify particular words in the sentence to which they are attached. Rather, they modify the whole sentence.

The whole family sat silent, *their eyes glued to the TV screen.*
Mortgage rates having risen drastically, Isabel gave up searching for a new house.
The old man lay sprawled on the sofa, *eyes closed, arms folded across his chest, his loud snores almost rousing the dog sleeping near him.*

In absolute phrases with the participle *being* followed by an adjective, *being* is often omitted so that the phrase itself consists simply of a noun followed by an adjective and any other modifiers.

Final examinations over, Linda returned to work.
The den was thoroughly inviting, *the lights low, the long sofa and overstuffed chairs luxuriously comfortable, the logs burning brightly in the fireplace,* and *our host open and friendly.*

EXERCISE 1c In the following sentences, identify the verbal phrases by underlining them once and the prepositional phrases by underlining them twice. Note that a prepositional phrase may sometimes be part of a verbal phrase, as in the verbal phrase *lying on the beach,* in which the verbal *lying* is modified by the prepositional phrase *on the beach.*

1 Pears are the most succulent fruit of winter.
2 Having worked late into the night, Mary went to bed.
3 To become independent is the desire of most young men and women.
4 Watching football on TV is the favorite sport of millions.
5 Rising in a graceful arc, the spaceship swung into orbit.
6 Smith wanted to hold the foreman to his promise.
7 Reports of flying saucers grew frequent in the summer.

8 Being loyal to her principles was more important to Jane than gaining approval from her friends.
9 For many years the gap between the rich and poor in South America has been widening.
10 The tornado struck the town, ripping roofs from houses and wrenching trees from the ground.

1d Recognizing clauses

A **clause** is a group of words containing a subject and a predicate. The relation of a clause to the rest of the sentence is shown by the position of the clause or by a conjunction. There are two kinds of clauses: (1) main, or independent, clauses and (2) subordinate, or dependent, clauses.

1 Main clauses. A main clause has both subject and verb, but it is not introduced by a subordinating word. A main clause makes an independent statement. It is not used as a noun or as a modifier.

2 Subordinate clauses. Subordinate clauses are usually introduced by a subordinating conjunction (*as, since, because,* etc.) or by a relative pronoun *(who, which, that)*. Subordinate clauses function as adjectives, adverbs, or nouns. They express ideas that are less important than the idea expressed in the main clause. The exact relationship between the two ideas is indicated by the subordinating conjunction or relative pronoun that joins the subordinate and the main clause.

A An ADJECTIVE CLAUSE modifies a noun or pronoun.

This is the jet *that broke the speed record.* [The subordinate clause modifies the noun *jet.*]
Anybody *who is tired* may leave. [The subordinate clause modifies the pronoun *anybody.*]
Canada is the nation *we made the treaty with.* [The subordinate clause modifies the noun *nation,* with the relative pronoun *that* understood.]

B An ADVERB CLAUSE modifies a verb, adjective, or adverb.

The child cried *when the dentist appeared.* [The subordinate clause modifies the verb *cried.*]
I am sorry *he is sick.* [The subordinate clause modifies the adjective *sorry,* with the subordinating conjunction *that* understood.]
He thinks more quickly *than you do.* [The subordinate clause modifies the adverb *quickly.*]

C A NOUN CLAUSE **functions as a noun. It may serve as subject, predicate noun, object of a verb, or object of a preposition.**

What John wants is a better job. [The subordinate clause is the subject of the verb *is*.]

This is *where we came in*. [The subordinate clause is a predicate noun.]

Please tell them *I will be late*. [The subordinate clause is the object of the verb *tell*.]

He has no interest in *what he is reading*. [The subordinate clause is the object of the preposition *in*.]

EXERCISE 1d(1) Underline the subordinate clauses in the following sentences and identify each as an adjective, adverb, or noun clause.

1 What one thinks at twenty often seems silly at thirty.
2 If success depended only on work, many would be rich.
3 Linda and her friends left before the party was over.
4 The apples that make the best pies are the sour ones.
5 When the lake was calm, we tried the outboard we had just bought.
6 Julie had the quality of intelligence that the director needed.
7 What a man promises is less important than what he does.
8 The clerks who annoyed him the most were those who seemed indifferent.
9 While he was telephoning, the repairman whom he had called knocked on the door.
10 Many people think that education is to be gotten only in school.

EXERCISE 1d(2) In the following sentences, identify the main and subordinate clauses. Indicate the function of each subordinate clause as adjective, adverb, or noun.

1 Platinum, which was discovered in 1750, is a very valuable metal.
2 The price that John paid for his car was too high.
3 Many unemployed men and women lack the skills that they need for jobs.
4 As the class ended, the teacher sighed with relief.
5 Many people who oppose capital punishment argue that it doesn't reduce crime.
6 Some parents let their children do whatever they please.
7 An educated person is one who knows the limits of his knowledge.
8 When a woman works, she should be paid whatever a man would be paid for the same work.
9 What we would like to do and what we can do are seldom the same thing.
10 One of the most valuable talents a writer can have is that of never using two words when one will do.

Clausal sentence classification. The number of main or subordinate clauses in a sentence determines its classification: simple, compound, complex, or compound-complex.

A **simple sentence** has a single main clause.

The wind blew.

Note that a sentence remains a simple sentence even though the subject, the verb, or both are compounded.

The cat and the dog fought.
The dog barked and growled.
The cat and the dog snarled and fought.

A **compound sentence** has two or more main clauses.

The wind blew and the leaves fell.

A **complex sentence** has one main clause and one or more subordinate clauses.

When the wind blew, the leaves fell.

A **compound-complex sentence** contains two or more main clauses and one or more subordinate clauses.

When the sky darkened, the wind blew and the leaves fell.

EXERCISE 1d(3)   In the following sentences, underline each main clause once, each subordinate clause twice, and indicate whether the sentence is simple, compound, complex, or compound-complex.

 1 When the professor told his class he was retiring, they applauded.
 2 Teachers advise against cramming for an exam, but it's better than flunking.
 3 Though I enjoy the country, bugs scare me and flowers make me sneeze.
 4 Before they are elected, politicians always promise to cut taxes, yet after they are elected, they seldom do.
 5 The judge wondered why the jury had deliberated so long.
 6 An addict needs more and more heroin, and needs it all the time.
 7 John and Judy, who enjoy skiing, are disappointed when the snowfall is light.
 8 The judge wondered why the members of the jury were deliberating so long and when they would return their verdict.
 9 Whenever you leave, please let me know where you are going.
10 Barking and wagging his tail violently, the dog exploded into the room and knocked everything off the table.

2

2 CASE **CA**

Case shows the function of nouns and pronouns in a sentence. In the sentence *He gave me a week's vacation,* the **subjective case** form *he* indicates that the pronoun is being used as the subject; the **objective case** form *me* shows that the pronoun is an object; the **possessive case** form *week's* indicates that the noun is a possessive.

Case endings were important in early English, but Modern English retains only a few remnants of this complicated system. Nouns have only two case forms, the possessive *(student's)* and a common form *(student)* that serves all other functions. The personal pronouns *I, we, he, she,* and *they* and the relative or interrogative pronoun *who* have three forms: subjective, possessive, and objective. The personal pronouns *you* and *it* have distinctive forms in the possessive.

PERSONAL PRONOUNS

	SUBJECTIVE	POSSESSIVE	OBJECTIVE
Singular			
FIRST PERSON	I	my, mine	me
SECOND PERSON	you	your, yours	you
THIRD PERSON	he, she, it	his, her, hers, its	him, her, it
Plural			
FIRST PERSON	we	our, ours	us
SECOND PERSON	you	your, yours	you
THIRD PERSON	they	their, theirs	them

RELATIVE OR INTERROGATIVE PRONOUN

Singular	who	whose	whom
Plural	who	whose	whom

2a

2a Subjective case

We use the subjective pronoun for the subjects of all verbs and for all pronouns after all forms of the verb *be* such as *is, are, were,* or *have been.* Speakers of English are unlikely to say or write "Us are happy" or "Him is going away." But compound subjects and some constructions in which the subject is not easily recognized sometimes cause problems.

1   Use the subjective pronoun form in all parts of a compound subject.

He and *she* wanted to go to the circus.
Jack and *she* went to the circus, but Bill and *I* worked.

2   After the conjunctions *than* and *as,* use the subjective form of the pronoun if it is the subject of an understood verb.

She gets her work done faster than *I.* [*I* is the subject of *get mine done,* which is understood by the reader.]
We are as rich as *they* [are].

3   Use the subjective form of a pronoun in an appositive describing a subject or a subject complement. An appositive is a word or phrase set beside a noun or pronoun that identifies or explains it by renaming it.

We three, *Joe, Mary, and I,* graduated together. [*Joe, Mary, and I* is an appositive describing the subject *We three.*]
We students had worked together for two years. [Not *Us students. Students* is an appositive defining the pronoun *we.*]

4   Use the subjective forms of the relative pronoun *who* and *whoever* when they serve as subjects of a clause.

The man *who* came to dinner stayed a month. [*Who* is the subject of *came* in the clause *who came to dinner.*]
Whoever sees the movie will enjoy it. [*Whoever* is the subject of the verb *sees* in the clause *whoever sees the movie.*]

The form of the pronoun is always determined by its function in its own clause. If it serves as subject of its clause, be sure to use the subjective form even though the whole clause may be the object of a verb or preposition.

No one can predict *who* will be appointed. [*Who* is the subject of *will be appointed.* The clause *who will be appointed* is the object of the verb *predict.*]
The owner offered a reward to *whoever* caught the escaped lion. [The entire clause is the object of the preposition *to. Whoever* is the subject of the clause.]

Note that the form of the pronoun used as subject will not be changed when such expressions as *I think* and *he says* come between the subject and its verb.

We invited only the people *who* he said were his friends. [*Who* is the subject of *were.*]

Barbara is a woman *who* I think deserves praise. [*Who* is the subject of *deserves.*]

Who do you think will buy Joe's car? [*Who* is the subject of *will buy.*]

If you are not sure which form to use in sentences such as these, try testing by temporarily omitting the interrupting words.

Barbara is a woman (who, whom) deserves praise.

(Who, whom) will buy Joe's car?

The test will help you determine in each case whether the pronoun *who* is the subject of the verb in the subordinate clause.

5   In writing, use the subjective case of the personal pronoun after forms of the verb *be*, except in dialogue.

It's me, using the objective form of the pronoun, is generally used by speakers in all but the most formal situations, and *it's him, her, us, them* are increasingly common. In writing, these simple conversational constructions seldom occur except in dialogue. When they do, choose between the formal *It's I* and the conversational *It's me* depending upon the character whose speech you are quoting.

Except in dialogue, standard written English requires the subjective case of pronouns after the forms of *be*.

It was *she* who determined the agenda of the committee, not *they*, the other committee members.

It was *they*, however, who determined the final committee recommendations.

6   In writing, use the subjective case for a pronoun following the infinitive *to be* when the infinitive has no expressed subject.

Spoken English commonly uses the objective case of the pronoun in this construction. (See **2c5** for the case of the pronoun after the infinitive when the subject is expressed.)

WRITTEN   I would not want to be *he*. [The infinitive *to be* has no expressed subject.]

SPOKEN   I would not want to be *him*.

EXERCISE 2a   In the following sentences, correct the errors of case in accordance with formal usage. Be ready to give reasons.

1 She and him were both born under the sign of Libra.

2 The senior cheerleaders, Jan, Eli, and me, attended the banquet.

3 After the flood, the Red Cross gave food to whomever needed it.
4 I would like to be them and camp in the mountains.
5 She may be stronger than me, but I'm smarter than her.
6 Aurelio is the kind of student whom is admired by everybody.
7 It was them who found the abandoned copper mine.
8 At the picnic Gary and me shared some ice cream with a stray bulldog.
9 There will be a place in the orchestra for whomever can play the violin as well as her.
10 The man in the blue sweater is him.

2b Possessive case

1 Generally, use the *s*-possessive *(boy's, Jane's)* with nouns naming living things. With nouns naming inanimate things, the *of*-phrase is sometimes preferred, but the *s*-form occurs very often.

ANIMATE   Jane's hair; an outsider's view; inspector's approval
INANIMATE the point of the joke; the wheel of the aircraft; the name of the paper; the city's newsstands; the magazine's tone

The *s*-possessive is commonly used in expressions that indicate time *(moment's notice, year's labor)* and in many familiar phrases *(life's blood, heart's content)*. Which possessive form to use may also depend on sound or rhythm: The *s*-possessive is more terse than the longer, more sonorous *of*-phrase (the President's signature, the signature of the President).

2 In formal English use the possessive case for a noun or pronoun preceding a gerund. In informal English, however, the objective case rather than the possessive case is often found before a gerund.

FORMAL   What was the excuse for *his* being late?
INFORMAL What was the excuse for *him* being late?

FORMAL   He complained of *Roy's* keeping the money.
INFORMAL He complained of *Roy* keeping the money.

Even in formal English the objective case is frequently used with plural nouns.

The police prohibited *children* playing in the street.

The choice of case sometimes depends on the meaning the writer intends to convey.

Imagine *his* playing the violin. [The act of playing the violin is empha-sized.]

Imagine *him* playing the violin. [The emphasis is on *him*. *Playing* is here used as a participle modifying *him*.]

And note the difference in the meaning of the following sentences:

I hate that *woman* riding a bicycle.
I hate that *woman's* riding a bicycle.

Revise such sentences to ensure clarity.

I hate that woman who is riding a bicycle.
I hate the way that woman rides a bicycle.

3   Use *which* to refer to impersonal antecedents. How-ever, substitute *whose* where the phrase *of which* would be awkward.

We saw a house *whose* roof was falling in. [Compare: *We saw a house the roof of which was falling in.*]

This is the car *whose* steering wheel broke off when the driver was going seventy miles an hour. [Compare: *This is the car the steering wheel of which broke off when the driver was going seventy miles an hour.*]

2c   Objective case

Objective pronoun forms are used for the objects of all verbs, verbals, and prepositions.

OBJECT OF VERB	The doctor sent *her* home.
	Our friends visited *us*.
OBJECT OF VERBAL	Visiting *them* was pleasant. [Object of ger-und *visiting*]
	I wanted to send *him* away. [Object of in-finitive *to send*]
OBJECT OF PREPOSITION	Forward the mail to *me*.
	She must choose between *us*.

Problems in the use of the objective pronoun forms are likely to occur only with the same kinds of constructions that cause problems in the use of the subjective pronouns. (See **2a.**)

1   Use the objective pronoun forms in all parts of a com-pound object.

He found Tom and *me* at home. [Not *Tom and I*. *Me* is a part of a compound object of the verb *found*.]

They must choose between you and *me*. [Not *between you and I*. *Me* is a part of a compound object of the preposition *between*.]

2 After the conjunctions *than* and *as,* use the objective pronoun if it is the object of an understood verb.

She needs him more than [she needs] *me*.
I notified him as well as [I notified] *her*.

3 Use the objective form of a pronoun in an appositive describing an object.

Their friends invited them—Jerry and *her*. [*Jerry and her* is an appositive describing *them*.]

4 Standard written English requires *whom* for all objects.

Whom are you discussing? [*Whom* is the object of the verb *are discussing*.]
Whom are you looking for? [*Whom* is the object of the preposition *for*.]

Speakers at all levels of usage commonly use *who* in such constructions unless it immediately follows a preposition.

SPOKEN   Who are you discussing?
SPOKEN   Who are you looking for?
SPOKEN   For whom are you looking?

In subordinate clauses, use *whom* and *whomever* for all objects. Remember that the case of the relative pronoun in a subordinate clause depends upon its function in the clause and not upon the function of the whole clause.

The visitors *whom* we had expected did not come. [*Whom* is the object of the verb *had expected*. The clause *whom we had expected* modifies visitors.]
Whomever we asked wanted more money than we could afford. [*Whomever* is the object of the verb *asked* in the clause *whomever we asked*. The entire clause is the subject of the sentence.]

5 When the infinitive *to be* has an expressed subject, both the subject and the object of the infinitive are in the objective case.

He took *him* to be *me*. [*Him* is the subject of the infinitive; *me* is the object.]

2c

EXERCISE 2b–c   In the following sentences, correct the errors of case in accordance with formal usage. Be ready to give reasons.

1 We appreciated him showing Jill and I the shortest route to Dallas.
2 The shortstop's error allowed Steve and I to score.
3 Just between you and I and the gatepost, her new dog has fleas.
4 The yoga teacher showed the three new students, Ian, Mary, and I, how to do a shoulder stand.
5 Who is Freda playing chess with?
6 Many of we birdwatchers were in the woods before daybreak.
7 I telephoned her as well as he.
8 We enjoyed seeing she and my cousin.
9 I thought them playing golf in a thunderstorm was foolish.
10 The rescue party found Rick and he in a hidden cave.

EXERCISE 2a–c   In the following paragraph, correct the errors in case forms in accordance with formal usage. Be prepared to give reasons for your revisions.

Last night three of we avid moviegoers, Ike, Len, and me, went to the Palace Theater to see Charlie Chaplin's last silent film, *City Lights*. Chaplin, whom Ike and me think is even funnier than Buster Keaton, makes friends with an eccentric millionaire, whom, it seems, is likable only when he is drunk. The other main character, who is more congenial than him, is a blind flower girl who wants a rich, respectable boyfriend and mistakenly takes Charlie, the poor tramp, to be he. There is a sentimental attachment between she and him, at least until she regains her eyesight and sees whom he really is. Ike disagreed with Len and I about which scene was the funniest. Ike liked the opening sequence in which several dignitaries, whom we think are city officials, unveil the Statue to Prosperity and find Charlie, the penniless tramp, asleep on the statue. They are humiliated by him spoiling the ceremony. Len and me liked the scene in which Charlie, whom is driving a Rolls-Royce belonging to the millionaire, stops the car and, not being as proud as him, picks up a discarded cigar butt.

3

3 ADJECTIVES AND ADVERBS **AD**

Adjectives and adverbs are modifying words; that is, they are words that limit or qualify the meaning of other words. Adjectives modify nouns, and they are usually placed either immediately before or immediately after the word they modify.

Adverbs normally modify verbs, adjectives, and other adverbs, although they may sometimes modify whole sentences. When they modify adjectives or other adverbs, they are adjacent to the words they modify. When they modify verbs, they are frequently, but not always, adjacent to the verbs.

Adverbs qualify the meaning of the words they modify by indicating such things as *when, where, how, why, in what order,* or *how often.*

The office closed *yesterday.* [*Yesterday* indicates when.]

Deliver all mail *here.* [*Here* indicates where.]

She replied *quickly* and *angrily.* [*Quickly* and *angrily* describe how she replied.]

Consequently, I left. [*Consequently* describes why.]

He *seldom* did any work. [*Seldom* indicates how often.]

Most adverbs are distinguished from their corresponding adjectives by the ending *-ly: strong-strongly, happy-happily, doubtful-doubtfully, hasty-hastily, mad-madly.* But the *-ly* ending is not a dependable indication of the adverb since some adverbs have two forms *(quick, quickly; slow, slowly);* others have the same form as adjectives *(fast, much, late, well);* and some adjectives also end in *-ly.* (See Section **39,** "Vocabulary," for a discussion of the ways adjectives are formed from nouns.)

Most uses of adjectives and adverbs are common to both standard and nonstandard English and to all levels. But formal English makes more frequent use of distinctive adverb forms than ordinary conversation does. Since certain distinctions in the use of adjectives and adverbs are especially clear markers of differences between standard and nonstandard, and between formal and informal English, they must be observed closely.

Where there is a choice between a form with *-ly* and a form without it, formal English prefers the *-ly* form—*runs quickly* rather than *runs quick, eats slowly* rather than *eats slow*—even though the shorter forms are widely used in informal English, particularly in such commands as *Drive slow.* Note particularly that *good* and *bad* as adverbs are nonstandard. The sentence *He talks good but writes bad* is nonstandard. Standard English requires *He talks well but writes badly.*

3a Use an adverb, not an adjective, to modify a verb.

INCORRECT   He writes *careless.*

CORRECT   He writes *carelessly.* [The adverb *carelessly* is needed to modify the verb *writes.*]

INCORRECT   She talks *modest.*

CORRECT   She talks *modestly.* [The adverb is needed to modify the verb.]

3b Use an adverb, not an adjective, to modify another adverb or an adjective.

INCORRECT	He was *terrible* wounded.
CORRECT	He was *terribly* wounded. [The adverb *terribly* is needed to modify the adjective *wounded*.]
INCORRECT	She works *considerable* harder than he does.
CORRECT	She works *considerably* harder than he does. [The adverb *considerably* is needed to modify the other adverb *harder*.]

The use of adjectives in place of adverbs is more common in conversation than in writing. The use of the adjective *real* as an emphatic *very* to modify adjectives and adverbs is heard at all levels of speech.

FORMAL	You will hear from me *very* soon.
COLLOQUIAL*	You will hear from me *real* soon.

3c Use an adjective to modify the subject after a linking verb.

The common **linking verbs** are *be, become, appear, seem* and the verbs pertaining to the senses: *look, smell, taste, sound, feel.* Predicate adjectives after such verbs refer back to the subject and should be in adjective form. In each of the following sentences, for example, the predicate adjective modifies the subject. The verb simply links the two.

Jane looks *tired* tonight. [*Tired* modifies *Jane*.]
The butter smells *sour*. [*Sour* modifies *butter*.]

One of the most frequent errors in this construction is *I feel badly* in place of the correct subject/linking-verb/predicate-adjective form *I feel bad.* Though *badly* is common even in educated speech, *bad* is strongly preferred by many speakers.

FORMAL	He feels *bad* [ill].
COLLOQUIAL	He feels *badly*.
FORMAL	He felt *bad* about it.
COLLOQUIAL	He felt *badly* about it.

*We use the term *colloquial* to signify the qualities of familiar spoken English.

3d Use an adverb after the verb if the modifier describes the manner of the action of the verb.

He looked *suspiciously* at me. [The adverb *suspiciously* modifies the verb *looked*. Contrast *He looked suspicious to me.*]

The thief felt *carefully* under the pillow. [The adverb *carefully* modifies the verb *felt*.]

In these examples the verbs *look* and *feel* express action, and must be modified by adverbs. But in constructions like *She looks tired* or *He feels well*, the verbs serve, not as words of action, but as links between the subject and the predicate adjective. The choice of adjective or adverb thus depends on the function and meaning of the verb—in other words, on whether or not the verb is being used as a linking verb. Ask yourself whether you want a modifier for the subject or for the verb.

EXERCISE 3a–d In the following sentences, correct in accordance with formal usage any errors in the use of adjectives and adverbs.

1 Tom is working regular at the shoe factory.
2 Some medicines taste bitterly.
3 We were reasonable careful using the chain saw.
4 Marie danced very graceful in the ballet.
5 The old couple were utter surprised by the anniversary party.
6 The defendant replied negative to the lawyer's questions.
7 The traffic sounds loudly to the residents of Main Street.
8 A Pawnee scout watched intent the wagon train in the valley.
9 The children were sure happy riding the carousel.
10 A young frog looked curious at the dragonfly.

3e Distinguish between the comparative and superlative forms of adjectives and adverbs.

Adjectives and adverbs show degrees of quality or quantity by means of their positive, comparative, and superlative forms. The **positive** form *(slow, quickly)* expresses no comparison at all. The **comparative,** formed by adding *-er* or by prefixing *more* to the positive form *(slower, more quickly)*, expresses a greater degree or makes a comparison. The **superlative,** formed by adding *-est* or by putting *most* before the positive form *(slowest, most quickly)*, indicates the greatest degree of a

3e

quality or quantity among three or more persons or things. Some common adjectives and adverbs retain old irregular forms (*good, better, best; badly, worse, worst*).

Whether to use *more* or *most* before the adjective or adverb or to add the *-er, -est* endings depends on the number of syllables in the word. Most adjectives and a few adverbs of one syllable form the comparative and superlative with *-er* and *-est*. Adjectives of two syllables often have variant forms (*fancier, more fancy; laziest, most lazy*). Adjectives and adverbs of three or more syllables always take *more* and *most* (*more beautiful, most regretfully*). Where there is a choice, select the form that sounds better or that is better suited to the rhythm of the sentence.

Some adjectives and adverbs, such as *unique, empty, dead, perfect, round,* are sometimes thought of as absolute in their meaning and thus not able to be logically compared. Logically, a room is either *empty* or *not empty,* a person is either *dead* or *alive.* Nevertheless, phrases such as "emptier than," "more perfect than," and "more dead than alive" are common in speech and very informal writing.

FORMAL	His diving form is *more nearly perfect* than mine.
INFORMAL	His diving form is *more perfect* than mine.
FORMAL	The new stadium is *more clearly circular* than the old one.
INFORMAL	The new stadium is *more circular* than the old one.

3f

3f In formal usage, use the comparative to refer only to one of two objects; use the superlative to refer only to one of three or more objects.

COMPARATIVE	His horse is the *faster* of the two.
SUPERLATIVE	His horse is the *fastest* in the country.
COMPARATIVE	Ruth is the *more* attractive but the *less* good-natured of the twins.
SUPERLATIVE	Ruth is the *most* attractive but the *least* good-natured of his three daughters.

EXERCISE 3e–f In the following sentences, correct in accordance with formal usage any errors in the use of the comparative and superlative forms of adjectives and adverbs.

1 The *Sea Sprite* was the faster of the nine sailboats in the regatta.
2 The Green Phantom's crime was more perfect than the police realized.
3 Sarah is reliabler than the other employees.
4 Your excuse for missing this meeting is the most impossible story I have ever heard.
5 Sanibel is the largest of the two offshore islands.

6 Old Granny Hawks says the more dignity people have, the deader they are.

7 The cars with front-wheel drive are successfuler than many earlier models.

8 Professor Blosser directs the world's most unique cyclotron laboratory.

9 Ruth is the best qualified of the two applicants for the job.

10 The reservoir is more empty than it was a year ago.

3g Avoid the excessive use of nouns to modify other nouns.

The use of nouns to modify other nouns in expressions such as *rock garden, steel mill, silver mine,* and *telephone booth* is very common in English. (See **40c.**) When there is no appropriate adjective form and when the nouns used to modify are short, such constructions are usually clear and concise. But when nouns are used to replace appropriate adjectives or when the series of nouns modifying other nouns is long, such expressions are awkward at best, confusing at worst.

1 Prefer an adjective if there is an appropriate one.

AWKWARD   *Siberia* railroad line

IMPROVED   *Siberian* railroad line

2 Avoid long series of nouns modifying other nouns.

CONFUSING   office management personnel report [A report about the management of office personnel? A report by personnel who are managing an office? Something else?]

CONFUSING   teacher education program analysis [An analysis of a program for educating teachers? An analysis by teachers of an educational program? Or something else?]

EXERCISE 3a–g In the following sentences, correct in accordance with formal usage any errors in the use of adjectives and adverbs.

1 He felt badly about losing his car keys.

2 Public servants should take their responsibilities serious.

3 According to Uncle Zed, the air didn't smell very well at the Garlic Festival.

4 We stopped at a Canada tourist office for information.

5 Our cat Daniel looks suspicious at all stray dogs.

6 The snow is not near as deep as it was last winter.

7 The tall ships sailed majestic into the harbor.

8 Of the two major types of Pacific storms, the typhoon is the most destructive.

9 This lake is called Round Lake because it is the roundest body of water in central Michigan.

10 I quit drinking the ginger ale very sudden when I saw the fly in the ice cube.

4 VERB FORMS **VB**

Of the several different parts of speech in English, verbs are the most complex. They have more forms than any other kind of word, and they can be divided into a number of different kinds according to their forms and uses. Since the terms used to describe these various forms and kinds are frequently used in discussing problems in their use, it is helpful to know them and to understand the distinctions they describe.

This section covers the various forms and kinds of verbs, their function, and some common problems in their use. Section **5** covers the forms, use, and problems of tense, mood, and voice in verbs.

Forms of the verb

All verbs except *be,* which we will discuss separately, have five forms. The first three of these—the plain form, the past tense, and the past participle—are called the **principal parts** of the verb.

A plain form or infinitive. The plain form, sometimes called the **base form,** of the verb is that listed in the dictionary *(work, begin, choose).* This is the form we use with the pronouns *I, we, you,* and *they,* and with all plural nouns to indicate present time or habitual action *(they work, days always end, we choose).* It is also the form we use after all the helping verbs, such as *will, can, must, should,* etc., except the forms of the verb *be.* When this form functions as an infinitive, it is usually preceded by *to: they wanted to work, we needed money to pay our bills.*

A past tense form. This is the form we use to indicate that the action or state of being indicated by the verb occurred at some time in the past. In most verbs it is formed simply by adding *-d* or *-ed* to the plain form: *smoked, planned, worked.* But in about two hundred verbs it is formed in some irregular way, usually by a vowel change: *grow, grew; swim, swam; drive, drove.* (See **4b.**)

A past participle. This is the form we use when we combine the verb with *has, have,* or *had: has worked, have grown, had driven.* It is also used with the forms of *be* to form the **passive voice:** *is defeated, was being driven, were discovered.* (See Section **5.**) In most verbs the past tense and the past participle have the same form: *played, have played; found, has found; slept, had slept.* But about forty-five verbs, including many very common ones such as *become, do, grow, speak,* and *write,* have separate forms for the past participle. (See **4b.**)

An -s form. This is the form we use with the pronouns *he, she,* and *it,* with all singular nouns, and with certain indefinite pronouns such as *each* or *someone* to indicate present time or habitual action: *she asks, the dog bites, someone always wins.* For all verbs except *be* and *have,* this form is made by adding *-s* to the plain form: *asks, bites, wins.* For the verbs *be* and *have* the *-s* forms are *is* and *has.*

A present participle. This is the form we use after *am, is, are, was,* or *were* to indicate action continuing at the time indicated: *I am working, he is playing, they are eating, the corn was growing.* For all verbs this form is made by adding *-ing* to the plain form.

The five forms of two verbs are summarized below:

		Regular verb	*Irregular verb*
PRINCIPAL PARTS	Plain form	work	begin
	Past tense	worked	began
	Past participle	worked	begun
	-s form	works	begins
	Present participle	working	beginning

The verb *be*. The verb *be* is different from any other in having eight forms, three more than any other English verb. Unlike any other verb, it has three present tense forms *(am, are,* and *is),* all different from the plain form *be;* and it has separate singular and plural forms *(was* and *were)* in the past tense. In addition, it has a present participle *(being)* and a past participle *(been).*

Kinds of verbs

Verbs can be divided into various kinds according to main forms and uses.

Regular and irregular verbs. Verbs are either regular or irregular according to the way they form their past tense and past participle.

A **regular verb** forms the past tense and past participle simply by adding *-d* or *-ed* to the plain form: *complete, completed, completed; repeat, repeated, repeated.*

An **irregular verb** forms the past tense and/or past participle in some unusual way, usually by changing an internal vowel. In many irregular verbs, although the internal vowel is changed, the past tense and past participle have the same form: *keep, kept, kept; sleep, slept, slept.* About forty-five, however, have three distinct forms: *freeze, froze, frozen; give, gave, given.* About twenty irregular verbs keep the same form for all three principal parts: *cut, cut, cut; hit, hit, hit.* Although there are in all only about two hundred irregular verbs in modern English, they include a great many we use most frequently. (See **4b** for a list of the most common.)

Main and auxiliary verbs. In a verb phrase such as *is going, had been winning, must have been found,* or *will be helped,* the last verb form indicates the principal meaning and is called the **main verb.** All other verb forms in the phrase indicate special shades of meaning, such as those of time, obligation, and possibility, and are called **auxiliary verbs** or helping verbs.

Auxiliary verbs make up a small group of function words that may be divided into subgroups according to the kinds of function they perform. All auxiliary or helping verbs except *be, have,* and *do* are marked by the fact that they have only one *form.*

1 The forms of *be (am, is, are, was, were, been,* and *being)* and of *have (has, have, had, having)* combine with main verbs to indicate tense and voice (see Section **5**) as in *have worked, were studying, is planned, had been defeated.* The auxiliaries *will* and *shall* are used to indicate future time as in *will go.*

2 The auxiliaries *can, could, may, might, must, ought (to), should,* and *would,* sometimes called **modal auxiliaries,** combine with main verbs to indicate ability, obligation, permission, possibility, etc.: *can go, could have gone, must go.*

3 The auxiliary *do* is used to form questions and negative statements and to give emphasis, as in *Does she work; She did not work yesterday; She does work hard.*

Transitive, intransitive, and linking verbs. Verbs may be grouped as intransitive, transitive, or linking according to whether they do or do not pass their action to another word, called their object, or whether they are followed by a word which refers back to the subject, called a subject complement. (See also Section **1.**)

Intransitive verbs are those that are not followed by any object or complement.

The church bells rang.
The book lay on the table.

Transitive verbs are those that are followed by one or more objects.

The hurricane struck the coast.
The company gave its workers notice. [*Workers* is an indirect object, *notice* a direct object.]
The storm made the roads impassable. [*Roads* is a direct object, *impassable* an object complement modifying *roads.*]

Linking verbs are those that are followed by a subject complement, that is, a word that renames or describes the subject.

Mata Hari was a German spy. [*Spy* describes *Mata Hari.*]
His allowance seems generous. [*Generous* describes *allowance.*]
The old man remained active. [*Active* describes *old man.*]

Many verbs may be used as either intransitive or transitive according to the sentence in which they are used.

He drove the car to work every day.
He always drives carefully.

Finite and nonfinite verbs. A **finite verb** can serve without an auxiliary as the main verb in a sentence; a **nonfinite verb** cannot. We can use *drive* as a main verb; *the men always drive.* But we cannot make a sentence with *infinitives* or *participles,* which are nonfinite verb forms: *the men to drive, the men driving,* and *the men driven* are not sentences. We must add an auxiliary to such forms to make them capable of forming sentences: *the men have to drive, the men are driving, the men were driven.*

It is usually possible to distinguish between finite and nonfinite verb forms by the fact that finite verbs change form in the present tense according to whether their subjects are singular or plural: *the bell rings* but *the bells ring.* In finite verb phrases, the auxiliaries *be, have* and *do* change form according to whether the subject is singular or plural: *the bell is ringing* but *the bells are ringing.* Compare the finite and nonfinite verbs in the following lists. Note particularly that all the word groups containing a finite verb are complete sentences but that none of those containing only nonfinite verbs are. Note also that the nonfinite verb forms remain unchanged.

FINITE	NONFINITE
The man plans his work.	The man planning his work. . .
The men plan their work.	The men planning their work. . .
The dog has eaten.	The dog having eaten. . .
The dogs have eaten.	The dogs having eaten. . .
She defeats her opponents.	The opponent to defeat. . .
They defeat their opponents.	The opponents to defeat. . .

Problems with verb forms

4a   **Be careful to use the -s and -ed forms of the verb when required.**

Standard English requires the *-s* ending on all present-tense verbs whenever the subject is *he, she,* or *it,* a singular noun, or an indefinite pronoun such as *someone.* Similarly, it requires the *-ed* ending on the past tense and the past participle of all regular verbs.

Writers sometimes fail to use these necessary endings, particularly on verbs in which the ending is not clearly pronounced in speaking. When such endings do not form a separate syllable, as in *attacks, attacked,* the final *-s* and *-d* sounds are likely to be almost entirely lost in speech. When the verb endings are immediately followed by a word beginning with a very similar sound, as in *used to, supposed to,* or *asks Steven,* the final sound of the verb is likely to be almost completely obscured.

While these endings may give any writer occasional difficulty, the *-s* ending is likely to be especially troublesome for speakers of dialects that regularly omit it, using such forms as *she go, he work, the man work.* All writers, in their proofreading, should be alert to the possible omission of these endings; speakers of dialects that regularly omit the *-s* ending may have to proofread their writing with special attention to the problem.

EXERCISE 4a   In the blank spaces in the following sentences, supply the correct form of the verb or verbs given in parentheses at the end of the sentence. If there are two blanks, use the correct form of the first verb in the first space and the second in the second space.

1. Now that Sally is working, it always _____ her father when she _____ him to have lunch with her. (please, ask)

2. Last year, when we _____ near the airport, the low-flying planes often _____ my mother. (live, frighten)

3. Now she _____ what she _____ to do. (do want)

4. Next year, she _____ to go to law school, so she _____
hard. (hope, work)

5. Bill _____ off during yesterday's lecture even though he
_____ hard to stay awake. (doze, try)

4b Distinguish carefully between the principal parts of irregular verbs.

Any writer may occasionally have to check a recent dictionary to be certain of the past tense or the past participle form of an irregular verb he or she seldom uses. But for writers whose spoken dialects regularly use nonstandard verb forms, irregular verbs can be especially troublesome. Such nonstandard forms seldom seriously interfere with meaning: the meaning of *I done, I have did,* or *I have took* is perfectly clear. But nonstandard forms of the irregular verbs are regarded as serious errors, and learning the correct forms is well worth the effort.

Remember that your dictionary lists the principal parts of all irregular verbs, that is, the plain form *(begin),* the past tense *(began),* and the past participle *(begun).* If your dictionary lists only the plain form and one other form *(bend, bent,* for example), the second form will be that of both the past tense and past participle. If the dictionary lists only the plain form, the verb is regular and forms both its past tense and past participle by adding *-d* or *-ed.*

The principal parts of many of the most commonly used irregular verbs are listed below. When two forms are listed, both are acceptable, although the first is that listed first in most dictionaries. Add to the list any other verbs you may have used incorrectly.

Present Infinitive (Plain Form)	Past Tense	Past Participle
beat	beat	beaten
become	became	become
begin	began	begun
bet	bet	bet
bid	bade, bid	bidden, bid
bite	bit	bitten
blow	blew	blown
break	broke	broken
bring	brought	brought
burst	burst	burst
buy	bought	bought
catch	caught	caught
choose	chose	chosen
come	came	come

Present Infinitive (Plain Form)	Past Tense	Past Participle
cut	cut	cut
dive	dived, dove	dived
do	did	done
draw	drew	drawn
drink	drank	drunk
drive	drove	driven
eat	ate	eaten
fall	fell	fallen
feel	felt	felt
find	found	found
fly	flew	flown
forget	forgot	forgot, forgotten
forgive	forgave	forgiven
freeze	froze	frozen
get	got	got, gotten
give	gave	given
go	went	gone
grow	grew	grown
hang (suspend)	hung	hung
hang (execute)	hanged	hanged
hid	hid	hidden
hit	hit	hit
hurt	hurt	hurt
keep	kept	kept
know	knew	known
lead	led	led
leave	left	left
let	let	let
lose	lost	lost
make	made	made
mean	meant	meant
read	read	read
ride	rode	ridden
ring	rang	rung
rise	rose	risen
run	ran	run
see	saw	seen
shake	shook	shaken
shine	shone	shone
sink	sank, sunk	sunk
speak	spoke	spoken
spin	spun	spun
spring	sprang, sprung	sprung
stand	stood	stood
steal	stole	stolen
stink	stank	stunk

Present Infinitive (Plain Form)	Past Tense	Past Participle
strike	struck	struck
swear	swore	sworn
swim	swam	swum
swing	swung	swung
take	took	taken
teach	taught	taught
tear	tore	torn
tell	told	told
think	thought	thought
throw	threw	thrown
wear	wore	worn
weave	wove, weaved	woven, weaved
weep	wept	wept
win	won	won
wind	wound	wound
write	wrote	written

EXERCISE 4b In the blanks in the following sentences, supply the correct forms of the verb or verbs in parentheses at the end of the sentence. If there are two blanks, use the correct form of the first verb in the first space and the second in the second space.

1 Plans for the space launch were _____ last spring. (begin)

2 The church bells _____ daily for two hundred years. (ring)

3 Shirley's friends had all _____ before she arrived. (eat)

4 Although many of the guests had _____ several glasses of beer, there was still plenty _____. (drink, leave)

5 Although Jack had _____ much about his topic, he was not satisfied with the report he had _____. (read, write)

6 Before they _____ in the morning, the pond had _____. (wake, freeze)

7 The child might have _____ if rescuers had not been near. (drown)

8 Soon after the fire started, the rats _____ out of the basement. (come)

9 On its first trial last week, the new speedboat _____ a record. (break)

10 Moses _____ his people follow the Ten Commandments. (bid)

4c Make the standard distinctions between *lie* and *lay*, *sit* and *set*.

These two pairs of irregular verbs are often bothersome. *Lie* and *sit* are always intransitive, which means that they cannot take objects or occur in the passive voice. *Lay* and *set* are always transitive and therefore always must either have objects or be in the passive. The distinction between the verbs in the two pairs continues to be carefully observed in written English, though not always in speech.

The principal parts of *lie*, meaning "recline," are *lie, lay, lain.* The principal parts of *lay*, meaning "place," are *lay, laid, laid.*

LIE

PRESENT	*Lie* down for a while and you will feel better.
PAST	The cat *lay* in the shade and watched the dog carefully.
PRESENT PARTICIPLE	His keys were *lying* on the table where he dropped them.
PAST PARTICIPLE	After he *had lain* down for a while, he felt better.

LAY

PRESENT	*Lay* the book on the table and come here.
PAST	He *laid* the book on the table and walked out the door.
PRESENT PARTICIPLE	*Laying* the book on the table, he walked out the door.
PAST PARTICIPLE	*Having laid* the book on the table, he walked out the door.

The principal parts of *sit* (meaning "occupy a seat") are *sit, sat, sat;* the principal parts of *set* (meaning "put in place") are *set, set, set.*

SIT

PRESENT	*Sit* down and keep quiet.
PAST	The little girl *sat* in the corner for half an hour.
PRESENT PARTICIPLE	*Sitting* down quickly, he failed to see the tack in the chair.

PAST PARTICIPLE	*Having sat* in the corner for an hour, the child was subdued and reasonable.

SET

PRESENT	*Set* the basket on the table and get out.
PAST	Yesterday he *set* the grocery cartons on the kitchen table; today he *set* them on the porch.
PRESENT PARTICIPLE	*Setting* his spectacles on the table, he challenged John to wrestle.
PAST PARTICIPLE	*Having set* the basket of turnips on the porch, Terry went to play the piano.

EXERCISE 4c In sentences 1, 2, and 3 below, supply the correct forms of *lie* or *lay* in the blanks provided. In sentences 4, 5, and 6, supply the correct forms of *sit* or *set*.

1 The trash _____ on the floor all last week; it has often _____ there before.

2 Every day when we came home from work, he _____ down for half an hour.

3 As they took them off the tree, they _____ the Christmas ornaments carefully on the table, but they did not want them to _____ there very long.

4 When he brought the groceries home, he _____ them on the counter and then _____ down at the table with his wife.

5 He said he was sure that he had _____ the vase on the shelf where his mother had told him to _____ it.

6 They had _____ down in the living room to discuss where they could _____ the new chair, which the delivery men had _____ in the garage.

4d Be sure that the main verb in every sentence you write is a finite verb.

Remember that only finite verbs or verb phrases can make assertions and serve as the main verbs of sentences. Nonfinite verb forms—infinitives *(to steal),* present participles *(stealing),* and past participles *(stolen)*—cannot serve as the main verbs of sentences unless they are accompanied by a helping verb. A group of words that has only a nonfinite verb will always be a sentence fragment. (See Section **6** for a full discussion of sentence fragments.)

EXERCISE 4a–c In the blanks in each of the following sentences, supply the correct form of the verb or verbs given in parentheses at the end of the sentence. If there is more than one blank, use the correct form of the first verb in the first blank, the second in the second blank, and so on. If there is more than one blank and only one verb given in parentheses, use the correct forms of that verb in the blanks.

1 Sally had _____ in the sun for an hour when Allen came and

_____ down nearby. (lie or lay)

2 His new shirt _____ badly when he washed it. (shrink)

3 Peter _____ every time he plays poker; he _____ again last night. (win)

4 Betty had _____ three miles daily for two months. (swim)

5 The thief had never _____ anyone where he had _____

the money after he _____ it. (tell, hide, steal)

6 Biff now throws his suit on the chair, but the first year he had it, every

time he _____ it, he _____ it up carefully as soon

as he _____ home. (wear, hang, come)

7 Yesterday I _____ my new car; I wish I could have _____ it last month. (get)

8 After the storm we _____ that the high wind had _____

limbs off several trees and _____ down two others. (find, break, blow)

9 Now she always _____ her father before she _____ the car. (ask, take)

10 The pipes had _____ even though we _____ the

plumber had _____ them when we _____ him to. (freeze, think, fix, ask)

5   VERBS: TENSE, MOOD, AND VOICE **T**

The form of a verb or verb phrase tells us three things about the action or state it names. It tells us what time the action occurs (tense); what the attitude of the speaker or writer is (mood); and whether the subject is performing the action or receiving it (voice).

Tense

Tense is the time of the action or state expressed by the verb. Almost all verbs show the difference between **present** and **past** time by a change in the verb form. All verbs show **future** time by using *shall* or *will* before the infinitive, or plain form, of the verb.

	Regular Verb	Irregular Verb
PRESENT	She walks today.	The sun rises today.
PAST	She walked yesterday.	The sun rose yesterday.
FUTURE	She will walk tomorrow.	The sun will rise tomorrow.

A few verbs have only one form for both present and past time: *burst, cast, hurt, split.* By themselves these verbs cannot show time; to do so, they must depend entirely on modifying words (*I split the wood yesterday*) or auxiliary verbs (*I was splitting the wood*).

In addition to the three tenses, which indicate the natural divisions of time into past, present, and future, all verbs have three **perfect tenses.** The perfect tenses indicate that the action named is completed or finished before a given point in time. Thus, for example, the past perfect tense (*had eaten*) indicates that the action named was completed before another past action: *He had eaten before his sister came home.* The three perfect tenses are formed by using the forms of the auxiliary *have* before the past participle of the main verb. The perfect tense forms of the verbs *work* and *see* are shown in the following:

	Regular Verb	Irregular Verb
PRESENT PERFECT	has or have worked	has or have seen
PAST PERFECT	had worked	had seen
FUTURE PERFECT	will have worked	will have seen

The six tenses, together with the way each is formed, are summarized in the following:

PRESENT	Plain form of verb with *I, we, you, they,* and all plural nouns; *-s* forms of verbs with *he, she, it,* and all singular nouns	I, we, you, they, the men eat he, she, it, the man eats
PAST	Plain form plus *-ed* in regular verbs; internal change in irregular verbs	talked, ate
FUTURE	*Shall* or *will* before plain form of verb	will talk, shall eat
PRESENT PERFECT	*Have* before past participle; *has* with *he, she, it,* and singular nouns	we, you, they, the men have talked/eaten; he, she, it, the man has talked/eaten

PAST PERFECT	*Had* before past participle	had talked/eaten
FUTURE PERFECT	*Shall/will have* before past participle	will have talked/eaten

All six tenses can have **progressive-tense** forms. These progressive forms indicate that the action named is continuing at the time indicated. They are made by using the forms of the auxiliary verb *be* with the *-ing* form of the main verb *(is giving, was winning, have been going)*.

The most common uses of the tenses of the active verb forms are as follows:

Tense	Use	Example
PRESENT	Expressing a present or habitual action	He is *is talking* to the students now. He *talks* to the students at least once every year.
PAST	Expressing an action that was completed in the past	He *talked* to the students yesterday.
FUTURE	Expressing an action yet to come	He *will talk* to the students tomorrow.
PRESENT PERFECT	Usually expressing an action carried out before the present and completed at the present; sometimes expressing an action begun in the past and continuing in the present	He *has talked* to the students before. [Action carried out before the present and now completed] He *has* always *talked* to the students. [Action begun in the past and continuing in the present]
PAST PERFECT	Expressing a past action completed before some other past action	This morning I saw the speaker who *had talked* to the students last month.
FUTURE PERFECT	Expressing an action that will be completed before some future time	He *will have talked* to the students before next Thursday.

For a full synopsis of a regular and an irregular verb, see *Conjugation* in the glossary, p. 516.

Problems with tense

In spite of the relatively complicated tense system, writers whose native language is English ordinarily have few problems in its use. The main problems that occur involve either special uses of the present tense or the choice of the appropriate tense in the subordinate clauses of some complex sentences.

5a Use the present tense to express general truths or accepted facts and to indicate habitual action. Use the present tense in critical writing about literature and the other arts.

GENERAL TRUTHS	All that glitters *is* not gold.
	Corn *grows* rapidly in warm, humid weather.
HABITUAL ACTION	The old man *exercises* daily.
	The bank *closes* at four o'clock.
CRITICAL WRITING	In Dickens' novel *David Copperfield,* David's harsh stepfather *sends* him to London where every day David *works* in a warehouse pasting labels on bottles.
	Jane Austen's use of ironic comment *is* highly effective.

Note that the present tense also often expresses future action, as in *Our trip begins tomorrow.*

5b Be sure that the tenses of verbs are in appropriate sequence.

The term **tense sequence** refers to the relation of the times expressed by the verbs in main and subordinate clauses in a complex sentence. When the verb in the main clause of a complex sentence is in any tense except the past or past perfect, the verb in the subordinate clause will be in whatever tense the meaning requires.

The weather service *predicts* that it *will be* hot again tomorrow. [The prediction occurs in the present but refers to the future.]
Our friends *will* not *know* that we *were* here unless we *leave* them a note. [Future, past, present]

If the verb in a main clause is in the past or past perfect tense, the verb in a subordinate clause following it will usually be in the past or past perfect tense, unless the subordinate clause states a general truth.

She *said* that she *wanted* [not *wants*] to live in an apartment.
He *thought* that he *had left* his coat in the car.

The owners *discovered* later that the fire *had destroyed* their house. [The destruction of the house occurred at a time before the owner's discovery of it.]

BUT   The child *discovered* painfully that fire *burns*. [Here *fire burns* states a general truth. Thus the verb is in the present even though the child's discovery occurred in the past.]

EXERCISE 5a–b In the following sentences, choose the verb form entered in parentheses that is in appropriate sequence. Be prepared to explain your choice.

1 He had never been told that the earth (revolved, revolves) around the sun.
2 They did not know what (has become, had become) of him, for he (has left, had left) over two hours before.
3 Joe made his way slowly down the steep slope, fearing that he (would fall, would have fallen) if he (moved, had moved) faster.
4 I (have been, had been) in college for three terms before I decided to major in computer science.
5 At the party we saw many people we (have seen, had seen) the week before.
6 Many people wished he never (made, had made) the speech.
7 He will be entitled to a vacation as soon as he (finished, has finished) his present assignment.
8 Of the movies I saw last year, *Holocaust* was the one I (enjoyed, have enjoyed) most.
9 We later learned that he (had, had had) to stay at the hospital for an hour even though he (had not been, has not been) injured.
10 In one of his most famous poems, Robert Frost says that good fences (make, made) good neighbors.

5c Use present infinitives and participles to express action occurring at the same time as or later than that of the main verb. Use perfect infinitives and past or perfect participles to express action earlier than that of the main verb.

The infinitive and participle forms are as follows:

	Infinitives	*Participles*
PRESENT	to begin	beginning
PAST	——	begun
PERFECT	to have begun	having begun

Infinitives and participles express only a time that is relative to the time indicated by the main verb of the sentence in which they are used. A present infinitive or participle expresses an action occurring at the same time as or later than that indicated by the main verb. A perfect infinitive or a past or perfect participle expresses a time that is earlier than that indicated by the main verb.

> She *wants* [*wanted, had wanted, will want*] *to study* law. [The present infinitive *to study* indicates the same time or time later than that of the main verb *want.*]
>
> She *would have* preferred *to study* [not *to have studied*] law.
>
> She *was* [*is, will be*] glad *to have studied* law. She would like *to have studied* law. [The perfect infinitive *to have studied* indicates that the study occurred earlier than the time indicated by the main verbs *was, is, will be*, or *would like.*]
>
> *Wanting* to study law, she *works* [*worked, had worked, will work*] hard. [The present participle *wanting* indicates the same time or a time later than that of the main verb.]
>
> *Having passed* the entrance exam, she is *celebrating* [*has celebrated, will celebrate*]. The perfect participle *having passed* indicates that passing the exam occurs before the celebrating.]
>
> *Defeated* in the election, the candidate *retired* [*has retired, had retired, will retire*] from politics. [The past participle *defeated* indicates that the defeat occurred before the time indicated by the main verb *retire.*]

EXERCISE 5c   In the following sentences, choose the infinitive or participle form that is in appropriate sequence. Be prepared to explain your choice.

1 He would have liked (to finish, to have finished) his work before going to bed.

2 They know him (to be, to have been) a concert pianist before his accident.

3 (Waving, Having waved) his arms wildly, the man standing by the road clearly wanted help.

4 In college, I hope (to study, to have studied) subjects which will be useful to me later.

5 They should not have tried (to drive, to have driven) the entire distance without stopping.

Mood

The mood of a verb indicates whether the speaker or writer regards the action named by the verb as a fact, a command, or a wish, request, or condition contrary to fact.

English has three moods: the **indicative,** used for ordinary statements and questions (*He is happy, Is he happy*); the **imperative,** used for commands (*Be happy*); and the **subjunctive,** used to express conditions contrary to fact (*If he were happy*) and in clauses following certain verbs. Except for the subjunctive, mood causes writers few problems.

Special forms for the subjunctive have almost disappeared from modern English. The few that do survive are those that appear in *if*

5c

clauses expressing unreal conditions; in *that* clauses after verbs expressing requests, recommendations, and demands; and in a few formal idioms.

5d

5d Use the subjunctive to express conditions contrary to fact.

If the rose bush *were* healthy, it would have more buds. [The bush is not healthy.]

Last year, the bush looked as though it *were* going to die. [But it didn't die.]

Helen could settle the argument if she *were* here. [But she isn't here.]

Note that not all clauses beginning with *if* automatically express a condition contrary to fact.

If my experiment is successful, I will prove my point. [Here the clause beginning with *if* merely states a condition that, if met, will prove the point.]

5e

5e Use the subjunctive in *that* clauses after verbs expressing wishes, commands, requests, or recommendations.

I wish I *were* younger. [*That* unexpressed]

The law requires that there *be* a prompt trial.

I move that the meeting *be* adjourned.

Resolved, that Mr. Smith *investigate* our finances.

His parents asked that he *remain* home.

5f

5f Be aware that the subjunctive is called for in a few surviving idioms.

Far be it from me.   Long live the Republic!
Suffice it to say.   Come what may.
Heaven help us!   Be that as it may.

Note that except in surviving idioms even the few remaining uses of the subjunctive observed above are often replaced in speech and informal writing by alternative forms. Compare *I wish I was taller, The law requires a prompt trial,* or *His parents asked him to remain at home* with the examples above. In more formal writing, the subjunctive remains quite firm.

EXERCISE 5d–f In the following sentences, choose the correct verb form. Be prepared to explain your choice.

1 The actor who played Roosevelt made the audience feel as if he (was, were) actually Roosevelt.

2 The crowd demanded that the criminal (is, be) executed.
3 If I (was, were) in Alaska, I would be colder than I am now.
4 If the bill (is, be) unpaid this month, our credit rating will be lowered.
5 My father urged that I (stay, stays) in college for the rest of the term.

Voice

Voice refers to the ability of transitive verbs to show whether the subject performs or receives the action named by the verb. When the subject performs the action, the verb is in the **active voice.** When it receives the action, the verb is in the **passive voice.**

ACTIVE   The elephant *dragged* his trainer.
         The poison *drove* its victim mad.
PASSIVE The trainer *was dragged* by the elephant.
         The victim *was driven* mad by the poison.

The passive voice is formed by using the appropriate form of the verb *be (am, is, are, was, were, been, being)* with the past participle of the main verb: *was driven, will have been driven, is being driven.* Note that although other auxiliaries may be included in the passive verb phrase, some form of the verb *be* must always come immediately before the past participle of the main verb.

Only **transitive verbs,** that is, verbs that can take an object, can show both active and passive voices. We can say *The student wrote the paper* or *The paper was written by the student,* but only *He talked,* not *He was talked.*

Most sentences in writing use verbs in the active voice, which is almost always more direct, more economical, and more forceful than the passive. But in two situations the passive voice is both useful and natural.

1   Use the passive when the actor is not known. Consider the following:

Peter L. Little was attacked and badly beaten while walking through Eastern Park about 11:15 last night.
The play was first performed in 1591.

In the first of these, since the writer presumably does not know who attacked Peter L. Little, he is forced to use the passive or to resort to some much less economical alternative such as *Some person or persons unknown attacked and badly beat. . . .* The second sentence suggests that though there is a record of the play's performance, there is none of its performers.

2   Use the passive when the receiver of the action is more important than the actor. Consider the following:

The new bridge was completed in April.

The experiment was finished on June 16; on June 17 the conclusions were reviewed by the advisory board and reported immediately to the Pentagon.

In such sentences as these, we have little interest in who completed the bridge or who performed the experiment and reported the results; the important things are the bridge and the experiment.

Problems in the use of voice include awkward and ineffective shifts from one voice to another, and the unnecessary or weak use of the passive. Both are problems of effectiveness in writing rather than of grammar. For awkward shifts in voice, see Section **10a.** For the weak use of the passive voice, see Section **36e.**

EXERCISE 5a–f   In each of the following sentences choose the correct form of the verbs, infinitives, or participles from each of the pairs given in parentheses.

1   The missing girl is reported (to be thumbing, to have been thumbing) a ride on the highway yesterday afternoon.

2   Though she hated (to go, to have gone) back to work, she should not (be, have been) too unhappy, since she (has had, had had) a full month's vacation.

3   Ever since I was ten years old, I (was, have been) riding horses.

4   The instructor will be very frustrated when he (finds, found) that five students have failed (to complete, to have completed) last week's assignment.

5   She was saving her money so that she (can go, could go) to California.

6   They thought it (is, was) better to drive than to go by train.

7   I wish I (was, were) going with you to Mexico.

8   Would he be as willing as he says, if he (was, were) being drafted?

9   The boy learned very early in life that some dogs (bite, bit).

10   (Having walked, walking) several miles, the old woman, exhausted, (decides, decided) to rest.

BASIC SENTENCE FAULTS
SEN FLT

The purpose of writing is to communicate facts, feelings, attitudes, and ideas clearly and effectively. Having something to say, thinking about it clearly, developing general ideas with ample fresh, specific, and accurate details—these are all indispensable to effective writing. So are many details of basic sentence structure and punctuation. Unless sentences observe the limits of English grammar and conform to the conventions of written English, they are not likely to be read, even if the ideas are interesting and the writing vivid. Readers confronted, for instance, with *In Yellowstone Park driving down the road some bears were seen having climbed down from the trees* don't judge effectiveness. They worry about basic grammatical difficulties that make the statement an incoherent mishmash. And writers who wish to be read must worry about them, too.

6   6   SENTENCE FRAGMENT **FRAG**

The usual sentence contains a subject and a verb and at least one independent clause. In writing, we indicate sentences by capitalizing the first word and placing appropriate end punctuation, usually a period, after the last. Any group of words that is set off as a sentence but that lacks a subject, a verb, or an independent clause is a **sentence fragment.**

Such fragments are common in speech, and they are sometimes used for certain special purposes in writing. But in most writing, incomplete sentences, or fragments, are very infrequent. The subject-verb sentence is what readers expect, and they will want some special effectiveness if that expectation is not met.

6a   Avoid punctuating phrases, dependent clauses, and other fragments as sentences.

Most fragments in student writing are phrases, clauses, and occasionally other constructions that depend for their meaning on independent clauses immediately preceding them. The most common types of fragments, together with revisions, are illustrated on pages 61–63. A fragment is usually an improperly punctuated part of the sentence that precedes or follows it. Thus the fragment can almost always be revised by joining it to that sentence, although other revisions may be possible and sometimes desirable.

1 Prepositional phrase. Prepositional phrases consist of a preposition, its object, and any modifiers of the object: *over the mountains, during the long intermission, after eating dinner.* Prepositional phrases usually serve as modifiers. (See **1c.**) The prepositional phrases in the following examples are italicized.

FRAGMENT   Lisa and Sally had just come home. *From their trip to New Orleans, Miami, and Atlanta.*

REVISED   Lisa and Sally had just come home *from their trip to New Orleans, Miami, and Atlanta.*

FRAGMENT   There must always be secrets. *Even between you and me.*

REVISED   There must always be secrets, *even between you and me.*

There must always be secrets—*even between you and me.*

[Here both revisions join the prepositional phrase introduced by *between* with the main statement, to which it clearly belongs. But the dash gives greater emphasis to the phrase. See **23b.**]

2 Verbal phrase. Verbal phrases consist of a verbal (infinitive, participle, or gerund), its object, and any modifiers of the object or verbal. (See **1c.**) The verbal phrases in the following examples are italicized.

FRAGMENT   The Dean finally agreed to see me. *To talk about my financial problems.* [Infinitive phrase]

REVISED   The Dean finally agreed to see me *to talk about my financial problems.*

FRAGMENT   The Egyptian pyramids are a remarkable accomplishment. *Showing much knowledge of the laws of physics.* [Participial phrase]

REVISED   The Egyptian pyramids are a remarkable accomplishment, *showing much knowledge of the laws of physics.*

FRAGMENT   The citizens voted against the proposed town budget. *Being angry at the continued tax increases.* [Participial phrase]

REVISED   The citizens voted against the proposed town budget, *being angry at the continued tax increases.*

The citizens voted against the proposed town budget; they were angry at the continued tax increases.

[This second revision changes the participial phrase beginning with *being* to an independent clause. Thus the two sentences could be separated by a period, but the semicolon suggests the close relationship between the clauses. See **21b.**]

3 Subordinate clause. Subordinate clauses are usually introduced by such subordinating conjunctions as *after, although, because, when, where, while,* or *until* or by a relative pronoun such as *who, which,* or *that.* Subordinate clauses that occur as fragments are almost always modifiers, which properly belong with the preceding or following sentence. (See **1d.**) Subordinate clauses in the following examples are italicized.

FRAGMENT	He took both English and mathematics. *Because both were required.*
REVISED	He took both English and mathematics *because both were required.*
	He took both English and mathematics; both were required. [Here the fragment has been made independent by dropping the subordinating conjunction *because,* but the close relationship of the second clause to the first is suggested by separating the two with a semicolon rather than a period.]
FRAGMENT	The resentment that his attack on the children caused lasted for many years. *Although it was seldom openly expressed.*
REVISED	The resentment that his attack on the children caused lasted for many years, *although it was seldom openly expressed.*
FRAGMENT	Prospectors invaded the newly discovered gold field. *Which was reported to be the richest yet found.*
REVISED	Prospectors invaded the newly discovered gold field, *which was reported to be the richest yet found.*

4 Appositives. Appositives are words or phrases that rename or explain a noun or a pronoun standing immediately before them. The appositives in the following examples are italicized.

FRAGMENT	The supervisor on my job was a kind person. *A thorough man, but always sympathetic and thoughtful.*
REVISED	The supervisor on my job was a kind person, *a thorough man, but always sympathetic and thoughtful.*
	The supervisor on my job was a kind person. He was thorough, but always sympathetic and thoughtful. [Here the fragment has been made independent by adding a subject and verb. This revision gives greater emphasis to the qualities of the supervisor.]
FRAGMENT	McBride knew better than to mix ten beers with driving. *Particularly driving in city traffic.*

REVISED   McBride knew better than to mix ten beers with driving, *particularly driving in city traffic.*

McBride knew better than to mix ten beers with driving—*particularly driving in city traffic.* [Here the dash
rather than the comma gives greater emphasis to what
follows. See **23b.**]

5   Other fragments.

FRAGMENT   She was offered one position in a law office. *And another
in the Bureau of Indian Affairs.*

REVISED   She was offered one position in a law office and another in the Bureau of Indian Affairs. [Here the fragment is the second part of a compound object of the
verb *offered.*]

FRAGMENT   After packing Saturday night, they left early Sunday
morning. *And reached Denver Monday evening.*

REVISED   After packing Saturday night, they left early Sunday
morning *and reached Denver Monday evening.*

[Here the fragment is the second part of a compound
predicate: *They left . . . and reached . . . .*]

FRAGMENT   *No rain for three months.* The reservoirs were low and the
streams were drying up.

REVISED   *With no rain for three months,* the reservoirs were low
and the streams were drying up. [This is an uncommon
form of fragment. Revision requires either giving the
disconnected initial phrase a beginning preposition and
joining it to the main clause, as illustrated, or making it
into an independent clause, as in *There had been no rain
for three months.*]

6b   Recognize acceptable incomplete sentences.

Exclamations, commands, and requests have no expressed subject; the
subject *you* is always understood. Such sentences as the following are
standard sentence patterns rather than incomplete sentences. (See **1a.**)

Look out!   Let the buyer beware!
Close the door.   Please pass the spinach.

Incomplete sentences are common in the questions and answers of
speech and in written dialogue, which imitates speech.

"Where do we go tonight?"
"To the movies."
"When?"
"In about an hour."

In most writing, except for the standard sentence patterns of exclamations and commands, incomplete sentences appear only in special situations.

1 Transitional phrases and a few familiar expressions. Sometimes experienced writers indicate the conclusion of one topic and the turning to another by using incomplete sentences.

So much for my first point. Now for my second.

In addition, a few familiar expressions such as *The quicker, the better* and *The more, the merrier* occur as incomplete sentences.

2 Answers to rhetorical questions. A rhetorical question is one to which the answer is obvious or one that the asker of the question intends to answer. Experienced writers sometimes follow such questions with incomplete sentences.

How much does welfare do for the poor? Not enough.
Who is to blame for accidents caused by drunk drivers? The drivers, always.

3 Experienced writers sometimes use incomplete sentences for special purposes. In description, particularly when recording *sense* impressions, writers occasionally rely on verbless sentences, as in the first example below. In expository writing, writers sometimes use a sentence fragment to gain special emphasis, as in the second example.

I watch the cars go by for a while on the highway. Something lonely about them. Not lonely—worse. Nothing. Like the attendant's expression when he filled the tank. Nothing. A nothing curb, by some nothing gravel, at a nothing intersection, going nowhere.

ROBERT M. PIRSIG, *Zen and the Art of Motorcycle Maintenance*

The voice in the ad is a highly fictitious created person, speaking as an individual in a particular situation. In a bathtub, for instance.

WALKER GIBSON, *Tough, Sweet & Stuffy*

EXERCISE 6(1) In the following sentences, eliminate ineffective fragments by (1) combining them with the main clause or (2) making them into complete sentences.

1 Many young people consider social work as a career. Not for the money, but for the satisfaction it provides.

2 The Beatles decided to stop giving concerts. Just as they were at the peak of their popularity.

3 Violence has become a tool of political dissent. Chiefly because non-violence can be so easily ignored.

4 He visited on Tuesday afternoon. Immediately after he had arrived from Los Angeles.

5 I think we should take the airport bus now. Or take a taxi later.

6 Linda has saved $700. Enough to make a down payment on a car.

7 Congress has investigated the Kennedy assassination several times. Trying to determine whether there was a conspiracy.

8 The hiking party should reach Porcupine Ridge before nightfall. Even with this heavy snow.

9 Winston Churchill is regarded as a great British leader. In war and in peace.

10 I left the Palace Bar when Desert Pete shot down the chandelier. Excusing myself first.

11 Ishmael finally arrived in Nantucket. To find a berth aboard a whaling ship.

12 Pedro has many hobbies. Collecting records, sailing, and skiing.

13 As a physician she had one major ambition. To alleviate pain.

14 Small, hand-held computers cannot handle complex data. Since they have little memory space.

15 The town marshal and the outlaw's daughter rode off into the sunset. And ended the movie.

EXERCISE 6(2)   In the following paragraph, eliminate ineffective fragments by (1) combining them with the main clause or (2) making them into complete sentences.

The Indians of the Great Lakes found many uses for the weeds and wildflowers of the region. Such as food, medicine, and dyes. Plants provided edible berries and seeds. Among them being the cranberry and the wild lily of the valley. And especially sunflower seeds, making a ground-up meal. Which when boiled was used in cooking. And by the Hurons as a hairdressing. Bulbs of the wood lily were eaten like potatoes. The plant also serving as a medicinal charm. White settlers copied the Indian practice of making tea from Labrador tea. An evergreen shrub. Especially during the Revolution. Imported tea being scarce in the war years. The Jack-in-the-pulpit, or Indian turnip, was used medicinally. To treat ulcers and sore eyes. There were many other medicinal plants. Wild iris, hepatica, and the cardinal flower, for example. Indians made a red dye from pokeweed. Sometimes called inkberry. Using the dye to stamp designs on baskets. Yellow dye was made from goldenrod. A weed growing profusely on rocky banks. And on the sand dunes of the Great Lakes. Other plants were useful as articles of trade or as charms. Cranberries and columbine seeds having value in intertribal commerce. The columbine and cardinal flower being prized as love charms. The wild lotus was thought to have mystic powers. Some tribes keeping it to protect against evil spirits.

7 COMMA SPLICE **CS**
RUN-TOGETHER OR FUSED SENTENCE **FS**

7a Comma splice   CS

Do not connect two main clauses with only a comma. Placing a comma between two main clauses without a coordinating conjunction (*and, but, for, or, nor, so, yet*) results in the **comma fault** or **comma splice.** If two main clauses are joined by a coordinating conjunction, a comma may precede the conjunction. If no conjunction is used, the two clauses must be separated by a semicolon or a period.

Comma splices may be corrected in one of the following ways:

1 Connect the main clauses with a coordinating conjunction.
2 Replace the comma with a semicolon.
3 Make a separate sentence of each main clause.
4 Change one of the main clauses to a subordinate clause.

COMMA SPLICE   I was unwilling to testify, I was afraid of the defendant.

REVISED   I was unwilling to testify, *for* I was afraid of the defendant.

I was unwilling to testify; I was afraid of the defendant.

I was unwilling to testify. I was afraid of the defendant.

Because I was afraid of the defendant, I was unwilling to testify.

The fourth revision would ordinarily be the most effective, for it not only corrects the comma splice but also indicates a specific relationship between the clauses. A good revision of a comma-splice error often entails reworking the sentence rather than merely inserting a punctuation mark. The kind of revision you choose will depend on the larger context in which the sentences occur.

A comma is sometimes used between main clauses not connected by a coordinating conjunction if two clauses are in balance or in contrast. Commas are also sometimes used between three or more brief and closely connected main clauses that have the same pattern.

A journalist's work is not important, it is indispensable. [Balanced main clauses]

Some people solve problems, others create them. [Contrasting main clauses]

I'm tired, I'm angry, I'm leaving! [Main clauses with the same pattern]

Although such sentences can be very effective, inexperienced writers would be wiser to use semicolons in them.

7b Use a semicolon or a period between two main clauses connected by a conjunctive adverb or a transitional phrase.

Conjunctive adverbs are words such as *accordingly, also, consequently, furthermore, however, instead, likewise, moreover, nevertheless, then, therefore,* and *thus.* Transitional phrases are phrases such as *for example, in fact, on the other hand, in conclusion, in the meantime.* When such words or phrases connect main clauses, they must always be preceded by a semicolon or a period.

Everything seemed quiet; then the explosion came.

John must be sick; otherwise he would be here.

He disliked college; however, he studied every day.

He wanted a job; in fact, he needed a job very badly.

7c Run-together or fused sentence   FS

Do not omit punctuation between main clauses. Such omission results in run-together or fused sentences—that is, two grammatically complete thoughts with no separating punctuation. Correct these errors in the same way as the comma splice.

FUSED   Balboa gazed upon the broad Pacific his heart was filled with awe.

REVISED   Balboa gazed upon the broad Pacific, *and* his heart was filled with awe.

Balboa gazed upon the broad Pacific; his heart was filled with awe.

Balboa gazed upon the broad Pacific. His heart was filled with awe.

When Balboa gazed upon the broad Pacific, his heart was filled with awe.

EXERCISE 7(1)   Eliminate comma splices and fused sentences from the following sentences.

1 The racing car crashed headlong into the wall then all was quiet.

2 One way to publicize a movie is to say it's restricted and intended for adults then everyone will want to see it.

3 After the blood transfusion, the patient was comfortable, the doctor left the hospital.

4 "I have not finished the painting," said the artist, "I hope to finish it soon."

5 My brother must be color-blind, he calls all colors blue.

6 General Eisenhower wrote a book about World War II, he called it *Crusade in Europe.*

7 Population continues to increase in most of the world we may not have enough food for all.

8 Most of Hemingway's novels have similar subjects, love and war are two of the most frequent.

9 Water is becoming scarce in many parts of the country, our children may have to ration it.

10 Russia and China were close allies for many years however they are now very suspicious of each other.

11 "The flood of '31 was the worst I can remember," remarked Granny Hawks, "The water in Bear Creek was so high you could walk under it."

12 Lefty Gomez shook his head when the catcher signaled for a fast ball he nodded when the catcher called for a slow curve.

13 Television comedies often emphasize tensions between parents and children, furthermore, they show how their problems can be solved by love and common sense.

14 We are seldom challenged by television, it's much easier to watch the screen than read a book.

15 "Smokey Bear's out to lunch," said the truck driver over his CB radio, "You can drive to the next water hole with the hammer down, this is Fiddle Cat out, good buddy."

EXERCISE 7(2)   In the following paragraph, eliminate comma splices and fused sentences.

Since 1965 Mexicans of all ages have enjoyed a comic book called *Kaliman, El hombre increible* (The incredible man) Kaliman is a handsome, powerful super-hero. Kaliman, whose native country is unspecified, became an orphan while a young boy, afterward he was educated by lamas in Tibet. But his adventures are not confined to Asia, in fact, he roams the universe crusading for justice. His adversaries are plunderers, mad scientists, vampires, and various other villians, they commit outrageous crimes against the innocent and oppressed, at times they plot to destroy Kaliman himself by using poison or deadly weapons. The victim whom he defends often has a beautiful daughter who falls in love with Kaliman, nevertheless he always treats women as innocent persons who should never be hurt or dishonored, occasionally, however, his life is threatened by an exotic villainess with magic powers. Kaliman is not a typical comic book hero defeating injustice with his physical strength or ability to dodge bullets and leap from mountains, instead, he depends mainly on his remarkable powers of mind and great learning to outwit his enemies. He never tries to kill a villain in the most desperate circumstances he uses a blowgun whose darts induce sleep for several hours.

8 FAULTY AGREEMENT **AGR**

Agreement is the grammatical relationship between a subject and a verb or a pronoun and its antecedent or a demonstrative adjective and the word it modifies. Since Modern English nouns and verbs have few inflections, or special endings, agreement usually presents few problems. However, there are some grammatical patterns, such as the agreement in number of a subject and verb, or a pronoun and its antecedent, that you must watch carefully.

8a Make every verb agree in number with its subject.

Sometimes a lack of agreement between subject and verb results from carelessness in composition or revision. But more often, writers use a singular subject with a plural verb or a plural subject with a singular verb, not because they misunderstand the general rule, but because they are uncertain of the number of the subject or because other words coming between the subject and the verb obscure the real subject.

1 Do not be confused by words or phrases that come between the subject and verb. Find the subject and make the verb agree with it.

The first two *chapters* of the book *were* exciting. [The verb agrees with the subject, *chapters,* not with the nearest noun, *book.*]
The *size* of the bears *startles* the spectators.

Singular subjects followed by such expressions as *with, together with, accompanied by,* and *as well as* take singular verbs. The phrases introduced by such expressions are not part of the subject, even though they do suggest a plural meaning.

FAULTY	The *coach,* as well as the players, *were* happy over the victory.
REVISED	The *coach,* as well as the players, *was* happy over the victory.
FAULTY	*Sally,* together with her friends, *were* here.
REVISED	*Sally,* together with her friends, *was* here.

2 Be alert to agreement problems with indefinite pronouns used as subjects.

Indefinite pronouns ending in *-one*, *-body*, and *-thing*, such as *anyone*, *everybody*, and *something*, always take singular verbs. The indefinite pronouns *another*, *each*, *either*, *neither*, and *one* always take a singular verb.

> *Everybody* in the audience *was* enthusiastic.
> *Another* of the pesticides *has* proved harmful to birds.
> *Each* of the students *needs* individual help.
> *Neither* of the books *was* available in the library.

The indefinite pronouns *all*, *any*, *most*, *more*, *none*, and *some* may take either a singular or a plural verb depending upon the noun they refer to.

> *Some* of the silver *is* missing. [*Some* refers to the singular noun *silver*.]
> *Some* of her ancestors *were* slaves. [*Some* refers to the plural noun *ancestors*.]
> *None* of the work *is* finished. [*None* refers to the singular *work*.]
> *None* of the birds *have* migrated yet. [*None* refers to the plural *birds*.]

A singular verb is sometimes used with *none* even when it refers to a plural noun. The plural is more common, however, in both spoken and written current English.

3 Use a plural verb with two or more subjects joined by *and*.

> A dog and a cat *are* seldom friends.
> The Ohio River and the Missouri River *empty* into the Mississippi.

However, use a singular verb when the two parts of a compound subject refer to the same person or thing.

> My friend and benefactor *was* there to help me.

4 Use a singular verb with two or more singular subjects joined by *or* or *nor*. If the subjects differ in number or person, make the verb agree with the subject nearer to it.

> Either the dean or his assistant *was* to have handled the matter.
> Either you or he *has* to be here.
> Neither the farmer nor the chickens *were* aware of the swooping hawk.

If one of the subjects joined by *or* or *nor* is singular and one plural, as in the last example above, place the plural subject second to avoid awkwardness.

5 When the verb precedes the subject of the sentence, be particularly careful to find the subject and make the verb agree with it.

Do not mistake the expletive *there* as the subject of the verb. (An expletive is a word that signals that the subject will follow the verb. See **1a**.)

> There *are* no *trees* in our yard. [*There* is an expletive. The subject is *trees: No trees are in our yard.*]
>
> On this question, there *remains* no *doubt.* [The subject is *doubt: No doubt remains on this question.*]

When a compound subject comes after the verb in a sentence beginning with the expletive *there,* the singular verb is sometimes used, particularly if the first item of the compound is singular.

> There *is* [or *are*] only a chair and a table left to auction. [The subject is the compound *a chair and a table.*]

Such sentences are best rewritten.

> Only a chair and a table are left to auction.

In some sentences beginning with the adverbs *here* and *there* or with an adverbial word group, the verb comes before the subject.

> There *goes* the *man* I was describing. [*There* is an adverb. The subject is the noun *man.*]
>
> Up the trail *race* the *motorcycles.* [The subject is *motorcycles.*]

6 Use a singular verb with collective nouns when the group is considered as a unit acting together. Use a plural verb when the individual members of the group are acting separately.

Collective nouns have a singular form but name a group of persons or things as a single unit: *audience, bunch, crowd, family, herd, jury,* and the like.

> Our family *goes* out to dinner weekly. [The family acts together as a single unit.]
>
> The family *have been* arriving all morning. [Members of the family arrived at different times.]

The committee *is* meeting today. [The singular verb *is* emphasizes the committee acting as a unit.]

The committee *are* unable to agree on a plan. [The plural verb *are* emphasizes the members of the committee acting separately.]

7   Make the verb agree with its subject, not with a predicate noun.

The best part of the program *is* the vocal duets.

Expensive cars *are* a necessity in his life.

8   When the relative pronouns *who, which,* and *that* are used as subjects, use a singular verb when the antecedent is singular, a plural verb when the antecedent is plural.

They are the women who *deserve* praise. [*Who* refers to the plural noun *women;* thus the verb is plural.]

The book that *was* lost belonged to the library. [*That* refers to the singular noun *book;* thus the verb is singular.]

The phrase *one of the* frequently causes problems in such sentences.

Sanderson is one of the councilmen who *oppose* the plan. [*Who* refers to the plural *councilmen;* several councilmen oppose the plan.]

Sanderson is the only one of the councilmen who *opposes* the plan. [*Who* refers to *one;* there is only one councilman, Sanderson, opposing the plan. Note that the meaning of the sentence would not be changed if the phrase *of the councilmen* were omitted.]

9   When the subject is the title of a novel, a play, or the like, or a word used as a word, use a singular verb even though the form of the subject is plural.

Romeo and Juliet is a Shakespearean play.

Songs and Satires is a book by Edgar Lee Masters.

Women is the plural of *woman.*

10   Use a singular verb with nouns that are plural in form but singular in meaning, such as *economics, news, physics.*

Mathematics *has* always been Betty's downfall.

The financial news *was* favorable last month.

11   Subjects indicating sums of money, distance, measurement, and the like ordinarily take singular verbs.

Three quarters of the money *is* already spent.

Forty years *is* a long time to live in one town.

Four miles *is* too much to jog.

If the items that make up the quantity are thought of as separate parts rather than as a single unit, the verb may be plural.

> Forty percent of the trees *were* damaged by the hurricane. [The trees were damaged separately.]
> One half of the students *have* finished the examination. [The students finished individually.]

The expression *the number* takes a singular verb, but *a number* takes a plural verb.

> *The number* of candidates for the position *was* large.
> *A number* of candidates *were* applying for the position.
> *The number* of people moving to the Southwest *is* increasing.
> *A number* of business firms *have* moved from New York.

EXERCISE 8a In the following sentences, correct any errors in agreement. Indicate any sentences that might be appropriate in informal English.

1 His only interest are his studies.
2 A fool and his money is soon parted.
3 Among my favorite plays are *Blues for Mister Charlie* by James Baldwin.
4 The burden of sales taxes fall most heavily on low-income families.
5 Taste in dress styles differ greatly.
6 None of his horses are entered in the Kentucky Derby.
7 The farmer and not the city dweller are hurt when food prices fall.
8 Thirty dollars are more than many can afford for a pair of shoes.
9 The white-throated sparrow is one of those field birds that loves to sing.
10 There is a good many reasons for tensions between Arabs and Israelis.

8b Use a singular pronoun in referring to a singular antecedent. Use a plural pronoun in referring to a plural antecedent.

8b

> *Helen* said that *she* wanted to work. [*She* refers to the singular antecedent *Helen.*]
> *Helium* is a tasteless and odorless gas; *it* is one of the most abundant elements. [*It* refers to the singular antecedent *helium.*]
> *Women* should be free to make *their* own decisions. [*Their* refers to the plural antecedent *women.*]

Most problems of agreement between pronouns and their antecedents occur with indefinite pronouns, collective nouns, and compound antecedents.

1   In writing, use singular pronouns to refer to indefinite antecedents such as *person, one, any, each, either, neither*

and compounds ending in *-one*, *-body*, and *-thing*, such as *someone*, *anybody*, and *everything*. (See also **8a2**.)

Spoken English frequently uses a plural pronoun to refer to indefinite antecedents, but the singular continues to be preferred in writing.

WRITTEN   *Everyone* should be allowed to speak *his* [or *his or her*] own mind.

SPOKEN   *Everyone* should be allowed to speak *their* own minds.

WRITTEN   He asked *each* of us to bring *his* [or *his or her*] own lunch.

SPOKEN   He asked *each* of us to bring *our* own lunch.

Historically *he* (*him*, *his*) has been used to refer to such antecedents as *one*, *none*, *everybody*, and similar indefinite pronouns that designate either male or female. This "common gender" use of the masculine pronouns has been widely criticized in recent years. Some critics have suggested coining new pronouns such as *himmer*, which would refer to both men and women. Others have urged the regular use of *he or she* (*him or her*, *his or hers*) when the reference is general. Language resists such changes as the first. Sometimes, using the second alternative is awkward, for it creates numerous pronoun references within a single sentence or paragraph. When awkwardness becomes a problem, writers who wish to avoid *he*, *him*, *his* for common gender can cast their sentences in the plural or rework sentences to eliminate gender references.

A careful writer will recast his sentences.
A careful writer will recast his or her sentences.
Careful writers will recast their sentences.

Recasting sentences will eliminate awkward gender references.

2   With a collective noun as an antecedent, use a singular pronoun if you are considering the group as a unit and a plural pronoun if you are considering the individual members of the group separately.

The *army* increased *its* watchfulness. [The army is acting as a unit.]
The *crew* are going about *their* duties without complaint. [The members of the crew have separate duties.]

3   If two or more antecedents are joined by *and*, use a plural pronoun to refer to them. If two or more singular antecedents are joined by *or* or *nor*, use a singular pronoun to

refer to them. **If one of two antecedents joined by *or* or *nor* is singular and one plural, make the pronoun agree with the nearer.**

Jack and Jim *have* finished *their* work.
Neither Jack nor Jim *has* finished *his* work.
Neither the instructor nor the students *have* finished *their* work.

EXERCISE 8b In the following sentences, make every pronoun agree with its antecedent in accordance with written usage. Indicate any sentence that would be acceptable in speech.

1 A person should be willing to defend their own principles.
2 Neither of the trucking companies could afford to compromise on their rates.
3 Every American should be free to live wherever they can afford.
4 The Vietnamese family has survived in spite of their tragedies.
5 Everybody has their own solution to the campus parking problem.
6 None of the students in the psychology class could analyze their own dreams.
7 If either a resident or a nonresident were qualified, they would get the job.
8 No child fully appreciates their parents until later in life.
9 The school board disagreed in its opinions about closing the Adams School.
10 The citizens' group submitted their complaint to the town council.

8c **Make sure that a demonstrative adjective *(this, that, these, those)* agrees in number with the noun it modifies.**

These adjective forms seldom cause difficulty. One frequent error, however, occurs when the demonstrative adjective is used with *kind of* or *sort of* followed by plural nouns. Here you must remember that the demonstrative adjective modifies the singular noun *kind* or *sort* and <u>not</u> the following plural noun. Thus a singular demonstrative is used.

NONSTANDARD	*These kind* of strawberries taste sweet.
STANDARD	*This kind* of strawberry tastes sweet.
NONSTANDARD	*These sort* of watches are expensive.
STANDARD	*This sort* of watch is expensive.

EXERCISE 8a–c In the following sentences, correct every error of agreement in accordance with written usage.

1 Poverty is one of the major forces that encourages crime.
2 If someone wants to "do their thing," they should be encouraged.
3 These sort of planes can exceed the speed of sound.

4 "Everybody is in a hurry to jump in their car and go some place," said Uncle Zed, "but they can't think of anything to do after they get there."

5 A person can live in a big city and still retain their warm feelings about life in a small town.

6 Two solutions to the state's energy problems have been offered, but neither have been tried.

7 After thirty, one loses both the rebelliousness and the inventiveness of their earlier years.

8 Although everyone wants the right to vote, they don't all exercise that right at election time.

9 If the house is to be sold, either the owner or the buyer must alter their price.

10 The committee on city planning do not approve the plan for a new shopping mall.

9

9   FAULTY REFERENCE OF PRONOUNS **REF**

A pronoun depends for its meaning upon its antecedent, the noun or other pronoun to which it refers. If the antecedents of the pronouns in your writing are not clear, your writing will not be clear. Place pronouns as close to their antecedents as possible and make all pronoun references exact.

9a

9a   Make sure that each pronoun refers clearly to a single antecedent.

Pronouns can, of course, refer to compound antecedents in such sentences as *Joan and Karen both believed they had been cheated,* where the pronoun *they* refers to *Joan and Karen.* If, however, a pronoun can refer to either of two possible antecedents, it will be ambiguous.

AMBIGUOUS	When Kathy visited her mother, she was angry. [Who was angry, Kathy or her mother?]
CLEAR	Kathy was angry when she visited her mother. Her mother was angry when Kathy visited her.
AMBIGUOUS	Arthur went with John to the airport, where he took a plane to Phoenix. [Who took the plane?]
CLEAR	After going to the airport with John, Arthur took a plane to Phoenix. After Arthur went to the airport with him, John took a plane to Phoenix.

EXERCISE 9a   Revise the following sentences by eliminating the ambiguous reference of pronouns.

1 Doris took the guppy out of the bowl while she washed it.
2 He took the shutters off the window frames and painted them.
3 I dropped the camera on the coffee table and damaged it.
4 Marilyn told Susan she should never have married Jim.
5 Andy gave his father a copy of *Huckleberry Finn,* which was one of his favorite books.

9b   Avoid making a pronoun refer to a remote antecedent.

In general, the nearer a pronoun is to its antecedent, the more likely it is to be immediately clear. The reader should never have to search for a pronoun's antecedent.

REMOTE   Champlain and his men could hear the sounds of the St. Lawrence rushing past boulders below their camp and the sighing of pines in the morning wind. In the distance was an ominous mountain range. *They* felt alone in the Canadian wilderness. [*Champlain and his men* is the only antecedent to which *They* can sensibly refer, but the pronoun is too remote from its antecedent for clear, easy reading.]

CLEAR   . . . *The explorers* felt alone in the Canadian wilderness. [This revision uses a noun that, in effect, repeats the subject.]

Champlain and his men, who felt alone in the Canadian wilderness, could hear the sounds . . . [The remote reference is eliminated by changing the third sentence into a subordinate clause.]

EXERCISE 9b   Revise all sentences in which pronouns are too remote from their antecedents.

1 Old Mission is a small village near the tip of a narrow peninsula that is covered with cherry orchards. Nearby are the east and west arms of Grand Traverse Bay. It has a post office and a grocery store.
2 The accident insurance policy lists the hazards covered and should be clear to the policyholder, since they are fully explained.
3 The delegates arrived in small groups for the emergency session of the UN. *The New York Times* printed a front-page story about the historic meeting. They stopped only to pose for press photographers at the entrance.
4 This house was built with fieldstones by my great-grandfather. The grounds cover several acres and include apple orchards and several outbuildings. It is filled with family heirlooms.
5 In the early spring many wildflowers, such as trillium, hepatica, and Dutchman's-breeches, grow in the woods near Walden Pond. Thoreau liked to ramble about this countryside. He often described them in his journals.

9c

9c Avoid the vague use of *this, that,* and *which* to refer to the general idea of a preceding clause or sentence.

The use of *this, that,* and *which* to refer to an idea stated in a preceding clause or sentence is common in informal English in such sentences as *They keep their promises, which is more than some people do.* Although such broad reference is often used by experienced writers when the meaning is unmistakably clear, it risks confusing the reader unless it is used with great care. Less experienced writers should ordinarily eliminate any vague use of *this, that,* and *which,* either by recasting the sentence to eliminate the pronoun or by supplying a specific antecedent for the pronoun.

VAGUE   Aid to African countries has been very limited, which has angered many black Africans.

REVISED   Aid to African countries has been very limited, a fact which has angered many black Africans. [*Fact* supplies a clear antecedent for *which.*]

That aid to African countries has been very limited has angered many black Africans. [The sentence has been recast to eliminate the vague *which.*]

VAGUE   Migrant workers are being exploited. Action to prevent this should be taken immediately.

REVISED   Action to prevent the exploitation of migrant workers should be taken immediately. [The sentence has been recast to eliminate the vague *this.*]

EXERCISE 9c   Revise all sentences in which the reference of pronouns is vague.

1 This is the most productive oil refinery in Louisiana. This was not built overnight.
2 She was self-conscious about her thick glasses, which didn't bother her friends.
3 Martin Luther King, Jr., was dedicated to nonviolence. That influenced his decision to become a minister.
4 The turn signals on this car do not operate, which should be repaired immediately.
5 He is going to a convention in Honolulu, which is exciting.

9d

9d Do not use a pronoun to refer to an unexpressed but implied noun.

To be clear, a pronoun must have a noun or the equivalent of a noun as its specific antecedent. Modifiers, possessives, and other words or phrases that merely suggest an appropriate noun do not provide clear and specific antecedents. Revise faulty sentences so that each pronoun has a specific noun or noun equivalent as antecedent, or otherwise recast the sentence.

FAULTY   Because we put a wire fence around the chicken yard, *they* cannot escape. [*Chicken* here is a noun modifying *yard*. It suggests but does not express the necessary antecedent *chickens*.]

REVISED   Because we put a wire fence around the chicken yard, the chickens cannot escape.

FAULTY   When the president's committee was established, she appointed several student representatives.
[The possessive *president's* implies but does not express the antecedent *president*.]

REVISED   When the president established the committee, she appointed several student representatives.

FAULTY   Tom's mother is an engineer, and that is the profession Tom wants to study. [The appropriate antecedent, *engineering*, is implied but needs to be specifically stated.]

REVISED   Tom's mother is an engineer, and engineering is the profession Tom wants to study.

EXERCISE 9d   In the following sentences, eliminate all references to unexpressed antecedents.

1 There is a fire station near the school, and we called them when we saw smoke.
2 He had a slight heart attack, but after a month's rest it was as good as ever.
3 When he was young he was a good chess player, but now he seldom has time to play it.
4 When the witness asked for police protection, two of them were assigned to guard him.
5 If children are irresponsible, some of it is probably the fault of their parents.

9e   In writing, avoid the indefinite use of *they* and *it*. Make sure any use of *you* is appropriate.

The indefinite use of *they, it,* and *you* is common at most levels of speech: *In Germany, they drink beer; it says in the dictionary that . . .; you can never find anything where you're looking for it.* In writing, these pronouns all have a much more restricted use.

1 *They* **always requires a specific antecedent in all but the most informal writing.** Correct its use in your writing by substituting an appropriate noun, or revise the sentence.

SPOKEN   In less industrialized areas, *they* do not understand the problems of the city.

WRITTEN   People living in less industrialized areas do not understand the problems of the city.

SPOKEN   *They* said on the late news that Mount St. Helens had erupted again.

WRITTEN   It was reported on the late news that Mount St. Helens had erupted again.

2 *It* **in the phrase** *it says* **referring to information in newspapers, magazines, books, and the like, though common in speech, is unacceptable in writing, except in dialogue.**

SPOKEN   *It* says in the newspaper that Monday will be warmer.

WRITTEN   The newspaper says that Monday will be warmer.

3 *You* **in the sense of people in general is common in informal writing:** *Differences of opinion among friends can be healthy if you don't take them too seriously,* **or** *When you're driving you should always be alert.* **More formal writing ordinarily prefers a general noun such as** *people* **or** *a person,* **or the pronoun** *one.*

INFORMAL   Many suburban towns do not permit *you* to drive more than twenty-five or thirty miles an hour.

FORMAL   Many suburban towns do not permit *people* [or *a person* or *one*] to drive more than twenty-five or thirty miles an hour.

You is always correct in writing directions or in other contexts where the meaning is clearly *you, the reader.*

Before turning on your air conditioner, be sure you have closed all your windows.

When using *you* in the sense of *you, the reader,* be sure that the context is appropriate to such use.

INAPPROPRIATE   In early colonial villages, you had to depend on wood for fuel. [The reader is unlikely to be living in an early colonial village.]

REVISED	In early colonial villages, *people* [or *a person* or *one*] had to depend on wood for fuel.
BETTER	Early colonial villagers had to depend on wood for fuel.

EXERCISE 9e   Revise the following sentences to avoid the indefinite use of *they, you,* and *it.*

1 In the first few verses of the Bible, it describes the creation of the world.
2 In every society you have to expect that some people will not be able to provide for themselves.
3 You find a generation gap in every generation.
4 In the Victorian era, they never talked about sex in public.
5 Throughout the development of the West, they drove back the Indians and took their land.

9f   Match the relative pronouns *who, which,* and *that* with appropriate antecedents.

In general, use *who* to refer to persons, *which* to refer to things, and *that* to refer to things and sometimes to persons.

Many *students who* major in mathematics today find employment with computer companies.

Arkansas, which became a state in 1836, was earlier a part of Louisiana.

Among the *flowers that* (or *which*) grow most easily are petunias and marigolds.

The possessive *whose* is frequently used to refer to things when the phrase *of which* would be awkward.

Cinderella is a story *whose* ending most of us know. [Compare *the ending of which.*]

The relative *that* can be used only in restrictive clauses, clauses necessary to meaning and thus not set off by commas. *Which* can be used in both restrictive and nonrestrictive clauses, clauses not necessary to meaning and thus set off by commas. (See **20c.**)

The *Equal Rights Amendment, which* was proposed by Congress in 1972, still had not been ratified by thirty-eight states in 1980.

The *amendment that* (or *which*) gave the right to vote to all citizens eighteen years old or older was ratified in less than four months.

Some writers prefer to introduce all restrictive clauses with *that* and to limit the use of *which* entirely to nonrestrictive clauses.

9g

9g Avoid the awkward use of *it* in two or more ways in a sentence.

We use *it* as an expletive to postpone a subject as in *It is sensible to be careful,* in certain idioms such as *it is cold* and such colloquial expressions as *He made it to the finish line,* and of course as a definite pronoun referring to specific antecedents. All of these uses are acceptable when appropriate, but sentences in which two different uses occur are likely to be confusing.

CONFUSING He put his *car* in the garage because he never leaves *it* out when *it* is bad weather. [The first *it* refers to *car;* the second is idiomatic.]

IMPROVED He put his car in the garage because he never leaves it out when the weather is bad [or *in bad weather*].

EXERCISE 9a–g Revise the following sentences by eliminating the faulty reference of pronouns.

1 Amy is studying hotel administration because her father owns one.
2 Mark told Bruce that he stayed up too late watching the televised hockey game.
3 We have an annual pumpkin show in my home town, which is open to the public.
4 Earl finished the roll of film by taking two pictures of a rusty Civil War cannon. Then he reloaded it.
5 Brad likes to talk about his wrestling ability, but he isn't a very good one.
6 In our textbook it says that pronouns should have clear antecedents.
7 She left her billfold in one of the stores and couldn't find it when she went back.
8 "The question is not whether God is on our side," said the army chaplain to the ragged band of patriots. They looked up in surprise as they prepared to meet the enemy in the hills near Boston. "It is whether we are on God's side."
9 The twins telephoned their parents nearly every day when they were vacationing in New Orleans.
10 After the hurricane's heavy damage in Haiti, it weakened to a tropical storm.

10

10 SHIFTS

A sentence is kept consistent by using one subject; one tense, voice, and mood in verbs; and one person and number in pronouns, as far as grammar and meaning allow. Unnecessary shifts in any of these elements tend to obscure meaning and make reading more difficult than it has to be. [See **32d(1)** for a discussion of consistency within paragraphs.]

10a Do not shift the subject or the voice of the verb within a sentence unnecessarily.

Particularly in compound and complex sentences, meaning frequently requires the writer to refer to more than one subject, as in the following sentence:

> When the *car* hit their dog, *John* ran home, and *Bill* held the dog until help arrived.

Here the writer is describing an accident involving two boys, their dog, and a car. Meaning clearly requires a shift of subject from one clause to another within the sentence. Such movement of a sentence from one subject to another is perfectly natural.

Less frequently, meaning may justify a shift from active to passive voice within a sentence.

> Three men *escaped* from the state prison yesterday but *were captured* before sundown.

Here the writer could have chosen to write *but the police captured them,* changing the subject but keeping the active voice in both main clauses of a compound sentence. But by choosing to use the compound predicate, *escaped . . . but were captured,* the writer keeps attention focused on the important subject, *three men.*

Unlike the shifts in subject and voice in these sentences, the shifts in the following sentences are unnecessary:

FAULTY As *the boys approached* the swamp, *frogs could be heard* croaking. [Here the focus of the sentence is on *the boys.* The shift of subject from *the boys* to *frogs* and of the voice of the verb from the active to the passive are unnecessary and distracting.]

REVISED As *the boys approached* the swamp, *they could hear* frogs croaking.

FAULTY *Ellen stayed* at a mountain resort, and her *time was spent* largely in reading. [The sentence is about Ellen. The shift of subject from *Ellen* to *time* and the resulting shift from active to passive voice blurs rather than sharpens the sentence.]

REVISED *Ellen stayed* at a mountain resort *and spent* her time largely in reading.

10a

EXERCISE 10a   In the following sentences, correct unnecessary shifts in subject or voice.

1 On the Fourth of July the people paraded down Main Street, and a fireworks display was also enjoyed.

2 Many unknown rings of Saturn were discovered when Voyager I sent back photographs to scientists.

3 If a person attends furniture auctions, bargains in antiques can sometimes be found.

4 The doctor told most patients to exercise daily, but the advice was largely ignored.

5 As we canoed toward the rapids, white water could be seen.

10b

10b   Do not shift person or number unnecessarily.

Just as meaning frequently requires us to refer to more than one subject in a single sentence, it may require us to refer to different persons or to combinations of singular and plural subjects, as in the following sentences:

> *I* stayed, but *they* left. [*I* is first person singular; *they* is third person plural.]
>
> The *snake* held its ground until the *coyotes* finally left. [*Snake* is singular, *coyotes* plural.]

But unless meaning clearly requires such changes, keep person and number within a given sentence consistent.

Unnecessary shifts in person are frequently shifts from the third person (the person being talked about) to the second person (the person being talked to). They occur principally because in English we can make general statements by using either the second person pronoun *you,* the third person pronoun *one,* or one of various third person general nouns such as the singular *a person* or the plural *people.* Thus any one of the following sentences is consistent:

> If *you* want to play games, *you* must learn the rules.
>
> If *a person* [or *one*] wants to play games, *he* [or *he or she*] must learn the rules.
>
> If *people* want to play games, *they* must learn the rules.

Failure to follow one of these possible patterns produces faulty shifts, as in the following:

> FAULTY   When *a person* has good health, *you* should feel fortunate.
>
> REVISED   When *a person* has good health, *he* [or *he or she*] should feel fortunate.
>
> When *you* have good health, *you* should feel fortunate.
>
> When *people* have good health, *they* should feel fortunate.

A second kind of unnecessary shift frequently occurs in sentences in which the writer starts with the first person and inconsistently shifts to the second. Such sentences are ordinarily more effective when the writer maintains the first-person point of view.

WEAK   I refuse to go to a movie where you can't buy popcorn.

IMPROVED   I refuse to go to a movie where I can't buy popcorn.

Faulty shifts in number within a sentence usually involve faulty agreement between pronouns and their antecedents. (See **8b.**)

FAULTY   I like *an occasional cup* of coffee, for *they* give me an added lift. [Shift from singular to plural. The pronoun should agree with the singular antecedent *cup*.]

REVISED   I like *an occasional cup* of coffee, for *it* gives me an added lift.

                     I like *occasional cups* of coffee, for *they* give me an added lift.

EXERCISE 10b   In the following sentences, correct unnecessary shifts in person or number.

1 I enjoy an exciting basketball game, but they leave me emotionally exhausted.
2 If a person lives in a democracy, you have a right to voice your opinions.
3 Sheila often studies in the library, where you can have peace and quiet.
4 Since you can get delicious chili at the Campus Diner, I often eat there.
5 Joyce and I visited the art museum because you could go free.

10c   Do not shift tense or mood unnecessarily.

10c

In a sentence such as *Nostalgia is a love of the way things were in our youth,* meaning requires a shift of tense from the present *is* to the past *were.* But except when the meaning or the grammar of a sentence requires such changes in tense, keep the same tense throughout all the verbs in a sentence.

FAULTY   He *sat* down at the desk and *begins* to write. [The verb shifts unnecessarily from past to present tense.]

REVISED   He *sat* down at the desk and *began* to write.

FAULTY   In chapter one of the book, Sally *accepts* her first job, but in chapter three she *resigned* it.

REVISED   In chapter one of the book, Sally *accepts* her first job, but in chapter three she *resigns* it. [In this sentence, the revision uses the present tense in both verbs because it is customary to use the present tense in describing actions in literature. See **5a.**]

10c

Shifts in mood within a single sentence or a series of related sentences are almost never justified. Such shifts most often occur in writing directions. Avoid them by casting directions consistently either in the imperative or the indicative mood.

> FAULTY   *Hold* the rifle firmly against your shoulder, and then you *should take* careful aim. [Shift from imperative to indicative mood]
>
> REVISED   *Hold* the rifle firmly against your shoulder and then *take* careful aim. [Both verbs are in the imperative mood.]
>
>   You *should hold* the rifle firmly against your shoulder and then (you should) take careful aim. [Both verbs are in the indicative. Note that here the second *you should* can be omitted since it will be understood by the reader.]

In general, directions are most economical and effective when they are written throughout in the imperative.

EXERCISE 10c   In the following sentences, correct needless shifts in tense or mood.

1 In the early innings the Tigers have a three-run lead, but in the seventh inning they lost it.
2 Henry jogged about a mile; then he sits on a park bench to rest.
3 *Gomer's Ghost* is an entertaining movie, even if the ghost overplayed his part.
4 Stand with your feet together; then you should raise your arms to shoulder height.
5 While shopping, Don saw Goldie Hawn at the frozen food counter, but she only gives him an icy stare.

10d

10d   Do not shift from indirect to direct quotation unnecessarily.

Direct quotation reports in quotation marks the exact words of a speaker or writer. Indirect quotation reports what someone has said or written, but not in the exact words.

> DIRECT   She said, "I'm tired and ready to leave."
>
> INDIRECT   She said that she was tired and ready to leave.

The tense in an indirect quotation should ordinarily be the same as the tense of the main verb. Unnecessary shifts between direct and indirect quotation often cause problems in tense.

> FAULTY   Lincoln asked the general *whether his army was well supplied* and *is it ready for battle.* [Shift from indirect to direct quotation. In such mixed constructions, the writer usually omits quotation marks from the direct quotation.]

REVISED   Lincoln asked the general whether his army was well supplied and whether it was ready for battle. [Indirect quo-
tation]

Lincoln asked the general, "Is your army well supplied? Is
it ready for battle?" [Direct quotation]

EXERCISE 10a–d Revise the following sentences, correcting all needless shifts
in tense, mood, voice, person, and number, and any shifts from indirect to direct
quotation. Be prepared to explain your changes.

1 First the surface should be carefully cleaned; then put the glue on.
2 The Sunday drivers were out in full force, and suddenly there is an
accident.
3 They said they had a copy of *Science,* and would I like to borrow it.
4 Great supplies of gold are found in South Africa, while Mexico leads
in silver mining.
5 A public opinion poll is based on a cross section of the population, but
sometimes they have been inaccurate.
6 Mr. Stein put a new fence around the yard, and then the wooden pick-
ets were painted.
7 Ruth wondered whether her mother had left and did she say when she
would be back.
8 The manager decided to offer free balloons, and the next day the store
is packed with children.
9 When one feels tired, a candy bar will give you quick energy.
10 Careful drivers check the pressure in the spare tire because it is sometimes needed.

11 MISPLACED PARTS **MIS PT**

Modern English relies heavily upon word order to show relations
among words. The Latin sentences *Puella amat agricolam* and *Agricolam
amat puella* have the same literal meaning: *The girl loves the farmer.* Even
though the subject and object are reversed, the special endings (-*a* and
-*am*) make the meaning of the sentence unmistakable. But if the English words are reversed, so is the English meaning: *The girl loves the
farmer; The farmer loves the girl.* Word order is crucial to meaning in
English.

Just as word order is the principal way to keep subject-verb-object
relations clear, so it is the principal way to keep many modifiers attached to the words they modify. Phrases and clauses that modify
nouns require special care, since they normally attach to the nearest
noun preceding them. Unless writers are alert, sentences such as these
can occur:

He bought a horse from a stranger with a lame hind leg.
We returned to Atlanta after a week's vacation on Monday.

SEN FLT

Context usually—though not always—allows readers to work out the intended meaning of such sentences. But at best a reader is distracted by the necessary effort.

11a

11a In writing, place adverbs such as *almost, even, hardly, just, only, nearly* immediately before the words they modify.

In speech we commonly put *only* and similar adverbs before the verb, regardless of what we mean them to modify. To avoid any possible ambiguity in writing, place such modifiers immediately before the words they modify.

SPOKEN	He *only* ran a mile.
WRITTEN	He ran *only* a mile.
SPOKEN	The team didn't *even* score once.
WRITTEN	The team didn't score *even* once.
SPOKEN	She *almost* read the whole book.
WRITTEN	She read *almost* the whole book.

EXERCISE 11a Revise the following sentences so that the limiting adverbs are placed immediately before the words they modify.

1 He almost seemed amused.
2 The oil spill just occurred off the French coast last week.
3 She only refused our offer of help because she wanted to be independent.
4 The earthquake victims needed the volunteers to bandage their wounds badly.
5 The legislature scarcely provided any funds for maintaining state parks.

11b

11b Be sure that modifying phrases refer clearly to the words they modify.

Phrases used to modify nouns must ordinarily be placed immediately after the words they are intended to modify.

CONFUSING	Who is the woman who gave you the candy *in the pink dress?* [The writer intends the phrase *in the pink dress* to modify woman, not candy.]
CLEAR	Who is the woman *in the pink dress* who gave you the candy?
CONFUSING	Joan borrowed a bicycle from a friend *with ten speeds.* [The writer intended the phrase *with ten speeds* to modify *bicycle,* not *friend.*]
CLEAR	Joan borrowed a bicycle *with ten speeds* from a friend.

Phrases used as adverbs may usually be placed either within the sentence close to the words they modify or at the beginning or end of the sentence. In some sentences, however, their placement requires special thought.

CONFUSING   The author claims the revolt was caused by corruption *in the first chapter*. [*In the first chapter* seems to modify the noun *corruption* although the writer surely intended it to modify the verb *claims*.]

CLEAR   *In the first chapter*, the author claims the revolt was caused by corruption.

CONFUSING   A huge boulder fell as we rounded the corner *with a crash*. [*With a crash* seems to modify the verb *rounded* although the writer intended it to modify the earlier verb, *fell*.]

CLEAR   A huge boulder fell *with a crash* as we rounded the corner.

EXERCISE 11b Revise the following sentences so that the modifying phrases refer clearly to the words they are intended to modify.

1 I kept thinking how religious my friends were for the rest of the day.
2 The astronauts looked forward to landing on the moon for several years.
3 The president announced that he would confer with his economic advisors at his press conference yesterday.
4 Hal dropped out of school after a semester's attendance over the weekend.
5 We were rescued after we were nearly drowned by a lifeguard.

11c Be sure that modifying clauses refer clearly to the words they modify.

Clauses that modify nouns usually begin with *who, which,* or *that* and follow immediately after the words they modify.

CONFUSING   He had a ribbon around his neck *that was tied in a bow*. [The ribbon, not his neck, was tied in a bow.]

CLEAR   Around his neck he had a ribbon *that was tied in a bow*.

CONFUSING   Susan cautiously approached the deserted house by a winding path, *which was said to be haunted*. [The house, not the path, was said to be haunted.]

CLEAR   By a winding path, Susan cautiously approached the house *that was said to be haunted*.

Adverb clauses are introduced by words such as *after, although,*

11c

because, since, and *until*. Like adverb phrases, they can usually be placed either within the sentence close to the words they modify or at the beginning or end of the sentence; but they can sometimes be confusing unless writers are careful.

CONFUSING   The police towed the stolen station wagon to the city garage *after it was abandoned*. [The clause *after it was abandoned* is intended to modify the verb *towed* but seems to modify the noun *garage*.]

CLEAR   *After the stolen station wagon was abandoned*, the police towed it to the city garage.

The police towed the stolen station wagon, *after it was abandoned*, to the city garage.

EXERCISE 11c   In the following sentences, place the modifying clauses in clear relationships to the words they modify.

1 She found a large apartment with two windows facing a garden that was well ventilated.
2 I suddenly realized that I had left the tickets at home after we reached the stadium.
3 Marty bought a Great Dane from a neighbor that was too big for the doghouse.
4 She gave an alarm clock to her cousin that was guaranteed for five years.
5 Nick sold his sports car to a used-car dealer that needed overhauling.

11d

11d   Avoid squinting modifiers.

A **squinting modifier** is one that may modify either a preceding word or a following word. It squints at the words on its right and left, and leaves the reader confused.

SQUINTING   His physician told him *frequently* to exercise.
CLEAR   His physician *frequently* told him to exercise.
His physician told him to exercise *frequently*.

SQUINTING   The committee which was studying the matter *yesterday* turned in its report.
CLEAR   The committee that was studying the matter turned in its report *yesterday*.
The committee, *which spent yesterday* studying the matter, turned in its report.

SQUINTING   She promised *on her way home* to visit him.
CLEAR   *On her way home*, she promised to visit him.
She promised to visit him *on her way home*.

EXERCISE 11d Recast the following sentences to eliminate squinting modifiers.

1 The pilot was told constantly to be prepared for emergencies.
2. The story he was reading slowly put Sarah to sleep.
3 A person who succeeds often is ambitious.
4 The speaker told the audience when the lecture was over they could ask questions.
5 The men who were beating on the wall wildly began shooting.

11e Do not split infinitives awkwardly.

An infinitive is split when an adverbial modifier separates the *to* from the verb. There is nothing ungrammatical about splitting an infinitive, and sometimes a split is useful to avoid awkwardness. But most split infinitives are unnecessary.

AWKWARD	She tried not *to* carelessly *hurt* the kitten.
CLEAR	She tried not *to hurt* the kitten carelessly.
AWKWARD	You should try *to*, if you can, *take* a walk every day.
CLEAR	If you can, you should try *to take* a walk every day.

On the other hand, note the following sentence:

The course is designed *to* better *equip* graduates to go into business.

In this case, if *better* is placed before *to equip* it will squint awkwardly between *designed* and the infinitive; after *to equip* it will modify graduates; at the end of the sentence it will be at best awkward and unnatural, if not entirely unclear.

EXERCISE 11e Revise the following sentences by eliminating awkward split infinitives.

1 We agreed to once and for all dissolve our business partnership.
2 The tennis team expects to, if the weather permits, play the match tomorrow.
3 The major nations of the world regularly decide to sometime in the near future reduce their armaments.
4 It's a relief to promptly send in your tax return after the first of the year.
5 You have to willingly accept the idea that you are responsible for the well-being of others, or the human condition will never improve.

11f

11f In general, avoid separating a subject from its predicate, a verb from its object, or the parts of a verb phrase unless separating them makes the sentence more effective.

EFFECTIVE SEPARATION   The captain, *seeing the ominous storm clouds gathering overhead,* ordered the crew to take in the sail.

And so Pilate, *willing to content the people,* released Barabbas unto them, and delivered Jesus, *when he had scourged him,* to be crucified.

MARK 15:15

Only when a man is safely ensconced under six feet of earth, *with several tons of enlauding granite upon his chest,* is he in a position to give advice with any certainty, and then he is silent.

EDWARD NEWTON

AWKWARD SEPARATION   She *found,* after an hour's search, the *money* hidden under the rug.

CLEAR   After an hour's search, she *found* the *money* hidden under the rug.

AWKWARD SEPARATION   At the convention I saw Mary Ward, whom I *had* many years ago *met* in Chicago.

CLEAR   At the convention I saw Mary Ward, whom I *had met* many years ago in Chicago.

EXERCISE 11f Revise the following sentences by eliminating the unnecessary separations of related sentence elements.

1 In a pleasant house in Concord, Emerson, who was a neighbor of Thoreau, lived.
2 Peggy is, despite strong objections from her parents, going to study music and painting.
3 John wrote, after discussing it with his sister, a letter resigning his position.
4 Swenson made, after years of smoking heavily, a great effort to stop.
5 Pollution, as many have discovered, is very hard to control.

EXERCISE 11a–f Revise the following sentences by eliminating all misplaced parts.

1 We watched the dog show on our TV, which was won by a golden retriever.
2 A farmer's market is located on the edge of the town, which always has fresh fruits and berries.
3 Charley even exercises during his lunch hour.
4 A salesperson who tries often makes a good profit.
5 The minister speaks out against sin every Sunday.
6 Everyone nearly suffers during an economic recession.
7 Linda is, despite her friends' confidence in her ability, going to give up studying music composition.
8 We had lunch at a drive-in, which cost more than it was worth.
9 Religious faith without doubt is a comfort to many people.
10 During the bombing the platoon leader ordered the men to immediately take cover.

12 DANGLING MODIFIERS **DGL**

A modifier must have something to modify. A **dangling modifier** is one that has nothing to modify because what it ought to modify has not been clearly stated in its sentence. For example:

Driving through the mountains, three bears were seen.

Driving through the mountains is a participial phrase that can modify anything that can drive. But there is nothing in the sentence that can do this. The sentence says that the bears were driving, but common sense tells us this can't be so. The writer surely meant that the bears were seen by some person who was driving.

Dangling modifiers may be verbal or prepositional phrases or elliptical clauses **(12d).** They most commonly come at the beginning of a sentence, but they can come at the end as well. To write *There were three bears, driving through the mountains* still leaves the bears apparently doing the driving. Nothing is expressed that *driving* can sensibly modify. Nor is *When a baby, my grandfather gave me a silver cup* improved by moving the clause to the end of the sentence.

Eliminate dangling modifiers by (1) reworking the sentence so that the modifier is clearly attached to the right word or (2) expanding the dangler into a full subordinate clause. The sentence in the illustration, for example, can be revised as follows:

Driving through the mountains, we saw three bears.
When we drove through the mountains, we saw three bears.

12a Avoid dangling participial phrases.

A **participle** is a verb form used as an adjective to modify a noun or pronoun. A participial phrase consists of a participle, its object, and any modifiers of the participle or object. (See **1b** and **1c**.)

DANGLING   Coming home late, the house was dark. [There is nothing in the sentence that can sensibly be coming home. A revision must identify some person.]

REVISED   Coming home late, we found the house dark.
            When we came home late, the house was dark.

DANGLING   Being made of glass, Horace handled the tabletop carefully.

REVISED   Because the tabletop was made of glass, Horace handled it carefully. [The participial phrase is expanded into a subordinate clause.]

EXERCISE 12a   Revise the following sentences to eliminate the dangling participial phrases.

1 Marinated in mustard sauce, the cook served a delicious ham.
2 Spanning the Straits of Mackinac, the engineers realized the bridge would be one of the world's longest suspension bridges.
3 Fierce and uncaged, visitors to wild game preserves must be careful not to arouse the animals.
4 Seated at an outdoor cafe, Paris reveals an exciting panorama.
5 Howling through the treetops, I could hear the wind.

12b Avoid dangling phrases containing gerunds.

A **gerund** is an *-ing* form of a verb used as a noun. A gerund phrase consists of a gerund, its object, and any modifiers of the gerund or object. (See **1b** and **1d**.) In typical dangling phrases containing gerunds, the gerund or gerund phrase serves as the object of a preposition.

DANGLING   Before exploring the desert, our water supply was replenished. [Who replenished it?]

REVISED   Before exploring the desert, we replenished our water supply.

DANGLING   After putting a worm on my hook, the fish began to bite. [A very accommodating fish that will bait the hook for you.]

REVISED   After I put a worm on my hook, the fish began to bite.

EXERCISE 12b Revise the following sentences to eliminate the dangling gerund phrases.

1 In deciding where to live, the distance to one's work should be considered.

2 After releasing the suspect, new evidence was submitted to the police.

3 In preparing the launch, Voyager II was inspected many times.

4 Before transferring to the new school, his mother took Bobby to meet his future teacher.

5 After getting up in the morning, the day began with a good breakfast.

12c Avoid dangling infinitive phrases.

An **infinitive** consists of the infinitive marker *to* followed by the plain form of the verb. An infinitive phrase consists of an infinitive, its object, and any modifiers of the infinitive or object.

> DANGLING   To take good pictures, a good camera must be used. [Who will use the camera?]
>
> REVISED   To take good pictures, you must use a good camera. If you wish to take good pictures, you must use a good camera.
>
> DANGLING   To write effectively, practice is necessary.
>
> REVISED   To write effectively, you [or *one*] must practice.

EXERCISE 12c Revise the following sentences to eliminate the dangling infinitive phrases.

1 To save fuel, the thermostat is turned down.

2 To be a good citizen, some knowledge of local government is necessary.

3 To plan a college program, career goals must be carefully considered.

4 To be a financial success, at least a hundred performances of a Broadway play are essential.

5 To be really secure, the lock on their office door was changed.

12d Avoid dangling elliptical clauses.

An **elliptical clause** is one in which the subject or verb is implied or understood rather than stated. The clause dangles if its implied subject is not the same as the subject of the main clause. Eliminate a dangling elliptical clause by (1) making the dangling clause agree with the subject of the main clause or (2) supplying the omitted subject or verb.

> DANGLING   *When a baby,* my grandfather gave me a silver cup.
>
> REVISED   *When a baby,* I was given a silver cup by my grandfather. [The subject of the main clause agrees with the implied subject of the elliptical clause.]
> *When I was a baby,* my grandfather gave me a silver cup. [The omitted subject and verb are supplied in the elliptical clause.]

12d

DANGLING	*While rowing on the lake,* the boat overturned.
REVISED	*While rowing on the lake,* we overturned the boat. [The subject of the main clause agrees with the implied subject of the elliptical clause.]
	While we were rowing on the lake, the boat overturned [*or* we overturned the boat]. [The elliptical clause is expanded into a subordinate clause.]

EXERCISE 12d   Revise the following sentences to eliminate the dangling elliptical clauses.

1 If sighted, astronauts could confirm that there is a man in the moon.
2 While combing her hair, someone knocked at the door.
3 A fish stole the bait off my hook while dozing.
4 If found, we will pay a reward for the lost ring.
5 You may slip on the floor, if highly polished.

EXERCISE 12a–d   Revise the following sentences to eliminate the dangling modifiers.

1 Pacing a mile in 1 minute, 52$^{1}/_{5}$ seconds, a world record in harness racing was set by Niatross.
2 When frightened, our thinking is controlled by our emotions.
3 After sharpening his claws on the waterbed, Uncle Zed saw our cat Daniel swimming to safety.
4 Waiting for the fog to lift, the flight to Louisville was finally cancelled.
5 To appreciate the music fully, the volume on the stereo should be high.
6 While riding my unicycle, a large dog chased me.
7 Being a minor, the judge suspended the sentence of the prowler.
8 Relaxing on the shore of the lake, his eyes followed the path of the speedboat.
9 To understand modern civilization, the past must be studied.
10 By collecting postage stamps, much history and geography are learned.

13

13   OMISSIONS **OM**
INCOMPLETE AND ILLOGICAL
COMPARISONS **COMP**

A sentence will be confusing if the writer omits words needed to insure clarity and accuracy. Sometimes, of course, writers omit words through haste or carelessness. This sort of omission can be caught with careful proofreading. Most omissions not caused by carelessness occur in three kinds of construction: (1) some constructions in which the omission of a preposition or conjunction is common in informal speech, (2) some kinds of compound constructions, and (3) comparisons.

13a Proofread your writing carefullly to avoid careless omissions.

The sample sentences below are confusing because they omit necessary words.

The opportunities for people television repair are varied.
Many millions people were unemployed last depression.
Learning by imitation is one of the most common in early life.

In the first two examples, the writer has simply failed to write the necessary words: *in* after *people* in the first, and *of* before *people* and *during the* before *last* in the second. The third sentence, although somewhat more complex, clearly requires something like *methods of learning* after *common*. Very probably the writer thought out the sentence with such a phrase and was merely careless in getting the idea down on paper.

13b In writing, spell out relationships left implied in speech.

Some constructions such as *He left Monday* are idiomatic. In speaking we often extend this pattern to such expressions as *We became friends spring semester,* or *The next few years we'll worry about prices.* In writing, such relationships need to be spelled out.

SPOKEN   Space travel *the last few years* has been exciting.
WRITTEN   Space travel *during the last few years* has been exciting.

The omission of *that* can often be confusing.

CONFUSING   He felt completely naked but totally private swimming was indecent.
REVISED   He felt that completely naked but totally private swimming was indecent.

The use of *type, make, brand* and some other similar words immediately before a noun (*this type show, this brand cereal*) is common in speech but is avoided by most writers.

COLLOQUIAL   I have never driven this *make car* before.
WRITTEN   I have never driven this *make of car* before.

13b

EXERCISE 13b In the following sentences, supply the omitted words that are implied but not stated.

1 Columbus Day, a special holiday for Americans of Italian ancestry, is celebrated October.
2 This model camera has an automatic film winder.
3 Rachel received several nice gifts the eight days of Hanukkah.
4 I understood French toast was provided with the American plan.
5 With this type metal detector you can find buried treasure, such as bottle caps and gum wrappers.

13c

13c Include all necessary words in compound constructions.

When we connect two items of the same kind with coordinating conjunctions such as *and* or *but,* we often omit words that unnecessarily duplicate each other: *She could [go] and did go; He was faithful [to] and devoted to his job.* But such omissions work only if the two items are in fact the same. If they are not, the resulting construction will be incomplete (see also the discussion of parallelism in Section **35**). Such incomplete constructions usually result from omitting necessary prepositions or parts of verb phrases.

INCOMPLETE	Martha was interested and skillful at photography.
REVISED	Martha was interested *in* and skillful *at* photography. [*Interested* idiomatically requires the preposition *in;* if it is not present, we tend to read *interested at.*]
INCOMPLETE	My cat never has and never will eat fish.
REVISED	My cat never has *eaten* and never will *eat* fish.
INCOMPLETE	Tom's ideas were sound and adopted without discussion.
REVISED	Tom's ideas were sound and *were* adopted without discussion. [*Were* needs to be repeated here since the two verbs are not parallel; the first *were* is used as the main verb; the second is used as an auxiliary with *adopted.*]

EXERCISE 13c Supply the omitted words in the following sentences.

1 Virginia always has and always will admire her Aunt Kate.
2 The concert was lively and appreciated by the audience.
3 Last year he determined to but finally gave up visiting Japan.
4 In China the major problem has and continues to be overpopulation.
5 He annually resolves to but fails in taking off excess weight.

13d

13d Make all comparisons complete and logical.

A comparison expresses a relation between two things: *A is larger than B.* To make a comparison complete and logical, include both items being compared, include all words necessary to make the relationship clear, and be sure that the two items are in fact comparable.

1 Avoid incomplete comparisons. Sentences such as *Cleanaid is better* or *Weatherall Paint lasts longer* are popular with advertisers because they let the advertiser avoid telling us what the product is better than or lasts longer than. To be complete, a comparison must state both items being compared.

INCOMPLETE	Our new Ford gets better mileage. [Better than what?]
REVISED	Our new Ford gets better mileage than our old one did.

2 Avoid ambiguous comparisons. In comparisons such as *He enjoys watching football more than [he enjoys watching] baseball,* we can omit *he enjoys watching* because only one meaning is reasonable. But when more than one meaning is possible in such sentences, the comparison will be ambiguous.

AMBIGUOUS	I admire her more than Jane. [More than Jane admires her? More than you admire Jane?]
CLEAR	I admire her more than I admire Jane.
	I admire her more than Jane does.

3 Avoid illogical comparisons. A comparison will be illogical if it compares or seems to compare two things that cannot be sensibly compared.

ILLOGICAL	A lawyer's income is greater than a doctor. [The sentence compares an income to a doctor. Logic requires the comparison of income to income or of lawyer to doctor.]
REVISED	A lawyer's income is greater than a doctor's.
	A lawyer's income is greater than that of a doctor.
	A lawyer has a greater income than a doctor does.

4 Avoid grammatically incomplete comparisons. Comparisons using the expression *as strong as, as good as,* and the like always require the second *as.*

INCOMPLETE	He is as strong, if not stronger than, Bob.
REVISED	He is as strong as, if not stronger than, Bob.
	He is as strong as Bob, if not stronger.

13d

In comparisons of items in the same class of things, use *other* or *any other*. In comparisons of items in different classes, use *any*.

INCORRECT	Mt. Everest is higher than *any* Asian mountain.
CORRECT	Mt. Everest is higher than *any other* Asian mountain.
	Mt. Everest is higher than *other* Asian mountains. [We are comparing Mt. Everest, one Asian mountain, to other Asian mountains.]
	Mt. Everest is higher than *any* American mountain. [We are comparing Mt. Everest, an Asian mountain, with American mountains, a different class.]

EXERCISE 13d   In the following sentences, make all comparisons complete and logical.

1 The population of Illinois is larger than Iowa.
2 Dennis telephones me more often than Jamie.
3 Graffiti, or words and pictures inscribed on walls, are as old, if not older than, ancient Roman civilization.
4 Lake Ontario is smaller than any of the Great Lakes.
5 For good eyesight, vitamin A is as essential, if not more essential than, other vitamins.

EXERCISE 13a–d   The following sentences all contain incomplete constructions. Revise each by supplying words that have been omitted.

1 His eyes are like a frightened chipmunk.
2 Ghetto children deserve to and should be getting better schools.
3 The Nile is longer than any African river.
4 In some countries the people are not as friendly as Italy.
5 His opinions were different from the other committee members.
6 Many people are both afraid and fascinated by snakes.
7 It seemed Thoreau wanted to avoid some of his Concord neighbors.
8 Jill is better than any rebounder on her basketball team.
9 Early Nebraska settlers found sod houses were warmer in winter.
10 Lee is both excited and experienced at mountain climbing.

14

14 AWKWARD OR CONFUSED SENTENCES **AWK**

Sometimes a sentence goes wrong because the predicate says something about the subject that cannot sensibly apply to that subject. Or a sentence goes wrong because it starts with one kind of construction and ends with a different kind of construction. The first of these faults is called **faulty predication;** the second, a **mixed construction.**

14a Make sure to combine only subjects and predicates that make sense together.

Not all subjects and verbs make sense together. For example, many living things can be subjects for the verb *eat—women, boys, ants, panthers.* Figuratively, we can speak of water *eating away* rock. But nouns like *bed, fence,* and *idea* are not likely subjects for *eat.* Sometimes, however, in haste or carelessness, writers construct sentences in which inappropriate verbs create faulty predications.

In each of the following sentences, the subject and the verb do not fit together.

> The *selection* of the committee *was chosen* by the students.

> Many *settlers,* moving into a new part of the country, *expanded* into towns.

> Any *member* who failed to do his job on the ship *meant* danger for the whole crew.

Illogical combinations of subject and verb are particularly likely to occur when the verb is the linking verb *to be* in its various forms. Linking verbs equate what comes before the verb with what comes after it—the subject with the complement. They say that something equals something else. Thus they cannot be used to connect things that are not equal. *My dog is a beagle* will do, but not *My dog is a reason.*

FAULTY	The first step in writing is spelling. [*Step* does not equal *spelling.*]
REVISED	The first step in writing is learning to spell.
FAULTY	His first trick was a pack of cards. [*Trick* does not equal *pack.*]
REVISED	His first trick was one with a pack of cards.
FAULTY	Schools are a serious quarrel today.

In the third example, *schools* clearly is not equivalent to *quarrel.* But revision is not really possible because the subject, *schools,* is itself so vague. Perhaps the writer meant something like *Increased taxes for schools cause serious quarrels today.*

A common kind of faulty equation occurs with predicates that begin with *is when* and *is where* and with the expression *the reason is because.* Definitions such as *Drunkenness is when you've had too much to drink* or *Subtraction is where you take one thing from another* are common in speech. Written English, however, ordinarily requires a noun or a word group functioning as a noun as both subject and complement in such definitions. Note the following sentences and their revisions.

FAULTY   A documentary is when a movie or a television drama analyzes news events or social conditions.

REVISED   A documentary is a movie or a television drama that analyzes news events or social conditions.

FAULTY   A hasty generalization is when you jump to conclusions.

REVISED   Hasty generalization involves jumping to conclusions.

To make a hasty generalization is to jump to conclusions.

Sentences such as *The reason he didn't come was because he was sick* are also common in speech, but *reason is that* is strongly preferred at all levels of writing. *Because* means *for the reason that;* therefore, the expression *the reason is because* is redundant.

FAULTY   The reason he went to Chicago was because he wanted to visit Kareem.

REVISED   The reason he went to Chicago was that he wanted to visit Kareem.

He went to Chicago because he wanted to visit Kareem.

EXERCISE 14a   Revise the following sentences to eliminate faulty predications.

1 People in the American sun belt, needing protection from intense summer heat, are many flat-roofed, Hispanic-styled houses.
2 Country music is sometimes broken dreams and lost loves.
3 A comic strip is when you have a series of drawings, usually with dialogue and stereotyped characters.
4 The reason some artists live in obscurity and die in poverty is because their work is boring as well as gaudy.
5 Mark Twain said that a camel was where a committee tried to plan a horse.

14b

14b   Do not mix constructions.

A mixed construction is one in which a writer begins a sentence in one construction and then shifts to another. The result is a derailed sentence that must be put back on its track to be clear.

MIXED   With every effort the student made to explain his problem got him more confused.

Here the writer began with a prepositional phrase, but by the time he arrived at his verb *got* he is thinking of *every effort* as his subject. We can untangle the sentence either by giving *got* the subject *he;* or by dropping the preposition *with* and making *every effort* his subject.

REVISED   With every effort the student made to explain his problem he got more confused.

Every effort the student made got him more confused.

Beginnings such as *the fact that, there are,* and *it is* often cause needless complexity and lead to mixed or confusing sentences.

MIXED   The fact that Ben was a good student he had many offers for good jobs. [*The fact that* as a beginning requires something like *results* or *leads to* as a main verb in the sentence. But the writer has forgotten that as the sentence develops.]

REVISED   The fact that Ben was a good student resulted in his having many offers for good jobs.

Because Ben was a good student, he had many offers for good jobs.

EXERCISE 14b   Revise the following sentences to eliminate the mixed constructions.

1 Some of the teams they play, it would make their season a success by beating Notre Dame.

2 Although he read some books about sailing does not mean he is an expert sailor.

3 The culture described by Chicano poets, they often reflect their Aztec origins.

4 By installing smoke alarms in houses will reduce the loss of life and property.

5 The fact that floodwaters covered the valley many farmers lost their wheat crop.

EXERCISE 14a–b   Correct the following sentences to eliminate faulty predications and mixed constructions.

1 By developing solar energy, it could reduce the need for other kinds of energy.

2 As a center for the performing arts, most young actors and actresses yearn to go to New York.

3 Because he forgot the date was why he missed the meeting.

4 My first reaction to being in a large class frightened me.

5 The price of the car cost her over $5,000.

6 The reason for her resignation is because she has been offered a higher salary.

7 Funky music is where the jazz style is derived from work songs, the blues, and gospel tunes.

8 He suffered from asthma is the main reason he moved to the Southwest.

9 Dandruff is when your scalp is dry and flakes off after you brush or comb your hair.

10 Having spent more than he expected for rent left him very little money for food.

REVIEW EXERCISE ON BASIC SENTENCE FAULTS (Sections 6–14) Indicate what strikes you as the principal error in each of the following sentences (faulty agreement, faulty reference, misplaced parts, etc.), and then revise the sentence.

1 Having been buried since the 14th century B.C., scientists found the tomb of Egyptian King Tutankhamen in 1922.

2 The letter was mailed an hour ago by the new clerk with the red sweater in the corner mailbox.

3 She likes Marie better than any of the other players.

4 Because Manhattan is an island, you have to take a bridge from New Jersey.

5 Millicent went to work in the theater after being graduated from college as an usherette.

6 When teenage children criticize their parents' friends, they usually feel uncomfortable.

7 In 1934 a well-known criminal wrote to Henry Ford saying he drove more Fords than others and stole them almost exclusively.

8 No matter how much he wanted to get there on time, and with several modes of transportation available.

9 Being too weak to answer the bell for the tenth round, the referee signaled the beaten challenger that the bout was over.

10 Most motorcycle riders consciously or unconsciously relate to their machines, they see them as extensions of their own personalities.

11 The years between 1865 and 1890 is the era of the cowboy, the trail town, and the great cattle drives.

12 The fairy tale is one of the early influences that helps children move from a fantasy world to reality.

13 In popular song lyrics an "outsider" is when a person is antisocial, unstable, arrogant, and often surviving through luck or violence.

14 Many housing projects for the elderly and low-income families are being built, which should emphasize open space and the human feelings of the occupants.

15 Since you can find great bargains at the flea market, I often go there.

16 They only bought a dog because their children wanted one.

17 Uncle Zed took our cat Daniel to a veterinarian that scratched his eye climbing a tree.

18 We intend to, if we can obtain tickets, see next year's Superbowl game.

19 In settling the New World, horses were first introduced by the Spaniards.

20 Children's toys are becoming safer, and some of it is a result of parents' complaints.

MANUSCRIPT MECHANICS
MS

It was very pleasant to me to get a letter from you the other day. Perhaps I should have found it pleasanter if I had been able to decipher it.

THOMAS BAILEY ALDRICH

Many practices of written English are merely conventions. Logic does not justify them; they represent standard ways of doing things. The mechanics of manuscript form, of writing numbers and abbreviations, of word division (syllabication) are such conventions. We observe them chiefly because readers expect writers to observe them. To be ignorant of these conventions or to violate them is not to commit a cardinal sin—it is only to be a nuisance to readers, who expect that any writer seeking their attention will have the graciousness to do the little things properly.

15 MANUSCRIPT FORM **MS**

15a Use suitable materials for your manuscripts.

1 Paper. Your instructor will probably require you to use standard theme paper ($8^{1}/_{2}$ by 11 inches) with lines about a half inch apart. Unless specifically told to, do not use narrow-lined notebook paper for themes. If you typewrite your manuscript, use either regular typewriter paper or the unruled side of theme paper. Do not use onionskin paper.

2 Typewriter. Use a black ribbon and keep the keys clean.

3 Pen and ink. Write on only one side of the paper. Use a good pen and black or blue-black ink. Do not write in pencil.

15b Make sure your manuscripts are legible.

1 Typewritten manuscripts. Use double spacing. Leave one space between words and two spaces between sentences.

2 Handwritten manuscripts. Provide adequate spacing between words and between lines. Avoid unnecessary breaks between letters and syllables at the ends of lines. Form all letters distinctly, with clear and conspicuous capitals. Cross all *t*'s. Dot all *i*'s with dots, not with decorative circles or other designs. Avoid artistic flourishes. If your handwriting tends to be large and sprawling or small and cramped or precariously tipped to right or left, make a conscious effort to improve it.

15c Keep your manuscripts physically uniform and orderly.

1   Margins. Leave a uniform one-and-a-half-inch margin at the top and at the left side of each page and about one inch at the right side and bottom. Resist the temptation to crowd words in at the right or bottom of the page.

2   Title. Center the title about two inches from the top of the page, or on the first line of a handwritten paper. Leave a blank line between the title and the first paragraph. Capitalize the entire title, or if your instructor prefers, capitalize the first word and all other words in the title except the articles, *a, an, the,* and short prepositions or conjunctions. Do not underline the title or put it in quotation marks unless it is an actual quotation. Use no punctuation after titles except when a question mark or exclamation point is required. Do not repeat the title after the first page.

3   Indenting. Indent the first line of each paragraph about an inch, or five spaces on the typewriter. Indent lines of poetry one inch from the regular margin, or center them on the page. If you are type-writing, use single spacing for poetry you are quoting.

4   Paging. Number all pages, after the first, in the upper right-hand corner. Use Arabic numerals (2, 3, 4, etc.).

5   Endorsement. The endorsement usually appears on the out-side sheet of the folded composition and includes your name, the course, and the date, plus any other information required by your instructor. Below is a specimen:

Fold ⟶   John Doe
here   English 101, Section A
                      October 18, 1981
                      Instructor: Mr. Brown
                      Class Paper 2

15d Carefully proofread your manuscripts before submitting them.

Give every manuscript a close, critical reading before turning it in. Allow a cooling-off period between composition and proofreading. If you know you are poor in spelling, punctuation, or some other skill,

15d

give your paper a separate reading for each kind of error. If your proofreading reveals a great many errors, recopy your composition. When recopying is not necessary, make specific changes as follows:

1   If you want to delete words, draw a horizontal line through them. Do not use a series of parentheses to cancel words.

2   If you want to begin a new paragraph within an existing paragraph, put the sign ¶ or *Par.* before the sentence that is to begin the new paragraph. When you want to remove a paragraph division, write *No* ¶ or *No Par.* in the margin.

3   If you want to make a brief insertion, write the new material above the line and indicate the point of insertion by placing a caret (∧) below the line.

15e

15e   After your instructor has returned a manuscript, make the necessary corrections and submit it again.

Correcting or rewriting your papers is invaluable practice. If your instructor indicates errors in your writing by using numbers or correction symbols that refer to specific sections of this handbook, study these sections before making revisions. Note that your instructor may not indicate all errors. Try to eliminate all faults before returning your corrected paper. Your instructor may want you to make corrections directly on your paper, particularly when these corrections involve grammar, punctuation, and mechanics. Or he or she may suggest that you try reworking a single paragraph or an entire brief paper.

On page 109 is an example of a paragraph marked by an instructor who has used the abbreviations and symbols listed on the front inside cover pages. The instructor asked the class to respond to the assertion that Freshman Composition should be a required course. Below it is the same paragraph after it has been corrected and revised by a student. Notice that the student has underlined those words and instructions that have been rewritten so that the instructor may easily check the accuracy of the corrections. (On pages 220–221 in Section **31,** "The Whole Composition," is an example of an essay that has been marked with the numbers that appear on the back endpapers of the handbook.)

16

16   NUMBERS **NOS**

Conventions governing the choice between spelling out numbers and using figures vary with the kind of writing. The more scientific or technical the writing, the greater the use of figures as opposed to spelled-out numbers. Most writing intended for the general reader

A paragraph marked with correction symbols

Glos

  Freshman Composition should be required of (each and every) student.

Shift (I) know that in (today's modern society) (I) will need to be able to write
         Dir   *NOS* *AB*

to get a good job. (You) would think that after (4) (yrs.) of high school

English / students would be able to write. But even students who (receive) *awk*
                   Ex   *T*

SUB good grades in high school have trouble (writing out) their ideas and

feelings. In college there are many other courses that (we) will be re- *Shift*

Frag quired to write in. [For example an essay exam in history.] So English

Cap (composition will help (me) pass these other courses. My English teachers

always said that writing was (something) which could be learned by anyone
           Ex

who really worked at it. *CS* I hope this is true. I think I have supported *Shift*
 SP

my (arguement) in this paragraph.

The same paragraph rewritten/revised

  Freshman Composition should be required of <u>all</u> students. <u>Today</u>
<u>a person needs to be able to write to get a good job.</u> Although
<u>students should be able to write after completing four years of high</u>
<u>school English</u>, even students who <u>received</u> good grades in high school
have trouble <u>expressing</u> their ideas and feelings <u>in writing</u>. In
college there are many other courses, <u>such as history, in which</u>
<u>students will be required to write essay exams</u>. English Composition
will help <u>them</u> pass these courses. My English teachers always said
that writing was <u>a skill that</u> could be learned by anyone who really
worked at it. <u>The experience of many students has proven this true.</u>
<u>These reasons support the argument that composition should be a re-</u>
<u>quired course.</u>

spells out numbers that can be written in two words or less except for special kinds of numbers such as those listed in 16b and 16c below. This is particularly true if the subject requires the use of only a few numbers. If a subject requires the extensive use of numbers, it will ordinarily be clearer if figures are used throughout. In any case, you should be consistent in your use of figures or spelled-out numbers in a given piece of writing. The following guidelines give common conventions for most general writing.

16a   **In nonscientific writing spell out numbers or amounts less than one hundred; use figures for other numbers or amounts.**

He spent ninety-seven dollars for a camera.

Miriam is twenty-two years old.

The boy saved $4.53.

On their vacation they drove 2,468 miles.

16b   **Use figures for dates and addresses.**

Dates	*Addresses*	
May 4, 1914	13 Milford Avenue	
July 2, 1847	57 East 121st Street	
1862–1924	Route 1 P.O. Box 353	Apartment 6A
17 B.C. to A.D. 21	Grinnell, Iowa 50122	

The ordinal numbers (first, third, ninth) or the forms 1st, 3rd, 9th may be used in dates if the year is not given: March 1, March first, March 1st.

In formal invitations dates are usually written out: Sunday, September ninth, nineteen hundred and eighty-one. (See **20i** for the punctuation of dates and addresses.)

16c   **Ordinarily, use figures for the following:**

decimals	8.72 13.27
percentages	72% or 72 percent
mixed numbers and fractions	$27\frac{1}{2}$ $19\frac{1}{4}$
scores and statistics	score of 35–10 a vote of 86–53
identification numbers	Channel 7 Flight number 523
volume, chapter, and page numbers	Volume V, Chapter 7, page 518
act, scene, and line numbers	Act II, scene 4, lines 18–47
figures followed by symbols or abbreviations	$18'' \times 23''$ $6' \times 9'$ 5 cu. ft. 72F 31C 55 mph.
exact amounts of money	$8.93 $29.95 53¢
times	4:30 P.M. 5:45 A.M. But *half past four, quarter of six, seven o'clock*

16d Except in legal or commercial writing, do not repeat in parentheses a number that has been spelled out.

COMMERCIAL   The original order was for fifty (50) pumps.

STANDARD   Carol has trained four sopranos in four years.

16e Spell out numbers that occur at the beginning of a sentence.

INAPPROPRIATE   217 bales of hay were lost in the fire.

REVISED   Two hundred seventeen bales of hay were lost in the fire.

If necessary, recast a sentence to eliminate numerals at the beginning.

INAPPROPRIATE   2,655 entries were received in the puzzle contest.

REVISED   In the puzzle contest 2,655 entries were received.

EXERCISE 16a–e In the following sentences, make any necessary corrections in the use of numbers.

1 John F. Kennedy was inaugurated on January 20th, 1961, at the age of 44.
2 The used stereo receiver was guaranteed for only ninety (90) days.
3 2 pounds of Kentucky bluegrass seed will sow 1,000 square feet of soil.
4 The satellite model measured eleven and nineteen-hundredths inches in circumference.
5 The bus left Mayfield at two-thirty P.M.
6 My breakfast at Pedro's Taco House cost $.95.
7 Labor Day is the 1st Monday in September.
8 There is a twenty percent chance of rain today.
9 Each of us consumers, on the average, uses one hundred and twenty-eight pounds of sugar a year.
10 Channel seven provides continuous television news coverage.

17 ABBREVIATIONS **AB**

With a few standard exceptions, abbreviations are avoided in ordinary writing. The following sections describe standard exceptions, as well as some forms that should not be used.

17a

1 Titles before proper nouns. Use such abbreviations as *Mr.*, *Mrs.*, *Ms.*, *Dr.* only when the surname is given: *Dr. Hart* or *Dr. F. D. Hart.*

INAPPROPRIATE He has gone to consult the Dr.

REVISED He has gone to consult Dr. Hart (*or* the doctor).

Use *St.* (Saint) with a Christian name: *St. James, St. Theresa.*
Use abbreviations such as *Hon., Rev., Prof., Sen.* only when both the surname and given name or initials are given: *The Hon. O. P. Jones,* but not *Hon. Jones.* In more formal usage, spell out these titles and use *The* before *Honorable* and *Reverend.*

INFORMAL Rev. W. C. Case delivered the sermon.

FORMAL The Reverend W. C. Case delivered the sermon.

2 Titles after proper names. Use the following abbreviations only when a name is given: *Jr., Sr., Esq., M.D., D.D., LL.D., Ph.D.* You may, however, use academic titles by themselves.

John Nash, Jr., received an M.A.

F. D. Hart, M.D., is now studying for his J.D.

3 Abbreviations with dates and numerals. Use the following abbreviations only when specific dates and numerals are given: B.C.; A.D.; A.M. or a.m.; P.M. or p.m.; No. or no.; $.

4 Latin abbreviations. Latin abbreviations such as *i.e.* (that is), *e.g.* (for example), *etc.* (and so forth) are common in most writing. In formal writing the English equivalent is increasingly used. Do not use *etc.* as a catch-all. It is meaningless unless the extension of ideas it implies is unmistakably clear. Do not write *and etc.;* the *and* becomes redundant.

CLEAR The citrus fruits—oranges, lemons, etc.—are rich in Vitamin C. [The reader has no difficulty in mentally listing the other citrus fruits.]

INEFFECTIVE We swam, fished, etc. [The reader has no clues to the implied ideas.]

REVISED We swam, fished, rode horses, and danced.

5 The names of agencies, organizations, corporations, and people ordinarily referred to by their initials.

Agencies	IRS, FBI, SEC
Organizations	AMA, YWCA, NOW
Corporations	NBC, IBM
People	JFK, FDR

If the name of an organization occurs frequently in a paper or article but is likely to be unfamiliar to readers, it should be spelled out in its first use and the abbreviation given in parentheses. Thereafter the abbreviation may be used: Zimbabwe African National Union (ZANU).

17b Spell out personal names; the names of countries and states; the names of days, months, and holidays; and the names of courses of instruction.

INAPPROPRIATE	Eliz., a student from Eng. who joined our bio class last Wed., expects to go home for Xmas.
REVISED	Elizabeth, a student from England who joined our biology class last Wednesday, expects to go home for Christmas.

The District of Columbia is spelled out when it is used alone but abbreviated, D.C., when it follows the city name, Washington. The United States and the Soviet Union are commonly abbreviated as the USA (or U.S.A.) or the US, and as the USSR (or U.S.S.R.)

17c Spell out the words *street, avenue, company,* and references to a subject, volume, chapter, or page, except in special contexts such as addresses and footnotes.

INAPPROPRIATE	The Perry Coal Co. has an office at Third Ave. and Mott St.
REVISED	The Perry Coal Company has an office at Third Avenue and Mott Street.
INAPPROPRIATE	The p.e. class is reading ch. 3 of the textbook.
REVISED	The physical education class is reading the third chapter (*or* Chapter 3) of the textbook.

Use such abbreviations as Bros., Inc., Co., and the ampersand (& for *and*) only in the names of firms where they are used in the official titles.

Barnes & Noble, Inc.
Sears, Roebuck and Co.

EXERCISE 17a–c In the following sentences correct all faulty abbreviations.

1 Mister Whitefeather is an artist who paints wildlife in the Cherokee Nat'l. Forest near the border of Tenn. and N. Carolina.
2 He enrolled in the U. of Me. because he wanted to study the culture of northern N. England.
3 The prof. in my comp. class explained how to write a letter of application.
4 The urban renewal project will cover the area between Main St. and Wisc. Ave.
5 Doctor Wilenski told the patient to take a tsp. of cough syrup every six hrs.
6 As we walked along Bourbon St. in N. Orleans we heard a Dixieland band playing "When the Sts. Go Marching In."
7 Gary & Jon Burns are bros. who own a business called Burns Bros. Car Sales.
8 Many writers, e.g. Benj. Franklin and Emma Goldman, have pointed out the dangers of the individual's being submerged in a mass society.
9 Wm. Shakespeare began writing plays during the reign of Queen Eliz. I of Eng.
10 Rev. Dean's sermons reflect her training in phil. and ancient hist.

18 SYLLABICATION **SYL**

When you find that you can write only part of a word at the end of a line and must complete the word on the next line, divide the word between syllables and use a hyphen to indicate the break. Always place the hyphen at the end of the line after the first part of a divided word, not at the beginning of the next line on which you complete the word.

When you are in doubt about the syllabication of a word, consult a good dictionary. Desk dictionaries normally use dots to divide words between syllables: *bank·rupt, col·lec·tive, ma·lig·nant, punc·ture.* Note that not every syllable marks an appropriate point at which to divide a word at the end of a line. (See **18b** and **18c**.)

18a Never divide words of one syllable.

WRONG   thr-ee, cl-own, yearn-ed, plough-ed
REVISED   three, clown, yearned, ploughed

18b Never divide a word so that a single letter stands alone on a line.

WRONG   wear-y, e-rupt, a-way, o-val
REVISED   weary, erupt, away, oval

18c When dividing a compound word that already contains a hyphen, make the break where the hyphen occurs.

AWKWARD   pre-Shake-spearean, well-in-formed, Pan-Amer-ican

REVISED   pre-Shakespearean, well-informed, Pan-American

EXERCISE 18a–c Which of the following words may be divided at the end of a line? Indicate permissible breaks with a hyphen. Refer to your dictionary if you are doubtful.

drowned	enough	walked
swimmer	twelve	automobile
learned	through	exercise
abrupt	acute	open
envelope	ex-President	preeminent

REVIEW EXERCISE ON MANUSCRIPT MECHANICS (Sections 15–18) Correct the errors in the following sentences.

1 Some stores add a service charge to bills that are not paid within thirty (30) days.

2 On Thursdays Betsy's classes are finished by ten forty-five A.M.

3 The vice-pres. of the Student Council sometimes acts as secy. of the mtgs.

4 The new Center of African Studies is located at the corner of Maple and Main Sts.

5 2 box tops must accompany every request for a free recipe booklet.

6 Paperback books, which once sold for a quarter, now cost as much as six dollars and ninety-five cents.

7 The Campus Theater will show a Bogart film on the 1st. Mon. of every mo.

8 Tourists in N.Y.C. often go to see the Empire State Bldg.

9 Most people voted to extend suffrage to 18 yr. olds.

10 A chimney sweep must have a variety of shovels, buckets, flue brushes, etc.

11 The Moore Mfg. Co. advertised a five percent discount on household appliances.

12 Heavyweight boxers must weigh over 175 lbs.

13 People fishing on Lake Mendota must throw back all perch measuring under five in.

14 Rev. Winters performed the marriage ceremony at the Lutheran Ch.

15 Mr. & Mrs. Hone entered their 3 yr. old filly in the race.

PUNCTUATION
P

Punctuation is far from being a mere mechanical device. It is mechanical as a matter of course, like word-spacing or the use of initial capitals; but punctuation is much more than that. It is an integral part of written composition.

GEORGE SUMMEY, JR.

When we speak, we use pauses and gestures to emphasize meaning, and we vary the tempo, stress, and pitch of our voices to mark the beginning and end of units of thought. In other words, we "punctuate" our speech. We punctuate writing for the same purposes, drawing on a whole set of conventional devices developed to give the reader clues to what we are trying to communicate.

The first of these devices is **spacing:** that is, closing up or enlarging the space between letters or words. For example, we do not runwordstogetherthisway. Instead, we identify a word as a word by setting if off from its neighbors. Spacing is the most basic of all punctuating devices. We use spacing also to set off paragraphs, to list items as in an outline, to mark lines of poetry, and the like.

But spacing, of course, is not the only punctuation we need. What, for example, can you understand from this string of words:

> yes madam jones was heard to say to the owl like old dowager without a doubt the taming of the shrew by shakespeare would be a most appropriate new years present for your husband

To make this passage intelligible, we need to add two other kinds of punctuation: (1) changes in the size and design of letters, namely, **capitals** and **italics;** and (2) marks or points, namely, **periods, commas, quotation marks, apostrophes,** and other special signs.

> "Yes, Madam," Jones was heard to say to the owl-like old dowager, "without a doubt, *The Taming of the Shrew* by Shakespeare would be a most appropriate New Year's present for your husband."

The example shows four functions of punctuation:

1   End punctuation. Capitals, periods, question marks, and exclamation points indicate sentence beginnings and endings.

2   Internal punctuation. Commas, semicolons, colons, dashes, and parentheses within sentences show the relationship of each word or group of words to the rest of the sentence.

3   Direct-quotation punctuation. Quotation marks and brackets indicate speakers and changes of speaker.

4   Word punctuation. Capitals, italics, quotation marks, apostrophes, and hyphens indicate words that have a special character or use.

In questions of punctuation there is often no absolute standard, no authoritative convention to which you can turn for a "correct" answer. But two general rules serve as reliable guides:

1 Punctuation is a part of meaning, not a substitute for clear and orderly sentence structure. Before you can punctuate a sentence properly, you must construct it properly. No number of commas, semicolons, and dashes can rescue a poorly written sentence.

2 Observe conventional practice in punctuation. Though many of the rules are not hard and fast, still there is a community of agreement about punctuating sentences. Learning and applying the punctuation rules that follow will help you observe these conventions.

19 END PUNCTUATION **END P**

19

Periods, question marks, and exclamation points signal the end of a sentence. Use a period after plain statements or commands; use a question mark after questions; use an exclamation point after strongly emotional expressions. Ordinarily, the character of the sentence dictates the proper end punctuation. Occasionally, however, you must determine for yourself what you intend the meaning of a sentence to be. Notice the different intentions behind these three sentences:

He struck out with the bases loaded.
He struck out with the bases loaded?
He struck out with the bases loaded!

The Period   .

19a   Use a period to signal the end of a statement, a mild command, or an indirect question.

19a

STATEMENT	She swam the mile with easy strokes.
COMMAND	Swim with easy strokes.
INDIRECT QUESTION	I asked her where she learned to swim with such easy strokes.

19b   Use a period after an abbreviation.

19b

Dr.   Mr.   Mrs.   Ms.   R.N.   C.P.A.   Sen.   B.A.

Omit the period after abbreviations that serve as names of organizations or government agencies (NEA, AFL, UNESCO, AMA, TVA).

P

If you are in doubt about whether to use periods in an abbreviation, consult a good dictionary for the standard practice.

The Question Mark   ?

19c   Use a question mark after a direct question.

Direct questions often begin with an interrogative pronoun or adverb *(who, when, what, etc.),* and usually have an inverted word order, with the verb before the subject.

> When did you study chemistry?
> Do you ever wonder what your future will be?
> You want to make a good impression, don't you?

19d   Use a question mark inside parentheses (?) to indicate doubt or uncertainty about the correctness of a statement.

The device shows that, even after research, you could not establish the accuracy of a fact. It does not serve as a substitute for checking facts.

> John Pomfret, an English poet, was born in 1667 (?) and died in 1702.

Rather than using (?), you may simply use *about:*

> John Pomfret, an English poet, was born about 1667 and died in 1702.

Do not use this mark as a form of sarcasm:

> It was a very charming (?) play.

19e   Do not use a question mark after an indirect question.

An **indirect question** is a statement implying a question but not actually asking one. Though the idea expressed is interrogative, the actual phrasing is not.

> They asked me whether I had studied chemistry in high school.
> He asked me whether I wished to make a good impression.
> I wonder what my future will be.

A polite request phrased as a direct question is often followed by a period rather than a question mark.

> Will you please return this book as soon as possible.
> May we hear from you at your earliest convenience.

The Exclamation Point **!**

19f   Use the exclamation point after an interjection or after a statement that is genuinely emphatic or exclamatory.

19f

Fire! Help!

What a vicious war!

The examination has been stolen!

19g   Do not overuse the exclamation point.

19g

Used sparingly, the exclamation point gives real emphasis to individual statements. Overused, it either deadens the emphasis or introduces an almost hysterical tone in your writing.

> War is hell! Think of what it does to young men to have their futures interrupted and sometimes cut off completely! Think of what it does to their families! Think of what it does to the nation!

EXERCISE 19a–g Supply the appropriate punctuation marks in each of the following sentences. If you feel that a choice of marks is possible, state why you chose the one you did.

1 Could you clarify that remark please
2 Every hotel guest should know where the fire exits are
3 Keep off the grass
4 He has an M A degree in horticulture and works for the U S D A
5 Those kids are hungry already
6 She asked whether our cat Daniel is a good mouser
7 A student group at M I T visited the Smithsonian Institution in Washington, D C
8 Will all passengers please collect their personal belongings before leaving the aircraft
9 Big John tooled his diesel van over to Pete's Diner and asked for the daily special of greasy pork chops and gravy
10 The management asks that people in the balcony refrain from throwing peanut shells on patrons in the lower seats
11 The real-estate investor bought a 450 ft lot on Rt 40
12 I wonder why Granny Hawks always describes anything she likes as "all wool and a yard wide"
13 Laurie has an A B degree and is studying for a Ph D at U C L A
14 The ship's captain ordered the crew to lower the lifeboats immediately
15 She asked the secretary whether there is a standard abbreviation for "chairperson"

20-24 INTERNAL PUNCTUATION **INT P**

End punctuation indicates whether a writer wants you to read a whole sentence as a question, a statement or an expression of emotion. Internal punctuation indicates the relationships and relative importance of elements within the sentence. Five punctuation marks are used for tnis purpose: commas, semicolons, colons, dashes, and parentheses.

The most important uses of these marks, like those of end punctuation, recur again and again. And like all uses of punctuation, they are a vital way of making the meaning of your sentences clear. In studying the following rules, notice not only how each mark is used but also how it contributes to the total meaning of the sentence.

20

20 THE COMMA ,

20a

20a Use a comma to separate main clauses joined by a coordinating conjunction.

The coordinating conjunctions are *and, but, or, nor, for, so,* and *yet.* When any one of these conjunctions is used to connect main clauses, it is always preceded by a comma.

> The Mayans of early Mexico were expert weavers, and some of their cotton textiles were mistaken for silk by Spanish explorers.

> Emerson said that youthful idealism is often misdirected and even comic, but sometimes young people see faults in society that are hidden from older people.

> The backpackers could follow the river valley, or they could risk finding a trail through the mountains.

> He lacks the sensitivity of an artist, nor does he have the patience of a scientist.

> In the spring thousands of hawks return north after wintering in the United States, for the Canadian forests are their hunting and nesting grounds.

> Thrifty housekeepers thaw frozen foods before cooking them, so they can save on utility bills.

> Engineers' squares should be completely accurate, yet they tend to get out of line and fail to measure a perfect 90 degrees.

There are, however, two exceptions.

1 Some writers omit the comma before the coordinating conjunction when one or both of the main clauses are very short: *Give a child enough rope and he'll trip you up.* But there is nothing wrong with a comma in such sentences, and since the comma is sometimes necessary for clarity, it is advisable simply to establish the habit of using it regularly.

2 When one or both of the main clauses joined by a coordinating conjunction are long or internally punctuated, use a semicolon before the coordinating conjunction.

> The Canadian Mounted Police were established in the 1870's to assure peaceful settlement of the northwest wilderness; and they became symbols of political and social order.

> The Mounties, dressed in red tunics and riding well-trained horses, were a familiar sight on the Canadian frontier; but few people in the United States saw Mounties except in the movies.

EXERCISE 20a In the following sentences, place a comma before each coordinating conjunction that joins main clauses.

1 In 1215 the Magna Carta became the law of England and it remains the basis for English civil liberties.
2 During the evening, storm clouds gathered overhead yet no rain fell.
3 I have a raspberry seed stuck between two teeth but I think a toothpick will dislodge it.
4 Helicopters are not relatively fast nor are they suited for long-distance travel.
5 The light wave is the transmission medium of the future for it has great message-carrying capacity because it uses glass fibers instead of copper wires.
6 We can walk to the stadium and arrive late for the game or we can take a taxi and see the kickoff.
7 Many young athletes call themselves joggers but others think of them as runners.
8 Solar energy is a promising field of research and many people are discovering its good employment prospects.
9 Dolphins have unusually good memories so they can be trained to perform amazing tricks.
10 The United States has vast reserves of coal and much of it may be converted into methane gas for energy.

20b Use a comma to separate introductory phrases and clauses from a main clause.

20b

Introductory phrases and clauses may be adverbial, modifying the verb in the main clause or the whole main clause; or they may serve as adjectives, modifying the subject of the main clause. Whatever their function, they should always be separated from the main clause by a comma unless they are very short and there is no possibility of misreading.

INTRODUCTORY PREPOSITIONAL PHRASES

According to legend, Hercules had enormous strength.
After his long exile to France, Charles II returned to England in 1660.
Like any man of sense and good feeling, I abominate work.
ALDOUS HUXLEY

INTRODUCTORY VERBAL PHRASES

To succeed as a long-distance runner, a person must have strong legs.
Announcing a recess, the judge retired to his chambers.
Exhausted by her effort, the swimmer fell back into the pool.
To be quite honest about it, that dog has been known to climb trees.

INTRODUCTORY CLAUSES

As soon as she had finished studying, she left the library.

If your job is to write every day, you learn to do it like every other job.
WILLIAM ZINSSER

Whenever I hear anyone arguing for slavery, I feel a strong impulse to see it tried on him personally. ABRAHAM LINCOLN

Do not confuse verbal modifiers with verbals used as subjects.

VERBAL MODIFIER	*Having been an arbitrator between labor and management for a decade,* he felt confident in tackling one more labor dispute.
VERBAL AS SUBJECT	*Having been an arbitrator between labor and management for a decade* made him feel confident in tackling one more labor dispute.

The comma is frequently omitted after very short introductory clauses or phrases. However, even when the introductory clause or phrase is very short, a comma is necessary if its omission can cause misreading.

CLEAR	When he arrived she was taking the cat out of the piano.
	After his defeat he retired from public life.
CONFUSING	When he returned home was not what it used to be.
	After dark fireflies came in large numbers.

EXERCISE 20b In the following sentences, insert commas after introductory elements whenever they are required.

1 According to Charlie Brown's philosophy you should dread only one day at a time.
2 Predicting the end of the world the self-styled prophet retired to a mountain cave.
3 To maintain our economic strength we must produce goods that can compete with products from other industrialized societies.
4 In winter storms are frequent in the Atlantic.
5 When people talk about ragtime they usually mean Afro-American folk music improvised on or composed for the piano.
6 As a symbol for modern America the novelist Ken Kesey chose a cuckoo's nest, or mental hospital.
7 To produce exciting or novel recordings rock groups are often dependent on electronic effects created in the sound studio.
8 In the American imagination the astronauts are a modern version of such early heroes as the explorers, pathfinders, and scouts.
9 Since we wanted to have a scenic vacation we traveled by boat from Vancouver through the inland waterways to Alaska.
10 Because of the fog all planes were grounded at the airport.

20c Use commas to set off nonrestrictive elements. Do not set off restrictive elements.

A **restrictive element**—which may be a clause, a phrase, or a word—is an essential modifier. It defines, limits, or identifies in some way the meaning of whatever it modifies. If it is removed from the sentence, the meaning is changed in some basic way. A **nonrestrictive element** may be interesting, but it is incidental to the basic meaning of the sentence.

An illustration will help make the difference clear.

RESTRICTIVE   A man *who is honest* will succeed.
NONRESTRICTIVE   Jacob North, who is honest, will succeed.

In the first sentence the clause *who is honest* identifies the kind of man who will succeed; it restricts the subject of *will succeed* to men *who are honest* as opposed to men *who are not honest*. In other words, the clause is restrictive. It is thus *not* set off with commas. In the second sentence, however, the proper noun *Jacob North* identifies or designates the particular man who *will succeed;* the fact that Jacob North *is honest* is merely amplifying information about a person already sufficiently identified. The clause is nonrestrictive. It *is* set off with commas.

In the illustration just discussed, the meaning is such that there is no question that the clause *who is honest* is restrictive in one sentence and not restrictive in the other. But sometimes whether a modifying element is restrictive or nonrestrictive depends upon your meaning. In such instances you must decide what you mean. Setting off the modifier or not setting it off is your only way of making your meaning clearer to your reader.

> The house, built by my grandfather, faced the mountain. [The phrase *built by my grandfather* is nonrestrictive and is thus set off by commas.]
>
> The house built by my grandfather faced the mountain, and the house built by my father stood only a hundred yards away. [In this compound sentence, the two phrases beginning with *built* limit and define the particular houses, distinguishing them from each other.]
>
> Texans, who have oil wells, can afford high prices. [All Texans have oil wells and can afford high prices.]
>
> Texans who have oil wells can afford high prices. [Some Texans have oil wells; only they can afford high prices.]

Always use *two* commas to set off a nonrestrictive element unless it begins or ends the sentence.

NOT	The old mare, half-blind and lame was hardly able to stand in the traces.
BUT	The old mare, half-blind and lame, was hardly able to stand in the traces.
	Half-blind and lame, the old mare was hardly able to stand in the traces.

1 Set off nonrestrictive clauses and phrases with commas. Do not set off restrictive clauses and phrases.

NONRESTRICTIVE CLAUSE	Elephants use their tusks, *which sometimes grow to ten feet or longer,* to fight, dig, or carry loads.
RESTRICTIVE CLAUSE	Elephants *that are sick or dying* often seek rivers or other water sources.
NONRESTRICTIVE CLAUSE	Akron, Iowa, *where my father grew up,* has a population of only 1242.
RESTRICTIVE CLAUSE	The town *where my father grew up* has a population of only 1242.
NONRESTRICTIVE PHRASE	My father, *on time for a change,* greeted us enthusiastically. [Prepositional]
RESTRICTIVE PHRASES	From the window *on the top floor* we could see the ships *in the harbor.* [Prepositional]
NONRESTRICTIVE PHRASES	Melinda, *determined to save enough money to buy a new car,* stayed home during her vacation. [Participial]
RESTRICTIVE PHRASES	Many houses *constructed with large windows exposed to the north* need a great deal of fuel. [Participial]

NONRESTRICTIVE PHRASES	The blizzard, *driving the heavy snow into deep drifts across the roads,* continued for twenty-seven hours. [Participial and prepositional]
RESTRICTIVE PHRASES	The economics text *lying on the table* was dog-eared. [Participial]

2   Set off nonrestrictive appositives with commas. Do not set off restrictive appositives. An appositive is a noun or a group of words used as a noun that describes or renames another noun, ordinarily the noun that comes immediately before it. Like clauses and phrases, appositives may be either restrictive or nonrestrictive, though appositives of more than one or two words are usually nonrestrictive and therefore set off by commas.

NONRESTRICTIVE APPOSITIVES

Davy Crockett, *the most famous man at the Alamo,* was a former Indian fighter.

No treatment, *not even hypnosis or acupuncture,* helped them stop smoking.

The whale, *a cold-water-dwelling mammal,* is protected by a thick layer of blubber.

"Hello, Mitty. We're having the devil's own time with McMillan, *the millionaire banker and close personal friend of Roosevelt."*   JAMES THURBER

Restrictive appositives limit, define, or designate the noun that they follow in such a way that their absence from the sentence would change its essential meaning. They are often, though by no means always, proper names following a more general noun or identifying phrase.

RESTRICTIVE APPOSITIVES

Robert Frost's poem *"Stopping by Woods on a Snowy Evening"* is one of his best-known poems.

The poet *Bryant* was a leader in New York literary circles.

Do you mean Napoli *the grocer* or Napoli *the doctor?*

The slang term *shrink* is often applied to psychiatrists.

The removal of the restrictive appositives from these sentences would leave such sentences as *Robert Frost's poem is one of his best-known poems* and *Do you mean Napoli or Napoli?*

EXERCISE 20c   In the following sentences, insert commas to set off nonrestrictive elements. Indicate which sentences are correct as written.

1 The expression "do your thing" was used by Emerson in the 1841 edition of his essay "Self-Reliance."

2 During the days of 19th century "Yellow Journalism," reporters who were unscrupulous created sensational events and paid witnesses to confirm them.

3 Pope John Paul II leader of the world's 563 million Catholics spoke strongly against political forces that degrade the poor.

4 Little Wolf a chief of the Cheyennes led a hunting party into the Powder River country.

5 Recent studies made by international economists predict that the gap between the wealthiest and poorest nations will continue to widen.

6 The heavy rain causing huge puddles on the streets delayed traffic.

7 By the year 2000, Mexico City which attracts many rural residents will have a population of thirty million.

8 In his journal, the voyager Christopher Columbus lamented that there were no nightingales in the New World.

9 Betsy eager to graduate and find a job enrolled in summer classes.

10 In the election of 1896, William McKinley the Governor of Ohio defeated William Jennings Bryan the silver-tongued orator from Nebraska.

20d

20d Use a comma to set off adverb phrases and clauses following the main clause and explaining, amplifying, or offering a contrast to it. Do not set off such clauses if they are closely related to the main clause.

Adverbial phrases and clauses usually *restrict* the meaning of the main clauses to which they are joined. They are therefore essential to the meaning of the main clause and are not set off by a comma when they follow the main clause. When they merely introduce additional *nonrestrictive* information, however, a comma is used to indicate that they are not essential to the meaning. The writer must be guided by the logic of his sentence and the meaning he intends. Note the following:

> You will not pass the examination unless you study carefully.
>
> You did not pass the examination, although I am sure you studied carefully.

The first of the examples sets up *unless you study carefully* as the condition for passing the examination. In the second, the main clause makes an unqualified statement of fact; the *although* clause adds some sympathy, but it doesn't qualify the fact of the main clause.

> Jane loves John because he tolerates her petty moodiness.
>
> Jane knows that she loves John, because she can tolerate his petty moodiness.

The first of the foregoing examples states that John's tolerance is an essential condition of Jane's love for him. In the second, the *because* clause merely introduces explanatory information about how Jane knows that she loves John.

Note that in some constructions a comma or the lack of one determines whether the reader will understand a phrase or a clause as a modifier of a final noun in the main clause or as an adverbial modifier.

> He has visited all the small towns in Pennsylvania.
>
> He has visited *all* the small towns, in Pennsylvania, in Ohio, in almost every state of the union.

In the first of these examples, *in Pennsylvania* restricts the location of the small towns and is an adjectival modifier of *towns*. In the second, however, the *in* phrase is additional information amplifying the assertion of the main clause but not essential to it.

EXERCISE 20d In the following sentences, insert commas wherever they are necessary to set off adverbial clauses or phrases.

1 We can get to the wedding on time if we hurry.
2 The hidden gold remains undiscovered since nobody can decipher the pirates' coded map.
3 We won't go out in this blizzard unless one of our neighbors needs help.
4 The climbers finally reached the top of Mt. Fuji although others had climbed to the summit before them.
5 Elisa went to the library after finishing her classes.

20e   Use commas to set off all absolute phrases.

Absolute phrases consist of a noun or a pronoun followed by a present or past participle. They modify the entire main clause in which they stand rather than any particular word or words in that clause. They are always nonrestrictive, supplying amplifying or explanatory detail rather than essential information. Thus they should always be set off by commas whether they appear at the beginning or end of a sentence or within it.

> He was stretched out on his reclining chair in the full sun, *his eyes covered, his head thrown back, his arms spread wide.*
>
> *Other things being equal,* short familiar words are better than long unfamiliar words.
>
> She was waiting for us, *her figure defined by the light from the half-open door.*
>
> The mastiff, *teeth bared, ears standing erect, body tensed,* refused to give ground.

P

EXERCISE 20e Insert commas in the following sentences to mark off absolute phrases.

1 Their faces lined with exhaustion the bicycle racers crossed the finish line.
2 The seagulls soared over the bay their wings spread against the wind.
3 All things considered gardening is a profitable hobby.
4 The bulldog his mouth watering with anticipation waited for the mail carrier to arrive.
5 Darkness rapidly approaching the children returned to their homes.

20f Use commas to set off elements that slightly interrupt the structure of a sentence.

Words, phrases, and clauses that slightly interrupt the structure of a sentence are often called *parenthetical elements.* Although such elements may add to the meaning of the sentence or serve to relate the sentence in which they stand to a preceding sentence or idea, they are not essential to its grammatical structure. Such elements include words of direct address, mild interjections, the words *yes* and *no,* transitional words and expressions, and phrases expressing contrast.

DIRECT ADDRESS	Can you show me, *Kathy,* how to punctuate this sentence?
	Will you speak a little louder, *George?*
MILD INTERJECTIONS	*Well,* no one can do more than his best.
	Oh, I never get A's—only C's and more C's.
TRANSITIONAL WORDS AND PHRASES	Sales taxes, *moreover,* hurt poor people severely.
	Christians, *on the other hand,* are opposed to violence.
	The judge ruled, *nevertheless,* that damages must be paid.
	The result, *in short,* was a complete breakdown of discipline.
CONTRASTED ELEMENTS	He had intended to write 1868, *not 1968.*
	Tractors, *unlike horses,* require gasoline.
	Insecticides and garden sprays now available are effective, *yet safe.*

Note that other elements of a sentence will interrupt its structure and require commas when they are inserted out of their normal grammatical order. Compare the following:

My grandmother always told me that work never killed anyone.
Work, *my grandmother always told me,* never killed anyone.

The exhausted and thirsty construction workers welcomed the cold beer.

The construction workers, *exhausted and thirsty,* welcomed the cold beer.

Always use two commas to set off a parenthetical element unless it begins or ends a sentence.

NOT	She insisted, however that they leave before midnight.
NOT	She insisted however, that they leave before midnight.
BUT	She insisted, however, that they leave before midnight.
	She insisted that they leave before midnight, however.

EXERCISE 20f Insert commas in the following sentences to set off parenthetical elements.

1 Sherlock Holmes to tell the truth was a very eccentric detective.
2 Well this is my bus stop, so I'll see you later Helen.
3 The main problem about exploring outer space Uncle Zed tells me is what people are going to do after they get there.
4 The traffic light was green officer when I drove through the intersection.
5 The Navaho tribe for instance are developing the energy resources on their reservations in the Southwest.
6 The world's poorer nations moreover must boost food production to sustain increasing numbers of urban industrial workers.
7 Excuse me sir but you are sitting on my hat.
8 Shrewd business management I think can yield profits even in bad times.
9 Peace in the Middle East according to some government experts is the key to solving American energy problems.
10 Radio unlike television cannot use cartoons and puppet shows to attract an audience of children.

20g Use commas to separate the items in a series.

A series consists of three or more words, phrases, or clauses of equal grammatical rank. The items of such a series are said to be coordinate: they have approximately equal importance. Typical series take the form *a, b,* and *c,* or the form *a, b,* or *c.*

She talked *fluently, wittily,* and *penetratingly.* [Three adverbs]

Some newspapers report sports events in *sailing, cross-country running, swimming,* and *tennis,* as well as other sports. [Four nouns]

Only a generation ago, the Navaho were *horsemen, nomads, keepers of flocks, painters in sand, weavers of wool, artists in silver,* and *singers of the yei-bie-chai.* [Seven nouns, some modified by prepositional phrases]

EDWARD ABBEY

Her sails ripped, her engines dead, and *her rudder broken,* the sailing vessel drifted helplessly. [Three absolute phrases]

The city couldn't *issue birth certificates on time, pay overtime when it was due, maintain its automotive fleets, deliver asphalt to men filling potholes, submit claims for federal and state aid payments, supply diaper pins to obstetric wards,* or *hire key staff.* [Seven predicates, each consisting of a verb and its object]   CHARLES R. MORRIS

After the accident, the driver of the car had no idea of *who he was, where he came from,* or *how the accident happened.* [Three dependent clauses]

Some writers treat three or more short, closely related independent clauses not joined by coordinate conjunctions as a series, separating them by commas rather than semicolons.

Some of the people said the elephant had gone in one direction, some said he had gone in another, some professed not even to have heard of any elephant.   GEORGE ORWELL

Less experienced writers will be safer using semicolons in such a series.

Some writers omit the comma before *and* in simple *a, b,* and *c* series: violins, flutes and cellos; men, women and children. But since the comma is sometimes vital for clarity, it is preferable to establish the habit of always including it.

Note how necessary the final comma is in the following:

Our resort is equipped with comfortable cabins, a large lake with boating facilities, and a nine-hole golf course.

I am interested in a modern, furnished apartment with two bedrooms, kitchenette, living room, bathroom with shower, and garage.

Without the comma after *facilities,* the first sentence seems to suggest that the resort has a lake with a golf course in it. Without the comma after *shower* in the second sentence, the writer seems to be asking for an apartment with a garage in the bathroom.

20h   Use commas to separate coordinate adjectives in a series; do not use commas to separate adjectives that are not coordinate.

Adjectives in a series are coordinate if each adjective modifies the noun separately. They are not coordinate if any adjective in the series modifies the total concept that follows it.

COORDINATE	You are a *greedy, thoughtless, insensitive* prig.
NOT COORDINATE	The boys are planning an *exciting holiday canoe* trip.

In the first sentence, each adjective is more or less independent of the other two; the three adjectives might be rearranged without seriously affecting the sense of the sentence: *thoughtless, insensitive, greedy prig; insensitive, greedy, thoughtless prig.* Moreover, the conjunction *and* could be inserted in place of the commas and the basic meaning would remain—*greedy* and *thoughtless* and *insensitive prig.*

But in the second sentence the adjectives are interdependent. Their order may not be changed, nor may *and* be substituted, without making hash of the original meaning—*canoe holiday exciting* trip; *holiday exciting canoe* trip; *exciting* and *holiday* and *canoe* trip. The adjectives in the second sentence constitute, in effect, a *restrictive* phrase, as distinct from the *nonrestrictive* quality of the adjectives in the first sentence, and therefore are not separated from one another by commas.

In actual usage, punctuating coordinate adjectives varies a great deal. Though few writers would punctuate the sentences above differently from the way we have punctuated them, many writers would be unable to choose between the punctuation of the following sentences:

He presented the ambassador with a *dirty, yellowed, gnarled* hand to shake.

He presented the ambassador with a *dirty yellowed gnarled* hand to shake.

Some writers feel that the meaning of the two sentences is slightly different: that the latter sentence suggests a more unified image than the former. That is, they feel that in the latter case the three adjectives intensify one another's qualities—*dirty-yellowed-gnarled* rather than *dirty and yellowed and gnarled.*

EXERCISE 20g–h In the following sentences, supply commas where they are needed to separate sentence elements in series.

1 Television advertising assures us that we can have skin that never wrinkles hair that always shines and dentures that never slip.
2 He brought a cup of strong steaming black coffee to the table.
3 Not all good citizens need endorse baseball hot dogs and apple pie.
4 To be healthy we should eat balanced meals sleep eight hours nightly and exercise daily.
5 Jean attended the Delta Gamma fall semester rush party.
6 Among the innovations brought into the world by Chinese civilization are the sailing ship the printing press and commercial banking.
7 Every year the engineering students sponsor an old time skunk rassle.
8 To the astronauts on the moon, the earth appeared fragile beautiful and alone in a dark universe.

9 Taking off his dingy old white cap lowering his battered black umbrella and scraping his tennis shoes on the doormat he rang the bell.

10 At the Navy swearing-in ceremony Nancy wore something old something new something borrowed and something blue.

20i Follow established conventions for the use of commas in dates, addresses, geographical names, titles, and long numbers.

1 Dates. If a date is written as month-date-year, use a comma between the date and the year. If such a date stands within a sentence, use a comma after the year.

> He left Detroit on July 19, 1967.
> He left Detroit on July 19, 1967, and never returned.

If only the month and year are given, use a comma neither between them nor after the year.

> He left Detroit in July 1967.
> He left Detroit in July 1967 and never returned.

If a date is written as day-month-year, use no commas.

> 17 July 1931   6 August 1982

2 Addresses. Standard comma punctuation of addresses is as follows:

> 205 Hayes Street, San Francisco, California 94102
> 39 West 46th Street, Olean, New York 71402

If geographical names or addresses appear within a sentence, use a comma after the final item. Note that no comma is used before the zip code.

ADDRESSES	He gave 39 West 46th Street, Olean, New York 71402 as his forwarding address.
GEOGRAPHICAL NAMES	He pretended to make the grand tour in three months, but he spent a whole month at Bremen, Germany, and the rest of his time in Tunbridge Wells, Kent, a small village in England.

3 Titles. Use commas to separate names from titles when the title follows the name. If the name followed by a title occurs within a sentence, use a comma after the title as well as between the name and the title.

Katherine Dugald, M.D.   William Harrington, Sr.

The university recently announced the appointment of Katherine Dugald, M.D., to the faculty of the medical school.

4 Large numbers. Ordinarily use commas in large numbers to indicate thousands, but do not use commas in social security numbers, telephone numbers, zip codes, and the like. These latter should be written as stated.

1,249	Social security number 391-07-4855
89,129	Telephone number 515-236-7669
1,722,843	Jamaica Plain, MA 02130

20j Use a comma to prevent misreading.

Sometimes in a sentence two words fall together so that they may be read two ways. In such instances, a comma may be necessary to prevent misreading even though no standard punctuation rule applies.

Long before, she had left everything to her brother.
Pilots who like to see sunbathers, fly low over apartment houses.
Inside the house, cats are sometimes a nuisance.

The omission of a comma after *before* in the first sentence would be momentarily confusing; we get off to a false start by reading *Long before she had left* without interruption. If there were no comma in the second sentence, we might think we were reading about flying sunbathers. A similar difficulty arises in the third sentence if *house* is not separated from *cats*. Often it is best to rewrite such sentences to avoid confusion.

The following sentences present similar problems:

To John, Smith was a puzzle. [Without the comma, the reader will take the introductory phrase to be *To John Smith*.]
People who can, take vacations in the summer. [Without the comma, the reader is likely to assume that the verb is *can take*.]

For the use of commas in quoted material, see **25d–f**.
For the misuse of the comma, see Section **24**.

EXERCISE 20i–j   In the following sentences, insert commas where conventional usage requires them or where they are needed to prevent misreading.

1 By age fifteen, the average American child has spent about 20000 hours in front of a television set.
2 Cautiously watching the cat spotted a field mouse in the deep grass.
3 The Great Depression began on Black Thursday October 24 1929 when the New York Stock Exchange began to collapse.
4 Tom made a down payment of $1200 on a new car.
5 On 6 May 1954 at Oxford England Roger Bannister became the first athlete to break the four-minute barrier in the mile run.
6 Above the clouds gathered ominously.
7 The public opinion poll asked 2304 people to name the most urgent problems facing the nation.
8 After July 1 her address will be 321 Rosewood Avenue Kilgore Texas.
9 My sister, who has always loved animals, now has an office with JANE SILVER D.V.M. painted on the door.
10 If you can wait for me after class.

REVIEW EXERCISE ON COMMA USAGE (Section 20)   Insert commas where they are needed in the following sentences. Indicate your reasons.

1 According to Benjamin Franklin success depended on practicing such virtues as industry frugality moderation and humility.
2 The Greek Parthenon built in the Fifth Century B.C. as a temple to the goddess Athena is threatened by pollution from countless Athenian automobiles.
3 We were surprised by the early spring snow shower.
4 The word *television* was used in *Scientific American* in 1907.
5 Among the signs of a good farmer are clean fence rows weedless fields and a well-painted barn.
6 *Adios amigo* until we meet again next fall.
7 On July 20 1969 Neil Armstrong and Edwin Aldrin made the first moon landing.
8 For directory assistance within your own telephone area dial 1 555 1212 and tell the operator the city and the name or place you want.
9 The hobo has many enemies including dogs and the police but his worst enemy is rain.
10 Many people criticize boxing as a brutal sport but some champions such as Jack Dempsey and Muhammad Ali have been seen as American folk heroes.
11 All contest entries must be postmarked by Saturday March 30 and mailed to P.O. Box 312 Atlanta Georgia 30300.
12 The college directory lists John A. Ward M.F.A. who teaches creative writing and John B. Ward Ph.D. who teaches biology.
13 Football is the only sport dependent on language for it uses play names color codes and formation numbers.
14 A migraine headache never kills doctors say.
15 As we walked across the dry field we could see the dust sticking to our clothes.

21 THE SEMICOLON ;

21a Use a semicolon to separate closely related main clauses not joined by a coordinating conjunction.

The main clauses of compound sentences are most commonly joined by a comma and one of the coordinating conjunctions: *and, but, or, nor, for, so,* and *yet.* (See **20a.**) When main clauses expressing closely related ideas are not joined by a comma and a coordinating conjunction, use a semicolon between them. (If the ideas in the main clauses are not closely related, or if you don't intend to direct the reader's attention to their relatedness, treat each main clause as a separate sentence.)

> The rabbit is the all-American game; it is everywhere, and everywhere hunted. JOHN RANDOLPH

> Good writing is not merely "correct writing"; it is clear, economical, and expressive writing.

> Initiative in the attack is not much in the nature of the tarantula; most species fight only when cornered so that escape is impossible. ALEXANDER PETRUNKEVITCH

> Children begin by loving their parents; as they grow older they judge them; sometimes they forgive them. OSCAR WILDE

> If employees were late or participated in job actions, the payroll system couldn't dock them; when they were hired, they weren't paid; and when they retired, they would as likely keep on being paid. CHARLES R. MORRIS

A comma is sometimes used to separate very short main clauses not joined by coordinating conjunctions, particularly if the clauses are parallel, as in *She is not a person, she is a legend* or *Some allow it, some don't.* But the semicolon is always correct in such sentences—and much safer for the inexperienced writer.

21b Use a semicolon to separate main clauses joined by a conjunctive adverb.

Conjunctive adverbs are words like *however, moreover, therefore, consequently, indeed,* and *then* that carry a thought from one main clause to the next. (See p. 517 for a more complete list.)

She applied for the position three weeks after the deadline for applications; *therefore,* she was not considered.

The meeting was long and boring; *nevertheless,* we stayed until the end.

An abnormally hot, dry growing season has parched crops throughout the plains; *consequently,* we may expect higher food prices in the near future.

You can recognize conjunctive adverbs and distinguish them from other kinds of joining words if you remember that they are the only kind of joining word that can be moved from the beginning of the clause in which they stand to another position in that clause without changing the sense.

We could survive without running water; *indeed,* our ancestors survived without any modern conveniences.

We could survive without running water; our ancestors, *indeed,* survived without any modern conveniences.

In contrast, coordinating conjunctions (*and, but,* etc.) or subordinating conjunctions (*although, because, if, since, when,* and the like) cannot move from their positions without changing or destroying meaning.

Coordinating conjunctions must stand between the clauses they connect.

Fido barked, *so* we knew he wanted to go out.

BUT NOT   Fido barked, we *so* knew he wanted to go out.

Similarly, subordinating conjunctions must stand at the beginning of the clauses they introduce.

Fido barked *because* he wanted to go out.

BUT NOT   Fido barked he *because* wanted to go out.

When a conjunctive adverb comes within the second main clause instead of at the beginning, the clauses still must be separated by a semicolon and the conjunctive adverb set off by commas.

Americans spend millions of dollars for road-building; our roads, however, are rapidly deteriorating.

21c **21c Use a semicolon to separate main clauses joined by a coordinating conjunction if the clauses are long or internally punctuated.**

The meeting last night, the most argumentative and confusing thus far, lasted until midnight; and unless something unexpected happens in the meantime, the next meeting may last even longer.

21c

When New England was first settled, lobsters were plentiful all along the coast; and since the settlers depended heavily on the sea for their food, especially in the early years, they certainly must have eaten lobster frequently.

In some instances, even when relatively short main clauses are joined by a coordinating conjunction, a semicolon instead of a comma may be used for emphasis.

He could hear the excitement of their talk from the next room; but he could not distinguish what they were saying.

21d **Use a semicolon to separate the items of a series if the items themselves contain commas.**

21d

The following people were present: John Smith, the doctor; Angelo Martinez, the dentist; and Alice Wilson, the psychiatrist.

The bureaucracy consists of functionaries; the aristocracy, of idols; the democracy, of idolators.
G. B. SHAW

EXERCISE 21a–d In the following sentences, insert semicolons or substitute them for commas wherever needed.

1 Rudy's Steak House is a very busy restaurant you need dinner reservations on the weekend.
2 The badger is only as big as a small dog, however, it is fearless and has sharp teeth and claws.
3 Several centuries before Christopher Columbus sailed to America, Irish sailors, exploring the Atlantic, reached Iceland, and they were followed by Norse sailors, who settled in Greenland.
4 In Latin America, carnivals are a popular form of entertainment they express both the old traditions and the modern culture of the region.
5 Detective-mystery stories are popular with readers of all ages, consequently, one of every four books published in the United States is a detective-mystery.
6 Louis Armstrong was not just a great jazz musician he was an emissary abroad for the creativeness of American music.
7 Older citizens remember the era of the railroad with nostalgia: the great black engines, steam hissing beneath their wheels, the dining car, where flawless waiters served ham soufflé and huckleberry pie, the brass-railed, open-air observation car, often the last car on the train.
8 Richard Cory was rich, handsome, and popular, nevertheless, he went home one summer night and put a bullet through his head.
9 Laurie manages the budget of the Flying Club, she is largely responsible for the group's sound financial practices.
10 Cedar trees are usually only about forty feet in height and about two feet in diameter, therefore, cedar lumber is seldom very long or wide.

11 The decade of the Twenties was the heyday of Babe Ruth, the Yankee slugger, Charles Lindbergh, the Atlantic flyer, and Rudolph Valentino, the movie matinee idol.

12 Some modern societies venerate the machine the automobile, especially, is often viewed as a symbol of efficiency and affluence.

13 Our canoe moved noiselessly across the calm lake, occasionally a splashing fish broke the silence.

14 Television has developed several kinds of western drama, the classic western, however, embodies the clash between frontier and civilization, lawlessness and order.

15 Public opinion polls have become a part of government, indeed, few governmental or political party decisions are made without consulting them.

22   THE COLON :

Whereas the semicolon always indicates a full stop, the colon indicates an addition or expectation. It indicates that what follows will explain, clarify, illustrate, specify detail.

22a   Use a colon to separate two main clauses when the second explains, illustrates, or amplifies the first.

It is safe to predict what prices will do in the next decade: they will go up.

Charm, in the abstract, has something of the quality of music: radiance, balance, and harmony.   LAURIE LEE

There are two times in a man's life when he should not speculate: when he can't afford it and when he can.   MARK TWAIN

22b   Use a colon to set off a list or series, including a list or series introduced by *the following* or *as follows.*

For the most part we are an intemperate people: we eat too much when we can, drink too much, indulge our senses too much.
                                                        JOHN STEINBECK

Anything is possible on a train: a great meal, a binge, a visit from card players, an intrigue, a good night's sleep, and strangers' monologues framed like Russian short stories.   PAUL THEROUX

If you are interested in reading further about usage, we recommend the following books: Evans, *A Dictionary of Contemporary American Usage;* Follet, *Modern American Usage;* and Bernstein, *The Careful Writer.*

22c Use a colon to introduce a formal quotation.

The sixteenth amendment set up the income tax: "The Congress shall have power to lay and collect taxes on incomes, from whatever source derived, without apportionment among the several states, and without regard to any census or enumeration."

22d Use a colon according to established conventions to separate items in biblical citations, subtitles and titles, and divisions of time.

BIBLICAL CITATION	Luke 3: 1–4
DIVISIONS OF TIME	9:20 a.m. 10:10 p.m.
SUBTITLES	*Evaluating Writing: Describing, Measuring, Judging*

EXERCISE 22a–d   In the following sentences, insert colons where they are needed.

1 The refugees left their homeland to search for three ideals peace, equality, and opportunity.
2 Thomas Paine stoutly defended the rights of the American colonies, as did others Franklin, Jefferson, John Adams.
3 Only one word can describe my first attempt to water ski splash.
4 One final question how do people learn to be self-confident?
5 Much of life is consumed by routine reading newspapers, riding to work, discussing the weather.
6 To make Paul Bunyan stew, combine the following one steer cut into two-inch cubes, one truckload of mixed carrots and potatoes, and one tanker of crushed tomatoes.
7 The "trouble" in Northern Ireland can be interpreted in an entirely nonreligious way it is a tragedy deriving from a lack of jobs in a dying economy.
8 To this I have made up my mind my own life is somehow related to the lives of all other human beings.
9 We need to preserve the distinct spheres of our environment the city, the rural countryside, and the wilderness.
10 To summarize belief in the magic power of music over the forces of nature prevailed in ancient China and still persists in India and Africa.

23   THE DASH AND PARENTHESES

Both dashes and parentheses are used to set off interrupting comments, explanations, examples, and other similar parenthetical elements from the main thought of the sentence. Commas are ordinarily used when parenthetical or other nonrestrictive elements are closely related in the main thought of the sentence. Dashes and parentheses are used when the interruption is abrupt and the element set off is only loosely related to the main thought of the sentence.

Though the choice between dashes and parentheses is sometimes a matter of taste, dashes emphasize more strongly the element being set off and give it greater importance than parentheses. Parentheses are more commonly used when the element enclosed is an incidental explanatory comment, an aside, or a nonessential bit of information.

A single dash is used following an introductory element or preceding a final sentence element. A pair of dashes is used to enclose an element within a sentence. Parentheses always are used in pairs around the enclosed element. In handwriting, distinguish the dash from the hyphen by making the dash longer. In typewritten copy, use two hyphens without spacing to indicate the dash.

The dash —

23a

23a Use the dash or a pair of dashes to mark abrupt shifts in sentence structure or thought.

Could he—should he even try to—borrow money from his father?

The police ordered the boys—their authority to do so has been questioned—to stop gathering in front of the store.

23b

23b Use the dash to set off nonrestrictive appositives and other parenthetical elements for emphasis.

At the end of the month, he will go on half time—and half pay.

In any fight against the sun, man—for all his technology—will come out the loser. *Newsweek*

Each person is born to one possession which overvalues all his others—his last breath. MARK TWAIN

The student wandered in at 9:30—half an hour after the class began.

The spoken language does not have the same standards as the written language—the tune you whistle is not the orchestra's score.

WILLIAM SAFIRE

23c

23c Use the dash for clarity to set off internally punctuated appositives or other parenthetical elements.

To prevent confusion, use dashes rather than commas to set off compound appositives. In the following sentence it is difficult to determine whether *Bill, Dave, and Blacky* are three additional men—or perhaps dogs or tame bears—or whether these are, in fact, the names of the men who were in the office.

Three men, Bill, Dave, and Blacky, were sitting in the office with their feet on the desk.

But when the commas are replaced by dashes, the meaning becomes clear:

Three men—Bill, Dave, and Blacky—were sitting in the office with their feet on the desk.

23d Use the dash to set off introductory lists or summary statements.

Gather data, tabulate, annotate, classify—the process seemed endless to Jane.

Black flies, horseflies, little triangular flies, ordinary house flies, unidentified kinds of flies—those are what I mean when I say I'm sick of flies.

Pound, Eliot, Williams—these were the poets the course devoted most attention to.

23e Use the dash to show interruption or hesitation in speech.

"Why don't you—" He stopped abruptly and looked away.

"Well, I—uh—we—some of us really want to drop your plan."

Parentheses ( )

23f Use parentheses to set off parenthetical information, explanation, or comment that is incidental or unimportant to the main thought of the sentence.

The lawyer contends (and we can see that the contention has some merit) that this client was convicted on doubtful evidence.

In our society (it's the only one I've experienced, so I can't speak for others) the razor of necessity cuts close.   STUDS TERKEL

More than 1,000 years ago, the Hopis (the word means "the peaceful ones") settled in the mesa-dotted farmland of northern Arizona. *Time*

Among the narratives in the text, Maya Angelou's (pp. 58–68) is my favorite.

23g

23g Use parentheses to enclose numerals or letters labeling items listed within sentences.

To check out a book from our library, proceed as follows: (1) check the catalog number carefully; (2) enter the catalog number in the upper left-hand corner of the call slip; (3) fill out the remainder of the call-slip information; and (4) hand in the call slip at the main desk.

EXERCISE 23a–g In the following sentences insert dashes or parentheses wherever needed.

1 They noticed or thought they noticed a figure disappearing in the darkness.
2 The Washington Mall, intended as a grand avenue, became instead oh, so obviously the backyard of official Washington.
3 This is a common impulse among all nations the quest for a happier way of life.
4 Gentleness, devotion, and playfulness all are requirements for a child's first dog.
5 The Wizard of Oz and his friends remember the Scarecrow and the Cowardly Lion? lived in a land of magic.
6 The Zen teacher told the students they should 1 eat when they are hungry, 2 sleep when they are tired, and 3 have quiet minds.
7 Several original plays a comedy, a tragedy, and a melodrama were presented by the Drama Club.
8 Well, I'm not sure that would you please repeat the question?
9 When it was officially designated as a town in 1833, Chicago had fewer than a hundred inhabitants.
10 Some seemingly valueless things old barn boards are an example can unexpectedly become popular and valuable.

24

24 SUPERFLUOUS INTERNAL PUNCTUATION

Careful punctuation helps readers separate words and ideas, helps group related words together, and enables writers to set off words or word groups for emphasis. Inadequate punctuation can force a reader to go over a passage several times to get its meaning. But too many marks of punctuation, marks inserted where they are not necessary or where they separate words that belong together, confuse a reader as much as too few marks.

The following sentence, for example, is jarring because of unnecessary and confusing punctuation.

> The people of this company, have, always, been aware, of the need, for products of better quality, and lower prices.

None of the commas in that sentence is necessary.

Use all the punctuation marks that will make the reader's work easier or that are required by convention. But do not insert marks that are superfluous. Especially avoid the misuses of the comma, the semicolon, and the colon described below.

24a Do not separate a single or final adjective from its noun.

NOT   He was a discourteous, greedy, deceitful, boy.
BUT   He was a discourteous, greedy, deceitful boy.

24b Do not separate a subject from its verb unless there are intervening words that require punctuation.

NOT   The worth of real estate, is determined by the demand for it.
BUT   The worth of real estate is determined by the demand for it.
       The worth of real estate, tangible property, is determined by the demand for it. [The commas set off an appositive.]

24c Do not separate a verb from its object unless there are intervening words that require punctuation.

NOT   Molly drove, her old car carefully down the road.
BUT   Molly drove her old car carefully down the road.

NOT   The boys always made Peanut, the butt of their pranks.
BUT   The boys always made Peanut the butt of their pranks.
       The boys always made Peanut, an undersized and immature smart aleck, the butt of their pranks.

24d Do not separate two words or phrases that are joined by a coordinating conjunction.

NOT   He is very honest, and patient.
BUT   He is very honest and patient.

NOT   I decided to work during the summer, and relax in the fall.
BUT   I decided to work during the summer and relax in the fall.

24e

24e Do not separate an introductory word, brief phrase, or short clause from the main body of the sentence unless clarity requires it.

NOT   On Wednesday, the ice in the river began to break up.

BUT   On Wednesday the ice in the river began to break up.

Occasionally, however, a comma must be inserted to prevent misreading. (See **20j**.)

NOT   Notwithstanding *Drums at Dusk* is a worthy successor to *Black Thunder*.

BUT   Notwithstanding, *Drums at Dusk* is a worthy successor to *Black Thunder*.

24f

24f Do not separate a restrictive modifier from the main body of the sentence. (See **20c**.)

NOT   The girl, who slapped my face, also kicked my shins.

BUT   The girl who slapped my face also kicked my shins.

NOT   The band, in the park, played the same tired old marches we had heard, for fifteen years.

BUT   The band in the park played the same tired old marches we had heard for fifteen years.

Note that adverbial phrases and clauses usually *restrict* the meaning of the word or clause to which they are attached. They are therefore essential to the meaning and should *not* be separated by a comma from what they modify. (See also **20d**.)

NOT   The product is available, in large and small sizes.

BUT   The product is available in large and small sizes. [The phrase *in large and small sizes* restricts the adjective *available* and is essential to the meaning.]

NOT   Once darkness fell, over the trees, the dogs began to bark.

BUT   Once darkness fell over the trees, the dogs began to bark. [The phrase *over the trees* restricts the meaning of the verb *fell*.]

24g Do not separate indirect quotations or directly quoted single words and short phrases from the rest of the sentence.

24g

CORRECT   After drinking ten bottles of pop, Henry said he could drink ten more.

Claude said he was "weary of it all" and that he had "absorbed" his "fill of monotony."

24h Do not separate a preposition from its object.

24h

NOT   Carol went to, New York, Washington, and Atlanta.
BUT   Carol went to New York, Washington, and Atlanta.

24i Do not use a semicolon to separate a main clause from a subordinate clause, a phrase from a clause, or other parts of unequal grammatical rank.

24i

NOT   Mortimer rushed out of the house in his shirt sleeves; although it was raining.

BUT   Mortimer rushed out of the house in his shirt sleeves although it was raining.

NOT   The speaker rambled on and on; making everyone increasingly restless.

BUT   The speaker rambled on and on, making everyone increasingly restless.

24j Do not use a semicolon before a direct quotation or before a list.

24j

NOT   She said to him; "Harry, you have to straighten up and fly right."

BUT   She said to him, "Harry, you have to straighten up and fly right."

NOT   On their trip to "rough it," they took the following; a propane cooking stove, two radios, a portable TV, and a supply of the latest paperbacks.

BUT   On their trip to "rough it," they took the following: a propane cooking stove, two radios, a portable TV, and a supply of the latest paperbacks.

24k

24k Do not use a colon between a verb and its object or complement, or between a preposition and its object.

NOT   My brother hates: snakes, caterpillars, worms, grubs, and all beetles.

BUT   My brother hates snakes, caterpillars, worms, grubs, and all beetles.

NOT   The driver was charged with: driving without a license, driving so as to endanger, and driving an unregistered vehicle.

BUT   The driver was charged with driving without a license, driving so as to endanger, and driving an unregistered vehicle.

EXERCISE 24a–k   Eliminate any superfluous commas in the sentences below.

1 The pilot, having received clearances, circled the airport, before landing.
2 Across the river was a protected cove, in which there were two rowboats, and one small sailboat.
3 The meeting began late, because Kelly was not sure where the Regency Hotel was, or when the meeting was scheduled.
4 Sherry decided she could not take the night job, and still take courses in chemistry, accounting, and history, in the mornings.
5 The ice, near the southern bank, was too thin, and soft, for ice skating.
6 Both robins, and phoebes, will build their nests in your backyard, on a shelf nailed to the house, or garage.
7 Chief Justice John Marshall, of Virginia, was a strong Federalist, who shaped our interpretation of the Constitution.
8 Penguins, in the Galapagos Islands, are unafraid of people on land, but they are terrified, if people join them, while swimming in the Pacific.
9 During the Irish Potato Famine, (1845–1849), thousands of Irish people found no food to buy, and fled to Boston, and other cities.
10 The speaker replied slowly, because he had not expected the question, and did not know what to say.

REVIEW EXERCISE ON INTERNAL PUNCTUATION (Sections 20–24)   In the following sentences, there are various errors in internal punctuation. Correct all errors, and be prepared to explain the reasons for your corrections.

1 Jeff went shopping Marty went to a movie and Louise stayed home to study.
2 Answering the defense attorney Robbins said angrily he was sure of his evidence.

3 Uranium which is important in atomic processes is found in parts of Africa.

4 Most novelists osteopaths paperhangers and funeral directors have something in common they are self-employed.

5 Every year more than thirteen million people visit the 2300 acre expanse of Walt Disney World in Lake Buena Vista Florida.

6 In the 17th century Newton Galileo and Descartes said that the universe operated according to a constant pattern moreover mathematics was the God-given key to understanding it.

7 Glenn our plumber who can bend iron pipe in his bare hands whistled songs from Gilbert and Sullivan operettas as he fixed our leaking pipes.

8 Common sense is not a common quality those who have it are often sought after.

9 Instead of buying costly pollution control devices some industrialists find it economical to redesign equipment improve products and recycle water and waste material.

10 A quiet stretch of Sudbury farmland, set behind a row of tidy typical colonials is the setting of the story.

11 According to American historians Elihu Burritt 1810–1879 the famous Learned Blacksmith carried a Greek grammar in his hat but they also report that he was not a very good blacksmith.

12 Words words words were all that came out of the meeting.

13 It's relatively easy to borrow money it's much harder to repay it.

14 The bones of birds zoologists report are hollow to improve flight and are much the same in all birds.

15 Jealousy a debilitating emotion can wreck a relationship for without genuine trust there can be no real love.

25–26 THE PUNCTUATION OF QUOTED MATERIAL **Q**

Direct speech and material quoted word for word from other written sources must always be set off distinctly from a writer's own words. Quotation marks usually indicate such distinction, although when quotations from written sources are long, the distinction may be shown with different spacing and indentation. Section 25 describes the conventional uses of quotation marks and special spacing to set off quoted material; the use and punctuation of explanatory words such as *he said;* the conventions controlling the placement of other marks of punctuation with quotation marks; and the special uses of quotation marks in certain titles and with words used as words.

An explanatory comment inserted in a quotation or the omission of some part of the original quotation calls for the use of brackets or the ellipsis mark. These are discussed in Section 26.

25   QUOTATION MARKS " "

Indicating quoted material

25a   Use double quotation marks to enclose a direct quotation from speech or writing.

"Don't dive from that rock," she told me.
It was Emerson who wrote, "A foolish consistency is the hobgoblin of little minds."

Note that in dialogue, each change of speaker is indicated by a new paragraph.

"I know I've been here before," he said.
"Don't you remember exactly when?" She looked at him questioningly, and she pointed to something behind and above him. He turned and saw the path into the woods.
"No, I don't remember. Can't you understand? I don't remember when!"

Remember not to set off indirect quotations.

She told me not to dive from that rock.
It was Emerson who wrote that foolish consistency is the hobgoblin of little minds.

25b   Use single quotation marks to enclose a quotation within a quotation.

She turned and said, "Remember Grandfather's advice, 'When other people run, you walk.' "

Notice that the end punctuation of the sentence within single quotation marks serves also as the end punctuation for the entire sentence unit of which it is a part.

25c Set off prose quotations of more than four lines and poetry quotations of more than three lines by spacing and indentation.

Long prose quotations. Prose quotations of more than four lines should be displayed—set off from the text of a paper and indented from the left-hand margin. In typewritten papers, leave three line-spaces between the text and the quotation, indent all lines of the quotation ten character-spaces from the left, and single-space it. Do not enclose a displayed quotation in quotation marks. If quotation marks occur *within* material you are setting off, use them as they are in the original: double for double, single for single.

> Professor George Summey's comment on the writer's responsibility for accuracy in reporting the words of others is worth quoting:
>
>> Anyone who quotes another person's words has the duty of keeping the words unchanged and continuous or of giving clear notice to the contrary. It is improper to alter wording or punctuation of quoted matter, to italicize words without due notice, or to make any other change. That would misrepresent the meaning of the quoted words in their context.
>
> No careful writer would question the need for such accuracy.

Quoted poetry. Single lines of poetry are ordinarily run into the text and enclosed in quotation marks unless the writer wishes to give them particular emphasis by setting them off.

> In the line "A spotted shaft is seen," the hissing *s* sounds echo Dickinson's subject: a snake.

Two or three lines of poetry may be either enclosed in quotation marks and run into the text or indented ten spaces from the left. If they are enclosed in quotation marks and run into the text, divisions between lines are indicated by a slash mark (/).

> Blake combines mystical and military images, as in the lines "Bring me my Spear: O clouds unfold! / Bring me my Chariot of fire."
>
> . . . as in the lines
>> Bring me my Spear: O clouds unfold!
>> Bring me my Chariot of fire.

Poetry quotations of more than three lines should always be set off from the text and indented ten spaces from the left.

EXERCISE 25a–c In the following sentences, insert double or single quotation marks or slash marks wherever needed.

1 I sometimes wonder what life will be like in the next century, Lee said.
2 She recalled, In his Nobel Prize acceptance speech, William Faulkner said, I believe that man will not merely endure: he will prevail.
3 Robert Herrick's lines, Gather ye rosebuds while ye may, Old Time is still a-flying remind us to make the most of our youth, for it passes quickly.
4 This large skylight is a collector to preheat our hot water supply, explained the owner of the solar house.
5 TV newscaster Jessica Savitch reported: When the space shuttle Columbia lifted off at Cape Canaveral, one witness said, It's like a hundred Fourth of Julys rolled into one.
6 The scientist predicted that cold water pumped from the ocean floor will someday be used to generate energy.
7 Uncle Zed smiled and began, Whenever old Buck Owen met a stranger, he would say, Let me tell you how I led a wagon train across the plains to Laramie.
8 For generations, American schoolchildren read Longfellow's poem beginning: Listen, my children, and you shall hear Of the midnight ride of Paul Revere.
9 The old Indian spoke: Listen to me, Little Fox, and I will teach you the good medicine songs of the Chippewas.
10 Geologists said that the eruption of Mount St. Helens in the spring of 1980 was one of the worst volcanic explosions in American history.

Punctuating explanatory words with quotations

25d   **25d In punctuating explanatory words preceding a quotation, be guided by the length and formality of the quotation.**

Explanatory words such as *he said* are ordinarily set off from quotations by a comma when they precede the quotation. However, when the quotation that follows is grammatically closely related, it may be followed by no punctuation, or when it is relatively long and formal it may be followed by a colon.

NO PUNCTUATION   He yelled "Stop!" and grabbed the wheel.

Auden's poem "In Memory of W. B. Yeats" begins with the line "He disappeared in dead of winter."

The Preamble begins with the words "We, the people of the United States."

It was President Franklin Roosevelt who said that "the only thing we have to fear is fear itself."

PUNCTUATION
WITH COMMA

The old man said very quietly, "Under no circumstances will I tell you where the money is
hidden."

The chairman asked him, "Have I stated your
motion correctly?"

PUNCTUATION
WITH COLON

The speaker rose to his feet and began: "The
party in power has betrayed us. It has not only
failed to keep its election promises but has sold
out to the moneyed powers."

**25e Use a comma to separate an opening quotation from the
rest of the sentence unless the quotation ends with a
question mark or an exclamation point.**

"The man is dead," he said with finality.

"Is the man dead?" he asked.

"Oh, no!" he screamed hysterically. "My brother can't be dead."

**25f When a quotation is interrupted by explanatory words (*he
said,* or their equivalent), use a comma after the first part of
the quotation. In choosing the proper punctuation mark to
place after the explanatory words, apply the rules for
punctuating clauses and phrases.**

"I am not unaware," he said, "of the dangers of iceboat racing."

"I have always worked hard," he declared. "I was peddling newspapers
when I was eight years old."

"Jean has great capacities," the supervisor said; "she has energy, brains,
and personality."

EXERCISE 25d–f In the following sentences, insert appropriate punctuation
marks where necessary to separate quotations from the rest of the sentence.

1 Woodrow Wilson's speech began "No matter how often we think of it,
the discovery of America must each time make a fresh appeal to our
imaginations."

2 When Ruth and Bill arrived at the party, we shouted "Surprise!" and
turned on the lights.

3 "When does the next bus leave for Oakland" he asked.

4 "I take the ecological view" she explained "that nature is a process in
which humans are involved with all other life forms."

5 "Look out for the bicycle!" somebody yelled, and the shortshop
dropped the fly ball.

6 "Do you believe in astrology" he inquired.

7 "You can have this rod and reel" the old man said "I never fish any
more."

8 Addressing the Birdwatchers Club, he asked "Did you know that a hummingbird weighs only one-tenth of an ounce?"

9 My favorite limerick begins with the words "There once was a man named Mehaffy."

10 "We intend" the hiker said "to follow the Alaska Pipeline along Richardson Highway to the Gulf of Alaska at Valdez."

Using other marks of punctuation with quotation marks

25g Follow established conventions in placing other punctuation with quotation marks.

1 Place commas and periods inside quotation marks. Commas are generally used to separate direct quotations from unquoted material.

> "There is no use in working," he complained, "when it only makes me more sleepy than usual."

Note that this rule *always* applies, regardless of the reason for using quotation marks.

> According to Shakespeare, the poet writes in a "fine frenzy."
> While he insisted that he was a "beatnik," I certainly got tired of hearing him say that everything was "cool."

2 Place semicolons and colons outside quotation marks.

> According to Shakespeare, the poet writes in a "fine frenzy"; by "fine frenzy" he meant a combination of energy, enthusiasm, imagination, and a certain madness.

3 Place a dash, question mark, or exclamation point inside the quotation marks when it applies only to the quotation; place it outside the quotation marks when it applies to the whole statement.

> He said, "Will I see you tomorrow?"
> Didn't he say, "I'll see you tomorrow"?
> "You may have the car tonight"—then he caught himself abruptly and said, "No, you can't have it; I need it myself."

When a mark applies to both quotation and sentence, use it only once.

> Has he ever asked, "May I come in?"

EXERCISE 25g   In the following sentences insert whatever punctuation marks are appropriate for use with quotation marks.

1 In his First Inaugural Address, Thomas Jefferson called for "a wise and frugal government"
2 The Dixieland band played "Do You Know What It Means to Miss New Orleans"
3 Did she say, "Acid rain has ruined the telescope lens"
4 "Excuse me, please" then he blushed with embarrassment and went on, "I know this is silly, but haven't I seen you in the movies"
5 This fishing lure is called the "Frivolous Fly" it is used mostly for trout fishing.

Other uses of quotation marks

25h   **Use quotation marks to set off titles of poems, songs, articles, short stories, and other titles that are parts of a longer work.** (For the use of italics to set off titles of longer works, see **27a** and **27b**.)

Theodore Roethke's poem "My Papa's Waltz" appeared in his book *The Lost Son and Other Poems.*
"The Talk of the Town" has for many years been the opening column of *The New Yorker.*
Bob Dylan's "A Hard Rain's A-Gonna Fall" is one of his most popular songs.
"Beowulf to Batman: The Epic Hero in Modern Culture," an article by Roger B. Rollin, originally appeared in the journal *College English.*

25i   **Words used in a special sense may be set off by quotation marks.**

When a new book comes into the library, it is first of all "accessioned."
Is this what you call "functional" architecture?

Do not use quotation marks around common nicknames. Do not use them for emphasis. And do not use them apologetically to enclose slang, colloquialisms, trite expressions, or for imprecise words or phrases when you cannot find the right word. If a word is appropriate, it will stand without apology. If it is not appropriate, it should be replaced.

EXERCISE 25h–i   In the following sentences, insert quotation marks wherever they are needed.

1 W. C. Handy's St. Louis Blues is one of the most popular jazz melodies ever composed.

2 *The Yale Review* begins each issue with a series of book reviews called Reader's Guide.

3 The word karate comes from the Japanese and means empty-handed or, to put it another way, the art of defense without a weapon.

4 Walt Whitman's When Lilacs Last in the Dooryard Bloomed is usually considered the best American poem about the death of Lincoln.

5 Expressions like Take it easy or Have a nice day soon become trite.

26 BRACKETS AND THE ELLIPSIS MARK [ ] . . .

The important uses of brackets and ellipsis marks are to indicate some change that a writer has made in material being quoted. Brackets are used to indicate that a writer has inserted into a quotation some information, comment, or explanation not in the original. The ellipsis mark is used to indicate that something has been omitted from the material being quoted.

26a Use brackets to set off editorial remarks in quoted material.

You will sometimes want to insert an explanatory comment in a statement you are quoting. By enclosing such comments in brackets, you let the reader know at once that *you* are speaking rather than the original author.

> John Dryden, a famous English poet, said, "Those who accuse him [Shakespeare] to have wanted knowledge, give him the greater commendation; he was naturally learned."

> The favorite phrase of their [English] law is "a custom whereof the memory of man runneth not back to the contrary."
>
> RALPH WALDO EMERSON

In bibliographical notations, use brackets to enclose the name of a writer *reputed* to be the author of the work in question.

> [Ned Ward], *A Trip to New England* (1699)

26b Use the word *sic* ("thus it is") in brackets to indicate that a mistake or peculiarity in the spelling or the grammar of a foregoing word appears in the original work.

> The high school paper reported, "The students spoke most respectively [sic] of Mrs. Higginbottom."

26c Use an ellipsis mark (three spaced periods . . .) to indicate an intentional omission from quoted material.

When you wish to quote from an author but wish to omit some word within a sentence or to omit one or more sentences, in fairness to the original author and your readers you must indicate that you have omitted material from the original. Such omissions are indicated by inserting an ellipsis mark at the point of omission. For an omission within a sentence, use three spaced periods, leaving a space before and after each period. When the omission comes at the end of a sentence, use four periods; the first is the usual sentence period, and the last three are the ellipsis mark.

For example, the first selection below is taken without any omission from Russel Nye's *The Unembarrassed Muse* (New York, 1971). It describes the comic-strip world of Walt Disney's Mickey Mouse. The second selection shows how a writer quoting from the original passage might use the ellipsis.

Mickey's is a child's world, safe (though occasionally scary), nonviolent, nonideological, where all the stories have happy endings. Characterization is strong and simple—Mickey is bright and friendly, Minnie eternally feminine, Goofy happily stupid, Donald of the terrible temper a raffish, likeable rascal. No Disney strip ever gave a child bad dreams or an adult anything to ponder.

Mickey's is a child's world, safe . . . nonviolent, nonideological, where all the stories have happy endings. Characterization is strong and simple—Mickey is bright and friendly, Minnie eternally feminine, Goofy happily stupid, Donald of the terrible temper a raffish, likeable rascal. No Disney strip ever gave a child bad dreams. . . .

EXERCISE 26 Supply the appropriate punctuation in each of the following sentences.

1 The letter said tartly, The fault is not with our product but with your skin; it appears to be supersensitive.
2 Perhaps you might like to do a study of Irish ghost stories the professor suggested.
3 How long have you noticed this condition the doctor asked.
4 The editor of the *Weekly Echo* reported that "The Martins recently celebrated their thirtieth year of martial *sic* bliss."
5 He said, When the policeman asked me Where's the fire? I felt like telling him it was in his garage.
6 The song Aquarius is from the musical *Hair.*

7 William Blake wrote the often-quoted lines To see a world in a grain of sand And a heaven in a wildflower Hold infinity in the palm of your hand And eternity in an hour.

8 The salesclerk said, Sir I would exchange this sweater, but he added, it has already been worn.

9 One day, just as I was going out to Rahul's house, I heard her shouting outside the door of the study. The director is a busy man! She was shouting. She had her back against the door and held her arms stretched out; M. stood in front of her and his head was lowered. Day after day you come and eat his life up! she said.

R. PRAWER JHABVALA, "My First Marriage"

10 I climbed up in the bar yelling, Walsh, I'm shot. I'm shot. I could feel the blood running down my leg. Walsh, the fellow who operated the fish-and-chips joint, pushed me off the bar and onto the floor. I couldn't move now, but I was still completely conscious. Walsh was saying, Git outta here, kid. I ain't got no time to play. A woman was screaming, mumbling something about the Lord, and saying, Somebody done shot that poor child.

CLAUDE BROWN, *Manchild in the Promised Land*

27–30   WORD PUNCTUATION **WORD P**

Italics, capitals, apostrophes, and hyphens identify words that have a special use or a particular grammatical function in a sentence.

> Our two-week reading program, assigned in Wednesday's class, is Shakespeare's *King Lear.*

Here the italics set off the words *King Lear* as a single title. The capitals identify *Wednesday, Shakespeare, King,* and *Lear* as proper names. The apostrophes indicate that *Shakespeare* and *Wednesday* are singular possessives and not plurals. The hyphen between *two* and *week* makes the two words function as a single adjective.

27   ITALICS

27

In printing, italics are typefaces that slope toward the right. In typed or handwritten manuscript, italics are indicated by underlining.

> On the printed page: *italics*

> In typewritten copy: `italics`

> In handwritten copy: *italics*

27a **Italicize the titles of books, newspapers, magazines, and all publications issued separately.**

"Issued separately" means published as a single work and not as an article or story in a magazine, nor as a chapter or section of a book. (For the proper punctuation of such titles, see **25h.**)

The New York Times   *Commentary*
The Lord of the Flies   *Death of a Salesman*
    Webster's New Collegiate Dictionary

Be careful not to add the word *The* to titles unless it belongs there and not to omit it if it does belong.

NOT	*The Reader's Digest*	NOT	the *Red Badge of Courage*
BUT	the *Reader's Digest*	BUT	*The Red Badge of Courage*

27b **Italicize the names of ships and aircraft, and the titles of works of art, movies, television and radio programs, and record albums.**

Titanic   *Spirit of St. Louis*
The Thinker   *The Empire Strikes Back*
Barney Miller   *Jethro Tull Live: Bursting Out*

27c **Italicize letters, words, and numbers used as words.**

Your *r*'s look very much like your *n*'s, and I can't tell your *7*'s from your *1*'s.
The early settlers borrowed Indian words like *moccasin, powwow,* and *wigwam.*

Quotation marks are also used to set off words as words in typewritten or handwritten manuscripts (see **25i**). However, if the subject you are writing about requires you to set off frequent words as words, underlining (italics) will make your manuscript look less cluttered.

27d **Italicize foreign words and phrases that have not yet been accepted into the English language.**

She graduated *magna cum laude.*
Many of the works of the *fin de siècle* that seemed so sensational when they were written appear to us now as innocent.

You may sometimes feel that a foreign word or phrase expresses your meaning more aptly or concisely than an English one. If you are sure that your readers will understand the expression, use it. But to overuse such words is pedantry. Many foreign words have been accepted into the English language and need no longer be italicized. The following words, for example, do not require italics:

bourgeois   milieu   denouement   liqueur

To determine whether a foreign word should be italiziced, consult a good dictionary. (See the discussion of spelling under "The Uses of a Dictionary," pp. 341–342.)

27e   Use italics to give a word special stress.

The idea that knowledge follows interest is a scandalous half-truth; it is a better-than-half-truth that *interest follows knowledge.*

I heard him say once that in a democracy (a *democracy,* mind you) a division of opinion cannot be permitted to exist.

27f   Avoid the overuse of italics.

Distinguish carefully between a real need for italicizing and the use of italics as a mechanical device to achieve emphasis. The best way to achieve emphasis is to write effective, well-constructed sentences. The overuse of italics will make your writing seem immature and amateurish, as in the following:

Any good education must be *liberal.*

America is a *true* democracy, in every sense of the word.

This book has what I call *real* depth of meaning.

EXERCISE 27a–f   Italicize words where necessary in the following sentences.

1 Robert Redford, who is best known as an actor, received an Oscar as best director for the movie Ordinary People.

2 H. M. S. Queen Elizabeth, for years the flagship of the Cunard Line, was finally retired from service.

3 Are you supposed to pronounce the p in coup de grâce?

4 Some Americans use the word simpatico as though it meant sympathetic, but its meaning is really closer to that of the English word charming.

5 Is T. S. Eliot's The Wasteland included in The Oxford Book of English Verse?

6 His travels had brought him greater understanding of himself and just a touch of savoir-faire.

7 Webster's Third New International Dictionary lists more than half a dozen pronunciations of lingerie.
8 I am constantly forgetting what eclectic means.
9 New Englanders tend to add an r to words that end in a and to omit the r in words that do end in r.
10 Thus, in Boston, Cuba becomes Cuber, while river becomes riva.

28 CAPITALS

Modern writers capitalize less frequently than did older writers, and informal writing permits less capitalization than formal writing. Two hundred years ago, a famous author wrote:

> Being ruined by the Inconstancy and Unkindness of a Lover, I hope a true and plain Relation of my Misfortune may be of Use and Warning to Credulous Maids, never to put much Trust in deceitful Men.
>
> JONATHAN SWIFT, "The Story of the Injured Lady"

A modern writer would eliminate all capitals but the initial *B* and the pronoun *I*.

28a Capitalize the first word of a sentence and the first word of a line of poetry.

Education is concerned not with knowledge but with the meaning of knowledge.

True ease in writing comes from art, not chance,
As those move easiest who have learned to dance.

ALEXANDER POPE, *Essay on Criticism*

Some modern poets ignore the convention of capitalizing each line of poetry, perhaps because they feel that an initial capital letter gives a word unwanted emphasis.

a man who had fallen among thieves
lay by the roadside on his back
dressed in fifteenthrate ideas
wearing a round jeer for a hat
     e. e. cummings, "a man who had fallen among thieves"

28b Capitalize the pronoun I and the interjection O.

Do not capitalize the interjection *oh* unless it is the first word of a sentence.

28c Capitalize proper nouns, their derivatives and abbreviations, and common nouns used as proper nouns.

1 Specific persons, races, nationalities, languages.

William	Bob	George A. Smith	Semitic
Asiatic	American	Mongolian	Cuban
Canadian	English	Swahili	Zulu

Usage varies for the term *black (blacks)* designating members of the Negro race. Although it is often not capitalized, and is never capitalized in the phrase "blacks and whites," many authors regularly capitalize other uses in current writing.

2 Specific places.

Dallas	Jamestown	California	Lake Erie
Newfoundland	Iran	Jerusalem	Ohio River

3 Specific organizations, historical events, and documents.

Daughters of the American Revolution   the French Revolution
the Locarno Pact   NAACP
Declaration of Independence

4 Days of the week, months, holidays, and holy days.

Thursday	April	Christmas	Sunday	Labor Day
Easter	Good Friday	Hanukkah	Ramadan	

5 Religious terms with sacred significance.

the Virgin   Allah   Holy Ghost   the Saviour

6 Titles of books, plays, magazines, newspapers, journals, articles, poems. Capitalize the first word and all others except articles, and conjunctions and prepositions of fewer than five letters. (See also **25h** and **27a**.)

Gone with the Wind	*The Country Wife*	*Pippa Passes*
Paradise Lost	*Atlantic Monthly*	*War and Peace*
Ebony	*Much Ado About Nothing*	

7 Titles, when they precede a proper noun. Such titles are an essential part of the name and are regularly capitalized.

Professor Wilson   Secretary Hawkins
Dr. Natalie Spence   Mr. Gottschalk
President Reagan   Judge Paul Perry

When titles follow a name, do not capitalize them unless they indicate high distinction:

Robert F. Jones, president of the National Bank
J. R. Derby, professor of English

BUT   Abraham Lincoln, President of the United States
John Marshall, Chief Justice, United States Supreme Court

"High distinction" is, however, becoming more and more broadly interpreted. Some people write forms such as the following:

Robert F. Jones, President of the National Bank
J. R. Derby, Professor of English

8 Common nouns used as an essential part of a proper noun. These are generic names such as *street, river, avenue, lake, county, ocean, college.*

Vine Street   Fifth Avenue   Pacific Ocean   Lake Huron
General Motors Corporation   Penn Central Railroad
Hamilton College   Mississippi River

When the generic term is used in the plural, it is not usually capitalized.

Vine and Mulberry streets   Hamilton and Lake counties
the Atlantic and Pacific oceans

28d   Avoid unnecessary capitalization.

A good general rule is not to capitalize unless a specific convention warrants it.

1 Capitalize north, east, south, west only when they come at the beginning of a sentence or refer to specific geographical locations.

Birds fly south in the winter.
BUT   She lives in the western part of the Old South.

2 The names of seasons need not be capitalized.

fall   autumn   winter   midwinter   spring   summer

3 Capitalize nouns indicating family relationships only when they are used as names or titles or in combination with proper names. Do not capitalize *mother* **and** *father* **when they are preceded by possessive adjectives.**

| | I wrote to my father | | My uncle has ten children. |
| BUT | I wrote Father | BUT | My Uncle Ben has ten children. |

4 Ordinarily, do not capitalize common nouns and adjectives used in place of proper nouns and adjectives.

	I went to high school in Cleveland.
BUT	I went to John Adams High School in Cleveland.
	I am a university graduate.
BUT	I am a Columbia University graduate.
	I took a psychology course in my senior year.
BUT	I took Psychology 653 in my senior year.

EXERCISE 28a–d Capitalize words as necessary in the following sentences. Remove unnecessary capitals.

1 After leaving detroit, we turned North toward Mackinac island for our Summer vacation with uncle Jim.
2 The reverend Martin Luther King, jr., first came to public attention as a leader of the Civil Rights sit-ins in the south.
3 The late Robert Kennedy had been attorney general of the United States before being elected senator from the state of New York.
4 It has been predicted that power in the un will eventually shift from the security council to the general assembly.
5 The Boston symphony orchestra is not to be confused with the Boston pops orchestra.
6 All Math Majors who were preparing to teach Elementary School students were required by the math department to take courses in the New Math.
7 The organization of American states is designed to encourage cooperation and understanding among the nations of the western hemisphere.
8 Annemarie O'hara, president of the student congress, addressed the meeting.
9 Many of the aberdeen angus cattle come from the state of Nebraska.
10 It was the fall of the Roman empire which ushered in the middle ages.

29 APOSTROPHE '

29a Use an apostrophe to show the possessive case of nouns and indefinite pronouns.

1 If a word (either singular or plural) does not end in *s*, add an apostrophe and *s* to form the possessive.

the woman's book	the women's books
the child's book	the children's books
the man's book	the men's book
someone's book	people's books

2 If the singular of a word ends in *s*, add an apostrophe and *s* unless the second *s* makes pronunciation difficult; in such cases, add only the apostrophe.

	Lois's book	James's book
BUT	Moses' leadership	Sophocles' dramas

(The addition of a second *s* would change the pronunciation of *Moses* to *Moseses* and *Sophocles* to *Sophocleses*.)

3 If the plural of a word ends in *s*, add only the apostrophe.

the girls' books
the boys' books
the Smiths' books [Referring to at least two persons named Smith]

4 In compounds, make only the last word possessive.

father-in-law's book [*Singular possessive*]
mothers-in-law's books [*Plural possessive*]
someone else's book

5 In nouns of joint possession, make only the last noun possessive; in nouns of individual possession, make both nouns possessive.

John and Paul's book [*Joint possession*]
John's and Paul's books [*Individual possession*]

29a

P

Here is a list showing standard singular and plural possessive forms:

Singular	Possessive Singular	Plural	Possessive Plural
child	child's	children	children's
man	man's	men	men's
lady	lady's	ladies	ladies'
father-in-law	father-in-law's	fathers-in-law	fathers-in-law's
passer-by	passer-by's	passers-by	passers-by's

29b

29b Use an apostrophe to indicate the omission of a letter or number.

can't	can not	o'clock	of the clock
doesn't	does not	blizzard of '89	blizzard of 1889
it's	it is	will-o'-the wisp	will of the wisp

In reproducing speech, writers frequently use an apostrophe to show that a word is given a colloquial, or dialectical pronunciation.

"An' one o' the boys is goin' t' be sick," he said.

A too frequent use of the apostrophe for such purposes, however, clutters up the page and annoys the reader.

29c

29c Use an apostrophe and s to form the plurals of letters, numbers, and words used as words.

In such cases, the letters, numbers, and words are also italicized, but the s is not.

Cross your *t*'s and dot your *i*'s.
Count to 10,000 by *2*'s.
Tighten your sentence structure by eliminating unnecessary *and*'s.

These are the only kinds of situations in which the apostrophe is used in forming plurals. It is never used in forming the plurals of proper names or other nouns.

29d

29d Do not use the apostrophe with the possessive form of personal pronouns.

The personal pronouns *his, hers, its, ours, yours, theirs* and the pronoun *whose* are possessives as they stand and do not require the apostrophe.

his father   a book of *hers*   a friend of *theirs*

Be particularly careful not to confuse the possessive pronoun *its* with the contraction *it's* (it is).

We couldn't find *its* nest.
We know *it's* a robin.

EXERCISE 29a–d Insert apostrophes or apostrophes plus *s* as necessary in the following sentences.

1 One of my most prized possessions is the Supremes first record album.
2 Its hard to believe that in a country as rich as ours, some people still go to bed hungry every night.
3 The chairpersons assistant has assured all members of the department that theyll have their class schedules in two weeks time.
4 Most modern cities havent the resources with which to keep up with their expanding populations.
5 He had asked for a months leave of absence, but he was allowed to take only the three days sick leave that were due him.
6 Hers was the better way, mine was the quicker.
7 Whats the point of experimenting with mind-expanding drugs when they can do terrible damage to ones mind?
8 A rock groups career, as show business goes, is relatively short.
9 The greatest years of *The New Yorker* were those under Harold Ross editorship.
10 Its hard to keep up with the Joneses when you dont have Mr. Jones income.

30 HYPHEN -

30

The hyphen has two distinct uses: (1) to form compound words, and (2) to indicate that a word is continued from one line to the next.

Convention in the latter use of the hyphen, called syllabication or *word division,* is arbitrarily fixed. (See Section **18.**) But convention in the use of hyphens with compounds not only shifts rapidly but is unpredictable. As a noun, *short circuit* is spelled as two words; but the verb *short-circuit* is hyphenated. *Shorthand, shortstop,* and *shortwave* are spelled as single words, but *short cut* is spelled as two words. *Short-term* in *short-term loan* is hyphenated, but in *the loan is short term* it is spelled as two words.

In such a rapidly changing and unpredictable matter, your only safe recourse is to consult a good, up-to-date dictionary. The following uses of the hyphen in forming compound words are widely accepted.

30a

30a   Use a hyphen to form compound words that are not yet accepted as single words.

The spelling of compound words that express a single idea passes through successive stages. Originally spelled as two separate words, then as a hyphenated word, a compound word finally emerges as a single word.

> *base ball* became *base-ball* became *baseball*
> *post mark* became *post-mark* became *postmark*

There is no way of determining the proper spelling of a compound at any given moment. Your dictionary is your most authoritative reference.

30b

30b   Use a hyphen to join two or more words serving as a single adjective before a noun.

Do not hyphenate such an adjective if it follows the verb as a predicate adjective.

	a well-known speaker
BUT	The speaker was well known.
	a grayish-green coat
BUT	The coat was grayish green.

Omit the hyphen when the first word is an adverb ending in -ly.

	a slow-curving ball		a quick-moving runner
BUT	a slowly curving ball	BUT	a quickly moving runner

30c

30c   Use a hyphen to avoid an ambiguous or awkward union of letters.

NOT	recreate [For "create again"]	NOT	belllike
BUT	re-create	BUT	bell-like

In commonly used words, the hyphen is omitted.

coeducational   coordinate   cooperate   readdress

30d Use a hyphen to form compound numbers from twenty-one through ninety-nine and to separate the numerator from the denominator in written fractions.

twenty-nine   fifty-five   two-thirds   four-fifths

30e Use a hyphen with the prefixes self-, all-, ex-, and the suffix -elect.

self-important   all-Conference   ex-mayor   governor-elect

Do not capitalize the prefix *ex-* or the suffix *-elect,* even when used in titles that are essential parts of a name.

ex-Mayor Kelley   Governor-elect Jones   ex-President Truman

EXERCISE 30   Insert hyphens as needed.

1 The editor in chief owns a well designed house.
2 He boasts that he is self made and self educated, but he forgets that he is also self centered.
3 My father in law once ran in the hundred meter relay; his team went as far as the semi finals.
4 The life long dream of many Americans is a four bedroom home with a two car garage.
5 He changed a twenty dollar bill into five dollar bills.

REVIEW EXERCISE ON WORD PUNCTUATION (Sections 27–30)   Supply the necessary italics, capitals, apostrophes, and hyphens in the sentences below.

1 magazines such as yankee and vermont life are popular with readers who idealize old time country life.
2 The item appeared in last mondays new york times.
3 its a well known fact that most old age pensions are inadequate for present day needs.
4 sarahs exhusband had been well meaning enough but too self effacing for an out going girls taste.
5 hes got too many ands in his sentences.
6 barbra streisands first big break in show business was in the broadway play i can get it for you wholesale.
7 the four american delegates carefully prepared proposal was rejected by the soviet unions spokesman.

8 although eighteen year olds can now vote, my brothers friend didn't vote until he was twenty-one.

9 the four cylinder sixty horse power car wasnt able to pull Jones custom built limousine out of the ditch.

10 roots, an eight part dramatic series based on alex haleys search for his long buried past, topped all previous tv programs in the nielson ratings.

REVIEW EXERCISES ON PUNCTUATION (Sections 19-30)

EXERCISE A Make all necessary corrections in internal punctuation and in the use of capitals, italics, apostrophes, and hyphens in the following sentences.

1 Her favorite writers joyce carol oates and james dickey are both contemporary.

2 Your faults are an uncontrollable temper inexperience and indifference to your work.

3 Since we had driven the car 87,000 miles we decided to turn it in.

4 If siege is spelled with an ie why is seize spelled with an ei?

5 What we need said mr. blevin the union spokesman is a good days pay for a good days work.

6 Many people perhaps most people do not know from what materials their clothing is made.

7 The government was faced with a difficult task it had to persuade a skeptical frustrated people that the energy shortage was real.

8 Her camera her new dress and her books all of which she left in her car were stolen.

9 I have just received an un-expected letter from the director of the bureau of internal revenue.

10 Ruth wanted a pontiac frances a ford donna a chrysler and alice a raleigh bicycle.

11 The late will rogers favorite saying was ive never met a man i did'nt like.

12 Judy garland is best remembered for her role in the 1930s film the wizard of oz.

13 Does anyone remember who said absolute power corrupts absolutely?

14 I make it a point to read the new york times every day and the new yorker every week only rarely however do i get around to time or newsweek.

15 You can't do that, they shouted from the balcony, you can't you can't.

EXERCISE B In the following sentences, determine which marks of punctuation are used correctly, which marks are used incorrectly, and what additional punctuation is needed. Be prepared to give reasons for your decisions.

1 I've seen the play *The Elephant Man* twice, but I still find it's plot fascinating.

2 We like to think that the spoils system went out with Andrew Jackson, but actually it's still in effect: in federal, state, and municipal government.

3 Is'nt it time we all ignored our own personal problems and cooperated with one another in making this world a better place to live in

4 You watch television all day long; and in the evening too.

5 Should one judge candidates from the speeches they make? from the printed matter they distribute? or from the ideas they generate?

6 Blacks and whites must learn to live and work together; otherwise, this country will suffer civil disorder.

7 The Presidents wifes activities are always reported in the press, so are his childrens.

8 I think I recognize that actor, wasn't he on the television show *The Jeffersons?*

9 I wanted to make that perfectly clear, the speaker said, Have I made it so?

10 D. W. Griffiths *The Birth of a Nation* 1915, was the most important movie in the early history of the film.

LARGER ELEMENTS

If you wish to be a writer, write.
EPICTETUS

Anyone who wishes to become a good writer should endeavor, before he allows himself to be tempted by the more showy qualities, to be direct, simple, brief, vigorous, and lucid.

H. W. FOWLER

31 THE WHOLE COMPOSITION **PLAN**

Whenever you undertake a specific piece of writing, you face two problems: saying what you really mean and making that meaning clear to your readers. For these two problems there are no easy solutions. One thing is certain, though. If a piece of writing is to be effective, you must decide at the outset *what* you want to say, *to whom* you want to say it, and *how* you want to say it. Once the writing is done— whether it be a letter home, or an application for a job, or a term paper—you must look at what you have produced and give honest answers to the following questions: Is the writing readable and clear? Does it convey a sense of purpose? Does it engage the reader in the way you want it to?

To be consistently satisfied with the answers to these questions, you need to develop a somewhat standardized approach to writing assignments, however different in form and purpose they may be. The procedure described in this section is one that many writers—professional and amateur—have found useful. Not all writing assignments require the use of each step in the procedure. Conversely, some assignments may require the addition of a step or two. The basic system provides a methodical way to approach any writing task, not in a rigid, lock-step manner but rather with a flexible framework you can adapt to the demands of the writing task confronting you.

Prewriting

1   Select a topic, then narrow it to fit the length of your writing assignment. (See Sections **31a** and **31b** on selecting and limiting a subject.)

2   Make a list of ideas, assertions, facts, and examples that are related to your subject and work this list into a preliminary outline. (See Section **31c** on taking notes and making a preliminary outline.)

3   Decide on the purpose of your piece of writing and frame a specific thesis statement for that purpose. (See Section **31d** on determining purpose and thesis.)

4   Think carefully about the kind of reader you are writing to; the identity of the reader largely determines *what* you want to say and *how* you want to say it. (See Section **31e** on considering audience.)

5   Decide on the pattern of organization and the methods of development that will best serve your purpose. (See Section **31f** on deciding on a pattern of organization and methods of development.)

6   Identify those items in the preliminary outline that fit your

purpose and support your thesis. Then work these items into an outline. (See Section **31g** on making an outline.)

Writing and revising

7   Begin to write and keep writing until you have completed a rough draft. Don't be concerned with problems of wording and phrasing or grammar and punctuation at this stage. (See Section **31i** on writing a preliminary draft.)

8   Try to think of an illustration, an anecdote, or an example to use for an interesting, engaging opening statement for this first draft. Once you have done so, go through the paper checking especially to make sure the ending is a complete summary of your topic and thesis. (See Section **31h** on beginning and ending the paper.)

9   Go over the entire draft, checking it for correct spelling, punctuation, and grammar. Then reread it carefully for clarity, organization, and sound reasoning. (See Section **31j** on revising the rough draft.)

10   Put your paper aside, if possible for a day or two but for as much time as you can afford. (You will gain perspective about the paper and be better able to spot weaknesses in logic or organization.) Then prepare the final copy. (See Section **31k** on preparing the final draft.)

These ten steps of the writing process comprise two phases: first, the prewriting or planning phase of the paper; second, the writing and revising phase of the paper. The prewriting process—the first six steps listed above—is as important to the quality and success of the final paper as are writing and revising—the final four steps in the list. Effective writing requires careful planning.

31a   Select a topic.

In college writing courses you are sometimes free to choose the topic for a paper; at other times you are assigned a topic. When you are asked to develop your own topic, look for one that interests you and about which you have some knowledge. Begin your search for a topic by examining your own experience, your abilities, your religious and political beliefs. Can you repair cars or lawnmowers? Are you knowledgeable about stereo components? Do you make your own clothes? Can you cook ethnic food? Do you play a sport or a musical instrument? What interesting people have you known as teachers, as religious leaders, as employers, or as fellow employees? Which ones have you liked or admired, and why? Have you recently read a book or seen a film that you liked? Why did you like it? What is your favorite television program, and why? Do you have any strong feelings, favorable or unfavorable, about courses you have taken in high school or college? Do you have political beliefs or allegiances? What are they, and why do you hold them? What kinds of jobs have you had? Which ones did you like or dislike, and why?

Examine your own experience. Every day you spend some time watching television, listening to the radio, perhaps reading a newspaper. What shows do you watch and why? What do you read first in the newspaper—the world news, the sports pages, the comics? Why? Perhaps you are dissatisfied with parking conditions on your campus or with the food served in the university grill. What remedies can you suggest for these problems? As these questions and the ones in the preceding paragraph suggest, the possibilities for finding topics in your own experience are limitless. Reflect on your experience and your interests in order to discover them.

Whether you choose your own topic or are assigned a single topic or a list of topics from which to choose one, the first step in the writing procedure is to select the topic and then narrow it down to fit the length of the paper required. Many students make the mistake of thinking that they have found a topic when, in fact, they have only thought of a general idea. Most of the papers you write in English courses will be 400 to 700 words long, or about 4 to 8 paragraphs. Topics such as "Prejudice is Evil" or "Equal Educational Opportunities for All" cannot be managed in papers of 400 to 700 words. Prejudice may be a good concept to think about, but you need a very limited aspect of prejudice for a short essay. Once you think of such topics as "My Roommate's Prejudices" or "My Prejudice Against Tall Blonds," you are approaching a manageable topic. Once you think of such possibilities as "Handicapped Students Need P.E. Courses Too" or "Why Not Women on the Football Team?" you have a topic you can discuss in a few well-developed paragraphs.

The following lists illustrate the difference between a general idea and a specific topic. Any topic in the *General* column can be narrowed to many different specific topics. Many of the topics in the *Specific* column are phrased as questions because questions often help to determine the purpose of a paper. Some of the specific topics might require further limiting, depending on the length of the paper assigned.

General	*Specific*
1. Controlling Pollution	1. The Cause of Three Recent Fish Kills in the Stones River
2. Technology Today	2. Bathroom Gadgets Unlimited
3. Television	3. The Glamorous Female Private Eye: Sexy and Savvy

General	Specific
4. Parents and Children	4. My Father's Unpredictable Moods
5. Advertising	5. "The Man Who Reads *Playboy*": Does He Really Exist?
6. Fashion in Clothes	6. Charlie Daniels: Boots, Jeans, and Big Cowboy Hats
7. Science Fiction	7. Why Ray Bradbury Is My Favorite Author
8. College Administration	8. Do Minority Students Really Need Minority Advisors?
9. College Life	9. Should Thursday Night Keg Parties Be Banned?
10. The College Newspaper	10. More Humor and Fewer Editorials, Please!
11. The Cost of Higher Education	11. Why I Can't Afford Not to Work Part-Time
12. Women's Athletics	12. Equal Funds for Equal Sports?
13. Popular Magazines	13. Why *Omni* Is Necessary to My Well-being
14. Soap Operas	14. The Soaps: How Clean Are They?
15. Military Service	15. Why Is Mom So Hostile Toward the Draft?
16. Solar Energy	16. The Advantages of a Solar Water Heater
17. Racial Prejudice in the U.S.	17. The Klan's Current Appeal to the Younger Generation
18. The Energy Crisis	18. The Economic Advantages of Owning a Subcompact
19. U.S. Middle East Policy	19. Could We Live Without Oil from the Middle East?
20. Urban Congestion	20. Catching a Taxi in New York City

EXERCISE 31a(1) Make a list of five general topics suggested by your interest in television, in movies, and in sports—for example, "Why Are Sitcoms so Popular?" "Why I Like Sci Fi Movies" or "My Weekly Date with Monday Night Football."

EXERCISE 31a(2) Make a list of five general topics suggested by your hobbies or your work—for example, "Refinishing Antique Furniture" or "Selling Ladies' Leisure Wear."

EXERCISE 31a(3) Make a list of five general topics suggested by your taste in music and in books—for example, "Is Country Music Just for Country Folks?" or "Why I Like the Novels of Ray Bradbury."

31b

31b Limit the topic.

Many students assume that writing a 500-word paper is an impossible task. ("How can I write 500 words about a topic? I don't know 500 words about anything.") Yet, as we have suggested, the experience of most freshmen is rich in potential topics. Finding these topics is the difficulty. Suppose your instructor gives you a list of general subjects such as the one in Section 31a and tells you to formulate a specific topic from one of the general subjects, frame a thesis statement about this specific topic, and then write a 500-word essay on the topic you chose. How do you begin? First, examine the list, looking for a subject that interests you or that you can relate to your own experience. With concentration and imagination, you almost certainly can come up with something.

But suppose you can't. You then face not so much the task of *finding* a topic as the challenge of *creating* or *inventing* one. You must go back over the list again, thinking about anything in your personal life that you might be able to connect to one of the general topic areas. Imagine college freshman Kevin McNeil in exactly that situation. An essay has been assigned, and Kevin is sitting in the library staring at the general subjects in Section 31a. Nothing exceptional has occurred in his life in the past few months, he is sure, except for the sporty little subcompact he purchased shortly after high-school graduation to get to work in the summer and to college in the fall. Kevin remembers worrying about whether he could afford a car and still assume some of the costs of college. He also recalls wondering if he would be able to afford gas for a car once he had one. As he thinks about his new car, Kevin suddenly realizes that connections exist between his reasons for buying it and topic 11, "The Cost of Higher Education" and topic 18, "The Energy Crisis." Both subjects were very much on his mind while he was considering what kind of car to buy.

Still, Kevin is uneasy about trying to write a paper that ties the cost of college to his new car or links his car and the high price of gas. Both ideas seem very general in scope and neither seems to have a clear direction or purpose to it. What Kevin recalls most vividly are the long hours he spent shopping for the car and the many conversations he and his parents had about financing the car and buying insurance for it. He feels that he learned a good deal about how to buy a car from the experience, and he thinks that this new knowledge might be best to write about.

So far, Kevin has isolated a subject that might be workable for him. The subject of buying a used car is still a very general one, and it needs further limiting if Kevin is to manage it in 500 words. No instructor wants you to write papers that are nothing more than series of vague generalizations lacking support. Good writing uses concrete details and examples to illustrate and support the main ideas in a paper. The next problem, then, is how to make a topic you have chosen even more specific. To limit a topic, you must define what *you* know about it.

What Kevin knows about used cars is how he shopped for and bought his car. To refresh his memory, he jots down a few notes about what he did when he decided to buy a car:

1   Asked parents for their permission and advice.
2   Stopped by some local dealers to look over their selection.
3   Called the bank to find out current interest rates and payment schedules.
4   Started reading the used car ads.

Looking over his notes, what Kevin sees is what *he* did when *he* wanted to buy a car, not necessarily what all people do when they set out to buy cars. He thinks that he might very well be able to write the following paper: "How I Selected the Used Car That Was Right for Me."

Kevin now has a topic drawn from his personal experience, one that he can write about effectively, one that may be instructive for someone who reads his paper. Kevin has not so much *found* this topic as *created* it. The paper is a long way from being finished, though. There is still much thinking to do about the topic, notes and at least a preliminary outline to prepare.

Thus far, Kevin has decided on a general subject and narrowed it to a manageable topic for a short essay. He has accomplished this much using his own experience and using his knowledge of that experience as it applies to the assignment in his English class. Kevin has discovered that a topic is not found, but rather made. He has engaged in a process called **invention,** a term applied to that aspect of the writing process involving the creation and development of a topic. He has, however, completed only the creation part of the process. Development comes next.

EXERCISE 31b(1)   Make a list of five specific topics from the list you made for Exercise 31a(1).

EXERCISE 31b(2)   Make a list of five specific topics from the list you made for Exercise 31a(2).

EXERCISE 31b(3)   Make a list of five specific topics from the list you made for Exercise 31a(3).

31c   Take notes and make a preliminary outline.

To develop a topic, you need to use the methods, **strategies of invention,** that are discussed and illustrated in this section. Invention strategies enable you to formulate a purpose (a thesis) and help you to organize the evidence you plan to use in your essay to support the thesis.

Finding out how much you really know about your selected topic, discovering how much information you can assemble that can be worked into your paper is the next step. Even with a good topic, one you are interested in and know something about, further crafting is necessary if you are to write an organized, coherent, adequately developed essay.

Many inexperienced writers think they are ready to write once they have selected their topics. They assume that all the examples and details an essay requires will spontaneously appear when they take pen in hand. In fact, very few people can simply pour forth coherent, well-constructed writing, even when they are writing about personal experiences. Accordingly, once you have selected a topic, set aside some time for making notes and for working up a preliminary outline or plan of your paper. Otherwise, you may discover too late that your topic is still too general or that you have insufficient information to develop the topic. Using one or more of the strategies of invention can make your work relatively easy.

Perhaps the most common method of inventing material for a topic is to make a list, an inventory of facts, examples, details—of practically anything relating to the topic. Some writers do this gradually, over a period of time. Some think about their topics while they enjoy a quiet cup of coffee, some while they travel to and from work or classes, some while they take an evening walk, jog, or bicycle ride. Other writers sit down with a blank piece of paper and write down ideas for thirty minutes or an hour. This latter technique, **brainstorming,** involves listing anything that comes to mind about the topic during a specified amount of time. One method is not superior to the other; discover for yourself which method you prefer.

Having selected a topic, Kevin needs to explore it further. When his roommate is out for a couple of hours in the morning, Kevin stays in the room and brainstorms. He gets a cup of coffee and sits at the desk to review the notes he made when he was narrowing the topic. Then he writes a list of everything he can remember. After an hour, he is surprised at how much he has written down. Here's what he has:

1   Asked parents for their permission.
2   Asked about methods of financing.

3 Asked about down payment: Should I earn it first? Could I borrow it?
4 Called bank to inquire about car loans and personal loans.
5 Inquired about interest rates and payment schedules.
6 Talked to Mom and Dad and some friends about what kind of car to buy.
7 Looked into advantages of subcompacts.
8 Discovered that some subcompacts were priced higher than many regular-sized cars.
9 Visited local dealers to look over their cars.
10 Inquired about the reputations of certain local dealers. Were they honest? Did they give warranties? What kind?
11 Started looking through the want ads for personal sales.
12 Learned how to check for condition of used cars; read *Consumer Reports*.
13 Learned about financing through a dealer.
14 Would be a cash purchase; no trade-in available.
15 Learned how to compare cars and prices.

As it is, the list looks pretty jumbled; but Kevin certainly has at hand enough information about buying the car to be able to write a 500-word essay. As he studies the notes, he sees a pattern in them—a chronological pattern that begins with his talking with his parents and ends with the actual financing and buying of the car. For the time being, he arranges this pattern into three major headings:

1 How I decided what kind of car to buy
2 How I shopped for and selected the car
3 How I bought and financed the car

This is not an outline for Kevin's paper, but it is a valuable first step toward a workable outline. It establishes at least temporary direction and order.

Another method that can help you to develop a topic is talking with people. Choose someone you can trust to give you an honest opinion about whether the topic is interesting, workable, and worth writing about. Have ready specific questions to ask your listener; it is likely, though, that the person will ask questions about the topic that you have not thought about yet. If possible, talk with someone who already knows something about the topic you have chosen. English instructors are always glad to talk about papers. They have been trained to give valuable assistance when you encounter such problems as developing a topic.

For his paper on buying a car, Kevin talks with his parents and with friends who have bought cars in the recent past. His father reminds him that he told Kevin never to offer a dealer the asking price of a car, but instead to start with a much lower bid. His mother mentions that she suggested having a reputable mechanic check the car before Kevin bought it. Kevin adds this additional information to his notes.

Once you have used one of the strategies of invention, you will realize what a valuable step it is as you prepare to write your paper. Invention results in specific information, and grouping specific information can produce a tentative plan of order for your paper.

EXERCISE 31c(1) Use one or two methods of invention to generate preliminary notes for two of the specific topics you listed in Exercises 31b(1), (2), or (3).

EXERCISE 31c(2) Which of the suggested specific topics listed on pp. 176–177 could you use without any further study or research for an essay of 300 to 500 words? Choose two of the topics and use one or two methods of invention to make preliminary notes for them.

31d Determine your paper's purpose and create a thesis statement reflecting that purpose.

After you have selected and narrowed your subject and listed your ideas on that subject, you have made real progress. But before you can start to write your paper, you need to decide upon a purpose for it. Then you need to frame a thesis; that is, you must create a statement that sums up the paper's controlling idea.

1 Determine a purpose. The purpose of a paper reflects your choice, as the writer, about what you want to do with the topic. But before you can sensibly decide on your purpose, you should know that, for centuries, writing has been categorized according to four types, or **modes:** narration, description, exposition, and argumentation. Each mode sets up its own promises and expectations between writer and reader, and each mode has certain characteristics that differentiate it from the others. This is not to say that the modes are mutually exclusive; in fact, most pieces of writing make use of two or more modes. For example, an attorney's brief may *narrate* the sequence of events in a crime, *describe* the actions of the alleged criminal, and *argue* for the conviction of the defendant. Before you can choose the mode (or modes) best suited to your essay, then, you must understand the uses and characteristics of all four.

A Narration. The purpose of narration is to tell a story, to recount in sequence a series of occurrences, to tell "what happened." Narration is the form most commonly given to writing meant to entertain: you experience it daily on television, in movies, and in short stories and novels. Its appeal is universal; narration is the first kind of discourse that children learn, in bedtime stories and in the yarns a grandfather spins about growing up long ago. If you have ever been asked to write an essay about what you did on your summer vacation—and who hasn't!—you were asked to write narration.

Usually, the purpose of a piece of narrative writing is not simply to relate a sequence of events. Storytellers almost always construct a story to make a point: to reveal character or to make a statement about human existence. Similarly, when you retell an experience of your own, you often do it in such a way that you reveal something about what you learned in the experience. You relate a certain historical event to compare it with a current political situation. You tell the story of a friend's death in an automobile accident to make a point about the uncertainty of life. See the first paper, p. 223, in the papers for analysis at the end of this chapter. As he recounts an unusual evening with his family, the writer discovers a meaning in the experience for himself and the other members of his family.

B **Description.** The purpose of description is to make readers see, feel, hear what the writer has seen or felt or heard. Description is often combined with exposition, argumentation and especially narration. In a narrative, for example, a writer may choose to describe a character's physical attributes in such a way as to suggest the character's moral attributes. In Melville's novel *Moby-Dick,* Captain Ahab's leg becomes a powerful symbol of his crippled moral nature, of his obsession to punish the whale that took part of his humanity from him. The descriptions of Ahab's physical appearance are meant to give insight into his moral nature.

Description can be of two kinds: objective (or technical) and suggestive (or impressionistic). The first requires writers to reproduce what they see as a camera would. An appraiser for a mortgage company provides an objective description of a house:

> Lot size 120 feet wide by 150 feet deep. Exterior dimensions of house: 84 feet by 27 feet. Living area 1,620 square feet; 648 additional square feet in two-car garage. Seven rooms: three bedrooms, living room, dining room, kitchen, den; two baths. One brick fireplace. Central heat (gas); central air (electric). R–19 insulation rating. Three years old.

The appraisal contains no emotional reaction or judgment of the house's appeal. The purpose of the appraiser's objective description is to enable the mortgage company to set a fair loan value on the house.

The homeowner who wishes to sell the same house writes up a description that reads as follows:

> Practically new three-bedroom, two-bath, ranch-style brick home situated on a shade-tree-covered half-acre lot. Over 1600 square feet of living area. Modern kitchen with built-in appliances. Cozy den with old-fashioned red brick fireplace and beamed ceiling. Formal living and

dining rooms for gracious entertaining. Master bedroom suite with adjoining full bath. Oversized two-car garage. Large patio with gas grill. All of this is nestled beneath stately maples and is available on a mortgage with a low $10^{1}/_{2}$% interest.

This description creates a much different impression than does the appraiser's. The latter description may not be merely the product of the owner's desire to sell the house; it no doubt reflects an emotional attachment to the house.

Another example of descriptive writing, especially of impressionistic description, can be found in the second paper, pp. 224–225, in the papers for analysis. In it the writer reveals the childhood fondness she felt for her uncle's country store as she describes a visit after an absence of several years. Notice how the attention to detail (objective description) intensifies the writer's reactions to and impressions of the old store. The best descriptive writing often fuses the two kinds of description in one piece of writing.

C Exposition. The purpose of exposition is to inform, to explain, to clarify—to make readers know or understand something about a subject. Your most frequent contact with exposition may be television news and the newspaper. The television program *Nova* is a good example of exposition. Exposition may sometimes appeal to emotions, as narration and description often do. For example, a news report of the death of a loved or hated person is likely to provoke strong feelings. But the primary purpose of exposition is to inform, fully and fairly. For this reason, good exposition is clear, concise, and straightforward.

Exposition is the mode used to write a manual for automobile owners, a recipe for southern fried chicken, a booklet on the rules of soccer, the format directions for preparing a paper. When you receive a booklet of instructions about how to register for your classes, you have been given expository prose. If the writers have failed in any of these instances to be clear and precise, the car owner, the cook, the soccer player, and the student suffer the consequences. Learning to write effective expository prose is the most important writing skill you can develop for daily life.

Even when exposition deals with controversial subject matter—gun control, for example—the writer or reporter in effect says to readers: "I'm simply trying to tell you something. I'm not trying to persuade you to believe what I believe or to lead you to value judgments, although there is the possibility that may happen. What I want to do is to make you know or understand something you didn't know or understand before—at least not so well or clearly." In the third paper, pp. 226–228, in the papers for analysis, the writer points out that the science-fiction film *Star Wars* makes use of certain conventions common in western stories and films. He is not arguing that *Star Wars* is a veiled copy of a western movie (although he may, in fact, think so); he is simply pointing out that some popular western elements are used in the film. The writer's purpose is certainly to interest and inform his readers; but he leaves it up to them to evaluate the significance of the information that such "western ingredients" as the "comical sidekick" and the "shoot-out" are a part of *Star Wars*.

D   Argumentation. The purpose of argumentation—or **persuasion,** as it is also called—is to convince readers (or listeners) of the rightness of your point of view (and, usually, the wrongness of an opposing viewpoint). You encounter argumentation in debates and editorials. Most, if not all, political speeches are a form of argumentation.

Because you are usually committed to the arguments you make, you must be careful not to lose control of your reasoning and your emotions when you intend to argue or persuade. Your purpose is to convince readers or listeners, and you can do so only if you present your case fully, objectively, and reasonably. Sound logic and a thorough understanding of the opposing position are prerequisites for effective argumentation.

In the fourth paper, pp. 229–230, in the papers for analysis, the writer uses careful logic as she constructs an interpretation of the E. A. Robinson poem "Richard Cory." She firmly believes that the author intended the story to be viewed in a certain way, and she supports her point of view with specific evidence from the poem itself. Similarly, a prosecuting attorney refers to the evidence of a crime to support an argument for a guilty verdict.

The difference between exposition and argumentation is this: in exposition you inform for the sake of informing, but in argumentation you inform in order to persuade. When you write argumentation, you say in effect: "I know what I believe. You may or may not find what I have to say interesting and informative, but my main purpose is not to inform. My main purpose is to persuade you to believe as I do." (See Section **33** for a discussion of writing persuasively.)

Taking into account the foregoing information on writing modes, Kevin is ready to decide the purpose for his paper on buying a car. Determining the purpose will help him frame a thesis statement for his paper. Remember that he proceeded through a chronology of events after he decided to buy a car. His notes and the very simple outline he made from them indicate the following sequence: he talked with his parents and others to decide what kind of car to buy; he shopped around and eventually found the car he wanted; he called the bank to inquire about loans and to make arrangements for financing the car.

Kevin's paper can certainly take the form of a narrative, but, just to be sure, he considers other possibilities. Description is out; Kevin sees no reason to include the appearance of the car. Argumentation seems unsuited to the topic; Kevin is unwilling to contend that the methods he used to buy a car ought to be followed by everyone who is shopping for a used car. Exposition, however, causes him to think further about what he wants the paper to accomplish. Kevin has to decide whether he simply wants to tell readers what he did or to inform them about a logical and systematic approach to a common dilemma. Kevin imagines a reader being able to use his paper as a guide to selecting a satisfactory used car. He decides that he is more interested in the essay's potential as exposition—informative writing—than as narration. Writing an expository paper will be a challenge, but Kevin feels that if he succeeds he will have written a better and more effective paper than if he were merely to tell the story of buying the car. Having decided to write an expository paper, he is now ready to frame a thesis statement, perhaps the most important step in the prewriting process.

2 Create a thesis statement. A thesis statement sets forth in a sentence the controlling idea and purpose of a paper. It answers the questions, What point does this paper make, what opinion does it offer, what stand does its writer take? A carefully stated thesis sentence introduces and summarizes the entire paper. Like any other sentence, a thesis sentence consists of a subject and a predicate. Once you have successfully limited your subject so that it is narrow and specific enough to manage in your paper, you have found the subject of your thesis sentence. Writing a thesis sentence is a matter of writing a predicate to go with that subject, a matter of deciding what assertion you wish to make about that subject.

For example, suppose you are given the general subject "Mass Media" as a topic to write about. After some thought, you narrow your interest down to television and, after still further thought, you decide to concentrate on television commercials. The next question is, what about television commercials? You need to state some central idea about commercials, to isolate what you wish to assert about them. You can make almost endless assertions about this topic (or any other). Here are a few examples:

> Television commercials are entertaining because of their music, their humor, and their scenery.
> Television commercials appeal to our desires for good health, good looks, and good living.
> Television commercials make us dissatisfied with our health, our appearance, and our income.
> Television commercials are at best misleading and at worst downright dishonest.

Television commercials make financially possible a far greater range of entertainment than would otherwise be possible without their financial support.

Each of the foregoing thesis sentences contains a clearly stated controlling idea, and each gives direction to the whole paper. The first two theses suggest overall expository purposes—to show in what ways commercials are entertaining and to explain how they appeal to certain desires; the last three suggest overall persuasive purposes—to convince the reader that commercials make viewers dissatisfied, to argue that commercials are dishonest, and to prove that they make possible variety in programming.

A well-formed thesis sentence not only gives a paper a clear purpose, it also helps you to keep a paper unified, provided that you stick to the purpose defined in the thesis statement. A good thesis sentence commits you to your purpose. Your task then is to support the thesis, to back it up with details and evidence, to explain what you mean by it, to convince your readers that it is a valid contention. The thesis sentence helps you to organize your paper because it provides the basis for decisions about what to include and what to exclude. What sponsors pay for TV advertising is crucial to your thesis if the point of your paper is that such payments support a broad range of entertainment. The same information, however, is clearly irrelevant to the four other examples of thesis statements; for them, it is information to exclude.

Most importantly, perhaps, a thesis sentence can give your paper an argumentative edge, a kind of dramatic interest. Even in a paper in which the general purpose is to explain or describe, a thesis sentence serves as the writer's commitment, a promise to make a clear point, to show that commercials are, after all, entertaining and not, as the reader thought, boring and frustrating. A good thesis sentence that defines a central idea clearly and precisely and gives a paper confident direction must meet three tests: it must be unified, limited, and specific.

A   A good thesis sentence is unified. A thesis sentence expresses only one central idea. Although it may include a secondary idea, it must subordinate any secondary idea to the central idea. You should be immediately suspicious of any thesis statement that is a compound sentence. Such sentences usually contain two central ideas, thereby defeating the unifying purpose of a thesis statement. Each of the following thesis sentences commits its writer to two main ideas, either of which requires a full paper for adequate development:

Television commercials are entertaining, *and* they help support a great range of programs.

Science fiction often anticipates new scientific developments, *but* it has never had as much appeal as detective stories.

The recent curriculum changes provide increased opportunities for students, *but* they also restrict the students' choices.

Intercollegiate football costs a disproportionate amount of money, *and* it involves many fewer students than other sports.

B A good thesis sentence is limited. Just as you need to narrow any general subject to a limited topic, so you need to narrow *your* assertion about the topic. In other words, just as the subject of a thesis sentence must be limited, so must its predicate. A good thesis must make an assertion that can be supported adequately in the time and space you have.

GENERAL | Good teachers have several different things in common.
LIMITED | Good teachers possess certain qualities: they are *competent* in their subjects, *fair* in their grading, and *imaginative* in presenting their materials.

GENERAL | Magazine advertising varies from magazine to magazine.
LIMITED | A magazine's advertising reflects the *social and economic desires* of its readers.

GENERAL | The selfishness of people can be seen in many ways.
LIMITED | The selfishness of people is at its worst *in a crowded subway.*

C A thesis sentence must be specific. A thesis sentence can be unified and restricted and yet not define a central idea usefully because the predicate is too vague and imprecise to give the paper any clear direction. Predicates that consist of *is* or *are* plus a vague complement such as *good, interesting,* or *a serious problem* are too imprecise to be useful. A sentence such as *The rising cost of higher education is a serious problem,* for example, does not state in what ways the problem is serious. The following examples show how thesis sentences with vague predicates can be made precise:

VAGUE | The rising cost of higher education is a serious problem.
SPECIFIC | The rising cost of higher education *may prevent many good students from attending college.*
 | The rising cost of higher education *makes it increasingly difficult for private colleges to survive.*

VAGUE | The neighborhood I grew up in was an unusual place to live.
SPECIFIC | Although the neighborhood in which I grew up was *crowded and noisy, it was always friendly.*

> Although the neighborhood in which I grew up *was open and quiet, it was very lonely.*

VAGUE   My difficulties in biology lab are unbelievable.

SPECIFIC   My difficulties in biology lab *amuse the other students, confuse my instructor, and frustrate me.*

> My difficulties in biology lab *are so serious that they provide a strong argument against requiring all students to take a laboratory science.*

The more unified, limited, and specific you can make a thesis sentence, the better you will have focused your central idea and controlled the purpose of your paper. The more clearly you state your purpose, the better prepared you are to determine what evidence should go in the paper to develop your central idea and how best that evidence should be organized.

Let's return to Kevin's paper on buying a car. Having decided that its purpose will be expository rather than narrative, Kevin must frame a thesis statement that clearly informs readers of the paper's central idea. Kevin should explain the systematic approach he followed in selecting and buying a used car so that anyone who reads his paper will learn this useful information. He also wants to make it clear that the procedure described in his paper is the result of his own experience in buying a used car. What he did in buying a car is going to serve as the supporting evidence for Kevin's thesis.

Kevin does not want to become argumentative about what he learned. He does not want a thesis statement that reads, "Based on my experience, I think that every potential used-car buyer should complete the following steps in purchasing a car." He is writing only from his own experience, too limited a base to prescribe what is best for all other used-car buyers. After several attempts, he finally writes the following thesis sentence: "I learned recently that buying a used car entails thoughtful planning, careful shopping, and sound financing." Something about this sentence satisfies him. Let's see what it is.

Kevin states, "I learned recently. . . ," which implies that his paper will inform readers of what he learned. What did he learn? He learned "that buying a used car entails thoughtful planning, careful shopping, and sound financing." The topic and organization of the paper are clearly stated in this clause. First, the paper will be about buying a *used car* only. Moreover, Kevin prepares readers for three paragraphs of development—on planning, shopping, and financing, in that order. He has composed an effective thesis statement, one that focuses the topic and establishes direction and control for his central idea and purpose.

And that is precisely the point. A good thesis sentence is certainly informative for readers; but at this stage its importance is that it helps the writer to organize and construct an effective essay.

31d

EXERCISE 31d(1)   Identify which writing mode seems most appropriate for each of the five specific topics you made for Exercise 31b(1), (2), (3). Explain what other modes, if any, you might use to supplement the primary mode for each topic.

EXERCISE 31d(2)   Read the papers for analysis, pp. 223–230, at the end of this chapter. Each paper represents one of the four writing modes. Identify the primary mode of each paper and tell what others have been combined with it to achieve the paper's purpose.

EXERCISE 31d(3)   Write two brief essays on the same subject but with different purposes. For example, write a factual, informative essay describing a dormitory room or an apartment, and then write a persuasive essay intended to convince a reader to live in the dormitory room or rent the apartment. Or write an objective report of an automobile accident, and then write a report about the same accident intended to prove that one of the drivers was clearly at fault.

EXERCISE 31d(4)   Some of the following thesis sentences define unified, limited, and specific central ideas. Others are not unified or are too broad or vague to be useful. Indicate which ones you think are satisfactory and explain why. Suggest revisions for those you think are unsuccessful.

1 Cigarette smoking is disgusting to those who don't smoke, harmful to those who do, and should be prohibited in public places.
2 A good coach has many different qualities.
3 Inflation is the most serious problem in the United States today.
4 Professional women athletes deserve benefits equal to those of men.
5 Shooting pool requires steady hands, keen eyes, and great patience.
6 Professor Winslow is a real human being.
7 Soccer is very different from football.
8 Objective examinations are unfair because they rely primarily on memory rather than on the ability to relate facts to one another.
9 There are several sure ways to lose a job.
10 Handicapped persons face many challenges every day.

EXERCISE 31d(5)   Write thesis sentences from the preliminary notes you made when you completed either Exercise 31c(1) or 31c(2).

31e

31e   Consider your reader.

Unless you are taking notes for yourself or writing a diary, your writing is aimed at a reader other than yourself. You must keep these readers in mind as you write, because they—your audience—influence what you write, the way you write, even why you write. Always try to picture a specific reader or some specific group or type of reader. Then ask yourself whether the best presentation for this specific audience is likely to be simple or complex, popular or technical, general or specific. If your intention is truly to communicate, you must adjust your subject matter, your point of view, the kind of detail and explanation you use, even the words you choose to the audience you are writing for.

When you write to parents, brothers or sisters, or close friends, you know their interests and the language they use. These are readers *familiar* to you. When you write to them you use a *personal* tone and style; you do so without even thinking about it. Generally, when you write to a familiar audience, you do so with ease and confidence. On the other hand, you may have experienced some difficulty writing to a reader *unfamiliar* to you. Did you, for example, find yourself uncertain about how to write letters of application to deans of admission when you were applying to college? Have you ever found it agonizing to write a letter of application for a job? If you have, it is because you are writing to an *unfamiliar* audience. When you write to such an audience, you are expected to do so in an *impersonal* tone and style. In such writing you want to appear as mature and responsible as you possibly can.

Imagine that near the end of the current semester Suellen Calley discovers that her grades are not going to be good. In fact, she is probably going to fail at least two courses. The reasons are painfully clear to her: excessive absences, incomplete work, and a lack of serious studying, combined with too many parties and a lot of time on the golf course practicing her game. To break the bad news, she writes the following letter home to her parents before the semester's end:

> Well, I know you're not going to like this one bit, but it looks as if I'm going down the tube in a couple of my courses. I think I told you before that my history instructor didn't like me from the first. And besides, the requirements are superhuman! I mean, how can anyone be expected to write two research papers in one semester, work part-time, study for other classes, and have any fun? As for biology, I think you have to be an Einstein to pass lab. I mean, how can they get away with requiring all that lab time? Half the time I was late for work because I had to stay over in lab to complete some stupid exercise on the circulation system of the great American toad. Don't worry, though, it looks like I'm going to get all A's and B's in my other courses. My PE teacher really likes me; he says I've shown more improvement than anyone else in my putting game.

Sure enough, the report card comes and along with it a notice that Suellen has been placed on academic suspension. If she chooses to appeal, she is told, she may do so by writing the Dean of Admissions and requesting a one-semester period of academic probation. Suellen knows a break when she sees one, so she sits down and writes the following letter to the dean:

> I would respectfully like to appeal my academic suspension and to request a semester's probation. I would like to point out that I only

failed two of the six courses that I took, and both are courses in which failures are common. I would like to emphasize that I made one A, two C's, and a D in my other classes. This should be evidence of my academic ability to do college-level work. I will frankly admit to you that I did not apply myself up to my ability in the two courses I failed. Moreover, I worked part-time last semester to help cover the cost of my education. I'm certain that you understand with today's economy the way it is why I need to help my parents with my college expenses. Maybe I worked too much; I plan to be more careful if I am permitted to return. Considering all these factors, I sincerely hope that you will allow me to return to school next semester.

The differences in the two letters are due to Suellen's perception of their different audiences. Despite the embarrassment of the revelation to her parents, she writes to them in a casual tone of confidence, knowing they will continue to love her despite her failures. To the Dean of Admissions, however, she sets forth her case in a respectful, impersonal tone. Her style is clearly self-conscious, even awkward at times because she is unsure of her audience. Otherwise, why would she write, "I will *frankly* admit *to you* that I did not *apply myself up to my ability*"? Writing to an unfamiliar audience need not result in such awkwardness; the rules and conventions of acceptable written English can help to ease the composition of even the most formal communications.

Specialized versus general audiences

In most of your writing, both for college courses and for later in your professional life, it is useful to think of two broadly different kinds of audience: specialized and general.

A **specialized reader** already knows a good deal about a subject. Attorneys who write articles for the *Harvard Law Review* do not have to define the legal terms they use: readers of the *Harvard Law Review*, other attorneys, already know them. Such writers do not have to attract readers' attention: the subject matter and the publication have already done that. Specialists, however, are not necessarily scholars or doctors or engineers. They can be enthusiasts for almost anything— drag racing, photography, country music, astrology, pottery making, or football. Today, numerous magazines court readers who have highly specialized hobbies and interests: *Antique Monthly, Big Bike Choppers, Fly Fisherman, Idaho Farmer-Stockman, Model Railroader, Nordic Skiing, The Plate Collector, Stamp Show News and Philatelic Review, Videography, Yoga Journal*, and so on.

Articles that appear in such magazines are written with a very specific and specialized audience in mind. Writers can take for granted the audience's interest in and knowledge of the subject matter. Such an audience can make sense of information, ideas, and sometimes even language that would be inappropriate for general readers.

A **general reader** is the reader to whom most writing is addressed. General readers may work in highly specialized professions or enjoy unusual hobbies; but when they turn to general-interest publications such as *Ebony, Psychology Today, Saturday Review,* and *Sports Illustrated,* they expect to be able to understand the articles. This is especially true of such widely read weekly magazines as *Newsweek, Time,* and *U.S. News and World Report.* Your English instructors may be highly educated readers of literature; but when they read *Newsweek,* they expect the section on law and medicine, for example, to be written in standard, nontechnical language that can be readily understood. Because their audience is made up of general readers, writers for such magazines must avoid technical, overspecialized terms. When such terms are used, writers must be careful to define them and to provide examples.

Most writing you do for college classes will be directed to a college-level audience. Admittedly, this is a mixed group, from new freshmen to well-seasoned professors. But this audience shares certain traits and interests. Such readers are interested in keeping up with current events and issues, in learning about new ideas and various life-styles, and in exploring new possibilities in technology. In other words, they are readers who are intelligent and curious, who will give what you write a fair hearing, but who will also scrutinize it carefully. They will expect what you write to be clear, to be specific, and to be honest or authentic. They will expect you to write coherently, to explain adequately, and to use concrete examples to illustrate general statements. Such expectations are not unreasonable; nor are they impossible for you to satisfy.

A word of warning to you in your college writing: do not waste time trying to write what you think the instructor wants. Any attempt to write what you think your instructor is looking for is almost certain to result in an artificial and unsuccessful piece of writing. Most instructors, whatever they teach, try their best to serve as sympathetic general or specialized readers of student papers. They try to judge how well a paper has met the needs of the readers to whom it was directed. The comments of your instructors are intended to explain to you how your paper might have been organized more clearly, how your style might have been sharpened, and how your paper might have been better suited to your readers. But, most of all, what your instructors want is *your* ideas, *your* explanations, *your* reasons. They want you to learn to speak your own mind so that others will listen and respect what you have to say.

31e

EXERCISE 31e(1)   Do any of the specific topics you listed for Exercise 31b (1), (2), or (3) seem aimed at specialized readers? What are they? Why are they appropriate for specialized readers?

EXERCISE 31e(2)   Write two letters in which you state the need for money. Write the first letter to your parents. Write the second to a loan officer at a local bank. Analyze the differences in the two letters and explain why you wrote them differently.

EXERCISE 31e(3)   Go to the library, find a magazine intended for general readers, and copy a paragraph from it. Then find a magazine or journal published for specialized readers and copy a paragraph from it. Analyze and explain the differences in the two paragraphs.

31f

31f   Decide on a pattern of organization and on one or more methods of development.

After you have narrowed your topic, used invention to generate a list of notes, decided on your purpose, and framed a thesis statement, the general shape of the paper should be clear to you. You have drawn up the paper's blueprint. You must now think about organization; that is, you must decide how you are going to give the paper internal order and coherence. You must also decide what method or methods of development to use in your paper.

1   Decide on a pattern of organization. The difference between a composition that is not planned and one that is carefully planned is the difference between a collection of parts for a motor and an assembled working motor. The collection of parts lacks organization; it is chaotic. The assembled motor is organized; the parts have been put together according to a design, and they function together as a whole.

Good organization in a composition results from your keeping purpose and thesis clearly in mind and from your arranging ideas and facts in an orderly pattern. Patterns of organization can be grouped into two kinds of order: natural order and logical order. **Natural order** is a pattern inherent in the topic itself. Narration, for example, normally requires that actions be told in the sequence in which they occurred. Description most often requires spatial order. **Logical order,** on the other hand, is imposed; the writer establishes the rationality of the arrangement of material.

A   Natural order. The two natural orders are (1) time, or chronological, order and (2) space order. They are the patterns most common to narrative and descriptive writing.

(1) *Time Order.* If your purpose is narration, time order will almost certainly be the pattern appropriate for your paper. If you write about an automobile accident, an athletic contest, or a historcal event, you will very probably relate the events in the same sequence in which they took place. Time order is also the pattern to use for writing instructions about how to set up a campsite, how to dissect a frog, or how to proceed through college registration. In using time order, you organize by laying out information in the sequence in which events occur or should occur. There can, of course, be departures from strict time sequence. For example, in an essay about an automobile accident, the writer might begin with an ambulance shrieking up to an emergency room, then retreat in time to narrate the events of the accident. But it is unlikely that the writer could compose a coherent paper without relying primarily on the order in which events occurred.

The first paper in the papers for analysis at the end of this chapter is an example of a narrative paper that uses time order. In it the writer carefully reconstructs the events at his home one Saturday night when the electricity failed during a storm.

(2) *Space Order.* If your purpose is description, spatial order is probably the appropriate pattern for your paper. If you write a description of your dormitory room, of your front yard, or of the view atop a ridge in the Great Smoky Mountains, you will want readers to develop a mental picture of what you are talking about. You may choose to focus the scene from where you stand and then move outward from left to right or right to left. In describing a house or building, you may first describe its exterior, then the interior. In describing both views, exterior and interior, you must maintain spatial control if the reader is to see the house clearly. Even the physical description of a person makes use of spatial pattern. If you were to write a description of your mother, for example, you would find it virtually impossible to create a sensible impression of her looks if you were to describe her dress, then her hair, then her fingernails, then her eyelashes, then her skin, then her shoes. Spatial order closely follows the order in which eyes see or movie cameras move. One bit of information relates to the next in terms of position.

The second paper in the papers for analysis at the end of this chapter is a descriptive paper that uses space order. In it the writer's focus moves from one side to the other as she describes the cluttered interior of her uncle's old country store. While the paper issues from the writer's experience, her primary purpose is to describe the store as she sees it once again after being away for several years.

B   Logical order. If your purpose is to explain an idea or to persuade a reader, a pattern of organization inherent in the topic itself may not exist. You must, therefore, impose an order on the topic.

You must decide how best to arrange your examples and your reasons. The most common and useful patterns for exposition and argumentation are as follows: (1) the order of climax; (2) general to particular; and (3) particular to general. If you are explaining an idea, you will most often state the *general* idea first in your thesis sentence and then support the general statement with *particular* details and examples that illustrate and develop the idea. The reverse is also possible: instances and examples first, summed up by a general statement. If you are writing to persuade a reader, you should arrange your reasons and evidence from least important to most important. This is order of climax; you save your most persuasive evidence or reason for the end of your argument.

The third of the papers for analysis at the end of this chapter is an example of general to particular order. In it the writer begins with the general statement (or thesis) that the film *Star Wars* contains many characteristics common to western stories and movies. He then lists and discusses particular features in *Star Wars* that bear striking similarities to the plot and characters in westerns.

Paper Four is an example of the order of climax. The writer arranges the reasons for her interpretation of the poem in a pattern of least important to most important, thus building to a logical climax. Note that she arranges the details from the poem to fit the order of her paper rather than simply following the order of their appearance in the poem.

Just as the modes of writing—narration, description, exposition, and argumentation—are often combined in a paper, so too the patterns of organization are often interwoven. Kevin's information about buying a car, for example, is laid out in a chronological series of steps. But he did not talk seriously with the loan officer at the bank or with the insurance agent until he had selected the car. There was no point in Kevin's talking to either party until he could provide the first with a specific amount to be borrowed and the second with a specific make, model, and year. Kevin's essay, then, will combine time order with logical order. He wants to inform readers not only that there are certain steps to take in buying a car, but that there are sound logical reasons to follow these steps in the order in which he presents them.

2 Decide on one or more patterns of development. No matter how coherently you organize a paper, if you hope to satisfy your readers you must develop the paper so that it seems both complete and convincing to them. If you are writing narration, you must recount all the events that are relevant to your thesis. If your paper is description, you must include sufficient details so that your readers have a clear, full picture of the scene or person that you are portraying. If you are writing exposition, you must provide sufficient examples or instructions so that readers can easily understand the idea or follow the steps outlined. If your purpose is argumentation, you must offer ample reasons and evidence if you expect to persuade your readers. Generally, you should provide a minimum of three examples, instances, or reasons to illustrate an idea or to support an argument. Fewer items of what is essentially proof of your thesis may seriously weaken the credibility of your paper.

Methods of development include the following: (1) detail and example; (2) comparison and contrast; (3) analysis and classification; and (4) cause and effect. Even though this discussion separates the processes of organization and development, the two go hand in hand. The choice of an organizational pattern leads quite naturally to a choice of one of these methods of development. The choice of both, of course, issues from your purpose and your thesis.

(1)   Detail and example. Many, if not most, papers you write in college will consist of a thesis supported by details and examples. A sharply defined thesis tends to reveal what details and examples you will need to develop the paper adequately. A specific thesis will control both the unity and the coherence (the pattern of order) of the details and examples. Suppose Kevin had decided on the following thesis: "Buying a used car is a time-consuming and frustrating experience." This thesis is not very helpful in identifying, ordering, and developing the details needed for support. On the other hand, the thesis statement that Kevin actually prepared contains the kinds of signals that direct a writer to the examples he or she needs. Look at it again: "I learned recently that buying a used car entails *thoughtful planning, careful shopping,* and *sound financing.*" This sentence calls for examples of how Kevin planned, shopped for, and financed the car. He can go back to the brainstorming list and find exactly the examples he will need to develop the paper.

Notice that all four papers for analysis, even though they have different purposes, contain examples and details. All the writers recognized the need to provide some details and examples in order to support and develop their respective theses adequately. Without such concrete development, a paper becomes merely a collection of general assertions. In the fourth paper, note how the writer uses direct quotations from a poem to support the general assertions about it.

(2)   Comparison and contrast. Another common type of development, comparison and contrast, may be more familiar to you than you realize. A history professor compares the causes of one war with the causes of another. An economics exam requires you to compare the economic conditions of the 1980's with those of the 1930's. You use comparison and contrast when you compare high-school courses with college courses or when you debate whether it's best to live in a dormitory or off campus.

31f

The third paper at the end of this chapter is an example of development by contrast and comparison. In it the writer discusses how *Star Wars* is similar to (has points of comparison with) western movies, especially in its characters and plot. The writer refers specifically to a number of western films and television series to support and develop his thesis. The writer has constructed his paper using comparision as a method of development.

(3) Analysis and classification. Analysis is the conscious process of trying to understand something, usually by taking it apart, breaking it down into its smaller parts. For example, if you have decided on a career in nursing, you must consider what kind of nursing you wish to practice: obstetrics, pediatrics, geriatrics, surgery. If you are assigned to write a paper on the government of the United States, you will quickly realize that the federal government has three parts: the legislative, executive, and judicial branches. It is impossible to understand much about an abstract concept like American government until you understand about the functions, responsibilities, procedures, and powers of these components, the three branches of federal government.

An important adjunct of analysis is classification; analysis, in fact, makes classification possible. You engage in classification when you group items according to a common principle or characteristic. Suppose you were assigned to write an essay on the student body at your university. You would first analyze, then classify. You would have to consider a variety of ways to distinguish one student from another. You could do so in terms of those who study diligently, those who study enough just to get by, and those who demonstrate no interest in their studies. When you assign several individuals to each of these categories, you are classifying according to study habits, a principle common to all students. Notice that a number of classifications are possible. For the same paper you could also divide students according to their place of residence or their choice of career. Whatever classification you select for a paper will depend on your purpose and must derive from careful analysis.

Classification without analysis is called **stereotyping.** You stereotype if you classify a person or a group without systematic and valid analysis. The outcome of stereotyping is often prejudice directed toward members of ethnic, political, racial, or religious groups. For example, almost all of Archie Bunker's opinions are instances of his stereotyping persons or groups rather than analyzing them in any rational manner.

The fourth paper at the end of this chapter shows how analysis and classification can be used to examine another person and his behavior. The writer observes that the townspeople have stereotyped Cory. The writer then examines Cory to try and explain why, since the townspeople thought him so privileged, he should wish to kill himself. The answer lies in a close analysis of what the reader can infer about Cory from the poem.

(4) Cause and effect. If your chemistry professor asks you to discuss the results of combining certain chemicals, you will develop your answer by the cause-and-effect method. You will state that a particular reaction occurs after various substances are combined. Similarly, if your economics professor wants you to discuss the likely consequences of restrictive fiscal policies, you are being asked to explore a cause-and-effect relationship. If your English instructor asks you to write a paper on why you selected the college you attend, you will be expected to develop the paper using an effect-to-cause relationship. The decision is an effect, an already accomplished action; the reasons for your decision are the causes.

Cause-and-effect development quite naturally falls into the pattern of (1) stating causes and describing or arguing what their consequences will be, or (2) identifying a problem or consequence and then explaining the causes. The fourth of the papers for analysis uses such development in the section where the writer states that Richard Cory has committed suicide. The effect is known; what must be explained are its causes. This paper, by the way, effectively incorporates all four methods of development discussed here.

The patterns of organization and the methods of development discussed in this unit are also explained and illustrated with sample paragraphs in Sections **32c** and **32g.**

EXERCISE 31f(1)   Read the papers for analysis, pp. 223–230. List the pattern of organization and the methods of development used in each paper. Then select one paper and write a paragraph in which you explain how the organization and development support the purpose of the paper.

EXERCISE 31f(2)   Study the list of specific topics you made for exercise 31b(1), (2), or (3). Which patterns of organization and methods of development seem best suited to the topics on the list? Explain how the organization and development would support the purpose of the paper.

EXERCISE 31f(3)   Study the thesis sentences that you composed for Exercise 31d(5). Which patterns of organization and methods of development seem appropriate to each statement? Explain how the organization and the development would support the purpose stated in the thesis.

31g   Make an outline or plan for your paper.

Make it a habit to construct an outline for every piece of writing you do. An outline provides you with a working blueprint of your paper's organization and development. An outline helps you to develop a topic in a logical and orderly way, and it enables you to distinguish clearly between more and less important ideas.

Outlines may vary from quickly jotted notes for an essay exam to carefully worked out topic or sentence outlines for long and complex papers. The kind of outline you choose will depend upon your writing assignment. For a brief in-class paper on your high-school English courses, for example, you might have time only for such brief notes as the following:

1. More literature than composition
2. Emphasis on grammar in 10th grade
3. Wrote most papers on literature
4. Research papers in 11th and 12th grades
5. Enjoyed literature more than papers
6. Lack of contemporary literature
7. Not much comment on papers except in 11th grade

Even this limited set of notes provides a guide for your paper. The notes suggest immediately two major divisions into composition and literature, and indicate that the main emphasis in high school was on literature. A glance at the notes suggests a grouping of topics 1, 3, 5, and 6 in one paragraph, 2 and 4 in another. Item 7 may not fit into this essay, or you may be able to use it as a supporting detail in one paragraph. The whole suggests some such thesis statement as *My high-school preparation in English included work in both composition and literature, but the latter was the more thorough as well as the more enjoyable.* With this kind of start and your notes before you as you write, even a brief paper is likely to go more smoothly and logically. Such preliminary outlines are, of course, especially valuable in writing examinations. The five or ten extra minutes you spend on a preliminary outline often pays off with a stronger answer.

The best place to begin an outline is with a carefully crafted thesis sentence because an effective statement of thesis announces the general divisions of your paper. Using the thesis sentence, you can thus establish the general divisions of your outline. In addition, the more notes you have, the easier it is for you to make an outline.

Examine your notes for some pattern of organization—time order, space order, general to specific, order of climax—and arrange your notes according to it. Next, think about what method or methods of development will complement the pattern of order, and arrange your notes according to it. If you follow these two steps, you will discover that making an outline is a much easier task than you supposed.

Make an outline for every paper whether or not your instructor requires one. The guidance an outline provides is especially valuable for in-class essays, which require you to work against a deadline. If you don't prepare an outline, you may discover too late that your paper lacks clear purpose, coherent order, and adequate development.

1 Use a consistent method for numbering and indenting major headings and subheadings. For most outlines, it is unnecessary to divide subheadings more than two degrees. Here is a conventional system of outline notation:

```
I.  . . . . . . . . . . . . . . . . . . . . . . . . . . . . . . . . . . . . . . .
    A.  . . . . . . . . . . . . . . . . . . . . . . . . . . . . . . . . . . . . .
        1.  . . . . . . . . . . . . . . . . . . . . . . . . . . . . . . . . . . .
            a.  . . . . . . . . . . . . . . . . . . . . . . . . . . . . . . . . .
            b.  . . . . . . . . . . . . . . . . . . . . . . . . . . . . . . . . .
        2.  . . . . . . . . . . . . . . . . . . . . . . . . . . . . . . . . . . .
    B.  . . . . . . . . . . . . . . . . . . . . . . . . . . . . . . . . . . . . .
II. . . . . . . . . . . . . . . . . . . . . . . . . . . . . . . . . . . . . . . .
```

2 Make your outline logical, clear, and consistent. Do not use single headings or single subheadings in your outline. Any category of heading or subheading must have at least two parts. If you have a I, you must also have a II. If you introduce an *A* under a roman numeral, you must also have a *B* under that roman numeral. If you put 1 under an *A*, you must also put a 2, and so on for any division. This procedure is logical since each new level of the outline is a division of a foregoing larger area, and you cannot logically divide something into just one part. A single subheading reflects poor organization; it should be incorporated into the heading of which it is logically a part. The following example illustrates correct divisions mathematically.

```
I.  One dollar
    A.  Fifty cents
    B.  Fifty cents
        1.  Twenty-five cents
        2.  Twenty-five cents
II. One dollar
```

The same principle requires that each group of subheadings be logically equal to the larger heading under which they fall. If you wish, for instance, to divide the general heading "dogs," you can do so with the subheadings "house dogs" and "working dogs" or "large dogs" and "small dogs" or "poodles," "collies," "spaniels." But each one of these groups represents a different principle of classification. If you were to make your major subheads "house dogs," "small dogs," and "poodles," for example, the outline would be illogical.

3 Use either the topic, the sentence, or the paragraph form throughout an outline. In a topic outline, use for each heading a noun (or a word or phrase used as a noun) and its modifiers. In a sentence outline, which has the same structure as the topic outline, use complete sentences as separate headings. Because it states ideas more fully, a sentence outline is more informative than a topic outline, but a topic outline is easier to read. A paragraph outline gives only a summary sentence for each paragraph in the theme. It does not divide and subdivide headings into subordinate parts. Sentence outlines are the most inclusive of the three types. Topic outlines, however, are probably the most popular with inexperienced writers because they take less time to prepare.

Before you start to outline, decide which type of outline you are going to use and then fulfill the requirements for that type consistently. If, for example, you choose to make a sentence outline, remember that *every* statement in the outline must be expressed as a complete sentence. Remember also to make all parts of the outline parallel in structure. The following outlines illustrate the types. Each one shows consistent structure. A thesis statement for these outlines might read as follows:

A study of printed advertisements from the eighteenth and nineteenth centuries reveals their rapid growth and changing character.

TOPIC OUTLINE

I. Colonial period
    A. Advertisements in Franklin's *Poor Richard's Almanack*
    B. Advertisements in newspapers
        1. Products and services
        2. Personals
II. Nineteenth century
    A. Appearance of mass circulation publications
        1. General audience newspapers and magazines
        2. Women's magazines
    B. Concentration of advertisements on particular products
        1. Soap and cosmetics
        2. Patent medicines
        3. Bicycles
    C. Introduction of sensational advertisements by P. T. Barnum

SENTENCE OUTLINE

I. Advertisements were printed during the colonial period.
    A. Benjamin Franklin both wrote and published advertisements.
    B. Advertisements appeared frequently in newspapers.
        1. A variety of products and services were advertised.
        2. Personal advertising was also very common.

II. Advertising flourished in the nineteenth century.
    A. Mass circulation publications made their appearance.
        1. Some newspapers and magazines appealed to general audiences.
        2. Some magazines appealed especially to women.
    B. A large proportion of advertisements were concentrated on a narrow range of products.
        1. Soap and cosmetics advertisements proliferated.
        2. Patent medicines were sold to millions as the result of mass advertising.
        3. As bicycles became popular toward the end of the century, competitive advertisements appeared by the hundreds.
    C. An analysis of P. T. Barnum's advertisements shows his introduction of sensational material.

PARAGRAPH OUTLINE

1. A variety of advertisements appeared frequently in newspapers of the colonial period.

2. With the development of mass circulation publications in the nineteenth century, advertisements proliferated in general audience and women's magazines.

3. An analysis of P. T. Barnum's advertisements shows his introduction of sensational material.

4 Use parallel grammatical construction for all items in the outline. Using consistent grammatical form emphasizes the logic of any outline you create and gives that outline clarity and smoothness. Inconsistent form, on the other hand, can make a perfectly rational ordering of items seem illogical. Of the following outlines on tennis, the one on the left is not in parallel grammatical form. The outline on the right is consistent both in form and logic.

THE GAME OF TENNIS *(nonparallel)*	THE GAME OF TENNIS *(parallel)*
I. The playing court	I. The court
A. The surface materials for it	A. Surfaces
1. Made of clay	1. Clay
2. Grass	2. Grass
3. Asphalt surfaces	3. Asphalt
B. Measuring the court	B. Measurements
1. For singles	1. Singles
2. Doubles	2. Doubles
C. Net	C. Net
D. Backstops necessary	D. Backstops

THE GAME OF TENNIS	THE GAME OF TENNIS
(nonparallel)	*(parallel)*

<table>
<tr><td>

II. Equipment needed
  A. Racket
  B. The tennis balls
  C. The wearing apparel
    of players
III. Rules for playing tennis
  A. The game of singles
  B. Doubles
IV. Principal strokes of tennis
  A. Serving the ball
  B. The forehand
    1. Drive
    2. Lobbing the ball
  C. The backhand stroke
    1. The drive
    2. Lob

</td><td>

II. The equipment
  A. Racket
  B. Ball
  C. Wearing apparel

III. The rules
  A. Singles
  B. Doubles
IV. The strokes
  A. Serve
  B. Forehand
    1. Drive
    2. Lob
  C. Backhand
    1. Drive
    2. Lob

</td></tr>
</table>

5 Avoid vague outline headings such as Introduction, Body, and Conclusion. Not only does the outline serve as a guide in your writing; submitted with your paper, it may also serve as a table of contents for your reader. To use such words as *Introduction, Body,* and *Conclusion* as outline headings gives no clue to what material is to come. If your paper is to have an introduction, indicate in the outline what it will include. If your paper is to have a formal conclusion, indicate in the outline what conclusion you will draw.

His composition instructor has not required Kevin McNeil to submit a formal outline with his paper on buying a used car. She has, however, strongly recommended the use of at least an informal outline to help in arranging the order of the paper. In the notes Kevin made while brainstorming, he discovered an arrangement that combines time order and logical order. He stated that order in his thesis sentence. Using the thesis, then, Kevin made these general divisions of his paper: (1) Selecting the car; (2) Shopping for the car; (3) Financing and insuring the car. Next, he arranged his notes according to these three divisions. When he finished putting the pieces together, Kevin's informal outline looked like this:

Thesis: I learned recently that buying a used car involves thoughtful planning, careful shopping, and sound financing.

    I. Selecting the car
      A. Sources of information
        1. Parents
        2. *Consumer Reports*

      B. Type of car
          1. Standard size
          2. Subcompact
  II. Shopping for the car
      A. Newspaper want ads
      B. Local auto dealers
          1. Types of cars sold
          2. Reputations of dealers
      C. Inspection by a reputable mechanic
 III. Financing the car
      A. Sources of loans
          1. Dealers
          2. Banks
      B. Types of payments
          1. Down payment
          2. Monthly payments
          3. Insurance premiums

Kevin now has a plan to follow as he writes the paper. His outline provides not only an order for the paper but also the details necessary to develop it adequately. With this outline, he is ready to write a rough draft. Kevin's prewriting process is complete.

EXERCISE 31g(1)   Study the following outlines. Are they organized consistently? Do you find any single headings or subheadings? Are all items in parallel grammatical construction? Be prepared to suggest appropriate revisions for each. Write a thesis sentence for one of the outlines; then revise that outline so that it is consistent with the principles of outlining.

THE ADVANTAGES AND DISADVANTAGES OF A CITY UNIVERSITY

   I. Convenience of location
      A. Transportation
      B. Hotels
      C. People
      D. Stores
      E. Theaters
  II. Advantages
      A. Center of travel
      B. Students learn to be more independent
      C. More types of people
      D. Those who have never been in city get new view
      E. Opportunities for work

III. Disadvantages
 A. Tendency to become interested in other things
 B. Too much for some to cope with
 C. Too close to other schools

THE VALUE OF PUBLIC OPINION POLLS

I. Introduction
 A. Operation of public opinion polls
  1. Selection of an important issue
  2. Constructing a set of questions
   a. Scientific nature of this construction
  3. A cross-section of the population is selected
 B. Replies are tabulated and results summarized
II. Importance of polls' results
  1. Attitudes of public revealed to lawmakers
  2. Power of present groups revealed
  3. Polls are a democratic process
   a. Polls reveal extent of people's knowledge

BAKING YOUR OWN BREAD

I. Introduction: Delicious taste, look, and feel of good bread
II. Bread-making in the past
 A. More difficult than now
 B. Necessary to make own yeast
 C. Kneading difficult
III. Bread-making today is popular
 A. Much easier
  1. Can make a few loaves at a time
  2. Gas and electric ovens are easier to control
 B. Making bread is enjoyable
  1. Sense of satisfaction in kneading own dough
  2. Bread baking in oven smells good
  3. More tasty than most bought breads
IV. Three easy recipes
 A. White bread
 B. Sweetened breads
  1. Raisin
V. Conclusion: Pleasure of sitting down to eat a slice of your own baked bread

EXERCISE 31g(2) Choose one of the papers for analysis (pp. 223–230) and make an outline for it that you think the writer could have followed to produce the paper he or she wrote.

EXERCISE 31g(3) Study the preliminary notes you made in Exercise 31c(1). Make an outline for each of the two sets of notes. Use the same style (topic, sentence, or paragraph) for both outlines. Be sure to construct the outlines in parallel form.

31h   Begin and end your paper effectively.

Begin your paper effectively.

The beginning of a paper serves as a springboard into the topic. It should inform as well as catch the reader's interest. These results are almost certain to follow if you write a strong, direct opening.

Important as a good beginning is, don't be concerned about it in your rough draft. After you have written the draft, you may find that your purpose is clearer to you, and writing an opener will then be much easier. You may discover that the first few sentences you wrote in the rough draft were warm-ups and that a little revising will transform the third or fourth sentence into a good beginning.

The length of the introduction depends on the size and the complexity of your subject. A paper of 1,000 or 1,500 words on, say, the merits of a career in the field of mass communications may require a paragraph to state the thesis and to outline the general plan of the paper. Papers of 500 to 600 words, the length you will normally write in your English classes, usually need no more than three to five sentences to get started effectively. You will find more helpful advice in the following comments about ineffective and effective beginnings.

A   Ineffective Beginnings

1   Avoid beginnings that are not self-explanatory. Do not make a reader refer to the title to find out the meaning of your paper's opening sentence. Do not begin a paper entitled "Nuclear Energy" with *Everyone is against it;* or a paper giving instructions for building a model airplane with *The first thing to do is to lay all the parts on the table.*

2   Avoid beginnings that start too far back. If you are writing a paper describing last Saturday's football game, get directly to the description; don't begin by explaining how you happened to go to the game. The writer of the following paragraphs meant well but should have begun with the second paragraph:

FATHER KNOWS BEST

You probably wonder from my title what I am going to write about. Well, it's a long story. It started back in 1964 when I was born. My mother announced to my father that I was a boy! "We're going to send

this statement: "If you have followed all the directions correctly, you should now have an assembled model ready to hang in your bedroom."

Just as the nature of an introduction depends on the length and the complexity of the paper, so too does the conclusion. A paper of 500 words may require no more than a sentence or two, while a paper two or three times that length will probably need a short paragraph to summarize its contents.

A   Ineffective Endings

1   Don't end your paper with an apology. Statements like the following harm a paper: "This is only my opinion, and I'm probably not really very well qualified to speak" or "I'm sorry this isn't a better paper, but I didn't have enough time." Such statements destroy the effect of whatever you have written. If you say that you have failed, your reader will probably agree with you.

2   Don't end your paper by branching off into another aspect of the topic or by introducing new material. The ending of a paper should conclude what you have said. Readers are distracted and frustrated when you introduce at the paper's end a new, undeveloped idea. Don't conclude a description of how autumn appeals to you with a statement that says: "Even though autumn is a beautiful and exhilarating time of year, spring is still my favorite season." Such a sentence only makes your reader wonder why you wrote about autumn in the first place.

B   Effective Endings

1   Conclude with a restatement of your thesis sentence. A paper called "Father Knows Best" might end: "Now that I have been here and have seen the school for myself, I am convinced that Father *does* know best. I have decided to enroll for the next term at State." Not only does this ending restate the thesis, it also shows that the student has learned something from writing the paper.

2   Summarize the major ideas that you developed in your paper. A summary serves the double purpose of bringing your paper to a conclusion and of reminding your readers once more of the major points that you discussed. A paper on building a model airplane might end: "As I have shown, all you need to build a model plane is a model to assemble, a little ingenuity, and a lot of patience. With these three ingredients you can fill the friendly skies of your bedroom."

3   Draw a conclusion from the facts you present. Especially if your purpose in a paper has been to argue a point of view, you need to write a conclusion that derives from the evidence or reasons you presented. Thus, if you write a paper in which you argue for passage of the Equal Rights Amendment, you might conclude it by saying: "As the foregoing examples and cases have illustrated, true equality and freedom for women will remain an illusion until they enjoy the same rights and privileges under the law as men do." Your conclusion is based squarely on the evidence presented in the paper.

EXERCISE 31h   Read the papers for analysis (pp. 223–230) and evaluate the beginning and ending of each paper. Explain why the beginnings and endings are effective or ineffective.

31i   Write a rough draft of a paper.

After you have completed the steps in the prewriting process, you are ready to write a rough draft of a paper. Writing a draft offers you the opportunity just to write. Do not concern yourself with grammar, mechanics, punctuation, or spelling. You can attend to these matters when you revise the draft. Take out your notes and your outline and write. Even when you are required to write rough and final drafts in class, most instructors will permit you to bring notes and a working outline with you to aid in writing your paper. Use your notes and your outline as you write a rough draft of your paper. Begin with your thesis sentence and use it as the controlling statement of order and purpose as you write. Start the rough draft as soon as possible after you have completed the prewriting process. You want to allow time to revise the rough draft at least once before you turn the paper in to your instructor.

As you write, give special attention to adequate development of your thesis. Include all the details and examples you can think of. Many papers fail because the writers fill the papers with unsupported general statements rather than with facts and evidence to support and illustrate the thesis. In your rough draft include everything that you can think of that is related to your thesis. You can go back later to rework the paper for unity and coherence.

For his paper on buying a used car, Kevin made numerous notes while brainstorming. Working with these notes and his outline at hand, he produces the following rough draft:

Rough draft

I learned recently that buying a used car involves thoughtful planning, careful shopping, and sound financing. Like any normal teen-ager who had just graduated from high school I wanted a car, my own set of wheels. Somehow my life just wasn't compleat without it. The question was, how do I go about getting it? I had almost no money saved, I had just started a summer job, and to make matters worse I was starting college in the fall. I needed money for that.

Mom and Dad thought a car would be okay for I was planning to work part time after I started college. They wanted me to buy a subcompact because of good gas mileage. They also told me to check out <u>Consumer Reports</u> for ratings on them. Being a teenager of the world, I sure didn't want a subcompact. I wanted a real set of wheels with bucket seats, a four on the floor, and an engine that really turned over the rpm's. But I knew I was being imature and impractical. In a small car I could get to the college and back on about a gallon of gas and work and back twice. Moneywise, a small car was what I needed, it just wasn't what I wanted. But I could afford the gas, go to school and work part-time. So I went to the library and read all I could find about subcompacts in <u>Consumer Reports</u>. I was really suprised at how much info was available. It told all about miles per gallon and how often different models needed to be repaired and what for. This info was sure helpful.

Shopping for the car turned out to be a lot tougher than I thought. I began reading the want ads for used cars and I spent every minute of my spare time on used car lots in town. Boy, subcompacts were sure hard to find. Where are all those imparts when you need one? I told each dealer how much money I could spend on a car and gave them my name and phone number and told them to call me when they got a car that fit the description of what I wanted. I talked to the people at the Better Business Burow to check into how long some dealers had been in business and their reputations. Finally, a salesman called me to say he had the car I wanted. I looked at what the salesman had and you can imagine how I felt when I saw a little red one with black bucket seats and only 23,000 miles on it! After driving it out, I knew it was the car for me, but to make sure it was in good condition I drove it over to the mechanic who took care of my folks car. He said everything was okay, no oil leaks, the breaks were okay, and the tires still had good rubber on them. So I drove it back and told the salesman it was the car I wanted.

As soon as I said that, the salesman asked me if I wanted to finance the car with them. I told him no, that I was going to finance it with the bank that had the loan on my folks car. So the next day I called the bank. I told the lady how much money I needed and she told me the interest rate (which I couldn't believe!) and the amounts of the payments depending on how long I financed the car. It was a recent model, so the bank let me finance it for four years which really helps keep my payments down. Then I called the insurance company and got another shock. Mom and Dad had told me insurance rates would be high, but that it would make me a better driver. Boy, were they right!

So here I am now going to school and work in my own set of wheels. I never guessed that buying a car could be so much work or so expensive. I will have to work hard to make all the payments and still go to school for the next four years.

Kevin's draft has considerable potential. It contains some basic errors and shows some weaknesses in unity and coherence. Rough drafts usually do have rough spots. Kevin's purpose is not clear because he narrates rather than explains what he learned. He has developed the essay well, however. He leaves hardly a stone unturned as he tells the story of the search for a car. The inclusion of so many details will be very helpful when Kevin revises the draft.

After you finish a rough draft, set it aside for at least a day. During this time, give some thought to the way you want to begin and end your paper.

EXERCISE 31i Study the notes you made for Exercise 31c(1) and the outlines you made for Exercise 31g(3). Using these, write a rough draft about one of the two topics.

31j

31j Revise your rough draft.

After you have let a rough draft sit for a day or two, revise it carefully. Important to producing successful papers is understanding that revision is much more than proofreading for and correcting errors in grammar, mechanics, punctuation, and spelling. True revision involves carefully examining your paper for unity, coherence, and adequate development—the principles discussed in this chapter. You should approach revision willing to rethink, restructure, and rewrite, when necessary, to accomplish your purpose.

Many students "revise" simply by copying the rough draft—often transferring the errors in the rough draft to the final draft. Revision requires not only correction of errors in grammar and punctuation but rearrangements and rewriting of phrases, sentences—whole paragraphs if necessary. Revision is thus a two-step process: (1) rethinking and reworking the rough draft and (2) editing and proofreading the rough draft. Applying the following lists of questions to each essay you write will make it relatively simple to revise your papers effectively.

Checklist for revising

1 Are the choice of topic and tone of the paper appropriate for your reader? See Section **31e.**

2 Does your paper have a clearly stated thesis sentence? See Section **31d.** Do all the paragraphs support and develop the thesis sentence? In other words, does the content of the paper show unity, a clear pattern of coherence, and adequate development? See Section **31f.**

3 Does your paper follow the outline you drew up for it? See Section **31g.** If you have departed from your original outline, are the

changes you have made logical, coherent, and effective improvements?

4   Does each paragraph contain a specific topic sentence? See Section **32a.** Do all the sentences in each paragraph relate logically to the topic sentence and support it? See Sections **32b, 32c,** and **32g.**

5   Are all terms clearly defined and all assertions supported? See Section **33.**

6   Do you have an effective opening and a strong conclusion for the paper? See Section **31h.**

Checklist for editing

1   Is each sentence grammatically correct? Are there errors in pronoun or in verb agreement? See Sections **8** and **9.** In tense? See Section **5.**

2   Are the sentences complete? See Section **6a.** Are any sentences joined by a comma or no punctuation at all? See Section **7.**

3   Are any sentences awkward or confusing because of dangling or misplaced phrases? See Sections **11–14.** Are all the sentences logical in their use of subordination, variety, parallelism, and emphasis? See Sections **34–37.**

4   Have you used correctly all commas, semicolons, periods, and other marks of punctuation? See Sections **19–24.**

5   Have you used correctly apostrophes, capitals, italics, abbreviations, and numbers? Are words hyphenated properly? See Sections **15–18** and **27–30.** If you used quoted material, did you quote it correctly? See Sections **25–26.**

6   Are any words misspelled? See Section **44.** Use the dictionary to check spelling! Are there any problems in usage—*lay* versus *lie,* for example? See Section **43.**

7   Are the words in your paper precise and appropriate to the topic? Have you used any slang expressions? See Sections **40–42.**

Not all these questions may apply to every paper you write—you may not have prepared an outline, for example—but most will. Failing to check even one or two of these matters could result in serious weaknesses in a paper.

Checking Kevin McNeil's rough draft for the items in the lists of questions reveals a number of problems. Kevin got carried away telling the story of how he bought the car—that is, with writing narration rather than exposition. Kevin had defined his purpose as wanting to explain what he learned as he went through the process of finding and buying a used car. With only minor shifts in sentences and in his point of view, Kevin can change the story-telling quality of his paper to what he had originally intended—informative explanation. Kevin

31j

also notices some problems in unity and coherence. Some sentences really aren't necessary; others need to be moved to conform to the sequence in his outline. He discovers some errors in grammar, especially in splicing sentences together with commas. He has made some spelling errors, too, in his haste to get his ideas down. None of the revisions Kevin needs to make is a cause for concern. No one, not even a professional writer, can produce a polished, finished essay in just one draft.

After Kevin has carefully examined and revised the rough draft, it looks like this:

Revised rough draft

discovered last summer   *requires*
I ~~learned recently~~ that buying a used car ~~involves~~ thoughtful

planning, careful shopping, and sound financing. Like any normal ~~teen-~~
high school graduate,
~~ager who had just graduated from high school~~ I wanted a car, my own set

   M   *complete*
~~of wheels.~~ Somehow ~~m~~my life ~~just~~ wasn't ~~compleat~~ without it. The

     But
~~question was, how do I go about getting it?~~ ∧I had almost no money

             comma 2
saved, ∧I had just started a summer job, and to make matters worse I was

        my education
starting college in the fall. I needed money for ~~that.~~

   gave their permission for a car since I planned
Mom and Dad ~~thought a car~~ would be okay for I was planning to work

     They advised me to shop for a
part time after I started college. ~~They wanted me to buy a subcompact~~

gas-saving subcompact and to go to the library and
~~because of good~~ gas mileage. ~~They also told me to check out Consumer~~

read about them in Consumer Reports. But
~~Reports~~ for ratings on them. ~~Being a teenager of the world,~~ ∧I sure

      a standard size sporty coupe
didn't want a subcompact. I wanted ~~a real set of wheels~~ with bucket

   gearshift   *with some real power.*
seats, a four on the floor, ∧And an engine that ~~really turned over the~~

     immature
rpm's. But I knew I was being ~~imature~~ and impractical. In a small car

               to
I could get to the college and back on about a gallon of gas and work

   I had to admit that
and back twice. ~~Moneywise,~~ a small car was what I needed, ~~it just~~

~~wasn't what I wanted. But I could afford the gas, go to school and~~

~~work part-time.~~ So I went to the library and read all I could find

         r   *to find that*
about subcompacts ~~in Consumer Reports.~~] I was ~~really~~ su~~r~~prised ~~at how~~

in addition to listing the mileage ratings they also gave
much info was available. ~~It told all about miles per gallon and how~~

you the repair record for the various models.
~~often different models needed to be repaired and what for.~~ This

information most
~~info~~ was ~~sure~~ helpful.

      proved to be more work than I thought it
Shopping for the car ~~turned out to be a lot tougher than I thought.~~ *would.*

I began reading the want ads for used cars and I spent every minute of

I couldn't find a suitable car in the want ads, so
my spare time on used car lots in town. ~~Boy, subcompacts were sure hard~~

          was willing to spend
~~to find. Where are all those imparts when you need one?~~ ∧I told each

The salesmen said they would call me when they traded for
dealer how much money I ~~could spend on a car~~ and gave them my name and
         a car
phone number ~~and told them to call me when they got a car~~ that fit the

description of what I wanted. I∧talked to the people at the Better *(also) (with)*

Business ~~Burow~~ to ~~check into~~ how long ~~some~~ dealers had been in business *(Bureau) (find out) (various)*

and∧their reputations. ~~Finally,~~ a salesman called me to say he had the *(how good) (were after about two weeks)*

car I wanted. ~~I looked at what the salesman had and you can imagine how~~

~~I felt when I saw~~∧a little red ~~one~~ with black bucket seats and only *(It was) (hatchback)*

23,000 miles on it! ~~After driving it out, I knew it was the car for me,~~

but to make sure it was in good condition∧I drove it over to the mechanic *(mechanical comma ?)*

who ~~took~~ care of my folks car. ~~He said everything was okay, no oil~~ *(takes) (He looked it over, drove it, and told me it looked okay to him.)*

~~leaks, the breaks were okay, and the tires still had good rubber on them.~~ *(Then worked out a deal with All that was left was)*

~~So~~ I drove it back and ~~told~~ the salesman. ~~it was the car I wanted.~~ *(to arrange the financing.T)*

~~As soon as I said that,~~ the salesman asked me if I wanted to finance *(the dealer)*

the car with∧them. I told him no, that I was going to finance it with

the bank that had the loan on my folks car. ~~So~~ the next day I∧~~called~~ *(T visited with a)* *(loan officer at)* *(her)* *(wanted to finance)* *(what)*

the bank. I told ~~the lady~~ how much money I ~~needed~~ and she told me ~~the~~ *(the monthly payments would be)*

~~interest rate (which I couldn't believe!) and the amounts of the pay-~~ *(Because it)*

~~ments~~ depending on how long I financed the car.∧ ~~It~~ was a recent model, *(was willing to) (lowered my)*

~~so the bank let me~~ finance it for four years which really ~~helps keep my~~ *(monthly payments. Finally)* *(to arrange for)*

~~payments down.~~ ~~Then~~ I called the insurance company ~~and got another~~ *(insurance.)* *(and they were right!)*

~~shock.~~ Mom and Dad had told me insurance rates would be high, ~~but that~~ *(I'm sure, though, that the high rates will)*

~~it would~~ make me a better driver. ~~Boy, were they right!~~ *(driving)* *(car.)*

So here I am ~~now going~~ to school and work in my own∧~~set of wheels.~~ *(Up until last summer)* *(dreamed)* *(involved)* *(planning.)*

∧I never ~~guessed~~ that buying a car ~~could be~~ so much work or ~~so expensive.~~ *(manage my money carefully to)*

I will have to ~~work hard to~~ make ~~all~~ the payments and still go to school

for the next four years. Even though I didn't get the sporty coupe I wanted, I do have bucket seats and a "four on the floor."

Study the reworked draft carefully. It shows that revision done correctly is a process requiring much more from a writer than just proofreading for grammar, punctuation, and spelling. Notice that both the beginning and the ending of the essay show improvement. Notice that the personal remarks, or "asides," have been deleted. Although not every item in Kevin's outline has been discussed, the revised draft adheres quite well to the plan and order of the outline. Thus the revision is better unified and more coherent than the rough draft. The essay now informs as well as narrates. It is briefer and more to the point. Even though the new version is not perfect, the revised draft is clearly a better essay than the rough draft.

EXERCISE 31j(1)   Read and analyze the papers for analysis (pp. 223–230) using the questions on pp. 214–215. Revise one of the papers according to the notes you make as you analyze.

EXERCISE 31j(2)   Use the questions listed on pp 214–215 to analyze the rough draft you wrote for Exercise 31i(1). Revise the draft according to the notes you make as you analyze it.

31k   Prepare and submit the final draft for evaluation.

When you have finished revising a paper, either recopy it neatly in your own handwriting or type it. Instructors read papers as editors and advisors. They mark errors in grammar and punctuation, and they suggest ways for you to improve your writing in the paper. Instructors read and evaluate your essays to help you become a more confident and competent writer.

On the following pages, Kevin's essay, marked and evaluated, is reproduced. The instructor has marked the essay with numbers that refer to sections of this handbook so that the precise nature of the errors can be identified and so that these errors can be avoided in future essays. In addition, the instructor has made several comments on the essay's unity, coherence, and development; on sentence structure and style; and on the paper's overall purpose. The instructor wrote these comments to point out the particular strengths of the essay and to encourage the continued development of these qualities in future essays.

Final draft

LEARNING TO WHEEL AND DEAL

I discovered last summer that buying a used car requires thoughtful planning, careful shopping, and sound financing. Like any ~~normal~~
high school graduate, ~~I wanted a car.~~ *I felt that my* My life wasn't complete without
a car. However, ~~it.~~ ~~But~~ ∧I had almost no money saved; I had just started a summer job;

41a

32d(4)

and to make matters worse, I was starting college in the fall. I

needed money for my education.

Mom and Dad gave their permission for a car~~;~~ since I planned to   *24i*

30b work part~~_~~time after I started college. They advised me to shop for

a gas-saving subcompact and ~~to go to the library and~~ *to* ∧read about (them)   *8b*

in <u>Consumer</u> <u>Reports</u>. [But I didn't want a subcompact. I wanted a

standard size sporty coupe with bucket seats, a "four on the floor"

23a gearshift(,)and an engine with some real power. But I knew I was being   *drive*

immature and impractical.] In a small car I could ~~get~~-to the college   *to (35a)*

and back on about a gallon of gas and∧work and back twice. I had to

admit that a small car was what I needed. ~~So~~ I went to the library)

and read all I could find in <u>Consumer</u> <u>Reports</u> about subcompacts. I

was ~~really~~ surprised to ~~find~~ *learn* that in addition to listing the mileage   *9e*

ratings(,)they also ~~gave~~(you) *listed* the repair record for the different models.

8b [This information was most helpful.] *unnecessary; delete.*

Shopping for the car proved to be more work than I thought it

would. I ~~began reading~~ *read* the want ads for used cars, and I spent every

minute of my spare time on used car lots in town. [∧ I couldn't find a   *Because/Since*

suitable car in the want ads, ~~so~~ I told ~~each dealer~~ *salesmen* how much I was

willing to spend and gave them my name and phone number.] ~~The salesmen~~

They promised to
~~said they would~~ call me when they traded for a car that fit the de-

41a scription of what I wanted. I also talked with the people at the

Better Business Bureau to find out how long various dealers had been

32d(4): Don't these remarks digress from the topic of thoughtful planning?

Reverse the order of these two sentences. therefore, 32d(4)

you might consider combining these into one sentence.

10c Keep tense consistent

34c Use logical subordination

You develop this paragraph well and you clearly organise the details and examples you use in it.

in business and how good their reputations were. (After) *a* about two

weeks *later* a salesman called me to say he had the car I wanted. It was

a little red hatchback with black bucket seats and *it had* only 23,000 miles

on it! To ~~make~~ *be* sure it was in good mechanical condition, I drove — 42b

it (over) to the mechanic who takes care of my *parents'* (folks') car. He looked (it) — 9a

over, drove (it), and told me (it) looked okay to him. Then I drove (it) *You use "it" too*

back and [worked out a deal] with the salesman. All that was left was *often here.*

to arrange the financing.

when
∧The salesman asked me if I wanted to finance the car with the

dealer(s) I told him ~~no,~~ *planned* that I ~~was going~~ to finance it with the bank

that had the loan on my (folks') car. The next day I visited with a

when
loan officer at the bank. ∧ I told her how much money I wanted to finance,

~~and~~ she told me what the monthly payments would be depending on how long

I financed the car.] Because it was a recent model, the bank was willing

in order to reduce
to finance it for four years [~~which really lowered~~ my monthly payments.]

Finally, I called the insurance company ~~to arrange for insurance.~~ [Mom

and Dad told me insurance rates would be high and they were right! I'm

sure, though, that the high rates will make me a better driver.]

to (35a)
So here I am driving to school and ∧work in my own car. Up until

last summer I never dreamed that buying a car involved so much work or

planning. I will have to manage my money carefully to make the payments

and still go to school for the next four years. Even though I didn't

get the sporty coupe I wanted, I do have bucket seats and a "four on the

floor."

Marginal notes: 41a, 42b, 12a, 34g — Combine into one sentence for logical subordination — 34b — 41c — 32b: again, don't these comments digress from the topic sentence? — 24d — 42a — Effective concluding sentence

Your thesis is clear, unified, and specific; you develop it well by using numerous details and examples. You carefully order the paper as you explain the process of buying the car. However, the second and fourth paragraphs lack topic sentences that are clearly related to the thesis sentence. Only the third paragraph contains a clear expository topic sentence. Your introductory and concluding paragraphs tie the paper together nicely. You need to be careful not to digress from the topic of a paragraph; see Section 32 b. In addition, you should study Section 34 to help you with logical subordination in sentences. This is an interesting essay. I enjoyed reading it.

31k

Instead of using numbers to mark the paper, the instructor could have used the correction symbols and abbreviations listed on the front inside cover pages of the book. A sample paragraph marked with these symbols appears on p. 109 in Section **15e.** No matter what method your instructor uses to mark papers, examine your papers carefully, note especially any comments about errors, and study the appropriate sections of the handbook in order to avoid repeating these errors in future papers. Pay close attention to the comments your instructor makes. Use them as guidelines to help you prepare and write other papers. If you do so, your writing will almost certainly improve with each paper you complete.

Writing a paper requires careful planning, and doing it well demands time and effort on your part. But the reward is worthwhile: a paper that you can be proud to call your own.

EXERCISE 31k(1)   Read the papers for analysis (pp. 223–230). Mark and analyze each paper as though you were the writer's composition instructor. Evaluate and comment on the qualities of unity, coherence, and development in each paper. Evaluate the four papers in terms of overall quality and effectiveness. Explain your ratings.

EXERCISE 31k(2)   Prepare for submission the revised draft that you wrote for Exercise 31j(2). Submit it to your instructor for evaluation. In addition, prepare a second copy of the paper; then mark and analyze it in a way similar to the sample paper on pp. 220–221. Give particular attention to the qualities of unity, coherence, and development in the paper. Comment on the essay's overall effectiveness.

Papers for analysis

Comments about the papers for analysis have been made throughout Section 31, and a number of exercises in this section make use of them. The papers may also be studied independently of the chapter. An analysis of each paper according to the questions on pp. 214–215 will point out differences in quality as well as purpose.

Each paper represents one of the four main types of writing discussed in Section 31d; it also uses at least one other type to support that purpose. The papers incorporate different patterns of organization and different methods of development. (See Section **31f.**) The first paper is narrative in its purpose. The second paper is descriptive; the writer makes use of some narration to clarify the description. The third paper is expository, but with a secondary argumentative purpose. The fourth paper tries to persuade the reader to view a character in a certain way as the basis for understanding the meaning of a poem.

Paper One

THE FAMILY REUNION

Over the past few years my family began to grow apart. Between school, hobbies, and work, there was never time for us as a family to spend together. We were a family that lacked communication. One Saturday something happened that brought my family together.

It was a typical Saturday evening. Both my parents were reading a magazine. My older brother was painting a picture in the basement, while my two younger sisters and brother were watching TV. I was writing a letter. Outside the rain was coming down so hard that I thought it was hailing. The sound of the rain was accompanied by harsh trembling of thunder and flashes of lightening. The lights in our house began to flicker off and on. Then about 8:00 the lights went off. Everything became real quiet. The voices from the TV died. The clocks stopped ticking.

Although we all became temporarily blind, each of us managed to get to the kitchen with only a couple of bruises from running into doors and walls. Each of us took a seat around the table where the candles were lit. My dad began to tell us stories about himself when he was a kid. Eventually, the conversation led up to our futures and what each of us planned to do with it. We all got so caught up with listening to everyone else that when the lights came back on we could not believe it was already 10:00. That night we all went to bed knowing a little more about ourselves and each other.

Paper Two

AN OLD COUNTRY STORE

As I walk up the wooden steps of the old store, I see Jasper, Uncle Ned's lazy hound, stretched out on the front porch basking in the afternoon sun. He raises his head as I pass and then continues his nap. The old men in faded overalls and flannel shirts whittle away at cedar sticks. The faded Coca-Cola sign still hangs on the front of the store. I realize that nothing has changed since I was a little girl scampering up the same steps in hopes of snitching one of Aunt Betty's oatmeal raisin cookoes from one of the big cookie jars on the shelf near the cash register.

As I open the squeaky screen door, I recognize the sweet musty scent which has always filled the room inside the old store. The first thing that catches my eye is the bulky old soft drink cooler under the front windows where Uncle Ned has always kept it. As I lift one of the heavy black lids on the top of the cooler, the cold air rushes out and cools my face. Uncle Ned still lays the bottles on their sides, and I still have to dig through the pile of bottles to get the drink I want. On the floor along the right wall of the store are bushel baskets of white onions, potatoes, fresh green beans, yellow squash, and green and red apples. On the shelves behind the bushels are cans of vegetables and jars of preserves, some of which were made by a lady who lives down the road from Uncle Ned and makes the best strawberry preserves I've ever tasted. Along side the jars of preserves are tins of sorghum molasses which Uncle Ned gets from a man on Sand Mountain. Cloth sacks of flour and sugar are piled on the bottom shelf just behind the bushel baskets.

As I walk toward the back of the store, I see the familiar old white meat case which holds slabs of hoop cheese, bologna, sausage and bacon. I notice that Uncle Ned has a new scale to weigh cheese and meat which is bright white and shiny compared to the dull color of the meat case. Above the meat case, hang several country hams. Next to the meat case in another cooler, Uncle Ned keeps a basket always filled with fresh country eggs and cartons of milk. Against the left wall are such things as catsup, homemade pickles and cans of coffee. Next to these on the wall near the screen door is the usual selection of odds and ends such as shoestrings, nail clippers, pocket knives, rain bonnets, and even a few fishing lures.

My favorite spot was always in the middle of the store where on one particular shelf near Uncle Ned's old antique cash register are boxes and boxes of loose candy in brightly colored wrappers of red, orange, blue, yellow, green, gold, and purple. The floor creaks under my feet just as it did when I was a little girl and tried to snitch a piece of candy before dinner. It was fun to creep across the creaking wooden planks to see if I could reach the candy undetected. And as usual, Uncle Ned spotted me peering over his little spectacles with that familiar grin on his face. Knowing that my sweet tooth has changed about as much as his store has over the years, he reaches for the jar of cookies, removes the lid and hands me a big oatmeal raisin cookie.

Paper Three

COWBOYS OR JEDI KNIGHTS?

The science fiction film Star Wars contains similarities to western movies and television series that do not seem purely coincidental. Even though the terrain of a planet in a distant galaxy and the badlands of the Old West are literally worlds apart, there are a number of coincidences in the settings, the characters, and the plots between Star Wars and westerns. This paper shows how Star Wars is like two of these westerns, True Grit and Gunsmoke.

In the typical western story, the setting is a place without law and order. Lawlessness prevails. The weak and innocent are at the mercy of ruthless outlaws. Similarly, in Star Wars the survival of the galaxy is endangered by the evil Darth Vader and his Imperial Storm Troopers. The opening scenes of both Star Wars and The Empire Strikes Back remind viewers of the Old West. The scenes are desert-like in their loneliness and their sandy, barren appearance. In The Empire Strikes Back Luke Skywalker and Hans Solo ride out like cowboys to patrol the territory on creatures that seem to be a cross-between a camel and a kangaroo. The opening scenes in both movies seem very familiar to the western fan.

In the typical western certain basic character types are evident. They include the "good guy" hero, a damsel in distress, and of course the villain. Very often there is also the humorous "sidekick" who is along to provide comic relief in the story. Luke Skywalker is clearly the "good guy" hero whose youth and innocence are balanced by the not so pure but heroic Hans Solo. It is interesting to note that modern heroes are not always saint-like in virtue, but are a combination of cunning and courage. Skywalker and Solo represent this type of modern hero as they bravely

fight for their damsel in distress, Princess Leia. Like Solo, Rooster
Cogburn in True Grit is something of an opportunist. He seems more interested in the reward than he is in justice when Mattie asks him to hunt
down her father's killer. Yet he does find the killer and even saves
Mattie's life after she's been bitten by a poisonous snake. In the ever-
popular Gunsmoke, Matt Dillon is frequently called upon to save Miss
Kitty from some dastardly and drunken renegade who has taken her hostage.

Whether science fiction or a western, the hero is usually a loner who
is handy with a weapon. In most westerns this particular weapon is a six-
gun or a rifle; in Star Wars Luke learns from the wise Kenobi to use "the
Force." Luke has already lost his parents at the beginning of the film,
then loses his aunt and uncle, finding himself alone. Hans Solo translated means "the lonely hand." Likewise, Cogburn and Dillon are men with
no family ties. This absence of ties, particularly to females, is important to the image of the science fiction hero as well as to the western
hero. However, this is not to say that these heroes aren't in some ways
enamored of their damsels in distress. Both Luke and Hans are fond of
Princess Leia, even though we know she only has eyes for Luke. Rooster
shows a gruff, paternal affection for Mattie, and Dillon's devotion to
Miss Kitty is never doubted. The true hero knows his place and keeps his
proper distance.

No western would be complete without the "sidekick" who always tags
along with the hero. This seems to be LaBoeuf's role in True Grit. And
where would Gunsmoke be without Festus? Star Wars has more than its share
of sidekicks. Chewbacca is the ever-faithful friend and companion to Hans
Solo. But the best moments in the movies go to the two robots, R2D2 and
CP30. They remind the viewers of Laurel and Hardy as they get into one

mess after another.

The plots of both science fiction stories and western stories depend on these basic character types. Sooner or later the hero must settle the conflict between the forces of good and evil by facing the villain alone in a "shoot-out," relying only on his skillful use of a weapon. Week after week on <u>Gunsmoke</u> Dillon faces a gunman or a gang single-handedly to preserve the law in Dodge City. In an unforgettable scene, Rooster puts his horse's reins in his mouth, a gun in one hand and a rifle in the other, and charges the group of outlaws that have kidnapped Mattie. Luke's courage and use of "the Force" as he rides down the center of the Death Star remind viewers of Rooster's ride into the blazing guns of the outlaws. Even though Luke is lucky to escape from Vader at the end of <u>The</u> <u>Empire</u> <u>Strikes</u> <u>Back</u>, we know that a fateful encounter will come when Luke will destroy Vader and his power once and for all. Until that day, Skywalker and Solo will continue to "ride the range" of space fighting for law and order in the badlands of the galaxy.

Paper Four

"ONE CALM SUMMER NIGHT" . . . BANG!

  The speaker of Edwin Arlington Robinson's "Richard Cory" leads us
to believe that Richard Cory is the personification of what every man
would like to be--the perfect gentleman--and that he has what every man
would like to have--unlimited wealth. From this characterization of
Richard Cory, we might assume that he is a very content man. However,
the surprise ending of the poem indicates differently. We can only deduce from the four stanzas of the poem what may have been Cory's reasons
for committing suicide. It is quite possible that despite Richard Cory's
calm, civilized appearance he was in reality very frustrated from con-
forming to the role of a perfect gentleman, having no goals for which to
strive, and most importantly, being alienated from those around him.

  The references in the poem to Cory's appearance suggest that he
looked as regal as a king: "He was a gentleman from sole to crown, /
Clean favored, and imperially slim." Although the speaker doesn't
actually say that Cory looked like a king, the words "crown" and "imperially" suggest royalty and support such an interpretation. The fact
that Cory was "admirably schooled in every grace" is evident in that "he
was always quietly arrayed, / And he was always human when he talked."
Just as a king is expected to behave in a certain manner, a person who
has been taught the social graces may feel compelled to behave as he
knows he should. In actuality, Cory may have longed to abandon his knowledge of the stifling rules of etiquette and behave just as those townspeople who so admired him. But having locked himself into this role of
"gentleman from sole to crown," he frustrates himself.

  Another frustrating aspect of Cory's existence is his wealth. In
addition to his perfect demeanor, we find that "he was rich--yes, richer
than a king." Had Cory tried to make a living like the townspeople, he

may not have been so frustrated with his predicament since there is admittedly a certain amount of satisfaction to be gained from doing a job and accomplishing a task. Receiving money for a job well done also promotes a feeling of self-sufficiency. Admittedly, any job has frustrations, but they seem minor in comparison to the frustration of an existence which seems pointless and futile like Cory's.

Both Richard Cory's social behavior and his wealth set him apart from the townspeople which leads us to perhaps the most significant source of his frustration--unintentional alienation. Although the townspeople admired Cory, they evidently were only aware of his appearance and set him on a pedestal. As the speaker states, "Whenever Richard Cory went down town, / We people on the pavement looked at him." The reference to "people on the pavement" suggests that Cory is not only higher in physical space but figuratively a person of "higher" or special qualities. He was seen as a person who "fluttered pulses when he said, 'Good Morning,' and he glittered when he walked." The townspeople are obviously awed by Cory's presence and "thought that he was eveything / To make us wish that we were in his place." It perhaps never occurs to the townspeople to look beneath Cory's outward appearance; they automatically assume that he is happy. Ironically, they "worked, and waited for the light, / And went without the meat, and cursed the bread," not realizing that compared to Cory who "one calm summer night, / Went home and put a bullet through his head" they were indeed fortunate in that they at least had each other to confide in. Richard Cory had no one.

Richard Cory's frustrations result in his suicide. He is locked behind the appearance of success, yet he is unhappy, and this unhappiness is intensified by his alienation from those who envy and admire him without really knowing him. We have to put ourselves in Richard Cory's place and try to understand him as "one calm summer night" about to explode into a tempestuous storm. When we do so, we become painfully aware of why he took his own life.

32 EFFECTIVE PARAGRAPHS ¶

A good paragraph has unity, coherence, and adequate development.

Unity requires that the paragraph have a single, clear, controlling idea, and that all the details introduced into the paragraph contribute to that controlling idea. The controlling or central idea is usually stated in a single sentence of the paragraph, called the **topic sentence**; this sentence often, though not always, is the first sentence of the paragraph. **Coherence** requires that all the sentences in a paragraph be connected in an orderly, clear way so that the reader can easily see how each sentence follows from the previous one, and how all relate to the controlling idea. **Adequate development** requires that there be enough details, facts, examples, evidence, or reasons included in the paragraph to make the controlling idea clear and meaningful to the reader.

For convenience, we discuss these three elements of a good paragraph separately, but all three are interrelated. A coherent paragraph is also unified and adequately developed. In other words, to support a topic sentence clearly and persuasively, you must develop a paragraph adequately and connect its sentences in an orderly way. Making a good paragraph calls for all three skills; no one is sufficient in itself.

UNITY IN THE PARAGRAPH ¶ UN

A unified paragraph is one that has a single, clear purpose, and one in which all sentences clearly relate to that purpose.

32a   State a paragraph's central idea in one sentence.

Most paragraphs have a **topic sentence**—a sentence that sums up the central idea of the paragraph. Topic sentences in paragraphs serve the same purpose as thesis sentences in papers. They insure that you have defined, both for yourself and your reader, the controlling idea of the paragraph. And by so doing, they serve as a guide to you in developing that idea.

The following paragraphs illustrate various ways of placing the topic sentence.

1   The topic sentence may be the first sentence of the paragraph. Such paragraphs state their central idea first and then add details supporting it. This kind of paragraph is the most common in expository writing, but it also occurs in persuasive and descriptive writing as well.

> *The tea-plant, a native of Southern China, was known from very early times to Chinese botany and medicine.* It is alluded to in the classics under the various names of Tou, Tseh, Chung, Kha, and Ming, and was highly prized for possessing the virtues of relieving fatigue, delighting the soul, strengthening the will, and repairing the eyesight. It was not only administered as an internal dose, but often applied externally in the form of paste to alleviate rheumatic pains. The Taoists claimed it as an important ingredient of the elixir of immortality. The Buddhists used it extensively to prevent drowsiness during their long hours of meditation.   OKAKURA KAKUZE, *The Book of Tea*

> *The* ENCYCLOPAEDIA BRITANNICA, *although a valuable research tool, is difficult to read and hard to handle—hardly designed for the hasty researcher.* Each article is thorough and detailed, but the tiny print is extremely hard to read. To be assured of getting every fact and detail, the researcher needs a strong light and, unless his eyes are keen, a magnifying glass. To pick up a volume in the first place, one needs both hands. One doesn't balance a *Britannica* volume in one hand while scribbling furiously with the other. A table or desk to lay the volume open on is absolutely necessary. But even sitting comfortably at a desk with a *Britannica* presents problems. To avoid crushing or tearing the onion-thin pages requires slow, deliberate, careful moves. Haste or carelessness could easily result in obliterating the whole article one wishes to read. Given these disadvantages to using the *Encyclopaedia Britannica*, fly-by-night researchers should consider other general reference books.
>
> *Student paragraph*

A paragraph's first sentence may combine a transition from the preceding paragraph with the topic statement of the new paragraph. In the example, the references to Dawson's location and size allude to topics in the paragraph preceding the one reproduced here; the clause in italics states the topic of the example paragraph.

Although it lay in the shadow of the Arctic Circle, more than four thousand miles from civilization, and although it was the only settlement of any size in a wilderness area that occupied hundreds of thousands of square miles, *Dawson was livelier, richer, and better equipped than many larger Canadian and American communities.* It had a telephone service, running water, steam heat, and electricity. It had dozens of hotels, many of them better appointed than those on the Pacific Coast. It had motion-picture theaters operating at a time when the projected motion picture was just three years old. It had restaurants where string orchestras played *Cavalleria Rusticana* for men in tailcoats who ate pâté de fois gras and drank vintage wines. It had fashions from Paris. It had dramatic societies, church choirs, glee clubs, and vaudeville companies. It had three hospitals, seventy physicians, and uncounted platoons of lawyers. Above all, it had people. PIERRE BERTON, *The Klondike Fever*

2 The topic sentence may be the last sentence of the paragraph. Such paragraphs give details first and lead up to the main point in the final sentence.

The true problem of city planning and rebuilding in a free society is how to cultivate more city districts that are free, lively and fertile places for the differing plans of thousands of individuals—not planners. Nothing could be farther from the aims of planners today. They have been trained to think of people as interchangeable statistics to be pushed around, to think of city vitality and mixture as a mess. Planners are the enemies of cities because they offer us only the poisonous promise of making every place in a city more like dull and standardized Morningside Heights. They have failed to pursue the main point: to study the success and failure of the real life of the cities. With their eyes on simple-minded panaceas, they destroy success and health. *Planners will become helpful only when they abandon what they have learned about what "ought" to be good for cities.*

JANE JACOBS, "How City Planners Hurt Cities"

Beginning at breakfast with flying globs of oatmeal, spilled juice, and toast that always lands jelly-side down, a day with small children grows into a nightmare of frantic activity, punctuated with shrieks, cries, and hyena-style laughs. The very act of playing turns the house into a disaster area: blankets and sheets that are thrown over tables and chairs to form caves, miniature cars and trucks that race endlessly up and down hallways, and a cat that becomes a caged tiger, imprisoned under the laundry basket. After supper, with more spilled milk, uneaten vegetables, and tidbits fed to the cat under the table, it's finally time for bed. But before they fall blissfully asleep, the children still have time to knock over one more bedtime glass of water, jump on the beds until the springs threaten to break, and demand a last ride to the bathroom on mother's back. *Constant confusion is a way of life for parents of small children.*

Student paragraph

3 The topic sentence may appear first and last. In such paragraphs the last sentence repeats the idea of the first, frequently restating it with some amplification or a slightly different emphasis in the light of the intervening details or discussion.

Clearly then, our first step is to convince our students of the importance of working from a thesis. The task is difficult, but we have their original motivation working for us. The students will easily understand that to work from a thesis is the way to please teacher, get a good grade, fulfill the assignment, and so on. If understanding the concept of thesis, finding an effective one, and organizing a paper about it were merely rote skills, this sort of motivation, superficial and temporary though it is, would be sufficient for our initial purposes. Full acceptance will come, and will *only* come, after personal experience has convinced each student that these procedures actually improve writing. Unfortunately for this simple solution, *thesis skills require a logical chain of reasoning and individual reflection.* They cannot be exercised effectively enough to achieve even the required preliminary success without some degree of real commitment on the part of the individual student. So our first task is to bring about in our students a real conversion of idea: *we must genuinely convince them of the persuasive purpose of the thesis and the essentially persuasive nature of all writing.*

BETH NEMAN, Teaching Students to Write

A metal garbage can lid has many uses. In the spring it can be used to catch rainwater in which a small boy can create a world of his own, a world of dead leaves and twigs inhabited by salamanders, small frogs, and worms. In the summer it can be turned on its top, the inside lined with aluminum foil, and used to hold charcoal for a barbecue. In the fall it can be used, with a similar lid, to frighten unsuspecting Halloween "trick-or-treaters." In the winter, if the handle is removed or flattened, the lid can be used by children to speed down snow-packed hills. *A garbage can lid covers garbage most of the time, but with a little imagination, one can uncover new uses for it.*

Student paragraph

4   The topic sentence may be implied. Narrative and descriptive paragraphs often do not have an explicitly stated topic sentence. But the controlling idea of such paragraphs is clearly implied by its details. In the following paragraph by Joan Didion, for example, the controlling idea might be stated thus: "Though the sources of one's childhood imaginings are long lost, the record of those imaginings perhaps reveals lifelong habits of mind."

My first notebook was a Big Five tablet, given to me by my mother with the sensible suggestion that I stop whining and learn to amuse myself by writing down my thoughts. She returned the tablet to me a few years ago; the first entry is an account of a woman who believed herself to be freezing to death in the Arctic night, only to find, when day broke, that she had stumbled onto the Sahara Desert, where she would die of the heat before lunch. I have no idea what turn of a five-year-old's mind could have prompted so insistently "ironic" and exotic a story, but it does reveal a certain predilection for the extreme which has dogged me into adult life; perhaps if I were analytically inclined I would find it a truer story than any I might have told about Donald Johnson's birthday party or the day my cousin Brenda put Kitty Litter in the aquarium.

JOAN DIDION, "On Keeping a Notebook"

EXERCISE 32a   What is the topic sentence, expressed or implied, in each of the following paragraphs?

1 Restaurants have always treated children badly. When I was small my family used to travel a lot, and waitresses were forever calling me "Butch" and pinching my cheeks and making me wear paper bibs with slogans on them. Restaurants still treat children badly; the difference is that restaurants have lately taken to treating us all as if we were children. We are obliged to order an Egg McMuffin when we want breakfast, a Fishamajig when we want a fish sandwich, a Fribble when we want a milkshake, a Whopper when we want a hamburger with all the fixings. Some of these names serve a certain purpose. By calling a milkshake a Fribble, for instance, the management need make no promise that it contains milk, or even that it was shaken.

ANDREW WARD, *"Yumbo"*

2 The Civil War was not won by the North; it was won by the South. The main objective of the South was to keep the land south of the Mason-Dixon line a white man's land—and they did just that. It is true that Lincoln, whose main goal was to preserve the Union, proclaimed the slaves free in 1862; but proclamations do not make people equal. That the South had achieved her goal was evident during the reconstruction period which followed the cease-fire. Although blacks were given the vote, they were too intimidated by the whites to cast their ballots. When they did vote, they voted the way the white men told them to—Democratic. The birth of the Ku Klux Klan after the Civil War also kept the black man "in his place." So strong were the South's commitments to the idea of a white man's land that blacks were still in an inferior position as late as 1964. It was not until the sixties, following the Supreme Court decisions on bus and school desegregation, that the black man finally achieved the status of an equal citizen. The South held fast to the idea of the white man's supremacy for one hundred years after the Civil War. *Student paragraph*

3 Through photographs, each family constructs a portrait-chronicle of itself—a portable kit of images that bears witness to its connectedness. It hardly matters what activities are photographed so long as photographs get taken and are cherished. Photography becomes a rite of family life just when, in the industrializing countries of Europe and America, the very institution of the family starts undergoing radical surgery. As that claustrophobic unit, the nuclear family, was being carved out of a much larger family aggregate, photography came along to memorialize, to restate symbolically, the imperiled continuity and vanishing extendedness of family life. Those ghostly traces, photographs, supply the token presence of the dispersed relatives. A family's photograph album is generally about the extended family—and, often, is all that remains of it. SUSAN SONTAG, *"In Plato's Cave"*

4 Every writer has his own ways of getting started, from sharpening pencils, to reading the Bible, to pacing the floor. I often rinse out my mind by reading something, and I sometimes manage to put off getting down to the hard struggle for an unconscionable time. Mostly I am helped through the barrier by music. I play records while I am writing and especially at the start of each day one particular record that accom-

panies the poem or chapter I am working at. During these last weeks it has been a record by Albinoni for strings and organ. I do not always play that key record, but it is there to draw on—the key to a certain piece of work, the key to that mood. The romantic composers, much as I enjoy listening to them at other times, are no help. Bach, Mozart, Vivaldi—they are what I need—clarity and structure.

MAY SARTON, *"The Art of Writing"*

5 An atmosphere that is a strange mixture of bleakness, tranquillity, and expectancy pervades the downstairs hall of the old gym early in the morning. As I walk from the chilly dawn outdoors into the basement of the old gym, I feel the dry heat on my face; although I assume that I am alone, I am surrounded by the impersonal noises of an antiquated steam-heating system. All the doors, which stand like sentries along the walls of the hallway, are locked, so that the deserted nature of that place and that hour are apparent; pipes hang from above, making the ceiling resemble the ugly, rarely viewed underside of a bizarre animal. I feel peaceful, however, in this lonely place, because of the silence. I know, moreover, that the desertlike heat is a sign that preparation has been made for my arrival and a signal that the day of work is about to begin. *Student paragraph*

32b

32b Be sure that every sentence in a paragraph bears on the central subject.

Not only must you have a clear purpose in writing a paragraph, you must also hold to that purpose throughout the paragraph. The writer of the following paragraph, for example, changes his purpose three times in the first three sentences, and he tacks on the last sentence as a kind of afterthought.

Henry James's extensive travel during his early years greatly influenced his later writings. Born in New York in 1843, Henry was destined to become one of the first novelists of the world. He received a remarkable education. His parents took him abroad for a year when he was only an infant. He was educated by tutors until he was twelve, and then taken abroad for three more years by his parents. His father wanted him to absorb French and German culture. His older brother, William, received the same education.

One way of revising this paragraph would be to restrict its subject matter to the one major topic of James's childhood.

Henry James, the novelist, had an unusual childhood. In 1844, while still an infant, he was taken abroad by his parents for a year. Upon his return, he and his older brother, William, were given private tutoring until Henry was twelve. At that time both boys were taken abroad to spend three years absorbing French and German culture.

Be careful not to violate the principle of unity by introducing new topics or points of view at the end of a paragraph. Notice in the following example how the last sentence, in which the writer deserts his earlier objectivity and takes sides in the argument, breaks the unity.

In the years following World War II there was much discussion on the question of lowering the minimum voting age to eighteen. Among people who believed that the age limit should be lowered, the favorite statement was, "If a boy is old enough to die for his country, he's old enough to vote in it." People who wanted the age limit to remain at twenty-one thought eighteen-year-olds would be unduly influenced by local wardheelers who would urge them to vote a "straight ticket." But the young voter who had not had a chance to become a "dyed-in-the-wool" party member tended to weigh the merits of the individual candidate rather than those of the party itself.

Revised, the paragraph might read:

In the years following World War II there was much discussion on the question of lowering the minimum voting age to eighteen. Among people who believed that the age limit should be lowered, the favorite statement was, "If a boy is old enough to die for his country, he's old enough to vote in it." People who wanted the age limit to remain at twenty-one thought eighteen-year-olds would be unduly influenced by the promises of dishonest politicians.

EXERCISE 32b(1)   Each of the following paragraphs opens with a topic sentence, but each violates unity by introducing information not related to the topic. Which sentences in each paragraph are not related to the topic of the paragraph? Could any of the sentences you identify as not related to the topic actually contribute to the topic if their position in the paragraph were changed?

1 (1) Racial discrimination has existed in the United States for many years. (2) It began when the first white settler decided that the Indians were an inferior breed. (3) It was given impetus by the arrival of the first Negro slaves. (4) A civil war was fought largely because the spokesman of the North, Abraham Lincoln, believed that all men are created equal. (5) Slavery was abolished and the Negro set free by act of Congress.

2 (1) The life of Thomas A. Edison illustrates the truth of the old saying "Genius is ten percent inspiration and ninety percent perspiration." (2) Edison was born in Milan, Ohio, and was expelled from school because his teachers thought he was a moron. (3) So Edison was educated at home by his mother, who helped him build a laboratory in the basement. (4) Edison spent long hours here, sometimes working as long as sixteen hours a day.

3 (1) Hardy's *The Return of the Native* is one of the finest novels I have ever read. (2) I was amazed to see how Hardy makes his major and minor episodes culminate in a great climax, and how inextricably he weaves the fortunes of his chief characters with those of his lesser characters. (3) Moreover, his handling of the landscape—gloomy Egdon Heath—is masterful. (4) He makes it a genuine, motivating force in the story. (5) My favorite character, however, was Diggory Venn.

4 (1) The advantages of modern transportation are many. (2) An enormous amount of time is saved by the great speeds at which vehicles of today travel. (3) Cross-country trips are much more comfortable than they were, and they can be made in days rather than months. (4) For land travel today the automobile, motorcycle, and bus have taken the place of the horse and wagon, stagecoach, and mule. (5) The railroad has been developed and extended since the use of the diesel. (6) Sailing ships are now chiefly a hobby and few consider them seriously as a means of transportation.

5 (1) If you intend to plant a strawberry bed, there are several things that you should consider. (2) Strawberries do best in a sandy loam or sandy clay that has been enriched with humus. (3) Blueberries and blackberries are better in acid soils. (4) Strawberries should be set out in an area that receives adequate drainage. (5) Too much moisture in the soil will kill them or interfere with their growth. (6) Other kinds of plants do better in marshy soils. (7) On account of frost dangers it is better to plant strawberries on a hillside or on a relatively high level area. (8) The effects of frost are rather peculiar; in general, plants in low-lying areas are more likely to be harmed by frost than those on hills. (9) The growth of young strawberries is actually increased if one pinches off the runners from the plants.

EXERCISE 32b(2)   Following are three topic sentences, each accompanied by a set of statements. Some of the statements are relevant to the topic, some are not. Eliminate the irrelevant ones, and organize the rest into a paragraph.

1 Given my choice I would sooner be in the Air Force than in any other service branch.

I am more interested in flying than in any other military occupation.

Opportunities for advancement are greater in the Air Force.

Wages in certain brackets of the Air Force are higher than in other branches.

There are many opportunities to travel.

My cousin has been in the Navy for two years, and has sailed around the whole world.

I think, though, that I still like the Air Force better.

2 The wreck on Route 64 at Mt. Nixon was caused entirely by careless and reckless driving by the driver of the Buick.

When the wreck occurred the lights were green for the cars coming off the side road.

A heavy truck loaded with hay was pulling out to cross the highway.

The Buick came speeding down the main road, went through the stoplight, and crashed into the truck.

You could hear the screeching of the tires and then the crashing and grinding of metal a quarter of a mile away.

You could hear it in our house up the road.

Both drivers were killed, and I will never forget how awful the accident was.

3 We owe some of our notions of radar to scientific observation of bats.

Most people hate bats.

Bats are commonly considered unattractive, ugly creatures.

They really look more like mice with wings than anything else.

Scientists noticed that bats rarely collided with anything in their erratic flight.

Keen eyesight could not be the reason for their flying the way they do, since bats are blind.

It was found that bats keep sending out noises inaudible to people and that they hear the echoes of those noises.

This principle whereby they fly safely was found to be similar to the main principle of radar.

COHERENCE IN THE PARAGRAPH ¶ **COH**

A paragraph may be unified without being coherent. Unity depends upon selecting details and ideas relevant to the paragraph topic. Coherence depends upon organizing these details and ideas so that the reader can easily see *how* they are relevant. Even though all the sentences of a paragraph bear upon a single point, unless they are knit together and flow into one another so that their relation to that single point is clear, they will not be coherent. A coherent paragraph leads readers easily from sentence to sentence. An incoherent paragraph confronts readers with puzzling jumps in thought, events out of sequence, facts illogically arranged, or points in a discussion omitted. Coherence requires that sentences be logically arranged and clearly connected.

32c   Arrange the sentences in a clear order.

32c

To insure coherence in a paragraph, arrange all sentences within the paragraph in some pattern that will create an orderly, natural flow of ideas. Like the arrangement you choose for an essay, the arrangement you choose for a particular paragraph will depend on your materials and your purpose. The common ways of ordering sentences are the methods of arrangement introduced in Section 31f: (1) time order, (2) space order, (3) order of climax, and (4) general to particular or particular to general.

1 Time order. Narrative paragraphs naturally arrange themselves in the order in which the events occur. The following simple paragraph recounts the death of a female eagle.

> On her own, one of the female's bold hunting trips was to prove fatal. The male saw from high above that she was making an attack on a ground squirrel in a dry arroyo. Her path would take her over an embankment at low altitude. Hidden from her view were two hunters walking close to the bluff. The male tensed as he saw his mate approach the men. As her black form swept over the hunters, they whirled and raised their guns. The female saw, but too late. As she banked sharply, two shots sang out and one slug tore through her body, sending her crashing in a crumpled mass. Helpless and distraught, the male watched from above as the hunters stretched out the wings of his mate and examined their prize. With the fear of man reinforced in his mind, he turned away and mounted up to return to the safety of the back country.   KENT DURDEN, *Flight to Freedom*

Specific directions and explanations of processes also arrange themselves naturally in time order. The following directions for mixing powdered clay proceed step by step through the process.

> Clay purchased in powder form is mixed with water to make it a plastic mass. To mix, fill a large dishpan or small tub about one-third full of water, sift clay over [the] water, one handful at a time, until [the] clay settles on top of the water to make a coating about 1 inch think. Cover [the] pan with paper or cloth and let the unstirred mixture set overnight. On the following day mix and stir it thoroughly. If [the] mass is too thick to knead, add more water. If too thin, add dry clay. Clay is in a state to store when it is soft and pliable but does not stick to the hands. Since clay improves with aging in a damp condition, mix as far ahead of time of use as you can. Wrap [the] clay in damp cloth and store in a covered crock for at least one week before using.
> HERBERT H. SANDERS, "How to Make Pottery and Ceramic Sculpture"

2 Space order. Many descriptive paragraphs arrange themselves easily according to some spatial order, from east to west, from bottom to top, from near to far, from the center outward, and the like. In the following paragraph, the author is standing at a high point overlooking a valley. The description moves first to the right, then to the left, then straight ahead (*before me),* and then farther and farther into the distance ahead (*beyond the creek* and *beyond that).*

> *On my right* a woods thickly overgrown with creeper descended the hill's slope to Tinker Creek. *On my left* was a planting of large shade

trees on the ridge of the hill. *Before me* the grassy hill pitched abruptly and gave way to a large, level field fringed in trees where it bordered the creek. *Beyond the creek* I could see with effort the vertical sliced rock where men had long ago quarried the mountain under the forest. *Beyond that* I saw Hollins Pond and all its woods and pastures; then I saw in a blue haze all the world poured flat and pale between the mountains.   ANNIE DILLARD, "Pilgrim at Tinker Creek"

In the following paragraph, the writer is describing the interior of her church's sanctuary. She carefully orders the details, always keeping the relative position of parts clear with such directional words and phrases as *over, above, on each side,* and with such descriptive verbs as *line, hang, guard, flank,* and *arching.*

The sanctuary of the First Presbyterian Church is a study in nineteenth century architecture. The sections of contoured, crescent-shaped oak pews separated by *two main aisles line the wedge-shaped main floor. Over the main floor in the rear hangs a balcony* supported by two Greek columns whose decorative gilt tops complement similar ornamentation at the front upper corners of the auditorium. *Brass rails guard the balcony seats and separate* the raised *podium from the choir loft behind* it. *Above and on each side of the podium* are opera-box windows of beveled glass and brass. *Three stained-glass windows flank each side* of the sanctuary and, gleaming in the sunlight, depict such simple religious subjects as lilies, the cross, and Christ in his roles of Shepherd and Comforter. The most distinctive feature, however, is the *huge fifteen-foot rotunda opening up the center* of the ceiling and arching its way to heaven.   *Student paragraph*

3 Order of climax. Many paragraphs can be made coherent as well as more effective by arranging details or examples in order of increasing importance. The writer of the following paragraph arranged its examples—kinds of jobs—in order of climax. Drucker's evidence moves from those jobs in which skill at expressing oneself (the paragraph's subject) is least important to those in which it is most important.

If you work as a soda jerker you will, of course, not need much skill in expressing yourself to be effective. If you work on a machine, your ability to express yourself will be of little importance. But as soon as you move one step up from the bottom, your effectiveness depends on your ability to reach others through the spoken or the written word. And the further away your job is from manual work, the larger the organization of which you are an employee, the more important it will be that you know how to convey your thoughts in writing or speaking. In the very large business organization, whether it is the government, the large corporation, or the Army, this ability to express oneself is perhaps the most important of all the skills a man can possess.

PETER F. DRUCKER, "How to Be an Employee"

4   General to particular or particular to general order. A great many paragraphs begin with a topic sentence that makes a general statement. Sentences that follow support the general statement with details, examples, evidence, and the like. Other paragraphs reverse this order, presenting first a series of details or reasons and concluding with a general statement that summarizes.

In the following paragraph the author begins with a general statement—that readers generally get lost through a writer's carelessness, which can take "any number of forms." The five successive sentences beginning with "perhaps" list five different forms that carelessness can take.

> If a reader is lost, it is generally because the writer has not been careful enough to keep him on the path. This carelessness can take any number of forms. Perhaps a sentence is so excessively cluttered that the reader, hacking his way through the verbiage, simply doesn't know what it means. Perhaps a sentence has been so shoddily constructed that the reader could read it in any of several ways. Perhaps the writer has switched pronouns in mid-sentence, or has switched tenses, so the reader loses track of who is talking or when the action took place. Perhaps sentence *B* is not a logical sequel to sentence *A*—the writer, in whose head the connection is clear, has not bothered to provide the missing link. Perhaps the writer has used an important word incorrectly by not taking the trouble to look it up. He may think that "sanguine" and "sanguinary" mean the same thing, but the difference is a bloody big one. The reader can only infer (speaking of big differences) what the writer is trying to imply.   WILLIAM ZINSSER, "On Writing Well"

In the following paragraph, the author begins by asserting that disasters may not be as widespread as records indicate. To support this statement, she contrasts the range of events reported in the news with the relative normalcy of most people's typical day. She then states the "law" she has formulated on the basis of her perception of the true situation. The paragraph thus moves from general to specific back to general.

> Disaster is rarely as pervasive as it seems from recorded accounts. The fact of being on the record makes it appear continuous and ubiquitous whereas it is more likely to have been sporadic both in time and place. Besides, persistence of the normal is usually greater than the effect of disturbance, as we know from our own times. After absorbing the news of today, one expects to face a world consisting entirely of strikes, crimes, power failures, broken water mains, stalled trains, school shutdowns, muggers, drug addicts, neo-Nazis, and rapists. The fact is that one can come home in the evening—on a lucky day—without having encountered more than one or two of these phenomena. This has led me to formulate Tuchman's Law, as follows: "The fact of

being reported multiplies the apparent extent of any deplorable development by five- to tenfold" (or any figure the reader would care to supply). BARBARA TUCHMAN, *A Distant Mirror*

In contrast to the two preceding paragraphs, the following paragraph moves from particular to general. The writer describes first her former cat, then her present cat, before her final general statement about the obvious difference between the two.

> I do not understand why people confuse my Siamese cat, Prissy, with the one I had several years ago, Henry. The two cats are only alike in breed. Prissy, a quiet, feminine feline, loves me dearly but not possessively. She likes to keep her distance from people, exert her independence, and uphold the cat's right to be finicky. She observes decorum and is never so rude as to beg, lick, or sniff unceremoniously. Her usual posture is sitting upright, eyes closed, perfectly still. Prissy is a very proper cat. Henry, on the other hand, was a disturbingly vocal tom cat who, before he died, loved me dearly but possessively. He was my shadow from morning until night. He expected me to constantly entertain him, and he was a crude, voracious eater. Henry never cared who saw him do anything, whether it was decorous or not, and he usually offended my friends in some way. The cat made himself quite comfortable, be it on top of the television, across strangers' feet or laps, in beds, drawers, sacks, closets, or nooks. The difference between Prissy and Henry is exactly the difference between Barbara Walters and Archie Bunker, and it would certainly take an imperceptive human to mistake those two. *Student paragraph*

EXERCISE 32c(1) Write a coherent paragraph that incorporates in your own words all the following information about Thomas Hardy.

He was an English novelist, short story writer, and poet.

He died in 1928, at the age of eighty-eight.

He is considered one of the most important of the writers who revolted against Victorian tradition at the end of the nineteenth century.

He is known for the pessimism of his ideas.

His most important prose works are novels of character and environment.

The Return of the Native, Tess of the D'Urbervilles, and *Jude the Obscure* are among his most important novels.

His best novels are studies of life in the bleak English countryside.

In his best novels individuals are defeated in their struggle against their physical and social environment.

Individuals in his best novels also struggle against the caprices of chance.

EXERCISE 32c(2) You can see how the order of sentences in a paragraph contributes to its coherence if you examine a paragraph in which the original order has been changed. The following paragraphs were coherent as they were originally written, but the order of sentences has been changed. Rearrange each group of sentences to make a coherent paragraph.

32c

1 (1) Landing a space capsule on Mars is technically complicated. (2) In 1971 one Soviet lander crashed and another stopped sending signals back after 20 seconds. (3) One of the Soviet 1974 attempts just flew past Mars. (4) Descending through Martian atmosphere is much trickier than landing on the airless moon. (5) The Soviets tried to land on Mars four times, twice in 1971 and twice in 1974. (6) Instruments on the second 1974 flight failed during descent, after transmitting usable signals for a few seconds.

2 (1) Language is full of symbols, but we also use signs or images that are not strictly descriptive. (2) Such things are not symbols. (3) We use spoken and written language to express the meaning we want to convey. (4) Although meaningless in themselves, signs have acquired a recognizable meaning through common usage or deliberate intention. (5) Some of these signs are mere abbreviations or strings of initials such as UN or UNESCO. (6) They are signs and do no more than denote the object to which they are attached. (7) Other signs are things such as familiar trademarks, badges, flags, and traffic lights.

3 (1) They fly in magnificent unison as they go further south to escape the cold. (2) The sight of the leaves covering the barren ground, additionally, indicates that cooler weather is approaching. (3) The fact that darkness arrives earlier in the evening makes one finally realize that the fall season has come. (4) There is nothing quite as visually exciting as noticing the signs which indicate fall is approaching. (5) Even during the day, the brisk wind compels a person to move at a quicker pace. (6) Obviously, the splendor of the fall season is unsurpassed. (7) Later in the afternoon, one notices that the birds, as well, are preparing for the onset of fall. (8) During the day one cannot help but notice the transformation in the leaves' colors from various shades of green to deep tones of red, gold, and brown.

32d

32d   Make clear the relationships among sentences.

Coherence requires not only that the sentences within a paragraph be related to each other, but also that their relationship be made clear. You can achieve clear relationships among sentences by the following means: (1) being consistent in point of view, (2) using parallel grammatical structure, (3) repeating words or ideas, and (4) using transitional words or phrases.

1   Maintain a consistent point of view. Avoid unnecessary shifts in person, tense, or number within a paragraph.

UNNECESSARY SHIFT IN PERSON

A pleasant and quiet place to live is essential for a serious-minded college student. If possible, you should rent a room from a landlady with a reputation for keeping order and discipline among her renters. Moreover, a student ought to pick a roommate with the same temperament as his own. Then you can agree to and keep a schedule of study hours.

UNNECESSARY SHIFT IN TENSE

Recently, I saw the movie *9 to 5*. The main characters are played by Jane Fonda, Dolly Parton, and Lily Tomlin. I particularly enjoyed the character who is played by Dolly Parton. She gives an excellent performance as an innocent, happily married woman who was suspected of having an immoral relationship with her boss. Lily Tomlin portrays an efficient, knowledgeable secretary who knew more about running an office than her boss does. Jane Fonda plays the role of a shy, somewhat confused country girl who was awed and rather frightened of the people she works with.

UNNECESSARY SHIFT IN NUMBER

Of great currency at the moment is the notion that education should prepare students for "life." A college graduate no longer goes out into the world as a cultivated gentleman. Instead students feel obliged to prepare themselves for places in the business world. Consequently, we are establishing courses on how to get and keep a mate, how to budget an income, and how to win friends and influence people—that is, how to sell yourself and your product. The study of things not obviously practical to a businessman is coming to be looked upon as unnecessary.

2 Use parallel grammatical structure. Using parallel grammatical structure in successive sentences is one of the most important ways of connecting them. Just as parallel grammatical form in coordinate parts of a single sentence emphasizes the coordinate relationship of the ideas, so parallel structure from sentence to sentence within a paragraph emphasizes the relationship of these sentences to the single idea of the paragraph.

Bowman had just happened to be looking at her. *He set* his cup back on the table in unbelieving protest. A pain pressed at his eyes. *He saw* that she was not an old woman. *She was* young, still young. *He could think* of no number of years for her. *She was* the same age as Sonny, and she belonged to him. *She stood* with the deep dark corner of the room behind her, the shifting yellow light scattering over her head and her grey formless dress, trembling over her tall body when it bent over them in its sudden communication. *She was* young. Her teeth were shining and her eyes glowed. *She turned and walked* slowly and heavily out of the room, and *he heard* her sit down on the cot and then lie down. The pattern on the quilt moved.

EUDORA WELTY, "Death of a Travelling Salesman"

Life has often been described as a game, and if one is to play any game successfully, *he must know how to balance his skills* and blend them into the combination most effective for transferring potential into actual performance. *Regardless of how many times* a guard has held his man scoreless, *if he himself has not scored* for his team, his effort is incomplete. *Regardless of how many points* a forward or center averages per game, *if he has not guarded the lane* at every attempt of penetration by the opposition, he is inefficient. The most valuable player trophy is awarded to the player *who scores considerably, who grabs rebounds mechanically* off the backboard, and *who hustles relentlessly* from the initial center jump until the final buzzer sounds. A successful player at his life's game *must also balance his skills. If he always leads, people may tire* of following; *if he always follows, others may consider* him unworthy of a leadership position when he desires it. The secret, then, is to incorporate the two so that a mediocre character is transformed into an exceptional one.

Student paragraph

3   Repeat key words and phrases. Many well-constructed paragraphs rely on the repetition of key words and phrases, often with slight modification, to emphasize major ideas and carry the thought from sentence to sentence. Pronouns referring back to clearly established antecedents in the previous sentence function in the same way. In the following paragraphs the words and phrases that are repeated to provide clear links from sentence to sentence and produce a closely integrated whole are in italics.

In discussing the pre-Civil War South, it *should be remembered* that the large plantation owners constituted only a small part of the *total Southern population.* By far the greater part of *that population* was made up of *small farmers,* and of course the Negro slaves themselves. Some *small farmers* had acquired substantial acreage, owned three or four slaves, and were relatively prosperous. But most of the *small farmers* were terribly poor. They rented their land and worked it themselves, sometimes side by side with the slaves of the great *landowners.* In everything but *social position* they were worse off than the Negro slaves. But it must *also be remembered* that they were as jealous of that superior *social position* as the wealthy *landowner* himself.   *Student paragraph*

Nonconformity is not only a desirable thing, it is an actual thing. One need only remark that all art is based upon *nonconformity*—a point that I shall undertake to establish—and that every great historic change has been based upon *nonconformity,* has been bought either with the blood or with the reputation of *nonconformists.* Without *nonconformity* we would have had no Bill of Rights nor Magna Carta, no public education system, no nation upon this continent, no continent, no science at all, no philosophy, and considerably fewer religions. All that is *pretty obvious.*

But it seems to be *less obvious* that to *create* anything at all in any field, and especially anything of outstanding worth, requires *nonconformity,* or a want of satisfaction with things as they are. The *creative* person—the *nonconformist*—may be in profound disagreement with the present way of things, or he may simply wish to add his views, to render a personal account of matters.   BEN SHAHN, *The Shape of Content*

4   Use transitional markers. A transitional marker is a word or a phrase placed at or near the beginning of a sentence to indicate its relation to the preceding sentence. The coordinating conjunctions *and, but, or, nor, so,* and *yet* are often used this way, particularly in informal writing, for they provide easy bridges from one sentence to another. But English provides a wide variety of transitional markers, as suggested in the lists below. Good modern writing uses the more formal markers sparingly. Be wary of cluttering your writing with unnecessary *however's, moreover's,* and *consequently's.* But you should be equally careful to know them and to use them when they create clarity.

Here is a list of many of the common transitional words and phrases:

TO INDICATE ADDITION

again, also, and, and then, besides, equally important, finally, first, further, furthermore, in addition, last, likewise, moreover, next, second, third, too

TO INDICATE CAUSE AND EFFECT

accordingly, as a result, consequently, hence, in short, otherwise, then, therefore, thus, truly

TO INDICATE COMPARISON

in a like manner, likewise, similarly

TO INDICATE CONCESSION

after all, although this may be true, at the same time, even though, I admit, naturally, of course

TO INDICATE CONTRAST

after all, although true, and yet, at the same time, but, for all that, however, in contrast, in spite of, nevertheless, notwithstanding, on the contrary, on the other hand, still, yet

TO INDICATE SPECIAL FEATURES OR EXAMPLES

for example, for instance, incidentally, indeed, in fact, in other words, in particular, specifically, that is, to illustrate

TO INDICATE SUMMARY

in brief, in conclusion, in short, on the whole, to conclude, to summarize, to sum up

TO INDICATE TIME RELATIONSHIPS

after a short time, afterwards, as long as, as soon as, at last, at length, at that time, at the same time, before, earlier, immediately, in the meantime, lately, later, meanwhile, of late, presently, shortly, since, soon, temporarily, thereafter, thereupon, until, when, while

Transitional words and phrases are italicized in the following:

As I have remarked, the pilots' association was now the compactest monopoly in the world, perhaps, and seemed simply indestructible. *And yet* the days of its glory were numbered. *First,* the new railroad stretching up through Mississippi, Tennessee, and Kentucky, to Northern railway-centers, began to divert the passenger travel from the steamboats; *next* the war came and almost entirely annihilated the steamboating industry during several years, leaving most of the pilots idle and the cost of living advancing all the time; *then* the treasurer of the St. Louis association put his hand into the till and walked off with every dollar of the ample fund; *and finally,* the railroads intruding everywhere, there was little for steamers to do, when the war was over, but carry freights; *so straightway* some genius from the Atlantic coast introduced the plan of towing a dozen steamer cargoes down to New Orleans at the tail of a vulgar little tugboat; and behold, in the twinkling of an eye, *as it were,* the association and the noble science of piloting were things of the dead and pathetic past!   MARK TWAIN, *Life on the Mississippi*

Sometimes a question may be made still more clear or precise by an indication of the circumstances in which it occurs. *Let us take an example.* I ask, "How wide is this bookcase?" This certainly appears to be a straightforward question that could be answered simply enough by specifying the number of inches across its front. *But* when one undertakes to find the answer, several perplexing considerations may arise. What dimension is wanted: the length of the shelf? the outside dimension? at the widest point? or at some other typical point? *Again,* how accurate a measure is wanted?—for no measurement is entirely accurate; all we can expect is greater or less accuracy. All these questions could be more or less cleared up by indicating the circumstances under which the problem arose. It might be, *for example,* that I contemplate placing the bookcase against a certain wall and desire to know whether or not it is too wide to fit into the position under consideration. *At once* I realize that the widest outside dimension is the one required, and that a relatively high degree of accuracy is necessary only if the width of the wall and that of the bookcase are found to be nearly the same.

HENRY S. LEONARD, *Principles of Right Reason*

EXERCISE 32d(1)   Make a coherent paragraph of the following statements. First, put them in logical order. Second, give them a consistent point of view and link them smoothly with transitional words or phrases. Revise the wording of the statements if necessary, but use all the information given.

(1) This attitude shows a naive faith in the competency of secretaries. (2) Practicing engineers and scientists say they spend half their time writing letters and reports. (3) Many of us foolishly object to taking courses in writing. (4) College students going into business think their secretaries will do their writing for them. (5) A student going into the technical or scientific fields may think that writing is something he seldom has to do. (6) Young businessmen seldom have private secretaries. (7) Our notion that only poets, novelists, and newspaper workers have to know how to write is unrealistic. (8) Other things being equal, a man in any field who can express himself effectively is sure to succeed more rapidly than a man whose command of language is poor.

EXERCISE 32d(2) The following paragraphs and paragraph parts are marred and made incoherent by shifts in person, tense, and number. Rewrite the paragraphs to insure consistency and coherence throughout.

1 Literature is a medium through which a person can convey his ideas toward or protests against different norms of society. Those works that deal with a moral issue are of particular importance in literature; they are written with a particular purpose in mind. A literary work such as Shakespeare's plays with a moral issue will live on to be reinterpreted by different generations. These works involve the reader for he forms his own moral judgment toward the issue. Arthur Miller's *Death of a Salesman* is a play which deals with moral issues.

2 It is difficult to feel compassion for people who do not deserve it. My neighbor, John Carroll, is a poor little rich boy who just can't find happiness and love. He had never been deprived of anything. The one thing he really wanted, a girl who had gone to high school with him, he couldn't get. His mother tells the story in such a way that you feel pity for this man because of this one thing that he couldn't attain. The people who least deserve compassion get more than their share of it.

3 Every time a nation is involved in a war it must face problems about its ex-soldiers after that war. The veteran is entitled to some special considerations from society, but how to treat them with complete fairness is a baffling problem. Livy reports that grants to the former soldier caused some troubles in the early history of Rome. There were many disagreements between them and the early Roman senators.

4 Preparing a surface for new paint is as important a step in the whole process as the application of paint itself. First, be sure that the surface is quite clean. You should wash any grease or grime from the woodwork. The painter may use turpentine or a detergent for this. One must be careful to clean off whatever cleanser they have used. Then sand off any rough or chipped paint.

5 One of the books I read in high school English was Dickens's *Tale of Two Cities*. In it the author tells of some of the horrors of the French Revolution. He spent several pages telling about how the French aristocrats suffered. The climax part of the book tells how a ne'er-do-well who had failed in life sacrifices himself for another. He took his place in a prison and went stoically to the guillotine for him.

PARAGRAPH DEVELOPMENT ¶ **DEV**

32e

32e   Develop every paragraph adequately.

If you do not pay attention to unity and coherence in writing your paragraphs (and your papers), you will lose your readers. No matter how willing they may be to stay with you, they will soon give up if you include details and reasons that they can't relate to your controlling ideas. And they will give up if they can't follow you from sentence to sentence. Paying attention to unity and coherence helps insure that your thinking is clear and orderly both to yourself and to your readers.

But no matter how careful you are not to introduce irrelevant details or to insure that one sentence follows another with shining clarity, you must develop central ideas with details, examples, evidence, and reasons if you are to inform, persuade, or simply interest your readers. Good topic sentences, no matter how carefully they are constructed to state the controlling ideas of the paragraphs, are relatively general statements. To make readers understand what those statements mean and to keep readers interested, you must explain or support such statements.

The following paragraph does not go far beyond its topic sentence:

It is not always true that a good picture is worth a thousand words. Often writing is much clearer than a picture. It is sometimes difficult to figure out what a picture means, but a careful writer can almost always explain it.

The writer of this paragraph has given us no details that explain why it is not true that pictures are worth more than words, or any reasons for believing his topic sentence. The second sentence merely restates the topic sentence, and the final sentence does very little more. Compare the following paragraph built on the same topic sentence.

It is not always true that a picture is worth a thousand words. Sometimes, in fact, pictures are pretty useless things. Far from being worth more than words, they can be downright frustrating. If you buy a new typewriter, would you rather have a glossy picture of it, or a 1000-word booklet explaining how it works? If your carburetor is clogged, do you need a picture of the carburetor, or an explanation of how to unclog it? If you can't swim and you fall in the river and start gulping water, will you be better off to hold up a picture of yourself drowning, or start screaming "Help!"?

In contrast to the first writer, this writer has given us three concrete examples of how words may in fact be worth more than pictures. We may object that pictures of both the typewriter and the clogged carburetor would be helpful along with the words. But we understand what the writer means. And we've been kept interested.

Each of the following sample paragraphs begins with a satisfactory topic sentence stating the writer's central idea. But each fails to give enough details or reasons to explain that idea to the reader, to make the idea concrete and clear. In short, these paragraphs are not adequately developed.

> The president should be elected for an eight-year term. In a four-year term the president has to spend too much of his time being a politician. He therefore can't carry out his plans.

A reader who is not already convinced that one eight-year presidential term is wiser and safer than two four-year terms is not likely to be persuaded by the two very general reasons the writer gives here.

> Work as a physical therapist is rewarding financially, but more important, it provides the satisfaction of helping others. For example, physical therapists can help handicapped children. They can also help others.

The reader expects more concrete details about the kind of work the physical therapist does, perhaps examples of the kinds of improvement brought to handicapped children, and certainly some more concrete information about who "others" are. He expects, too, some clearer explanation of the idea of satisfaction, which the topic sentence promises.

EXERCISE 32e   Choose two of the following topic sentences and develop each into a meaningful paragraph by supporting it with details, examples, evidence, and reasons.

1 A first impression is not always a reliable basis for judgment.
2 A book that is one man's meat may be another man's poison.
3 The first day of college is a nerve-shattering experience.
4 Making homemade furniture is less difficult than it appears.
5 Words are the most powerful drugs used by mankind.
6 There are three great advantages to air travel—speed, comfort, and thrills.
7 Harmony seldom makes the headlines.
8 Keeping a detailed budget is more trouble than it's worth.

32e

9 A good hitter is far more valuable to a baseball team than a good fielder.

10 Fashions in clothes (books, drama, hairdress, slang, etc.) change from one year (decade, century) to the next.

32f

32f Avoid excessively long and excessively short paragraphs.

The length of a paragraph is determined by the nature of the subject, the type of topic sentence, the intention of the writer, and the character of the audience. Ultimately, the length of a paragraph is a matter that you must determine for yourself. In general, however, avoid paragraphs that contain less than six or more than twelve sentences. Too short a paragraph may indicate that you are not developing your topic sentence adequately. Too long a paragraph may indicate that you are permitting excessive detail to obscure your central aim.

Excessively long paragraphs may be revised either by a rigorous pruning of details or by division into two or more paragraphs. Insufficiently developed paragraphs usually show lack of attention to detail and an imperfect command of the full idea of the paragraph. The paragraphs below, for example, are all insufficiently developed. The arguments are undirected, and the generalizations are inadequately supported by reasons, examples, and details. Simply stitching these fragments together would not produce a coherent, unified statement; instead, the entire statement would have to be thought through again and then rewritten.

> I am in favor of lowering the minimum voting age to eighteen. I think the average eighteen-year-old has more good judgment to put to use at the polls than the average middle-aged person.
>
> Among the members of the two major parties there is too much straight-ticket voting. I think the candidate himself and not his party should be voted on. The young voter would weigh the virtues of the candidate and not his party.
>
> It is unlikely that the young voter would be influenced by corrupt politicians. The majority of eighteen-year-olds are high school graduates and would surely have learned enough about current affairs to use good judgment.
>
> If the question of lowering the voting age were put to a nationwide vote, I am sure it would pass.
>
> In conclusion I say give young Americans a chance. I am sure they will make good.

EXERCISE 32f Group the following sentences into two paragraphs. Provide some transitional markers for the sentences, and, when possible, combine sentences.

> Martin Luther King was an ordained minister from Atlanta, Georgia. He gained prominence as a civil-rights leader during the 1950's

and 1960's. In 1956 he led a boycott by Montgomery, Alabama, blacks against segregated city bus lines. After his success in Montgomery, he founded the Southern Christian Leadership Conference. This gave him a base to expand the civil-rights movement in the South and throughout the nation. In 1963 he organized a massive civil-rights march on Washington, D.C., which brought together more than 200,000 people. It was there that he delivered his famous "I Have a Dream" speech. In the years that followed, King broadened his political involvement. He continued to work for civil rights, but he also became an outspoken critic of the Vietnam war. His criticism of the war was based on his belief that the war was contributing to poverty in America. He argued that our valuable national resources were being used to finance the war rather than to fight poverty at home. In 1968 he planned another large-scale march to Washington. It was to be called the Poor People's March. He never fulfilled his wish though. In April of 1968 he went to Memphis, Tennessee, to help settle a strike by sanitation workers. While there he was assassinated.

32g Choose a method of paragraph development suitable to your subject matter and your purpose.

Paragraphs are clear, convincing, and complete to the degree that they are packed with specific, relevant information fleshing out their general controlling ideas, that is, to the degree that those ideas are *developed*. There are many ways of developing paragraphs, and a "best" way depends on the paragraph topic and the way it is related to the other paragraphs in the paper. Most paragraphs can be developed by one of the following methods: (1) by using details, examples, or illustration, (2) by comparing or contrasting, (3) by defining, (4) by explaining causes and effects, or (5) by analyzing or classifying.

1 **Details, examples, and illustrations.** One of the most common and convincing ways to develop a general statement is to provide concrete and specific details or illustrations that will convey to the reader a clear impression of what the general statement really means to the writer. In fact, a good many of the other methods of development depend more or less on the use of detail and example, for these are virtually indispensable to clear and lively writing.

You may support a topic sentence either by amassing a variety of specific details, by providing a few examples, each stated in a sentence or two, or by describing at greater length a single extended illustration of your topic.

The author of the following paragraph gives us his controlling idea in the first and last sentences: the freedom of Americans today is a limited and licensed freedom. If you don't believe me, he says in effect, look at this list of thirty or forty different things you must have certificates or licenses for. Note how the writer gains coherence in his long list of details by ordering them roughly in the sequence in which they occur from birth to death.

> Americans are still born free but their freedom neither lasts as long nor goes as far as it used to. Once the infant is smacked on the bottom and lets out his first taxable howl, he is immediately tagged, foot-printed, blood-tested, classified, certificated, and generally taken in census. By the time that squawler has drawn the breath of adulthood he must have some clerk's permission to go to school or stay away, ride a bike, drive a car, collect his salary, carry a gun, fish, get married, go into the army or stay out, leave or re-enter the country, fly a plane, operate a power boat or a ham radio, buy a piece of land, build a house or knock one down, add a room to the house he has bought, burn his trash, park his car, keep a dog, run his business, go bankrupt, practice a profession, pick the wildflowers, bury the garbage, beg in the streets, sell whiskey in his store, peddle magazines from house to house, walk across a turnpike from one of his fields to another now that the state has divided him—the list is endless. Even in death his corpse must be certified and licensed before the earth may swallow him legally. Freedom is no longer free but licensed.
>
> JOHN CIARDI, "Confessions of a Crackpot"

In the following paragraph, the writer explains the pitfalls that await the unsuspecting student in a freshman composition course. She arranges the details she uses in the order she meets them in the course of the semester.

> A student rarely becomes convinced in school that he is an accomplished writer. The student must overcome major errors, only to deal with punctuation problems, poor topic sentences, weak structure, and faulty logic. The unsuspecting freshman believes that when he eliminates from his papers comma splices, fragments, faulty agreement, and misspellings, he merits an A. That student has merely reached the point at which his teacher can check his "respectfully submitted" papers for superfluous internal punctuation, misplaced parts, dangling modifiers, and awkwardness. After dealing with these seemingly insurmountable problems, the student is only held accountable for heavier burdens: paragraph unity and coherence, adequate development, consistency of tone, and variety of sentence structure. Should the student write a paper in English 101 that is worthy of being a model, he would only learn that the demands of 102 are more rigorous. No sooner does the student reach the top of one mountain than he sees a taller one before him.   *Student paragraph*

The following paragraph supports its central idea with a discussion of nine brief examples, each consisting of a quotation. All are selected to support the general assertion that popular magazine biographies of celebrities overflow with superlatives.

> We can hear ourselves straining. "He's the greatest!" Our descriptions of celebrities overflow with superlatives. In popular magazine biographies we learn that a *Dr. Brinkley* is the "best-advertised doctor in the United States"; *an actor* is the "luckiest man in the movies today"; *a Ringling* is "not only the greatest, but the first real showman in the Ringling family"; *a general* is "one of the best mathematicians this side of Einstein"; *a columnist* has "one of the strangest of courtships"; *a statesman* has "the world's most exciting job"; *a sportsman* is "the loudest and by all odds the most abusive"; *a newsman* is "one of the most consistently resentful men in the country"; *a certain ex-King's mistress* is "one of the unhappiest women that ever lived." But, despite the "supercolossal" on the label, the contents are very ordinary. The lives of celebrities which we like to read, as Leo Lowenthal remarks, are a mere catalogue of "hardships" and "breaks." These men and women are "the proved specimens of the average." DANIEL J. BOORSTIN, *The Image*

In the following paragraph, the writer supports her central idea that college students and graduates with their first job have much in common by citing several ways in which the circumstances of the two are alike.

> Why is it that college students envy graduates with full-time jobs, and graduates with full-time jobs envy college students? Except for the direction that the money flows, the two have much in common. Whether a person is beginning college or beginning his first full-time job, he discovers that he is at the lowest level of the institution and that movement toward the top is a slow process. Meanwhile, he must report regularly and monotonously to a given place at a given time. He finds himself besieged with deadlines and relentless demands, and he must continuously fulfill another person's expectations of him. Either as college student or new employee, he is penalized for absences, late work, and indifference to his tasks. His vacation time is fixed by someone in a superior position. When the college student finally graduates and the employee is finally promoted, both sadly discover that the process begins again: the college student needs a Master's degree; the vice-president lacks seniority. Both are again the lowest in the new rank; for both, the next move toward the top again seems a difficult and remote possibility. *Student paragraph*

The central idea of the next paragraph is that scientists who experiment with the world's living space take irresponsible risks with our future. Here the author does not offer several relatively brief examples to support his assertion. Rather he describes more fully a single illustration—an experiment with the little-understood Van Allen

Belt—in which scientists have acted without any foreknowledge of the consequences.

> When the mad professor of fiction blows up his laboratory and then himself, that's O.K., but when scientists and decision-makers act out of ignorance and pretend it is knowledge, they are using the biosphere, the living space, as an experimental laboratory. The whole world is put in hazard. And they do it even when they are told not to. During the International Geophysical Year, *the Van Allen Belt was discovered. The Van Allen Belt* is a region of magnetic phenomena. *Immediately the bright boys decided* to carry out an experiment and explode a hydrogen bomb in the Belt to see if they could produce an artificial aurora. The colorful draperies, the luminous skirts of the aurora, are caused by drawing cosmic particles magnetically through the rare gases of the upper atmosphere. It is called ionization and is like passing electrons through the vacuum tubes of our familiar neon lighting. It was called the Rainbow Bomb. Every responsible scientist in cosmology, radio-astronomy, and physics of the atmosphere protested against this tampering with a system we did not understand. They exploded their bomb. They got their pyrotechnics. We still do not know the price we may have to pay for this artificial magnetic disturbance.
>
> LORD RITCHIE-CALDER, *Polluting the Environment*

2   Comparison and contrast. Some controlling ideas naturally suggest development by comparison and contrast. Consider these topic sentences:

> My brother is a natural student; I am a natural nonstudent.
>
> Women have a long way to go before they have genuinely equal opportunity and recognition, but they have gone some of the distance since my mother finished high school.
>
> Foreign small cars may have virtues, but if we compare them carefully to their American counterparts, we'll choose the American.

Such sentences either directly assert or imply a contrast and almost require the writer to fill out the details of that contrast.

The paragraph that follows compares poetry and advertising, developing the assertion that they are alike in many ways by giving three examples of their similarity. The parallel constructions that mark the successive points of comparison and help give the paragraph coherence are in italics.

> Nevertheless, poetry and advertising have much in common. To begin with, *they both make extensive use* of rhyme and rhythm ("What's the word? Thunderbird!"). *They both use words chosen* for their affective and connotative values rather than for their denotative content ("Take a puff . . . it's springtime! Gray rocks and the fresh green leaves of springtime reflected in a mountain pool. . . . Where else can you find

air so refreshing? And where can you find a smoke as refreshing as Salem's?"). William Empson, the English critic, said in his *Seven Types of Ambiguity* that *the best poems are ambiguous;* they are richest when they have two or three or more levels of meaning at once. *Advertising, too,* although on a much more primitive level, *deliberately exploits ambiguities* and plays on words: a vodka is advertised with the slogan "Leaves you breathless"; an automobile is described as "Hot, Handsome, a Honey to Handle." S. I. HAYAKAWA, *Language in Thought and Action*

In the following paragraph, the writer compares modern astronauts and the ocean voyagers of centuries ago.

Our modern astronauts are much like the ocean voyagers who sailed the seas five hundred years ago. Like the ocean voyagers, today's astronauts are adventurous men who want to experience the thrill of exploring unconquered areas. After blast-off, the astronauts sail into an unexplored sea of space to find new information about other planets and to contribute to man's understanding of space and of distant planets. Similarly, the ocean voyagers contributed to man's understanding of this planet. They chartered the oceans of the world, discovered its continents, and brought back to the Europeans new knowledge of the world and of other cultures. It takes the same kind of adventurous spirit to explore the unknown seas of outer space that it took to explore the unknown seas of this world. *Student paragraph*

In the two preceding paragraphs, the similarities between two things constitute the central ideas of the paragraphs. But in many paragraphs the controlling idea, while not stating a comparison or contrast, nonetheless may require some development of a comparison or contrast. In the following paragraph, for example, the author contends that because beginning writers do not know how writing differs from speech, they proceed under false assumptions. Her assertion requires her to explain some of the contrasts between writing and speaking.

Here the problem of unfamiliar forms merges with the second pedagogical problem—that *the beginning writer does not know how writers behave.* Unaware of the ways in which writing is different from speaking, he imposes the conditions of speech upon writing. As an extension of speech, writing does, of course, draw heavily upon a writer's competencies as a speaker—his grammatical intuitions, his vocabulary, his strategies for making and ordering statements, etc., but it also demands new competencies, namely the skills of the encoding process (handwriting, spelling, punctuation) and the skill of objectifying a statement, of looking at it, changing it by additions, subtractions, substitutions, or inversions, taking the time to get as close a fit as possible between what he means and what he says on paper. Writers who are not aware of this tend to think that the point in writing is to get everything right the first time and that the need to change things is a mark of the amateur. (Thus a student who saw a manuscript page of Richard Wright's *Native Son*, with all its original deletions and substitutions, concluded that Wright couldn't have been much of a writer if he made all those "mistakes.") MINA SHAUGHNESSY, *Errors and Expectations*

In any comparison or contrast, it is important to give your careful attention to the clear arrangement of the points of similarity or difference. The more extended the comparison, the more crucial such clear ordering becomes. Note how careful the writer of the two following paragraphs is to keep the same order within the two paragraphs. In each, he speaks first of Roosevelt, then of Churchill; in each he moves back, at the end of the paragraph, to a telling final point of comparison. The careful ordering of the paragraphs helps keep them coherent.

> *Roosevelt,* as a public personality, was a spontaneous, optimistic, pleasure-loving ruler who dismayed his assistants by the gay and apparently heedless abandon with which he seemed to delight in pursuing two or more totally incompatible policies, and astonished them even more by the swiftness and ease with which he managed to throw off the cares of office during the darkest and most dangerous moments. *Churchill* too loves pleasure, and he lacks neither gaiety nor a capacity for exuberant self-expression, together with the habit of blithely cutting Gordian knots in a manner which often upsets his experts; but he is not a frivolous man. *His nature possesses a dimension of depth—and a corresponding sense of tragic possibilities, which Roosevelt's lighthearted genius instinctively passed by.*
>
> *Roosevelt* played the game of politics with virtuosity, and both his successes and his failures were carried off in splendid style; his performance seemed to flow with effortless skill. *Churchill* is acquainted with darkness as well as light. Like all inhabitants and even transient visitors of inner worlds, he gives evidence of seasons of agonized brooding and slow recovery. *Roosevelt might have spoken of sweat and blood, but when Churchill offered his people tears, he spoke a word which might have been uttered by Lincoln or Mazzini or Cromwell but not Roosevelt, greathearted, generous, and perceptive as he was.* ISAIAH BERLIN, "Mr. Churchill"

A special kind of comparison is **analogy.** An analogy draws a parallel between two things that have some resemblance on the basis of which other resemblances are to be inferred. When a comparison is drawn between a large city and an anthill or between a college and a factory or between the human nervous system and a telephone system, that is analogy. Parallels of this sort, although they may be quite inexact in many respects, enable us to visualize ideas or relationships and therefore to understand them better.

In the first of the two paragraphs that follow, the writer compares having a manuscript dissected by a gifted editor to having a skilled mechanic work on one's car. In the second, the writer compares the student's job of managing time to that of the juggler's coordinating multiple tennis balls or Indian clubs.

> Having a manuscript under Ross's scrutiny was like putting your car in the hands of a skilled mechanic, not an automotive engineer with a bachelor of science degree, but a guy who knows what makes a motor go, and sputter, and wheeze, and sometimes come to a dead stop; a man with an ear for the faintest body squeak as well as the loudest engine rattle. When you first gazed, appalled, upon an uncorrected proof of one of your stories or articles, each margin had a thicket of queries and complaints—one writer got a hundred and forty-four on one profile. It was as though you beheld the works of your car spread all over the garage floor, and the job of getting the thing together again and making it work seemed impossible. Then you realized that Ross was trying to make your Model T or old Stutz Bearcat into a Cadillac or Rolls-Royce. He was at work with the tools of his unflagging perfectionism, and, after an exchange of growls or snarls, you set to work to join him in his enterprise. JAMES THURBER, *The Years with Ross*

A college student trying to organize his studies and activities is like a juggler trying to manage several tennis balls or Indian clubs at once. Each student takes several courses that have varying types and amounts of required work. He must learn to manage his time so that he can get all his work for each course done on schedule. The task of the student in managing the work of four or five different courses alone is similar to that of the juggler coordinating four or five tennis balls at once. But in addition to his four or five courses, the student must also fulfill his responsibilities to perhaps two or three organizations and manage his social activities with friends. If the student cannot learn to distribute his time wisely among all these different demands, he may begin to feel like the juggler who has lost his coordination; his work and activities may begin to scatter in disarray, like the juggler's tennis balls which fall to the ground around him. In contrast, the student who learns to manage his time effectively keeps his studies and varied activities flowing smoothly, just as the juggler who successfully creates a smooth circle of six or eight flying tennis balls or Indian clubs. *Student paragraph*

3 Definition. The logic of a paragraph sometimes requires that key objects or terms be defined. Definition is necessary to set the limits within which a topic or a term is used, especially in dealing with abstract matters. Full and exact paragraphs of definition are frequently important parts of papers, essays, and articles. Note that paragraphs of definition many times make use of details and examples, of comparison and contrast, and of restatement, in order to insure clarity.

The following definition first states the two basic elements of the fairy story—"a human hero and a happy ending." The author develops the paragraph by describing the kind of hero and the kind of story pattern that are the special marks of the fairy tale. Italics show the movement of the paragraph, a movement basically controlled by the progress of the hero from beginning to end of the tale.

> *A fairy story,* as distinct from a merry tale, or an animal story, *is a serious tale with a human hero and a happy ending. The progression of its hero is the reverse of the tragic hero's: at the beginning* he is either socially obscure or despised as being stupid or untalented, lacking in the heroic virtues, *but at the end,* he has surprised everyone by demonstrating his heroism and winning fame, riches, and love. *Though ultimately he succeeds, he does not do so without a struggle* in which his success is in doubt, for opposed to him are not only natural difficulties like glass mountains, or barriers of flame, but also hostile wicked powers, stepmothers, jealous brothers, and witches. *In many cases indeed, he would fail were he not* assisted by friendly powers who give him instructions or perform tasks for him which he cannot do himself; that is, in addition to his own powers, he needs luck, but this luck is not fortuitous but dependent upon his character and his actions. *The tale ends with the establishment of justice;* not only are the good rewarded but also the evil are punished.
>
> W. H. AUDEN, Introduction to *Tales of Grimm and Andersen*

In the two paragraphs that follow, John Holt develops a definition of intelligence. Holt relies upon contrast to develop his definition: intelligence is not, Holt tells us, what it is often said to be—an ability to score well or do well. Rather, it is a "way of behaving" in certain situations. We might call the development here a not-this-but-that development.

The three-sentence first paragraph sets the general contrast between the two definitions. The second moves initially to the more specific but quickly returns to the basic pattern. The italicized phrases will help you follow the controlling, not-this-but-that flow of the definition. The two paragraphs here could have been combined. By using two paragraphs, however, Holt is better able to draw attention to his description of how a person acts in a new situation—a description that is very important in clarifying his definition.

> *When we talk about intelligence, we do not mean* the ability to get a good score on a certain kind of test, or even the ability to do well in school; these are at best only indicators of something larger, deeper, and far more important. *By intelligence we mean* a style of life, a way of behaving in various situations, and particularly in new, strange, and perplexing situations. *The true test of intelligence is not how* much we know how to do, *but how* we behave when we don't know what to do.
>
> *The intelligent person, young or old, meeting a new situation or problem,* opens himself up to it; he tries to take in with mind and senses everything he can about it; he thinks about *it,* instead of about himself or what it might cause to happen to him; he grapples with it boldly, imaginatively, resourcefully, and if not confidently at least hopefully; if he fails to master it, he looks without shame or fear at his mistakes and

learns what he can from them. *This is intelligence.* Clearly its roots lie in a certain feeling about life, and one's self with respect to life. *Just as clearly, unintelligence is not* what most psychologists seem to suppose, the same thing as intelligence only less of it. *It is an entirely different* style of behavior, arising out of an entirely different set of attitudes.

JOHN HOLT, *Why Children Fail*

4   Causes and effects. Some kinds of central ideas invite development by an examination of causes or effects. Pollution and poverty exist. What causes them? What are their effects? What are the effects of television? Of the widespread use of computers? What are the causes behind the movements for equality of women, the popularity of football, the high rate of unemployment?

The initial topic sentence of the following paragraph by Margaret Mead states a general *effect*—that in our society women suffer from lack of stimulation, from loneliness, dullness. Mead then develops the paragraph by detailing specific causes. The paragraph gains clarity and order by the author's division of detailed causes into two main groups—those associated with the pattern of relationships with children and husbands, and those associated with certain "conditions of modern life." The sentence that begins with *Moreover* marks this division.

> *Women in our society complain of the lack of stimulation, of the loneliness, of the dullness of staying at home.* Little babies are poor conversationalists, husbands come home tired and sit reading the paper, and women who used to pride themselves on their ability to talk find on the rare evening they can go out that their words clot on their tongues. As the children go to school, the mother is left to the companionship of the Frigidaire and the washing machine. Yet she can't go out because the delivery man might come, or a child might be sent home sick from school. The boredom of long hours of solitary one-sided communication with things, no matter how shining and streamlined and new, descends upon her. *Moreover,* the conditions of modern life, apartment living, and especially the enormous amount of moving about, all serve to rob women of neighborhood ties. The better her electric equipment, the better she organizes her ordering, the less reason she has to run out for a bit of gossipy shopping at the corner store. The department stores and the moving-picture houses cater to women—alone—on their few hours out. Meanwhile, efficient mending services and cheap ready-made clothes have taken most sensible busy work out of women's hands and left women—still at home—listening to the radio, watching television.   MARGARET MEAD, "What Women Want"

The central idea of the next paragraph, by Jerzy Kosinski, is that television has turned today's students into spectators. Television is the cause, says Kosinski; I have just described the effects. Here the topic sentence—the statement of *cause*—comes in the middle of the paragraph. Kosinski leads up to it by detailing the *effects* he has observed and follows it with his speculative explanation.

> During the last four years, I have taught at Wesleyan, Princeton, and at Yale University. I have often lectured at many schools throughout the country. I am appalled by what I think emerges as the dominant trait of the students of today—their short span of attention, their inability to know or believe anything for more than half an hour. *I feel it was television which turned them into spectators,* since by comparison with the world of television, their own lives are slow and uneventful. When they first believed that what they saw on TV was real, they overreacted, only to feel cheated when the next program demanded a new emotion. Later, they felt simply manipulated by whatever drama they witnessed. By now, they have become hostile, and so they either refuse to watch the TV altogether or they dissect the medium and throw out all that upsets them. JERZY KOSINSKI, NBC *Comment*

In the paragraph that follows, the writer discusses the causes of a problem faced by his father, a high-school teacher, and other teachers. Note how many examples the writer gives of the causes of the "shell shock" that teachers experience every day. The writer makes good use of parallel grammatical structure to reinforce the impact of the examples on the reader.

> My father is a public high-school teacher. He and the other teachers face a growing number of problems that seem to have no solutions. Having observed my father's behavior for several years, I have concluded that high-school teachers are suffering from a disorder formerly associated with war veterans—shell shock. Besides teaching five or six classes a day, teachers are also expected to sponsor clubs, coach athletic teams, raise money, head committees, chaperone dances, arrange parades, light bonfires, publish newspapers, and sell pictures. In my father's work, paper work means more than just grading papers. It also means filling out a never-ending stream of forms that insure racial equality in the classroom, that provide free lunches to the needy, that reassure administrators that everything is in its place, and that even request more forms to be filled out. Discipline has also taken on a new meaning in public schools. Today, discipline means searching for drugs, putting out fires, disarming students, and breaking up gang fights. Faced with these daily problems and demands, it is no wonder that teachers like my father are becoming less like educators and more like soldiers suffering from combat fatigue. *Student paragraph*

5 Analysis and classification. Analysis takes things apart. Classification groups things together on the basis of their differences or similarities. You use them both every day. You break your days into morning, noon, and night; in the supermarket you look for pepper among the spices and hamburger in the meat department, because you know that's the way they're classified. Similarly in writing, both in individual paragraphs and in entire essays, analysis and classification frequently can serve as guides to development and to organization.

In the following paragraph, Lynes develops his explanation of bores by setting up three different classes: the Crashing Bore, the Tinkling Bore, and the Still Waters Run Deep Bore. He also suggests two broader classes: the militant, to which the first two kinds belong, and the passive. The classification provides the pattern for the development of his paragraph and serves as a guide to the kind of detail he will select in describing each.

> The common variety of bores is well known to everyone. Ambrose Bierce said that a bore is "a person who talks when you want him to listen," but as apt as the definition is, the species is a good deal more complicated than that. There are, for example, many gradations of boredom, such as the Crashing Bore whose conversation weighs on you like an actual physical burden that you want to throw off because it is stifling you, and quite a different kind, the Tinkling Bore whose conversation bothers you in the way that an insistent fly does, annoying but not dangerous. There are such types as the Still Waters Run Deep variety who defy you to say anything that will change the expression on their faces much less elicit an encouraging word from them. There you are on the sofa with them, their intense eyes peering at you wth something between hopelessness and scorn, impressing on you the deep reservoir of their self-sufficiency and challenging you to ruffle the waters that lurk there. I cite this merely as an example of the passive as opposed to the militant type (both the Crashing and the Tinkling are militant), for it is those who make you feel like a bore who are the most boring of all. RUSSELL LYNES, *Guests: or How to Survive Hospitality*

In the following paragraph, the writer humorously analyzes the types of assignments that college students are asked to do during a semester. She classifies each assignment on the basis of the emotional effect it has on the student.

> After his first semester at a university, a student may notice that his assignments can be categorized according to the various emotional states they produce. For example, "The I'll-Do-It-Later-Tonight" assignment is a relatively easy assignment which takes no more than five or ten minutes and causes the student little inconvenience or worry. Related to this type is "The-I-Thought-I-Could-Do-It-Later-Tonight" assignment, which seems simple but is in reality much more than the student bargained for. This type often causes a sleepless night for the panicking student. "The-Impossible-Dream" assignment also causes the student a certain amount of panic. These assignments, also known as semester projects, are designed to take the majority of the semester to complete, and they seem to hang over the student's head like a dark cloud of doom. Much like this assignment, but perhaps even more traumatic, is "The-I'm-Going-To-Fail-This-Course" assignment. The pur-

pose of this one is to rid the instructor of half the class. This assignment may be seriously pursued with genuine interest and yet remain incomprehensible. The student must face the fear of a low grade-point average if he encounters many assignments of this type. Of all the types of assignments, this is the most dreaded.   *Student paragraph*

In the next paragraph, Lionel Ruby divides language into three classes on the basis of three different functions that language performs. From such a paragraph, the author could clearly develop successive paragraphs illustrating each function by example or by further subdivision.

Language has more than one purpose. We might say that language operates on different levels, except that the word "levels" suggests higher and lower planes in a scale of value, and this is not intended here. We shall deal with three functions: the informative, the expressive, and the directive. To say that language has these three functions is to say that there are three different reasons for speaking. One reason, or purpose, is to communicate factual information. This is the informative function. We speak also in order to express our feelings, to "blow off steam," or to stir the feelings and attitudes of the person we are talking to. We shall call this the expressive or "emotive" function. And, finally, we speak in order to get people to act. This is the directive function.   LIONEL RUBY, *The Art of Making Sense*

EXERCISE 32g(1)   Which of the methods of paragraph development discussed in this section seems to be the most appropriate method of developing each of the following topic sentences into a paragraph? Why? After you have answered this question briefly, choose one of the topics and write a paragraph using it. Is your paragraph developed according to your original notion?

1 Attending a small college has disadvantages as well as advantages.
2 To watch a college mixer is to see every type of human being.
3 Wit and humor are not the same thing.
4 Contemporary society places too much emphasis on test scores.
5 Good government begins at the local level.
6 Fraternities have to watch carefully the line between fellowship and snobbishness.
7 Some people come to college wanting to learn, but refusing, at the same time, to change a single idea they came with.
8 A distinction should be drawn between liberty and license.
9 Campus slang is a puzzle to the uninitiated.
10 The differences in education and social conditioning for boys and girls in our society result in the waste of many talented women.
11 If we must reduce the amount of energy we use, we must expect to make great changes in the way we live.
12 We are too much inclined to measure progress by the number of television sets rather than by the quality of television programs.

EXERCISE 32g(2) *You cannot do wrong without suffering wrong.* Write two separate and unrelated paragraphs to develop this topic sentence. In the first paragraph, define as clearly as you can what you think is meant by *wrong* and *suffering wrong*. In the second, demonstrate the truth or falsity of the statement by giving examples.

EXERCISE 32g(3) *My reading tastes have changed since I came to college.* Write three separate and unrelated paragraphs to develop this topic sentence. In the first paragraph, show why your tastes have changed. In the second, demonstrate how they have changed. In the third, contrast specifically your reading tastes in high school with your reading tastes in college.

CONSISTENCY OF TONE IN THE PARAGRAPH ¶ **CON**

When you read effective writing, you may be struck by the fact that what seems to hold the sentences together is more than mere adherence to an organizational principle. There is about such writing some inner consistency that unites everything into an authoritative whole. What you are responding to is a kind of consistency of **tone** that pervades the whole of a passage of good writing.

Tone is one of those matters that are clear enough until you try to define them. You know well enough what you mean when, if your neighbor has complained about your barking beagle, you remark that you don't mind his complaining but you don't like his tone. But when you try to describe exactly what it is you don't like, you find it extremely difficult. Tone is produced by an interplay of many elements in speech and writing. Sentence structure, diction, the mode of organization and development chosen, the kinds of examples, illustrations, and details drawn on—these and many other factors are involved in tone.

The best way to increase your awareness of tone in writing is to study carefully a variety of effective paragraphs, asking yourself how you would describe their tone and then trying to determine how the writer has conveyed that tone. A writer's tone can be impersonal or personal, formal or informal, literal or ironic, sentimental or sarcastic, sincere or insincere, enthusiastic or indifferent, dogmatic or doubtful, hostile or friendly, condescending or respectful, modest or authoritative, serious or humorous, and the like. Obviously it can be a level in between any of these extreme pairs, or it can be a complex quality that can be adequately described only by a combination of several of these terms. By careful study of good writing, you can increase your awareness of the many factors that contribute to the control of tone.

32h 32h **Choose an appropriate tone and maintain it consistently.**

1 Appropriate tone. An appropriate tone is one that reflects the writer's understanding of and respect for the needs and feelings of readers. It is not easy to state what will create such appropriateness in any particular paragraph or paper; but some things are generally to be avoided. Among them, these are the most important: talking down to your audience by repeating the obvious; talking over the heads of your audience, merely to impress them, by using words or allusions or examples they are unlikely to understand; being excessively dogmatic or sarcastic; being excessively or falsely enthusiastic.

This opening sentence of a student paper illustrates an extreme of inappropriate tone: *No one can tell me that people who vote for the characters on the Democratic ticket aren't putting their own selfish interests ahead of the true good of the country.* Whatever readers may think of the thesis of the writer, his expression of it is offensive. The language is emotional, the writer's attitude dogmatic. Readers have the immediate feeling that there is no point in reading further, since they cannot hope, apparently, for any sort of balanced or reasoned discussion of the sort appropriate to the topic.

2 Consistent tone. Consistency requires that once you have set a particular tone, you maintain it. A jarring shift in tone may ruin the effect of a paragraph even though it otherwise meets the tests of unity, coherence, and adequate development. The following paragraph from a student theme illustrates the point:

> Curiosity has developed ideas that have been vastly beneficial to mankind. We have seen mankind emerge from the age of great darkness into the age of great light. Today every hotrod artist profits from the ideas of past inventors and every housewife has a kitchen full of push-button gadgets that she couldn't have without ideas. Above all, modern scientific theory leads us to a clearer and deeper comprehension of the universe. So we see curiosity is really a helpful tool.

The principal fault of this paragraph is its jarring shifts of tone. The first two sentences and the next to last sentence set a serious, somewhat formal tone by such phrases as *vastly beneficial, we have seen mankind emerge,* the parallel phrases *great age of darkness* and *great age of light,* and *clearer and deeper comprehension of the universe.* But the language of both the third and last sentences, and the examples cited in the third sentence, depart completely from this tone of seriousness and formality. Having been prepared for comment about the great concepts of religion, politics, education, or science, readers are offered *hotrod artists* and *push-button gadgets.* The effect is something like that of a cat meowing in a church service.

EXERCISE 32h Study the following paragraphs. Describe the tone of each and discuss the factors that contribute to it.

1 Have you ever noticed the detail of the plants in the backgrounds of some Albrecht Dürer prints? They are perfect and finished, as finished as though they are as important as Death or Virtue in the foreground. The ferns have countless lacy fronds, the grasses are heavy-headed with seeds, the succulents are fleshy and ready to ooze viscous fluid if they're grazed by the tip of a lance.   *Student paragraph*

2 For we're always out of luck here. That's just how it is—for instance in the winter. The sides of the buildings, the roofs, the limbs of the trees are gray. Streets, sidewalks, faces, feelings—they are gray. Speech is gray, and the grass where it shows. Every flank and front, each top is gray. Everything is gray: hair, eyes, window glass, the hawkers' bills and touters' posters, lips, teeth, poles and metal signs—they're gray, quite gray. Cars are gray. Boots, shoes, suits, hats, gloves are gray. Horses, sheep, and cows, cats killed in the road, squirrels in the same way, sparrows, doves, and pigeons, all are gray, everything is gray, and everyone is out of luck who lives here.

         WILLIAM H. GASS, "In the Heart of the Heart of the Country"

3 Even though large tracts of Europe and many old and famous States have fallen or may fall into the grip of the Gestapo and all the odious apparatus of Nazi rule, we shall not flag or fail. We shall go on to the end. We shall fight in France, we shall fight in the seas and oceans, we shall fight with growing confidence and growing strength in the air; we shall defend our Island, whatever the cost may be. We shall fight on the beaches, we shall fight on the landing grounds, we shall fight in the fields and in the streets, we shall fight in the hills; we shall never surrender; and even if, which I do not for a moment believe, this Island or a large part of it were subjugated and starving, then our Empire beyond the seas, armed and guarded by the British Fleet, would carry on the struggle, until, in God's good time, the New World, with all its power and might, steps forth to the rescue and liberation of the Old.

         WINSTON CHURCHILL, *Speech at Dunkerque*

4 At one point or another in their college careers, many students find themselves having to cope with the insensitive professor. This creature abounds with irritating habits of disregard. He continually begins class late, leaving the students to wonder whether or not class will indeed be held. When he does arrive, he fills the room with the smoke of the cigar that he chews the duration of the period. He smiles as his students groan over the impossible questions on the mid-term, a test that he assured them would be no problem. He returns papers that bleed with his nasty comments which show no regard for the student ego. And perhaps most irritating to the student, he is never to be found outside of class. When a lucky student does find this professor, he doesn't hesitate to make the student aware of the inconvenience created by him. Obviously not all professors suffer the disease of disregard. If they did, college would be intolerable.   *Student paragraph*

5 My education and that of my Black associates were quite different from the education of our white schoolmates. In the classroom we all learned past participles, but in the streets and in our homes the Blacks learned to drop *s*'s from plurals and suffixes from past-tense verbs. We were alert to the gap separating the written word from the colloquial. We learned to slide out of one language and into another without being conscious of the effort. At school, in a given situation, we might respond with "That's not unusual." But in the street, meeting the same situation, we easily said, "It be's like that sometimes."

MAYA ANGELOU, *I Know Why the Caged Bird Sings*

Paragraphs for study

No one can learn to write well simply by following general prescriptions. One of the best ways to develop skill in writing is to develop skill in observing how others write. Reading is an integral part of the process of learning to write, not something entirely separate from it. Test your understanding of the principles of good paragraphs by a close study of the following paragraphs. Analyze each to determine the main points, the topic sentence, the transitions from sentence to sentence, the method or methods of paragraph development and organization, and the tone.

1. By day it [the kitchen] was the scene of intense bustle. The kitchen-maid was down by five o'clock to light the fire; the laborers crept down in stockinged feet and drew on their heavy boots; they lit candles in their horn lanthorns and went out to the cattle. Breakfast was at seven, dinner at twelve, tea at five. Each morning of the week had its appropriate activity: Monday was washing day, Tuesday, ironing, Wednesday and Saturday baking, Thursday "turning out" upstairs and churning, Friday "turning out" downstairs. Every day there was the milk to skim in the dairy—the dairy was to the left of the kitchen, and as big as any other room in the house. The milk was poured into large flat pans and allowed to settle; it was skimmed with horn scoops, like toothless combs.   HERBERT READ, *The Eye of Memory*

2. The whole aim of good teaching is to turn the young learner, by nature a little copycat, into an independent, self-propelling creature, who cannot merely learn but study—that is, work as his own boss to the limit of his powers. This is to turn pupils into students, and it can be done on any rung of the ladder of learning. When I was a child, the multiplication table was taught from a printed sheet which had to be memorized one "square" at a time—the one's and the two's and so on

up to nine. It never occurred to the teacher to show us how the answers could be arrived at also by addition, which we already knew. No one said, "Look: if four times four is sixteen, you ought to be able to figure out, without aid from memory, what five times four is, because that amounts to four more one's added to the sixteen." This would at first have been puzzling, *more* complicated and difficult than memory work, but once explained and grasped, it would have been an instrument for learning and checking the whole business of multiplication. We could temporarily have dispensed with the teacher and cut loose from the printed table.   JACQUES BARZUN, *Teacher in America*

3.   Registration is a very frustrating experience for the college freshman. First, a student has to find her advisor to get help in deciding what courses to take and to get the advisor to sign the trial schedule. Usually, the advisor is not in the office because he is either at home, in the gym helping with registration, on a coffee break, or out for an early lunch. After one finally finds her advisor or forges the advisor's signature, the second step is to wait with hundreds of other students for the assigned registration time to arrive. When the right time arrives, the third step is to secure class cards from the different tables on the gym floor. Getting class cards requires standing in long lines, sometimes for an hour. Frequently, the class cards that one needs most are unavailable, in which case one has to make an entirely new schedule. Sometimes, one must even return some class cards already secured and begin to secure new cards. After finally getting the class cards needed, the last step in registration is spending another hour standing in lines to pay fees, get an identification card, and register a car. Having survived registration, the new student usually leaves the gym completely exhausted.   *Student paragraph*

4.   One of the earliest forms of the story that we made up in Africa was the fable. A fable is a tale about animals . . . but really about people. It instructs us; it teaches us something about human behavior. But people do not like to be told straight out about themselves, so the storyteller acts as if he's just talking about buzzards or rabbits or something. When we came to these shores years ago, we brought these tales along. We even made up new ones, for there was much peculiar behavior on the part of people here to talk about and to teach about. So often, while drumming in the yard, we would tell stories about crafty foxes or sly monkeys or big dumb bears. We were often talking about our situation as slaves, trying to survive through our wits, trying to instruct each other through a "code" language.

      TONI CADE BAMBERA, "Rappin' About Story Forms"

5.   What men, in their egoism, constantly mistake for a deficiency of intelligence in woman is merely an incapacity for mastering that mass of small intellectual tricks, that complex of petty knowledges, that collection of cerebral rubber-stamps, which constitute the chief mental equipment of the average male. A man thinks that he is more intelligent than his wife because he can add up a column of figures more accurately, or because he is able to distinguish between the ideas of

rival politicians, or because he is privy to the minutiae of some sordid and degrading business or profession. But these empty talents, of course, are not really signs of intelligence; they are, in fact, merely a congeries of petty tricks and antics, and their acquirement puts little more strain on the mental powers than a chimpanzee suffers in learning how to catch a penny or scratch a match.

H. L. MENCKEN, *In Defense of Women*

6.   It was all over though. The big cat lay tangled in the willows: his head and shoulder raised against the red stems, his legs reaching and his back arched downward, in the caricature of a leap, but loose and motionless. The great, yellow eyes glared balefully up through the willows. The mouth was a little open, the tongue hanging down from it behind the fangs. The blood was still dripping from the tongue into the red stain it had already made in the snow. High behind the shoulder, the black pelt was wet too, and one place farther down, on the ribs. Standing there, looking at it, Harold felt compassion for the long, wicked beauty rendered motionless, and even a little shame that it should have passed so hard.   WALTER V. T. CLARK, *The Track of the Cat*

7.   The world does not much like curiosity. The world says that curiosity killed the cat. The world dismisses curiosity by calling it idle, or *mere* idle, curiosity—even though curious persons are seldom idle. Parents do their best to extinguish curiosity in their children, because it makes life difficult to be faced every day with a string of unanswerable questions about what makes fire hot or why grass grows, or to have to halt junior's investigations before they end in explosion and sudden death. Children whose curiosity survives parental discipline and who manage to grow up before they blow up are invited to join the Yale faculty. Within the university they go on asking their questions and trying to find the answers. In the eyes of a scholar, that is mainly what a university is for. It is a place where the world's hostility to curiosity can be defied.

EDMUND S. MORGAN, "What Every Yale Freshman Should Know"

8.   As man proceeds toward his announced goal of the conquest of nature, he has written a depressing record of destruction, directed not only against the earth he inhabits but against the life that shares it with him. The history of the recent centuries has its black passages—the slaughter of the buffalo on the western plains, the massacre of the shorebirds by the market gunners, the near-extermination of the egrets for their plumage. Now, to these and others like them, we are adding a new chapter, and a new kind of havoc—the direct killing of birds, mammals, fishes, and indeed practically every form of wildlife by chemical insecticides indiscriminately sprayed on the land.

RACHEL CARSON, *Silent Spring*

9.   For years, nuclear-power advocates have claimed that nuclear power is the most economical form of energy available; but in light of a few facts, one begins to doubt this claim. The cost of building the Sequoiah nuclear plant, for example, exceeded a billion dollars. For

this astronomical amount of money, one can expect this reactor to be out of operation approximately thirty percent of the time. After thirty or forty years, it will become too "hot" to operate and will be shut down permanently. Even though the reactor will be shut down, it will still be highly radioactive and will have to be totally encased in concrete and lead—all at a cost of another few million dollars—and guarded virtually forever. Nuclear power is neither cheap nor economical; it is both expensive and wasteful.   *Student paragraph*

10. My boyhood was spent in a world made tranquil by two invisible catastrophes: the Depression and World War II. Between 1932, when I was born, and 1945, when we moved away, the town of Shillington changed, as far as I could see, very little. The vacant lot beside our home on Philadelphia Avenue remained vacant. The houses along the street were neither altered nor replaced. The high-school grounds, season after season, continued to make a placid plain visible from our rear windows. The softball field, with its triptych backstop, was nearest us. A little beyond, on the left, were the school and its boiler house, built in the late 1920's of the same ochre brick. In the center a cinder track circumscribed the football field. At a greater distance there were the tennis courts and the poor farm fields and the tall double rows of trees marking the Poorhouse Lane. The horizon was the blue cloud, scarred by a gravel pit's orange slash, of Mount Penn, which overlooked the city of Reading.   JOHN UPDIKE, *Five Boyhoods*

11. The definition of equality varies from woman to woman. For some women, equality means being equal to men politically and socially. They feel that the traditional codes of chivalry are no longer applicable and resent men who open their doors, pull out their chairs, and help them with their coats. On the other hand, for some women, equality means that they should have the same opportunities and benefits as men yet also enjoy the tradition of chivalry. These women, although they may hold prestigious positions in government, education or medicine, don't resent a man who opens the door for them. Still for other women, equality is little more than a public interest story which has no effect upon their lives. They are secure in their lifestyles, whether domestic or not, and tend not to question the issue. Perhaps there is no one definition of equality for women but many, since each woman must decide how important equality is to her own self-esteem before she can determine what equality means.   *Student paragraph*

12. A sign is anything that announces the existence or the imminence of some event, the presence of a thing or a person, or a change in a state of affairs. There are signs of the weather, signs of danger, signs of future good or evil, signs of what the past has been. In every case a sign is closely bound up with something to be noted or expected in experience. It is always a part of the situation to which it refers, though the reference may be remote in space and time. In so far as we are led to note or expect the signified event we are making correct use of a sign. This is the essence of rational behavior, which animals show in varying degrees. It is entirely realistic, being closely bound up with the

actual objective course of history—learned by experience, and cashed in or voided by further experience.

SUSANNE K. LANGER, "The Lord of Creation"

33 WRITING PERSUASIVELY **LOG**

During your lifetime most of your writing, whether in school or on the job, will have a distinctly argumentative character. Your U.S. history exam may require that you write a short essay answering the question "What were the major causes of the Civil War?" Your English professor, explaining possible topics for a research paper, may say, "I don't want to read papers 'all about' a topic. I want you to digest your research and draw your own conclusions about the subject." Your company's regional manager may ask you for a proposal assessing several new sales strategies. The school board may decide to close your child's school, sending her to one in another neighborhood, and you and your neighbors want to write a letter of protest.

All these writing tasks require more than assembling facts and information. They require analysis and logical evaluation so that the information builds a case, so that a stand on the issues can be formed. In short, few of us put words on paper, whether by desire or request, unless we have some point to make, some assertion to present [see Section **31d(2)**]. Making an assertion places us in the realm of argument, because an assertion is a statement that can (or should) be supported with facts, with reasons—in other words, with evidence.

In each of the situations cited above, the audience evaluating the assertion and the supporting argument is clear: the professors, the regional manager, the school board. But even when you do not personally know your readers, making educated guesses about them and assessing their probable characteristics can be as important as thinking about the points you want to present (see Section **31e**).

Assessing the audience helps you decide on an effective approach. What is your readers' average age and level of education? What other factors such as sex, life style, income, type of employment, political or geographic affiliation may make them more or less receptive to your point of view? Most important of all, is your audience likely to agree with you or disagree with you?

If your audience already agrees with you, your problem is clearly not to persuade them further. It is rather to get them to act. When Thoreau delivered his address "Civil Disobedience," he knew his audience was already opposed to slavery; his task was not to convince them of the evils of slavery but to inspire them to act on behalf of the antislavery cause. Thoreau's essay is full of emotionally charged language, passionate in its call for action.

How much emotion you can effectively communicate to readers will depend on the topic and the intensity of belief you and your readers share. Clearly, a fist-shaking, tear-streaming appeal to vote down a proposed $2 increase in club dues is inappropriate. On the other hand, if you fail to express deep feelings when the occasion demands, your appeal will be equally ineffective. "Move us," the audience says to you, "don't talk about a serious problem as if it were a minor inconvenience."

If readers are likely to disagree with you, you must take a different approach. No matter how strongly you believe that abortion is wrong or that welfare should be increased or that writing courses should not be required in college, there are nonetheless persuasive arguments for believing the opposite. You can assume that many of your readers will start out disagreeing with your point of view. If you want these readers to listen to your position, start out by recognizing theirs. If you begin by acknowledging their arguments, even admitting the strength of some of those arguments, you can then move on to suggest their weaknesses, and finally to set your own arguments against them (see Section **33e**).

If you go about the task of persuading with respect for readers' convictions, you will be much more likely to get them to listen. Your purpose is, after all, to persuade. If you say (or even suggest) that your readers are ignorant, stupid, or ridiculous to believe as they do, you will only antagonize them. You will never persuade them.

An effective argument is more, then, than an attempt to persuade readers that what you do or believe is right or just—or what others do or believe is wrong or unjust. At its most fundamental level, an effective argument is a statement of judgment or opinion that is supported with logical and persuasive evidence.

33a Learn to recognize arguable assertions.

It is important to recognize which assertions are arguable and which are not. Trying to argue some assertions is pointless because not all assertions can be supported with valid reasons.

1 *A priori* is a term of logic meaning, roughly, "before examination." Assertions based on an *a priori* premise cannot be argued because such a premise can be neither proved nor disproved; people are simply convinced of its truth or untruth. *A priori* premises are beliefs so deeply held that they have the force of fact, although they cannot be supported by factual evidence.

Many deeply held and widely shared assumptions about human nature are *a priori* premises with cultural, racial, social, and moral or religious roots. If you argue from an *a priori* premise with someone who does not share that premise, you will find yourself arguing in circles or along parallel lines—but never toward resolution—because legitimate proof is not possible. For instance, when people passionately argue that one governmental or social system is better than another, they are often basing their position on different *a priori* premises. If one person believes, *a priori,* that human beings are basically good, altruistic, and trustworthy while the other person believes human nature essentially wicked, selfish, and dishonest, then the two can reach no final conclusion. The premises are not provable, no matter how many examples each person cites.

A priori premises may change or be replaced over time. Such change can be seen in emerging attitudes toward women's roles in American society. *A priori* assumptions underlying assertions about the "weaker sex," a woman's "place," or inherently masculine and feminine characteristics are not nearly as widely shared today.

2   Subjective expressions of taste and nonrational reactions cannot be argued. The Latin *de gustibus non disputandum est,* "there is no disputing about tastes," is another way of saying subjective reactions do not lend themselves to reasoning. No matter how sound your logic that there is no lack of oxygen in an elevator stalled between floors, to a claustrophobic the sense of suffocation is very real. No matter how good for you spinach may be, if you can't stand its taste, nutritional reasons won't convince you to eat it.

3   Matters of fact cannot be argued. If a fact is verifiable, there is no point in debating it. It can either be true (a *bona fide* fact) or false (not a fact), but in neither case is it a matter for argument because the record can be checked. The earth is round, or nearly so. This fact was verified by fifteenth-century explorers and more recently by means of space flights.

4   Statements involving unverifiable facts cannot be argued. While it is interesting to speculate about whether there is life after death, the answer is simply unknowable.

5   Statements based on insufficient facts cannot be argued conclusively. For instance, people enjoy arguing that life exists on other planets. Statistically, the odds favor extraterrestrial life forms. But we have no hard evidence at this point to prove the assertions. All we can say is perhaps; the jury is still out. Should information pointing one way or the other come to light, a conclusion may eventually be drawn. In the meantime, logical reasoning on the topic won't carry us very far.

6   On the other hand, facts are slippery and not necessarily static. What may be accepted as verifiably true this year may be proven false by next. Before sailors circled the globe, the populace accepted as fact that the world was flat. During the Middle Ages the plague that killed

millions was attributed to God's wrath. People had no knowledge that fleas could transmit microorganisms from rats to humans and thus infect the population. What was once the "fact" of God's wrath is now regarded as a lack of adequate hygiene. Correspondingly, what serves as fact today may be tomorrow's quaint, ignorant notion. Time and scientific inquiry have taught us that very little is immutably certain. The best we can do is draw conclusions from available data, deciding to formulate an argument when the supporting data warrant it.

EXERCISE 33a Decide which of the following assertions are arguable and which are not. Be prepared to explain why each assertion does or does not lend itself to argument.

1 The television series "Roots" was watched by more viewers than any network program in television history.
2 Peanut butter cookies taste better than chocolate chip cookies.
3 Killing is wrong.
4 Not all high-school graduates should attend college.
5 One should always tell the truth.
6 Americans own more cars and television sets per capita than citizens of any other country.
7 God created the universe and everything in it in six days.
8 Blue is a prettier, more restful color than orange.
9 A good first-grade teacher is one who keeps the children quiet and in their seats.
10 If the people of this country had believed the Vietnam war was right, we would have won it.

33b Learn the parts of an argument.

Because an **assertion** states the stand or point of view on a topic [see Section **31d(2)**], it is sometimes called a thesis, claim, or proposition. But whatever it may be called, it must be supported by valid evidence if the reader is going to believe it.

Evidence is the part of an argument the reader is willing to accept as true without further proof. Most evidence can be categorized as either fact or opinion: that is, (1) a verifiable occurrence or experience or (2) a trusted judgment believed reliable because the source is knowledgeable, prestigious, and authoritative. We have already noted that facts can be slippery **[33a(6)]**. In a later section **[33e(l)]**, you will see that prestigious opinion also has its pitfalls if the source is not truly knowledgeable. Nevertheless, a plausible argument depends on evidence that is accurate, pertinent to the main assertion, and sufficient to support it.

Evidence often comprises a major portion of an argument, especially if the topic is controversial or complex. There are no hard and fast rules for determining how much evidence is enough. It depends on the nature of your topic and the characteristics of your audience—how likely the readers are to agree or disagree with your assertion.

You have probably experienced the frustration of reading on your English compositions the comments "not enough support" or "more examples needed." Bear in mind the benchmark of shared experience; that is, the more widely shared or commonly acknowledged an experience, the fewer examples you need to convince readers. The sun rises in the east. No one is going to argue with you. If in a paper on the value of home remedies, however, you offer as fact the statement that mustard-plasters are good for curing colds, you will have to cite a wide and representative sampling of incidents as well as testimony from respected medical authorities to convince your audience. Most readers would view your statement not as fact but as an assertion needing proof.

Evidence is only as good as its accuracy and your audience's willingness to accept it. Consequently, persuading the reader means looking at the evidence from the reader's point of view and then supplying an appropriate combination of statistics, illustrations, specific examples, personal experience, or occurences reported by authorities to validate the evidence in your reader's eyes—and thus to support your argument's assertion.

Arguments also contain a third element, sometimes implied rather than stated, that shows the connection between the truth of the supporting evidence and the truth of the assertion. This third element is often called the **warrant.**

ASSERTION:	We can expect college tuition to increase.
EVIDENCE:	The cost of living keeps going up.
WARRANT:	Since colleges are subject to the same economic pressures as everyone else, tuition increases will be necessary to meet rising costs.

Using an implied warrant, and a different order of presentation, the same argument might be written:

EVIDENCE:	Because the cost of living keeps going up,
ASSERTION:	we can expect college tuition to increase as well.

The words "because" and "as well" serve as the warrant, clearly implying the reason why or connection between the truth of the evidence and the truth of the assertion.

EXERCISE 33b   Find the assertion, evidence, and warrant in each of the following passages. If any of the parts is implied, point out the words that indicate the implied part or supply the missing words.

1 I have a terrible sinus headache. Whenever the weather changes, I get one of these headaches, so we can expect rain before the day is over.

2 Most people are indifferent to local politics. Oh, they complain a lot about things, but only a minority of registered voters bothers to go to the polls when national candidates are not on the ballot.

3 And they lived happily ever after.

4 America's love affair with the big, flashy, luxury car is over. The energy crisis has seen to that.

5 If you don't behave yourself, Santa Claus won't bring you any presents.

6 The Surgeon General has determined that cigarette smoking is dangerous to your health.

7 National political conventions are merely ritualistic pageants. Their intended function, selecting the party's presidential candidate, has been taken over by the state primaries.

8 Some acreage in California's San Joaquin Valley is suffering from a build-up of salt deposits, the result of irrigation without adequate drainage. Irrigation can bring life to crop lands, but it can also bring slow death.

9 I must be out of shape. Yesterday I painted the bathroom, and this morning I feel as if I had been run over by a truck.

10 Don't touch the baby birds in that nest or their mother will abandon them.

33c Define terms whose exact meaning is essential to clear communication.

Much senseless argument arises because people fail to agree on meanings. Readers have to understand your terms before they can follow your reasonings. The assertion *If the people of this country had believed the Vietnam war was right, we would have won it* is unsatisfactory on several counts, not the least of which is the slippery term *right*. The reader is bound to ask, "What do you mean by 'right'?"

The word *right* is an abstraction, and abstract terms are among the most difficult to define. However, the assertion itself could have provided some useful clues. Consider the statement *A good first-grade teacher is one who keeps the children quiet and in their seats.* This assertion defines *good* by using a concrete example: a teacher whose class is quiet and in place. Definitions, then, supply words or examples more easily understood than the term being defined and show what items should be included or excluded from the category the term covers.

Definition by word substitution. Many terms can be satisfactorily defined by merely offering a synonym the reader is likely to know. This is particularly true for technical or other little-known terms. Often an **appositive**—another noun or a group of words used as a noun—placed immediately after the term will be useful for such a definition.

cardiac arrest, stopping of the heart
aerobic (oxygen-requiring) bacteria

aquifer, a natural underground water reservoir
layette, clothing or equipment for a newborn child

Formal definition. We learn about something new by discovering it resembles things we already know and then noting how it differs from them. Constructing a **formal definition**—sometimes called an *Aristotelian, logical,* or *sentence definition*—requires exactly the same steps. First, we explain the class of things—the **genus**—to which a term belongs, and then we determine how it differs from other things in that class—its **differentiation.** Formal definitions characteristically take the form *x is y;* that is why they are termed *sentence definitions.*

1 The first step in formal definition is to put the term into the class of items to which it belongs. This process is called **classification.**

Term		*Genus*
A carpet	is	a floor covering.
A crumpet	is	a light, soft bread similar to a muffin.

In general, the narrower the classification, the clearer the eventual definition.

NOT	A crumpet is a bread.
BUT	A crumpet is a light, soft bread similar to a muffin.
NOT	A rifle is a weapon.
BUT	A rifle is a firearm.

Indeed, a crumpet is classified as bread, but so is pumpernickel. Though *weapon* is a legitimate classification for *rifle,* the class includes more than is necessary (knives, spears, clubs, and so on).

2 Distinguish the term from other members of its class. This process is called **differentiation.**

Term		*Genus*	*Differentiation*
A carpet	is	a floor covering	of woven or felted fabric usually tacked to a floor.
A crumpet	is	a light, soft bread similar to a muffin	baked on a griddle, often toasted and served with tea.

Defining a term by genus and differentiation is analogous to the comparison and contrast methods of paragraph and essay development (see Sections **31f** and **32g**). The term is first classified according to similarity and then differentiated according to dissimilarity.

3   Use parallel form in stating the term to be defined and its definition. Do not use the phrases *is when* or *is where* in definitions.

NOT   A debate *is when* two people or sides argue a given proposition in a regulated discussion.

BUT   A debate is a regulated discussion of a given proposition between two matched sides.

4   Be sure the definition itself does not contain the name of the thing defined or any derivative of it. John Keats's line "Beauty is truth, truth beauty" is poetic, but not very helpful as a definition. Nothing is achieved when definitions are **circular,** when words are defined in terms of themselves.

NOT   A rifle is a firearm with *rifling* inside its barrel to impart rotary motion to its projectile.

BUT   A rifle is a firearm with spiral grooves inside its barrel to impart rotary motion to its projectile.

NOT   Traditionally, masculinity has been defined as the behavioral *characteristics of men.*

BUT   Traditionally, masculinity has been defined as the behavioral characteristics of courage, forcefulness, and strength.

5   Whenever possible, define a term in words that are familiar to the reader. It doesn't do much good to describe a truffle as "a fleshy, subterranean fungus, chiefly of the genus *Tuber,* often esteemed as food" if your reader won't know the meaning of *subterranean* or *fungus.* This example illustrates why dictionary definitions can sometimes be frustrating and unhelpful. Readers might find "an edible, lumpy plant that grows underground and is related to the mushroom" a much more understandable definition of *truffle.* The complexity of Dr. Samuel Johnson's definition of the simple word *network* is a notorious illustration:

Network: anything reticulated or decussated, at equal distances, with interstices between the intersections.

Ordinarily, of course, you will define terms without being aware of giving them a genus and a differentiation. But it is always possible to check your definition against the criteria given above. Consider the following example from a student paper:

Finally, college is valuable to a person interested in success. By *success* I don't mean what is usually thought of when that word is used. I mean achieving one's goals. Everybody has his own goals to achieve, all of them very different. But whatever they are, college will give one the know-how and the contacts he needs to achieve them successfully.

33c

This definition is obviously unsatisfactory; but the specifications for definition will help clarify why and how it breaks down. If the statement that this paragraph makes about *success* is isolated, it comes out like this: *Success is the successful achievement of goals that know-how and contacts gained at college help one achieve.* First, this statement violates one of the principles of definition because it defines the word in terms of itself: *success is the successful achievement.* Next, the writer does not make clear what he means by *goals,* and the qualifying clause *that know-how and contacts gained at college help one achieve* does nothing to help us grasp his intended meaning because we do not know how he defines *know-how* and *contacts.* Hence, he has failed in both aspects of good definition: he has neither put the terms into an understandable class nor made a real differentiation. What he says is that success means being successful, which is not a definition.

Extended definition. A good many terms, particularly abstract words like *propaganda, democracy, happiness, religion, justice,* and *satisfaction,* require considerably more than a formal definition if their meaning is to be clear. Extended definitions usually have a formal definition at their core but expand upon it using synonyms, examples, analogies, descriptions of operations and results, and various other explanations to show the reader more precisely what is meant. Extended definitions may be one paragraph long or longer; entire articles or even books can be structured as extended definitions.

The following paragraph illustrates a simple extended definition. (For further examples see the sample paper at the end of this section, pp. 292–294.) Note that the first sentence in this definition gives a kind of dictionary definition of *induction. Induction* is put into a class of things—in this case *the art of reasoning.* It differs from other things in that class—in this case by being that kind of reasoning in which we first examine particulars and then draw a conclusion from them. This general definition is then developed in two parts: (1) by explaining the kind of scientific reasoning that is inductive, and (2) by explaining, through a series of specific examples, how our everyday reasoning is inductive.

Induction is the kind of reasoning by which we examine a number of particulars or specific instances and on the basis of them arrive at a conclusion. The scientific method is inductive when the scientist observes a recurrent phenomenon and arrives at the conclusion or hypothesis that under certain conditions this phenomenon will always take place; if in the course of time further observation supports his hypothesis and if no exceptions are observed, his conclusion is generally accepted as truth and is sometimes called a law. In everyday living, too, we arrive at conclusions by induction. Every cat we encounter has claws; we conclude that all cats have claws. Every rose we smell is fragrant; we conclude that all roses are fragrant. An acquaintance has, on various occasions, paid back money he has borrowed; we conclude that he is frequently out of funds but that he pays his debts. Every Saturday morning for six weeks the new paper boy is late in delivering the paper; we conclude that he sleeps on Saturday mornings and we no longer look for the paper before nine o'clock. In each case we have reasoned inductively from a number of instances; we have moved from an observation of some things to a generalization about all things in the same category.

NEWMAN AND GENEVIEVE BIRK, *Understanding and Using English*

Extended definition can be used to clarify terms in an argument, but frequently it constitutes a whole argument—in and of itself—used not only to inform but also to persuade. In such a case the writer is trying to convince readers to share his or her beliefs in addition to clarifying a term. Thoreau wrote "Civil Disobedience" not only to explain the concept but also to justify it as a course of action. Alvin Toffler's book *Future Shock* provided our language with a new term, and the book is an extended definition of that term. But *Future Shock* does more than identify and describe a phenomenon: in Toffler's words, the book's purpose is "to help us cope more effectively with both personal and social change. . . . Toward this end, it puts forward a broad new theory of adaptation." In short, *Future Shock* argues for a set of new attitudes and behavioral patterns.

EXERCISE 33c(1)   Examine the following definitions and be prepared to answer the following questions about each. Is the class (genus) to which the term belongs clearly named? Is the class narrow enough to be satisfactory? Does the definition clearly differentiate the term from other things in the class? Does the definition repeat the term it is defining? Is it stated in parallel form?

1 An expert is one who guesses right.
2 A pot party is where everyone is smoking pot.
3 A thermometer measures temperature.
4 Religion is emotion seasoned with morality.
5 A touchdown pass is when the player throws the ball for a touchdown.
6 Analysis means to break something down into its parts.
7 Passive resistance is when people simply refuse to follow orders.
8 A frying pan is a cooking utensil that is large and flat.
9 Inflation is rising prices.
10 "Home is the place where, when you have to go there, they have to take you in."   ROBERT FROST

EXERCISE 33c(2)   Write formal definitions of two of the following terms.

1 rain check
2 guerrilla
3 jukebox
4 chair
5 examination

33c

EXERCISE 33c(3) Select one of the following terms and write a paragraph of extended definition. Use your first sentence to state a formal definition of the term and then clarify it in the rest of the paragraph.

1 mass media
2 inflation
3 pornography
4 underemployment
5 freedom

33d

33d **Be sure your argument is well supported and logically sound. Sound arguments are usually constructed using two major logical processes: induction and deduction.**

Inductive reasoning (as you learned from the example of extended definition) proceeds from the particular to the general. If particular facts are shown to be true time after time or if a laboratory experiment yields the same result whenever it is run or if people in a wide and varied sampling respond the same way to a given question, *then* a general conclusion may be drawn. Repeated experimentation and testing led to the conclusion that the Sabin vaccine would prevent polio. Scientists use induction when they test and retest a hypothesis before stating it as a general truth. The whole scientific method proceeds by inductive reasoning.

Deductive reasoning proceeds from the general to the particular. From a general conclusion other facts are deduced. The validity of the deduction, naturally, depends on the truth of the initial conclusion. Because you know that penicillin is an effective weapon against infection, seeking a doctor to administer it to you if you have an infection is valid deductive reasoning.

You should also be aware that there is an induction-deduction cycle of reasoning. Sound conclusions reached through induction may in turn serve as the basis for deduction. For example, over many years the National Safety Council has kept careful records of the occurrence and circumstances of highway accidents and has reached the valid conclusion that the proportion of accidents to cars on the road on holiday weekends is the same as the proportion on weekends that are not holidays. From this conclusion, arrived at inductively, you may deduce that you can travel safely by car to your grandmother's house next Thanksgiving.

In this way, the arguments you construct may use both induction and deduction. Sometimes you reason from conclusions a reader accepts as true; sometimes you must prove the truth of the conclusions themselves. In either case, the assertions you make in the course of the argument should be adequately supported, and there should be no errors in the logic.

A convincing argument presents sufficient evidence to support its assertions and presents it in a manner that is logically error-free. Errors of logic in argument, called **fallacies,** weaken an argument, making it unreliable. Most fallacies fall into two categories: fallacies of oversimplification and fallacies of distortion. Common fallacies of oversimplification are **hasty generalizations, inadequate cause-and-effect relationships, false analogies,** and **either/or fallacies.**

1   Support and qualify all generalizations. A **generalization** asserts that what is true of several particulars (objects, experiences, people) of the same class (genus) is true of most or all particulars of that class. For example, the statement *Drinking coffee in the evening always keeps me awake at night* is a generalization based on several particular experiences on separate evenings. Generalization is essential to thinking; without it, we could not evaluate experience—only accumulate isolated facts. Similarly, generalization is essential to argument, since evaluation is part of the argumentative process. In fact, generalizations often appear as topic sentences in paragraphs (see Section **32a**).

An argument's main assertion may be presented as a generalization: *Most people are indifferent to local politics.* Moreover, because arguments of any length or complexity are comprised of clusters or chains of smaller, related arguments whose proof supports the main assertion, the writer typically uses a number of generalizations in the course of convincing the reader. Thus, generalization is very important—but it has its dangers, as the following discussion reveals.

Avoid hasty generalizations. Do not leap to conclusions on the basis of insufficient evidence. We all tend to generalize from a few striking examples, especially when they accord with what we want to believe. But unless examples are irrefutably typical, they can lead to fallacies, even absurd assertions.

PARTICULAR *A*	Mrs. Jones's son never gets home when his mother tells him to.
PARTICULAR *B*	Sally, the girl down the street, won't go to college though her father wants her to.
PARTICULAR *C*	My brother keeps telling his daughter not to go out with that boy, but she keeps right on doing it.
HASTY GENERALIZATION	Young people today don't obey their parents. [Does this generalization include Henry and John and Mike, who are always home on time? Or Katie, who is in college though she doesn't want to be? Or the brother's other daughter, who married the son of her father's best friend?]

33d

PARTICULAR *A*	I know an Italian who is a bookie.
PARTICULAR *B*	The Italian who runs our neighborhood grocery once short-changed my neighbor.
PARTICULAR *C*	A man named Valenti was a gangster.
HASTY GENERALIZATION	Italians are crooks.

Hasty generalizations are dangerous because they make assertions about groups containing millions of individuals on the basis of three or four examples. And more often than not, the writer knows of examples that don't fit the generalizations but, giving in to the temptation to oversimplify, leaves them out.

To protect an argument's validity, as well as to be fair to your readers, never advance a generalization unless you can support it with sufficient evidence. Sometimes two or three examples may be enough, but sometimes you will need to analyze the evidence in detail. If you can think of exceptions to the generalization, you can be sure your readers will too; so you should prepare a counterargument to handle them (see Section **33e**).

Avoid broad generalizations. Be cautious in using words such as *always, never, all, none, right, wrong* in generalizations. Broad generalizations, like hasty generalizations, arise from inadequate evidence. Sweeping statements invite readers to start thinking of exceptions, to start picking apart your argument even before you've presented your evidence. Many an otherwise reasonable assertion has foundered for lack of *seldom* instead of *never, usually* instead of *always.*

OVERSTATED	Playing football always results in injury.
	Playing football results in injury.
QUALIFIED	Playing football sometimes results in injury.
	Playing football can result in injury.

Note that an overstated generalization need not specifically state that it applies to *all* people. By not making a qualification it clearly implies *all,* as in the second overstatement above. Similarly, words other than modifiers can act as qualifiers. For example, the verbs *can* and *may* prevent overstatements, as in the second qualification above, where *can* implies possibility rather than certainty.

2 Do not assume that a cause-and-effect relationship exists between two facts merely because one follows the other in time. This inadequate assessment of cause and effect results in the fallacy of oversimplification known as **post hoc, ergo propter hoc** ("after this, therefore because of this").

The Navy began allowing women to serve on its ships in the 1970's, and its preparedness has decreased steadily since then. [The newspaper columnist who made this statement ignored other important factors such as cuts in defense spending and a shortage of new vessels and equipment, all of which adversely affected the Navy's military strength.]

I'm not surprised George had a heart attack. We warned him not to take that high-pressure job at company X. [While a connection between stress and heart disease has been established, physicians point to diets high in cholesterol, lack of exercise, and smoking—long-term behavior that can contribute to heart attack. George's life style more than likely made him a good candidate for a heart attack long before he changed jobs.]

3   Do not assume that because two circumstances or ideas are alike in some respects, they are alike in all respects. This fallacy, **false analogy**, shares some characteristics of broad generalizations. Because one or two points are analogous, it is very tempting to go overboard and claim two situations or concepts are wholly analogous. Political speeches are full of oversimplified, faulty analogies, and so are moral diatribes.

Of course he'll make a good Secretary of Agriculture. He's lived on a farm all his life and turned a healthy profit raising livestock. [Undoubtedly farming experience is an asset, but success as a cattle grower does not guarantee success as a governmental administrator dealing with a wide variety of agricultural concerns.]

The United States is headed right down the road to oblivion, following in the footsteps of ancient Rome: too much luxury and leisure, too much sex and violence. The Roman orgy and bloody circus have their modern counterparts in American promiscuity and violent television programs. Like the Romans, we'll be conquered by stronger invaders one day. [This analogy fails to take into account vast differences between ancient Rome and modern America—imperial dictatorship versus representative democracy, to mention just one.]

Analogy can be a useful persuasive tool, but keep in mind that while it can clarify, it can never prove a point. Analogy's value increases in direct proportion to the number of parallels you cite and decreases with every difference your reader thinks of.

4   Do not claim there are only two alternatives if, in fact, there are several. Either/or fallacies result if you oversimplify choices, proposing only two when several actually exist. Truth sometimes is an either/or sort of thing: either you passed the examination, or you failed it. But most things about which we argue aren't as clear-cut. Arguing as if only two possibilities exist when the facts justify a variety of possibilities is also known as the **all-or-nothing fallacy** or

33d

false dilemma. (These two fallacies are frequently distinguished from each other, but both involve ignoring alternatives.)

> Students come to college for one of two reasons: they come either to study or to party. Judging by Mack's attendance at campus mixers, I'd say he didn't come to study. [It's possible Mack studies very little, if at all. It's also possible he studies very efficiently and thus has free time to go to dances. Clearly, many combinations of studying and partying, to say nothing of the endless possibilities that include neither studying nor partying, are available to both the prudent and the not-so-prudent college student.]

> A woman can't have it both ways. She has to choose between career and family. [Statistics show that a significant proportion of married women and mothers in this country hold jobs. Somebody obviously has seen through the false dilemma to at least a third alternative.]

EXERCISE 33d Explain what is wrong with the reasoning in the following statements, and try to identify the fallacies of oversimplification that occur.

1 Television is responsible for the violence in society today.
2 That girl my brother is seeing is a very bad influence on him; he met her at Christmas time and within a year he had dropped out of college.
3 Sex education gives kids too many ideas. There has been an increase in teenage pregnancies in our town every year since they started those sex education classes at the high school.
4 Your repeated failure to show up for work on time suggests either you don't like your job or you're lazy.
5 Welfare recipients are a lot like drones in a beehive. While the rest of us work to produce society's goods and services, they just consume and breed.
6 Any member of Congress who goes on a junket is just taking a vacation at the taxpayers' expense.
7 All this emphasis on "career training" has turned the university into an assembly line. Poke the students in at one end, keep piling on the required courses, and out they pop at the other end with a diploma but no individuality or ability to think creatively.
8 If you really loved me, you'd spend our anniversary here at home instead of going on that business trip.
9 World War I started during Wilson's term, World War II started during Roosevelt's term, and the Vietnam War escalated during Johnson's term; if we elect another Democratic president, he'll start another war.
10 Anyone who heads a large corporation got to the top by ruthless maneuvering and looking out for "number one."

33e

33e   Be sure your argument answers objections from the opposition without resorting to distortion.

A successful argument takes into account counterarguments the reader is likely to raise and tries to refute them fairly and reasonably. If counterpoints are indeed valid, the best procedure is to recognize their validity but provide sufficient evidence to substantiate the truth of your assertions over all. The surest way to damage your own position is to ignore counterarguments or, worse yet, divert attention from them by trying to appeal to your reader's prejudices and emotions. You may be successful in your diversion, but you will have avoided the real issues being discussed and failed the test of logical reasoning. In short, your argument will have been distorted and unfair.

One of the most common kinds of argumentative distortion is **slanted language,** words using **connotation** to appeal to emotion and prejudice (see Section **40**). Slanted language "twists out of shape," distorts meaning. For example, today words like *radical, permissive,* and *cover-up* produce negative responses from many people, while words like *freedom, responsibility,* and *efficiency* produce positive responses.

Consequently, the calculated—or careless—use of such words in argument tends to evoke emotional rather than reasoned reactions. If Candidate Jones is described as standing for "free, responsible, and efficient government" while Candidate Smith is described as "a radical with a permissive philosophy," voters are likely to favor Jones over Smith without attempting to learn either candidate's actual position on inflation, government spending, unemployment, or anything else. It's not unusual to find diametrically opposed positions described by the same connotative language. "Fiscal responsibility" can mean a tax cut in one politician's campaign and a tax increase in another's.

Arguments can also be twisted and bent by **fallacies of distortion,** errors that misrepresent all or part of an argument's meaning. Among distortion techniques are **transfer, argument to the man, argument to the people, non sequitur, begging the question,** and **red herring.**

1 Do not associate an idea or term with a famous name in the hope of imbuing the former with characteristics of the latter. The erroneous technique of **transfer (argumentum ad verecundiam)** uses positive or negative association rather than reason as a basis for conclusion. When used negatively, transfer becomes a form of **name calling.** In either case, the hope is that characteristics will transfer, even when logically there is no connection—which explains the notable incongruity of professional football players' endorsing women's pantyhose or popcorn poppers.

We are the political party of Franklin D. Roosevelt and John Kennedy. Our campaign platform follows in that great democratic tradition.

Schmaltz believes the federal government should decide the issue. He stands for big government, which is just another name for creeping socialism.

If Miss America can get beautiful hair like this using X shampoo, you can too.

33e

2 Do not sidestep an argument by trying to discredit the person who proposed it. Argument to the man (**argumentum ad hominem**) ignores the point being argued and attacks a person's character instead. This distortion technique is similar to that of red herring [see Section **33e(6)**] because it substitutes a false issue for *bona fide* proof. Furthermore, even though discredited for one thing, a person may be right about others.

> Why should you believe what Hartwell says about the needs of our schools? He is suspected of taking bribes. [Quite apart from the fact that Hartwell is only "suspected of taking bribes," what he has to say about school needs may be based upon extensive study and analysis.]
>
> Don't listen to Collins's arguments for abortion. She doesn't even like children. [That Collins doesn't like children says something about her. But her arguments for abortion may stem from deep conviction reached after long experience as a doctor.]

3 Do not sidestep an argument by appealing to the instincts and prejudices of the crowd. Argument to the people (**argumentum ad populum**) arouses emotions people have about institutions and ideas. When politicians evoke God, country, family, or motherhood, they are making such an appeal—as, for example, when candidates say they will protect the interests of the American family.

A slightly different fallacy that uses similar crowd appeal is the **bandwagon** approach. This fallacy says that what is right for the masses is right for the individual: one must go along with the crowd in belief or action. Obviously this is not true, as many incidents of mob rule have shown. Nevertheless, the bandwagon is a favorite ploy among advertisers (and children) who claim "everyone" is buying or doing something.

> Fifty million people can't be wrong! Drink Slurp-o!
> But Mom, all the kids are wearing shorts (*or* roller-skates *or* green wigs) to the prom!
> The responsible citizens of this state know that a vote for Jenkins is a vote for open and honest government.

4 Do not substitute inference for a logically sound conclusion. A **non sequitur** ("it does not follow") attempts a fallacious leap in logic, omitting proof.

> This is the best play I have seen this year, and it should win the Pulitzer prize. [Unless you have seen all the plays produced this year and are qualified to judge the qualities that make one a Pulitzer prize winner, it doesn't follow that the one you like best should win.]
>
> The problems we face today have been caused by Washington. Elect Green to Congress. [Not only is the first assertion offered without evi-

dence, but certainly we are given no proof that Green can solve the problems. Perhaps his strength lies in the fact that he has been in Omaha rather than Washington for the past four years.]

5 Do not assume the truth of something you are trying to prove. Begging the question is a fallacy that occurs when a premise requiring proof is put forward as true. A related fallacy is called **circular argument.**

This insurance policy is a wise purchase. It covers all expenses related to cancer treatment. [While the policy may pay cancer-related expenses, the statement assumes the buyer will get cancer. If he or she does not, the policy will not have been a wise purchase.]

His handwriting is hard to read because it is illegible. [This argument does not move from premise to conclusion but merely moves in a circle. *Illegible* means "difficult or impossible to read," so the author has said only that the handwriting is hard to read because it is hard to read.]

6 Do not introduce a false issue in the hope of leading your reader away from a real one. A most graphically termed fallacy, a **red herring,** supplies a false scent in an argument, diverting the hounds from their quarry and leading them down an irrelevant trail. Usually the false issue elicits an emotional reaction, side-tracking the reader's attention from the real issue and the proof it needs.

American cars really are superior to Japanese imports. After all, we should "buy American" and support our own economy rather than sending our dollars overseas. ["Buying American," a disguised appeal to patriotism, diverts attention from real issues such as mileage ratings, repair records, safety, and so on, exhibited generally by American cars as compared with Japanese cars.]

I don't think Mary Ann should have been expelled from school for cheating on Professor Thompson's calculus text. Lots of people cheat on exams—they just don't get caught. Besides, everybody knows Thompson's tests are too hard anyway. [Neither the pervasiveness of academic cheating nor the difficulty of calculus tests is relevant to the issue. The author tries to justify Mary Ann's action with two red herrings—a bandwagon appeal and an attack on Thompson—both of which are beside the point.]

EXERCISE 33e Explain the errors in reasoning in the following statements and try to identify the fallacies of distortion that occur.

1 My father raised his children with an iron hand, and we turned out all right. I intend to raise my son the same way. What was good enough for Dad is good enough for me.

2 Norma's house is always a mess. Anyone who's that disorganized at home couldn't possibly organize city government. I certainly wouldn't vote for her for mayor.

3 If you believe in the sanctity of the family, you'll agree that the books used in our schools should be chosen by us parents and not by the teachers. We are the ones who should decide what our children read.

4 He made very good grades in college so he's bound to do well in the business world.

5 The government must cut spending because economy in government is essential.

6 He knew how to run a lathe, but I didn't hire him because he spent a year in reform school and once a criminal, always a criminal.

7 How can you support the Equal Rights Amendment? Do you want women and men sharing the same restrooms?

8 In that TV commercial for Uppity Airlines, Herman Hero says their plane is the safest thing in the sky. He used to be an astronaut, so he must know what he's talking about.

9 Obviously a good golf game is the key to success in this company. Most of the rising young executives play golf, so I'd better practice my putting.

10 Senator Graft wouldn't have been charged with accepting bribes if there weren't some truth to it.

REVIEW EXERCISES ON WRITING PERSUASIVELY (Section 33)

EXERCISE A Prepare a counterargument for at least one of the arguments stated below. Be sure your counterargument exposes any fallacious reasoning you find in the statements and does not itself contain fallacies. Also be sure to anticipate and defuse objections likely to be raised by the opposition.

1 I have been trying to help my nephew with his arithmetic assignments, but he's still getting failing grades on his tests. He must not be paying attention, or else he's just stupid in math.

2 All these unnecessary environmental regulations are really not essential. Besides, the costs of pollution control are aggravating the national decline in productivity and the rise in inflation. The auto industry has suffered severe financial losses in recent years, and the energy crisis has made our country's deposits of high-sulfur coal crucial to our energy supply. What we need now is less environmental regulation, not more.

3 Since 1964 scores on Scholastic Aptitude Tests have been dropping. What's more, students graduating from high school today can neither read nor write nor do arithmetic at their grade level. Clearly, the minimum competency testing program used in Jacksonville, Florida, should be instituted nationwide. If a student can't pass these standardized tests, he or she shouldn't graduate.

4 My roommate will make a terrific veterinarian. She just loves animals. She's always bringing home stray dogs and cats. It really upsets her to see an animal suffer.

5 If a coat or suit becomes old, ragged, and out of style, we don't continue to wear it. We replace it with a new one. Similarly, employees who reach age 65 should be forced to retire to make way for younger people with energy and fresh ideas.

EXERCISE B The following problems are designed to direct your attention to some of the violations of logic that you encounter every day.

1 Analyze several automobile advertisements, several cosmetic or drug advertisements, and several cigarette advertisements in current magazines or on television on the basis of the following questions:

   a What specific appeals are made? (For example, automobile advertising makes wide use of the bandwagon approach; cosmetic advertising often uses transfer methods.) How logical are these appeals?

   b Are all terms clearly defined?

   c What kinds of generalizations are used or assumed? Are these generalizations adequately supported?

   d Is evidence honestly and fairly presented?

   e Are cause-and-effect relationships clear and indisputable?

   f Is slanted, loaded language used? What is the advertiser trying to achieve with the connotative language?

2 Look through copies of your daily newspaper and bring to class letters to the editor or excerpts from political speeches that contain examples of fallacious reasoning. Look for false analogies, unsupported generalizations, name-calling, and prejudices.

3 Read an opinion article in a popular magazine and write a report analyzing the logic underlying the opinions and conclusions it states.

EXERCISE C Read "Disporting at the Olympics," the student paper at the end of this section, and answer the following questions.

1 Which of the four types of writing (narration, description, exposition, argumentation) are represented? (See Section **31d.**)

2 Which type matches the author's apparent purpose?

3 Where does the author use definition?

4 In your own words, what is the essay's main assertion? Which sentence(s) in the essay states this assertion?

5 What generalizations does the author make? Are they supported with adequate evidence?

6 Do any parts of the argument rest on shaky assumptions or *a priori* premises?

7 Does the essay include counterarguments to handle objections likely to be raised by the opposition?

8 Is the author's reasoning sound?

9 Is any of the language unfairly slanted?

10 Do you find the essay persuasive? Why or why not?

Paper for analysis

DISPORTING AT THE OLYMPICS

The word <u>sport</u>, which for most of us means some kind of organized athletic activity like football or tennis, is a shortened form of the word <u>disport</u>, meaning to occupy oneself with diversion or amusement. <u>Disport</u> has its roots in a Latin verb, <u>disporter</u>--to carry away. Every four years sports fans act out the intent if not the knowledge of the Latin root, getting "carried away" by the Olympic Games. In modern times, the Olympics have certainly provided diversion; however, frequently they have not been all that amusing. All too often the Olympics have been a showcase for politics rather than athletics.

Nevertheless, the International Olympic Committee tries to put on a brave face and continues to declare the Olympics apolitical: the old "it's not whether you win or lose, but how you play the game" spirit. This sentiment echoes the words of Baron Pierre de Coubertin, who founded the modern Olympics in 1896: "The essential thing in life is not conquering, but fighting well." Noble sentiments indeed, but the youngest Little Leaguer will tell you they just don't wash. When athletes gather to compete, winning is everything. When athletes representing their nations gather to compete every four years at the Olympics, winning is also political.

But need politics spoil the Olympics? Not necessarily. Not if audiences and the International Olympic Committee stop worrying so much about politics and focus on the true center of the games--the athletes and their skill. We can't ignore the politics, but if we stop paying so much attention to them, we may be able to adjust our perspective so the sports predominate.

The first step in adjusting our perspective is to recognize that the Olympics--both ancient and modern--have always been political. The ancient games were a display of martial strength and ability--running, boxing, wrestling, chariot racing were all combat skills. From 380 B.C. the games even featured a race run in armor. In 364 B.C. the Eleians "forgot" it was "only a game" and actually attacked the Pisates during the Olympics, trouncing them.

The modern Olympics had their own savage counterpart in 1968 at Munich when Arab terrorists kidnapped and killed nine Israeli athletes in the Olympic Village. Less violent incidents include Hitler's use of the 1936 Berlin games to propagandize for Naziism; African boycotts in 1972 and 1976 protesting Rhodesian participation; and the summer games boycott by the United States and 30 other nations in 1980 to protest Russia's invasion of Afghanistan. It's pretty hard to ignore politics like that.

On the other hand, we can stop stewing about it and concentrate on the sports themselves. Every time our news media, the Olympic Committee, or anyone else dwells on politics rather than athletics, the people who would use the games for political ends benefit. The attention feeds on itself and creates more attention, more politics. The cry that the Olympics are too political becomes self-fulfilling prophesy.

Instead, the real story, the real media event, is the athletes, their skill, and the demands of their sport. The mind in concentration, the body in motion--these things are basic and satisfying no matter what training program, sports medicine staff, government, or political persuasion attends them. Athletic ability is fundamentally individual and personal; we can respond to it in an individual and personal way.

A good example is the Russian figure-skating pair, Rodnina and Zeitzev. They participated in the 1980 winter games at Lake Placid, after the Russian invasion of Afghanistan but before the American boycott. As they skated into the ice rink, the television commentator noted the pair had been nervous about their reception by the American crowd. The crowd was polite, but as the pair executed their routine, people became enthusiastic. The audience knew that Irina Rodnina would never skate at another Olympics: she was retiring after these winter games. They also knew her performance was thrilling, nearly flawless. Spinning, jumping, whirling through lifts and spirals with her husband-partner, Rodnina personified grace on ice. That was what brought the crowd to its feet in applause.

Human grace, skill, and achievement—personal talent, endurance, and triumph—these carried Rodnina and Zeitzev beyond politics. If the Olympic Committee, and media, and American audiences focus on these, every four years we can still get "carried away" at the Olympics.

EFFECTIVE SENTENCES
EF

Every sentence is the result of a long probation [and] should read as if its author, had he held a plough instead of a pen, could have drawn a furrow deep and straight to the end.

HENRY DAVID THOREAU

A sentence may be perfectly clear and grammatical without being *effective*. Most effective sentences not only communicate simple facts and ideas, they bring together a number of facts and ideas in ways that show the relationship among them. Such sentences enable the writer to knit into the basic subject-verb-object pattern of a sentence the modifiers that give interest and full meaning to ideas. And the skillful use of such sentences together, in carefully thought out sequence, allows writers to express meaning more exactly.

34 COORDINATION AND SUBORDINATION **SUB**

Most effective sentences bring together two or more ideas that they relate to one another by **coordination** and **subordination.** Broadly, **coordination** expresses equality: two things that are coordinate have roughly the same importance, the same rank, the same value. **Subordination** expresses some sort of inequality: when one thing is subordinate, or dependent, upon another, it is in some way of lesser importance or rank or value.

Coordination

When you coordinate two or more words, phrases, or clauses, you tell your reader that they go together and that they are equally important, or approximately so. The simplest kind of coordination occurs when you join two or more phrases or clauses by *and, but, or,* or by one of the other coordinating conjunctions: *workers and managers, working in the city but living in the suburbs, wherever you go or whatever you do.* Like other coordinating conjunctions, **correlative conjunctions**—coordinating conjunctions that work in pairs—indicate that the single words and phrases they link are equally important. The most important of these pairs are *both . . . and, either . . . or, neither . . . nor, not . . . but,* and *not only . . . but also*—as in *both successful and satisfied, neither chemistry nor biology, she not only practiced medicine but also raised English spaniels.* Conjunctive adverbs—words like *consequently, however,* and *nonetheless*—can never connect words, phrases, or dependent clauses, but they allow you to coordinate whole sentences: *He had been warned that a severe storm was coming; nonetheless, he insisted on starting his trip.*

34a   Coordinate to bring equal related ideas together.

Coordination allows you to bring equal parts of separate sentences together into single sentences by creating compound subjects, objects, modifiers, or whole predicates. By so connecting them and by putting them in the same grammatical form, you emphasize their equal meaning and importance and express your ideas more clearly and without needless repetition.

John wanted a new suit. He wanted a new coat. He wanted a new hat. He couldn't afford them.

John wanted a new suit, coat, and hat, but couldn't afford them. [Coordinate objects, *suit, coat,* and *hat;* coordinate verbs, *wanted* and *couldn't afford*]

Susan applied to graduate school. Elaine applied to graduate school. Ted applied to graduate school.

Susan, Elaine, and *Ted* all applied to graduate school. [Coordinate subjects]

During the morning the students were studying for their biology exam. They were also studying throughout the afternoon and evening.

The students were studying for their biology exam *not only during the morning but also throughout the afternoon and evening.* [Adverbial phrases coordinated by correlative conjunctions *not only* and *but also*]

But coordination not only allows you to bring together equal parts within sentences; it also allows you to express equal relationships among more complex ideas and information among a series of sentences. Although a series of sentences may set out facts and ideas of roughly equal importance, those sentences often leave readers to puzzle out exact relationships. When the ideas in such sentences are equal and closely related, they can often be brought together by coordination into a single, easy-to-follow sentence that clearly reveals those relationships.

Compare the following:

Winter is the season when animals get stripped down to the marrow. Humans also do. Animals can take the winter easy by hibernating. Humans are exposed naked to the currents of elation and depression.

Winter is the season when *both* animals *and* humans get stripped down to the marrow, *but* many animals can hibernate, take the winter easy, as it were; we humans are exposed naked to the currents of elation and depression.   MAY SARTON, *Plant Dreaming Deep*

The information in both versions is much the same. But the first forces the reader to work much harder to discover that animals and humans share the same exposure to winter, but with different effects. May Sarton's original single sentence pulls all the relationships tightly and clearly together by first linking *animals* and *humans* with the co-ordinating pair *both . . . and,* then by establishing the idea of contrast between them with *but,* and carries out the contrast by linking her statements about animals on the one hand and humans on the other by the semicolon, itself a kind of coordinating link.

EXERCISE 34a Combine the following sentences, using coordinating conjunctions either to link the two sentences as a single compound sentence or to link similar elements of the two sentences as compound subjects, objects, predicates, or modifiers.

1 Ryan has made a great deal of money. He still lives simply and unpretentiously.
2 I planned my paper carefully. I wrote it hastily.
3 The four roommates had decorated the fine old Victorian house with furniture that looked expensive. It was inexpensive.
4 You may remain outside in the hot sun. You can go inside and watch TV in an air-conditioned room.
5 The Senator said that he disapproved of the legislation. The Senator said that he would support the legislation.
6 The program indicated that Dr. Thomas would speak at 11:00 A.M. She spoke at 9:30 A.M. We missed her talk.
7 You had better not annoy Bowser, Chuck's dog. You'll wish you hadn't.
8 The bobcat was fearless. The bobcat was vicious.
9 The field was full of rattlesnakes. We were afraid to walk through it.
10 Lois and Guido could afford a trip to Europe. They could afford a new car. They couldn't afford both.

Subordination

Subordination allows you to build into sentences details, qualifications, and other lesser information and ideas while keeping the main statement of the sentence clear and sharply focused. When you coordinate two or more pieces of information, you indicate that they are equally important. When you put information into subordinate constructions—modifying words, phrases, subordinate clauses, and other modifying word groups—you indicate that they are less important than the main statement, even though they may still be vital to the full meaning of the sentence. Subordinating conjunctions, particularly, enable you to express exact relationships among your ideas.

Take a simple example of two factual statements. *He was late. I was angry.* If these two sentences stand as they are or if they are joined coordinately with *and—He was late, and I was angry—*readers will probably guess that the lateness caused the anger. But they can't be sure. They can be sure, however, if the two sentences are combined with a subordinating conjunction that expresses the intended relationship.

> Because he was late, I was angry.
> When he was late, I was angry.
> If he was late, I was angry.

Each of these expresses a different kind of relationship between the two events, but each of them makes the intended relationship explicit. None of them leave the reader to guess at the meaning the writer had in mind.

34b Put your main idea in the main clause; subordinate other information.

The main clause of a sentence should carry your central idea; details, qualifications, and other relevant information that is closely related but less important than that central idea should be put into subordinate constructions.

Consider the following sentence as a possible topic sentence for a paragraph:

> Gorillas have often been killed to permit the capture of their young for zoos, and men have recently been occupying more and more of their habitat and gorillas are now threatened with extinction.

Although the information in that sentence is perfectly clear, it is unclear whether the central concern is with the gorilla's threatened extinction or with the causes for that threat. Readers will probably assume that the principal concern is the threat to the gorilla's existence. But neither writer nor readers can be sure what direction the paragraph that this sentence introduces will take.

Either of the following versions, however, makes the central idea of the writer unmistakably clear:

> Because gorillas have often been killed to permit the capture of their young for zoos and men have recently been occupying more and more of their habitat, *they are now threatened with extinction.*

> Even though gorillas have often been killed to permit the capture of their young and are now threatened with extinction, *men have recently been occupying more and more of their habitat.*

The first version of the sentence makes it clear that the writer's focus is on the threatened extinction of the gorillas; the second, that the writer's focus is on the current increasing encroachment on the gorilla's habitat.

Here is another example.

> An arms race will be very costly, but we may be forced into one, and many people think it is necessary.

Which is the writer's main idea? That an arms race will be costly? That we may be forced into one? That many people think it is necessary? The following revisions establish one idea as the main idea by expressing it in a main clause and subordinating the other related ideas:

> Although we may be forced into an arms race because many people think it is necessary, *such a race will be very costly.*
>
> Although an arms race may be very costly, *we may be forced into one,* because many people think it is necessary.

Each of these revisions establishes a slightly different idea as the writer's central one, but both knit the three originally separate ideas into a single sentence that clearly distinguishes the writer's main point from subordinate ones. Neither of these sentences is intrinsically better than the other. Which of them the writer chooses must be determined by which point the writer sees as most important.

EXERCISE 34b Revise the following sentences by making one idea the main clause and subordinating other ideas.

1 We drove onto a gravel road. It led into the woods. It was narrow. We wondered whether it was safe.
2 The house was very old. It was painted yellow. The paint was faded. In some places it was cracked.
3 The bookshelves were too expensive. I went to a lumber yard. I bought some boards. I bought some brackets. I put them up myself.
4 I got up late this morning. I had to wait for a bus. I was late to class.
5 One of the early experimenters with submarines was Robert Fulton. He built the first successful steamboat. He also experimented with torpedoes.
6 I had never smoked marijuana before. I was invited to a pot party. I went. Someone offered me a joint. I took it. The effect was not quite what I had expected. I didn't finish it. I left the party.
7 Late-night TV talk shows are very popular. The hosts are usually very funny. The guests are from many walks of life. Some of them are politicians. Some are show-business celebrities. They talk about various things. The mixture makes for interesting conversation.
8 TV documentaries are very interesting. One showed the plight of the migrant workers. Another showed conditions in the ghetto. Still another showed the helplessness of neglected senior citizens. The one I liked best was entitled "Birth and Death."

9 We decided to take the subway. We didn't know the way. We asked directions. The train agent was very helpful.

10 I studied hard. I read the textbook. I read outside sources. I wrote a 15-page paper. I bought the instructor a Christmas present. I flunked the course.

34c Be aware of the different relationships subordinating words express.

Subordinating conjunctions allow you to express a variety of relationships. The most important of these are cause, condition, concession, purpose, time, and location. These relationships, together with the most common subordinating conjunctions expressing them and examples of their use, are shown below:

CAUSE

because, since
We now controlled the minority vote. We felt sure we could win.
Because we now controlled the minority vote, we felt sure we could win.

CONDITION

if, even if, provided, unless
Many serious diseases can be controlled. We must identify them early enough.
If we identify them early enough, we can control many serious diseases.
Unless we identify them early enough, many serious diseases cannot be controlled.

CONCESSION

although, though, even though
Morgan has always worked conscientiously and carefully. He has never received a very high salary.
Although Morgan has always worked conscientiously and carefully, he has never received a very high salary.

PURPOSE

in order that, so that, that
Shelley had prepared carefully for her bar examination. She wanted to be sure of passing it on her first attempt.
Shelley had prepared carefully for her bar examination so that she could be sure of passing it on her first attempt.

TIME

as long as, after, before, when, whenever, while, until

Terry and Lee were confronted with the evidence and they admitted that they had taken part in the robbery.

After Terry and Lee were confronted with the evidence, they admitted that they had taken part in the robbery.

LOCATION

where, wherever

A new office building stands on the corner of High and Federal Streets. A small cigar factory stood on that corner for years.

A new office building stands on the corner of High and Federal Streets where a small cigar factory stood for years.

The relative pronouns—*who (whose, whom), which,* and *that*—allow you to use adjective clauses for information and details about nouns.

Susan brought me a beautiful piece of jade. She just returned from Mexico.

Susan, who just returned from Mexico, brought me a beautiful piece of jade.

Hemenway was a big burly man. His face was tough and belligerent.

Hemenway, whose face was tough and belligerent, was a big burly man.

The tomb of Tutankhamen was filled with spectacular treasures. It was among the greatest archaeological finds of all time.

The tomb of Tutankhamen, which was among the greatest archaeological finds of all time, was filled with spectacular treasures.

EXERCISE 34c   Combine the following pairs of sentences, using a subordinate conjunction that will expess the relationship indicated in parentheses.

1 He rested over the weekend. He would be ready to go back to work on Monday. (purpose)

2 Manuel was given the award. He had the highest score. (cause)

3 Sally will go to college. She can borrow the necessary money. (condition)

4 The children washed the car. Their father was sleeping. (time)

5 Karen had been saving as much money as she could for a year. She still could not afford to go to San Francisco for her vacation. (concession)

6 My neighbors the Cavalettis prefer to heat by gas. They believe it is cheaper and cleaner. (cause)

7 Compensation for women has improved significantly. It is still far from equal to that of men. (concession)

8 The river reaches flood level. Those people living along its banks have to be evacuated. (time)

9 Jim has been betting on the horse races. He needs to borrow money from all his friends. (result)

10 All students must have their schedules approved by an advisor. Then they can get their admission cards for each of their courses. (time)

34d Learn to use such subordinating constructions as appositives, participial phrases, and absolute phrases.

Subordinate clauses, together with single-word modifiers and simple prepositional phrases, are the most common means of subordinating ideas and detail. But writing often uses other constructions that seldom occur in speech. Three of the most useful of these are appositives, participial phrases, and absolute phrases. Understanding these structures and learning to use them when appropriate can help you to improve your sentences.

Appositives

Appositives are words or word groups that rename, further identify, or describe another word. Appositives rename, clarify, identify, or expand the meaning of the word or phrase to which they are attached, but unlike clauses or whole sentences, they have the same grammatical function as the word or phrase they clarify. That is, a word group that serves as an appositive to a sentence subject could also serve as the subject; an appositive to a verb object could also serve as its object. Appositives most often function as nouns or noun word groups, but they may also serve as adjectives.

Appositives often offer an economical alternative to subordinate clauses. You can, for example, combine the following two sentences by putting the information of the second sentence either in a relative clause or in an appositive:

Sven Nilssen has told me much about Sweden.
He is my close friend and an accomplished pianist.
Sven Nilssen, who is my close friend and an accomplished pianist, has told me much about Sweden.

But the combination with an appositive is briefer and moves more quickly:

Sven Nilssen, a close friend and an accomplished pianist, has told me much about Sweden.

In general, any nonrestrictive clause that consists of *who* or *which* as the subject, some form of the verb *to be,* and a complement can be reduced to an appositive, as in the following:

My mother was born in Lincoln, Nebraska.
She was the oldest of seven children.
My mother, the oldest of seven children, was born in Lincoln, Nebraska.

Jim Slade, who is a militant labor organizer, has been repeatedly denied admission to the factory.
Jim Slade, a militant labor organizer, has been repeatedly denied admission to the factory.

Often a series of appositives can be used to bring together several details in a single sentence. In the following passage, each of the last three sentences states a separate observation about the way in which keepers of notebooks are a "different breed altogether."

Keepers of private notebooks are a different breed altogether. They are lonely and resistant rearrangers of things. They are anxious malcontents. They are children afflicted at birth with some presentiment of loss.

But in Joan Didion's original sentence, she has used a series of appositives to combine all these observations into a single smooth, clear, yet packed sentence.

Keepers of private notebooks are a different breed altogether, lonely and resistant rearrangers of things, anxious malcontents, children afflicted at birth with some presentiment of loss.

JOAN DIDION, *On Keeping a Notebook*

Although appositives are most commonly noun groups, they can also be used as adjectives, as in the following:

A lovely hand tentatively rose.
The hand was almost too thin to be seen.

A lovely hand, almost too thin to be seen,
tentatively rose.   HERBERT KOHL, *36 Children*

She was about thirty-five years old.
She was dissipated.
She was gentle.

She was about thirty-five years old, dissipated and gentle.

JOHN CHEEVER, "The Sutton Place Story"

Participles and participial phrases

Participles are nonfinite verb forms that can help form verb phrases or function as adjectives. Like finite verbs, they can take objects and modifiers to form participial phrases. Present participles end in *-ing* (living, studying, flowing, driving, eating). Past participles of regular verbs end in *-ed* (lived, studied, wasted); past participles of irregular verbs often end in *-n* or *-en* (blown, driven, eaten) but sometimes have other irregular forms (slept, clung, swum). Together with objects or modifiers, participles may form phrases, as in the following:

Eating their way into the sills of the house, the termites caused great damage.

Dressed in the warmest clothes they could find, Kathie and Mark stepped out into the driving wind.

Participial phrases often provide an alternative way of expressing information or ideas that can be expressed in sentences or dependent clauses. Compare the following:

Writing is a slow process. It requires considerable thought, time and effort.

Writing is a slow process, *which requires considerable thought, time, and effort.*

Writing is a slow process, *requiring considerable thought, time, and effort.*

In contrast to relative clauses, which ordinarily must follow immediately after the nouns they modify, participial phrases can precede the nouns they modify. A participial phrase can usually be placed at more than one point in a sentence.

The old house, *which was deserted twenty years ago and said to be haunted by the ghost of its former owner,* stood halfway up the hill.

Deserted twenty years ago and said to be haunted by the ghost of its former owner, the old house stood halfway up the hill.

The old house, *deserted twenty years ago and said to be haunted by the ghost of its former owner,* stood halfway up the hill.

Since participial phrases are somewhat flexible in their position, they often permit you to vary sentence structure to fit a particular purpose in a given paragraph. You must, however, be careful not to create misplaced modifiers with participial phrases (see Section **12a**).

Participial constructions are especially useful for suggesting action and for describing events that occur at the same time as those in the main clause. Compare the following:

The hikers struggled to the top of the ridge. They were gasping for breath and nearly exhausted.

The hikers, gasping for breath and nearly exhausted, struggled to the top of the ridge.

In the following sentence, notice how Updike uses a pair of present participial phrases to suggest that his walking through the yard and his clutching the child's hand both occur at the same time as his thinking that "It was all superstition."

[It was all] superstition, I thought, walking back through my yard, and clutching my child's hand tightly as a good luck token.

JOHN UPDIKE, "Eclipse"

Absolute phrases

Absolute phrases consist of a subject, usually a noun or a pronoun, and a participle together with any objects or modifiers of the participle. They may be formed from any sentence in which the verb is a verb phrase that contains a form of the verb *be* followed by a present or past participle simply by omitting the *be* form. In other sentences they may be formed by changing the main verb of a sentence into its *-ing* form. Note the following:

SENTENCE	Her lips were trembling.
ABSOLUTE	Her lips trembling . . .
SENTENCE	The wind blew with increased fury, and the drifts rose ever higher.
ABSOLUTE	The wind blowing with increased fury, and the drifts rising ever higher . . .

When the participle of an absolute phrase is a form of the verb *be,* the verb is frequently omitted entirely, so that the absolute consists simply of a noun followed by adjectives.

The pianist played beautifully, her technique flawless, her interpretation sure and sensitive.

The advantages of the absolute phrase are its speed and compression. It allows you to add specific, concrete detail to a general statement with greater economy than most alternative constructions. In addition, its placement in a sentence is extremely flexible. It can be placed at the beginning or end of a sentence, or often in the middle. Note the following examples:

The rain having stopped, we went to the beach.

Their dinner finished, the two industrialists were ready to talk business.

We ran into the house, *eyes averted.*

The little boy stood crying beside the road, *his bicycle broken, his knees bruised,* and *his confidence badly shaken.*

The driver of the wrecked car, *one leg trapped beneath the dashboard, body pinned firmly against the steering wheel,* had to be extricated by the rescue squad.

EXERCISE 34d   Revise the following passages, expressing what you consider to be the most important idea in the main clause and using appositives, participial phrases, or absolute phrases to subordinate other ideas.

1 Mrs. James will chair this year's Community Fund drive. She is a vice-president of the City Savings Bank.

2 Jane left home at seven o'clock this morning so that she could avoid the heavy traffic, because she wanted to get to work early.

3 As Jack ran back to throw a pass, he slipped and fell on a patch of gravel.

4 Anne Frank's diary, which she began in 1943 and kept faithfully until her death two years later, became one of the most humane accounts of one of history's least humane periods.

5 Aspirin was first commercially produced in 1899. It is the most common pain reliever known today.

6 Millie Luce was a freshman at State University. She was sitting at her desk. The writing pad before her was blank. The pencil in her hand was badly chewed. The waste basket beside her was overflowing with crumpled sheets of paper.

7 Houdini was the undisputed champion of escapes. He successfully challenged audiences around the world to construct traps from which he could not escape.

8 They were accused of cheating. They tried to lie their way out of it because they had succeeded in doing so once before.

9 The patient quickly got into the dentist's chair. Her jaw was badly swollen and her tooth was aching horribly.

10 The 1974 red Toyota stood in the driveway. Its engine was running smoothly. Its body was dented a bit here and there but it was polished mirror-bright. Inside, the upholstery was carefully protected by covers.

34e   Avoid excessive coordination.

A series of short, simple sentences all of the same or very similar structure will give all your facts and ideas equal weight and importance. Such sentences are sometimes called "primer" sentences because they are like those of children's first reading books. If you find yourself relying heavily on such sentences, examine them, try to determine which ideas are important and which are minor, and rework them into more complex sentences, making appropriate use of both coordination and subordination.

CHOPPY He stood on a street corner. The wind was blowing. He peered into the darkness. He was a stranger. He realized that he had no place to go.

REVISED Standing on a windy street corner and peering into the darkness, the stranger realized that he had no place to go.

CHOPPY A plane far off broke the sound barrier. Several windows on the avenue were shattered. The landlords were angry. They complained to the authorities.

REVISED When several windows on the avenue were shattered by a distant plane breaking the sound barrier, the angry landlords complained to the authorities.

Avoid trying to solve the problem of excessively simple sentences by stringing them together with a series of *and's* and *but's*. Such strings are just as ineffective as a choppy series of simple sentences.

INEFFECTIVE We approached the river and we looked down from the bluff, and we could see the silvery stream and it wound below in the valley.

REVISED When we approached the river and looked down from the bluff, we could see the silvery stream winding below in the valley.

34f Avoid faulty coordination.

Faulty coordination occurs when two or more facts or ideas that have no apparent logical connection are coordinated.

FAULTY The poet John Keats wrote "The Eve of St. Agnes," and he died of tuberculosis.

Two such unrelated facts would make strange bedfellows even if one were subordinated to the other, unless perhaps they were given some such meaningful context as the following.

He could remember only two facts about John Keats: He wrote "The Eve of St. Agnes" and he died of tuberculosis.

Sometimes faulty coordination occurs when writers leave out important information that is evident to them but not to a reader.

FAULTY My father was in the army in World War II, but he didn't have enough money to finish college.

CLEAR   Although my father's service in World War II entitled him to some education under the G.I. bill for veterans, he didn't have enough money to finish college.

A somewhat different kind of faulty coordination occurs when a writer coordinates items from overlapping classes. In the following sentence, for example, the four-item coordinate series makes it appear that there are four different kinds of animals or birds in the pet show the writer is describing. But clearly there are only three: dogs, parrots, and monkeys. The "mangy cocker spaniel" belongs among the dogs.

CONFUSING   Entered in the pet show were several dogs, two parrots, three monkeys, and a mangy cocker spaniel.

CLEAR   Entered in the pet show were two parrots, three monkeys, and several dogs, one of which was a mangy cocker spaniel.

EXERCISE 34e–f(1)   Revise the following sentences to eliminate excessive or faulty coordination.

1 Their father was an accountant and he worked for the Chase Manhattan Bank and he had moved to New York in 1980.
2 Olson bought his new car only three months ago and he has already had two accidents.
3 John Ciardi published his first book of poems in 1940 and he has written several books of poems and for some years he wrote a column for the *Saturday Review* and he has translated Dante's *Divine Comedy* and has written several other books.
4 Unemployment and declining productivity in our industry are our greatest problems, and we are spending billions for new weapons.
5 He dropped out of high school and he decided to get a job but he couldn't find one and then he decided to go back to school and later he went to college.
6 Her grandfather's will left her a collection of old glass, three clocks, an antique car, and several broken bottles.
7 New York has a first-class harbor and has become the leading American port, and the city has had many financial problems.
8 Hilda has not read the assigned books, so she will not be ready for the examination, so she may have trouble with the course.
9 *Funny Girl* had a long run on Broadway and broke many box office records and was later made into a movie and Barbra Streisand played the leading role.
10 The Indian Highway was formerly an Indian trail, but it is now a major highway, and it is a scenic and important route.

EXERCISE 34e–f(2)   Rewrite the following passages, using both coordination and subordination as appropriate to eliminate choppy sentences.

1 I arrived home at quarter past four. Then I began my reading for the next day. My first assignment took two hours. Then it was time to have

34f

dinner. I was tired. I could not enjoy the steak that we had for dinner. I finished dinner. I went back to finish my reading. At eleven o'clock I went to bed.

2 The setting of most of Edith Wharton's stories is New York or Paris. These cities are world capitals. Their society is wealthy and aristocratic. Perhaps, however, Edith Wharton's best novel is *Ethan Frome*. The story tells the tragic story of a poor farmer. He lived in a remote section of Massachusetts.

34g

34g   Avoid excessive subordination.

Excessive subordination occurs when you include in a sentence details that are unessential or only loosely related to the main line of thought in the sentence. It also occurs when successive dependent clauses are strung together, each attached to the preceding one without clear relationship to the main clause. In the following sentence, for example, the italicized clauses are only remotely related to the main direction of the sentence. They clutter rather than clarify what the writer is saying.

EXCESSIVE SUBORDINATION	My fishing equipment includes a casting rod *which my Uncle Henry gave me many years ago* and which is nearly worn out, and an assortment of lines, hooks, and bass flies, which make good bait *when I can get time off from work to go bass fishing* at Hardwood Lake.
REVISED	My fishing equipment includes an old casting rod and an assortment of lines, hooks, and bass flies. The flies make good bait when I can go bass fishing at Hardwood Lake.

In the following sentence, the successive details are all essential, but the structure of successive dependent clauses makes their relationship hard to grasp.

AWKWARD	We walked down Fifth Avenue, which led us to Washington Square, where we saw the memorial arch, which resembles the *Arc de Triomphe* which is in Paris.

Such sentences can often be improved by changing some of the clauses to modifying phrases. Sometimes clarity requires that the sentence be reworked as two separate sentences.

REVISED	We walked down Fifth Avenue to Washington Square, where we saw the memorial arch resembling the *Arc de Triomphe* in Paris.

34h Avoid faulty subordination.

Faulty subordination, sometimes called "upside-down" subordination, occurs when the idea that the reader would normally expect to be the more important is placed in a subordinate clause. In many sentences, determining which ideas to place in a main clause and which to subordinate depends entirely on context. In one context, you might want to write, *While Lincoln was still President, he was shot,* thus emphasizing the assassination itself. In another, you might want to write, *When he was shot, Lincoln was still in office,* thereby making more prominent the fact that he was still in office. There is no way of determining, aside from context, which of these versions is the better sentence.

But in many sentences, the logic of normal expectation works on the reader. A sentence such as *He happened to glance at the sidewalk, noticing a large diamond at his feet* contradicts the reader's sense of the relative importance of the two ideas, glancing at the sidewalk and noticing a diamond. Except in a very unusual situation, the finding of a diamond would be the logically more important fact, and a reader would expect the sentence to say *Happening to glance at the sidewalk, he noticed a large diamond at his feet.*

INEFFECTIVE	The octopus momentarily released its grip, when the diver escaped.
REVISED	The octopus momentarily releasing its grip, the diver escaped.
INEFFECTIVE	He was playing his first major league game, being a better first baseman than some who had been playing for years.
REVISED	Although he was playing his first major league game, he was a better first baseman than some who had been playing for years.
INEFFECTIVE	I visited my home town after being away twenty years, when I was astonished at the change in its appearance.
REVISED	When I visited my home town after being away twenty years, I was astonished at the change in its appearance.
	After being away twenty years, I visited my home town and was astonished at the change in its appearance.

EXERCISE 34g–h Some of the following sentences subordinate their more important ideas. Others contain excessive subordination. Rewrite them, using both coordination and subordination to make them more effective.

1 She pulled the emergency cord, averting a train wreck.
2 According to the popular ballad, Casey Jones attempted to arrive on schedule, being prevented by a head-on collision with another train.
3 The reporters, many of them wearing their press cards pinned to their lapels, flocked to the launch site, where the technicians were giving a last check to the spaceship that was to carry three astronauts, who were just then walking up the ramp, to the moon.
4 Ralph Waldo Emerson was an individualist because he said, "Whoso would be a man must be a nonconformist."
5 *A Clockwork Orange*, which was written by Anthony Burgess, and which was a best seller for many months, was made into a motion picture, directed by Stanley Kubrick, which was very well received by film critics who thought it was one of the year's best movies.
6 Although their salaries remained the same, prices continued to rise.
7 Mrs. Wood opened the door of the cage, when her pet parrot escaped.
8 My sports car, which I bought from a friend of mine, a car enthusiast who buys old cars and then rebuilds them as a hobby, had developed a rumble in the engine which has begun to worry me for I know nothing about repairing cars and haven't the money to go to a mechanic.
9 He fell seven stories and broke eight ribs, puncturing one lung, although he lived to tell the tale.
10 Although Marion graduated with honors, she had to pay most of her own expenses.

35

35 PARALLELISM ∥

Grammar requires that when you coordinate two or more elements in a sentence, you make them *parallel*, that is, you state them in the same grammatical form. Noun must be matched with noun, verb with verb, phrase with phrase, and clause with clause.

A lawyer must be *articulate* and *logical*. [Parallel and coordinate adjectives]
She *closed the door, opened the window,* and *threw herself* into the chair. [Three coordinate and parallel predicates, each consisting of verb plus direct object]
The otter's fur is dark-chocolate brown, and *its eyes are small and black.* [Two coordinate and parallel independent clauses]

But parallelism is more than a grammatical requirement; it is a basic rhetorical principle. Equal form reinforces equal meaning. By putting equally important parts of a sentence or of successive sentences into equal grammatical constructions, you emphasize their relationship to one another. Grammar requires the parallelism in each of the examples above. But in each, the parallelism confirms the coordinate relationship, the equal importance of the coordinate parts.

35a   Use parallelism to make coordinate relationships clear.

1   In single sentences. Putting equal ideas in a sentence in parallel constructions will help you make their coordinate relationship more immediately clear to your reader. Compare the following sentences:

> If they buy the assigned books, students can usually be successful, but they must read them and careful notes must be taken.
>
> Students can usually be successful if they *buy the assigned books, read them,* and *take careful notes.*

The first sentence really sets three conditions for a student's success: buying the books, reading them, and taking notes. But the sentence muddies this equal relationship by putting the first in an *if* clause separate from the other two; and although the last two conditions—reading the books and taking notes—are coordinated by *and,* the first is active and the second passive, thus further weakening their coordinate relationship. The revised sentence brings the three conditions neatly and clearly together in a single parallel series of predicates.

2   Among successive sentences. Many times you can increase the coherence of your writing by combining several successive sentences into a single sentence that uses parallelism carefully.

Suppose you are trying to get together your ideas about the things necessary for good writing and that you have written the following in a first draft:

> Logical thinking is one of the things necessary for good writing. Good writers also have to organize their ideas coherently. And finally, anyone who wants to write well must express his ideas clearly.

Look at this closely; *thinking, organizing,* and *expressing* are the main related processes here. Parallel structure can help you knit these together tightly and emphasize them clearly. Compare the following single sentences with the three original sentences:

Thinking logically,		
organizing ideas coherently,		
and	are three requirements of good	
expressing ideas clearly	writing.	

or

Logical thought,		
coherent organization,		
and	are the major ingredients of good	
clear expression	writing.	

or

	to think logically,	
	to organize ideas	
	coherently,	
Anyone who wishes to write well must	and	
learn	to express them	
	clearly.	

Any of these versions of the first draft pulls the ideas together into a single economical unit and gives emphasis to the three major items.

Notice how parallelism helps to keep the following sentences clear and to emphasize the relation between the ideas.

	loss of wages for
	workers,
	interference with
	production for
Strikes, though sometimes necessary,	managers,
mean	and
	disruption of services
	for consumers.

	to make	lies sound truthful
		and
		murder respectable
Political language is		
designed	and	
	to give an appearance of	
	solidity to pure wind.	

3   In whole paragraphs. Just as you can often make single sentences clearer by coordinating equal ideas and putting them in parallel constructions, so you can often use roughly parallel sentences to increase the coherence of an entire paragraph. [See also Section **32d(2)**.] Study the following paragraph:

> Otters seem to improvise. *When swimming along* in a lake or a stream, *one may push* a leaf or twig ahead of it. *Or it may drop* a pebble, then chase it through the sparkling water, catching it before it touches bottom, only to bring it to the surface and drop it again. *Underwater, it may balance* a rock or mussel on its head as it swims, *or play* cat and mouse games with its prey. *In captivity, it plays* games with every moving object and explores all corners and crevices for string to pull, wires to loosen, latches to open, and new mysteries to solve.
>
> <div align="right">GEORGE LAYCOCK, "Games Otters Play," <i>Audubon</i></div>

The structure of this paragraph is kept unmistakably clear by its careful coordinating and confirming parallelism throughout. The simple topic sentence, "Otters seem to improvise," is developed by a series of details of their improvisation in three situations: in the water, underwater, or in captivity.

EXERCISE 35a   Using parallelism and subordination, revise and improve the following passages.

1 The cat is a domestic animal. It is clean. It is also intelligent. Cats like to stay at home. They are fond of playing with people and like to sleep. It enjoys catching mice, too.
2 How she sleeps on that bed is a mystery. The bed is hard. It is lumpy and it slopes. Her diet is also a mystery. And no one understands where she gets her money.
3 Walking in the rain is one way Dan relaxes. He also likes to relax by listening to music. He likes to listen to selections from his large record collection. He also likes classical music on his favorite FM station. In the summer he sometimes gets his relaxation by reading while he sits on the sun deck.
4 Ann Jenkins strode through the lobby of the Warner Building. Next she walked into the elevator. She got off at the sixteenth floor after which she walked into her office. During that whole time she couldn't remember why she was going to her office.
5 Burdo dresses neatly. He does not dress flashily. He always thinks clearly. He has a record of being honest. What's more, he has considerable influence with several of our excellent customers. That's why we hired him—all those things and especially the last one.

35b Use parallelism for elements joined by coordinating or correlative conjunctions.

Coordinating conjunctions. Just as the careful use of parallelism can be an aid to constructing effective sentences, to combining successive sentences for economy and clarity, and to maintaining coherence throughout an entire paragraph, lack of parallelism can throw a reader off and make for particularly ineffective sentences. To keep your sentences clear as well as grammatically correct, let the structure of the first of two or more coordinate elements in a sentence set the pattern for the structure of the remaining elements.

AWKWARD	Mollie enjoys *her work* as a marketing manager during the day and *going* to the theatre in the evening.
PARALLEL	Mollie enjoys *working* as a marketing manager during the day and *going* to the theatre in the evening.
AWKWARD	Desmond is tall, with blue eyes, and has a congenial manner.
PARALLEL	Desmond is tall, blue-eyed, and congenial.

When you are coordinating prepositional phrases or infinitives, clarity will sometimes require you to point up parallel structure by repeating prepositions.

AMBIGUOUS	Sam helps with the work around the house by cooking and ironing his own shirts.
CLEAR	Sam helps with the work around the house *by* cooking and *by* ironing his own shirts.
AMBIGUOUS	Maria wants to write stories that describe the South and study the habits of the Creoles. [stories that study the habits of the Creoles?]
CLEAR	Maria wants *to* write stories that describe the South and *to* study the habits of the Creoles.

Correlative conjunctions. Correlative conjunctions are coordinating pairs: *either . . . or, neither . . . nor, both . . . and, not . . . but, not only . . . but also.* Parallelism requires that the structure following the second part of the correlative be the same as that following the first part.

FAULTY	You are either *late* or *I am early.* [The writer has connected the adjective *late* and the clause *I am early.* Parallelism requires the connection of the two clauses beginning with *You* and *I.*]
PARALLEL	*Either you are late* or *I am early.*
FAULTY	Ellen not only has been outstanding in her studies but also in athletics.
PARALLEL	Ellen has been outstanding not only in her studies but also in athletics.

If you are uncertain of the parallelism with correlative conjunctions, try recasting your sentence as two sentences. Take, for example, the sentence *Not only is Shakespeare famous for his plays but also his sonnets.* Recast as separate sentences, this becomes

> Shakespeare is famous for his plays.
> Shakespeare is famous for his sonnets.

When you combine the common parts of these two sentences to get *Shakespeare is famous for,* it is clear that the two distinct parts that belong in parallel form are *his plays* and *his sonnets.* The correct forms of the sentence are thus either

> Shakespeare is famous for not only his plays but also his sonnets.

or

> Shakespeare is famous not only for his plays but also for his sonnets.

35c Avoid faulty parallelism with *and who, and which, and that.*

Do not use an *and who, and which,* or *and that* clause in a sentence unless you have already used a parallel *who, which,* or *that* clause. (So too with *but* and *who, which,* or *that.*)

FAULTY	We met Abner Fulton, a brilliant biologist and who is also an excellent pianist.
REVISED	We met Abner Fulton, who is a brilliant biologist and who is also an excellent pianist.
REVISED	We met Abner Fulton, who is both a brilliant biologist and an excellent pianist.
FAULTY	I like a romantic novel with exciting action and which keeps me guessing.
REVISED	I like a romantic novel that has exciting action and that keeps me guessing.

EXERCISE 35b–c(1) Revise the following sentences to express coordinate ideas in parallel form.

1 The navy promoted all officers who had served two years at sea, or if they had been on shore duty for five years.
2 Hilda has spent three summers in Europe, but she neither speaks German nor French.
3 You make many of your friends angry not only because you cheat but you are such a hypocrite.
4 She is a person who knows how to play tennis and having a knack for dancing.

5 My work consisted of planning the menus, purchasing the food, and supervision of the employees.

6 The students were told to obtain a transcript of their grades and that they could apply for admission.

7 To be a good teacher, one must have patience, liking to help others, and to show a great capacity for learning.

8 Ann not only had applied for the position, but also Warren had applied for it.

9 You must either pass this examination, or you will fail the course.

10 Marcia moved into a new apartment with more space and having air conditioning.

EXERCISE 35b–c(2) Revise the following sentences to express coordinate ideas in parallel form.

1 Being too early, even if it wastes valuable time, is better than to arrive too late.

2 The biography of Stilwell is interesting, lively, and also an informative piece of writing.

3 She bought a new Volvo having a standard transmission and with a radio and heater.

4 Mary has a full-time career, is a member of the school committee, and doing her own yard work.

5 Good politicians not only work well with the public but also they do not compromise their own ideals.

6 The reviewer could not decide whether he should ignore the book or to write an unfavorable review of it.

7 Hemingway's early short stories and novels not only were fresh and vigorous, but he also influenced other writers.

8 The lecture was long, tiresome, and could not be easily understood.

9 They put out the oil well fire by tunneling under the surface, planting some dynamite, and then they exploded it from a distance.

10 Some people neither like popular music or classical music.

36 EMPHASIS **EMP**

Effective sentences emphasize main ideas and keep related details in the background. The careful use of coordination, parallelism, and subordination enables you to stress your most important ideas without losing track of less important, related ideas and information. Variety enables you to emphasize important ideas by stating them in sentences that are brief and simple in relation to the other sentences around them. In addition to all these useful strategies, you can also emphasize ideas within a single sentence by controlling the arrangement of elements within the sentence and by the careful use of repetition.

As you revise sentences to achieve the emphasis you want, always keep in mind that any sentence is part of a paragraph and of a larger whole. To determine what to emphasize in a given sentence, you must always think of the sentence in its context.

36a   Put important ideas in emphatic positions in the sentence.

The position of a word or idea within a sentence usually determines the emphasis it receives. Generally, the most emphatic place in the sentence is its end; the next most emphatic, its beginning; the least emphatic, its middle. Consider the following sentence:

> Mr. Ellicott, our new plant manager, was inefficient from the start, but always agreeable.

The end position of *always agreeable* gives that fact the heaviest stress in the sentence, a stress further heightened by separating *but always agreeable* with the slight pause of a comma. As, say, a topic sentence of a paragraph that explains Ellicott's combination of inefficiency and agreeableness, with emphasis on the latter, the sentence is well suited to its purpose.

If, however, the sentence introduces a paragraph explaining Ellicott's inefficiency, it must be revised.

> Mr. Ellicott, our new plant manager, though always agreeable, was from the start inefficient.

In this version of the sentence, the statement of Ellicott's agreeableness is subordinated and placed in the middle of the sentence, and the statement of his inefficiency is held for the most emphatic position.

Compare the emphasis in the following pairs of sentences:

> Fields was arrested for fraud after he escaped from prison recently.
> Fields, who escaped from prison recently, was arrested for fraud.

> Hispanic-speaking people want to be understood, just as much as other minorities in the country.
> Hispanic-speaking people, just as much as other minorities in the country, want to be understood.

In the latter of each of these pairs of sentences, emphasis on the main clause is increased by placing lesser information within the main clause. Such placement of modifying phrases and clauses delays the predicate for the final emphatic position in the sentence.

Sometimes you can increase the emphasis on a single-word adverb or a brief adverb phrase by moving it to the initial position in a sentence.

Debra reached sleepily for the alarm clock.
Sleepily, Debra reached for the alarm clock.

Be careful not to weaken emphasis by placing minor qualifying phrases before your subject or at the end of the sentence.

Such matters as incorrect spelling and unconventional punctuation can distract a reader from otherwise good writing.
Incorrect spelling and unconventional punctuation can distract a reader from otherwise good writing.

Be aware, too, that weak qualifying phrases such as *in my opinion, by and large,* and *for the ~st part* are usually unnecessary. When they are necessary for accuracy, it is usually better to place them within the sentence than at the beginning or end of the sentence.

WEAK The history of English vocabulary is the history of English civilization, in many ways.

BETTER The history of English vocabulary is in many ways the history of English civilization.

EXERCISE 36a Revise the following sentences by putting important words in an emphatic position.

1 He is an overbearing, egotistical bore, in my opinion.
2 The results of the flood were disastrous, by and large.
3 You are more perceptive and far more sensitive than I am, as a rule.
4 Tolstoy had a profound understanding of people and of the passions that drive them, for the most part.
5 This university would be closed and its faculty fired, if I had my way.
6 Teddy Roosevelt was dynamic and full of life, I have read.
7 Test results prove that smoking seriously impairs the health, in most cases.
8 The lawyer shirked his responsibility and the judge was biased, it seems to me.
9 The day was clear, the sun was shining, and the snow was packed hard; it was a great day for skiing, in my opinion.
10 With its superior technology and its single-minded determination, the United States will definitely win the space race, if everything goes right.

36b **36b Use periodic sentences for emphasis.**

A **periodic sentence** holds its main idea until the end. A **loose sentence,** sometimes called a **cumulative sentence,** completes its main statement and then adds subordinate details.

Strictly speaking, any sentence consisting of a main clause followed by an adverbial phrase or clause is loose and can be made periodic simply by moving the adverbial modifier to the beginning.

LOOSE   Brenda showed great courage and kindness when her mother was in the hospital for two months and her father was on the edge of a breakdown.

PERIODIC   When her mother was in the hospital for two months and her father was on the edge of a breakdown, Brenda showed great courage and kindness.

The balanced sentence is a compound sentence in which the independent clauses are exactly, or very nearly, parallel in all elements.

We always like those who admire us; we do not always like those whom we admire.   LA ROCHEFOUCAULD, *Maxims*

Grammar maps out the possible; rhetoric narrows the possible down to the desirable and effective.

FRANCIS CHRISTENSEN, *Notes Toward a New Rhetoric*

As these two examples illustrate, the balanced sentence is useful in stating contrasts and distinctions.

Both the long periodic sentence and the balanced sentence are planned sentences, the product of careful revision rather than of first drafts. They carry considerable emphasis and should be used only when your subject matter warrants them. Be careful not to fall into the error of the following sentence, in which the writer creates a degree of suspense completely disproportionate to the subject matter.

PERIODIC AND   At the end of a dark alley, three flights down in a
INEFFECTIVE   dark basement full of grim and evil-looking sailors, I ate my lunch.

Often, periodic and loose constructions are more or less equally effective. Your choice must be guided by the particular emphasis you want, and by the relation of your sentence to those before it and after it.

LOOSE   Balboa reached the Pacific after a long, hazardous journey.

PERIODIC   After a long, hazardous journey, Balboa reached the Pacific.

LOOSE   He will be a good kindergarten teacher if enthusiasm is a guarantee of success.

PERIODIC   If enthusiasm is a guarantee of success, he will be a good kindergarten teacher.

EXERCISE 36b   Change these loose sentences into periodic ones.

1 I began seeing a psychiatrist regularly after my marriage broke up.
2 They started a new business and made a million dollars after their first business failed.
3 The wine turned to vinegar, although we tried to keep it in a cool place.
4 The boat neared the finish line, the rowers bending rhythmically and the oars flashing in the sun.
5 They stood the cold for an hour, stamping their feet and blowing on their fingers.
6 I saw two cars crash head-on several years ago on a three-lane highway in Minnesota.
7 Aretha's doctor insisted that she take a vacation after she suffered a severe shoulder dislocation.
8 Your research paper will be accepted if, after you have finished typing it, the footnotes are in good order.
9 I had still not balanced my accounts, although I had checked my figures and added again.
10 Three miles of rough water lay between the ship and the shore.

36c   **Be aware of the arrangement of items in a parallel series.**

When items are arranged in a parallel series, emphasis tends to fall on the last item, simply because it is last. Compare the following:

> You are a coward, a thief, a murderer, and a liar.
> You are a liar, a coward, a thief, and a murderer.

Of these two, the first, by placing *a liar* in the end position, tends to suggest that lying is more important than thievery and murder. The second sentence, in contrast, moves in the order that fits our usual sense of values, suggesting by its arrangement that of all the items named, murder is the most serious. Note that in each of the following sentences the items in the series are arranged in the order of their increasing importance:

> Their lives were brief and tragic.
> I was broke, lonely, and thoroughly discouraged.
> The city was famous for clear signs, wide clean streets, beautiful parks, and well-planned museums.

The arrangement of a series in descending order of importance can sometimes be used for its humor.

> If once a man indulges himself in murder, very soon he comes to think little of robbery; and from robbing he next comes to drinking and Sabbath-breaking, and from that to incivility and procrastination.
>
> THOMAS DE QUINCY

In many series some other principle works together with that of increasing importance to dictate the arrangement of items in a series. In the following sentences, for example, the controlling principle of arrangement is simply the order of events; in the first sentence, events occur in the order we would normally expect, but, as the second sentence illustrates, they might well have occurred in the reverse order.

> At first they were perplexed by the unusual noises, then disturbed, and at last terror-stricken.

> At first they were terror-stricken by the unusual noises, then as time wore on merely disturbed, and finally merely perplexed.

In the following sentence, the order of items in each of the series is from large to small, an order that is consistent with the writer's intention to show that even the smallest detail reflected "orderliness."

> The orderliness of their house and their yard mirrored the orderliness of their lives: inside, each chair, each painting, each book had its assigned place; outside, each tree, shrub, and flower seemed planted by design.

EXERCISE 36c Revise the following sentences by arranging ideas in more logical order.

1 He moved away from the city because he was ill, his rent was high, and he wanted to let his dog run.
2 Most students get bored with school after years of college, high school, and elementary school.
3 They inherited a million dollars, a house, and some jewelry.
4 The play closed after the first week and received terrible reviews.
5 The candidate promised a guaranteed income for all, mingled with people in the street, and smiled at children.
6 Charles is a capable gardener, a famous athlete and a poker player.
7 We find similar psychological reactions in frogs, in guinea pigs, in men, and in rats.
8 During his vacation David acquired some souvenirs, a thoroughbred racehorse, and a bad sunburn.
9 The earthquake caused 100 deaths and toppled several of the buildings in the area.
10 Laurence Olivier is one of the great Shakespearean actors of all time and a director and producer as well.

36d Repeat key words and ideas for emphasis.

36d

Careless and awkward repetition of words makes sentences weak and flabby (see Section **41d**), but careful repetition of key words can be an effective way of gaining emphasis, as in the following sentences:

> A *moderately* honest man with a *moderately* faithful wife, *moderate* drinkers both, in a *moderately* healthy home: that is the true middle class unit.
>
> G. B. SHAW

36d

Don't *join* too many gangs. *Join* few if any. *Join* the United States and *join* a family—but not much in between, unless a college.

ROBERT FROST

It is the *dull* man who is always *sure,* and the *sure* man who is always *dull.*

H. L. MENCKEN

(For a discussion of ways in which repetition of words and ideas links sentences within a paragraph, see Section **32d.**)

EXERCISE 36d Discuss the effectiveness of the repetition of words and phrases in each of the sentences below. (Note how frequently effective repetition and effective parallelism reinforce each other.)

1 No one can be perfectly free till all are free; no one can be perfectly moral till all are moral; no one can be perfectly happy till all are happy.

HERBERT SPENCER

2 There is no mistake; there has been no mistake; and there shall be no mistake.

DUKE OF WELLINGTON

3 To know how to say what others only know how to think is what makes men poets or sages; and to dare to say what others only dare to think makes men martyrs or reformers or both.

ELIZABETH CHARLES

4 It is true that you may fool all the people some of the time; you can even fool some of the people all the time; but you can't fool all of the people all the time.

ABRAHAM LINCOLN

36e

36e   Prefer the active to the passive voice.

The **active voice** puts the subject (the actor) first, and follows it with the active verb, and then the object (the receiver of the action): *The cat killed the rat.* The **passive voice** turns things around, putting the receiver in front, then the verb, and finally the original subject: *The rat was killed by the cat.* (See Section **5.**)

Of the two, the active is almost always more direct, more forceful, and more economical. Always prefer it to the passive unless you have good reason not to. When you find yourself using the passive, check yourself to be sure you really need it, that what you want to say cannot in fact be better said in the active voice. More often than not, you will find that you gain both economy and emphasis with the active voice. Note the following examples:

PASSIVE   The pump has been installed in several medical centers and will be tested next week. [15 words]

ACTIVE   Several medical centers have installed the pump and will test it next week. [13 words]

PASSIVE   Two devices for insuring safety are shown in the accompanying illustrations. [11 words]

ACTIVE	The accompanying illustrations show two safety devices. [7 words]
PASSIVE	It was voted by the faculty that all students should be required to take mathematics. [15 words]
ACTIVE	The faculty voted to require mathematics. [6 words]
PASSIVE	Your request has been received and reviewed by the department, but it has been decided that it does not meet the requirement as stated by departmental rules. [27 words]
ACTIVE	We have reviewed your request; it does not meet requirements stated by the department. [14 words]

Careless and unnecessary use of the passive sometimes leads to a shift in a voice that makes your sentences inconsistent (see Section **10a**). Note the following:

FAULTY	He boiled the water, and then the spaghetti was added.
REVISED	He boiled the water and then added the spaghetti.
FAULTY	When weasels suck eggs, both yolk and white are sucked out of the shell.
REVISED	When weasels suck eggs, they suck both yolk and white out of the shell.

For situations in which the passive voice is useful and natural, see Section **5.**

EXERCISE 36e   In the following sentences replace the passive voice with the active.

1 A boomerang can be made to do amazing stunts by a skillful thrower.
2 My ankles were snapped at by an angry dog.
3 The radiator of my car became frozen during the cold spell.
4 Extreme caution is needed if we are to experiment with genetic change.
5 Police procedures were scrutinized by the press.
6 An addition to the house was planned by my parents.
7 The returned astronauts were interviewed by reporters.
8 The menu was selected by the chairman of the refreshments committee.
9 Many major accidents are caused by drunken drivers.
10 Polio vaccine is distributed by the local Department of Health.

37   VARIETY **VAR**

37

A long series of sentences identical or very similar in length and structure is monotonous. But a series of well-written sentences provides more than mere absence of monotony. It reflects the careful molding of form to the writer's thought and the careful choice of length and structure to gain emphasis where the writer wants it.

37a Vary sentence structure and length to create emphasis and accentuate meaning.

Consider the following paragraph by Jane Howard. Notice the variety in length and structure of the eight sentences that make up the paragraph.

> The trouble with the families many of us were born into is not that they consist of meddlesome ogres but that they are too far away. In emergencies we rush across continents and if need be oceans to their sides, as they do to ours. Maybe we even make a habit of seeing them, once or twice a year, for the sheer pleasure of it. But blood ties seldom dictate our addresses. Our blood kin are often too remote to ease us from our Tuesdays to our Wednesdays. For this we must rely on our families of friends. If our relatives are not, do not wish to be, or for whatever reasons cannot be our friends, then by some complex alchemy we must try to transform our friends into our relatives. If blood and roots don't do the job, then we must look to water and branches.
>
> JANE HOWARD, *Families*

The length of these eight sentences ranges from the seven-word *But blood ties seldom dictate our addresses* to the long thirty-three-word sentence beginning *If our relatives are not.* Structure varies from the simple subject-verb-object pattern of the crisp fourth, fifth, and sixth sentences to the much greater complexity of the opening twenty-six-word sentence and the two closing sentences of thirty-three and sixteen words respectively.

Such variety of length and structure is by no means accidental. In the paragraph immediately before this one, Howard has set her thesis: all of us need to belong to a clan, a tribe; if our families don't fit that need, we will find a substitute that does. The quoted paragraph develops that thesis. Its pivotal point falls at the cluster of three sentences—seven, sixteen, and ten words, respectively—that comes at the approximate center of the paragraph: we need "kin . . . to ease us from our Tuesdays to our Wednesdays"; our blood families are usually too remote; for this we need friends.

There is no formula for such a "right" variety of length and form among the sentences of a paragraph or a paper. The variety of Jane Howard's paragraph above comes not from some predetermined pattern she worked out for the paragraph. It comes, rather, from choosing the length and form best suited to the meaning and emphasis she intended.

Such fitting of form to meaning is not likely to come in the first draft of a paragraph or paper. It comes with revision. When you turn to revising the early drafts of your writing, be suspicious if many or most of your sentences are either short or long or if some single structure seems to recur overfrequently. You will need relatively long and complex sentences to relate ideas clearly to one another and to subordinate minor detail; short sentences to give you emphasis where you want it; variety to avoid monotony. Be aware, too, that the kind of sentences that will be appropriate if you are writing a sports column or a set of simple directions will differ from the kind you will need to explain a complex idea. Remember that short sentences can be vigorous and emphatic, but that they are more likely to be effective when placed in contrast to longer sentences.

Most important, always keep in mind that sentence variety is not an end in itself. If you set out to make your sentences alternately short and long, you will end with awkward and artificial writing. If you set out to shift structure with each new sentence without regard to the relationship of one to another, you are more likely to destroy the coherence of the whole than to achieve effective variety. Your choice of length and structure for any one sentence must always depend upon your meaning and upon the relationship of that sentence to those that stand before and after it.

Ways of achieving variety

37b Use coordination and subordination to combine several short sentences or to improve long compound sentences.

If you find that many of your sentences tend to be short and simple or to fall into strings of short sentences connected by *and*'s and *but*'s, review Sections **34** and **35** and practice using subordination and parallelism to improve your sentences.

INEFFECTIVE	Gail approached the stallion warily. He saw the bridle in her hand. She stood still and the stallion waited. Then she tried to toss the reins over his head. But he galloped away.
REVISED	Gail warily approached the stallion, who saw the bridle in her hand. She stood still, the stallion waiting. But when she tried to toss the reins over his head, the stallion galloped away.
INEFFECTIVE	Gilman was the chief of the volunteer fire department, and he was also the town's only grocer, but he was never too busy in his store to attend a fire.
REVISED	Gilman, the chief of the volunteer fire department and the town's only grocer, was never too busy in his store to attend a fire. [Facts about Gilman in the first two clauses are reduced to an appositive; the last becomes the main clause.]

37b

For practice in combining short sentences and improving long compound sentences, see Exercises **34a** and **34b**.

37c

37c Vary the position of free modifiers.

A modifier that can be moved from one position to another within a sentence without interfering with clarity or meaning is called a **free modifier.** Prepositional phrases, clauses, and single words that modify nouns must ordinarily be placed next to or very close to the nouns they modify; their position is relatively fixed. But adverbs, adverb phrases and clauses, many participial phrases, and absolute phrases can often be placed at different positions in a sentence; these are free modifiers. Moving such modifiers into varying positions in your sentences can help you place the emphasis of your sentence where you want it and increase sentence variety.

ADVERB PHRASES AND CLAUSES

Westerners and Arabs still do not understand each other, *in spite of two thousand years of contact.*

In spite of two thousand years of contact, Westerners and Arabs still do not understand each other.

Westerners and Arabs, *in spite of two thousand years of contact,* still do not understand each other.

The defendant changed his plea to guilty *because the prosecutor had built up such convincing evidence against him.*

Because the prosecutor had built up such convincing evidence against him, the defendant changed his plea to guilty.

The defendant, *because the prosecutor had built up such convincing evidence against him,* changed his plea to guilty.

The bank's vice president kept juggling several customers' large deposits *to cover his own embezzlement.*

To cover his own embezzlement, the bank's vice president kept juggling several customers' large deposits.

The bank's vice president, *to cover his own embezzlement,* kept juggling several customers' large deposits.

PARTICIPIAL PHRASES

The deer, *grazing peacefully in the valley,* were unaware of the approaching hunters.

Grazing peacefully in the valley, the deer were unaware of approaching hunters.

[Being] unaware of the approaching hunters, the deer were grazing peacefully in the valley.

Gasping for air, the diver came to the surface.

The diver, *gasping for air,* came to the surface.

The diver came to the surface, *gasping for air.*

Note that in placing participial modifiers, you must be alert to the possibility of creating a misplaced modifier (see Section **12a**). Participial phrases can almost always be placed either before or after the nouns they modify. But whether they can be more widely separated will depend upon the sentence. In the example above, *gasping for air* can logically modify only *diver,* not *surface;* and since the sentence is brief, the phrase can comfortably be placed at its end. But in the previous example, if the *grazing* phrase were moved to the end of the sentence, it would modify *hunters* rather than *deer.*

Absolute phrases, since they always modify the entire sentence in which they stand, can usually be placed either at the beginning or end of a sentence or within it.

ABSOLUTE PHRASES

His hair cut close, his arms and legs tanned, his face freckled, Jonathan seemed the typical country boy in summer.

Jonathan, *his hair cut close, his arms and legs tanned, his face freckled,* seemed the typical country boy in summer.

Jonathan seemed the typical country boy in summer—*his hair cut close, his arms and legs tanned, his face freckled.*

Sarah settled back for a quiet evening, *the work day over, the bills paid, some letters written.*

The work day over, the bills paid, some letters written, Sarah settled back for a quiet evening.

Sarah, *the work day over, the bills paid, some letters written,* settled back for a quiet evening.

EXERCISE 37c In the following sentences, underline the modifier or modifiers that could be placed in a different position. Write one or if possible two revisions of each sentence. In some sentences you may have to make slight changes in wording when you change the position of the modifier.

1 The workers discovered a leak in the twelve-inch pipeline late last night, after searching for two days.

2 Examining each apple in the bin one by one, Henry chose only the ripest and the reddest ones.

3 Emily, lingering at the window of her apartment, watched the last boat sail out of the harbor.

4 The zebras, warned by the hunter's shots, stampeded across the plain.

5 Their membership expired and their credit exhausted, the four couples were in no position to argue with the club manager.

6 Audrey looked around the living room one last time, her suitcases already packed and her mind firmly made up.

7 To prevent Oswald from complaining and making an unpleasant scene, Doris exchanged seats with him.

8 Ellen had decided that borrowing money was not the answer to their financial troubles, even before Susan brought up the question.

9 Although millions of dollars were expended in one eight-block area of the city's slums, living conditions changed little for most of those living there.

10 Buried for two centuries or more, valuable relics of the early inhabitants' daily life were unearthed when the new subway was constructed.

37d Occasionally vary the normal subject-verb-object sentence pattern.

The subject-verb-object pattern of the basic English sentence is so strongly established that any shift in it causes unusually heavy emphasis. Sentences such as *Over the fence jumped Oscar* or *Siamese cats she adores* are rare in most modern writing. But such **inversion** is possible, and when context justifies it, it can be useful. Consider the following, for example:

> Throughout Dawson's life his great obsession had been to secure wealth, great wealth, wealth that would enable him to indulge his wildest fantasies. Such wealth he constantly dreamed of; and such wealth he was determined to get at all costs.

A more common and much less emphatic inversion occurs when the subject and verb of a sentence are reversed in a sentence opening with a long adverbial modifier, as in the following:

> Across the boulevard where a milk truck scurries to more lucrative fields lies the sea and miles of empty beach.
> JOHN J. ROWLAND, *Spindrift*

37e Occasionally vary the types of sentences.

Except in dialogue, the overwhelming majority of sentences in writing are statements. But questions, commands, and occasionally even exclamations are sometimes useful.

Questions at the beginning of a paragraph can point its direction. The following sentence opens a paragraph in which the author argues that TV news coverage is superior to that of all but the best newspapers:

> Why do I think network TV does a better job of informing than [most] newspapers?   MARYA MANNES, "What's Wrong with the Press?"

Or a question may open a paragraph of definition.

> What is civilized man? By derivation, he is one who lives and thinks in a city.
> BERNARD IDDINGS BELL

Imperative sentences are the staple sentences of writing that gives directions. But occasionally they are useful in other contexts.

Observations indicate that the different clusters of galaxies are constantly moving apart from one another. To illustrate by a homely analogy, think of a raisin cake baking in an oven.

EXERCISE 37a–e(1) Rewrite each of the following sentences twice, using the methods suggested in this section to vary the structure.

1 We came home sullen and irritable after fighting traffic for an hour and a half.
2 The child had lost her way but was brought home by a thoughtful neighbor.
3 The coach rushed out on the field to protest the umpire's decision.
4 I knew my hangover had begun because my head ached and my mouth felt dry.
5 The upholsterer, his mouth full of tacks and his magnetic hammer swinging like a piece of machinery, stretched and fastened the chair cover with amazing speed.
6 The Surgeon General has determined that cigarette smoking is dangerous to your health, and that warning is printed on every package of cigarettes.
7 The earthquake caused much loss of life and devastation in the villages and cities of Nicaragua, and the United States quickly offered assistance.
8 Black writers have made important contributions to American literature for more than 150 years, but many educated people are still not aware of that fact.
9 They wanted to dance, and the record player was broken.
10 They bought only old furniture, which they refinished themselves, and were able to furnish their new home at relatively little cost.

EXERCISE 37a–e(2) Revise the following paragraph by introducing greater variety in sentence structure.

Mark felt better as he slammed the front door. He did not even glance over his shoulder to see if his parents were watching him. He walked to a nearby park. He sat down on a bench. He knew why his parents had yelled at him. He didn't blame them. They had both worked hard at their restaurant to keep him in comfort. They wanted him to have the opportunities that they had missed. They wanted him to be a doctor. But he couldn't seem to concentrate at school. He wanted to sleep in class. He liked most of his teachers but he didn't really hear them. He brought home very poor marks. He wanted to work with automobiles. He didn't want to be a doctor. The smell of gasoline, the sound of the motor, the shine of the chrome all fascinated him. He would have to face them and tell them that he couldn't be something he didn't want to be. He delayed returning home to tell them and he did not look forward to the scene they would make and the lack of understanding they would show.

REVIEW EXERCISE ON EFFECTIVE SENTENCES (Sections 34–37) Indicate what strikes you as the principal detraction from the effectiveness of each of the following sentences (faulty subordination, lack of emphasis, lack of parallelism, etc.), and then revise the sentence.

1 While Mario was still deeply in debt, he felt that the bargain was too good to let pass.
2 The children were terrified and confused and they fell exhausted on the wet leaves.
3 Robert Frost was a poet. He wrote about rural New England. He also wrote about the human condition.
4 After reading the book, I decided to change my way of life, and my plans for the future also changed.
5 The fighter was very strong and in excellent condition and he was knocked out in the fifth round.
6 Poverty still exists in the United States, and it's a shame because we are the wealthiest nation on earth, and there is no excuse for it, and it's about time we eradicated it.
7 Many countries are suffering badly from overpopulation, and India and Pakistan are but two examples.
8 Some college students regard their education as irrelevant, and not being useful.
9 After working in the Peace Corps for two years, Elizabeth returned to school after refusing several job offers.
10 He leaned back in his chair, closed his eyes, rested his hands on his lap, and sleep came to him.
11 While Chekhov was the principal support of his family, he attended medical school and wrote short stories.
12 The substitute teacher was a married man with a good sense of humor and who loved Russian ardently and conveyed this to his classes.
13 To a naughty child, a scolding parent seems like a giant standing seven feet tall with a large mouth, and having eyes that glared in the dark.
14 Our love of colonial arts and crafts is reflected in our homes and in our home magazines but our love of modern technological skills is also reflected in our homes and magazines.
15 Arizona has the largest United States Indian population and the Hopi, Navajo, and Apache are the names of the Indian tribes there.
16 To become a responsible voter you should know the issues. You should listen to the candidates. You should become familiar with their views. You should learn their weaknesses. You should also come to know their strengths. Then you can make a wise choice.
17 Rachel Carson wrote a great deal about the problems that arise when insecticide is used and she was vigorously opposed by insecticide com-

panies and some people who find insecticides helpful but what about the people who have been poisoned by them?

18 Harlem is reached by walking up Fifth Avenue, the most glamorous street in the richest city in the world, and it is infested with rats and disease.

19 Terror gripped the city of Boston when the Boston Strangler roamed free, and later a movie was made that recalled those days.

20 The space trip was an unqualified success, and the astronauts had been kept in seclusion for weeks before it to guard them against infection.

WORDS
WDS

Dictionaries are like watches; the worst is better than none, and the best cannot be expected to go quite true.

SAMUEL JOHNSON

38 THE DICTIONARY

The study of words begins with the dictionary. A good dictionary is a biography of words. It records spelling, pronunciation, word history, meaning, part of speech, and, when necessary, principal parts, or plurals, or other forms. Frequently it records the level of current usage. Very often the dictionary includes other information as well—lists of abbreviations, rules for punctuation and spelling, condensed biographical and geographical information, the pronunciation and source of many given names, and a vocabulary of rhymes. For writers and readers a dictionary is an indispensable tool.

Unabridged dictionaries

Unabridged dictionaries contain the most complete and scholarly description of English words available. The three most often referred to today are described below.

> *The Oxford English Dictionary.* 13 vols., plus supplements. New York: Oxford Univ. Press, 1933, 1972, 1977. Now also available in a photographically reduced edition of two volumes published in 1971.

Commonly referred to as the *OED,* this is the greatest dictionary of the English language. Containing over 500,000 entries, it traces the progress of each word through the language, giving dated quotations to illustrate its meaning and spelling at particular times in its history. A single word may occupy several pages. *Set,* for example, occupies twenty-three pages, and a single one of its more than 150 definitions is illustrated by thirteen quotations from writings beginning in 1056 and extending to 1893.

> *Webster's New International Dictionary of the English Language.* 3rd ed. Springfield, Mass.: G. & C. Merriam, 1976.

This is the unabridged dictionary that people who live in the United States are most likely to be familiar with. Issued originally in 1909, it was revised in 1934. The current edition, thoroughly revised, was first published in 1961. Though not as exhaustive as the *OED,* its definitions are scholarly and exact and frequently supported by illustrative quotations. Since the 1961 edition uses style labels such as *slang* infrequently and does not use the label *colloquial,* some readers continue to prefer the second edition.

Random House Dictionary of the English Language. New York: Random House, 1966.

With only 260,000 entries, the *Random House Dictionary* is considerably briefer than most unabridged dictionaries. But it is a sound and scholarly dictionary with especially up-to-date entries. It is the only entirely new unabridged dictionary to be published in recent years.

Other unabridged dictionaries of English are the *New Standard Dictionary of the English Language* and the *Dictionary of American English* (four volumes), which is made on the same plan as the *OED* and follows the history of words as they were used by American writers between 1620 and 1900.

The wide resources of an unabridged dictionary are suggested by the entry below. Since dictionaries must say much in little space, they use a great number of abbreviations and seemingly cryptic entries. You will find these troublesome unless you take time to read the explanatory pages and acquaint yourself with the symbols used. It will also be useful to follow through the sample entry below:

> ¹**howl** \\'haŭl, *esp before pause or consonant* -aŭəl\\ *vb* -ED/-ING/ -S [ME *houlen;* akin to MD *hūlen* to howl, MHG *hiulen, hiuweln* to howl, OHG *hūwila* owl, Gk *kōkyein* to shriek, wail, lament, Skt *kauti* he cries out] *vi* **1 :** to utter or emit a loud sustained doleful sound or outcry characteristic of dogs and wolves ⟨wolves ~*ing* in the arctic night⟩ ⟨the only sound is a melancholy wind ~*ing* —John Buchan⟩ **2 :** to cry out or exclaim with lack of restraint and prolonged loudness through strong impulse, feeling, or emotion ⟨the scalded men ~*ing* in agony⟩ ⟨the hungry mob ~*ed* about the Senate house, threatening fire and massacre —J.A.Froude⟩ ⟨proctors ~*ing* at the blunder⟩ **3 :** to go on a spree or rampage ⟨this is my night to ~⟩ ~ *vt* **1 :** to utter or announce noisily with unrestrained demonstrative outcry ⟨newsboys ~*ing* the news⟩ **2 :** to affect, effect, or drive by adverse outcry — used esp. with *down* ⟨supporters of the Administration ... ready to ~ down any suggestion of criticism —*Wall Street Jour.*⟩ **syn** see ROAR
> ²**howl** \\"\\ *n* -S **1 :** a loud protracted mournful rising and falling cry characteristic of a dog or a wolf **2 a :** a prolonged cry of distress **:** WAIL **b :** a yell or outcry of disappointment, rage, or protest **3 :** PROTEST, COMPLAINT ⟨raise a ~ over high taxes⟩ ⟨set up a ~ that he was being cheated⟩ **4 :** something that provokes laughter ⟨his act was a ~⟩ **5 :** a noise produced in an electronic amplifier usu. by undesired regeneration of alternating currents of audio frequency **:** OSCILLATION — called also *squeal*
>
> By permission. From *Webster's Third New International Dictionary.* © 1981 by G. & C. Merriam Co., Publishers of the Merriam-Webster Dictionaries.

In the example, from *Webster's Third New International,* the two main entries are printed in boldface type and preceded by the superscripts ¹ and ². The first is labeled *vb* for *verb,* the second *n* for *noun.* The -ED/-ING/-S in the first entry and the -S in the second show that the endings of *howl* as verb and as noun are regular. The pronunciation is indicated between slant lines, called **reverse virgules.** For the verb, it is given as follows: \\haŭl or haŭəl\\. The note before the second pronunciation explains that it occurs especially when the word is pronounced before a pause (at the end of a sentence, for example) or before a word beginning with a consonant. Inside the front cover or in the prefatory material of the dictionary, a key shows that *aù* is pronounced like the *ow* in *now* or the *ou* in *loud,* and that ə is a symbol representing the sound of the first and last *a* in *banana.*

The material between the brackets shows the origin or etymology of the word: *howl* comes from a word in Middle English (ME) spelled *houlen,* and is related to Middle Dutch (MD) *hūlen* and Middle High German (MHG) *hiulen* or *hiuweln,* all meaning "to howl"; to the Old High German (OHG) word *hūwila* meaning "owl"; to the Greek (Gk) *kōkyein* meaning "to wail" *or* "lament"; and to the Sanskrit (Skt) word *kauti* meaning "he cries out."

The definitions that follow are divided into various senses by bold-face numerals 1, 2, etc. The first group of these senses under ¹**howl** is preceded by the label *vi,* indicating that these are senses in which the verb is intransitive (not followed by an object). The second group of two meanings is preceded by the label *vt,* indicating that these are meanings in which the verb is transitive (followed by an object). For each sense, enclosed in angle brackets (⟨ ⟩) are quotations typical of the contexts in which the word occurs in the meaning given. These verbal illustrations become a major part of the definition itself by showing an actual context for the word. Those labeled by authors' names or by sources are actual quotations; those not so labeled are typical phrases offered by the dictionary editors. Under meaning 2 as a transitive verb, a usage note states that in this meaning *howl* is used especially with *down* in the phrase *howl down.* A swung dash (~) replaces the word itself in all such illustrations of the word. The final information, after **syn,** means that in the entry for *roar* is a discussion of the synonyms of *howl.* (See pp. 353–356 for illustration and discussion.)

In the second boldface entry, ²**howl,** the pattern is repeated for the senses in which *howl* occurs as a noun. Since no separate pronunciation or etymology is given, each of these is the same as for the verb. Under *a* and *b* of meaning 2, two different but related senses of that meaning are given. The words in small capitals (WAIL in meaning 2, PROTEST and COMPLAINT in meaning 3, and OSCILLATION in meaning 5) are the other main entries where further related definitions are given.

You can see something of the ways in which dictionaries must change if they are to be contemporary by comparing with the foregoing entry the following entry for the noun *howl* from the second edition, first issued in 1934.

howl, *n.* **1.** The loud, protracted, mournful cry of a dog or a wolf, or other like sound.
2. A prolonged cry of distress; a wail; also, a wild yell of disappointment, rage, or the like; as, *howls* of derision.

As you can see at a glance, the two meanings offered here are very close to those numbered 1 and 2 in the *Third New International.* But meanings 3, 4, and 5 listed in the *Third International* are all missing. They developed after the second edition was compiled.

Desk dictionaries

Although occasionally you may wish or need to refer to an unabridged dictionary in the library, particularly if you are reading older literature or older writing in other fields, a good abridged, or desk, dictionary will ordinarily serve all your needs in daily reading and writing. Although the five desk dictionaries briefly described below differ in important ways, they all contain 150,000 or more entries, provide careful etymologies and basic grammatical information about each entry, and specify distinctions among synonyms. All but *Webster's Collegiate* provide helpful style or usage labels.

1 *Webster's New Collegiate Dictionary.* **8th ed. Springfield, Mass.: G. & C. Merriam Co., 1981.** Based upon the *Third New International,* this desk dictionary profits from its extensive scholarship. The order of definitions under any one word is historical. It has relatively full etymologies, a wide range of synonymies, and full prefatory material. Abbreviations, biographical names, and place names are listed separately at the end of the dictionary. Some users find inconvenient the lack of the label *colloquial* or its equivalent, *informal,* and sparse use of the label *slang.*

> **howl** \'hau̇(ə)l\ *vb* [ME *houlen;* akin to MHG *hiulen* to howl, Gk *kōkyein* to shriek] *vi* **1 :** to emit a loud sustained doleful sound characteristic of dogs **2 :** to cry loudly and without restraint under strong impulse (as pain or grief) **3 :** to go on a spree or rampage ~ *vt* **1 :** to utter with unrestrained outcry **2 :** to affect, effect, or drive by adverse outcry — used esp. with *down* <~*ed* down the speaker> — **howl** *n*

2 *Webster's New World Dictionary.* **2nd college ed. New York: Simon & Schuster Inc., 1981.** This dictionary emphasizes simplified definitions even of technical terms and includes a large number of words and phrases that are relatively informal. Usage labels are generously used. Synonymies and etymologies are full and thorough. Common meanings are placed first in the definitions. All words are contained in the main alphabetical list. Identification of Americanisms and attention to the origin of American place names are special features.

howl (houl) *vi.* [ME. *hulen*, akin to G. *heulen* < IE. echoic base **kāu-*, whence Sans. *kāuti*, (it) cries, OHG. *hūwila*, owl] **1.** to utter the long, loud, wailing cry of wolves, dogs, etc. **2.** to utter a similar cry of pain, anger, grief, etc. **3.** to make a sound like this *[a howling wind]* **4.** to shout or laugh in scorn, mirth, etc. —*vt.* **1.** to utter with a howl or howls **2.** to drive or effect by howling —*n.* **1.** a long, loud, wailing cry of a wolf, dog, etc. **2.** any similar sound **3.** [Colloq.] something hilarious; joke —**howl down** to drown out with shouts of scorn, anger, etc. —**one's night to howl** one's time for unrestrained pleasure

3 *The American Heritage Dictionary of the English Language.* **New York: American Heritage Publishing Company, Inc.; Boston: Houghton Mifflin Company, 1981.** The distinguishing features of this dictionary are its generous illustrations and its usage notes based upon a consensus of a panel of some 100 writers, editors, poets, and public speakers. Definitions are arranged in this order: the initial definition offers what the editors judge to be the central meaning, and it serves as the base for the arrangement of other senses of the word. Synonymies are generous; etymologies are made somewhat more readable by avoidance of all abbreviations. The single alphabetical listing incorporates abbreviations and biographical and geographical entries. An appendix of Indo-European roots is a special feature.

howl (houl) *v.* **howled, howling, howls.** —*intr.* **1.** To utter or emit a long, mournful, plaintive sound characteristic of wolves or dogs. **2.** To cry or wail loudly and uncontrollably in pain, sorrow, or anger. **3.** *Slang.* **a.** To laugh uproariously. **b.** To go on a carousal or spree. —*tr.* **1.** To express or utter with a howl or howls. **2.** To effect, drive, or force by or as if by howling. —*n.* **1.** The sound of one that howls. **2.** *Slang.* Something uproariously funny or absurd. [Middle English *houlen, howlen,* perhaps from Middle Dutch *hūlen.* See *ul-* in Appendix.*]

4 *The Random House Dictionary of the English Language.* **College ed. New York: Random House, 1980.** This dictionary is based on the unabridged *Random House Dictionary of the English Language.* Definitions are arranged with the most common given first; recent technical words receive careful attention. A single alphabetical listing incorporates all biographical and geographical as well as other entries. Among its prefaces, that by Raven I. McDavid, Jr., on usage, dialects, and functional varieties of English, is a particularly valuable summary.

howl (houl), *v.i.* **1.** to utter a loud, prolonged, mournful cry, as that of a dog or wolf. **2.** to utter a similar cry in distress, pain, rage, etc.; wail. **3.** to make a sound like an animal howling: *The wind howls through the trees.* **4.** *Informal.* to laugh loudly. —*v.t.* **5.** to utter with howls. **6.** to drive or force by howls (often fol. by *down*): *to howl down the opposition.* —*n.* **7.** the cry of a dog, wolf, etc. **8.** a cry or wail, as of pain, rage, protest, etc. **9.** a sound like wailing: *the howl of the wind.* **10.** a loud, scornful laugh or yell. **11.** something that causes a laugh or a scornful yell, as a joke or funny or embarrassing situation. [ME *hul(en)*, *houle*; c. D *huilen*, G *heulen*, LG *hülen*, Dan *hyle*; with loss of *h*, Icel *ȳla*]

From *The Random House College Dictionary*, Revised Edition. Copyright © 1980, 1979, and 1975 by Random House, Inc. Reprinted by permission.

5 *Funk & Wagnalls Standard College Dictionary.* **New York: Funk & Wagnalls, 1977.** The reliability of this dictionary is insured by an impressive advisory board, many members of which are leading linguists. It is marked by a convenient type size, by relatively simple and natural definitions, and by particular attention to usage labels for words termed *informal* (which replaces the term *colloquial*) and *slang*. Material on usage is incorporated in some 260 notes. Common meanings are placed first in each entry. The *Standard* runs biographical names and place names into the main body of the dictionary rather than listing them separately. Introductory material in the text edition includes valuable summaries of the history of the language, English grammar, and regional variations in American pronunciation.

howl (houl) *v.i.* **1.** To utter the loud, mournful wail of a dog, wolf, or other animal. **2.** To utter such a cry in pain, grief, or rage. **3.** To make a sound similar to this: The storm *howled* all night. **4.** To laugh loudly: The audience *howled*. — *v.t.* **5.** To utter or express with howling: to *howl* one's disapproval. **6.** To condemn, suppress, or drive away by howling: often with *down*. — *n.* **1.** The wailing cry of a wolf, dog, or other animal. **2.** Any howling sound. [ME *houlen*. Cf. G *heulen*.]

From *Funk & Wagnalls Standard College Dictionary.* Copyright © 1977 by Harper & Row Publishers, Inc. Reprinted by permission of the publisher.

The uses of a dictionary

1 Spelling. The spelling entry of a word in the dictionary uses centered dots between syllables, showing how to separate it properly at the ends of lines (see "Syllabication," Section **18**). It also gives the proper spelling of compound words—properness depending on whether the editors found them more often written as two single words *(half brother)*, as a hyphenated compound *(quarter-hour)*, or as one word *(drugstore)*. Dictionaries also indicate foreign words that require italics (in manuscript, underlining). The *American Heritage* and the *Standard* label such words or phrases as Latin, German, etc.; *Webster's New World* uses a double dagger (‡). *The Random House Dictionary* indicates such words by printing the main entry word in boldface italic type. All dictionaries also indicate whether a word is always or usually capitalized in a particular meaning.

All modern dictionaries list variant spellings of many words, though not all by any means list the same variants or give the same comments about them. For example, all five list *centre* and *theatre* as well as the more common *center* and *theater*. But while *centre* is cited as the British spelling by all, only *Random House* and the *Standard* cite *theatre* as British; the other three leave it unqualified. And all five dictionaries list *licence* as a variant spelling of *license*, but whereas *Webster's Collegiate* and *Random House* have no qualifying note, all others cite *licence* as British. The spelling *knowledgeable* is the first entry in all five dictionaries, but only *Random House* lists the variant spelling *knowledgable*.

Such variation among dictionaries is common, and you must be careful to examine the explanatory material at the front of a dictionary to know exactly what policy is followed. Frequently, though by no means always, if variant spellings are listed, the first will be somewhat more common; the most carefully edited dictionaries sometimes adopt some means of indicating that this is so. *Webster's New Collegiate,* for example, indicates that two variants are equally common by joining them with *or (caddie* or *caddy)* but joins variants the second of which is less common by *also (woolly* also *wooly)*. In general, if there is a question about spelling, choose the first listed variant unless there is a special reason for choosing the second.

Whatever dictionary you choose, it will be your authority on all questions of spelling. Refer to it whenever you have any doubt about a correct spelling.

EXERCISE 38(1)   Give the preferred spelling of each word.

aesthetic	enclose	liquorice
catalogue	favour	modeled
catsup	judgement	Shakspere

EXERCISE 38(2)   Rewrite the following compounds, showing which should be written as they are, which hyphenated, and which written as two or more separate words.

castoff	jazzmen	uptodate
easygoing	passkey	wellmarked
horserace	showdown	worldwide

EXERCISE 38(3)   Copy the following foreign words, underlining those that require italics and supplying accents where needed.

bon voyage	dramatis personae	resume
coup d'etat	matinee	sine qua non
creche	nouveau riche	Weltschmertz

2 Pronunciation. Dictionaries indicate the pronunciation of words by respelling them with special symbols and letters. Explanation of the symbols is given either at the bottom of the page on which the entry appears or in the prefatory pages or both.

Dictionaries show frequently occurring variant pronunciations as they do variant spellings. In the sample entry from *Webster's Third New International*, for example, you can see that an unabridged dictionary may even show variant pronunciations for such a simple word as *howl*. Again, as with variant spellings, though the first listed is sometimes said to be "preferred," the statements about pronunciation in most carefully edited modern dictionaries do not bear this out. Usually, unless there is a limiting label or comment attached to one or more variants, they are all equally "correct." Your preference should be determined by the pronunciation you hear in the conversation around you.

EXERCISE 38(4) What is the pronunciation of the following words? If usage is divided for any, which pronunciation seems more acceptable to you? Why? Copy the dictionary pronunciation for each.

adult	exquisite	impotent
cerebral	formidable	mischievous
despicable	greasy	route

3 Etymology. The **etymology** of a word—that is, origin and derivation—often helps clarify its present meaning and spelling. Because the course of history changes, restricts, or extends the meanings of words, however, many original meanings have been lost completely. *Presently*, for example, formerly meant *at once, immediately;* it now usually means *shortly, in a little while.*

EXERCISE 38(5) Trace the etymology of each of the following:

assassin	familiar	neighbor	shirt
bedlam	fedora	organization	skirt
draggle	lampoon	sandwich	squelch

EXERCISE 38(6) From what specific names have the following words been derived?

ampere	gardenia	shrapnel
boycott	macadam	ulster
chauvinism	quisling	watt

EXERCISE 38(7) From what language did each of the following words come?

almanac	dory	jute	mukluk	trek
cherub	goulash	kerosene	piano	tulip
cockatoo	huckster	moccasin	squadron	typhoon

4 Meaning. Strictly speaking, dictionaries do not *define* words; they record the meaning or meanings that actual usage, past and present, has attached to words. When more than one meaning is recorded for a single word, *Webster's Collegiate* lists them in order of historical use. Most other dictionaries list the more general and present meaning first. Special and technical meanings are clearly labeled. Choosing the appropriate meaning out of the many offered is not difficult if you read them *all* and understand their order of arrangement as indicated in the prefatory pages of the dictionary.

EXERCISE 38(8) How many different meanings can you find for each of the following words?

call	land	run
get	light	set
go	out	turn

EXERCISE 38(9) Trace the changes in meaning that have taken place in each of the following words:

bounty	gossip	machine
complexion	humor	manufacture
engine	intern	sincere
fond	knave	starve
generous	lozenge	virtue

5 Synonyms and antonyms. A **synonym** is a word having the same or almost the same general meaning as the vocabulary entry. An **antonym** is a word having approximately the opposite meaning. In dictionaries, for practical reasons, not all entries show synonyms and antonyms. Well-edited desk dictionaries include paragraph-length discussions of groups of synonyms, defining the different shades of meaning associated with each member of the group. These discussions are located usually at the end of certain entries and cross-referenced at related entries. (For full illustration of synonym entries from various dictionaries, see pp. 354–356.)

6 Grammar. Dictionaries give a good deal of grammatical information about a word. All dictionaries indicate the part of speech to which each word belongs. If a particular word can serve as more than one part of speech, most dictionaries include all its functions and meaning under a single entry, grouping the meanings separately for each function. Thus under the entry for *minor*, *Webster's New World* and *American Heritage* list its meanings first as an adjective *(adj)*, then as a noun *(n)*, and last as an intransitive verb *(vi* or *intran)*. *Webster's Collegiate*, however, has a separate entry for each part of speech.

Dictionaries also list the inflected forms of words if they are irregular in any way or if they might cause spelling problems. Thus in the entry for the verb *drink*, all dictionaries list the irregular past tense *drank* and past participle *drunk*. Similarly, dictionaries list irregular plural forms of nouns, as in *child, children,* or *alumna, alumnae.* Usually the principal parts of verbs, noun plurals, and the comparative and superlative forms of adjectives are not given if they are formed regularly. Thus verbs that form both their past tense and their past participles by adding *-ed (walk, walked)* are not given unless they raise a spelling question, as in *travel, traveled, traveling* or *travelled, -lling.* Similarly, plurals ending in *-s* or *-es (cats, dishes)* are often not given. And comparatives and superlatives formed by adding *more, most,* or *less, least,* or *-er, -est* are not given unless the addition of the *-er, -est* endings presents a spelling difficulty *(heavy, heavier, heaviest).*

EXERCISE 38(10) What are the past tense and the present participle of each of these verbs?

broadcast	get	set
focus	lend	teach
dive	shrink	wake

EXERCISE 38(11) What is the plural (or plurals) of each of the following?

alumnus	crisis	index
bear	daisy	madame
court-martial	fish	stratum

EXERCISE 38(12) Write the comparative and superlative forms of each of the following:

bad	lengthy	red
ill	much	shyly
little	often	well

7   Labels. Dictionaries label words or particular meanings of words to indicate that they are in some way restricted. Words and meanings not so labeled are appropriate for general use. Although the particular labels dictionaries use vary somewhat, all labels can be divided into four general categories: *geographic* labels, *time* labels, *occupational* or *subject* labels, and *usage* or *style* labels.

Geographic labels indicate that the word or meaning so labeled is limited to a particular area. Typical labels of this sort are *British, Australian, New England, Southern U.S.,* and the like. Thus *Webster's Collegiate* labels *lift,* in the meaning of *elevator, British,* and *outbye,* meaning *a short distance away, Scottish. Webster's New World* labels *corn pone,* a kind of corn bread, *Southern U.S.* The label *dialectal* or *regional* usually suggests a specialized local or provincial word, often traditional. Thus *larrap,* meaning a *blow* or *to flog,* is labeled *dialectal* by *Webster's Collegiate* and *regional* by *American Heritage.*

Time labels indicate that the labeled word has passed out of use entirely or no longer occurs in ordinary contexts. *Obsolete* means that a word has passed out of use entirely, as *absume* and *enwheel,* words that have not been used for two hundred years. *Archaic* means that the labeled word or meaning is no longer generally used although it may still be seen occasionally in older writing, as *belike,* meaning "probably," or *outland,* meaning "a foreign land."

Subject labels indicate that a word or a particular meaning belongs to a special field such as law, medicine, baseball, finance, mathematics, or psychology. Thus *Webster's New World* identifies *projection* as a psychiatric term *(Psychiatry)* when used to mean the process of assigning one's own undesirable impulses to others and as a photographic term *(Photog.)* when used to mean projecting an image on a screen. *American Heritage* labels as *law* the meaning of *domain* in the sense of ownership and rights of disposal of property.

Style labels indicate that a word or meaning is restricted to a particular level of usage. Typical style labels are *slang, colloquial, informal, nonstandard, substandard, illiterate,* and *vulgar.* Variations among dictionaries are greatest in their choice of labels and in the words and meanings to which they apply them. Nonetheless, there is broad agreement on the meanings of the labels themselves.

Slang indicates that a word, though widely used, has not yet been accepted in the general vocabulary. Slang terms and meanings often are used humorously; are likely to be short-lived, limited to a particular group of people; and are used almost entirely in speech rather than writing. Typical examples are *hangup* (a fixation, an intense preoccupation), *shades* (sunglasses), *snow* (cocaine or heroin), and *megabuck* (a million dollars). Of the dictionaries described, *Webster's Collegiate* is by far the most sparing in its use of the label, allowing many entries labeled *slang* by others to pass without any label.

Colloquial and informal are almost synonymous terms. They both indicate that a word is characteristic of speech or of quite informal, rather than more formal, writing. The *Standard* and the *American Heritage* use the label *informal; Webster's New World* uses *colloquial. Webster's Collegiate* uses neither label and thus may be less useful for those who need to determine how appropriate a word is for a particular writing context. *Webster's New World,* for example, says *fizzle* is colloquial, the *Standard* says it is informal, and *Webster's Collegiate* gives it no label.

Illiterate, substandard, and some other similar terms are labels indicating that a word is limited to uneducated speech, as *drownded* for the past tense of *drown.* Though dictionaries vary somewhat in the particular labels they use (the *Standard* uses *illiterate* to mean about the same thing as *Webster's substandard,* for example), their agreement in classifying a word as being limited to uneducated speech is much greater than their agreement in labeling a word *slang, colloquial,* and so on.

To use your dictionary wisely as a guide to usage, you will have to examine the explanatory notes in it carefully to determine exactly what labels are applied and how they are interpreted by the editors.

EXERCISE 38(13)   Which of the following are standard English, which colloquial or informal, and which slang, according to your dictionary? If possible, check more than one dictionary to determine if they agree.

corny	goof	moll
cool	hipster	snollygoster
flap	jerk	wise-up
foul-up	kibitzer	yak

EXERCISE 38(14)   In what areas of the world would you be likely to hear the following?

billabong	hoecake	potlatch
chuckwagon	laager	pukka
coulee	petrol	sharpie

EXERCISE 38(15)   The following questions are designed to test your ability to use the whole dictionary, not only its vocabulary entries, but also its various appendices. Any of the desk dictionaries discussed in this section will help you find the answers. Look up the meanings of *etymology, homonym, antonym, syllabication,* and *synonym,* if necessary, before answering the questions.

1 What is the etymology of the word *precise?*
2 What are two homonyms for the word *reign?*
3 What are some antonyms for the word *concise?*
4 What is the syllabication of the word *redundant?*
5 What are some synonyms for the adjective *correct?*
6 Give the meanings of these abbreviations: *syn., v. mus., R.C.Ch.*
7 What do the following phrases mean: *finem respice, ars longa vita brevis, de profundis, honi soit qui mal y pense?*
8 What is the population of Birmingham, Michigan?
9 Who was the oldest of the Brontë sisters?
10 From what language does the proper name *Nahum* come?

Special dictionaries

General dictionaries bring together in a single reference all of the information you ordinarily need about a word. Special dictionaries, because they limit their attention to a single kind of information about words or to a single category of words, can give more complete information. Thus a dictionary of slang can devote an entire page to the word *hip,* in contrast to the general dictionary, which can afford no more than four or five lines. Similarly, dictionaries of usage and of synonyms can provide much more complete information of a particular kind than space allows in general dictionaries. Such dictionaries are no substitute for the daily usefulness of a good desk dictionary, but they are extremely useful supplements.

When you need specialized information about words, check one of the following dictionaries:*

Bernstein, Stuart M. *The Careful Writer: A Modern Guide to Usage.* New York: Atheneum, 1977.

Fowler, H. W. *Dictionary of Modern English Usage.* 2nd ed. Rev. and ed. Sir Ernest Gowers. London: Oxford Univ. Press, 1965.

Partridge, Eric. *Origins: A Short Etymological Dictionary of Modern English.* 4th ed. New York: MacMillan, 1966.

Webster's New Dictionary of Synonyms. Springfield, Mass: G. & C. Merriam, 1973.

Wentworth, Harold, and Stuart Berg Flexner. *Dictionary of American Slang.* 2nd supp. ed. New York: Crowell, 1975.

The difference between the right word and the almost-right word is the difference between lightning and the lightning bug.

Attributed to MARK TWAIN

39

39 VOCABULARY

The English language contains well over a million words. Of these, about two-fifths belong almost exclusively to special fields: e.g., zoology, electronics, psychiatry. Of the remaining, the large dictionaries list about 500,000, the desk dictionaries about 150,000. Such wealth is both a blessing and a curse. On the one hand, many English words are loosely synonymous, sometimes interchangeable, as in *buy* a book or *purchase* a book. On the other hand, the distinctions between synonyms are fully as important as their similarities. For example, a family may be said to be living in *poverty,* or in *penury,* or in *want,* or in *destitution.* All these words are loosely synonymous, but only one will describe the family exactly as you see it and wish your reader to see it. In short, as a writer of English you must use words carefully.

Passive and active vocabulary

In a sense, you have two vocabularies: a **passive,** or **recognition, vocabulary,** which is made up of the words you recognize in the context of reading matter but do not actually use yourself; and an **active** vocabulary, which consists of "working" words—those you use daily in

*See also the lists of reference books in "The Library," Section **45.**

your own writing and speaking. In the passage below, the meaning of the italicized words is fairly clear, or can at least be guessed at, from the context. But how many belong in your *active* vocabulary?

> Has it been duly marked by historians that the late William Jennings Bryan's last *secular* act on this globe of sin was to catch flies? A curious detail, and not without its *sardonic overtones.* He was the most *sedulous* flycatcher in American history, and in many ways the most successful. His *quarry,* of course, was not *Musca domestica* but *Homo neandertalensis.* For forty years he tracked it with coo and bellow, up and down the *rustic* backways of the Republic. Wherever the *flambeau* of Chautauqua smoked and guttered, and the bilge of idealism ran in the veins, the Baptist pastors damned the brooks with the *sanctified,* and men gathered who were weary and heavy laden, and their wives who were full of Peruna and as *fecund* as the shad (*Alosa sapidissima*)—there the *indefatigable* Jennings set up his traps and spread his bait.
>
> H. L. MENCKEN, *Selected Prejudices*

Increasing your vocabulary

There are no shortcuts to word power. A good vocabulary is the product of years of serious reading, of listening to intelligent talk, and of seeking to speak and write forcefully and clearly. All this does not mean that devices and methods for building up your vocabulary are useless. But it does mean that acquiring a good vocabulary is inseparable from acquiring an education.

1   Increasing your recognition vocabulary. English has many words based on a common root form, to which different prefixes or suffixes have been added. The root form *spec-,* for example, from the Latin *specere (to look),* appears in *specter, inspection, perspective, aspect, introspection, circumspect, specimen, spectator.* Knowing the common prefixes and suffixes will help you detect the meaning of many words whose roots are familiar.

Prefixes

Prefix	*Meaning*	*Example*
ab-	away from	absent
ad-*	to *or* for	adverb
com-*	with	combine
de-	down, away from, *or* undoing	degrade, depart, dehumanize
dis-*	separation *or* reversal	disparate, disappoint
ex-*	out of *or* former	extend, ex-president
in-*	in *or* on	input
in-*	not	inhuman

Prefix	Meaning	Example
mis-	wrong	mistake
non-	not	non-Christian, nonsense
ob-*	against	obtuse
pre-	before	prevent
pro-	for *or* forward	proceed
re-	back *or* again	repeat
sub-*	under	subcommittee
trans-	across	transcribe
un-	not	unclean

EXERCISE 39(1) Write words denoting *negation* from the following.

EXAMPLE movable—able to be moved
immovable—*not* able to be moved

accuracy	conformity	mutable
adorned	distinctive	rational
agreeable	explicable	workable

EXERCISE 39(2) Write words denoting *reversal* from the following.

EXAMPLE accelerate—to move at increasing speed
decelerate—to move at decreasing speed
increase—to grow larger
decrease—to grow smaller

centralize	integrate	please
do	magnetize	qualify
inherit	persuade	ravel

Suffixes. These fall into three groups: noun suffixes, verb suffixes, adjectival suffixes.

Noun suffixes denoting *act of, state of, quality of* include the following:

Suffix	Example	Meaning
-dom	freedom	*state of* being free
-hood	manhood	*state of* being a man
-ness	dimness	*state of* being dim
-ice	cowardice	*quality of* being a coward
-ation	flirtation	*act of* flirting

*The spelling of these prefixes varies, usually to make pronunciation easier. *Ad* becomes *ac* in *accuse*, *ag* in *aggregate*, *at* in *attack*. Similarly, the final consonant in the other prefixes is assimilated by the initial letter of the root word: *colleague (com + league); illicit (in + licit); offend (ob + fend); succeed (sub + ceed).*

Suffix	Example	Meaning
-ion	intercession	*act of* interceding
⎡-sion	scansion	*act of* scanning
⎣-tion	corruption	*state of* being corrupt
-ment	argument	*act of* arguing
-ship	friendship	*state of* being friends
⎡-ance	continuance	*act of* continuing
-ence	precedence	*act of* preceding
-ancy	flippancy	*state of* being flippant
⎣-ency	currency	*state of* being current
-ism	baptism	*act of* baptizing
-ery	bravery	*quality of* being brave

Noun suffixes denoting *doer, one who* include the following:

Suffix	Example	Meaning
-eer (general)	auctioneer	*one who* auctions
-ist	fascist	*one who* believes in fascism
⎡-or	debtor	*one who* is in debt
⎣-er	worker	*one who* works

Verb suffixes denoting *to make* or *to perform the act of* include the following:

Suffix	Example	Meaning
-ate	perpetuate	*to make* perpetual
-en	soften	*to make* soft
-fy	dignify	*to make* dignified
-ize, -ise	sterilize	*to make* sterile

Adjectival suffixes include the following:

Suffix	Meaning	Example
-ful	full of	hateful
-ish	resembling	foolish
-ate	having	affectionate
-ic, -ical	resembling	angelic
-ive	having	prospective
-ous	full of	zealous
-ulent	full of	fraudulent
-less	without	fatherless
-able, -ible	capable of	peaceable
-ed	having	spirited
-ly	resembling	womanly
-like	resembling	childlike

EXERCISE 39(3)   Write words indicating *act of, state of,* or *quality of* from the following words.

advance	deny	promote
calculate	helpless	rebel
disappear	judge	statesman

EXERCISE 39(4)   Write nouns indicating *doer* from the following.

advise	communicate	profit
boast	disturb	sail
command	preach	save

EXERCISE 39(5)   Write verbs indicating *to make* or *to perform the act of* from the following nouns and adjectives.

beauty	idol	moral
black	liquid	peace
captive	modern	victim

EXERCISE 39(6)   Make adjectives of the following words by adding a suffix.

humor	rest	thwart
irony	speed	wasp
mule	talk	whimsey

Combining forms. Linguists refer to the following as **bound forms;** they appear generally, but not always, as prefixes:

Combining Form	Meaning	Example
anthropo	man	*anthropo*logy
arch	rule	*arch*duke, mon*arch*
auto	self	*auto*mobile
bene	well	*bene*ficial
eu	well	*eu*logy
graph	writing	*graph*ic, biog*raphy*
log, logue	word, speech	mono*logue*
magni	great	*magni*ficent
mal	bad	*mal*ady
mono	one	*mono*tone
multi	many	*multi*plication
neo	new	*neo*-classic
omni	all	*omni*bus
pan, pant	all	*pan*hellenic
philo	loving	*philo*sophy
phono	sound	*phono*graph
poly	many	*poly*gamy
pseudo	false	*pseudo*nym
semi	half	*semi*formal

2 Increasing your active vocabulary. Another way to increase word power is to keep transferring words from your recognition vocabulary to your active vocabulary. Make a conscious effort to introduce at least one new word a day into your active vocabulary. At the same time, be alert to opportunities for increasing your recognition vocabulary. A good system is to enter each new word on a small card: write the word on one side, the definition and a sentence illustrating its correct use on the other. Then you can quickly test yourself on the meaning of all the new words you collect.

EXERCISE 39(7) Define each of the following words and use it correctly in a sentence.

compatible	malign	estrangement
demagogue	unscrupulous	promiscuous
intimidate	officious	euphoria
disparage	facetious	corpulent
ostentatious	incentive	transcend
altruistic	ambiguous	pompous
taciturn	pragmatic	finite

3 Strengthening your active vocabulary. Are you sure that *enthusiast, fanatic, zealot,* and *bigot* mean what you think they mean? You know that *deadly, mortal,* and *fatal* are very much alike in meaning—but do you know the exact distinctions among them? All the desk dictionaries listed in Section 38 group synonyms and point out their differences. Unabridged dictionaries carry quite exhaustive discussions of synonyms. The Merriam-Webster *New Dictionary of Synonyms* is devoted exclusively to the grouping and differentiating of synonyms. The various editions of Roget's *Thesaurus* are valuable for the long lists of closely related words they provide, though they must be used cautiously because they give no discussion of distinctions in meaning and offer no guiding examples.

One of the most valuable ways to strengthen your vocabulary is to cultivate the habit of studying dictionary discussions of synonyms. The following examples will give you an idea of the extent to which various dictionaries explore synonyms. The numerals in synonym entries refer to numbered meanings in the definition part of a main entry. For example, "**4.** alleviate, cure, heal" in the *Random House* example means that *alleviate, cure,* and *heal* are all synonyms for *help* when it is used in the sense numbered **4** in the definition part of the main entry. Similarly, *afflict* is an **antonym,** or opposite, for this fourth defined sense of *help.*

From the *Random House,* for *help:*

—**Syn. 1.** encourage, befriend; support, uphold, back, abet. HELP, AID, ASSIST, SUCCOR agree in the idea of furnishing another with something needed, esp. when the need comes at a particular time. HELP implies furnishing anything that furthers another's efforts or relieves his wants or necessities. AID and ASSIST, somewhat more formal, imply esp. a furthering or seconding of another's efforts. AID implies a more active helping; ASSIST implies less need and less help. To SUCCOR, still more formal and literary, is to give timely help and relief in difficulty or distress: *Succor him in his hour of need.* **4.** alleviate, cure, heal. **10.** support, backing. —**Ant. 4.** afflict. **8.** hinder.

From *Webster's Third,* for *howl:*

syn HOWL, ULULATE, BELLOW, BAWL, BLUSTER, CLAMOR, VOCIFERATE: ROAR suggests the full loud reverberating sound made by lions or the booming sea or by persons in rage or boisterous merriment ⟨far away guns *roar* —Virginia Woolf⟩ ⟨the harsh north wind . . . *roared* in the piazzas —Osbert Sitwell⟩ ⟨*roared* the blacksmith, his face black with rage —T.B.Costain⟩ HOWL indicates a higher, less reverberant sound often suggesting the doleful or agonized or the sounds of unrestrained laughter ⟨frequent *howling* of jackals and hyenas —James Stevenson-Hamilton⟩ ⟨how the wind does *howl* —J.C.Powys⟩ ⟨*roared* at his subject . . . *howled* at . . . inconsistencies —Martin Gardner⟩ ULULATE is a literary synonym for HOWL but may suggest mournful protraction and rhythmical delivery ⟨an *ululating* baritone mushy with pumped-up pity —E.B.White⟩ BELLOW suggests the loud, abrupt, hollow sound made typically by bulls or any similar loud, reverberating sound ⟨most of them were drunk. They went *bellowing* through the town —Kenneth Roberts⟩ BAWL suggests a somewhat lighter, less reverberant, unmodulated sound made typically by calves ⟨a woman *bawling* abuse from the door of an inn —C.E.Montague⟩ ⟨the old judge was in the hall *bawling* hasty orders —Sheridan Le Fanu⟩ BLUSTER suggests the turbulent noisiness of gusts of wind; it often suggests swaggering and noisy threats or protests ⟨expressed her opinion gently but firmly, while he *blustered* for a time and then gave in —Sherwood Anderson⟩ ⟨swagger and *bluster* and take the limelight —Margaret Mead⟩ CLAMOR suggests sustained, mixed and confused noisy outcry as from a number of agitated persons ⟨half-starved men and women *clamoring* for food —Kenneth Roberts⟩ ⟨easy . . . for critics . . . to *clamor* for action —Sir Winston Churchill⟩ VOCIFERATE suggests loud vehement insistence in speaking ⟨was not willing to break off his talk; so he continued to *vociferate* his remarks —James Boswell⟩

From *Webster's New Collegiate,* for *wit:*

syn WIT. HUMOR. IRONY. SARCASM. SATIRE. REPARTEE *shared meaning element* : a mode of expression intended to arouse amused interest or evoke attention and laughter or a quality of mind that predisposes to such expression. WIT suggests the power to evoke laughing attention by remarks showing verbal felicity or ingenuity and swift perception, especially of the incongruous <true *wit* is nature to advantage dressed, what oft was thought, but ne'er so well expressed —Alexander Pope> HUMOR implies an ability to perceive and effectively express the ludicrous, the comical, or the absurd, especially in human life <the modern sense of *humor* is the quiet enjoyment and implicit expression of the fun of things —Louis Cazamian> IRONY applies to a manner of presentation in which an intended meaning is subtly emphasized by appropriate expression of its opposite <*irony* properly suggests the opposite of what is explicitly stated, by means of peripheral clues — tone of voice, accompanying gestures, stylistic exaggeration . . . thus, for "Brutus is an honorable man" we understand "Brutus is a traitor" —Jacob Brackman> SARCASM applies to savagely humorous expression, frequently in the form of irony, intended to cut and wound <the arrows of *sarcasm* are barbed with contempt —Washington Gladden> SATIRE applies primarily to writing that holds up vices or follies to ridicule and reprobation often by use of irony or caricature <his dry wit and his easy, good-natured *satire* on the follies of the day —Eleanor M. Sickels> REPARTEE applies to the power or art of responding quickly, smoothly, pointedly, and wittily or to an interchange of such response <as for *repartee* . . . , as it is the very soul of conversation, so it is the greatest grace of comedy —John Dryden>

From *Webster's New World,* for *destroy:*

SYN.—destroy implies a tearing down or bringing to an end by wrecking, ruining, killing, eradicating, etc. and is the term of broadest application here *[to destroy* a city, one's influence, etc.*]*; **demolish** implies such destructive force as to completely smash to pieces *[* the bombs *demolished* the factories*]*; **raze** means to level to the ground, either destructively or by systematic wrecking with a salvaging of useful parts; to **annihilate** is to destroy so completely as to blot out of existence *[* rights that cannot be *annihilated]*

From *Funk & Wagnalls Standard,* for *speech:*

— Syn. 4. *Speech, address, talk, oration, harangue, lecture, discourse, sermon,* and *homily* denote something said to an audience. Any public speaking may be called a *speech.* An *address* is a formal *speech,* as on a ceremonial occasion. *Talk,* on the other hand, suggests informality. An *oration* is an eloquent *address* that appeals to the emotions, while a *harangue* is a vehement *speech,* appealing to the emotions and often intended to spur the audience to action of some sort. A *lecture* is directed to the listener's intellect; it gives information, explanation, or counsel. Any carefully prepared *speech* or writing is a *discourse. Sermon* and *homily* are concerned with religious instruction; a *sermon* is usually an interpretation of Scripture, and a *homily* gives ethical guidance.

From the *American Heritage,* for *curious:*

> **Synonyms:** *curious, inquisitive, snoopy, nosy, intrusive.* These adjectives apply to persons who show a marked desire for information or knowledge. *Curious* more often implies a legitimate desire to enlarge one's knowledge, but can suggest a less commendable urge to concern oneself in others' affairs. *Inquisitive* frequently suggests excessive curiosity and the asking of many questions. *Snoopy* implies an unworthy motive and underhandedness in implementing it. *Nosy* suggests excessive curiosity and impertinence in an adult; applied to a child, it may refer less unfavorably to habitual curiosity. *Intrusive* stresses unwarranted and unwelcome concern with another's affairs.
>
> © 1981, Houghton Mifflin Company. Reprinted by permission from *The American Heritage Dictionary of the English Language.*

EXERCISE 39(8)   Indicate the distinctions in meaning among the words in each of the following groups.

1 neglect, omit, disregard, ignore, overlook
2 costly, expensive, valuable, precious, priceless
3 calm, tranquil, serene, placid, peaceful
4 puzzle, perplex, bewilder, dumbfound
5 fashion, style, vogue, fad, rage, craze
6 conform, adjust, reconcile
7 correct, accurate, exact, precise
8 obstruct, hinder, impede, bar, block, dam
9 design, plan, scheme, plot
10 mock, mimic, copy, ape

Care should be taken, not that the reader may understand, but that he must understand.

QUINTILIAN

40   EXACTNESS **EX**

To write with precision, you must know both the denotation and the connotation of words. **Denotation** is the core of a word's meaning, sometimes called the "dictionary," or literal, meaning; for example, a *tree* is *a woody perennial plant having a single main axis or stem commonly exceeding ten feet in height.* **Connotation** refers to the reader's emotional response to a word and to the associations the word carries with it. Thus, *tree* connotes *shade* or *coolness* or *shelter* or *stillness.*

You can fail to write what you mean by misunderstanding the denotation of a word you choose. For example, the student who wrote *In thinking biology would be an easy course, I was thinking wistfully* simply chose a wrong word. She meant *wishfully,* not *wistfully.* To write *The men who had risked their lives to rescue the child were praised for their heroics* will not do. *Heroics* means something quite different from *heroism,* and if you use one when you mean the other, you will simply be wrong.

But you are more likely to miss saying exactly what you mean by missing the connotations of the words you use than by missing their denotations. Connotations cannot be fixed precisely, for individual responses to a word differ. But many words nonetheless have quite stable connotations. *Home* generally suggests security, a sense of one's own place. Most of us would prefer a *convertible* to a *jalopy* and would be suspicious of buying either from a *scheming* seller of used cars.

You must take care, of course, that the connotations of the individual words you choose are those you intend. But you must also make sure that your words fit the associations called up by other words in both the individual sentence and the larger context in which they are used. Sentences such as the following go wrong because the words don't fit connotatively:

> *Brandishing* his gun and *angrily demanding* the money, the thief *gaped* at the frightened clerk.
> The *timid little* man *sidled* up to the policeman and *glared* at him.

In the first example, the verb *gaped* suggests awe, stupidity, or astonishment, any of which clash sharply with the meaning associated with words like *brandishing* and *angrily demanded.* In the second sentence, *timid* and *sidle* suggest a hesitancy and lack of confidence that don't jibe with the choice of *glare,* which suggests hardness and hostility. Both sentences go wrong because they set up conflicting connotations.

Many words stand for abstractions: *democracy, truth, beauty.* Because the connotations of such words are both vague and numerous, state specifically what you mean when you use them, or make sure that the context clarifies their meaning. Otherwise, readers will misunderstand, or—worse—will think they understand your terms when they do not. (See Section **33a**.)

40a Distinguish carefully among synonyms.

English is rich in synonyms, groups of words that have nearly the same meaning: *begin, start, commence; female, feminine, womanly; funny, comic, laughable.* But most synonyms differ in connotation, and exact writers choose carefully among them, observing their precise shades of meaning. Occasionally, the difference in meaning between two synonyms is so slight that it makes little difference which you choose: you can *begin a vacation* or *start a vacation*—either will do. But usually the differences will be much greater. To *commence a vacation,* for example, will not do; *commence* means *begin,* but it connotes far more formality than ordinarily goes with vacations. And it makes a much more important difference whether you describe a woman as *female, feminine,* or *womanly,* or a movie as *funny, comic,* or *laughable.*

Exact writing requires that you both increase the number of synonyms you can draw from in writing (see pp. 353–356), and distinguish carefully among them. Knowing that *fashion* and *vogue* are synonyms for *fad,* or that *renowned* and *notorious* are synonyms for *famous,* gives you the chance to make writing more exact. Choosing the synonyms that connote the precise shade of meaning you want makes it more exact.

The careless use of synonyms not only makes writing inexact; it often actually distorts meaning.

> Capone was a *renowned* gangster. [*Renowned* has favorable connotations that the writer probably did not intend. *Famous* would do, but it is not very exact. *Notorious* would be exact.]

EXERCISE 40a(1)   Replace the italicized words in the following sentences with more exact ones. Explain why each italicized word is inappropriate.

1 His characters are *garish* and alive; they are people you will remember as old friends.
2 His *obstinacy* in the face of danger saved us all.
3 The ambassador, being treated like a common tourist, sputtered in *displeasure.*
4 We can't blame Margaret for leaving him; certainly she had an ample *pretext.*
5 The school's most honored professor was without fault: a wise mentor to her students, and in addition a scholar recognized as *pedantic* and profound.

EXERCISE 40a(2)   Explain the differences in meaning among the italicized words in each of the following groups.

1 an *ignorant,* an *illiterate,* an *unlettered,* an *uneducated* person
2 a *detached,* a *disinterested,* an *indifferent,* an *unconcerned* attitude
3 *to condone, to excuse, to forgive, to pardon* a person's actions
4 an *insurrection,* a *mutiny,* a *rebellion,* a *revolution*
5 a *barbarous,* a *cruel,* a *fierce,* a *ferocious,* an *inhuman,* a *savage* character

40b   Be careful not to confuse words with similar sound or spelling but with different meanings.

Some words are **homonyms,** that is, they have the same pronunciation but different meanings and different spellings (*idol, idle, idyll; aisle, isle*). Other words are sufficiently similar in sound and spelling to be confusing. Treat all these words as you would any other unfamiliar term: learn the correct spelling and meaning of each as an individual word.

EXERCISE 40b What are the differences in meaning in each of the following groups of words?

1	adapt, adept, adopt	**16**	confidently, confidentially
2	alley, ally	**17**	costume, custom
3	allude, elude	**18**	elicit, illicit
4	anecdote, antidote	**19**	epic, epoch
5	anesthetic, antiseptic	**20**	flaunt, flout
6	angel, angle	**21**	genteel, gentile
7	arraign, arrange	**22**	historic, historical
8	block, bloc	**23**	human, humane
9	borne, born	**24**	ingenious, ingenuous
10	Calvary, cavalry	**25**	marital, martial
11	cannon, canon	**26**	morality, mortality
12	canvas, canvass	**27**	prescribe, proscribe
13	carton, cartoon	**28**	receipt, recipe
14	chord, cord	**29**	statue, statute
15	climactic, climatic	**30**	waive, wave

40c Generally, avoid invented words.

A **coined** word is a new and outright creation (like *gobbledegook, blurb*). A **neologism** is either a new word or a new use of an old word or words (like Madison Avenue's *package plans*). A **nonce-word,** literally **once-word,** is a word made up to suit a special situation and generally not used more than once (*"My son,"* he said, *"suffers from an acute case of televisionitis"*). Though the great majority of neologisms and nonce-words are short-lived, they are among the ways by which new words and new functions for old words are constantly working their way into a changing language.

English is relatively free in shifting words from one part of speech to another. The process is called **functional shift** and is one of the many ways in which our language grows. The noun *iron* is used as an adjective in *iron bar,* and as a verb in *iron the sheets.* The space age gives us *All systems are go,* using the verb *go* as a modifier. *River, paper,* and *sea* are clearly nouns in form (they make plurals with *-s*), but we commonly use them as modifiers in *river bank, paper bag,* and *sea water.*

But the fact that such changes are common in English does not mean that words can freely shift from one function to another. In *He opinioned that Edward was guilty, opinion* is used as a verb, a grammatical function to which it is entirely unaccustomed. The meaning may be roughly clear, but the use is not accepted. We *punish* a person. There is perhaps no good reason why we should not speak of *a punish.* But we don't; if we want a noun, we use *punishment.*

You should devote most of your attention to learning the meanings of words already established by usage, but you should not be afraid to try a new coinage if it seems to suit your purpose. Your instructor will judge whether the experiment is successful. Be careful, however, to avoid "unconscious" inventions—words that you "invent" because of spelling errors or an inexact knowledge of word forms (*understandment* for *understanding, multification* for *multiplication*). If you have any doubt about the accepted grammatical functions of a word, consult your dictionary.

EXERCISE 40c In the following sentences correct the italicized words that seem to you needlessly invented. Check your dictionary when necessary to determine whether a particular word is an accepted form or whether it is used in the way it appears in the sentence in the exercise.

1 One glimpse of the activities of the police or the mobs in urban riots reveals the *savagism* of human nature.
2 Teachers should be strictly *unpolitical;* they should not try to influence their students.
3 Even in our computer age, human behavior is largely *unpredictable.*
4 He displayed *liberalistic* tendencies in economic affairs.
5 That highway is *stoplighted* all the way to town; let's take the turnpike.
6 The cottage is nearly finished; we're going *to roof* it tomorrow.
7 Before we started building it, we had *to bulldoze* a clearing.
8 As each of the kids came out of the pool, I *toweled* him or her dry.
9 This year we're going *to holiday* in Bermuda.
10 Next summer Janine is going *to jeep* her way cross-country.

40d   **Be alert to changes in meaning from one form of a word to another.**

A roommate whom you *like* is not necessarily a *likable* roommate, nor is a *matter of agreement* an *agreeable matter.* Many words have two, sometimes three, adjectival forms: e.g., a *changeable* personality, a *changing* personality, a *changed* personality. Be careful not to substitute one form for another.

FAULTY	The cook served our *favorable* dessert last night.
STANDARD	The cook served our *favorite* dessert last night.
FAULTY	He is a good student; he has a very *questionable* mind.
STANDARD	He is a good student; he has a very *questioning* mind.

EXERCISE 40d Point out the differences in meaning between the italicized words in each of the following groups.

1 an *arguable* point
   an *argued* point
2 a *practical* solution
   a *practicable* solution
3 a *hated* person
   a *hateful* person

4 a *liberal* foreign minister
   a *liberated* foreign minister
5 a *single* effect
   a *singular* effect
6 an *intelligible* writer
   an *intelligent* writer

7 a *godly* person	**10** a *workable* arrangement
a *godlike* person	a *working* arrangement
8 an *informed* teacher	**11** an *amicable* neighbor
an *informative* teacher	an *amiable* neighbor
9 a *peaceful* nation	**12** a *yellow* piece of paper
a *peaceable* nation	a *yellowed* piece of paper

40e Use accepted idioms.

An **idiom** is an expression that does not follow the normal pattern of the language or that has a total meaning not suggested by its separate words: *to catch fire, strike a bargain, ride it out, lose one's head, hold the bag.** Such expressions are a part of the vocabulary of native speakers. In fact, we learn them in the same way we learn new words—by hearing them in the speech around us, and by reading them in context. For the most part they give no more, and no less, difficulty than vocabulary itself gives us. Dictionaries usually give the common idiomatic expressions at the end of the definition of a word entry.

For many writers the most troublesome idioms in English are those that require a particular preposition after a given verb or adjective according to the meaning intended. The following list contains a number of such combinations that frequently cause trouble.

ABSOLVED BY, FROM	I was *absolved by* the dean *from* all blame.
ACCEDE TO	He *acceded to* his father's demands.
ACCOMPANY BY, WITH	I was *accompanied by* George. The terms were *accompanied with* a plea for immediate peace.
ACQUITTED OF	He was *acquitted of* the crime.
ADAPTED TO, FROM	This machine can be *adapted to* farm work. The design was *adapted from* a previous invention.
ADMIT TO, OF	He *admitted to* the error. The plan will *admit of* no alternative.
AGREE TO, WITH, IN	They *agreed to* the plan but *disagreed with* us. They *agreed* only *in* principle.
ANGRY WITH, AT	She was *angry with* me and *angry at* the treatment she had received.
CAPABLE OF	He is *capable of* every vice of the ignorant.
CHARGE FOR, WITH	He expected to be *charged for his* purchase, but he didn't expect to be *charged with* stealing something.
COMPARE TO, WITH	He *compared* the roundness of the baseball *to* that of the earth. He *compared* the economy of the Ford *with* that of the Plymouth.

---

*The term *idiom* is also used to mean the characteristic expression or pattern of a dialect or language. In this sense of the word, we can speak of the *idiom* of speakers from South Boston, or we can compare English *idiom* with German or French.

CONCUR WITH, IN	I *concur with* you *in* your desire to use the revised edition.
CONFIDE IN, TO	He *confided in* me. He *confided to* me that he had stolen the car.
CONFORM TO, WITH CONFORMITY WITH	The specifications *conformed to* (or *with*) his original plans. You must act in *conformity with* our demands.
CONNECT BY, WITH	The rooms are *connected by* a corridor. He is officially *connected with* this university.
CONTEND FOR, WITH	Because she needed to *contend for* her principles, she found herself *contending with* her parents.
DIFFER ABOUT, FROM, WITH	We *differ about* our tastes in clothes. My clothes *differ from* yours. We *differ with* one another.
DIFFERENT FROM*	Our grading system is *different from* yours.
ENTER INTO, ON, UPON	She *entered into* a new agreement and thereby *entered on* (or *upon*†) a new career.
FREE FROM, OF	He was *freed from* his mother's domination and now he is *free of* her.
IDENTICAL WITH	Your reasons are *identical with* his.
JOIN IN, WITH, TO	He *joined in* the fun *with* the others. He *joined* the wire cables *to* each other.
LIVE AT, IN, ON	He *lives at* 14 Neil Avenue *in* a Dutch colonial house. He *lives on* Neil Avenue.
NECESSITY FOR, OF NEED FOR, OF	There was no *necessity (need) for* you to lose your temper. There was no *necessity (need) of* your losing your temper.
OBJECT TO	I *object to* the statement in the third paragraph.
OBLIVIOUS OF	When he held her hand he was *oblivious of* the passing of time.
OVERCOME BY, WITH	I was *overcome by* the heat. I was *overcome with* grief.
PARALLEL BETWEEN, TO, WITH	There is a *parallel between* your attitude and his. This line is *parallel to* (or *with*) that one.
PREFERABLE TO	A leisurely walk is *preferable to* violent exercise.
REASON WITH, ABOUT	Why not *reason with* them *about* the matter?

Different than is colloquially idiomatic when the object of the prepositional phrase is a clause:

FORMAL	This town looks *different from* what I had remembered.
COLLOQUIAL	This town looks *different than* I had remembered it.

†In many phrases, *on* and *upon* are interchangeable: *depend on* or *depend upon; enter on* or *enter upon.*

REWARD BY, WITH, FOR	They were *rewarded by* their employer *with* a raise *for* their work.
VARIANCE WITH	This conclusion is at *variance with* your facts.
VARY FROM, IN, WITH	The houses *vary from* one another *in* size. People's tastes *vary with* their personalities.
WAIT FOR, ON	They *waited for* someone to *wait on* them.
WORTHY OF	That candidate is not *worthy of* your trust.

EXERCISE 40e Provide the idiomatic prepositions needed in the following sentences.

1 The students acceded _____ the increased need to conform _____ security regulations.

2 The men were acquitted _____ the charge and absolved _____ all blame for the damage to the building.

3 Price control seems preferable _____ excessive inflation but many businesspeople differ _____ this conclusion.

4 Some critics argue that there was no necessity _____ the resumption of bombing North Vietnam, and that the United States could have entered _____ a ceasefire agreement earlier.

5 I agreed _____ his proposal, which had been adapted _____ one I had made previously.

6 Lois Bowers said she was angry _____ him because his actions did not conform _____ those of a responsible citizen.

7 The fence was built parallel _____ the street and connected _____ their neighbor's stone wall.

8 Having been freed _____ his parents' supervision, he saw no necessity _____ keep (*or* keeping) them informed of his whereabouts.

9 I am not capable _____ budget (*or* budgeting) my own income for I am unable to add 4 and 4 and get 8.

10 We entered _____ a contract to buy the house after Mr. Jones agreed _____ our request for a twenty-year mortgage.

40f Prefer concrete and specific to abstract and general words.

Abstract words name qualities, ideas, concepts: *honesty, virtue, poverty, education, wisdom, love, democracy*. **Concrete** words name things we can see, hear, feel, touch, smell. *Sweetness* is abstract; *candy, honey, molasses,* and *sugar* are concrete. To describe people as *reckless* is to describe them abstractly; to say *they ran two traffic lights in the center of* *town, and they drove eighty-five miles an hour in a restricted zone* is to pin that recklessness down, to make it concrete.

General words refer to all members of a class or group. **Specific words** refer to the individual members of a class. *Vegetation* is general; *grass, shrubs, trees, flowers,* and *weeds* are specific. *Animal* is general; *lions, elephants, monkeys, zebras, cats, dogs, mice,* and *rabbits* are specific.

The classes abstract and concrete, and general and specific overlap with each other, and both are relative. The verb *communicate* is both abstract and general. *Speak* is concrete and specific relative to *communicate,* but it is general compared to *gasp, murmur, rant, rave, shout,* and *whisper. Music* is concrete and specific relative to *sound* but general compared to *classical music,* which in turn is general compared to *Beethoven's Fifth Symphony. Dwelling* is a general word; *apartment, cabin, barracks, house, hut, mansion, shack,* and *tent* are specific. But *dwelling* is more specific than *building,* which includes not only *dwelling* but also *church, factory, garage, school,* and *store.*

All effective writing will use both abstract and concrete words, both general and specific. There are no substitutes for such abstractions as *fairness, friendship, love,* and *loyalty.* But all abstractions need to be pinned down by details, examples, and illustrations. When not so pinned down, they remain vague and always potentially confusing. We can all quickly agree that taxes and justice should be *fair.* But until each of us has narrowed down by detail and example what he or she means by *fairness* in these matters, we will not understand each other in any useful way.

Similarly, we cannot do without general terms. We would be hard-pressed to define *cat* if we could not begin by putting cats in the general class *animal.* But immediately we have done so, we must name the specific characteristics and qualities that distinguish cats from, say, armadillos or raccoons. To say *Tom enjoys reading* tells readers very little until they know whether the reading consists of *Sports Illustrated, Popular Mechanics,* and *Wonder Woman* or of Dickens and Dostoyevsky.

Effective writing constantly weaves back and forth between abstract and concrete, between general and specific. It is the writer's use of the abstract and general that guides the reader, but it is the concrete and specific that allow the reader to see, feel, understand, and believe. *This lamp supplies insufficient light* informs us; *this fifteen-watt bulb gives no more light than a firefly in a jam jar* makes us understand what the writer means by *insufficient.*

Whenever you use abstract words, give them meaning with concrete details and examples. Whenever you use general words, tie them down with specific ones. Try constantly to express yourself and your ideas in concrete terms; search for the most specific words you can find.

GENERAL	The flowers were of different colors.
SPECIFIC	The chrysanthemums were bronze, gold, and white.
GENERAL	The cost of education has increased greatly.
SPECIFIC	Tuition at many private universities has increased as much as 1,000 percent in the past three decades.
MORE SPECIFIC	Tuition at Boston University was $300 in 1947; it was $6,200 in 1982.
SPECIFIC	Mateo was a stocky man, with clear eyes and a deeply tanned face. His skill as a marksman was extraordinary, even in Corsica, where everyone is a good shot. He could kill a ram at one hundred and twenty paces, and his aim was as accurate at night as in the daytime.
MORE SPECIFIC	Picture a small, sturdy man, with jet-black, curly hair, a Roman nose, thin lips, large piercing eyes, and a weather-beaten complexion. His skill as a marksman was extraordinary, even in this country, where everyone is a good shot. For instance, Mateo would never fire on a wild ram with small shot, but at a hundred and twenty paces he would bring it down with a bullet in its head or shoulder, just as he fancied. He used his rifle at night as easily as in the daytime, and I was given the following illustration of his skill, which may seem incredible, perhaps, to those who have never travelled in Corsica. He placed a lighted candle behind a piece of transparent paper as big as a plate, and aimed at it from eighty paces away. He extinguished the candle, and a moment later, in utter darkness, fired and pierced the paper three times out of four.

PROSPER MÉRIMÉE, *Mateo Falcone*

40g Use figurative language.

Inexperienced writers are likely to think that figurative language is the monopoly of poets. In fact, it plays an important part in much prose and is one of the most effective ways of making meaning concrete. The basis of most figurative language lies in the comparison or association of two things essentially different but nonetheless alike in some underlying and surprising way. The two most common figures of speech are simile and metaphor. **Similes** make direct and explicit comparisons, usually introduced by *like, as, as if,* or *as when,* as in *Jess is as changeable as the New England weather.* **Metaphors** imply comparisons, as in *Prisoned in her laboratory, she ignored the world.*

Both simile and metaphor require that the the two things compared be from different classes so that their likeness, when pointed out, will be fresh and surprising. If they are extended, as in the second example below, they must be consistent.

The teacher shook her finger in my face as she might shake a clogged fountain pen.

Up scrambles the car, on all its four legs, like a black beetle straddling past the schoolhouse and the store down below, up the bare rock and over the changeless boulders, with a surge and a sickening lurch to the skybrim, where stands the foolish church.

D. H. LAWRENCE, *Mornings in Mexico*

Apt figures of speech can do much to make writing concrete and vivid, and by making one experience understandable in terms of another, they can often help clarify abstractions. But take care in creating figures of speech. When they strain too hard, as in the first example below, they will miss their mark and fall flat. When two figures get mixed so that they create clashing images in the eye of the reader, they will not only miss their mark, they will be ludicrous, as in the second and third examples below.

Her smile was as warm as an electric blanket.

He had to be on the rocks before he would turn over a new leaf.

Grandmother's tiny fingers seemed to stitch the material with the speed of a pneumatic drill.

EXERCISE 40g Replace the mixed or incongruous figures of speech in the following sentences with fresher, more appropriate comparisons.

1 While he was battling his way through the sea of life, fate stepped in and tripped him up.
2 John brought his big guns to the debate and stifled his opponent.
3 The odor of the flowers on the table shouted a welcome.
4 The young teacher is rapidly gaining a foothold in the eyes of the students.
5 We're skating on thin ice, and if anybody upsets the applecart, we'll all lose our bread and butter.
6 The Senate wanted to plug the loopholes in the tax bill, but they couldn't because too many important people had their fingers in the pie.
7 He worked as busily as a beaver, but one day he got as sick as a dog and decided to turn over a new leaf.
8 I'm as blind as a bat without my glasses, even in my apartment, which I know like the back of my hand.
9 She was head over heels in love with him, but she kept her feet firmly on the ground.
10 He had his back to the wall when he finally hit the nail on the head.

In composing, as a general rule, run your pen through every other word you have written; you have no idea what vigor it will give your style.

SIDNEY SMITH

41   DIRECTNESS **DIR**

The challenge to directness comes from two fronts—wordiness and vagueness. A wordy writer uses more words than are necessary to convey meaning.

WORDY   He attacks the practice of making a profitable business out of college athletics from the standpoint that it has a detrimental and harmful influence on the college students and, to a certain degree and extent, on the colleges and universities themselves.

IMPROVED   He attacks commercialization of college athletics as harmful to the students and even to the universities themselves.

A vague writer fails to convey meaning sharply and clearly.

VAGUE   The report asserts the danger from unguarded machines which may lessen the usefulness of workers in later life as well as reducing their life expectancy.

IMPROVED   The report asserts that unguarded machines may severely injure or even kill workers.

Vagueness and wordiness are sometimes indistinguishable, as in the preceding examples. The weight of unnecessary words tends to obscure meaning. But very often wordiness is just awkwardness; the meaning is clear, but the expression is clumsy.

AWKWARD   The notion that Communists are people who wear long black beards is a very common notion.

IMPROVED   The notion is common that Communists are people who wear long black beards.

41a   Eliminate words and phrases that do not add to your meaning.

Good writing says things in as few words as possible without losing clarity or completeness. It makes every word count. You can often make your writing more direct and economical by (1) cutting unnecessary words and phrases and (2) reducing clauses to phrases, and phrases to single words.

1 Cutting unnecessary words and phrases. Often as you revise your writing you will be able to strike out words that are clearly unnecessary, or gain directness by slight changes.

WORDY	When the time to go had arrived, Molly left.
REVISED	When it was time to go, Molly left.
WORDY	After the close of the war, Bob went to college.
REVISED	After the war, Bob went to college.
WORDY	She is attractive in appearance, but she is a rather selfish person.
REVISED	She is attractive, but rather selfish.

Words such as *angle, aspect, factor,* and *situation,* and phrases such as *in the case of, in the line of, in the field of* are almost never necessary. They are common obstacles to directness.

WORDY	John is majoring in the field of biology.
REVISED	John is majoring in biology.
WORDY	Another aspect of the situation that needs to be examined is the matter of advertising.
REVISED	We should also examine advertising.

Be suspicious of sentences beginning with *there are, there is, it is.* They are often roundabout statements.

WORDY	There are many reasons why we have pollution.
REVISED	Pollution has many causes.
WORDY	It is a fact that many students read very little.
REVISED	Many students read very little.

Phrases such as *I believe, I think,* and *in my opinion* are usually unnecessary.

WORDY	In my opinion, we must reduce violence on television.
REVISED	We must reduce violence on television.
WORDY	I believe that nuclear power plants are dangerous.
REVISED	Nuclear power plants are dangerous.

2 Reducing clauses to phrases and phrases to single words. Wordiness often results from using a clause when a phrase will do, or a phrase when a single word will do.

WORDY	There were instances of aggression on the country's frontier in many cases.
REVISED	There were many instances of aggression on the country's frontier.
	Aggression was frequent on the country's frontier. [In the first revision the phrase *in many instances* has been reduced to a single adjective modifying *instances*. But note that the second revision is made even more direct by eliminating the *there are* construction.]
WORDY	The shirt, which is made of wool, has worn well for eight years.
REVISED	The woolen shirt has worn well for eight years. [The clause *which was made of wool* has been reduced to the single modifier *woolen*.]
WORDY	The snow that fell yesterday is already melting.
REVISED	Yesterday's snow is already melting. [The clause *that fell yesterday* has been reduced to the single modifier *yesterday's*.]
WORDY	The conclusions that the committee of students reached are summarized in the newspaper of the college that was published today.
REVISED	The conclusions reached by the student committee are summarized in today's college newspaper. [The first *that* clause has been reduced to a participial phrase beginning with *reached*. The second *that* clause has become the single word *today's*. The phrases *of students, in the newspaper,* and *of the college* have all been reduced.]
WORDY	The football captain, who is an All-American player, played his last game today.
REVISED	The football captain, an All-American, played his last game today. [The clause has been reduced to a descriptive noun phrase—an appositive.]

EXERCISE 41a Rewrite the following sentences to reduce their wordiness.

1 He is an expert in the field of labor relations.
2 The fastest kind of automobile requires the best quality of gasoline.
3 Most Congressmen spend a majority of the hours which they have in each working day attending committtee meetings.
4 In my opinion, Dr. Mackenzie is of greater ability and of greater experience than Dr. Smith.
5 People have to be educated as to how to plan good, inexpensive menus that will meet their nutritional needs.
6 The rain, which has been coming down steadily for two weeks now, is washing away the seeds I planted in the ground at an earlier time.
7 Mrs. Armstrong, who was my history teacher, had a classroom manner that was very dynamic.

8 There are two reasons that I have for not going: the first is that I have an examination to study for; the second is that I have no money.

9 Love and understanding of them are two of the most important things young children need.

10 After several hours of shopping around to buy my niece a gift, I finally decided to give her a check to buy whatever she decided she preferred.

41b

41b Prefer one exact word to two or more approximate words.

Many groups of words are simply roundabout ways of expressing what a single exact word expresses more directly.

Wordy	*Direct*
this day and age	today
of an indefinite nature	indefinite
at this point in time	now
by means of	by
call up on the telephone	telephone
destroy by fire	burn
was made the recipient of	was given

Often we can substitute one precise word for two or more approximate synonyms.

WORDY His *temperament* and *disposition* are unpleasant.

REVISED His *disposition* is unpleasant

WORDY She described her *deeds* and *doings* as a foreign correspondent.

REVISED She described her *adventures* as a foreign correspondent.

41c

41c Avoid redundancy.

Expressions such as *visible to the eyes* and *audible to the ears* are said to be **redundant;** they say the same thing twice. Typical examples include the following:

Redundant	*Direct*
advance forward	advance
continue on	continue
refer back	refer
combine together	combine
circle around	circle
small in size	small
disappear from view	disappear
throughout the whole	throughout
basic fundamentals	fundamentals
important essentials	essentials

Sometimes sentences become wordy through the writer's careless repetition of the same meaning in slightly different words.

WORDY	As a rule, Susan usually woke up early.
REVISED	Susan usually woke up early.

WORDY	We planned to go at 3 o'clock P.M. in the afternoon.
REVISED	We planned to go at 3 P.M.

WORDY	In their opinion, they think they are right.
REVISED	They think they are right.

41d Avoid awkward repetition.

Repetition of important words is a useful way of gaining emphasis (see Section **3d**). But careless repetition is awkward and wordy.

AWKWARD	The investigation revealed that the *average teachers teaching* industrial arts in California have an *average* working and *teaching* experience of five years.
REVISED	The investigation revealed that teachers of industrial arts in California have an average of five years experience.

AWKWARD	Gas mileage in the American car is being *improved* constantly in order to *improve* efficiency.
REVISED	Gas mileage in the American car is being improved constantly to increase efficiency.

AWKWARD	The *important subject* on which I am going to speak is career opportunities, a *subject* of *great importance* to college students.
REVISED	I am going to speak on career opportunities, a subject of great importance to college students.

EXERCISE 41b–d   Eliminate redundancies and unnecessary repetition from the following sentences.

1 Because Jill believed exercise was a necessary requirement, her habitual custom was to jog every morning at 7 A.M.
2 This book is intended and designed to explain the basic fundamentals of English.
3 Barbara Linger's limousine sedan, black in color, has been seen a countless number of times parked in front of Blickel's market.
4 It was the consensus of opinion among the students that grades should be abandoned.
5 Teachers should provide several examples to illustrate the grammatical rules they are trying to teach.
6 So far as understanding his meaning is concerned, I would classify Joyce in the category of writers who are very difficult to read.

41d

7 He is an industrial engineering student studying the principles of time-and-motion study.

8 As far as I'm concerned, government should keep out of intervening in private business, in my opinion.

9 A reckless driver is no better than a murderer who goes around killing people.

10 Last night we had to circle all around the block before finding a parking space in which to park the car.

41e

41e   Prefer simple, direct expressions to needlessly complex ones.

Never be ashamed to express a simple idea in simple language. The use of complicated language is not in itself a sign of superior intelligence (see Sections **42d** and **42e**).

NEEDLESSLY COMPLEX	Not a year passes without some evidence of the fundamental truth of the statement that the procedures and techniques of education are more complicated and complex than they were two decades ago.
DIRECT	Each year shows that methods of education are more complex than they were twenty years ago.

If alternative forms of the same word exist, prefer the shorter. Choose *truth* and *virtue* rather than *truthfulness* and *virtuousness*. Choose *preventive* rather than *preventative*.

To prefer simplicity does not mean to make *all* writing simple. Naturally, highly complex or technical subjects call at times for complex and technical language.

One of the simplest ways of evolving a favorable environment concurrently with the development of the individual organism, is that the influence of each organism on the environment should be favorable to the *endurance* of other organisms of the same type. Further, if the organism also favors *development* of other organisms of the same type, you have then obtained a mechanism of evolution adapted to produce the observed state of large multitudes of analogous entities, with high powers of endurance. For the environment automatically develops with the species, and the species with the environment.

A. N. WHITEHEAD, Science and the Modern World [his italics]

EXERCISE 41e   Find a paragraph or two of needlessly complex writing in one of your textbooks. Explain in one or two paragraphs how you think the writing might be made more direct.

41f   Use euphemisms sparingly.

Euphemisms substitute a more pleasant word or phrase for one that is, for any reason, objectionable. They express unpleasant things in less harsh and direct ways: *pass away* for *die, perspire* for *sweat, mortal remains* for *corpse, intoxicated* for *drunk.* Most common euphemisms are associated with the basic facts of existence—birth, age, death, sex, the bodily functions—and often seem necessary for politeness or tact. We are more comfortable describing a good friend as one who *is stout* and *likes to drink* than as a *fat drunk.* And in such contexts these terms are harmless.

But the use of euphemisms to distract us from the realities of work, unemployment, poverty, and war is at best misleading and at worst dishonest and dangerous. Today we take for granted such terms as "sanitation engineer" (plumber), "funeral director" (undertaker), and "maintenance people" (janitors). Such terms perhaps help protect the feelings of individuals and give them status. But the individuals themselves still have to sweat pipes, prepare bodies for burial, and sweep floors—in short, do work that is hard or unpleasant. And if the terms make us forget that reality, they are misleading. It is a short step further to language consciously intended to deceive. Such language gives us "protective reaction" (bombing), "strategic withdrawal" (retreat), "visual surveillance" (spying), and "inoperative statements" (lies). Such phrases are downright dishonest. They are created for the sole purpose of distracting us from realities that we need to know about. Slums and ghettos are no less slums and ghettos because we call them the "inner city." And if you're fired, you're out of a job even if you've been "terminated" or "deselected."

Keep your own writing honest, and be alert to dishonesty in the writing of others. Use euphemism when tact and genuine respect for the feelings of your audience warrant it. Do not use it to deceive.

EXERCISE 41a–f   Each of the sentences below violates a principal of directness. Find and then correct the error.

1. We of the United States cannot expect to spread peace throughout other nations and countries until we can teach and educate our own people to respect each other as equal individuals.
2. Their capacity for hard work makes them capable of working long hours each day.
3. The integration of public schools is a major step forward toward complete equality of all groups.
4. During the entirety of my whole college career, I continually went on thinking about my plan to work my way around the world.

5 It has just been in the past couple of years that black Americans have begun to make clear that they wish to develop their own racial identity by themselves without outside interference.

6 The reason for Nixon's choice of Agnew as a running mate for vice-president stemmed from the fact that he wanted a Southern candidate as nominee.

7 The first settlers in the West were prospectors who explored the new land as they prospected for gold.

8 The actress acted very badly, but the play was played through to the very end and conclusion.

9 He was the handsomest-looking Irish wolfhound I had ever seen before in my life.

10 The increasing filth in our waterways through pollution has bothered and troubled scientists for a period of one and a half decades.

A speech is composed of three things: the speaker, the subject on which he speaks, and the audience he is addressing.

ARISTOTLE, *Rhetoric*

42 APPROPRIATENESS **APPR**

Because the English language is constantly growing, it continues to be a useful vehicle for conveying thought accurately and effectively. Fortunately, words appear, disappear, or shift their meanings slowly so that there is always available a large core of stable, generally used words. Beyond this core are wide ranges of usage: slang, regional expressions, profanity, clichés, jargon, stilted diction. Words from these categories must be used sparingly if at all.

There are no words in the English language that cannot be used somewhere at some time. But when a piece of writing is overloaded with slang or clichés, the question of *appropriateness* arises. You may consider yourself such a casual, easy-going person that you think casual, easy-going language is appropriate to you. It may be—in a letter to close friends about an exciting summer holiday. Even in letter-writing, however, you must also consider your audience and your subject: that letter to friends would necessarily be different if you were expressing your sympathy for an illness in their family. But when you sit down to write papers for your courses, keep your eye on that core of stable, generally used and generally understood words. If you do depart from those words, have a good reason.

42a Ordinarily, avoid slang.

Slang consists of the rapidly changing words and phrases in popular speech that people invent to give language novelty and vigor. Slang often is created by the same processes we use to create most new words: by combining two words (*ferretface, blockhead*); by shortening words (*pro, prof, vet*); by borrowing from other languages (*kaput, spiel*); and by generalizing a proper name (*the real McCoy*). Often slang simply extends the meaning of phrases borrowed from other activities (*lower the boom* from sailing; *tune in, tune out* from radio; *cash in your chips* from poker). A great deal of slang gives a new range of meaning to existing words (*tough, cool, bread, heavy, crash, turned on, joint*).

Slang is a part of the current language. It is spontaneous and direct and helps give color and liveliness to the language. It often contributes directly to the growth of the language as slang terms move gradually into general use. Words like *rascal* and *sham* were originally slang terms; shortened forms such as *A-bomb, ad, gym,* and *phone* are now appropriate to most informal writing. In informal writing, a carefully chosen slang word can be effective:

Has Harold Wilson *Lost His Cool?*   *New York Times* headline

Heaven knows there are large areas where a shrewd eye for the *quick buck* is dominant.   FREDERICK LEWIS ALLEN, *The Big Change*

But slang has serious limitations in writing, and even much conversation. It is imprecise, is often understandable only to a narrow social or age group, and usually changes very rapidly. You may be familiar with the latest slang, but who knows *lollapalooza, balloon juice,* or *twerp?* The fact that *hep* became *hip* within a few years suggests how shortlived slang can be.

Enjoy slang for the life it sometimes gives to speech. But even in conversation, remember that slang expressions may not be understood, that at best a little of it goes a long way, and that if you rely on *hot, cool, lousy,* and *tough* to describe all objects, events, and ideas, you don't communicate much. In writing, use slang only when it serves some special purpose. Except in carefully controlled contexts, slang and standard language make an inappropriate mixture.

Persuading Mrs. McGinnis to be seated, the chairman of the Committee on Indian Affairs asked her politely not to foul up the state's plans to hit pay dirt on Ishimago's claim.

EXERCISE 42a(1)   Almost everyone has favorite slang terms. Make a list of your own slang expressions and compare the list with those of your classmates to see how "original" your own slang is.

EXERCISE 42a(2)   Can you think of a situation or general context in which the following sentences might be appropriate? Explain.

1 We were invited to a party last night but we couldn't make the scene.
2 The trouble was that my boyfriend was all uptight about his car and I got hung up on a TV show I was watching.

42a

3 I finally told him that he should do his thing and I'd do mine.
4 Anyway, I never got a chance to show off my crazy new hairdo and my really cool fur coat.
5 My boyfriend finally showed up when I was all decked out and he said I was real foxy.
6 I asked him how he was making out with the car and he told me everything was coming up roses.
7 So we decided to blast off and go to a movie.
8 The movie was like dullsville so my boyfriend asked if I wanted to go and tie one on.

42b

42b   Avoid regional and nonstandard language.

Regional words (sometimes called **provincialisms** or **localisms**) are words whose use is generally restricted to a particular geographical area. Examples are *tote* for *carry, poke* for *bag, spider* for *frying pan, gumshoes* for *overshoes, draw* for *small valley,* and *woodpussy* for *skunk.* **Nonstandard** words and expressions generally occur only in the speech of uneducated speakers. Examples are *ain't, could of, he done,* and double negatives such as *can't never, scarcely none,* and *don't have no.* Dictionaries label such words *nonstandard* or *illiterate.*

REGIONAL	She *redded up* the house for our *kinfolk.*
GENERAL	She cleaned the house for our relatives.
NONSTANDARD	He *didn't ought to have* spent the money.
STANDARD	He shouldn't have spent the money.
NONSTANDARD	I wish Irving *had of drove more careful.*
STANDARD	I wish Irving had driven more carefully.

EXERCISE 42b(1)   List at least five examples of regionalisms (as *The cat wants in*) and describe circumstances under which they could be used appropriately.

EXERCISE 42b(2)   If you are a native of the region in which your college is located, ask a classmate from another region to give you a list of ten words or expressions that strike him or her as being regionalisms in your speech. If you come from another region yourself, make up your own list of regionalisms of the college area and compare it with a classmate's.

42c

42c   Avoid trite expressions.

A trite expression, sometimes called a **cliché,** or a **stereotyped** or **hackneyed phrase,** is an expression that has been worn out by constant use, as *burning the midnight oil, Father Time, raving beauties, man about town.* Words in themselves are never trite—they are only used tritely. We cannot avoid trite expressions entirely, for they sometimes describe a situation accurately. But writers who burden their language with clichés run the risk of being regarded as trite thinkers. What would be your estimate of the person who wrote this?

> A college education develops a *well-rounded personality* and gives the student an appreciation of *the finer things of life.*

Effectively used, triteness can be humorous. The string of trite expressions in the example below explodes into absurdity when the writer transposes the words in the two clichés in the last clause.

> A pair of pigeons were cooing gently directly beneath my window; two squirrels plighted their troth in a branch overhead; at the corner a handsome member of New York's finest twirled his night stick and cast roguish glances at the saucy-eyed flower vendor. The scene could have been staged only by a Lubitsch; in fact Lubitsch himself was seated on a bench across the street, smoking a cucumber and looking as cool as a cigar. — S. J. PERELMAN, *Keep It Crisp*

Watch for trite words and phrases in your own writing, and replace them with new, original ways of expressing yourself. As you proofread your manuscripts, be as sensitive to clichés as you are to misspellings.

EXERCISE 42c Copy the following passage. Circle all clichés and all expressions that are longer or more involved than they need be. Suggest more appropriate wordings for each.

> The American Way is the only feasible route for educational personnel to tread in our educational institutions of learning. Despite its humble origins, this child of adversity, born in a log cabin, has beyond a shadow of a doubt reached the summits in this fair country of ours.
>
> There is too much of a tendency to view this great institution with alarm. But on the other hand people who live in glass houses, which is the type most inclined to cast aspersions and generally be wet blankets, are usually the ones by whom the criticisms are made.
>
> Now I'm just an ordinary schoolteacher, and don't have any complicated ideas on how our schools should be run, but I know that Abe Lincoln, if he were alive, would disapprove of the newfangled techniques that are making a shambles of our educational system.
>
> Foreigners are at the bottom of the attack on our American heritage and the American Way in education. These notorious radicals have wreaked havoc with our boys and girls.

42d Avoid jargon in writing for a general audience.

42d

The term **jargon** has several meanings. In a famous essay, "On Jargon," Sir Arthur Quiller-Couch defined the term as vague and "woolly" speech or writing that consists of abstract words, elegant variation, and "circumlocution rather than short straight speech." Linguists often define jargon as hybrid speech or dialect formed by a mixture of languages. An example would be the English-Chinese jargon known as pidgin English.

To most people, however, jargon is the technical or specialized vocabulary of a particular trade or profession—for example, engineering jargon or educational jargon. Members of the profession, of course, can use their jargon when they are communicating with one another, for it is their language, so to speak. But the use of technical jargon is inappropriate when you are writing for a general audience.

Unfortunately, jargon impresses a great many people simply because it sounds involved and learned. We are all reluctant to admit that we do not understand what we are reading. What, for example, can you make of the following passage?

THE TURBO-ENCABULATOR IN INDUSTRY

. . . Work has been proceeding in order to bring to perfection the crudely conceived idea of a machine that would not only supply inverse reactive current for use in unilateral phase detractors, but would also be capable of automatically synchronizing cardinal grammeters. Such a machine is the Turbo-Encabulator. . . . The original machine had a base plate of prefabulated amulite surmounted by a malleable logarithmic casing in such a way that the two spurving bearings were in a direct line with the pentametric fan. . . . The main winding was of the normal lotus-o-delta type placed in a panendermic semiboloid slot in the stator, every seventh conductor being connected by a non-reversible tremie pipe to the differential girdlespring on the "up" end of the grammeters. . . .

> Reprinted by permission of the publishers,
> Arthur D. Little, Inc., Cambridge, Mass.

This new mechanical marvel was a joke, the linquistic creation of a research engineer who was tired of reading jargon.

EXERCISE 42d Make a list of twenty words, terms, or phrases that constitute the jargon in a field that you know. Define these terms in a way that a general reader could understand; then justify the use of the terms among the people in your field.

42e Avoid artificial diction and "fine writing."

Artificiality is not inherent in words themselves but in the use that we make of them. State simple facts and assertions simply and directly, or you run the risk of making your writing sound pompous and self-conscious, as in the following examples.

| ARTIFICIAL | The edifice was consumed by fire. |
| NATURAL | The house burned down. |

| ARTIFICIAL | We were unable to commence our journey to your place of residence because of inclement weather conditions. |
| NATURAL | We could not come because it was snowing. |

Many inexperienced writers believe, mistakenly, that an artificial diction makes for "good writing." They shift gears when they go from speaking to writing. They try to make their writing sound like the speech of Hollywood's version of a college professor, and once again the results sound stilted.

| ARTIFICIAL | The athletic contest commenced at the stipulated time. |
| NATURAL | The game began on time. |

| ARTIFICIAL | I informed him that his advice was unsolicited. |
| NATURAL | I told him to mind his own business. |

Your writing may become artificial simply because you are trying too hard to write effectively, because you have grown more concerned with *how* you write than with *what* you write. Writing marked by a continuously artificial diction is called "fine writing."

| FINE WRITING | Whenever the press of daily events and duties relaxes its iron grip on me, whenever the turmoil of my private world subsides and leaves me in quiet and solitide, then it is that I feel my crying responsibility as one of God's creatures and recognize the need to speak out loudly and boldly against the greed and intolerance that carry humanity into the terrible destruction of armed conflict. |
| NATURAL | I am a crusader for international peace. |

EXERCISE 42e Find an example of "fine writing" in a newspaper or magazine and explain in a short paper why you think it ineffective.

EXERCISE 42a–e First assume a specific audience (e.g., classmates, group of businesspeople, parents, etc.); then comment on the appropriateness of the language in the following selection in terms of that audience.

Like many other just plain "guys," I just graduated from high school. Being like most of these other guys, I naturally didn't really accomplish much during my previous school years. Yes, I got fair grades, met lots of swell kids, played football. I guess I'm just one of those guys who had the run of the school and never bothered to study.

No, I'm not bragging. I'm just telling you why high school was never like college.

A lot of people graduate from high school every year. A good percentage go to college and the rest go out and get a job. Four years later, the college student graduates. Does that mean he's going to get a better job than the fellow who went from high school directly to a job?

No. It doesn't mean a thing unless the guy in college really studied and hit the books. What I'm trying to bring out is that a person who goes to college and doesn't study is no better off than a guy who goes out and gets a job immediately after high school graduation.

So college for me is the "big jump." I fooled around in high school, and if I don't get right down and study now, I might as well quit school and start that $150.00 a week job.

Now, I don't have anything against a $150.00 a week job. It's just that twenty years from now, I'd probably still be there getting the same $150.00. This is it, so I guess it's time for me to bear down and study hard. I think this will be the "big jump."

REVIEW EXERCISE ON WORDS (Sections 40–42) Revise each of the following sentences according to what you have learned in the sections on exactness, directness, and appropriateness.

1 He was trying to keep abreast of company development when the tide turned against him and his reputation ebbed.

2 College students have to invest most of their time with studying if they are going to be successful students.

3 C. B. Brown must have really been on the stick when he polished off six Gothic novels in less than four years.

4 Many neophyte pedagogues in the area of bilingual education are substandard in instructional methodology of teaching.

5 The authorship of the novel has not been authenticated, but the evidence of the extant material that survives points to one Joshua Fiddings.

6 The campus police opinionated that the burglary attempters had entranced through the caf.

7 Although my little subcompact is cute as a button, my face becomes red as a beet when someone leaves me in the dust at a stoplight.

8 Mr. Smith's frequent disregard of his wife's bridge bids was the bane of her existence.

9 It is our intention to supply all your wants, and we intend to make you so comfortable here that you will not be afraid to tell us what you want in the way of comforts.

10 Professor Caitlin's life was poor in terms of meager remunerative values, but more students in the college remember her than any other teacher.

11 Coaches are paid for the type of teams they produce or for the number of winning games per season.

12 The house was square in shape and blue in color, and he decided in his mind that price-wise it was a real good buy.

13 I thought I was doing the best thing when I signed up for the army.

14 I was filled with anger and rage when my precious and expensive stereo equipment was destroyed and ruined by the vandals.

15 By reading *Yachting* I am able to keep abreast with the tide of affairs in the sailing world.

"Awfully nice" is an expression than which few could be sillier: but to have succeeded in going through life without saying it a certain number of times is as bad as to have no redeeming vice.

H. W. FOWLER

43 GLOSSARY OF USAGE **GLOS**

Choosing the right word—or not choosing the wrong one—is one of the most difficult problems for writers. General guidelines—such as, be idiomatic, confine colloquial words to speech and very informal writing, avoid nonstandard words—can be helpful, but only if you know the idiom and know what is colloquial and nonstandard. And that knowledge often comes only slowly and with much reading and experience. This glossary is intended to help you with some of the most commonly troublesome words and phrases. But it is necessarily brief; you should keep a good college dictionary at hand and consult it both for words not listed here and for additional information about words that are listed.

For information about labels used in dictionaries, see pp. 345–346. The following two labels are used in this glossary:

COLLOQUIAL   Commonly used in speech but inappropriate in all but the most informal writing

NONSTANDARD   Generally agreed not to be standard English

In addition to specifically labeled words, some words and phrases are included here because, although widely used, they are wordy or redundant (e.g., *but that, inside of, in the case of*); vague and overused (e.g., *level, overall*); or objected to by many readers (e.g., *center around, hopefully* meaning *it is hoped, -wise* as a suffix). A few word pairs often confused (e.g., *imply, infer*) are included, but Section **40b** has a more complete list of such pairs.

a, an *A* is used before words beginning with a consonant sound, even when the sound is spelled with a vowel (*a dog, a European, a unicorn, a habit*). *An* is used before words beginning with a vowel sound or a silent *h* (*an apple, an Indian, an hour, an uproar*).

above, below *Above* and *below* are standard ways of referring to material preceding or following a particular passage in writing *(the paragraph above, the statistics below)*. Some readers object to the use as stilted and overly formal.

accept, except To *accept* is to receive. To *except* is to exclude. As a preposition *except* means "with the exclusion of." (He *accepted the list from the chairman. The list excepted George from the slate of candidates. He asked why it included all except George.*)

actually Like *really*, frequently overworked as an intensifier.

ad A shortened form of *advertisement*, inappropriate in formal writing. Other clipped forms include *auto, exam, math, phone, photo*.

affect, effect As verbs, to *affect* is to influence, to *effect* is to bring about. *Effect* is more commonly used as a noun meaning "result." *(Recent tax reforms affect everyone. They are intended to effect a fairer distribution of taxes. The effects have yet to be felt.)*

aggravate To *aggravate* is to intensify, to make worse *(The hot sun aggravated his sunburn)*. Colloquially it is often used to mean "to annoy, provoke" *(My teasing aggravated him)*.

agree to, agree with To *agree to* is to consent; to *agree with* means "to concur" *(I agree with Gail's opinion, and will therefore agree to the contract)*.

ain't A contraction of *am not*, extended to *is not, are not, has not, have not*. Though often used in speech, it is strongly disapproved by the majority of speakers and writers.

a lot, alot The correct spelling is *a lot*.

all, all of Constructions with *all of* followed by a noun can frequently be made more concise by omitting the *of*; usually the *of* is retained before a pronoun or a proper noun; *all of Illinois*, but *all the money, all this confusion*.

allude, refer To *allude to* is to refer to indirectly; to *refer to* is to direct attention to *(When he spoke of family difficulties, we knew he was alluding to his wife's illness even though he did not refer directly to that)*.

allusion, illusion An *allusion* is an indirect reference; an *illusion* is a false impression *(He was making an allusion to magicians when he spoke of people who were apt at creating illusions)*.

already, all ready *Already* is an adverb meaning "previously" *(We had already left)* or "even now" *(We are already late)*. In the phrase *all ready, all* modifies *ready;* the phrase means "completely prepared" *(We were all ready by eight o'clock)*.

alright, all right   *All right* remains the only established spelling. *Alright* is labeled nonstandard in both the *New World* and *Random House* dictionaries, although *Webster's* lists it without a usage label.

also, likewise   Not acceptable substitutes for *and* (*We packed our clothes, our food, and* [not *also* or *likewise*] *our books*).

altogether, all together   *Altogether* means "wholly, completely"; *all together* means "in a group," "everyone assembled" (*She was altogether pleased with her new piano, which she played when we were all together for our reunion*).

alumnus, alumna   An *alumnus* (plural *alumni*) is a male graduate. An *alumna* (plural *alumnae*) is a female graduate. *Alumni* is now usually used for groups including both men and women.

among, between   *Among* implies more than two persons or things; *between* implies only two. To express a reciprocal relationship, or the relationship of one thing to several other things, however, *between* is commonly used for more than two (*She divided the toys among the three children. Jerry could choose between pie and cake for dessert. An agreement was reached between the four companies. The surveyors drove a stake at a point between three trees.*)

amount, number   *Amount* refers to quantity or mass; *number* refers to countable objects (*Large numbers of guests require a great amount of food*).

an   See *a, an*.

and etc.   *Etc.* (Latin *et cetera*) means "and so forth." The redundant *and etc.* means literally "and and so forth." See **17a4.**

and/or   A legalism to which some readers object.

and which, and who   Use only when *which* or *who* is introducing a clause that coordinates with an earlier clause introduced by *which* or *who* (*John is a man who has opinions and who often expresses them*).

ante-, anti-   *Ante-* means "before," as in *antedate*. *Anti-* means "against," as in *anti-American*. The hyphen is used after *anti-* before capital letters, and before *i*, as in *anti-intellectual*.

any more, anymore   Either spelling is correct. Meaning *now* or *nowadays*, the expression is used only in negative contexts (*He doesn't live here any more*). Used in affirmative contexts the expression is regional and should be avoided in writing (*What's the matter with you anymore?*).

anyone, everyone, someone   Not the same as *any one, every one, some one*. *Anyone* means "any person" (*He will talk to anyone who visits him*). *Any one* means "any single person or thing" (*He will talk to any one of his neighbors at a time, but not more than one at a time*).

anyplace   Colloquial for *any place*.

43

anyway, any way, anyways *Anyway* means "nevertheless, no matter what else may be true" *(They're going to leave school anyway, no matter what we say).* Do not confuse it with *any way (I do not see any way to stop them). Anyways* is a colloquial form of *anyway.*

anywheres Colloquial for *anywhere.*

apt See *liable.*

around Colloquial as used in *stay around* meaning "stay nearby" and in *come around to see me.* As a synonym for the preposition *about, around* is informal and objected to by some in writing; write *about one hundred* rather than *around one hundred.*

as In introducing adverbial clauses, *as* may mean either "when" or "because." Thus it is best avoided if there is any possibility of confusion. As a substitute for *that* or *whether (He didn't know as he could go)* or for *who (Those as want them can have them), as* is nonstandard. For confusion between *as* and *like*, see *like, as, as if.*

as . . . as, so . . . as In negative comparisons, some authorities prefer *not so . . . as* to *not as . . . as,* but both are generally considered acceptable.

as, like See *like, as.*

as to A wordy substitute for *about (He questioned me about* [not *as to*] *my plans).* At the beginning of sentences, *as to* is standard for emphasizing *(As to writing, the more he worked, the less successful he was).*

at Wordy in such constructions as *"Where are you eating at?"* and *"Where is he at now?"*

athletics Plural in form, but often treated as singular in number. See **8a10.**

awful, awfully In formal English *awful* means "inspiring awe" or "causing fear." Colloquially it is used to mean "very bad" or "unpleasant" *(an awful joke, an awful examination). Awfully* is colloquial as an intensifier *(awfully hard, awfully pretty).*

bad, badly Often confused. *Bad* is an adjective and should be used only to modify nouns and as a predicate adjective after linking verbs *(She had a bad cold and felt bad* [not *badly*]). *Badly* is an adverb *(She hurt her leg badly* [not *bad*]).

being that, being as (how) Nonstandard substitutions for the appropriate subordinating conjunctions *as, because, since.*

below See *above, below.*

beside, besides *Beside* is a preposition meaning "by the side of." *Besides* is an adverb or a preposition meaning "moreover" or "in addition to." *(He sat beside her. Besides, he had to wait for John.)*

better See *had better*.

between, among See *among, between*.

blame for, blame on Both are standard idioms, although some writers prefer the first. *(They blamed him for it. They blamed it on him.)*

bunch Colloquial when used to mean a group of people or things *(a bunch of dishes, a bunch of money)*. Used in writing to refer only to things growing or fastened together *(a bunch of bananas, a bunch of celery)*.

bursted, bust, busted The principal parts of the verb are *burst, burst, burst*. *Bursted* is an old form of the past and past participle, which is no longer considered good usage. *Bust* and *busted* are nonstandard.

but, hardly, scarcely All are negative and should not be used with other negatives. *(He had only* [not *didn't have but*] *one hour. He had scarcely* [not *hadn't scarcely*] *finished. He could hardly* [not *couldn't hardly*] *see.)*

but however, but yet Redundant. Use *but, however,* or *yet* but not two together (I was ill, *but* [not *but yet*] I attended).

but that, but what Wordy equivalents of *that* as a conjunction or relative pronoun *(I don't doubt that* [not *but that* or *but what*] *you are right).*

calculate, figure, reckon Colloquial when used to mean "to think" or "to expect."

can, may Informally *can* is used to indicate both ability *(I can drive a car)* and permission *(Can I use the car?)*. In formal English, *may* is reserved by some for permission *(May I use the car?)*. *May* is also used to indicate possibility *(I can go to the movies, but I may not)*.

case, in the case of Wordy and usually unnecessary. See **41al.**

censor, censure To *censor* means "to examine in order to delete or suppress objectionable material." *Censure* means "to reprimand or condemn."

center around, center about Common expressions, but objected to by many as illogical. Prefer *center on (The debate centered on* [not *centered around* or *centered about*] *the rights of students).*

character Wordy. *He had an illness of a serious character* means *He had a serious illness.*

complected   A colloquial or dialect equivalent of *complexioned* as in *light-complected*. Prefer *light-* or *dark-complexioned* in writing.

complete   See *unique*.

consensus of opinion   Redundant; omit *of opinion*. *Consensus* means "a general harmony of opinion."

considerable   Standard as an adjective *(considerable success, a considerable crowd)*. Colloquial as a noun *(They lost considerable in the flood)*. Nonstandard as an adverb *(They were considerable hurt in the accident)*.

contact   Overused as a vague verb meaning "to meet, to talk with, write," etc. Prefer a more specific word such as *interview, consult, write to, telephone*.

continual, continuous   *Continual* means "frequently repeated" *(He was distracted by continual telephone calls)*. *Continuous* means "without interruption" *(We heard the continuous sound of the waves)*.

continue on   Redundant; omit *on*.

convince, persuade   Widely used interchangeably, but many careful writers *convince* people that something is so, but *persuade* them to do something. The distinction seems worth preserving.

could of   Nonstandard for *could have*.

couple   Colloquial when used to mean "a few" or "several." When used before a plural noun, it is nonstandard unless followed by *of (We had a couple of* [not *couple*] *minutes)*.

credible, creditable, credulous   Sometimes confused. *Credible* means "believable" *(Their story seemed credible to the jury)*. *Creditable* means "praiseworthy" *(You gave a creditable violin recital)*. *Credulous* means "inclined to believe on slight evidence" *(The credulous child really believed the moon was made of cheese)*.

criteria   See *data*.

cute, great, lovely, wonderful   Overworked as vague words of approval. Find a more specific word *(It was an attractive, spacious, compact, convenient, or comfortable house)*.

data, criteria, phenomena   Historically *data* is a plural form, but the singular *datum* is now rare. *Data* is often treated as singular, but careful writing still often treats it as plural *(These data* [not *this*] *are* [not *is*] *the most recent)*. *Criteria* and *phenomena* are plurals of the same kind for the singular forms *criterion* and *phenomenon*.

deal   Colloquial in the sense of *bargain* or *transaction (the best deal in town);* of *secret arrangement (I made a deal with the gangsters);* and of *treatment (I had a rough deal from the Dean).* Currently overworked as a slang term referring to any kind of arrangement or situation.

definite, definitely   Colloquial as vague intensifiers *(That suit is a definite bargain; it is definitely handsome).* Prefer a more specific word.

differ from, differ with   To *differ from* means "to be unlike." To *differ with* means "to disagree."

different from, different than   *From* is idiomatic when a preposition is required; *than* introduces a clause. See **40e.**

disinterested, uninterested   Now frequently used interchangeably to mean "having no interest." The distinction between the two, however, is real and valuable. *Uninterested* means "without interest"; *disinterested* means "impartial" *(Good judges are disinterested but not uninterested).*

don't   A contraction for *do not,* but not for *does not (She doesn't* [not *don't*] *want a new dress).*

doubt but what   See *but that.*

due to   Some writers object to *due to* as a preposition meaning "because of" or "owing to" *(The festival was postponed because of* [or *owing to,* not *due to*] *rain).* Acceptable when used as an adjective *(My failure was due to laziness).*

due to the fact that   Wordy for *because.*

each and every   Unnecessarily wordy.

effect   See *affect, effect.*

enthuse   Colloquial for *show enthusiasm* or *make enthusiastic.*

equally as good   The *as* is unnecessary. *Equally good* is more precise.

etc.   See *and etc.* and **17a4.**

everyone, every one   See *anyone.*

everywheres   Nonstandard for *everywhere.*

every which way   Colloquial for *in every direction, in great disorder.*

except   See *accept, except.*

expect   Colloquial when used to mean "suppose" or "believe" *(I suppose* [not *expect*] *I should do the dishes now).*

43

extra   Colloquial when used as an adverb meaning *especially* or *particularly* (*It was a particularly* [not *extra*] *hot summer*).

fact, the fact that   Usually wordy for *that* (*I was unaware that* [not *of the fact that*] *they had left*).

factor   Wordy and overworked. See **41a1.**

farther, further   Some writers prefer to use *farther* to refer to distance and restrict *further* to mean "in addition" (*It was two miles farther to go the way you wished, but I wanted no further trouble*). Dictionaries recognize the forms as interchangeable.

fewer, less   *Fewer* refers to numbers, *less* to amounts, degree, or value (*We sold fewer tickets than last year, but our expenses were less*).

field   Wordy and overworked. Say, for example, *in atomic energy* not *in the field of atomic energy. See* **41a1.**

figure   See *calculate.*

fine   As an adjective to express approval (*a fine person*) *fine* is vague and overused. As an adverb meaning "well" (*works fine*) *fine* is colloquial.

flunk   Colloquial for *fail.*

folks   Colloquial when used to mean *relatives,* and in the phrase *just folks,* meaning "unassuming, not snobbish." Standard in the sense of people in general, or of a specific group (*folks differ, young folks*).

former, latter   *Former* refers to the first-named of two; *latter* refers to the last-named of two. *First* and *last* are used to refer to one of a group of more than two.

function   As a noun meaning "event" or "occasion," *function* is appropriate only when the event is formal (*a presidential function*). As a verb meaning "work," "operate," *function* is currently overused and jargonish (*I work* [not *function*] *best after I've had a cup of coffee*).

further   See *farther, further.*

get   A standard verb, but used colloquially in many idioms inappropriate in most writing. (*Get wise to yourself. That whistling gets me. You can't get away with it.*)

good, well   *Good* is colloquial as an adverb (*The motor runs well* [not *good*]). *You look good* means "'You look attractive, well dressed," or the like. *You look well* means "You look healthy."

good and   Colloquial as a synonym for *very* (*good and hot, good and angry*).

great   See *cute.*

graduate   Either I *graduated from* college or I *was graduated from* college is acceptable, but I *graduated college* is nonstandard.

had better, had best, better   Standard idioms for *ought* and *should,* which are more formal *(You had better* [or *had best] plan carefully).* More formally: *You ought to* [or *should] plan carefully). Better* alone *(You better plan carefully)* is colloquial.

had ought, hadn't ought   Nonstandard for *ought* and *ought not.*

hang, hung   The principal parts of the verb are *hang, hung, hung,* but when referring to death by hanging, formal English uses *hang, hanged, hanged (We hung the pictures. The prisoners hanged themselves.)*

hardly   See *but.*

have, of   See *of, have*

he or she   See **8b1.**

himself   See *myself.*

hisself   Nonstandard for *himself.*

hopefully   *Hopefully* means "in a hopeful manner" *(They waited hopefully for money).* It is now widely used in the sense of "it is hoped" *(Hopefully, you can send me money).* Some readers object to this use.

hung   See *hang, hung.*

idea   Often used vaguely for *intention, plan, purpose,* and other more exact words. Prefer a more exact choice. *(My intention* [not *idea] is to become an engineer. The theme* [not *idea] of the movie is that justice is colorblind.)*

ignorant, stupid   The distinction is important. An *ignorant* child is one who has been taught very little; a *stupid* child is one who is unable to learn.

illusion   See *allusion, illusion.*

imply, infer   To *imply* means to suggest without stating; to *infer* means to draw a conclusion. Speakers *imply;* listeners *infer (They implied that I was ungrateful; I inferred that they didn't like me).*

in, into   *In* indicates "inside, enclosed, within." *Into* is more exact when the meaning is "toward, from the outside in," although *in* is common in both meanings. *(I left the book in the room, and went back into the room to get it.)*

in back of, in behind, in between   Wordy for *back of, behind, between.*

individual, party, person   *Individual* refers to one particular person. *Person* refers to any human being as a distinct personality. *Party* refers to a group of people, except in legal language (*Jefferson defended the rights of the individual. Lee is a person* [not *an individual*] *of strong character. You are the person* [not *party*] *I am looking for.*)

infer   See *imply, infer*.

ingenious, ingenuous   *Ingenious* means "clever"; *ingenuous* means "naive" (*Inventors are usually ingenious, but some are too ingenuous to know when they have been cheated*).

in regards to   Nonstandard for *as regards* or *in regard to*.

inside of, outside of   The *of* is unnecessary (*He stayed inside* [not *inside of*] *the house*).

in the case of, in the line of   See *case*.

into   See *in, into*.

irregardless   Nonstandard for *regardless*.

is when, is where, is because   Faulty predications in such sentences as: *A first down is when the football is advanced ten yards in four plays or fewer. A garage is where. . . . The reason is because. . . .* See **14a.**

its, it's   The possessive pronoun has no apostrophe. *It's* is a contraction of *it is*.

-ize   The suffix *-ize* is one of several used to form verbs from nouns and adjectives (*hospitalize, criticize, sterilize*). Writers in government, business, and other institutions have often used it excessively and unnecessarily in such coinages as *finalize, concretize, permanize*. Such coinages are widely objected to; it is best to limit your use of *-ize* words to those that are well established, and resist the temptation to coin new ones.

kind, sort   These are frequently treated as plural in such constructions as *these kind of books* and *those sort of dogs*. Preferred usage in both speech and writing requires singular or plural throughout the construction, as in *this kind of book* or *these kinds of books*.

kind of, sort of   Colloquial when used to mean *somewhat, rather* (*I was rather* [not *kind of*] *pleased*).

kind of a, sort of a   Omit the *a*.

latter   See *former, latter*.

lay, lie   To *lay* means "to place, put down" (*Lay the book on the table*). To *lie* means "to recline" (*The dog lies on the floor*). See **4c.**

learn, teach   To *learn* means "to gain knowledge"; to *teach* means "to give knowledge" (*We learn from experience; experience teaches us much*).

leave, let   To *leave* is to depart; to *let* is to permit or allow *(I must leave now. Will you let me go?)*.

less   See *fewer, less*.

let   See *leave, let*.

level   Overworked and unnecessary in such phrases as *at the retail level, at the particular level*. Use only when the idea of rank or degree is clearly meant *(We speak of our education as divided into three levels: elementary, secondary, and college)*.

liable, apt, likely   Often used interchangeably. But careful writing reserves *liable* for "legally responsible," or "subject to," *likely* for "probably," and *apt* for "having an aptitude for" *(I am likely to drive carefully, for I am not an apt driver, and I know I am liable for any damages)*.

lie, lay   See *lay, lie*, and see **4d**.

like, as, as if   *Like* is a preposition; *as* and *as if* are conjunctions. Though *like* is often used as a conjunction in speech, writing preserves the distinction *(He looks as if* [not *like*] *he were tired)*. Note that *as if* is followed by the subjunctive *were*.

likely   See *liable*.

loose, lose   Loose means "to free." *Lose* means "to be deprived of." *(He will lose the dog if he looses him from his leash.)*

lots, lots of, a lot of   Colloquial for *much, many*, or *a great deal (I had a great deal of* [not *lots of*] *money and bought many* [not *lots of* or *a lot of*] *cars)*.

lovely   See *cute*.

mad   Dictionaries recognize *mad* as a synonym for *angry*, or *very enthusiastic*, but some readers object to its use in these meanings.

manner   Often unnecessary in phrases like *in a precise manner* where a single adverb *(precisely)* or a "with" phrase *(with precision)* would do.

may   See *can, may*.

may of   Nonstandard for *may have*.

media   A plural form (singular *medium*) requiring a plural verb *(The mass media are* [not *is*] *sometimes guilty of distorting the news)*.

maybe, may be   *Maybe* means "perhaps"; *may be* is a verb form. Be careful to distinguish between the two.

might of   Nonstandard for *might have*.

mighty   Colloquial as an intensifier meaning "very" or "extremely" *(mighty tasty, mighty expensive)*.

most   Colloquial as a substitute for *almost* or *nearly*.

must of   Nonstandard for *must have*.

myself, yourself, himself   *Myself* is often used in speech as a substitute for *I* or *me* but is not standard in written English. Reserve *myself* for emphatic *(I myself will do the work)* or reflexive use *(I hurt myself)*. The same applies to the forms *yourself, himself, herself,* etc.

nice, nice and   *Nice* is overused as a vague word of approval meaning "attractive, agreeable, friendly, pleasant," and the like. Use a more exact word. *Nice and* as an intensifier *(The beer was nice and cold)* is colloquial.

nohow   Nonstandard for *not at all, in no way*.

none   The indefinite pronoun *none* may take either a singular or a plural verb, depending on its context *(None of the gold was stolen; None of the men were absent)*. See **8a2.**

nothing like, nowhere near   Colloquial for *not nearly (I was not nearly [not nowhere near] as sick as you)*.

nowheres   Nonstandard for *nowhere*.

number   See *amount, number*.

of, have   In speech the auxiliary *have* in such combinations as *could have, might have,* etc., sounds very much like *of,* leading some people to write *could of, might of,* etc. All such combinations with *of* are nonstandard. In writing be careful to use *have*.

off of, off from   Wordy and colloquial *(The paper slid off* [not *off of*] *the table*.

OK, O.K., okay   All are standard forms, but formal writing prefers a more exact word.

on account of   Wordy for *because of*. Regional for *because (She bought the car because* [not *on account of*] *she needed it)*.

outside of   Colloquial for *except (Nobody was there except* [not *outside of*] *Henry)*. See also *inside of*.

overall   An overused synonym for *general, complete,* as in *overall prices, overall policy*. Often meaningless, as in *Our overall decision was to buy the car*.

over with   Colloquial for *ended, finished, completed*.

party   See *individual*.

per Appropriate in business and technical writing (*per diem, per capita, feet per second, pounds per square inch*). In ordinary writing prefer *a* or *an* (*ninety cents a dozen, twice a day*).

percent, percentage Both mean "rate per hundred." *Percent* (sometimes written *per cent*) is used with numbers (*fifty percent, 23 percent*). *Percentage* is used without numbers (*a small percentage*). Avoid using either as a synonym for *part* (*A small part* [not *percentage*] *of the money was lost*).

perfect See *unique*.

person See *individual*.

persuade See *convince, persuade*.

phenomena See *data*.

phone Colloquial for *telephone*. In formal writing use the full word.

photo Colloquial for *photograph*. In formal writing use the full word.

plan on Colloquial in such phrases as *plan on going, plan on seeing,* for *plan to go, plan to see*.

plenty Colloquial as an adverb meaning "very, amply" (*I was very* [not *plenty*] *angry*). Note that as a noun meaning "enough, a large number," *plenty* must be followed by *of* (*I've had plenty of money*).

poorly Colloquial or dialectal for *ill, in poor health*.

practical, practicable *Practical* means "useful, not theoretical." *Practicable* means "capable of being put into practice" (*Franklin was a practical statesman; his schemes were practicable*).

pretty Colloquial and overused as an adverb meaning "somewhat, moderately" (*pretty difficult, pretty sick*). Use a more specific word.

principal, principle As an adjective *principal* means "chief, main"; as a noun it means "leader, chief officer," or, in finance, "a capital sum, as distinguished from interest or profit." The noun *principle* means "fundamental truth" or "basic law or doctrine." (*What is my principal reason for being here? I am the principal of the local elementary school. That bank pays 5 percent interest on your principal. The textbook explained the underlying principle.*)

provided, providing Both are acceptable as subordinating conjunctions meaning "on the condition" (*I will move to Washington, providing* [or *provided*] *the salary is adequate*).

raise, rise *Raise, raised, raised* is a transitive verb (*They raised potatoes*). *Rise, rose, risen* is intransitive (*They rose at daybreak*).

real Colloquial for *really* or *very* (*real cloudy, real economical*).

reason is because   See *is when* and **14a**.

reason why   Usually redundant *(The reason* [not *reason why*] *we failed is clear)*.

reckon   See *calculate*.

refer   See *allude, refer*.

regarding, in regard to, with regard to   Overused and wordy for *on, about,* or *concerning (We have not decided on* [not *with regard to*] *your admission)*.

right   Colloquial or dialectal when used to mean "very" *(right fresh, right happy)*. *Right along* and *right away* are colloquial for *continuously, immediately*.

rise, raise   See *raise, rise*.

round   See *unique*.

said   *Said* in such phrases as *the said paragraph, the said person* occurs frequently in legal writing. Avoid the use in ordinary writing.

scarcely   See *but, hardly, scarcely*.

set, sit   Often confused. See **4c**.

shall, will, should, would   *Will* is now commonly used for all persons *(I, you he, she, it)* except in the first person for questions *(Shall I go?)* and in formal contexts *(We shall consider each of your reasons)*. *Should* is used for all persons when condition or obligation is being expressed *(If he should stay. . . . We should go)*. *Would* is used for all persons to express a wish or customary action *(Would that I had listened! I would ride the same bus every day.)*

shape up   Colloquial for *proceed satisfactorily (Our plans are shaping up)*.

should   See *shall*.

should of   Nonstandard for *should have*.

show up   Colloquial when used to mean "appear" *(They did not show up)* or to mean "expose" *(You showed them up for the liars they are)*.

since, because   The subordinating conjunction *because* always indicates cause. *Since* may indicate either cause or time *(It has rained since yesterday. Since you need money, I'll lend you some)*. Be careful to avoid using *since* in sentences where it could indicate either cause or time and thus be ambiguous. In *since we moved, we have been working longer hours,* it is unclear whether *because we moved* or *from the time we moved* is meant.

sit, set   See *set, sit*.

situation Wordy and unnecessary in expressions like *We have an examination situation.*

so *So* is a loose and often imprecise conjunction. Avoid using it excessively to join independent clauses. For clauses of purpose, *so that* is preferable (*They left so that* [not *so*] *I could study*). *Because* is preferable when cause is clearly intended (*Because it began to rain, we left* [not *It began to rain, so we left*]).

some Colloquial and vague when used to mean "unusual, remarkable, exciting" (*That was some party. This is some car.*). In writing use a more specific word.

someone, some one See *anyone.*

sometime, some time Use one word in the sense of a time not specified; use two words in the sense of a period of time (*Sometime we shall spend some time together*).

somewheres Nonstandard for *somewhere.*

sort See *kind, sort.*

sort of See *kind of, sort of.*

sort of a See *kind of a.*

straight See *unique.*

stupid See *ignorant, stupid.*

such Colloquial and overused as a vague intensifier (*It was a very* [not *such a*] *hot day*).

sure Colloquial for *surely, certainly* (*I was surely* [not *sure*] *sick*).

sure and, try and Colloquial for *sure to, try to.*

suspicion Dialectal when used in place of the verb *suspect.*

take and Nonstandard in most uses (*Lou slammed* [not *took and slammed*] *the book down*).

teach, learn See *learn, teach.*

than, then Don't confuse these. *Than* is a conjunction (*younger than John*). *Then* is an adverb indicating time (*then, not now*).

that Colloquial when used as an adverb (*She's that poor she can't buy food. I didn't like the book that much.*)

that, which *That* always introduces restrictive clauses; *which* may introduce either restrictive or nonrestrictive clauses. See **20c.** Some writers and editors prefer to limit *which* entirely to nonrestrictive clauses (*This is the car that I bought yesterday. This car, which I bought yesterday, is very economical.*)

theirselves Nonstandard for *themselves.*

then, than See *than, then.*

there, their, they're Don't confuse these. *There* is an adverb or an expletive (*He walks there. There are six.*). *Their* is a pronoun (*their rooms*). *They're* is a contraction for *they are* (*They're too eager*).

these kind, these sort See *kind, sort.*

this here, that there, these here, them there Nonstandard for *this, that, these, those.*

thusly Nonstandard for *thus.*

to, too *To* is a preposition. *Too* is an adverb meaning *also* (*She laughed too*) or *more than enough* (*You worked too hard*). In the sense of *indeed* it is colloquial (*She did too laugh*).

toward, towards Both are correct, though *toward* is more common in the United States, *towards* in Britain.

try and See *sure and.*

type Colloquial for *type of* (*This type of* [not *type*] *research is expensive*). Often used, but usually in hyphenated compounds (*colonial-type architecture, tile-type floors, scholarly-type text*). Omit *type* for such expressions wherever possible.

uninterested See *disinterested, uninterested.*

unique Several adjectives such as *unique, perfect, round, straight,* and *complete* name qualities that do not vary in degree. Logically, therefore, they cannot be compared. Formal use requires *more nearly round, more nearly perfect* and the like. The comparative and superlative forms, however, are widely used colloquially in such phrases as *the most unique house, most complete examination, most perfect day.* Their occurrence even in formal English is exemplified by the phrase *more perfect union* in the Constitution. See **3c.**

used to In writing be careful to preserve the *d* (*We used to* [not *use to*] *get up at six every morning*).

used to could Nonstandard for *used to be able.*

wait on Colloquial when used to mean "wait for"; *wait on* means "to serve, attend" (*We waited for* [not *waited on*] *the clerk to wait on us*).

that you should go. The expressions *want off, want in, want out* are regional and should not be used in writing.

wait on   Colloquial when used to mean "wait for"; *wait on* means "to serve, attend" *(We waited for* [not *waited on*] *the clerk to wait on us).*

ways   Colloquial when used for *way* meaning "distance" *(It is a long way* [not *ways*] *to Brownsville).*

well   See *good, well.*

where   Colloquial when used as a substitute for *that (I read in the mayor's report that* [not *where*] *many local crimes are unsolved).*

which   For *and which,* see *and which;* for the distinction between *that* and *which,* see *that, which.*

while   Used most precisely to indicate time *(He had the radio on while he was studying).* It can also be used with the meaning of *although (While she was always willing to work, she seldom was paid well).* Because both these meanings are possible, be careful not to use *while* when the meaning could be ambiguous. In *While we both worked for the same company, we did not often meet* it is not clear whether the meaning is *when* or *although.*

   While is not generally acceptable in the meaning of *and* or *but (Susan is a doctor, and* or *but* [not *while*] *Ray is an engineer).*

will   See *shall.*

wise   A long-established adverb suffix, *-wise* is used to mean "in a specific direction" *(lengthwise, sidewise)* or "in the manner of" *(crabwise, clockwise).* More recently *-wise* has been widely overworked as a suffix meaning "with regard to, in connection with" *(dollarwise, educationwise).* Many object to the use as jargon and unnecessary, and it is best avoided.

wonderful   See *cute.*

would   See *shall.*

would of   Nonstandard for *would have.*

you all   Informal Southern dialect form used as a plural of *you.*

yourself   See *myself.*

44

44 SPELLING **SP**

Language existed first as speech, and the alphabet is basically a device to represent speech on paper. When letters of the alphabet have definite values and are used consistently, as in Polish or Spanish, the spelling of a word is an accurate index to its pronunciation, and vice versa. Not so with English. The alphabet does not represent English sounds consistently. The letter *a* may stand for the sound of the vowel in *may, can, care,* or *car; c* for the initial consonant of *carry* or city; *th* for the diphthong in *both* or in *bother.* Different combinations of letters are often sounded alike, as in *rec(ei)ve, l(ea)ve,* or *p(ee)ve.* In many words, moreover, some letters appear to perform no function at all, as in *i(s)land, de(b)t, of(t)en, recei(p)t.* Finally, the relationship between the spelling and the pronunciation of some words seems downright capricious, as in *through, enough, colonel, right.*

Much of the inconsistency of English spelling may be explained historically. English spelling has been a poor index to pronunciation ever since the Norman conquest, when French scribes gave written English a French spelling. Subsequent tampering with English spelling has made it even more complex. Early classical scholars with a flair for etymology added the unvoiced *b* to early English *det* and *dout* because they mistakenly traced these words directly from the Latin *debitum* and *dubitum* when actually both the English and the Latin had derived independently from a common Indo-European origin. Dutch printers working in England were responsible for changing early English *gost* to *ghost.* More complications arose when the pronunciation of many words changed more rapidly than their spelling. The *gh* in *right* and *through,* and in similar words, was once pronounced much like the German *ch* in *nicht. Colonel* was once pronounced *col-o-nel.* The final *e* in words like *wife* and *time* was long ago dropped from actual speech, but it still remains as a proper spelling form.

The English tendency to borrow words freely from Latin and French has given us groups like the native English *sight,* the French *site,* and the Latin *cite.* Our word *regal,* with its hard *g,* comes from the Norman French. Our word *regent,* with *g* sounded as a *j,* comes from Parisian French. Words like *machine, burlesque,* and *suite* come directly from the French, with little change in spelling or pronunciation. *Envelope,* on the other hand, maintains its French spelling but is given an English pronunciation. From Spanish comes the proper noun *Don Quixote;* its Spanish pronunciation (dōn kē·hō′tä) is still frequently heard, but the English adjective *quixotic* is pronounced kwĭks · ot′ĭk.

The complex history of the English language may help to explain why our spelling is illogical, but it does not justify misspelling. Society tends to equate bad spelling with incompetent writing. In fact, only the misspellings tend to be noticed, not the quality of the writing, and correct spellings sometimes render faulty constructions invisible. That particularly American institution, the spelling bee, has for generations put a higher premium on the correct spelling of *phthisis* than on a clearly constructed sentence. To illustrate, test your own attitude. Which of the two selections below seems better?

> Parants should teech children the importence of puntuallity.

> The condition of unpunctuality which exists in the character of a great many members of the younger generation should be eliminated by every means that lies at the disposal of parents who are responsible for them.

On first reading, the first sentence seems inferior to the second. Actually the former is the better sentence—more direct and succinct. But the misspellings make it difficult to take the sentence seriously. Readers have been conditioned to treat misspellings as one of the greatest sins a writer can commit.

44a Avoid secondary and British spellings.

Many words have a secondary spelling, generally British. Though the secondary spelling is not incorrect, as an American writer you should avoid it. Here is a brief list of preferred and secondary spelling forms; consult a good dictionary for others.

1. *American **-e***

   anemia
   anesthetic
   encyclopedia
   fetus

   *British **-ae, -oe***

   anaemia
   anaesthetic
   encyclopaedia
   foetus

2. *American **im-, in-***

   impanel
   incase
   inquiry

   *British **em-, en-***

   empanel
   encase
   enquiry

3. American ***-ize***

   apologize

   *British **-ise***

   apologise

4. *American **-or***

   armor
   clamor
   color
   flavor

   *British **-our***

   armour
   clamour
   colour
   flavour

4. American **-or** (cont.)	British **-our** (cont.)
labor	labour
odor	odour
vigor	vigour

5. American **-er**	British **-re**
center	centre
fiber	fibre
somber	sombre
theater	theatre

6. American **-o**	British **-ou**
mold	mould
plow	plough
smolder	smoulder

7. American **-ction**	British **-xion**
connection	connexion
inflection	inflexion

8. American **-l**	British **-ll**
leveled	levelled
quarreled	quarrelled
traveled	travelled

9. American **-e** omitted	British **-e**
acknowledgment	acknowledgement
judgment	judgement

44b

44b Proofread your manuscripts carefully to eliminate misspelling.

In writing a first draft, you are forming words into sentences faster than you can write them down. You are concentrating, not on the words you are actually writing, but on the words to come. A few mistakes in spelling may easily creep into a first draft. Always take five or ten minutes to proofread your final draft to make sure that you do not let misspellings stand uncorrected.

The failure to proofread accounts for the fact that the words most often misspelled are not, for example, *baccalaureate* and *connoisseur,* but *too, its, lose, receive,* and *occurred.* Not trusting ourselves to spell hard words correctly, we consult a dictionary and take pains to get the correct spelling on paper. But most of us think we can spell a familiar word. Either we never bother to check the spelling, or we assume that a word pictured correctly in our minds must automatically spell itself correctly on the paper in front of us. This thinking accounts for such errors as omitting the final *o* in *too,* confusing the possessive *its* with the contraction *it's,* and spelling *loose* when *lose* is meant. You will never forget how to spell *receive* and *occurred* if you will devote just a few moments to memorizing their correct spelling.

On pages 408–410 is a list of 350 words often misspelled. Almost every one of them is a common word; to misspell any of them in a finished paper denotes carelessness.

44c Cultivate careful pronunciation as an aid to correct spelling.

Some words are commonly misspelled because they are mispronounced. The following list of frequently mispronounced words will help you overcome this source of spelling error.

accident*a*lly		note the *al*
acc*u*rate		note the *u*
can*d*idate		note the first *d*
envir*o*nment		note the *on*
gover*n*ment		note the *n*
incident*a*lly		note the *al*
math*e*matics		note the *e*
prob*ab*ly		note the *ab*
quan*t*ity		note the first *t*
represen*ta*tive		note the *ta*
soph*o*more		note the second *o*
su*r*prise		note the first *r*
*ath*l*e*tics	NOT	ath*ele*tics
disas*t*rous	NOT	disas*t*erous
heigh*t*	NOT	heigh*th*
gri*e*-vous	NOT	gr*e*-*vi*-ous
ir-r*el*-e-*v*ant	NOT	ir-re*v*-e-*l*ant
mis-ch*ie*-vous	NOT	mis-ch*e*-*vi*-ous

However, pronunciation is not an infallible guide to correct spelling. Although, for example, the last syllables of *adviser, beggar,* and *doctor* all are pronounced as the same unstressed *ur,* all are spelled differently. Proceed cautiously in using pronunciation as a spelling aid.

44d Distinguish carefully between the spellings of words that are similar in sound.

English abounds in words whose sound is similar to that of other words but whose spelling is different: for example, *rain, rein, reign.* The most troublesome of such words are listed below.

all ready: everyone is ready
already: by this time

all together: as a group
altogether: entirely, completely

altar: a structure used in worship
alter: to change

ascent: climbing, a way sloping up
assent: agreement; to agree

breath: air taken into the lungs
breathe: to exhale and inhale

capital: chief; leading or governing city; wealth, resources
capitol: a building that houses the state or national lawmakers

cite: to use as an example, to quote
site: location

clothes: wearing apparel
cloths: two or more pieces of cloth

complement: that which completes; to supply a lack
compliment: praise, flattering remark; to praise

corps: a military group or unit
corpse: a dead body

council: an assembly of lawmakers
counsel: advice; one who advises; to give advice

dairy: a factory or farm engaged in milk production
diary: a daily record of experiences or observations

descent: a way sloping down
dissent: disagreement; to disagree

dining: eating
dinning: making a continuing noise

dying: ceasing to live
dyeing: process of coloring fabrics

forth: forward in place or space, onward in time
fourth: the ordinal equivalent of the number 4

loose: free from bonds
lose: to suffer a loss

personal: pertaining to a particular person; individual
personnel: body of persons employed in same work or service

principal: chief, most important; a school official; a capital sum (as distinguished from interest or profit)
principle: a belief, rule of conduct or thought

respectfully: with respect
respectively: in order, in turn

stationery: writing paper
stationary: not moving

their: possessive form of *they*
they're: contraction of *they are*
there: adverb of place

whose: possessive form of *who*
who's: contraction of *who is*
your: possessive form of *you*
you're: contraction of *you are*

44e Familiarize yourself with spelling rules as an aid to correct spelling.

1   Carefully distinguish between *ie* and *ei*. Remember this jingle:

Write *i* before *e*
Except after *c*
Or when sounded like *a*
As in *eighty* and *sleigh*.

i before e	*ei after c*	*ei when sounded like a*
thief	receive	weigh
believe	deceive	freight
wield	ceiling	vein

Some exceptions

leisure
financier
weird

2   Drop the final *e* before a suffix beginning with a vowel but not before a suffix beginning with a consonant.

a. Suffix beginning with a vowel, final *e* dropped:

please + ure = *pleasure*
ride + ing   = *riding*
locate + ion = *location*
guide + ance = *guidance*

EXCEPTIONS:

In some words the final *e* is retained to prevent confusion with other words.

dyeing (to distinguish it from *dying*)

Final *e* is retained to keep *c* or *g* soft before *a* or *o*.

	notice + able	= *noticeable*
	change + able	= *changeable*
BUT	practice + able	= *practicable* (*c* has sound of *k*)

44e

b. Suffix beginning with a consonant, final *e* retained:

sure + ly	= *surely*
arrange + ment	= *arrangement*
like + ness	= *likeness*
entire + ly	= *entirely*
entire + ty	= *entirety*
hate + ful	= *hateful*

EXCEPTIONS:

Some words taking the suffix *-ful* or *-ly* drop final *e:*

awe + ful	= *awful*
due + ly	= *duly*
true + ly	= *truly*

Some words taking the suffix *-ment* drop final *e:*

judge + ment	= *judgment*
acknowledge + ment	= *acknowledgment*

The ordinal numbers of *five, nine,* and *twelve,* formed with *-th,* drop the final *e. Five* and *twelve* change *v* to *f.*

fifth	ninth	twelfth

3 Final *y* is usually changed to *i* before a suffix, unless the suffix begins with *i.*

	defy + ance	= *defiance*
	forty + eth	= *fortieth*
	ninety + eth	= *ninetieth*
	rectify + er	= *rectifier*
BUT	cry + ing	= *crying* (suffix begins with *i*)

4 A final single consonant is doubled before a suffix beginning with a vowel when (a) a single vowel precedes the consonant, and (b) the consonant ends an accented syllable or a one-syllable word. Unless both these conditions exist, the final consonant is not doubled.

stop + ing	= *stopping* (*o* is a single vowel before consonant *p* which ends word of one syllable.)
admit + ed	= *admitted* (*i* is single vowel before consonant *t* which ends an accented syllable.)

stoop + ing = *stooping* (*p* ends a word of one syllable but is preceded by double vowel *oo*.)

benefit + ed = *benefited* (*t* is preceded by a single vowel *i* but does not end the accented syllable.)

EXERCISE 44e(1) Spell each of the following words correctly and explain what spelling rule applies. Note any exceptions to the rules.

argue + ment	= ?	change + able	= ?
beg + ar	= ?	change + ing	= ?
bury + ed	= ?	awe + ful	= ?
conceive + able	= ?	precede + ence	= ?
eighty + eth	= ?	shine + ing	= ?
associate + ion	= ?	busy + ness	= ?
hop + ing	= ?	defer + ed	= ?
droop + ing	= ?	peace + able	= ?

5 **Nouns ending in a sound that can be smoothly united with -*s* usually form their plurals by adding -*s*. Verbs ending in a sound that can be smoothly united with -*s* form their third person singular by adding -*s*.**

Singular	*Plural*	*Some Exceptions*		*Verbs*	
picture	pictures	buffalo	buffaloes	blacken	blackens
radio	radios	Negro	Negroes	criticize	criticizes
flower	flowers	zero	zeroes	radiate	radiates
chair	chairs				
ache	aches				
fan	fans				

6 **Nouns ending in a sound that cannot be smoothly united with -*s* form their plurals by adding -*es*. Verbs ending in a sound that cannot be smoothly united with -*s* form their third person singular by adding -*es*.**

Singular	*Plural*
porch	porches
bush	bushes
pass	passes
tax	taxes

7 **Nouns ending in *y* preceded by a consonant form their plurals by changing *y* to *i* and adding -*es*. Verbs ending in *y* preceded by a consonant form their third person singular in the same way.**

Singular	Plural
pity	pities
nursery	nurseries
carry	carries
mercy	mercies
body	bodies

EXCEPTIONS:

The plural of proper nouns ending in *y* is formed by adding *-s* (*There are three Marys in my history class*).

8   Nouns ending in *y* preceded by *a*, *e*, *o*, or *u* form their plurals by adding *-s* only. Verbs ending in *y* preceded by *a*, *e*, *o*, or *u* form their third person singular in the same way.

Singular	Plural
day	days
key	keys
buy	buys
guy	guys
enjoy	enjoys

9   The spelling of plural nouns borrowed from French, Greek, and Latin frequently retains the plural of the original language.

Singular	Plural
alumna (*feminine*)	alumnae
alumnus (*masculine*)	alumni
analysis	analyses
basis	bases
crisis	crises
datum	data
hypothesis	hypotheses
phenomenon	phenomena

The tendency now, however, is to give many such words an anglicized plural. The result is that many words have two plural forms, one foreign, the other anglicized. Either is correct.

Singular	Plural (foreign)	Plural (anglicized)
appendix	appendices	appendixes
beau	beaux	beaus
focus	foci	focuses
index	indices	indexes

Singular	Plural (foreign)	Plural (anglicized)
memorandum	memoranda	memorandums
radius	radii	radiuses
stadium	stadia	stadiums

EXERCISE 44e(2)   Spell the plural of each of the following words correctly and explain what spelling rule applies. Note any exceptions to the rules.

1 frame	6 branch	11 echo	16 Charles
2 rose	7 bass	12 stratum	17 no
3 dash	8 cameo	13 church	18 potato
4 maze	9 fly	14 lady	19 play
5 table	10 box	15 mass	20 pain

44f   Spell compound words in accordance with current usage.

Compound words usually progress by stages from being written as two words, to being hyphenated, to being written as one word. Since these stages often overlap, the correct spelling of a compound word may vary. For the spelling of a compound at any particular moment, take the advice of a good dictionary. (For the general use of the hyphen in compounds, see "Hyphen," Section **30**.)

44g   Use drills to help cultivate the habit of correct spelling.

Spelling is primarily a habit. Once you learn to spell a word correctly, you no longer need to think about it; its correct spelling becomes an automatic skill. But if you are a chronic misspeller you have the task not only of learning correct spellings but of unlearning the incorrect spellings you now employ. You must train your fingers to write the word correctly until they do so almost without your thinking about it. Here is a suggested drill that will aid you in learning correct spellings.

1   Look carefully at a word whose spelling bothers you and say it to yourself. If it has more than one syllable, examine each syllable.
2   Look at the individual letters, dividing the word into syllables as you say the letters.
3   Try to visualize the correct spelling before you write the word. If you have trouble, begin again with the *first* step.
4   Write the word without looking at your book or list.
5   Look at your book or list and see whether you wrote the word correctly. If you did, cover the word and write it again. If you write the word correctly the third time, you have probably learned it and will not have to think about it again.
6   If you spell the word incorrectly any one of the three times, look very carefully at the letters you missed. Then start over again and keep on until you have spelled it correctly three times.

44g Spelling lists

The following lists contain many words you are likely to use in writing whose spelling is troublesome. The words are arranged in alphabetized groups for easy reference and for drill.

Group 1

1. accidentally
2. accommodate
3. accompanied
4. achieved
5. address
6. aggravate
7. anxiety
8. barren
9. believe
10. ceiling
11. confident
12. course
13. disappear
14. disappoint
15. dissipate
16. efficiency
17. emphasize
18. exaggerate
19. exceed
20. fiery
21. finally
22. financial
23. forehead
24. foreign
25. forfeit
26. grief
27. handkerchief
28. hurriedly
29. hypocrisy
30. imminent
31. incidentally
32. innocence
33. intentionally
34. interest
35. legitimate
36. likely
37. manual
38. mattress
39. misspell
40. niece
41. occasion

Group 2

1. arctic
2. auxiliary
3. business
4. candidate
5. characteristic
6. chauffeur
7. colonel
8. column
9. cylinder
10. environment
11. especially
12. exhaust
13. exhilaration
14. February
15. foremost
16. ghost
17. government
18. grievous
19. hygiene
20. intercede
21. leisure
22. library
23. lightning
24. literature
25. mathematics
26. medicine
27. mortgage
28. muscle
29. notoriety
30. optimistic
31. pamphlet
32. parliament
33. physically
34. physician
35. prairie
36. prejudice
37. pronunciation
38. recede
39. recognize
40. reign
41. rhetoric

Group 3

1. apparent
2. appearance
3. attendance
4. beggar
5. brilliant
6. calendar
7. carriage
8. conqueror
9. contemptible
10. coolly
11. descent
12. desirable
13. dictionary
14. disastrous
15. eligible
16. equivalent
17. existence
18. familiar
19. grammar
20. guidance
21. hindrance
22. hoping
23. imaginary
24. incredible
25. indigestible
26. indispensable
27. inevitable
28. influential
29. irresistible
30. liable
31. marriage
32. momentous
33. naturally
34. nickel
35. noticeable
36. nucleus
37. obedience
38. outrageous
39. pageant
40. permissible
41. perseverance

Group 1 (cont.)

42. organization
43. parallel
44. piece
45. psychiatrist
46. psychology
47. receive
48. religious
49. severely
50. villain

Group 2 (cont.)

42. rhythm
43. schedule
44. sentinel
45. soliloquy
46. sophomore
47. studying
48. surprise
49. twelfth
50. Wednesday

Group 3 (cont.)

42. persistent
43. pleasant
44. possible
45. prevalent
46. resistance
47. secede
48. strenuous
49. vengeance
50. vigilance

Group 4

1. allot
2. allotted
3. barbarian
4. barbarous
5. beneficial
6. benefited
7. changeable
8. changing
9. commit
10. committed
11. committee
12. comparative
13. comparatively
14. comparison
15. compel
16. compelled
17. competent
18. competition
19. compulsion
20. conceivable
21. conceive
22. conception
23. conscience
24. conscientious
25. conscious
26. courteous
27. courtesy
28. deceit
29. deceive
30. deception
31. decide
32. decision
33. defer
34. deference
35. deferred
36. describe
37. description

Group 5

1. hesitancy
2. hesitate
3. instance
4. instant
5. intellectual
6. intelligence
7. intelligent
8. intelligible
9. maintain
10. maintenance
11. miniature
12. minute
13. ninetieth
14. ninety
15. ninth
16. obligation
17. oblige
18. obliged
19. occur
20. occurred
21. occurrence
22. omission
23. omit
24. omitted
25. picnic
26. picnicking
27. possess
28. possession
29. precede
30. precedence
31. preceding
32. prefer
33. preference
34. preferred
35. procedure
36. proceed
37. realize

Group 6

1. obstacle
2. operate
3. opinion
4. pastime
5. persuade
6. piece
7. politician
8. practically
9. presence
10. professor
11. propeller
12. quantity
13. recommend
14. region
15. relieve
16. representative
17. reservoir
18. restaurant
19. ridiculous
20. sacrifice
21. sacrilegious
22. safety
23. salary
24. scarcely
25. science
26. secretary
27. seize
28. separate
29. shriek
30. siege
31. similar
32. suffrage
33. supersede
34. suppress
35. syllable
36. symmetry
37. temperament

Group 4 (cont.)

38. device
39. devise
40. discuss
41. discussion
42. dissatisfied
43. dissatisfy
44. equip
45. equipment
46. equipped
47. excel
48. excellent
49. explain
50. explanation

Group 5 (cont.)

38. really
39. refer
40. reference
41. referred
42. repeat
43. repetition
44. transfer
45. transferred
46. tried
47. tries
48. try
49. writing
50. written

Group 6 (cont.)

38. temperature
39. tendency
40. tournament
41. tragedy
42. truly
43. tyranny
44. unanimous
45. unusual
46. usage
47. valuable
48. wholly
49. yoke
50. yolk

Group 7

1. accept
2. across
3. aisle
4. all right
5. amateur
6. annual
7. appropriate
8. argument
9. arrangement
10. association
11. awkward
12. bachelor
13. biscuit
14. cafeteria
15. career
16. cemetery
17. completely

18. convenient
19. cruelty
20. curiosity
21. definite
22. desperate
23. diphtheria
24. discipline
25. disease
26. distribute
27. dormitories
28. drudgery
29. ecstasy
30. eighth
31. eliminate
32. eminent
33. enemy
34. except

35. exercise
36. extraordinary
37. fascinate
38. fraternity
39. furniture
40. grandeur
41. height
42. hypocrite
43. imitation
44. interest
45. livelihood
46. loneliness
47. magazine
48. material
49. messenger
50. mischievous

THE LIBRARY
AND THE
RESEARCH PAPER

Knowledge is of two kinds: We know a subject ourselves, or we know where we can find information
upon it.

A man will turn over half a library to make one book.

SAMUEL JOHNSON

The processes of **research** range from simple fact-digging to the most abstruse speculations. Consequently, there is no one generally accepted definition of the word. *Webster's Dictionary* emphasizes the meaning of the first syllable, *re-:* "critical and exhaustive investigation . . . having for its aim the revision of accepted conclusions, in the light of newly discovered facts." The *New World Dictionary* stresses the meaning of the second syllable, *-search:* "systematic, patient study and investigation in some field of knowledge, undertaken to establish facts or principles." The second definition more closely describes what is expected of you in your first years in college. You will not often revise accepted conclusions or establish new principles. But you can learn to collect, sift, evaluate, and organize information or evidence and come to sound conclusions about its meaning. In doing so you will learn some of the basic methods of modern research, and the ethics and etiquette that govern the use the researcher makes of other people's facts and ideas.

When instructors ask you to prepare a research paper, they are concerned less with the intrinsic value of your findings than with the value you derive from the experience. Writing a research paper demands a sense of responsibility, because you must account for all your facts and assertions. If your results are to be accepted—and that is a large part of your purpose—you must be prepared to show how you got those results.

The citing of sources distinguishes the research paper from the expository essay in popular magazines. Good journalists undertake research to assemble their materials, but readers of magazines or newspapers are primarily concerned with the results of that research. Journalists expect to be accepted on faith. Researchers, however, write for their peers—for readers who can critically evaluate findings; for this reason researchers use footnotes to help readers check the evidence if they wish to do so.

In a research paper, your audience expects you to indicate your sources. It expects you to be thorough—to find and sift the relevant evidence; to be critical of the evidence—to test the reliability of your authorities; to be accurate—to present your facts and cite your sources with precision; to be objective—to distinguish clearly between facts and opinions or generalizations related to those facts.

45 THE LIBRARY

The library is one of the most valuable resources on the college campus. Every successful student draws constantly on its facilities. To use the library efficiently, you must know about its resources: what they are, how to find them, how to use them. Many libraries provide guided tours as well as printed information about their resources and the location of different kinds of books. There is always a reference librarian whose special assignment is to help you. Never feel embarrassed to ask him or her for help if you are confused.

Once you have learned to use the library, you will be able to spend your time on productive study and research rather than in wandering about in the hope of finding random bits of information. Section 45 is designed to help you become familiar with what is in your library and with the ways of finding what you want.

Knowing the library resources

Libraries have three principal kinds of holdings: a general collection of books; a collection of reference works; and a collection of periodicals, bulletins, and pamphlets.

General collection of books. The general collection includes most of the books in the library—all those that are available for general circulation. Small libraries usually place these books on open shelves and make them available to people who have library privileges. Most large university libraries, however, keep these books in stacks, which are closed to everyone except librarians, graduate students, faculty members, and persons holding special permits. If you want to borrow a book from such a library, you submit a call slip bearing the call number of the book you want, the name of its author, and its title to library personnel. (The information that goes on the call slip you obtain from the **card catalog,** which will be discussed later.)

Reference books. Reference books include encyclopedias, dictionaries, indexes, directories, handbooks, yearbooks, atlases, and guides. Most libraries place these books on open shelves in the main reading room and do not allow their removal from the room.

Periodicals, bulletins, pamphlets. A **periodical** is a publication that appears at regular (periodic) intervals. **Bulletins** and **pamphlets** may or may not be periodicals, depending on whether they are issued as parts of a series of publications or as separate, single publications. They are usually kept in the stacks with the main collection of books. Recent issues of magazines and newspapers are usually kept in the open shelves of the reading room. Older issues are bound in volumes and shelved in the stacks.

Finding your way among the library resources

Even a small library may have fifty or sixty thousand books—far too many for you ever to hope to search through for what you need. A large university library will have several hundred thousand books, and perhaps a million or more. The directories and guides that libraries provide will help you find the particular books and articles you want. These include (1) the card catalog, (2) the collection of reference books, and (3) the various indexes to periodicals. With a knowledge of how to use these and occasional help from the reference librarian, you can find your way to the books and articles on any subject.

Using the card catalog. The heart of the library is its **card catalog,** an alphabetical list of all the books and periodicals the library contains. Most libraries have a separate catalog that describes all periodical holdings in detail.

The **classification system** on which a card catalog is based serves as a kind of map of library holdings. In libraries where you have direct access to the shelves, familiarity with the classification system enables you to find classes of books in which you are interested without using the catalog. But the chief purpose of a classification system is to supply a **call number** for every item in the library. When you fill out a slip for a book, be sure to copy the call number exactly as it appears on the card.

American libraries generally follow either the Dewey decimal system or the Library of Congress system in classifying books. The system in use determines the call number of any book.

The Dewey system, used by most smaller libraries, divides books into ten numbered classes:

000–099	General works	500–599	Pure science
100–199	Philosophy	600–699	Useful arts
200–299	Religion	700–799	Fine arts
300–399	Social sciences	800–899	Literature
400–499	Philology	900–999	History

Each of these divisions is further divided into ten parts, as:

800	General literature	850	Italian literature
810	American literature	860	Spanish literature
820	English literature	870	Latin literature
830	German literature	880	Greek literature
840	French literature	890	Other literatures

Each of these divisions is further divided, as:

821	English poetry		826	English letters
822	English drama		827	English satire
823	English fiction		828	English miscellany
824	English essays		829	Anglo-Saxon
825	English oratory			

Further subdivisions are indicated by decimals. *The Romantic Rebels,* a book about Keats, Byron, and Shelley, is numbered 821.09, indicating a subdivision of the 821 English poetry category.

The Library of Congress classification system, used by large libraries, divides books into lettered classes: ·

A	General works
B	Philosophy, Religion
C	History, Auxiliary sciences
D	Foreign history and topography
E–F	American history
G	Geography, Anthropology
H	Social sciences
J	Political science
K	Law
L	Education
M	Music
N	Fine arts
P	Language and literature
Q	Science
R	Medicine
S	Agriculture
T	Technology
U	Military science
V	Naval science
Z	Bibliography, Library science

Each of these sections is further divided by letters and numbers that show the specific call number of a book. *English Composition in Theory and Practice* by Henry Seidel Canby and others is classified in this system as PE 1408.E5. (In the Dewey decimal system this same volume is numbered 808 C214.)

For most books (not periodicals) you will find at least three cards in the library catalog: an **author card;** a **title card** (no title card is used when the title begins with words as common as "A History of . . ."); and at least one **subject card.** On the following page is a specimen **author card** in the Dewey system; it is filed according to the surname of the author:

```
  820.903
1 W54
    2  Wilson, John Harold, 1900–
            The court wits of the Restoration, an introduction.
      3  Princeton, Princeton Univ. Press, 1948.

         4  vi, 264 p.   ports.   23 cm.

         5  Bibliography : p. [218]–222.




             1. English literature—Early modern (to 1700)—Hist. & crit.
      6  2. English wit and humor—Hist. & crit.    I. Title.

      7  PR437.W54              8  820.903          9  48—4835*

      10  Library of Congress        [60b²1]
                                      11
```

1 $\begin{array}{l} 820.903 \\ W54 \end{array}$ gives you the call number of the book.

2   "Wilson, John Harold, 1900–" gives the name of the author and the date of his birth and, because no date follows 1900–, indicates that he was living at the time this card was printed.

3   "The court wits . . . 1948" gives the full title of the book, the place of publication, the name of the publisher, and the date of publication. (Note that library practice in capitalizing titles differs from general practice.)

4   "vi, 264 p. ports. 23 cm." indicates that the book contains 6 introductory pages numbered in Roman numerals and 264 pages numbered in Arabic numerals; that portraits appear in the book; and that the book is 23 centimeters high (an inch is 2.54 centimeters).

5   "Bibliography: p. [218]–222" indicates that the book contains a bibliography that begins on page 218 and ends on page 222. The brackets around 218 mean that the page is not actually numbered but appears between numbered pages 217 and 219.

6   "1. English literature . . . Title" indicates that the book is also listed in the card catalog under two subject headings—English Literature, and English Wit and Humor—and under one title heading, "Court wits of the Restoration. . . ." Notice that the subject heading "English literature" has the subdivision "Early modern (to 1700)" and that this latter heading has the subdivision "Hist. & crit.," the heading under which the first subject card is located. The second subject card comes under a division of "English wit and humor" called "Hist. & crit." The Arabic numerals indicate subject headings; the Roman numeral ("I. Title") indicates a title heading.

7   "PR437.W54" is the Library of Congress call number.

8   "820.903" is the class number under the Dewey system.

9 "48–4835*" is the order number used by librarians when they wish to order a copy of the card itself.

10 "Library of Congress" tells you that a copy of the book is housed in, and has been cataloged by, the Library of Congress.

11 "[60b²1]" is a printer's key to the card.

A **title card** is simply a copy of the author card with the title typed just above the author's name. The title card is filed in the catalog according to the first word of the title that is not an article.

A **subject card** is also a copy of the author card, with the subject typed just above the author's name. It is filed in the catalog alphabetically according to the subject heading (see item 6 above). The subject cards, which are gathered together in one place in the catalog, help you find all or most books on a particular subject. (To find articles on a subject, use the reference tools described on pages 423–426.)

Title and subject cards for Wilson's *The Court Wits* are illustrated below.

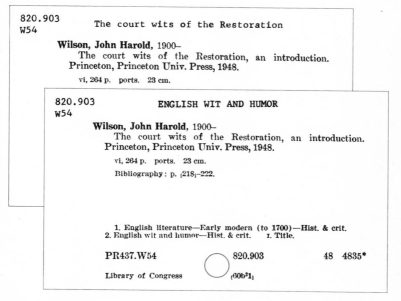

Except for the difference in the call number, catalog cards in libraries that use the Library of Congress system are identical with those in libraries that use the Dewey system. The Library of Congress call number and the Dewey system number appear in the lower line of the card illustrated (items 7 and 8), whereas only that of the system a given library uses is typed in the upper left corner of its catalog cards.

Finding the right reference book. Explore the reference section of your library. Become familiar with the kinds of reference works available and with the most important works of each kind. If you cannot find the book you want or if you do not know what book will help you most, consult the reference librarian.

Following is a representative list of reference books available in most libraries.

GUIDES TO REFERENCE BOOKS

Galin, Saul, and Peter Spielberg. *Reference Books: How to Select and Use Them.* 1969.

Gates, Jean Key. *Guide to the Use of Books and Libraries.* 3rd ed. 1973.

Sheehy, Eugene P. *Guide to Reference Books.* 9th ed. 1976.

Shove, Raymond H., *et al. The Use of Books and Libraries.* 10th ed. 1967.

CATALOGS

Books in Print. Author and title indexes for *Publishers' Trade List Annual. Subject Guide to Books in Print.* 2 vols.

Cumulative Book Index. Monthly listing of published books in English. Cumulated annually.

Monthly Catalog of U.S. Government Publications. 1895 to date.

National Union Catalog. Subject and author listings of Library of Congress holdings as well as titles from other libraries, motion pictures, recordings, and film strips.

Union List of Serials in Libraries of the United States and Canada. Lists of periodicals and newspapers. Supplemented monthly by *New Serial Titles.*

Vertical File Index. 1935–. Supplements to date. (Formerly called *Vertical File Service Catalog,* 1935–54.) Monthly, with annual cumulations. Subject and title index to selected pamphlet material.

GENERAL ENCYCLOPEDIAS

Chambers Encyclopedia. New rev. ed. 15 vols. 1975.

Collier's Encyclopedia. 24 vols. 1977.

Encyclopedia Americana. 30 vols. 1977.

Encyclopaedia Britannica. 15th ed. 30 vols. 1979.

Encyclopedia International. 20 vols. 1963–64.

New Columbia Encyclopedia. 1 vol. 1975.

DICTIONARIES, WORD BOOKS

Dictionary of American English on Historical Principles. 4 vols. 1936–44.

Evans, Bergen and Cornelia. *A Dictionary of Contemporary American Usage.* 1957.

Fowler, Henry W. *Dictionary of Modern English Usage.* 2nd ed. Rev. by Sir Ernest Gowers. 1965.

Funk & Wagnalls New Standard Dictionary. Unabridged. 1964.

Oxford Dictionary of English Etymology. 1966.

Oxford English Dictionary. 12 vols. and supplement. 1888–1933. Also known as *New English Dictionary.*

Partridge, Eric. *A Dictionary of Slang and Unconventional English.* 7th ed. 1970.

Random House Dictionary of the English Language. Unabridged. 1973.

Roget's International Thesaurus. Several editions available.

Webster's Dictionary of Proper Names. 1970.

Webster's New Dictionary of Synonyms. 1973.

Webster's Third New International Dictionary. Unabridged. 1976.

Wentworth, Harold, and Stuart B. Flexner. *Dictionary of American Slang.* 2nd ed. 1975.

YEARBOOKS

Americana Annual. 1924–.

Britannica Book of the Year. 1938–.

CBS News Almanac. 1976–.

Congressional Record. 1873–. Issued daily while Congress is in session; revised and issued in bound form at end of the session.

Facts on File. A weekly digest of world events. 1940–.

Information Please Almanac. 1947–.

Negro Almanac. 1967–.

New International Year Book. 1907–.

Reader's Digest Almanac and Yearbook. 1966–.

Statesman's Year Book. 1864–.

Statistical Abstract of the United States. 1878–.

United Nations Statistical Yearbook. 1945–1968. Monthly supplements.

World Almanac and Book of Facts. 1868–.

Year Book of World Affairs. 1947–.

ATLASES AND GAZETTEERS

Columbia-Lippincott Gazetteer of the World. 1962.

Commercial and Library Atlas of the World. Frequently revised.

Encyclopaedia Britannica World Atlas. Frequently revised.

National Geographic Atlas of the World. 4th ed. 1975.

New Cosmopolitan World Atlas. Issued annually.

The Times Atlas of the World. 1975.

Webster's New Geographical Dictionary. 1972.

GENERAL BIOGRAPHY

American Men and Women of Science. 13th ed. 1976.

Biography Index. 1946–. Quarterly. Cumulated annually, with permanent volumes every three years.

Current Biography: Who's News and Why. 1940–. Published monthly with semiannual and annual cumulations.

Dictionary of American Biography. 24 vols. 1922–76.

Dictionary of American Scholars. 6th ed. 1974.

Dictionary of National Biography. (British) 22 vols. 1938. Reprinted 1966 with corrections and additions 1923–63.

Dictionary of Scientific Biography. 1970–.

International Who's Who. 1936–.

Webster's Biographical Dictionary. 1976.

Who's Who. (British) 1849–.

Who's Who in America. 1899–.

Who's Who of American Women. 1958–.

Who Was Who. 1897–1960.

Who Was Who in America, Historical Volume. 1607–1896.

World Who's Who in Science. 1968.

BOOKS OF QUOTATIONS

Bartlett, John. *Familiar Quotations.* 15th ed. 1981.

Evans, Bergen. *Dictionary of Quotations.* 1968.

The Macmillan Book of Proverbs, Maxims, and Famous Phrases. 1965.

Mencken, H. O. *A New Dictionary of Quotations on Historical Principles from Ancient and Modern Sources.* 1942.

Oxford Dictionary of Quotations. 1953.

Stevenson, Burton. *The Home Book of Bible Quotations.* 1949.

——————. *The Home Book of Quotations.* 10th rev. ed. 1967.

MYTHOLOGY AND FOLKLORE

Bullfinch, Thomas. *Bullfinch's Mythology.* 2nd rev. ed. 1970.

Funk & Wagnalls Standard Dictionary of Folklore, Mythology, and Legend. 2 vols. 1949.

Gray, Louis H., ed. *The Mythology of All Races.* 1916–32. Reprinted 1964.

Hammond, N. G., and H. H. Scullord. *The Oxford Classical Dictionary.* 2nd ed. 1970.

Larousse World Mythology. 1968.

LITERATURE, DRAMA, FILM, AND TELEVISION

Aaronson, C. S., ed. *International Television Almanac.* 1956–.

Adelman, Irving, and R. Dworkin. *Modern Drama: A Checklist of Critical Literature on Twentieth Century Plays.* 1967.

Benét, William Rose. *The Reader's Encyclopedia.* 2nd ed. 1965.

Bukalski, Peter J. *Film Research: A Critical Bibliography.* 1972.

Cassell's *Encyclopedia of World Literature.* Rev. ed. 1973.

Cawkwell, Tim, and John Milton Smith, eds. *World Encyclopedia of the Film.* 1972.

Columbia Dictionary of Modern European Literature. 1947.

Dictionary of World Literary Terms. 3rd ed. 1970.

Etheridge, J. M., and Barbara Kopala. *Contemporary Authors.* 1967.

Hart, J. D. *Oxford Companion to American Literature.* 4th ed. 1965.

Hartnoll, Phyllis. *The Oxford Companion to the Theatre.* 3rd ed. 1967.

Harvey, Sir Paul, and J. E. Heseltine. *Oxford Companion to Classical Literature.* 2nd ed. 1937.

——————. *Oxford Companion to English Literature.* 4th ed. 1967.

Hoffman, Daniel, ed. *Harvard Guide to Contemporary American Writing.* 1979.

Hornstein, Lillian H., ed. *The Reader's Companion to World Literature.* Rev. ed. 1973.

International Encyclopedia of the Film. 1972.

Kunitz, S. J., and Vineta Colby. *European Authors, 1000–1900.* 1967.

Kunitz, S. J., and Howard Haycraft. *American Authors, 1600–1900.* 1952.

——————. *British Authors Before 1800.* 1952.

——————. *British Authors of the Nineteenth Century.* 1936.

——————. *Twentieth Century Authors.* 1942. Supplement, 1955.

Literary History of England. 2nd ed. 4 vols. 1967.

Literary History of the United States. 4th ed. 2 vols. 1974.

Millett, Fred B. *Contemporary American Authors.* 1970.

Manly, John M., and Edith Rickert. *Contemporary British Literature.* 1974.

New Cambridge Bibliography of English Literature. 4 vols. 1969–74.

New York Times Film Reviews, 1913–1968. 1970–71.

Whitlow, Roger. *Black American Literature.* 1973.

Woodress, James, ed. *American Fiction 1900–1950: A Guide to Information Sources.* 1974.

HISTORY, POLITICAL SCIENCE

Cambridge Ancient History. Rev. ed. 5 vols. Plates. 1970–75.

Cambridge Medieval History. Rev. ed. 1967–.

Cyclopedia of American Government. 3 vols, 1949.

Dictionary of American History. 3rd ed. 8 vols. 1976.

Encyclopedia of American History. 5th ed. 1976.

Harvard Guide to American History. Rev. ed. 2 vols. 1974.

Johnson, Thomas H. *Oxford Companion to American History.* 1966.

Langer, William L. *An Encyclopedia of World History.* 5th ed. 1972.

New Cambridge Modern History. 14 vols. 1975.

Political Handbook and Atlas of the World. Published annually.

Political Science: A Bibliographical Guide to the Literature. 1965.

Schlesinger, Arthur M., and D. R. Fox, eds. *A History of American Life.* 13 vols. 1927–48.

Smith, Edward C., and Arnold J. Zurcher, eds. *Dictionary of American Politics.* 2nd ed. 1968.

Webster's Guide to American History. 1971.

THE ARTS

Apel, Willi. *Harvard Dictionary of Music.* 2nd ed. 1969.

Bryan, Michael. *Bryan's Dictionary of Painters and Engravers.* 5 vols. 1971.

Canaday, John C. *The Lives of the Painters.* 4 vols. 1969.

Chujoy, Anatole, and P. W. Manchester. *The Dance Encyclopedia.* Rev. ed. 1967.

Dictionary of Contemporary Music. 1974.

Dictionary of Contemporary Photography. 1974.

Encyclopedia of Painting. 3rd ed. 1970.

Encyclopedia of World Art. 15 vols. 1959–1968.

Feather, Leonard. *Encyclopedia of Jazz.* Rev. ed. 1960.

Fletcher, Sir Banister F. *A History of Architecture.* Rev. ed. 1975.

Focal Encyclopedia of Photography. Rev. ed. 2 vols. 1969.

Grove's Dictionary of Music and Musicians. 5th ed. 9 vols. and supplement. 1954.

Myers, Bernard S. *McGraw-Hill Dictionary of Art.* 5 vols. 1969.

Osborne, Harold. *Oxford Companion to Art.* 1970.

Popular Music: An Annotated List of American Popular Songs. 6 vols. 1973.

Scholes, Percy A. *Oxford Companion to Music.* 10th ed. 1970.

Stambler, Eric. *Encyclopedia of Pop, Rock, and Soul.* 1975.

Thompson, Oscar, and N. Slonimsky. *International Cyclopedia of Music and Musicians.* 10th ed. 1975.

Westrup, Jack A., and F. C. Harrison. *The New College Encyclopedia of Music.* 1960.

PHILOSOPHY, RELIGION

Adams, Charles, ed. *A Reader's Guide to the Great Religions.* 1977.

The Concise Encyclopedia of Western Philosophy and Philosophers. 1960.

Encyclopedia Judaica. 16 vols. 1972.

Encyclopedia of Philosophy. 4 vols. 1973.

Encyclopedia of Religion and Ethics. 1908–27. 12 vols. and index. Reissued 1951.

Ferm, Vergilius. *Encyclopedia of Religion.* 1976.

Grant, Frederick C., and H. H. Rowley. *Dictionary of the Bible.* Rev. ed. 1963..

New Catholic Encyclopedia. 15 vols. 1967.

New Schaff-Herzog Encyclopedia of Religious Knowledge. 1949–50. 12 vols. and index.

Twentieth-Century Encyclopedia of Religious Knowledge. 2 vols. 1955.

Universal Jewish Encyclopedia. 10 vols. 1948.

SCIENCE, TECHNOLOGY

Chamber's Technical Dictionary. 3rd ed. Revised with supplement. 1974.

Dictionary of Physics. 1975.

Encyclopedia of Chemistry. 3rd ed. 1973.

Encyclopedia of Physics. 1974.

Gray, Peter, ed. *The Encyclopedia of the Biological Sciences.* 1970.

Handbook of Chemistry and Physics. 1914–.

Harper Encyclopedia of Science. Rev. ed. 1967.

McGraw-Hill Encyclopedia of Science and Technology. 15 vols. 1971.

Speck, G., and B. Jaffe. *A Dictionary of Science Terms.* 1965.

Universal Encyclopedia of Mathematics. 1964.

Van Nostrand's Scientific Encyclopedia. 5th ed. 1978.

SOCIAL SCIENCES

Davis, John P., ed. *The American Negro Reference Book.* 1966.

A Dictionary of Psychology. Rev. ed. 1964.

Encyclopedia of Educational Research. 4th ed. 1969.

Encyclopedia of Human Behavior: Psychology, Psychiatry, and Mental Health. 1975.

Encyclopedia of Social Work. 1965. (Formerly *Social Work Yearbook,* 1929–1960.)

Encyclopedia of the Social Sciences. 15 vols. 1930–35.

Good, Carter V. *Dictionary of Education.* 3rd ed. 1973.

Handbook of Business Administration. 1967.

Handbook of Forms and Model Letters. 1971.

International Encyclopedia of the Social Sciences. 17 vols. 1968.

Klein, Barry T., ed. *Reference Encyclopedia of the American Indians.* 1973–74.

Mitchell, Geoffrey D. *A Dictionary of Sociology.* 1968.

Munn, G. G. *Encyclopedia of Banking and Finance.* 7th ed. 1973.

White, Carl M., et al. *Sources of Information in the Social Sciences.* 2nd ed. 1973.

Using general and special periodical indexes. A library's catalog merely shows what periodicals are available. To locate the articles you may need in those periodicals you must be acquainted with and know how to use the periodical indexes, which are usually shelved in the reference section of the library. Such indexes are usually classed as general or special indexes. **General indexes** list articles on many different kinds of subjects. **Special indexes** limit themselves to articles in specific areas. Representative lists of both kinds of indexes follow.

GENERAL INDEXES

Readers' Guide to Periodical Literature, 1900 to date. Published semimonthly; cumulated every three months and annually. The *Readers' Guide* gives entries under author, title, and subject.

This is the most widely known and used of the general indexes. Because many periodical indexes use systems very similar to that of the *Readers' Guide,* it is worth examining some sample entries below.

The headings for 1 through 5 are **subject entries;** 6 and 7 are **author entries.** Entry 8, a subject entry, indicates that an article indexed under the subject heading *Graffiti* was published in the June 1969 issue of *Science Digest,* volume 65, pages 31 through 33. Titled "Walls Remember," it was illustrated and unsigned. (All abbreviations and symbols used are explained in the first pages of any issue of the *Readers' Guide.*)

The second listing under entry 1 refers the user to a series of articles by D. Wolfle published in *Science* on the subject "Are Grades Necessary?" The first article appeared in the issue of November 15, 1968 (volume 162, pages 745–746); the second and third appeared, respectively, in the issues for April 18 and June 6, 1969. Entry 2, under the subject heading *Graduate students,* indexes a review by D. Zinberg and P. Doty in the May 1969 issue of *Scientific American* of a book, *New Brahmins: Scientific Life in America,* by S. Klaw. The + that follows the page references is an indication that the review is continued on a page or pages past 140. Entries 3, 4, and 7 are cross-references to the places in the *Guide* at which the user can find the subject or author listed.

1 **GRADING and marking (students)**
Answer to Sally; multiple-choice tests. **W. R.** Link. Ed Digest 34:24-7 My '69
Are grades necessary? D. Wolfle; discussion. Science 162:745-6; 164:245. 1117-18 N 15 '68. Ap 18. Je 6 '69
ROTC: under fire but doing fine. il U S News 66:38 My 19 '69
2 **GRADUATE students**
New Brahmins: scientific life in America, by S. Klaw. Review
Sci Am 220:139-40+ My '69. D. Zinberg and P. Doty
3 **GRADUATION.** See Commencements
4 **GRADUATION addresses.** See Baccalaureate addresses
5 **GRAEBNER, Clark**
Profiles. J. McPhee. por New Yorker 45:45-8+ Je 7; 44-8+ Je 14 '69
6 **GRAEF, Hilda**
Why I remain a Catholic. Cath World 209:77-80 My '69
7 **GRAF, Rudolf F.** See Whalen. G. J. jt. auth.
8 **GRAFFITI**
Walls remember. il Sci Digest 65:31-3 Je '69

From *Readers' Guide to Periodical Literature,* July 1969, p. 73. Reproduced by permission of The H. W. Wilson Company.

Two other general indexes are valuable supplements to the *Readers' Guide:*

International Index. 1907–65. Became *Social Sciences and Humanities Index.* 1965–73. Divided into *Social Sciences Index.* 1974–, and *Humanities Index.* 1974–.

Poole's Index to Periodical Literature, 1802–81. Supplements through January 1, 1907. This is a subject index to American and English periodicals.

SPECIAL INDEXES

These indexes list articles published in periodicals devoted to special concerns or fields.

The Bibliographic Index. 1938–. Indexes current bibliographies by subject; includes both bibliographies published *as* books and pamphlets and those that appear *in* books, periodical articles, and pamphlets.

Book Review Digest. 1905–. Monthly, cumulated annually. Lists books by author and quotes from several reviews for each.

Essay and General Literature Index. 1934–. Indexes collections of essays, articles, and speeches.

New York Times Index. 1913–. Semimonthly, with annual cumulation. Since this index provides dates on which important events, speeches, and the like, occurred, it serves indirectly as an index to records of the same events in the other newspapers.

Ulrich's International Periodicals Directory. 13th ed. 2 vols. 1969–70. Lists periodicals under the subjects they contain, with detailed cross-references and index, thus indicating what periodicals are in a particular field. Also indicates in what other guide or index each periodical is indexed, thus serving indirectly as a master index.

The titles of most of the following special indexes are self-explanatory.

Agricultural Index. 1916 to date. A subject index, appearing nine times a year and cumulated annually.

Applied Science and Technology Index. 1958 to date. (Formerly *Industrial Arts Index.*)

The Art Index. 1929 to date. An author and subject index.

Articles on American Literature. 1900–1950. 1950–1967.

Biological and Agricultural Index. 1964–. (Formerly *Agricultural Index.* 1907–64)

Boyd, Anne M. *United States Government Publications.* 3rd ed. 1949.

Business Periodicals Index. 1958 to date. Monthly. (Formerly *Industrial Arts Index.*)

Catholic Periodical Index. 1930–1933. 1939–. An author and subject index.

Dramatic Index. 1909–1949. Continued in *Bulletin of Bibliography,* 1950 to date. Annual index to drama and theater.

The Education Index. 1929 to date. An author and subject index.

Engineering Index. 1884 to date. An author and subject index.

Granger's Index to Poetry. 6th ed. 1973.

Index to Legal Periodicals. 1908 to date. A quarterly author and subject index.

Industrial Arts Index. 1913–1957. An author and subject index, monthly, with annual cumulations. (In 1958 this index was split into *Applied Science and Technology Index* and *Business Periodicals Index.*)

Monthly Catalog of United States Government Publications. 1905–.

Play Index. 1968.

Popular Periodical Index. 1973. Author and subject guide to about 25 periodicals not otherwise indexed.

Public Affairs Information Service Bulletin. 1915 to date. Weekly, with bimonthly and annual cumulations. An index to materials on economics, politics, and sociology.

Quarterly Cumulative Index Medicus. 1927 to date. A continuation of the *Index Medicus,* 1899–1926. Indexes books as well as periodicals.

Short Story Index. 1953–. Supplements.

Song Index. 1926. Supplement.

United Nations Documents Index. 1950–.

EXERCISE 45(1)   Draw a diagram of the reference room of your library, indicating on it the position of the following reference books and indexes.

1 *Encyclopaedia Britannica*
2 *Encyclopedia of Religion and Ethics*
3 *Jewish Encyclopedia*
4 *Dictionary of American History* (DAH)
5 *Dictionary of American Biography* (DAB)
6 *American Authors, 1600–1900*
7 *Who's Who*
8 *Facts on File*
9 *World Almanac*
10 *New English Dictionary* (NED), often referred to as *Oxford English Dictionary* (OED)
11 *General Card Catalog*
12 *Readers' Guide to Periodical Literature*
13 *The New York Times Index*
14 *The Art Index*
15 *Dramatic Index*

EXERCISE 45(2)   Answer each of the following questions by consulting one of the standard reference guides listed in Exercise 45(1).

1 Where can you find information on the significance of the Menorah in Jewish history?

2 Among which tribe of American Indians is the highest development of shamanism found?

3 What did the word *gossip* mean in twelfth-century England?

4 Where can you find listed articles on French stained glass, printed in 1957 and 1958?

5 What was the first invention of Peter Cooper, American inventor, manufacturer, and philanthropist (d. 1883)?

EXERCISE 45(3)   Write a brief paper on one of the following subjects. Be sure to answer all the questions raised. Read the prefaces or introductions to the reference works you are asked to describe, check to see how each work is organized, and make a special point of finding out how to use the works efficiently and effectively. If you have difficulty deciding what particular advantage each work has for research, consult Eugene P. Sheehy, *A Guide to Reference Books*.

1 Compare the *Dictionary of National Biography* and *Who's Who in America*. On what basis does each work include biographical data about an individual? Nationality? Contemporaneity? Prominence? What kinds of prominence? What kinds of information can you get about an individual in each work? Which work is more detailed? What particular research value does each have?

2 Compare the *World Almanac* and *Facts on File*. Both works are known as "yearbooks." How do they differ in methods of compilation of material? How does this difference affect the way in which they are organized? How does it determine the types of information included in each? How do you look up an item in each one? Under what circumstances would you consult the *World Almanac* rather than *Facts on File*? *Facts on File* rather than the *World Almanac*?

3 Compare the *Oxford English Dictionary* (OED) with the *Heritage Dictionary* or *Webster's New World Dictionary*. For illustrative purposes look up the word *kind* in each. What does each work tell you about the derivation of the word? About its history in the English language? How up-to-date is each dictionary? When would you use each one and for what purpose? What does each work tell you about the meaning of *devil* in the phrase *between the devil and the deep blue sea*? What does each work tell you about the sense in which Shakespeare meant the word *prevent*? What does each work tell you about *turbojet*? About *chemist*? About *fancy*?

46   THE RESEARCH PAPER

Choose and limit a subject.

Although your own interest in or curiosity about a topic is a good motivation in choosing a subject for a research paper, common sense requires that you choose a subject appropriate for research and limit it so that you can cope with it satisfactorily in the space and time at your disposal. Subjects developed largely from personal experience will not make satisfactory research topics since they do not require the acquaintance with library resources and the practice of note-taking that are part of the purpose of a research paper. Topics such as "The History of Medicine," "The American Indian," or "Modern Warfare" are far too broad and general for, say, a 1,500-word paper. If they are to be made at all workable, they have to be narrowed to such topics as "The Discovery of Anesthesia," "The Relation of the Mohicans to the Five Nations," "The Rival Claims of Types of Army Rifles in World War II," or similar relatively specific subjects.

Certain other kinds of topic will prove unsatisfactory for less obvious reasons. Some topics offer little practice because all necessary information can easily be found in a single authoritative source. Descriptions of technical or industrial processes ("The Production of Coffee"), narratives of a person's life ("Napoleon's Military Career"), or relatively simple narrative histories ("The History of Baseball") usually fall in this group. Some topics are so controversial and complex that the time and space allowed for a student research paper are not sufficient to permit a careful weighing of evidence for both sides leading to a reasonably objective conclusion. Topics such as "Is the Supreme Court Too Powerful?" and "The Relative Merits of Federal and Local Support of Education" are of this kind.

The most satisfactory topics, then, are those that encourage you to explore the resources of the library and to develop habits of meaningful note-taking. They give you practice in organizing and unifying information drawn from several sources. In your preliminary consideration of possible topics, avoid those that are too personal, too broad, too simple, or too complex to accomplish these aims.

Choosing and limiting a topic require more preliminary work than merely choosing a general topic you are interested in and arbitrarily narrowing it down to something you think you can manage. Unless you have already read widely about the topic you choose, you will need to begin your search for material, discover what material is available in your library, and skim several articles or chapters of books before the direction you will wish to take becomes very clear to you. Even after you have made a preliminary outline and started taking notes, you will still be engaged in more and more clearly limiting and defining your topic as you read. In fact, until you have made a preliminary survey of what is available about your topic, you may have only a very general sense of how you can limit it wisely.

EXERCISE 46(1)   If you do not have a topic you are already interested in or curious about and have not been assigned a specific topic, one good way to get started is to select a question and then search out the most accurate possible answer to it. If you lack a topic, select one of the following questions and begin working on a research paper in which you will answer it—or another question to which it leads you. Use your ingenuity to discover exactly what the question means. Check the rest of this section for guidance in finding material and getting it in order.

1 Why did Benedict Arnold turn traitor?
2 Was Billy the Kid a desperado?
3 What progress have women made in securing improved wages and salaries in the past decade?
4 How extensively did the early Algonquins engage in agriculture?
5 Where did American Indians come from?
6 How was Lincoln's "Gettysburg Address" received by his contemporaries?
7 What are some of the important changes that have taken place in the Roman Catholic Church in recent years?
8 Can a pitcher curve a baseball?
9 How are Spanish-speaking children taught English?
10 What happened in the Scopes trial?
11 What are the present theories on the migratory instincts of birds?
12 Have employment opportunities improved for black Americans?
13 What happened to the settlers on Roanoke Island?
14 What was the Teapot Dome scandal?
15 Is the climate growing warmer?
16 What was learned about the moon in the Apollo program?
17 What are the plausible explanations for the statues on Easter Island?
18 Does the legend that Pocahontas saved John Smith's life square with the probable facts in the case?
19 Did Fulton invent the steamboat?
20 Has football supplanted baseball as the national game?
21 Did the Norse make voyages to America before Columbus?
22 What is the present ideological makeup of the Supreme Court?
23 Were Sacco and Vanzetti convicted on the basis of circumstantial evidence?
24 Did Edgar Allan Poe die insane?
25 What are the reasons for the disappearance of the dinosaur?
26 What effects has television had on professional sports?
27 What are the future prospects for a practical electric car?
28 To what extent was politics involved in the 1980 Olympics?
29 What is disco dancing and how did it develop?
30 What accounts for the popularity of country music?

Begin your search for information and start tentative planning.

Make use of bibliographical aids. After your initial choice of subject, research begins with a preliminary search for material and the preparation of a preliminary bibliography—that is, a list of articles, books, newspaper reports, or the like, that you think are relevant to your subject. The sources for your preliminary bibliography are such reference works as the following:

Subject cards in the main card catalog.
Bibliographies at the end of pertinent articles in various encyclopedias.

Readers' Guide to Periodical Literature.

Appropriate special periodical indexes (*Engineering Index, Education Index,* etc.).

The New York Times Index.

Guides to reference books, such as those listed on pages 418–423.

For the research paper reproduced later in this chapter, Annie Guzman decided to investigate the predictions of futurists about life in the year 2000. She began her search for material with the most recent issues of the *Readers' Guide,* and since her interest was in current predictions, she limited herself to the most recently published sources. (If she had been writing about, say, the Great Depression, she probably would have looked through the bound volumes of the *Readers' Guide* starting with 1929.) Annie looked for appropriate articles not only under the heading *Future* but also under likely cross-reference headings such as *Twenty-first century* and *Forecasting.* She then skimmed through five or six articles with promising titles to get a general sense of the topic. Within two or three hours, Annie had decided that at least part of her paper would be concerned with the possibility of some kind of worldwide disaster. She had also realized that there were many aspects of the topic she simply couldn't handle and some she didn't care to pursue. Annie was thus beginning to *limit* her topic intelligently. What had been a vague idea and a hazy interest was now beginning to take a more specific preliminary shape.

In her next visit to the library, after skimming through a few more articles with promising titles, Annie sat back, thought about her topic, and jotted down a very rough outline on a note card:

   I. Possible disasters (Bundy)
      A. War—compare Bradbury story
      B. Famine—controversy re supply of food
      C. Overpopulation—get more data
  II. Optimistic futurists—Buckminster Fuller?—get book
III. Pessimistic futurists—???

The reminders "get more data" and "get book," as well as the question marks, are indications that Annie is learning how in research one thing leads to another and that it is a mistake to depend on one's memory. As you will see, Annie later decided not to categorize the futurists as optimistic and pessimistic, although she did use those adjectives once or twice. But this very rough outline did lead her to Buckminster Fuller and, in turn, to some important new ideas.

The next session at the library Annie devoted primarily to books. Searching the subject catalog led to several promising titles. Annie jotted down the call numbers, gave them to the desk, and eventually collected the books. She did not make the mistake of starting to read immediately. Instead, she looked first at *all* the tables of contents and indexes, and she skimmed through the prefaces, introductions, and one or two chapters. On this basis she was able to determine that several books had little value for her topic, so she returned them. She did not waste time reading books and articles that later turned out to be useless. As you become a practiced researcher, you will learn not only what to hold on to but also what to send back.

Prepare exact bibliography cards for each source. Annie was careful throughout her preliminary search to make an individual bibliography card for each article, book, or pamphlet she thought she might use. Follow this procedure consistently, even though it may sometimes seem unnecessary. Failure to get all the necessary bibliographic information at the time you are consulting a book or article can delay and inconvenience you later. Return trips to the library, time-consuming in themselves, sometimes result only in finding that a periodical is at the bindery or that a book is not available. At best, omission of a particularly useful piece of information may make it necessary to look through several books or periodicals to relocate an exact source.

The best method of keeping an accurate and useful record of your sources is to make out bibliography cards. The common sizes of cards are $3'' \times 5''$, $4'' \times 6''$, and $5'' \times 8''$. Researchers often use larger sizes for note-taking and the $3'' \times 5''$ size for bibliographic entries.

Make out a separate bibliography card for each source you consult. Although the exact information for various kinds of sources varies, all entries require three basic kinds of information: author, title, and publication information. For magazines, journals, newspapers, and the like, "publication information" includes the title of the magazine or journal, its date, and the pages on which the article you are citing occurs. If your source is a translation or an edited book, you will need the name of the translator or editor as well as that of the author. If your source is a selection in an anthology or a collection, you will need the name of the editor and the title of the collection in addition to the title of your selection and the name of its author.

For your use in later locating each source, place the library call number in the lower left-hand corner of each bibliography card.

The exact details of form for both bibliography entries and documentation notes (footnotes or endnotes) vary among disciplines. The forms given following, as well as those given for documentation on pages 445–453, are those established by the Modern Language Association and described in the *MLA Handbook* (1977), which is the style guide for some eighty professional journals in the languages, humanities, and some social sciences. Use these forms unless your instructor requires otherwise.

FORM FOR BIBLIOGRAPHIC ENTRIES

Books

A BOOK WITH ONE AUTHOR	Roszak, Theodore. <u>The Making of a Counter-Culture</u>. Garden City, N.Y.: Anchor Books, 1969.
A BOOK WITH TWO OR THREE AUTHORS	Bryan, Margaret B., and Boyd H. Davis. <u>Writing About Literature and Film</u>. New York: Harcourt Brace Jovano-vich, 1975.
A BOOK WITH MORE THAN THREE AUTHORS	Lauer, Janice, et al. <u>Four Worlds of Writing</u>. New York: Harper & Row, 1981.
A BOOK IN AN EDITION OTHER THAN THE FIRST	Ferguson, Mary Anne. <u>Images of Women in Literature</u>. 2nd ed. Boston: Hough-ton Mifflin, 1973.
A BOOK IN A SERIES	Ryf, Robert S. <u>Henry Green</u>. Columbia Essays on Modern Writers, No. 29. Ed. William York Tindall. New York: Columbia Univ. Press, 1967.
A WORK OF TWO OR MORE VOLUMES	Morison, S. E., and H. S. Commager. <u>The Growth of the American Republic</u>. 3rd ed. 2 vols. New York: Oxford University Press, 1942.
A TRANSLATION	Kazantzakis, Nikos. <u>Zorba the Greek</u>. Trans. Carl Wildman. New York: Simon & Schuster, 1952.
A REPRINT OF AN OLDER EDITION	Lowes, John Livingston. <u>The Road to Xanadu: A Study in the Ways of the Imagination</u>. 2nd ed. 1930; rpt. New York: Vintage-Knopf, 1959.
AN EDITED BOOK	Timko, Michael, ed. <u>Twenty-Nine Short Stories</u>. New York: Knopf, 1975.

A BOOK WITH AN AUTHOR AND EDITOR	Melville, Herman. <u>Billy Budd, Sailor</u>. Ed. Harrison Hayford and Merton M. Sealts, Jr. Chicago: Univ. of Chicago Press, 1962.

A SELECTION IN AN ANTHOLOGY OR COLLECTION	Wills, Gary. "The Making of the Yippie Culture." In <u>Perspectives for the 70's</u>. Ed. Robert G. Noreen and Walter Graffin. New York: Dodd, Mead, 1971.

Encyclopedia Articles

AN UNSIGNED ARTICLE	"Universities." <u>Encyclopaedia Britannica: Macropaedia</u>. 1974 ed.

SIGNED ARTICLE	J[ones], J. K[nox], and D[avid] M. A[rmstrong]. "Mammalia." <u>Encyclopaedia Britannica: Macropaedia</u>. 1974 ed.
	Goodwin, George G. "Mammals." <u>Collier's Encyclopaedia</u>. 1976 ed.

Magazine, Journal, and Newspaper Articles

AN ARTICLE FROM A WEEKLY MAGAZINE	Farrell, Barry. "Second Reading: Bad Vibrations from Woodstock." <u>Life</u>, 5 Sept. 1969, pp. 4–7.

AN ARTICLE FROM A MONTHLY MAGAZINE	DeMott, Benjamin. "Looking Back on the Seventies: Notes Toward a Cultural History." <u>The Atlantic</u>, March 1971, pp. 58–64.

AN ARTICLE FROM A JOURNAL WITH CONTINUOUS PAGINATION THROUGHOUT THE VOLUME	Tracy, Philip. "Birth of a Culture." <u>Commonweal</u>, 90 (1969), 529–33.

AN ARTICLE FROM
A JOURNAL THAT
PAGES EACH ISSUE
SEPARATELY

Kopkind, Andrew. "A New Culture of
Opposition." Current, 111 (October
1969), pp. 54-57.

AN ARTICLE FROM
A DAILY NEWSPAPER

Hartnett, Ken. "The Alternative Society,
Part Two: Disaffected Depend on
Society They Shun." Boston Evening
Globe, 27 April 1971, p. 2 cols 2-5.

A BOOK REVIEW

Morris, Jan. "Visions in the Wilderness."
Rev. of Sands River, by Peter Matt-
hiessen. Saturday Review, April
1981, pp. 68-69.

AN UNSIGNED ARTICLE
OR REVIEW

"Form and Function in a Post and Beam
House." Early American Life, Oct.
1980, pp. 41-43.

A PUBLIC DOCUMENT

U.S. Department of Health, Education, and
Welfare. National Center for Educa-
tional Statistics. Digest of
Educational Statistics. Washington,
D.C.: Government Printing Office, 1968.

AN UNPUBLISHED THESIS
OR DISSERTATION

Stein, Robert A. "Paradise Regained in
the Light of Classical and Christian
Traditions of Criticism and Rhetoric." Diss. Brandeis 1968.

*Films, Television,
and Radio Programs*

Boorman, John, dir. Excalibur. With
Nigel Terry, Helen Mirren, Nicholas
Clay, Cherie Lunghi, Paul Geoffrey,
and Nicol Williamson. Orion Pictures, 1981.

Casey Stengel. Writ. Sidney and David
Carroll. Perf. Charles Durning.
PBS, Boston, 6 May 1981.

Recordings

> Thomas, Dylan. <u>Dylan Thomas Reading</u>.
>
>   Caedmon, TC-1002, 2 vols., 1952.
>
> Moussorgsky, Modeste. <u>Pictures at an</u>
>
>   <u>Exhibition</u>. Leonard Pennario,
>
>   piano. Capitol Records, P-8323,
>
>   n.d.

Letters

A PUBLISHED LETTER

> Mills, Ralph J. Jr., ed. <u>Selected</u>
>
>   <u>Letters of Theodore Roethke</u>.
>
>   Seattle: Univ. of Washington
>
>   Press, 1968.

A PERSONAL LETTER

> Hall, Donald. Letter to author. 18
>
>   Sept. 1980

INTERVIEWS

> Silber, John R. Personal interview. 5
>
>   June 1979.
>
> Kennedy, Senator Edward. Telephone
>
>   interview. 3 May 1980.

EXERCISE 46(2)   Select one or more of the following subjects and list all the likely sources in which you would look for (1) preliminary information and (2) periodical articles on the subject.

1 Bilingual Education for Spanish-Speaking Americans
2 The India-Pakistan Wars
3 Women's Magazines
4 "Black Capitalism"
5 The "Jewish Novel"
6 Acupuncture
7 The Poetry of Robert Frost
8 Jazz in the 1920's
9 The Early Plays of G. B. Shaw
10 Religious Rites of the Navaho Indians
11 The Use of Hypnosis in Medicine
12 Migratory Habits of Birds
13 The Early History of the Teamster's Union
14 Viking Exploration of America
15 Migratory Workers in the Southwest

46

EXERCISE 46(3)   Prepare a short bibliography (on cards) for one of the following topics.

1 Negro Colleges
2 Color Television
3 The Development of Solar Energy
4 The Theatre of the Absurd
5 Organic Foods
6 Medicare
7 Bluegrass Music
8 Pop Art
9 The Assassination of Lincoln
10 Rockets and Interplanetary Travel

EXERCISE 46(4)   Prepare a short working bibliography for one of the following persons and hand in a brief biographical sketch with it.

Martin Luther King	Joe Louis
Margaret Fuller	Charles Steinmetz
Henry Kissinger	Anwar Sadat
Marilyn Monroe	Tennessee Williams
Susan B. Anthony	Charles Chaplin
Harry Truman	Georgia O'Keeffe
Pope John XXIII	Louis Armstrong
Winston Churchill	Frank Lloyd Wright
Ralph Nader	Eudora Welty

Start planning your paper.

The processes of choosing and limiting a subject, making a preliminary search of materials available, and gathering bibliographic entries all help you bring your subject gradually into focus. As you begin to read sources, even at the preliminary stage of your research, your plan should slowly become more and more definite and clear. Try to crystallize it into some sort of outline.

Your early outlines may be quite general and will eventually be reworked as you make additions, deletions, even outright changes in direction. Outlines are useful to let you review your own thinking about your topic, to suggest kinds of information you have and do not have, and to help you see possible patterns of final organization that you can work toward.

Annie Guzman was able to expand and refine her preliminary outline after several days of reading, note-taking, and thinking:

I. Summary of Ray Bradbury's "August 2026 . . ."
  A. Technological advances
  B. Nuclear disaster
II. View of Futurists
  A. Technological advances
    1. Automation in home (plenty in Kahn and Wiener)
    2. Transportation—get more
    3. Energy sources—(too complex?)
    4. Daily life—maybe something on family structure
  B. Possibility of disaster
    1. Nuclear war—need for international control
    2. Overpopulation
      a. Optimistic view
      b. Pessimistic view—get Ehrlich book?
    3. Famine—control over food production
III. Cooperation among nations
  A. Energy—????? (too complex?)
  B. Agriculture
  C. Armaments
  D. Population
IV. Conclusion—Buckminster Fuller

This second outline differs greatly both from the first one (p. 430) and from the final one (pp. 458–459). At this point, Annie was satisfied that she knew where she was going. There were still question marks and reminders, and there would be additions, deletions, and revisions, but the paper was nearing the rough-draft stage.

Take careful notes on your reading. Once you have finished the preliminary search to assure yourself that you have a workable subject, have established some sense of the directions you may take, and have jotted down an initial list of possible headings, you will begin to take notes on everything you read that seems at all pertinent to your topic. Do not be afraid of taking too many notes. It is much easier to lay aside notes that turn out to be superfluous than it is to return to the library to search again for sources you have already gone to the trouble of finding once.

Develop the habit of entering your reading notes on standard-size cards. They are easier to carry than a notebook, easier to refer to than full sheets of paper, and easy to rearrange as you experiment with various possible structures. In taking notes, observe the same principles that you observed in writing out your bibliography cards: Make sure that all your notes are accurate and complete. Be especially careful that you know the exact source from which you took each piece of information. Be *very* careful to distinguish between information you are summarizing or paraphrasing and information you are quoting. Place quotation marks around *all* material you take word for word from any source. In general, force yourself to summarize, paraphrase, and record relevant facts rather than quote. Reserve exact quotation for particularly telling phrases or for information that must be rendered exactly as you found it.

Use a separate card for each note. Each card should contain notes from only one source, and all notes on any one card should be about a single subject. Do not include on a single card notes on more than one subtopic in your outline. The usefulness of your cards depends greatly on the convenience with which they can be arranged in differing sequences.

To make arrangements and rearrangements easier, place a subject heading on each card. Think of a heading as a title for what you have just read. Carefully expressing the heading in your own words, not in words copied from the source, will help you be certain that you understand the material you have read.

Cards with separate notes can easily be combined when you are experimenting with arrangements for your first draft. Cards that combine two or more notes on somewhat different items will prevent you from doing this.

Annie Guzman prepared the note cards on page 439 for her research paper. The first is an exact quotation. The second is a brief summary of several pages of her reading. The third records a short quotation and then summarizes the article's conclusion. Study these cards as well as those given with the text of the research paper. They do not represent the only way to take notes, but they are good notes and, more than anything else, are responsible for the success of the paper itself.

Understand what to acknowledge. One of the purposes of keeping accurate bibliography cards and careful notes that record all your sources and distinguish carefully between direct quotation and paraphrase is to provide you with all the information you will need for documenting in footnotes or endnotes all the material you have gathered in researching your topic. Your own contributions in a research paper are your exact definition of the topic or problem you are studying; the order you impose upon the material you have collected; and the insights, interpretations, judgments, and conclusions you arrive at through your reading in a variety of sources. But in the nature of research, your own final judgments and conclusions grow out of the facts, ideas, and opinions of the various authors whose books and articles you have read and taken notes on. And all those facts, ideas, interpretations, opinions, and conclusions of others that you incorpo-

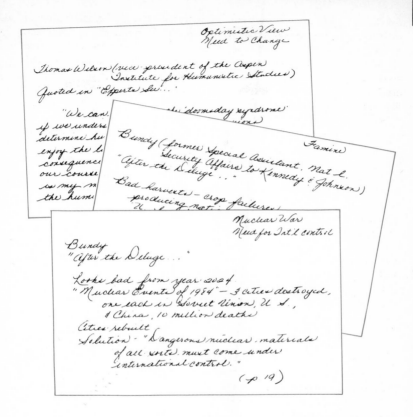

Optimistic View
Need to Change

Thomas Wilson (vice-president of the Aspen
Institute for Humanistic Studies)
Quoted in "Experts See..."

"We can... ...the 'doomsday syndrome'...
if we unders... ...ions
determine he...
enjoy the l...
consequence...
our course...
is my m...
the hum...

Bundy (former Special Assistant.   Famine
Security Affairs) to Kennedy & Johnson)
"After the Deluge..."
Bad harvests — crop failures
producing nat...
U...

Nuclear War
Need for Int'l control

Bundy
"After the Deluge..."

Looks bad from year 2024
"Nuclear Events of 1984" — 3 cities destroyed,
one each in Soviet Union, U.S.,
& China, 10 million deaths
Cities rebuilt
Solution — "Dangerous nuclear materials
of all sorts must come under
international control."
(p. 19)

rate in your own paper you must always acknowledge by documenting the sources.

Always acknowledge in documentation notes all direct quotations, charts, diagrams, tables, and the like, that you reproduce wholly or in part in your paper. Always acknowledge also your paraphrases and summaries of the interpretations, opinions, and conclusions of authors you have read. Keep in mind that the interpretations and conclusions reached by other writers are in many ways more important contributions on their part than the bald facts they may have gathered and therefore even more deserving of acknowledgment.

You do not have to provide documentation for facts that are common knowledge. "Common knowledge" consists of standard historical and literary information available in many different reference books— the date of Lincoln's assassination, the birth and death dates of John F. Kennedy, the fact that Charles Dickens created such characters as Uriah Heep and Mr. Micawber, or that Faulkner's novels are set in the South, or that Darwin's theory of evolution was the subject of great intellectual debate in the nineteenth century. Such information is considered common knowledge as far as documentation is concerned, even though it may be far from the tip of your tongue at the moment, even though you may, in fact, have learned it for the first time when you began your research. In contrast, common sense will tell you that highly specialized facts—the cost of a six-room house in the 1830's, the number of Polaroid cameras sold between 1970 and 1980, the estimated population of Mongolia in 1950, the highest recorded tide in San Francisco Bay, or the number of earthquakes in Peru during the nineteenth century—are unlikely to be common knowledge.

In addition to information that is widely available and undisputed, facts agreed upon by nearly all writers discussing a particular subject are considered common knowledge. As soon as you read in any subject to some depth, you will quickly come to see that certain material is taken as established fact while other material is disputed or has been established by some special investigation. A student writing on Wordsworth for the first time, for example, may not have known at the start that the *Preface to the Lyrical Ballads* was first published in 1800. But it will not take long to discover that everyone writing on the subject accepts this as an established fact. Such information will not need to be acknowledged. In contrast, the exact date of a particular poem may be a matter of dispute or may have been established by a scholar's diligent research. Information of this kind must be acknowledged.

Be careful to avoid plagiarism. Plagiarism consists of passing off other people's ideas, opinions, conclusions, facts, and words as your own. Always acknowledge direct quotations, charts, diagrams, tables, and discussions that paraphrase or summarize the ideas, interpretations, opinions, and conclusions of others.

The most obvious kind of plagiarism occurs when you appropriate whole paragraphs or longer passages from another writer into your own paper. Long word-for-word quotations are rarely appropriate to a paper, but if they ever are, you must indicate clearly that they *are* quotations and indicate their exact source in a note. No less dishonest is the use of all or most of a single sentence or an apt figure of speech appropriated without acknowledgment from another writer.

Suppose, for example, that you are working on a paper about families and have read a book by Jane Howard entitled *Families.* You have a note card on which you have written the partial sentence "Good families have a switchboard operator—someone who cannot help but keep track of what all the others are up to . . ." Your notes indicate that this is a quotation. But when you turn to writing your paper, this and other phrases from the same source seem so apt to your purposes in a slightly different context that you yield to temptation and write, as if in your own words, "All families need at least two things: someone around whom others cluster and someone who cannot help but keep track of what all the others are up to—a kind of switchboard operator." You have plagiarized just as badly as the writer who has appropriated a whole paragraph. The words are not yours, they are Jane Howard's, and honesty requires that you give her credit for them.

You are unlikely to copy directly from another writer without being consciously dishonest as you do so. But even though you acknowledge the source in a note, you are also plagiarizing when you incorporate in your paper faultily paraphrased or summarized passages from another author in which you follow almost exactly the original's sentence patterns and phrasing. Paraphrasing and summarizing require that you fully digest an author's ideas and interpretations and restate them in your own words. It is not enough simply to modify the original author's sentences slightly, to change a word here and there. Consider the following original together with the sample paraphrases and summary:

ORIGINAL   The craft of hurricane forecasting advanced rapidly in the Sixties and early Seventies, thanks to fast computers and new atmospheric modeling techniques. Now there is a lull in the progress, strangely parallel to the lull in the storm cycle. The Center shoots for a 24-hour warning period, with 12 daylight hours for evacuation. At that remove, it can usually predict landfall within 100 miles either way. Longer lead times mean much larger landfall error and that is counterproductive. He who misses his predictions cries wolf.

WILLIAM H. MACLEISH, "Our Barrier Islands," *Smithsonian*, Sept. 1980, p. 54.

FAULTY   Hurricane forecasting made rapid progress in the
PARAPHRASE   sixties and seventies due to fast computers and new atmospheric techniques, but there is now a lull in the progress. The Warning Center tries for a 24-hour warning period, including 12 hours of daylight. That close to a storm, it can usually predict landfall within 100 miles either way. If lead times are longer, there will be a much larger error, which will be counterproductive.[7]

Even though the writer acknowledges the author, as indicated by the footnote at the end of the paragraph, this is a clear example of plagiarism. The author has combined the first two sentences of the original and changed a few words here and there but in no way indicated that most of the paragraph's structure and phrasing is almost exactly that of the original.

IMPROVED
PARAPHRASE

New techniques, together with computers, have significantly increased the accuracy of hurricane forecasting. Now it is possible to predict where a hurricane will hit land with an error of not more than 100 miles if a warning of 24 hours is allowed. If more than 24 hours is required, the error will be proportionately greater.[7]

This paraphrase successfully puts the information in the words of the researcher. Both the sentence structure and the phrasing are clearly the researcher's, not the original author's. But such a full paraphrase of a relatively simple passage is probably much more complete than someone researching hurricane warning problems and developments in a variety of sources would need. In many contexts, a simple, brief summary statement like the following might well be sufficient:

SUMMARY

With computers and new techniques, forecasters can now provide a 24-hour hurricane warning and predict within 100 miles either way where a storm will hit.[7]

Learn when and how to use quotations. A research paper sprinkled with quotations or consisting of long quotations stitched loosely together with brief comments will almost always be an unsatisfactory paper. The point of research is to present in your own words the interpretations and judgments you have come to as a result of your reading, making clear and accurate references to the sources you have learned from.

Nonetheless, since such a paper requires evidence from your sources for the conclusions you have reached, it is likely to lead to more frequent direct quotations than you would ordinarily use in an essay presenting your personal, unresearched views. A carefully researched paper on the changing roles of the family in the past three decades will present more occasions for quotation from outside sources than a personal essay on your changing relationship with your own family.

Learning to use quotations wisely when you have good reason and learning how to fit them easily, naturally, and logically into your own writing are the tricks of effective use of quotation. Your *use* of a quotation, not the quotation itself, is your research contribution. When readers come upon a quotation, they should never feel that it has been dropped upon them suddenly, but rather that it is an intrinsic part of the whole weave of what they are reading.

Many contexts can justify the use of brief and—less frequently—long quotations. But the contexts in which they are most likely to be preferable to paraphrase or summary are those in which the original phrasing is striking or memorable; the force of the writer's statement is important and would be lost in paraphrase; the quotation is an example of what is being discussed; or, in writing about a writer or a literary work, the quotations exemplify the writer's style or typify a character, theme, or the like.

In general, long quotations are less useful and less justified than short ones. Annie Guzman, the writer of the research paper in this section, uses two quotations long enough to require setting off by indentation (see Section **25c**). The two present typical situations in which such quotations are useful. The first gives Ray Bradbury's portrait of a frightening future, which Annie quotes in the opening paragraph of her paper. Here, the quotation immediately establishes a scenario— one kind of possible future—a description it would have been difficult, perhaps impossible, to paraphrase without losing the force of Bradbury's original.

The second long quotation in the paper comes on p. 467, where Annie reproduces some nine lines of direct quotation from Paul Ehrlich, an authority who sees overpopulation as the greatest threat to the future. Although perhaps less well justified than the quotation from Bradbury, the force of Ehrlich's language is important to the paper's purpose and would have been hard to preserve in paraphrase.

Annie provides a fairly formal introduction to each of her long quotations, making clear the purpose of each. Annie has also been selective in both long quotations: as the ellipses indicate, she has left out material by the original authors that is extraneous to her purpose. Such omissions are permissible as long as they do not change the meaning of the original.

In most papers, you are likely to have more occasion to use brief quotations than long ones. Short quotations, well used and not over-used, can often give concreteness and a sense of authenticity to your research. Occasional short quotations, carefully chosen and wisely used in a paper in which paraphrase and summary predominate, testify to the fact that you have read thoroughly and carefully, digested your sources well, and identified telling phrases and statements. Such brief quotations need always to be fitted naturally into the syntax of your own sentences and the flow of your thought.

Study the following examples, noticing how their student writers have worked the quotations smoothly into their own sentences or introduced them with such natural phrases as "John Frederick Nims remarks," "reports that," "in Mary McCarthy's words," or "in the words of one man."

> Not all Victorian women were the shy, timid, modest beings they are sometimes imagined to be. Elizabeth Barrett Browning once submitted a poem about women as sex objects which her editor rejected "for indecency."[6] As John Frederick Nims remarks, "Who would have expected such a poem from a Victorian lady with three names?"[7]

Any study of the music of Bela Bartok can well begin by taking note of the commanding presence of the man himself. Yehudi Menuhin, describing his first meeting with the composer, reports than he "felt at once that I was facing someone pared down to the essential core."[1]

The book which is most informative about Mary McCarthy as a person is perhaps her *Memories of a Catholic Girlhood,* which reflects, in part, her early life with her great-aunt, who, in McCarthy's words, "had a gift for turning everything sour and ugly."[5]

Distrust of and distaste for "new-fangled inventions" is long. English writers of the nineteenth century denounced the arrival of the railroad in their beloved Lake country. Fifty years ago, H. L. Mencken recorded in characteristically pungent language his dislike for automobiles, phonographs, and movies, and observed that although he saw "potentialities" for the radio, he was convinced they would never be realized "so long as the air is laden and debauched by jazz, idiotic harangues by frauds who do not know what they are talking about, and the horrible garglings of ninth-rate singers."[6]

There is nothing like a time of inflation, declining productivity, burgeoning government expenditures, and increasing taxes to unleash a flood of conflicting economic theory. Our own period is fertile ground for such debate, and we find ourselves choosing sides between those who believe that only a return to the virtues of old-line capitalism can save us, preaching that we must untax the rich so that they may invest, since "the creation of wealth is the only salvation of the poor,"[1] and those who tell us that only a "fundamental restructuring of American society"[2] will keep us from going down.

Whenever you make use of direct quotations in your writing, be sure to transcribe them accurately. Make it a rule to check and recheck each quotation, including its punctuation. Make sure that you understand the mechanical conventions of quoting material. Indicate omissions from a quotation by using ellipses (see **26c**), and make sure that what you retain is grammatically coherent. If you insert words of your own in the original, indicate your insertion by placing brackets around it (see **26a**). If the quotation contains a mistake or peculiarity of spelling or grammar, retain it in your quotation but indicate that it appears in the original by using *sic* (thus it is) in brackets immediately following it (see **26b**).

Follow standard forms for documentation notes. Note form, as used in professional scholarship and research, is complex and varied. Most forms have evolved in meeting the demands of formal scholarship, itself a precise and exacting business. Furthermore, conventions of documentation differ from discipline to discipline. If you have occasion to write research papers in a field other than English, you are likely to find that the discipline has its own established conventions that you will be expected to follow. Consult the style of the publications in the field, study the conventions, and adhere to them exactly.

Even though you are now chiefly concerned with adding to your *own* knowledge, you are expected to adopt the habits of the professional scholar and follow an established set of conventions. The conventions described here, like those for bibliographic entries on pp. 432–435, are based on those established by the Modern Language Association and set forth in the *MLA Handbook* (1977).

Number notes consecutively throughout a paper. Indicate that you are providing a note by placing a raised number at the end of the statement to be documented. Always place the raised note number outside whatever punctuation goes with the sentence or paragraph to which it refers, and always at the end of the statement, never at the beginning. Then repeat the raised figure at the beginning of the note itself. Do not use periods, other marks of punctuation, diagonals, or parentheses with note numbers. After the raised numeral, leave a space (one space, if you are typing), then begin the note.

In typewritten papers, double-space all notes. Start each note on a new line, indented five spaces. If the note extends for more than one line, begin the second and later lines flush to the margin.

TEXT

> of these about 100 were independent, over 106 more were church-related, and more than 500 were public institutions.[1]

NOTE

> [1] Paul Woodring, The Higher Learning in America: A Reassessment (New York: McGraw T. McGraw, 1968), p. 32.

In the first full draft of your paper, it sometimes helps you keep track of notes if you include each one as you write, directly after the reference to it, setting it off from the text itself by lines, as in the following. Then in the final draft you can place the notes in their correct position.

TEXT

> "College teachers," writes Professor Seymour E. Harris, "do not primarily seek high economic rewards, or they would not have chosen teaching in the first place."[2]

NOTE

> [2] Higher Education: Resources and Finance (New York: McGraw-Hill, 1962), p. 637.

TEXT

> It becomes increasingly apparent, however, that many who might otherwise have

In the final copy of your paper, notes may be placed either at the bottom of pages on which references fall—**footnotes**—or collected at the end of the paper on a separate page or pages. Placed at the end, they are called **endnotes** or simply **notes.** The *MLA Handbook,* whose guidelines we are following, recommends that in research papers of the sort you are doing, all notes be collected at the end of the paper, as in Annie Guzman's paper in this section. Notes gathered at the end of the paper begin on a separate page entitled *Notes.* These notes are typed consecutively, double-spaced, on as many pages as are necessary; the note pages are numbered consecutively with those of the paper; the first page is often not numbered. The same is true for the bibliography (see also p. 480–481).

Footnotes, too, are typed in consecutive order, double-spaced, with at least a two-line space separating text from footnote. Some instructors prefer you to use a straight line to separate text from footnotes (see an example on p. 445).

The sample note forms that follow are the forms you should use the first time you refer to a particular source you are using in your paper. If you refer to the same source again in your paper, you may often use a shorter form (see pp. 450–451).

FORM FOR NOTES CITING A REFERENCE FOR THE FIRST TIME

Books

A BOOK WITH ONE AUTHOR

[1] Theodore Roszak, The Making of a Counter-Culture (Garden City, N.Y.: Anchor Books, 1969), pp. 47–48.

A BOOK WITH TWO OR THREE AUTHORS

[2] Margaret B. Bryan and Boyd H. Davis, Writing About Literature and Film (New York: Harcourt Brace Jovanovich, 1975), pp. 37–38.

A BOOK WITH MORE THAN THREE AUTHORS

[3] Janice Lauer et al., Four Worlds of Writing (New York: Harper & Row, 1981), pp. 170–71.

A BOOK IN AN EDITION OTHER THAN THE FIRST

[4] Mary Anne Ferguson, Images of Women in Literature, 2nd ed. (Boston: Houghton Mifflin, 1973), p. 268.

A BOOK IN A SERIES

[5] Robert S. Ryf, <u>Henry Green</u>, Columbia Essays on Modern Writers, No. 29, ed. William York Tindall (New York, Columbia Univ. Press, 1967), pp. 22-23.

A WORK OF TWO OR MORE VOLUMES

[6] S. E. Morison and H. S. Commager, <u>The Growth of the American Republic,</u> 3rd ed. (New York: Oxford Univ. Press, 1942), II, 75.

A TRANSLATION

[7] Nikos Kazantzakis, <u>Zorba the Greek</u>, trans. Carl Wildman (New York: Simon & Schuster, 1952), pp. 121-22.

A REPRINT OF AN OLDER EDITION

[8] John Livingston Lowes, <u>The Road to Xanadu: A Study in the Ways of the Imagination</u>, 2nd ed. (1930; rpt. New York: Vintage-Knopf, 1959), p. 231.

AN EDITED BOOK

[9] Michael Timko, ed., <u>Twenty-Nine Short Stories</u> (New York: Knopf, 1975), p. ix.

A BOOK WITH AN AUTHOR AND AN EDITOR

[10] Herman Melville, <u>Billy Budd, Sailor</u>, ed. Harrison Hayford and Merton M. Sealts, Jr. (Chicago: Univ. of Chicago Press, 1962), pp. 27-29.

A SELECTION IN AN ANTHOLOGY OR COLLECTION

[11] Gary Wills, "The Making of the Yippie Culture," in <u>Perspectives for the 70's</u>, ed. Robert G. Noreen and Walter Graffin (New York: Dodd, Mead, 1971), p. 57.

Encyclopedia Articles

AN UNSIGNED ARTICLE

[12] "Universities," <u>Encyclopaedia Britannica: Macropaedia</u>, 1974 ed.

A SIGNED ARTICLE

[13] J. K[nox] J[ones], Jr., and D[avid] M. A[rmstrong],
"Mammalia," <u>Encyclopaedia Britannica: Macropaedia</u>, 1974
ed.

[14] George G. Goodwin, "Mammals," <u>Collier's Ency-
clopaedia</u>, 1976 ed.

Magazine, Journal, and Newspaper Articles

AN ARTICLE FROM A WEEKLY MAGAZINE

[15] Barry Farrell, "Second Reading: Bad Vibrations
from Woodstock," <u>Life</u>, 5 September 1969, p. 4.

AN ARTICLE FROM A MONTHLY MAGAZINE

[16] Benjamin DeMott, "Looking Back on the Seventies:
Notes Toward a Cultural History," <u>The Atlantic</u>, March
1971, p. 60.

AN ARTICLE FROM A JOURNAL WITH CONTINUOUS
PAGINATION THROUGHOUT THE VOLUME

[17] Philip Tracy, "Birth of a Culture," <u>Commonweal</u>,
90 (1969), 532.

AN ARTICLE FROM A JOURNAL THAT PAGES EACH ISSUE
SEPARATELY

[18] Andrew Kopkind, "A New Culture of Opposition,"
<u>Current</u>, 111 (October 1969), 56.

AN ARTICLE FROM A DAILY NEWSPAPER

[19] Ken Hartnett, "The Alternative Society, Part
Two: Disaffected Depend on Society They Shun," <u>Boston
Evening Globe</u>, 27 April 1971, Sec. 3, p. 2, col. 2.

A BOOK REVIEW

[20] Jan Morris, "Visions in the Wilderness," rev. of
<u>Sands River</u>, by Peter Matthiessen, <u>Saturday Review</u>,
April, 1981, p. 69.

AN UNSIGNED ARTICLE OR REVIEW

21 "Form and Function in a Post and Beam House,"
Early American Life, October, 1980, p. 42.

A PUBLIC DOCUMENT

22 U.S. Department of Health, Education, and Welfare, National Center for Educational Statistics, Digest of Educational Statistics (Washington, D.C.: Government Printing Office, 1968), p. 69.

AN UNPUBLISHED THESIS OR DISSERTATION

23 Robert A. Stein, "Paradise Regained in the Light of Classical and Christian Traditions of Criticism and Rhetoric," Diss. Brandeis 1968, p. 73.

Films, Television, and Radio Programs

24 John Boorman, dir., Excalibur, with Nigel Terry, Helen Mirren, Nicholas Clay, Cherie Lunghi, Paul Geoffrey, and Nicol Williamson, Orion Pictures, 1981.

25 Casey Stengel, writ. Sidney and David Carroll, performed by Charles Durning, PBS, Boston, 6 May, 1981.

Recordings

26 Dylan Thomas, "Fern Hill," Dylan Thomas Reading, Vol, I, Caedmon, TC-1002, 1952.

27 Modeste Moussorgsky, Pictures at an Exhibition, Leonard Pennario, piano, Capitol Records, P-8323, n.d.

Letters

A PUBLISHED LETTER

28 "To Kenneth Burke," 6 Sept. 1949, Selected Letters of Theodore Roethke, ed. Ralph J. Mills, Jr. (Seattle: Univ. of Washington Press, 1968), pp. 154-55.

46

A PERSONAL LETTER

^{29} Letter received from Donald Hall, 18 Sept. 1980.

Interviews

^{30} Personal Interview with John Silber, President, Boston University, 5 June 1979.

^{31} Telephone interview with Senator Edward Kennedy, 3 May 1980.

FORM FOR SECOND AND SUBSEQUENT REFERENCES TO A SOURCE

A first note must be detailed because certain information is necessary to distinguish one source from all others. Later notes can—and should—be brief and simple.

Current practice, as encouraged by the *MLA Handbook,* is as follows:

1 If only one work by a given author is used, cite only the author's last name and the appropriate page reference in subsequent notes.

^{1} Theodore Roszak, <u>The Making of a Counter-Culture</u> (Garden City, N.Y.: Anchor Books, 1969), p. 61.

^{4} Roszak, p. 110.

2 If two or more works by the same author are used, cite the author's last name and a shortened title, as follows:

^{1} Benjamin DeMott, "Looking Back on the Seventies: Notes Toward a Cultural History," <u>The Atlantic</u>, March 1971, p. 60.

^{3} Benjamin DeMott, "The Sixties: A Cultural Revolution," <u>New York Times Magazine</u>, 14 December 1969, p. 4.

^{5} DeMott, "Looking Back," p. 62.

^{8} DeMott, "The Sixties," p. 4.

If your reference is to one volume of a work in two or more volumes be careful to indicate the volume number in subsequent notes, even if the reference is to the same volume.

⁴ S. E. Morison and H. S. Commager, <u>The Growth of</u> <u>the American Republic,</u> 3rd ed. (New York: Oxford Univ. Press, 1942), II, 75.

⁹ Morison and Commager, II, 183.

Although the forms described above for note references after the first are now widely used, some editors and instructors continue to prefer the use of the Latin abbreviation *ibid.,* meaning "the same title as the one cited in the previous note," when a subsequent reference to a given work immediately follows the first citation.

¹ Mary Anne Ferguson, <u>Images of Women in Litera-</u> <u>ture,</u> 2nd ed. (Boston: Houghton Mifflin, 1973), p. 268.

² Ibid., p. 249.

If the second reference in the example above were to a work other than Ferguson's *Images of Women in Literature, ibid.* could not be used.

When a second reference cites exactly the same page, only *ibid.* is used; otherwise the appropriate page number is given.

Be aware that documentation forms vary among disciplines. The preferred forms of notes and bibliographic entries vary considerably among disciplines. The style described in the *Publication Manual of the American Psychological Association* describes the style used in psychology and, with slight differences, in several other fields. Each of the natural sciences, the American Medical Association, such fields as linguistics, and many other groups and disciplines have their own preferred styles, each of which is described in detail in the particular group's style manual.

Although these manuals differ in exact detail from discipline to discipline, all sciences use basically one of two systems that may be described as the name and year system and the number system. In both of these systems, the work cited is referenced parenthetically within the text, and the full description of the work appears only at the end of the paper in a *List of References* or *Literature Cited* section.

The **name and year system** places, in parentheses, the last name of the author and the year of publication at the point a source is mentioned in the text. If the author's name is mentioned in the text itself, only the year of publication is given in parentheses.

Bilkovsky (1979) finds no correlation between the growth of the spores and temperature changes of no more than 10°. Therien (1981), however, finds slight changes in the growth rate with changes greater than 7°.

If the author's name is not mentioned in the text itself, it is enclosed in parentheses together with the publication date.

One study (Speisman, 1978) showed Nardil to produce significant changes in the depressive patterns of men over 40, even when the drug was given in a dosage no greater than 30 mg daily.

When page numbers are important, they may be inserted within the parentheses.

Gonzales (1977: 23–25) has calculated the memory properties of the alloy Nitinol.

When this system is used, all references are listed alphabetically by the author's last name at the end of the paper. If two or more studies by the same author are cited, they are listed in chronological sequence by year. The information given on each work in the listing is essentially the same as that required by the MLA form exemplified in this text—author, title, and publication information—but the entries differ in the order in which the information is arranged and in some mechanical details. Only the last name and initials of the author are given, and only the first word of the title is capitalized.

Perkins, J. <u>Neurotic characteristics as predictors of</u>

    <u>author success</u>. Englewood Cliffs, N.J.: Prentice-

    Hall, 1981.

Strethman, C. P. <u>Achievement and longevity</u>. New York:

    John Wiley, 1978.

In the **number system** of documentation, if the author's name is mentioned in the text itself, the reference is indicated only by a number in parentheses. If the author's name is not mentioned, the reference given parenthetically includes the author's last name followed by the appropriate number. References are numbered in this way sequentially throughout the text. In the *List of References* or *Works Cited* section at the end of the paper, each item is given a corresponding number and listed in the order of its occurrence in the text. In the text the reference will appear as follows:

Oliver (11) finds that only one type of halophyte, *Salicornia europa,* or pickleweed, will germinate in water with a saline content of 36 parts per thousand.

The list of references would then show this entry:

11. Oliver, W. H. <u>Salinity tolerance among halophytes</u>.

New York: Academic Press, 1978.

Abbreviations

As recommended by the *MLA Handbook* and other style manuals, researchers currently use many fewer abbreviations than they once did. Several abbreviations, however, such as ed., rev., n.d., and the like, are still commonly used, and others occur frequently in earlier research you may read. The following list contains most of those you are likely to meet:

anon.	anonymous
art., arts.	article(s)
c., ca.	*circa* (about); used with approximate dates
cf.	*confer* (compare)
ch., chs. (*or* chap., chaps.)	chapter(s)
col., cols.	column(s)
diss.	dissertation
ed., edn.	edition
ed., eds.	editor(s)
e.g.	*exempli gratia* (for example)
et al.	*et alii* (and others)
f., ff.	and the following page(s)
ibid.	*ibidem* (in the same place)
i.e.	*id est* (that is)
illus.	illustrator, illustrated by, illustration
introd.	introduction
l., ll.	line(s)
loc. cit.	*loco citato* (in the place cited)
ms, mss	manuscript(s)
n.b.	*nota bene* (take notice, mark well)
n.d.	no date (of publication) given
n.p.	no place (of publication) given
n. pag.	no pagination
no., nos.	number, numbers
numb.	numbered
op. cit.	*opere citato* (in the work cited)
p., pp.	page(s)
passim	throughout the work, here and there
q.v.	*quod vide* (which see)
rev.	revised

rpt.	reprint, reprinted
trans., tr.,	translator, translated, translation
univ.	university
v.	*vide* (see)
vol., vols.	volume(s)

Prepare your final bibliography.

Your last task, when you have completed the final draft of your paper and made sure your notes are all in proper order, is to prepare your final bibliography. Use the cards you prepared as you were working on your paper. Arrange them in alphabetical order by the last name of each author. If you have sources for which no author is given, their position in your alphabetical listing should be determined by the first word of their titles, excluding initial articles *a, an,* and *the.* That is, "A Guide to Course Studies" should be included at its appropriate position under the letter *G.*

Begin your bibliography on a separate page headed *Works Cited, Bibliography,* or *Bibliography of Works Cited* according to your instructor's requirement. Include all items you have referred to in notes or in your text, but unless your instructor requests, do not include any works you may have consulted but have not referred to. Begin each item of your bibliography flush with the left-hand margin. Whenever an item runs to more than one line, indent the second and later lines five spaces. Double-space the bibliography throughout. See the bibliography at the end of the sample research paper for an example.

Sample research paper

Annie Guzman's research paper, presented in this section, is a successful student paper. For this assignment Annie had to choose a topic that interested her, gather authoritative information about it from a number of sources, and organize the information clearly in a paper of about 1,500 words that would both report the information and make some evaluation of it. She was also required to submit a thesis statement, a sentence outline, a bibliography in proper form, and endnotes to document all evidence in appropriate note form. The Commentary accompanying this paper directs attention to some of the problems of writing and documentation Annie faced and solved.

The format. The title of each part (outline, paper, bibliography, endnotes) is centered one inch below the top of the page. The text is double-spaced, with well-balanced left and right margins of about one inch. Small Roman numerals number the thesis and outline pages. Consecutive Arabic numerals number the pages of the paper itself, including the bibliography and endnotes.

The title page, thesis statement, and sentence outline. The first three sections give a quick summary of this research paper. This prefatory material falls into three divisions: (1) *the title,* which is a very general statement; (2) *the thesis statement,* which explains briefly what the paper attempts to do; and (3) *the outline,* which is a rather full statement.

THE FASCINATING AND FRIGHTENING WORLD

OF THE FUTURISTS

By

Annie Guzman

English 101, Section Q

Mr. G. Lapin

April 4, 1982

i

Outline

Thesis: Although all those studying the future recognize the threat
of worldwide disaster, often portraying it vividly, many
believe that through cooperation and technology we can escape doomsday and enjoy major innovations in the ways we live.

I. Ray Bradbury's science-fiction story "August 2026: There Will
Come Soft Rains" gives a fascinating and frightening glimpse
into the future.

II. Most futurists believe we can escape doomsday through technology and cooperation among nations.

A. We can escape the doomsday threats of nuclear war, famine,
and overpopulation through technology and cooperation.

1. Nuclear war: Such a war would have nightmarish consequences, but international control of nuclear
weapons can prevent it.

2. Famine: Crop failures could result in the death of
many millions, but some futurists believe that advanced technology can provide enough food for everyone.

3. Overpopulation: Uncontrolled population growth could
bring humanity to "the brink of extinction," but most
futurists believe we still have time to institute
population control, and may be able to do so without
restricting individual freedom.

B. Cooperation among nations will be an absolute necessity if we are to solve our problems.

    1. We can expect more global interdependence in the future.

    2. We in the United States may have to cut back on our standard of living, but life will be far from unpleasant.

III. Futurists predict major changes in our daily lives.

A. In our daily lives we will make use of many technical innovations, for which we will find the necessary resources and energy sources.

B. We can expect other changes in family size and housing.

C. We will be healthier and live longer as medical science makes major breakthroughs.

IV. There is still time to avert oblivion and instead fulfill the dream of a peaceful, prosperous world, and even dare to work toward a future Utopia.

Commentary

Paragraph 1

This introductory paragraph, the summary of the science-fiction story, not only is interesting—research papers do not have to be boring—but it also serves as a framework to the paper as a whole. It leads to the two key questions asked in paragraph 2 and it serves as a continuing motif in paragraphs 8, 9, and 11. Annie summarizes the story effectively in a few sentences and selects a good quotation to dramatize the situation.

The long quotation is indented ten spaces from the left and double-spaced and does not use quotation marks at beginning and end. Note also the use of ellipsis—three spaced periods after the sentence period.

THE FASCINATING AND FRIGHTENING WORLD

OF THE FUTURISTS

In 1950 Ray Bradbury, the famous science-fiction writer, published
the short story "August 2026: There Will Come Soft Rains." The main
character is a fully automated, almost human house full of mechanical
devices. Meals are prepared automatically according to an established
schedule; listening devices are programmed to recognize and respond to
people's voices; and the house's own "voice" entertains by reading
poetry aloud. Bridge tables miraculously appear in time for card games,
and tiny automated cleaning animals resembling robot mice continually
keep the house spotless. The house seems to function without the aid
of any human beings, and early in the story we are told that that is
indeed the case:

> The house stood alone in a city of rubble and ashes. . . .
> At night the ruined city gave off a radioactive glow which
> could be seen for miles. . . . The entire west face of the
> house was black, save for five places. Here the silhouette
> in paint of a man mowing a lawn. Here, as in a photograph,
> a woman bent to pick flowers. Still farther over, their
> images burned on wood in one titanic instant, a small boy,
> hands flung into the air; higher up, the image of a thrown
> ball, and opposite him a girl, hands raised to catch a ball
> which never came down.[1]

Paragraph 2

Using the story as a link, Annie introduces the two questions she will answer in her paper. Paragraphs 3, 4, 5, and 6 will deal with the possibility of disaster, and paragraphs 8, 9, and 10 will deal with possible technological advances. Annie has divided her paper into two parts—"the fascinating" and "the frightening," or "the hopes" and "the fears." The reader, given a good direct statement about the intention and limits of the paper, knows exactly what to expect.

Paragraph 3

This paragraph is a general answer to the first question and will be developed in greater detail in the following three paragraphs. Some readers might question Annie's statement about "most futurists." How can she arrive at such a conclusion on the basis of necessarily limited reading? Her defense would be that she felt she had looked at a reasonably large body of material, had noted that a few authorities had also written that "most" futurists felt that way, and that her judgment was based on objective reading of what she believed were representative viewpoints.

Annie tells us something about the authorities she cites—Wilson is "of the Aspen Institute"; in paragraph 4 Bundy is "a former White House aide"; in paragraph 5 Abelson is "editor of *Science Magazine*." Such identification is important because it provides evidence that the authorities cited are really authorities.

Paragraph 4

In a good opening sentence, Annie introduces the three elements of the first part of her paper—the answer to the first question. She then begins discussion of the first element, "nuclear war." In her research, Annie had gathered a good deal of material about the horrors of nuclear war, and in the first draft of the paper she had devoted a complete paragraph to that subject. But then she decided that she was belaboring the point and was in danger of losing sight of her thesis statement.

Her decision to remove the paragraph from the final draft was a good one. Writers must learn to resist the temptation to include all their researched material; and they must learn to be discriminating in their revisions.

2

Bradbury's imaginative glimpse into the future is both fascinating and frightening. The future, the story seems to say, holds out the possibility of tremendous technological advances, but also the threat of total destruction. Today both the hopes and the fears concern not only the science-fiction writers but also the scientists and scholars-- "futurists"--whose studies cover a very wide range of interests. My own interest in this subject I have limited to the two questions raised by Bradbury's story: How real is the threat of worldwide disaster? And if we do have a future, what kind of technological and other advances can the average American really expect?

As for the first question, most futurists believe we can avoid the kind of catastrophe described in the story. Thomas Wilson, of the Aspen Institute for Humanistic Studies, seems to sum up this view: "We can ward off the 'doomsday syndrome' if we understand that human decisions determine human conditions. . . . We have the ability to change our course--our social values--and this is my main cause for optimism about the human predicament."[2]

The three most frequently mentioned causes of a future doomsday are nuclear war, famine, and overpopulation. Former White House aide McGeorge Bundy, taking an imaginative look backward from the year 2024, speaks of the "Nuclear Events of 1984" in which three great cities were destroyed, one each in the Soviet Union, China, and the United States, with the loss of ten million lives. But he sees this nightmarish pro-

Paragraph 5

Annie moves neatly to the second element, and again cites Bundy to point out the possible consequences. This time, however, Annie presents the views of two additional authorities. She felt she had to do so because she herself was surprised to read that experts were so optimistic about food production. Again, she exercised good judgment. (There is no need to belabor a point, to indulge in "documentation overkill"; but when it is necessary to prove a point, do not hesitate to use more than one source.) In addition, Annie realized that she had relied entirely on Bundy in her discussion of nuclear disaster. Though he had proved a good authority, she recognzed the need to support her point with additional authorities.

By comparing the note cards below with the text, you can see how effectively Annie paraphrases the Piel quotation and how she works the Abelson statement into the structure of her sentence.

3

phesy not as leading to the end of the world but as a terrible lesson that teaches the leaders of the nations to do something about international control of nuclear weapons.[3] Certainly such a scenario can by no means be described as "optimistic"--although other possibilities in thermonuclear, gas, and biological warfare are more horrifying. What futurists are saying is that if we realize how utterly destructive future wars can be, perhaps we will learn in time to prevent such wars.

The second doomsday nightmare is famine in large parts of the world. In Bundy's scenario, famines resulting from crop failures in the grain-producing countries cause a death toll of sixty-five million.[4] Bundy then imagines the creation of an international "World Food Commission" with the power to prevent future famines.[5] But other futurists are even more confident that famine can be averted. Gerard Piel, keynote speaker at the 1976 annual meeting of the American Institute of Biological Sciences, was optimistic about the ability of advanced technology to provide enough food for everyone, and he cited one agricultural expert who estimated that India alone could feed the world.[6] Philip H. Abelson, editor of <u>Science Magazine</u>, believes that the United States is technically capable of feeding a "population ten to one hundred times as great as our present one." But as do others, Abelson recognizes that the basic problem is not insufficient food but overpopulation.[7]

Paragraph 6

Annie introduces the third element, but this time she gives the first words to the more pessimistic view of Ehrlich. Ideally, she should have gone to Ehrlich's book, since Hilsman in his footnote tells us where he got the quotation. The reason the original source is better is that readers can then go to the source and make a judgment about whether or not the quoted writer has been treated fairly. Does the quotation truly represent his view? Is it taken out of context? Have important ideas or modifications been left out?

Annie's defense was, "What am I supposed to do—spend my whole life in the library?" It's hard to argue with the writer of a good paper, but still . . .

In the last sentence, Annie recapitulates the three doomsday possibilities by mentioning once again the Bundy scenario.

Note the *three* spaced periods indicating ellipsis within a sentence in the quoted paragraph, and the use of brackets to indicate a change Annie made in the Hilsman quotation.

4

6

And here the futurists come to the third possible doomsday--
overpopulation. But again the views of most futurists are more optimistic than one might expect. Roger Hilsman, for example, does not see the
future as bleakly as Paul R. Ehrlich, who wrote in 1970:

> The explosive growth of the human population is the most
> significant terrestrial event of the past million millennia.
> Three and one half billion people now inhabit the Earth, and
> every year this number increases by 70 million. . . . Man-
> kind itself may stand on the brink of extinction; in its
> death throes it could take with it most of the other passen-
> gers of Spaceship Earth. No geological event in a billion
> years . . . has posed a threat to terrestrial life comparable
> to that of human overpopulation.[8]

Hilsman believes that mankind can solve this problem, and that even
with a population of seven billion in the year 2000, there is still
hope to slow down the rate of growth and to find the food, resources,
and energy to support that population. Hilsman admits he is "alarmed"
by the present threat of overpopulation, but he believes that humans
"will <u>eventually</u> solve [the] problem."[9] And Dennis Gabor believes this
can be done "without any dictatorial interference with the family and
with the institutionalized religions."[10] It is interesting to note

Paragraph 7

This paragraph serves both as a commentary on the doomsday section and as a transition to the second part of the paper—the answer to the second question. Here again, Annie had much more material than she used. She put in the Waldheim quotation because of his authoritative position as Secretary General of the United Nations, and she summarized Barber's ideas because he said so succinctly what other futurists were saying. Here are some of the cards she worked with:

5

that in Bundy's futuristic scenario, population control is tied to the program to end hunger, and thus, together with international control of nuclear weapons, the world finds solutions to the three major problems it faces.[11]

7   If there is one thing that futurists agree upon, it is that cooperation among nations will be an absolute necessity. Kurt Waldheim, Secretary General of the United Nations, states, "It is this fact of global interdependence which is the dominant reality of our times, and it will become increasingly so over the next fifty years."[12] Such interdependence may very well result, as one authority pointed out in an interview, in the need for us in the United States to cut back on our standard of living. A nation that has six percent of the world's population cannot continue to use forty percent of the world's resources.[13] But, although life may change in a number of ways, future inhabitants of the United States will find life not at all unpleasant.

8   According to at least one prediction, the automation described in Bradbury's science-fiction story will probably be part of daily life in the United States by the year 2000. In a list of one hundred "very likely" technical innovations, the authors include such items as "Automated or more mechanized housekeeping and home maintenance . . . automated grocery and department stores . . . extensive use of robots

Paragraph 8

Annie begins discussion of the second part of the report. Here the three elements are not so clearly marked as in the first part, but material does not always lend itself to clear-cut divisions or categories. Annie does well in organizing and condensing what she does have. Wisely, she anticipates a question from the reader: Where will the energy for all this automation come from? And wisely, she resists the temptation to get deeply involved in the controversy over energy resources, not because she cannot find any answers but because there are just too many for her to make use of in this paper.

Paragraph 9

Annie continues with the discussion by presenting material from several sources. This catch-all paragraph could have been strengthened by the introduction of more sociological data, more predictions about "the home" rather than the house of the future. But the paragraph is well organized and begins and ends with effective transitional devices.

The bit about the contoured bathtub Annie did not find in the library. She just ran across it while reading the newspaper. This is not unusual, since good researchers give themselves plenty of time and often happen upon useful material in unexpected places.

and machines 'slaved' to humans."[14] Such large-scale mechanization would of course require unprecedented demands for energy and resources, but futurists seem to be optimistic about the possibility of discovering new resources and energy sources. Rene Dubos stated in an interview that "resources don't exist until we invent them. . . . A resource is something that each generation learns to extract and use." For example, he suggests that new technologies will make it possible for us to make use of much that we now consider industrial and domestic waste.[15] In addition, we will make considerable use of new sources of energy such as solar electrical power and geothermic energy.[16]

9

But of course a house--even a science-fiction house--is not a home. And here, too, futurists see changes in the years to come. Families will be smaller; there will be more single people and childless couples.[17] Actually, the citizen of the future is unlikely to live in a single-family dwelling, as in the Bradbury story, since such housing will not only be too expensive for the average person but will also become a symbol of wastefulness and thus "socially unacceptable."[18] Instead, the condominium will replace the single-family home.[19] Heating of buildings will be made more efficient, and even bathtubs may be contoured to the body to avoid wasting hot water.[20]

Paragraph 10

This is a well-written paragraph. It begins with a good topic sentence, provides links between sentences, and contains a good mix of paraphrase, summary, and direct quotation. The information is derived from five different sources, but the paragraph flows smoothly from beginning to end.

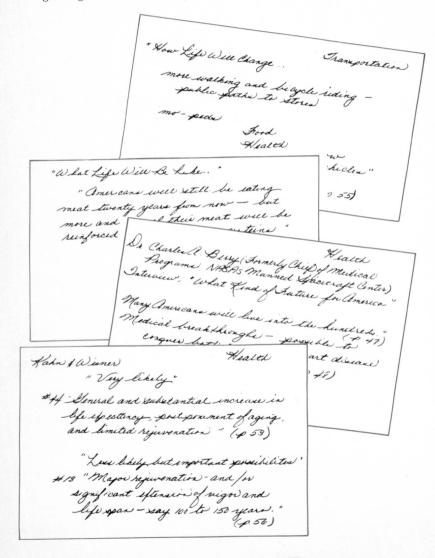

7

Conservation of energy will also probably result in a healthier lifestyle. Since we will be less likely to use automobiles--we will see more bicycles, mopeds, and trolleys[21]--people will do more walking. A reduction of meat in our diet will also be healthier for us, and the meat we do eat will be reinforced with vegetable proteins.[22] The fact that we will be eating less and less meat is suggested by a headline "Remember Chickens?" in "Clippings from Tomorrow's Newpaper: News Stories of 2024" by scientist and science-fictionist Isaac Asimov.[23] More important, Kahn and Wiener list as "very likely" such advancements as "general substantial increase in life expectancy, postponement of aging, and limited rejuvenation" and as an "important possibility" a life span of between 100 and 150 years.[24] Dr. Charles A. Berry, the "astronauts' doctor," stated in an interview that he believes many people will have a life span of one hundred years, and the future will also bring major medical breakthroughs, including the conquest of both cancer and heart disease.[25]

Number 87 in Kahn and Wiener's list of one hundred very likely innovations is "stimulated and planned and perhaps programmed dreams."[26] This sounds like science-fiction material (what Andrew A. Spekke calls "Buck Rogers stuff"),[27] but in a way it summarizes what most futurists

Paragraph 11

Annie spent a great deal of time on her final paragraph. It is a good one. It summarizes the paper; it reminds us of the science-fiction story and contrasts the story's conclusion with the vision of Buckminster Fuller. Annie came across his name many times while doing her research, and she decided very early that she would end her paper with a quotation from his works.

It is worthwhile comparing Annie's final draft of the last four sentences with her first two drafts. The time she spent on the rewriting was clearly worth it.

FIRST DRAFT

R. Buckminster Fuller, who is regarded by many as the "prophet" among futurists, is more optimistic than Ray Bradbury. Bradbury seems to say that even if we attain a technical Utopia we will end in oblivion. But Fuller writes: "This moment of realization that it soon must be Utopia or Oblivion coincides exactly with the discovery by man that for the first time in history Utopia is, at least, physically possible of human attainment." Not only futurists but all people hope that he is right.

SECOND DRAFT

R. Buckminster Fuller, the "Prophet," is optimistic about making the dream come true. He believes that Utopia is possible, but it will not come unless we choose it. Bradbury offers Utopia and then Oblivion, but Fuller speaks for the many futurists who feel there is still time for mankind to come to its senses. He believes that "for the first time in history Utopia is, at least, physically possible of human attainment."

8

are saying. If we hope to achieve the dream of a peaceful, prosperous world, we will have to stimulate our imaginations and plan and program our course of action. R. Buckminster Fuller, perhaps the most respected "prophet" among the futurists, believes that the chances of fulfilling that dream are good. He is not afraid to speak of a future Utopia. Whereas Bradbury seems to offer both Utopia and oblivion, Fuller speaks for those who feel there is still time for us to come to our senses and choose our future. He writes: "This moment of realization that it soon must be Utopia or Oblivion coincides exactly with the discovery by man that for the first time in history Utopia is, at least, physically possible of human attainment."[28]

Documentation notes. Note 1 follows MLA style for a first reference to a short story in an edited collection. The author's name is not given in the note since it was mentioned in the text. Giving the edition makes it possible for the reader to find the documented material; editions often differ considerably.

Note 2 follows MLA style for an unsigned article in a weekly magazine. "Quoted in" makes clear that Thomas Wilson is not the author of the article.

Note 3, like note 2, follows the form for a weekly magazine. Since the author was identified in the text, his name is omitted from the note.

Notes 4 and 5 require only the name of the author and the page references since they refer to the source cited in note 3.

Note 6 is in MLA style for an article in a journal with continuous pagination throughout the volume.

Note 7 is MLA form for a signed article in a book by several contributors and an editor.

Note 10 refers to the publisher, Alfred A. Knopf, simply as Knopf. MLA style recommends the use of shortened forms of publisher names. Such shortened forms may be used in bibliographic entries too.

Note 14 follows MLA form for a book written by two authors. It also contains a brief documented comment that Annie did not incorporate into the text. Editors and teachers disagree about notes of this type, called **substantive notes.** Some readers of research papers find substantive notes a useful way to include material that is relevant but too digressive to include in the text itself. Others feel that if material is not significant enough to be in the text, it should not appear in the paper at all. Check with an instructor before you use substantive notes, and never use them simply to cram in all the leftover bits of your research.

9

NOTES

1 An Introduction to Literature, ed. Sylvan Barnet, Morton Berman, and William Burto, 6th ed. (Boston: Little, Brown, 1977), pp. 270-71.

2 Quoted in "Experts See World Perils Ahead—But 'Humanity Will Survive,'" U. S. News & World Report, 23 June 1975, p. 64.

3 "After the Deluge, the Covenant," Saturday Review/World, 24 Aug. 1974, p. 19.

4 Bundy, pp. 18-19.

5 Bundy, p. 20.

6 Quoted in "The Next 200 Could Be Best," BioScience, 26 (1976), 431.

7 "The Continuing Scientific Revolution," in Man and the Future, ed. James E. Gunn (Lawrence, Kansas: The Univ. Press of Kansas, 1968), p. 57.

8 Quoted in Roger Hilsman, The Crouching Future (Garden City, N. Y.: Doubleday, 1975), pp. 503-04.

9 Hilsman, p. 504.

10 Inventing the Future (New York: Knopf, 1964), p. 210.

11 Bundy, p. 20.

12 "Toward Global Interdependence," Saturday Review/World, 24 Aug. 1974, p. 63,

13 Benjamin R. Barber, in "What Kind of Future for America?" U. S. News & World Report, 7 July 1975, p. 46.

14 Herman Kahn and Anthony J. Wiener, The Year 2000: A Framework for Speculation on the Next Thirty-Three Years (New York: Macmillan, 1967), pp. 52, 53, 54. Some of these predictions seem to have come

Note 16 indicates a summary of six pages. Annie had four separate note cards with information about various sources of energy but ultimately decided that all she could spare was a one-sentence statement.

Note 19 gives a shortened form of the title first documented in note 17.

Note 20 provides information about the columns the newspaper article can be found in as well as the page and section.

In note 28, Annie refers to a work she did not actually use in her paper. Although she took notes from this collection, she found no direct use for the material. She did feel, however, that the book was interesting enough to mention to readers of her research paper who might want to look deeper into the topic for themselves.

true already. Robot mail carts and an electronic library are in use.
A. R. Roalman, "A Practical Approach to Predicting the Future," Science
Digest, Nov. 1976, 75.

[15] "Looking into the Future," Current, 171 (Mar. 1975), 40.

[16] Gabor, pp. 95-100.

[17] "How Life Will Change for Americans in Years Ahead," U. S. News
& World Report, 12 Jan. 1976, p. 54.

[18] Rene Dubos, "Recycling Social Man," Saturday Review/World, 24
Aug. 1974, p. 10.

[19] "How Life Will Change . . .," p. 54.

[20] "Contoured Bathtub--Energy Saver of the Future," The Boston
Globe, 14 Feb. 1977, Sec. 2, p. 6, cols. 3-7.

[21] "How Life Will Change . . .," p. 55.

[22] "What Life Will Be Like 20 Years in the Future," U. S. News &
World Report, 14 Jan. 1974, p. 74.

[23] Saturday Review/World, 24 Aug. 1974, p. 78.

[24] Kahn and Wiener, pp. 53, 56.

[25] "What Kind of Future for America?" pp. 47-48.

[26] Kahn and Wiener, p. 55.

[27] "America: The Next 200 Years," Intellect, 105 (1976), 50.

[28] Utopia or Oblivion: The Prospects for Humanity (New York:
Bantam, 1969), p. 292. For some informative discussion about Buckmin-
ster Fuller's ideas as well as selections from his writings, see
Patricia Wallace Garlan, Maryjane Dunstan, and Dyan Howell Pike, Star
Sight: Visions of the Future (Englewood Cliffs, N.J.: Prentice-Hall,
1977), pp. 107-45.

WORKS CITED

Asimov, Isaac. "Clippings from Tomorrow's Newspapers: News Stories
    of 2024." Saturday Review/World, 24 Aug. 1974, pp. 78, 80.

Bradbury, Ray. "August 2026: There Will Come Soft Rains." An Intro-
    duction to Literature. Ed. Sylvan Barnet, Morton Berman, and
    William Burto. 6th ed. Boston: Little, Brown, 1977.

Bundy, McGeorge. "After the Deluge, the Covenant." Saturday Review/
    World, 24 Aug. 1974, pp. 18-20, 112-114.

"Contoured Bathtub--Energy Saver of the Future." The Boston Globe, 14
    Feb. 1977, Sec. 2, p. 6, cols. 3-7.

Dubos, Rene. "Recycling Social Man." Saturday Review/World, 24 Aug.
    1974, pp. 8-10. 102-06.

"Experts See World Perils Ahead--But 'Humanity Will Survive.'" U. S.
    News & World Report, 23 June 1975, pp. 64-65.

Fuller, R. Buckminster. Utopia or Oblivion: The Prospects for Human-
    ity. New York: Bantam, 1969.

Gabor, Dennis. Inventing the Future. New York: Knopf, 1964.

Garlan, Patricia Wallace, Maryjane Dunstan, and Dyan Howell Pike.
    Star Sight: Visions of the Future. Englewood Cliffs, N.J.:
    Prentice-Hall, 1977.

12

Gunn, James E., ed. Man and the Future. Lawrence, Kansas: The Univ. Press of Kansas, 1968.

Hilsman, Roger. The Crouching Future. Garden City, N. Y.: Doubleday, 1975.

"How Life Will Change for Americans in Years Ahead." U. S. News & World Report, 12 Jan. 1976, pp. 54-56.

Kahn, Herman, and Anthony J. Wiener. The Year 2000: A Framework for Speculation on the Next Thirty-Three Years. New York: Macmillan, 1967.

"Looking Into the Future." Current, 171 (Mar. 1975), 24-46.

Roalman, A. R. "A Practical Approach to Predicting the Future." Science Digest, Nov. 1976, pp. 74-79.

Spekke, Andrew A. "America: The Next 200 Years." Intellect, 105 (1976), 49-50.

Waldheim, Kurt. "Toward Global Interdependence." Saturday Review/ World, 24 Aug. 1974, pp. 63-64, 122.

"What Kind of Future for America?" U. S. News & World Report, 7 July 1975, pp. 44-50.

"What Life Will Be Like 20 Years in the Future." U. S. News & World Report, 14 Jan. 1974, pp. 72-75.

WRITING SUMMARIES AND ESSAY EXAMS

47 SUMMARIES

The ability to summarize effectively—to strip a paragraph or a chapter down to its central meaning without distorting the author's original thought and approach—is extremely useful. Writing such summaries is an excellent way to study. Having such summaries available is invaluable for later reference and review.

Preparing summaries can also help you to read with greater accuracy and to write with greater conciseness and directness. You cannot summarize effectively if you have not read carefully, discriminating between principal and subordinate ideas. Such discrimination, in turn, will help you to sharpen your own style and to avoid the wordiness that creeps into careless writing.

Before you try to summarize a passage, read it carefully to discover the author's purpose and point of view. As you read, pick out the central ideas and notice how they are arranged. Be on the lookout for the author's own compact summaries, either at the beginning or end of a passage or at points of transition.

After studying the passage, you are ready to organize your summary, or **précis.** Ordinarily you will be able to reduce a paragraph—or sometimes a whole group of paragraphs—to a single sentence. Very complex paragraphs, however, may require more than one sentence.

Use a simple or complex sentence rather than a compound sentence to summarize a paragraph—unless the original paragraph itself is poorly organized. A compound sentence implies that there are two or more equally dominant ideas in the paragraph. If you find that you have written a compound summarizing sentence, recheck the paragraph to make sure that the author did not imply some subordinating relationship that you have missed. In determining the author's intent, be alert to such writing techniques as parallel clauses and phrases, which indicate ideas of equal weight, and transitional words and phrases, which show relationships among ideas.

Summarize the author's ideas in the order in which they have been presented, but avoid following the exact wording too closely. If you are overly scrupulous in trying to preserve the flavor of the original, your summary will be far too long. Do not hesitate, however, to pick up the author's key terms and phrases, for they are useful in binding the précis together. Discard any figures of speech, digressions, or discussions that are not essential to the "trunk and main branches." When you are all through, you should find that you have reduced the material to not over one-third of its original length. Study the following example:

We very rarely consider, however, the process by which we gained our convictions. If we did so, we could hardly fail to see that there was usually little ground for our confidence in them. Here and there, in this department of knowledge or that, some one of us might make a fair claim to have taken some trouble to get correct ideas of, let us say, the situation in Russia, the sources of our food supply, the origin of the Constitution, the revision of the tariff, the policy of the Holy Roman Apostolic Church, modern business organization, trade unions, birth control, socialism, the League of Nations, the excess-profits tax, preparedness, advertising in its social bearings; but only a very exceptional person would be entitled to opinions on all of even these few matters. And yet most of us have opinions on all these, and on many other questions of equal importance, of which we may know even less. We feel compelled, as self-respecting persons, to take sides when they come up for discussion. We even surprise ourselves by our omniscience. Without taking thought we see in a flash that it is most righteous and expedient to discourage birth control by legislative enactment, or that one who decries intervention in Mexico is clearly wrong, or that big advertising is essential to big business and that big business is the pride of the land. As godlike beings why should we not rejoice in our omniscience? JAMES HARVEY ROBINSON, *The Mind in the Making*

Notice that this paragraph hinges on the sentence beginning *And yet most of us have opinions on all these. . . .* This sentence suggests the pattern that your summarizing sentence should probably take. The central idea of the paragraph is that we do not ordinarily take pains in forming our convictions on important matters, but we nevertheless express our opinions as a matter of right and even take delight in our apparent omniscience. The main clause of your summarizing sentence will express the second part of the central idea, retaining the author's ironic approach.

We are godlike beings who delight in our ability to form and express convictions on birth control, on intervention in Mexico, or on the role of big business, without a moment's thought.

To preserve the author's qualification in the first part of the paragraph, however, you must precede the main clause with a subordinate clause.

Although the few pains we take to understand such things as the situation in Russia, the sources of our food supply, the origin of the Constitution, the revision of the tariff, the policy of the Holy Roman Apostolic Church, modern business organization, trade unions, birth control, socialism, the League of Nations, the excess-profits tax, preparedness, and advertising in its social bearings give us little reason to have confidence in our opinions on these matters, we are godlike beings who delight in our ability to form and express convictions on birth control, on intervention in Mexico or on the role of big business, without a moment's thought.

But this "summary" is almost half as long as the original. To reduce it further, replace the specific examples with general terms.

Although the few pains we take to understand such things as social, political, economic, religious, and medical issues give us little reason to have confidence in our convictions on these matters, we are godlike beings who delight in our ability to form and express such convictions without a moment's thought.

This summary, less than one-third the length of the original, would be acceptable for most purposes, but occasionally even a shorter summary is desirable.

Although we have little reason to trust our convictions on the important issues of life, we delight in forming and expressing such opinions without a moment's thought.

Clearly this last sentence does not express everything in Robinson's paragraph, where the concreteness and the vigor of the short sentences are perhaps even more striking than its central thought. But a summary is concerned only with the central thought, not necessarily with retaining the author's style, and the central thought is preserved even in the shortest statement above.

EXERCISE 47(1)   Write a two-sentence summary of the paragraph by Jacques Barzun, on pp. 268–69, beginning "The whole aim of good teaching."

EXERCISE 47(2)   Write a one-sentence summary of the same paragraph.

EXERCISE 47(3)   Try to write a one-sentence summary of the following paragraph. Does the effort tell you anything about the weakness of the paragraph itself?

Among the many interesting aspects of dietary training is the living together of the students. This allows each to get acquainted with people from all over the States and to exchange ideas and viewpoints from different sections of the country. By living in such a home, many girls grow into more mature individuals. It proves a good chance for girls who have always lived at home to become more independent. It also helps to establish feelings of self-sufficiency in those who have never before been on their own.

EXERCISE 47(4)   Write the briefest summary you can of the paragraph below.

Great care and attention is given in the organization of pageants and other popular feasts, and of these a Russian crowd is particularly appreciative, throwing itself wholeheartedly into the enjoyment of every detail. The "crowd sense," which is just another expression of the corporate instinct, is peculiarly strong in Russia, and it is often curiously reminiscent of an English crowd, particularly in its broad and jolly sense of humor. But Russians of any class have a much stronger artistic sense than we have. This was so before the revolution, and it comes out in the organization of these festivals. They are all out to enjoy themselves, and anything particularly clever or pretty gets them at once. In Kiev, still as always a beautiful city on its lovely site, in the late summer of 1936, I saw a march past of all the wards in turn. They swung past with splendid vigor, squads of men or of women—one squad of women had in the middle of it a fine old man with a long beard who looked very pleased with his company. There were flowers and dancing everywhere; each ward was preceded by a dancing band of girl skirmishers in the picturesque Ukrainian costume, sometimes singing the charming Ukrainian folk songs. At one point various forms of recreation and amusement were represented: the fishermen carrying long fishing rods with colored paper fish hooked to them, the chess players carrying enormous cardboard knights, bishops, and castles. Interspersed between the detachments came curious and fanciful constructions, sometimes very ingenious; an effigy of Trotsky with long nose and black eyes and curls made an excellent Mephistopheles. It was a family feast of old and young, and we all exchanged our comments as each new surprise went past. With the usual courtesy to guests there was a chair set for me, and when I wanted to let a lady have it, I was genially told "that I had to submit to the will of the majority." At one time a torrent of rain came down, but the marchers swung past with all the more vigor and enjoyment. And so it was with the on-lookers. After several hours of it, I asked a neighboring policeman whether I couldn't go away: "No," he said very nicely, "you must stay and enjoy it." And enjoy it they certainly did, for in spite of more downpours of rain, from my room in the hotel I could hear them singing and dancing on the square outside till two in the morning. The one thing that fell below the level of all the rest was the exhausting reiteration of the portraits of Stalin and the other "big noises" of Communism. There must have been about forty of Stalin alone: one ten foot high, of the face alone. I noticed a sympathetic cheer when there came past a single portrait of Lenin.   BERNARD PARES, *Russia: Its Past and Present*

48   ESSAY EXAMS

What you have learned from this handbook about effective writing applies to the special problem of writing essays for exams. You will be expected to write standard English, to organize material intelligently, and to provide evidence and detail to support generalizations. When you have several days to write a paper or a take-home exam, you spend a good part of the time on prewriting—choosing and limiting your subject, thinking about it, gathering material, and outlining. You also have time to make important changes after your first draft—revising paragraphs and sentences, substituting more precise words, and proofreading. You cannot expect to do all this in the half-hour, hour, or even two hours you have for an in-class exam. You are writing under pressure; you have so much time and no more. Therefore, it saves time to go into essay exams knowing how to proceed.

Preparation

Most of your prewriting must be done before you go to the exam. How can you accomplish that when you don't know what questions will be asked? You will not be able to choose a subject; it will be chosen for you—or, at best, you will be allowed to choose from among two or three. You know the *general subject* of the exam, however: it is the subject matter of the course or of part of the course. Your goal, then, is to go to the exam having in mind a rough outline of the course segments. This process of outlining begins with the first lecture or reading assignment and continues uninterrupted to the day of the exam. Take notes during lectures, underline key passages and make marginal notations in your textbooks, summarize your reading, look over your gathered material from time to time, evaluate it, and structure it. You will then be ready to study and review for the exam. As you study, prepare a more formal outline based on an overview of the course material and any guidelines suggested by your instructor. Writing such an outline and studying it helps fix the general subject in your mind.

Prewriting

As soon as you see the specific questions in an exam, your subject is limited for you. Say, for example, your general subject was the history of Europe from 1815 to 1848—the segment of the course on which you are being examined. Now you are given fifty minutes to answer four questions, the first of which is: *What were the four major political and social developments in Europe during the period of 1815–1848?* Or, your general subject was three stories by Nathaniel Hawthorne and two by Herman Melville—the stories you discussed in class. Now you are given fifty minutes to answer two questions, the first of which is: *Hawthorne has been called a "moralist-psychologist." Define the term and eval-*

uate Hawthorne's effectiveness as moralist-psychologist by making specific reference to two of his tales.

Read the examination question carefully. Never start writing without thinking about what you are being asked to do. Are you being asked to summarize or to analyze? Are you expected to present information or to interpret? Are you being asked to comment on a given statement, possibly disagree with it, or to prove it by providing supporting evidence?

The European history question directs you to furnish information (what *are* the four major developments?). You have only about ten minutes to answer the question, so you will not be able to go into great detail. Don't try to fill up half a blue book with everything you know about the subject. In the second question, you are asked to define and evaluate; you must make a critical judgment on the basis of specific evidence in Hawthorne's stories. You have approximately twenty-five minutes to organize and write the essay. Make it a rule to take a minute or two to think about the question, and answering it will be easier.

Having done this, gather material and prepare a rough outline of the limited topic. Typical notes for the history question could include the following:

> 1815—Congress of Vienna
> 1848—Revolutions
> Nationalism—C. of V. denied rights to Poles, Belgians, Greeks, etc.
> Conservative—Liberal Conflict—Cons. anti-reform. Lib. underground
> Industrial Expansion—Intro. of machines. Transportation—railroads, steam transport, etc.
> Class conflict—Lower class vs. middle class

An answer to the question on Hawthorne could develop from the following notes:

> How human beings behave (psych.) and how they ought/ought not to (moral)
> "Ambitious Guest"—psychological study of human ambitions—moralistic application
> "Wakefield"—integration of psych. and moral—people tied to systems

After briefly studying such notes, you have only to number them in the order you wish to present them—and you have an outline.

As in all outlining, you should not feel rigidly bound to the material and its structure. As you write, other ideas may come to you and a better structure may suggest itself. The student who answered the Hawthorne question, for example, decided to write on "Egotism" rather than "The Ambitious Guest." With time looking over your shoulder, though, you probably cannot afford to change your plans more than once.

Cover statement

On the basis of your notes you should now be able to begin your examination essay by writing a sentence or two that will serve as a thesis statement. The students who answered the above questions began as follows:

> Although there were no major conflicts among the European powers between the Congress of Vienna (1814–1815) and the Revolutions of 1848, important developments were taking place that would affect the future history of Europe. Four of these developments were the rise of nationalism, the conflict between the conservatives and the liberals, the conflict between the lower and middle classes, and the expansion of industry.

> Hawthorne is a moralist-psychologist who is concerned not only with *how* people behave but also with how they *ought* or *ought not* to behave. He is most successful when he integrates the two approaches, as in "Wakefield," and least successful when his moralizing gets away from him, as in "Egotism; or, The Bosom Serpent."

Often, of course, the pressure of the exam keeps you from composing such a thorough cover statement. If coming up with a good cover statement is delaying you, limit your opening to what is specifically required by the question (e.g., Define "moralist-psychologist"), then develop your ideas, and then conclude, after looking over what you have written, with the summary or evaluation (e.g., "Hawthorne, then, is most successful when. . . ."). In some examinations you will not be in the position to summarize or evaluate until you have addressed yourself to a number of particulars in the body of your answer. Whether you begin your answer with a cover statement or not, resist the temptation, so powerful during the first few minutes of an exam, to start writing down everything you know. Don't begin to write until you know what direction you want your answer to take. And remember, your audience is your instructor: he or she knows the subject, so don't waste valuable time on writing background information or overexplaining facts.

Development

Provide supporting evidence, reasoning, detail, or example. Nothing weakens a paper so much as vagueness, unsupported generalizations, and wordiness. Don't talk about "how beautiful Hawthorne's images are and what a pleasure it was to read such great stories," etc., etc. If necessary, go back to your jotted notes to add supporting material. If you have written a cover statement, look at it again and then jot down some hard evidence in the space at the top of the page.

Say you have been asked to discuss the proper use of the I.Q. score by a teacher. Your notes read: *Intelligence—capacity for learning. Must interpret carefully. Also child's personality. Score not permanent. Measures verbal ability.* You have formulated this cover statement: *"Intelligence" is a vague term used to describe an individual's capacity for learning. The teacher must remember that I.Q. scores tell only part of the story and that they are subject to change.* Now you must provide the material for development. Think about specific I.Q. tests, specific studies that support your generalizations. Such notes as the following will help you develop your essay:

> 10% of children significant change after 6 to 8 years
> High motivation often more important than high I.Q.
> Stanford-Binet—aptitude rather than intelligence
> Verbal ability—children from non-English-speaking families—culturally deprived—low verbal score
> N.Y. study—remedial courses, etc.—40% improvement in scores

You now have some raw material to work with, material you can organize and clearly relate to your cover statement.

You still have some hard thinking to do, but at least you have something to think about. Even if you do not fully succeed in integrating your data into a perfectly coherent and unified essay, you will have demonstrated that you read the material and have some understanding of it. Padding, wordiness, and irrelevancies prove only that you can fill up pages.

Must you never toss in a few interesting tidbits not specifically called for by the question? There is nothing wrong with beginning a discussion of the significance of the Jefferson-Adams correspondence with: "In their 'sunset' correspondence of more than 150 letters, Jefferson and Adams exchanged their ideas on world issues, religion, and the nature and future of American democratic society, almost until the day they both died—July 4, 1826." While only the middle third of this sentence is a direct response to the question, the other information is both relevant and interesting. Such details cannot *substitute* for your answer, but they can enhance it, just as they would an out-of-class essay.

Last look

Try to leave time at the end of the exam to read what you've written. Check to see if you have left out words or phrases. See if you can add an additional bit of detail or evidence; you can make insertions in the margins. Correct misspellings and awkward sentences. See if your cover statement can be improved. You are not expected to write a perfectly polished essay in an exam, but make your essay as readable as you can in the time you have left.

EXERCISE 48 Evaluate an essay exam answer you have written. Place pluses ($+$) and minuses ($-$) in the margins, and make a list of strengths and weaknesses. Look over your lecture notes, textbooks, and other material, and then revise your examination until you are satisfied it merits a higher grade.

WRITING ON THE JOB: BUSINESS CORRESPONDENCE

49

49 WRITING ON THE JOB: BUSINESS CORRESPONDENCE

A frequent complaint voiced by college students goes like this: "What good will knowing how to write a 500-word essay do me after I've graduated? How does my research paper on Hawthorne's short stories prepare me to compose a business letter to a customer or a memo to my boss?"

These are reasonable questions, and they deserve a thoughtful reply. The assumption is that if you write well in one context, let's say the research paper on Hawthorne, you will be able to write well in other contexts, too. The assumption is generally correct. Your ability to construct clear, purposeful, effective sentences and paragraphs will stand the test of almost any writing task. The organizing and writing skills you need to construct a 500-word essay are those you need, on the job, to write letters, memos, and reports.

Another way of saying it is that both academic and business writing require attention to the same elements of composition: purpose, audience, tone, style, grammar, mechanics, and organization. Business correspondence may *look* special because it uses a special format (with headings, salutations, and so forth), but it is really governed by the same principles as your college writing assignments. Indeed, the biggest difference between academic and business writing is that your business associates, if anything, will be *less* tolerant than your teachers of errors, poor organization, windy language, and time-wasting failure to present ideas clearly. Because its fundamental purpose is to help get things done, the hallmark of good business writing is its efficiency.

Memos and letters

The most common types of business correspondence are the memorandum (memo) and the letter. The principal difference between the two is really only a matter of audience: a memo is *internal* correspondence written to your fellow employees; a letter is *external* correspondence written to someone outside your company or organization. A memo reflects this difference in its **routing information.** Instead of the return and inside addresses, salutation, complimentary close, and signature found on a letter, a memo provides this "sender-receiver" information in abbreviated form at the upper left of its first page.

```
TO:       Marian Kaufman
FROM:     Jon Carter  JC.
DATE:     March 13, 1982
SUBJECT:  April Sales Meeting Agenda

As we agreed on the phone yesterday, the April
meeting should be used to develop strategies
for improving sales of our summer sportswear
line. Historically, the most unprofitable
territory has been New England, even though
```

Because people in the same organization ordinarily have the same address, full addresses are superfluous. When writer and recipient know each other, titles and departments can be omitted, though they may be used if the writer and the recipient have not corresponded often.

```
TO:       William H. Whalen, Director of
          University Publications
FROM:     Cinda Brandt, Management Business
          Representative
DATE:     December 5, 1983
SUBJECT:  Bid for Undergraduate Catalog
```

You may have noticed that Jon Carter's memo contains his signed initials next to his name. Although initialing a memo is not mandatory, to do so indicates that the sender has reread and approved the memo after it was typed.

In most other respects, memos differ little from letters. Both are single-spaced with double-spacing between paragraphs and sections, both may use block or indented paragraphs, and both may contain headings and enumeration as visual cues to guide the reader through the contents.

Visual cues are important in business correspondence. As the sample letters illustrate, paragraphs tend to be shorter than in an essay, research paper, or novel. Lists are sometimes presented vertically, and series may include bullets (see sample letter 1) or numbers that would probably be omitted in an essay. The reason has to do with the way business letters and memos are used. As part of its function of getting a job done, business correspondence often serves as a reference document. Consequently, the reader must be able to find items quickly. By dividing the discussion more frequently into subtopics and by providing more visual cues, the writer aids not only the reader's understanding but also a fast, easy reference to specific portions of the document.

49

Parts of a business letter

The standard business letter has six parts: (1) the heading, which includes the return address and date; (2) the inside address; (3) the salutation; (4) the body; (5) the complimentary close; and (6) the signature. The first sample letter (p. 502) illustrates a widely used format for these parts and provides a model you can follow. The content of that letter describes the arrangement of the parts and the special conventions of punctuation.

A more unusual business letter format, but one that is growing in popularity, is known as the simplified letter format. Simplified letters use full block style, with all parts flush at the left margin. The salutation and complimentary close are eliminated. A subject line appears where the salutation ordinarily would be placed. This format is easy to type because no tab stops are needed, the subject is immediately clear, and the lack of salutation resolves problems when the name of the recipient is not known. Sample letter 3 (p. 504) shows the simplified format.

The following comments explain appropriate selection of the heading, salutation, complimentary close, and other details pertaining to the parts of business letters.

The heading. Two parts comprise the heading of a business letter: the return address and the date. Although you may have seen a writer's name included as part of the heading, usually the first line, this practice is incorrect. It may be the result of the writer's copying the appearance of letterhead stationary.

Most businesses use letterhead stationery on which the company's name, address, and sometimes the writer's name have been printed or engraved. When using letterhead stationery, you need supply only the date portion of the heading. Sample letter 4 (p. 505) illustrates correspondence typed on letterhead stationery.

The salutation. The content of the salutation, or greeting, depends somewhat on the relationship between writer and reader. Commonly the title and last name of the addressee are used: *Dear Mr. Meade, Dear Professor Connelly, Dear Miss* [or *Mrs.*] *Shearer. Dear Ms. Shearer* is now widely used, not only when a woman's title is not known, but also because many women prefer it. If a woman to whom you are writing identifies herself as Miss or Mrs., however, always address her in the same way.

What if you know the recipient's name but not whether that person is male or female, as may happen if a letter is signed with initials *(S.S. Fleming)* or with a name popular for both sexes *(Lee Hunter)*? Rather than annoying your recipient by guessing incorrectly, it is better—and never wrong—to use the addressee's full name in the salutation: *Dear Lee Hunter*.

Formerly, the conventions governing standard business letters called for *Dear Sir* or *Gentlemen* when writing to organizations or persons you do not know. Because the reader may very likely be a woman, this greeting is inappropriate. Although *Dear Sir or Madame* or *Dear Ladies and/or Gentlemen* is acceptable, another alternative is to use the recipient's title, avoiding gender-specific designations entirely: *Dear Personnel Director; Dear Department Manager*. Avoid *To whom it may concern*.

For appropriate forms of salutation and inside addresses for letters to government officials, military personnel, and the like, check your desk dictionary for guidance. If you are answering a letter, use the same forms as those in the letter to which you are replying.

How should you address a person you know well or with whom you have corresponded before? If you would address that person by his or her first name when speaking face to face or on the telephone, it is more than likely appropriate to use the first name in your letter's salutation as well.

The complimentary close. The majority of business letters close simply and courteously with *Sincerely*. Less common but quite acceptable are the following closes: *Yours truly; Very truly yours; Sincerely yours*. Business letters addressed to people with whom there is frequent and friendly correspondence often use *Cordially* or *Cordially yours*. Closings such as *Respectfully yours* and *Yours respectfully* are reserved for formal circumstances where they seem appropriate as, for example, in addressing a letter to the president of your university or to a high government official.

Note that the first word of a complimentary close is always capitalized, but *only* the first.

The signature. Both the handwritten and the typewritten signature are important. If appropriate, the typewritten signature may be followed by the writer's official capacity, but neither professional titles nor degrees should be used with the signature.

Sincerely yours,

William H. Oliver

William H. Oliver
Editor

A woman may, if she wishes, place *(Ms.), (Miss)*, or *(Mrs.)* before her typed name. A married woman may choose to add, in parentheses, below her typed name *Mrs.* followed by her husband's name.

Sincerely,

Katherine Carlone

(Ms.) Katherine Carlone

Yours truly,

Elizabeth Phillips

Elizabeth Phillips
(Mrs. Charles Phillips)

As with the salutation, in letters to people with whom you are on a first-name basis, it is perfectly appropriate to sign only your first name. The typewritten signature should use your full professional name.

Cordially,

Melinda

Melinda G. Kramer
Communications Director

Reference initials. Business letters that have been typed by someone other than the sender frequently identify the sender and the typist by their initials. In the same area—the lower left—you will find information about other material enclosed with the letter and the names of people who have received copies of the letter. Such information is typed flush with the left margin, as follows:

INITIALS OF SENDER AND OF TYPIST	RLW/cwm
ENCLOSURE	Enc.: Color chart
RECIPIENT OF A COPY	cc: Patrick Q. Jay, Manager

Kinds of business letters*

Request letters. Perhaps the most common kind of business letter most of us write is that asking someone to do something: give us information, send us something we have seen advertised, or correct a mistake. Such letters should be direct, businesslike, and courteous, even when you are registering a complaint.

Above all they must be clear. They must directly state what you want the reader to do, and they must give the exact information the reader needs to meet your request. You will notice that sample letters 2 and 3 (pp. 503 and 504) conclude by telling the readers just what the writers want, what results Kevin Lawry and Marilyn Conway expect. Conclusions of this type are appropriately called **action endings.**

Request letters can be grouped into two categories: (1) those with reader benefit and (2) those without reader benefit. In other words, if fulfilling the sender's request does the recipient some good, the request has reader benefit. Sample letter 3, although registering a complaint, falls in the reader-benefit category because the company clearly

---

*Some of the sample letters on pp. 502–507 are adapted from P.D. Hemphill, *Business Communications* (Englewood Cliffs, N.J.: Prentice-Hall, 1976).

gains when its customers are satisfied and loses when they are un-happy.

Requests without reader benefit are somewhat problematic. Why should your reader do what you want if he or she has nothing to gain from it? In such cases you are really relying on your reader's good will. Besides writing clearly, you should take up as little of the reader's time as possible, make your request reasonable, and—if you can—encourage the reader's good will, perhaps by paying an honest compliment. Requests for information can frequently be handled in this way, as sample letter 2 shows.

Verification letters and letters of transmittal. The purpose of much business correspondence is to let readers know information has been received or is being sent and to ensure that it has been understood accurately. Verification letters do what their name suggests: they verify. If an associate telephones you to arrange a meeting, you may want to send him or her a verification letter confirming time and place and the topics to be discussed. Following that meeting, either of you might write another letter summarizing the discussion and substantiating any agreement reached. Participants thus have a record of pertinent information and can verify mutual understanding.

Letters of transmittal (also called **cover letters**) typically accompany other materials, especially documents such as reports. A transmittal letter identifies for the reader the material it accompanies and explains why the sender is transmitting the material to the recipient. When a report or document is involved, a transmittal letter may briefly summarize its contents—highlighting the most important findings, conclusions, and recommendations.

A transmittal letter is not nearly as superfluous as it may seem. Consider the number and variety of tasks confronting a business person in the course of a week or month, and imagine what could happen if a fifty-page report appeared in the morning mail without its transmittal letter: "Now what in the world is this?" Eventually the recipient would remember he or she had commissioned a study to be passed along to Jones in Consumer Affairs—but not before wasting time in puzzlement and frustration. Meanwhile, the report idles between the sender and the people who need it. Sample letter 4 (p. 505) shows an example of a transmittal letter.

Letters of application. Though letters requesting information, registering complaints, and the like, are probably those you will write most often, letters in which you apply for a job you want are almost certainly among the most important you will write. When writing such letters, keep the following advice in mind:

1   Application letters usually fit either of two categories: solicited

applications and prospecting applications. When you know an opening for a position actually exists because you have heard about the vacancy or seen it advertised, you will write a solicited application letter (see sample letter 5). In addition to specifying the position, in this case identify the advertisement or mention the source from whom you obtained the information about the job opening. If a specific person suggested you write, mention that fact. When you have no direct knowledge that a job opening exists but you want to be considered if a position is available, your application letter is a prospecting application (see sample letter 6). In this case you will identify the type of position you desire and mention why you are interested in working for the company you are addressing.

2　Describe any part of your education or previous work experience that you believe prepares you for the job you want. Be brief, direct, and factual, but at the same time present the information to your advantage. Use your education and experience to show the prospective employer how you are qualified to contribute to the company. Remember that the employer is the "buyer," and you are "marketing" your credentials and skills. Although the tone of your letter should not be egotistical, neither should it sound apologetic or pleading. Do not beg. Write a letter that is informative, courteous, and confident.

3　Provide references if at all possible, but remember that useful and relevant references must come from people who actually know your work at first hand. People for whom you have worked successfully and instructors with whom you have taken relevant courses are often among your best references. Remember that a potential employer consulting one of your references will want to know specific things about the quality of your work, your overall ability—and your reliability. Be sure to get permission from persons whose names you intend to use before you list them as references.

4　An application letter is similar to a request letter: you are asking the reader to do something—consider you for a job. Consequently, you should use an action ending. Since the next step in the employment process is typically a job interview, you can end your letter by asking the reader to let you know when it would be convenient for you to come for an interview. Always tell the reader when, where, and how you can be reached if you are not available at your return address during business hours.

5　For many part-time or temporary positions, it is sufficient to describe your experience and other qualifications in the body of your letter, as the writer of sample letter 5 does. But for full-time positions, and particularly if your background, qualifications, and references are fairly extensive, it is wiser to present information in clear, quickly readable form on a personal data sheet, or resumé, as does the writer of sample letter 6. This enables you to use your application letter to highlight in summary form particularly important information and to provide any additional persuasive details, while conveniently presenting necessary factual information on the resumé. Be sure to mention your resumé in your letter.

Following the sample letters are two resumés showing effective formats. The first format is widely used and fairly traditional. The second format organizes information according to skills and may be a good choice if you want to emphasize your capabilities. For people whose work experience is varied or not continuous, or whose education is not obviously applicable to the job they are seeking, the format of the second resumé is the more effective.

Remember, too, that experience need not be only jobs for which you received pay. Volunteer work, community service, and other activities may have added skills relevant to the job you are seeking. Similarly, you may want to list education that did not result in a degree. Consider for your resumé and your application letter evening classes, classes taken at the YMCA or community center—in fact, any training that is relevant to the employment you desire.

Use action verbs to describe your experience: *organized, developed, assisted,* instead of *duties included.* . . . Talk about what you accomplished, goals you met or exceeded, skills you learned or demonstrated. Like your application letter, your resumé should be persuasive.

The personal data you include on your resumé should be only that which is pertinent to the job. For example, height and weight, hair or eye color are not likely to be the least bit relevant. Laws forbidding job discrimination based on marital status, age, sex, race, or religion have also changed the personal data appearing on resumés; employers cannot require this type of information from job applicants. For instance, if you are seeking a sales position that involves extended periods on the road or a job with a company that routinely transfers managers among its several plants around the country, you might list willingness to travel or relocate under personal data; but you need not indicate whether you are male or female, single or married.

Sample letter 1: modified block style without indented paragraphs

521 Lake Street
Tucson, Arizona 85702
April 29, 1983

Mr. Peter B. McHenry
Business Manager
University of Texas
Austin, Texas 78752

Dear Mr. McHenry:

Business letters appear in several formats. The most common ones are
full block style, modified block style either with or without indented
paragraphs, and simplified style. This letter uses modified block
style without indented paragraphs.

- All parts of the letter except the heading, the complimentary
  close, and the signature are placed flush with the left margin.

- Paragraphs are not indented.

- Within the body of the letter, portions for which special emphasis is desired may be indented.

- The heading is placed approximately flush with the right margin;
  note that it includes the date.

- The complimentary close is aligned with the heading.

If you are using letterhead stationary, the date may be typed three or
four spaces below the letterhead and either centered or placed flush
with either margin. In what is called the full block style, all parts
of the letter are placed flush with the left margin.

The punctuation in the heading and inside address of this letter is
open. That is, no punctuation is placed at the end of lines, although
internal punctuation between city and state and between day and year is
retained. The salutation and complimentary close, however, are followed
by a colon and a comma, respectively. In fully open punctuation, no
punctuation is used after the salutation and close.

Note that spacing in the letter is an important part of its appearance.
Two or three spaces should be left between the date and the inside
address. Double spacing should be used between all other main parts
of the letter, and always between paragraphs. It is wise to allow
four spaces between the complimentary close and your typed signature.

The appearance is well served also by the picture frame placement used
in this letter, which maintains uniform and generous margins. In addition, the bullets denoting the principal characteristics of modified
block style draw the reader's attention to the information, making it
easy to spot. The purpose of a business letter format is to increase
efficiency and effectiveness in transmitting information.

Sincerely,

Dan Portillo

Dan Portillo

Sample letter 2: full block style

416 Wabash Avenue
West Point, Indiana 47963
April 23, 1983

Clark Equipment Company
Public Relations Department
Circle Drive
Buchanan, Michigan 49107

Dear Sir or Madam:

An assignment for my college business-writing class requires that I
write a research report on a company for whom I might like to work
after graduation. Clark Equipment Company is my choice for this
report.

Preliminary research in our business school's library has convinced me
that Clark is a solid performer in the heavy equipment industry. Because I am a construction management major, I am familiar with your
construction machinery and its excellent reputation.

Please send me a copy of Clark's 1982 annual report together with any
other descriptive information you may have about Clark Equipment Company, particularly the construction machinery division. I would also
appreciate a few issues of the company's employee magazine. Thank you.

Sincerely,

Kevin Lawry

Kevin Lawry

Sample letter 3: simplified style

444 West Wilson Street
Madison, Wisconsin 53715
July 9, 1982

Cambridge Camera Exchange, Inc.
7th Avenue and 13th Street
New York, N.Y. 10011

INCOMPLETE SHIPMENT

The Minolta SRT 201 camera outfit I ordered from you on June 21 arrived today and appears to be in good working order. However, your advertisement in <u>The New York Times</u> for Sunday, June 16, listed six items as being supplied with this outfit, including a film holder and a sun shade. Neither of these items was included in the package I have just received, nor do I find any notice that they will be sent at a later date.

I am sure that this omission is unintentional and that you will correct it. Will you please let me know when I may expect to receive the film holder and sun shade, as advertised. If there is a dealer in the immediate area, I would be happy to get them from him if you will authorize me to do so at your expense.

Marilyn S. Conway

Marilyn S. Conway

Sample letter 4: modified block style with indented paragraphs

November 10, 1981

Ms. Roberta Basave
Employee Training and Development
Precision Engineering Incorporated
3116 Garson Blvd.
Greenbelt, Tennessee 37401

Dear Ms. Basave:

  The enclosed proposal outlines a six-week training program to assist your staff with technical writing. Following your request on October 1 that I evaluate Precision Engineering's technical publications, reports, and correspondence, I reviewed writing samples collected by the company's six department heads. Besides analyzing the samples for grammatical correctness, clarity, tone, style, and organization, I also used the Gunning-Fogg Index to assess the readability level.

  The conclusions detailed in the proposal indicate that your employees write correct, grammatical English. However, they need to work on reducing their use of jargon, editing for wordiness, and simplifying their sentence structure--particularly in the company's instruction manuals.

  The proposal describes a training program designed to help your staff improve specific skills, enabling them to communicate more effectively with your customers.

  Working with you and your staff during the past month has been a pleasure. I look forward to continued association with Precision Engineering. Once the proposal is approved, we can begin arrangements for the training program, perhaps holding the initial session shortly after the first of the year.

Cordially,

Ruthann Schlar

(Mrs.) Ruthann Schlar

RS/bo
Enc. proposal

Sample letter 5: modified block style without indented paragraphs

3481 Mountain Road
Bellevue, Washington   98004
April 14, 1982

Dr. Winthrop D. Pierce
Professor of Marketing
University of Washington
Seattle, Washington   98105

Dear Professor Pierce:

Through your bulletin posted at the University of Washington placement service I learned that you are looking for students to work part time for you next year in various marketing research projects. I think my educational background and my experience working with people could be put to good advantage in such work.

In early June I expect to receive my A.A. degree with a marketing specialty from Bellevue Community College. Courses I have taken include Marketing, Advertising, Business Writing, Business Law, Accounting, and Computer Programming. I plan to continue my study at the University of Washington next year.

I have been holding two part-time jobs, one as an assistant to Professor John Leonard in the Business Department at Bellevue Community College, and one as a night dispatch clerk in the Bellevue Trucking Company. I believe I work well with people. In my position with Professor Leonard I supervise three other part-time students, and my work at the Bellevue Trucking Company requires me to deal constantly with other workers.

Both Professor John Leonard and Mr. Oscar Malenko, manager of the Bellevue Trucking Company, have assured me they could recommend me to you. I believe you know Professor Leonard. Mr. Malenko can be reached by telephone at (206) 555-5437.

Please let me know when we can meet for an interview. I can arrange to come to Seattle at your convenience. You can reach me or leave a message for me at my home phone (206) 555-7654.

Sincerely,

Ralston Phillips

Ralston Phillips

Sample letter 6: modified block style with indented paragraphs

848 Plains Street
Fort Pierre, South Dakota   57067
August 15, 1982

John Stafford
Curator
W.H. Over Museum
University of South Dakota
Vermillion, South Dakota   57069

Dear Mr. Stafford:

    I have been an active volunteer at museums throughout most of my adult life and am now looking for permanent employment in a museum. As the enclosed resume shows, I have experience in many areas of museum operations ranging from collecting and cataloging specimens to arranging exhibits to managing funds and staff.

    My love for museum work began in college when I helped with children's programs at a small natural history museum. Later I served a very exciting six years on the governing board of the Tippecanoe County Historical Association in Indiana.

    During that time we supervised the County Historical Museum, located in the Victorian home of the city's founder, and oversaw the archeological exploration of a seventeenth-century settlement along the Wabash River. In addition, the Association-sponsored Feast of the Hunter's Moon, a re-creation of a frontier harvest festival, doubled its annual attendance while I was handling its publicity.

    Since moving to South Dakota, I have visited your museum several times and am impressed by the quality of its exhibits, particularly those on mining and native Americans. While participating in the Fort Quiatenon archeological excavations, I gained expertise in Indian artifacts, which I want to broaden.

    I would like to talk with you about employment possibilities at the W.H. Over Museum. Please call me at (605) 555-30859.

Sincerely yours,

Joanne Lewkowski

Joanne Lewkowski

PERSONAL DATA SHEET

JOANNE LEWKOWSKI

848 Plains Street
Fort Pierre, South Dakota   57067
(605) 555-0859

POSITION SOUGHT: MUSEUM CURATOR'S ASSISTANT

Education	B.A., Earlham College, Richmond, Indiana, 1970
	Major: history Minor: biology
	Graduate study, State University of New York,
	1971-72. Courses in researching, cataloging,
	mounting exibits.

Experience   Board of governors, Tippecanoe County Historical
Association (TCHA), Lafayette, Indiana, 1975-81.
Association owns and operates County Historical
Museum; operates block house at Fort Quiatenon;
sponsors and organizes annual Feast of the Hunter's
Moon, a two-day re-enactment of the 17th-century
French settlers' life; is granting agency for
archeological dig at original Quiatenon site.

Chairwoman, TCHA Quiatenon Committee, 1976-80.
Handled major funds and grants, worked with federal
and local agencies and Michigan State University
anthropology faculty and students. Excavation
volunteer at Quiatenon dig, summers 1976-80.

Docent, Tippecanoe County Historical Museum, 1974-75.
Researched and prepared exhibits, presented historical
lectures and guided tours.

Student volunteer, Joseph Moore Museum, Earlham
College, 1968-70. Assisted director of small
natural history museum, identified and cataloged
specimens, maintained exhibits, organized museum
tours for school children.

Personal Data   Speak and write French. Interests include travel
and photography.

References   Martin Ferguson, administrative assistant, Tippecanoe County Historical Association, 909 South St.,
Lafayette, Indiana 47905

Professor Norris Vernon, Department of Anthropology,
Michigan State University, East Lansing, Michigan 48824

Professor Jack Copeland, Biology Department, Earlham
College, Richmond, Indiana 47374

RESUME

JOANNE LEWKOWSKI   OBJECTIVE: MUSEUM MANAGEMENT

848 Plains Street
Fort Pierre, South Dakote   57067
(605) 555-0859

Qualifications   Familiar with all aspects of museum work from pre-
                  paring exhibits to fund-raising and publicity. Proven
                  skills in research, exhibit design, financial management,
                  staff supervision, and communications.

Museum   As member of Tippecanoe County Historical Association
Management   (TCHA) board of governors, 1975-80, directly involved
                  in operation of County Historical Museum: preparing
                  annual budget, approving acquisitions and events,
                  hiring staff.

Research   Learned research methods and field techniques during
and Field Work   two years as undergraduate volunteer at Earlham Col-
                  lege's Joseph Moore Museum and during part-time graduate
                  study in New York. Applied these skills while a docent
                  at County Historical Museum, 1974-75. Researched and
                  mounted Museum's highly successful "Victorian Christmas"
                  exhibit in 1975. Gained further experience at Fort
                  Quiatenon archeological digs run by TCHA and anthro-
                  pologists from Michigan State University, summers
                  1976-80.

Fundraising   Obtained four major federal grants and raised over
                  $15,000 locally when chairing TCHA Quiatenon Committee,
                  1976-80.

Public   Prepared publicity campaign for Feast of the Hunter's
Relations   Moon, annual re-enactment of 17th century settler's
                  life at Fort Quiatenon, 1976-77. Wrote news releases,
                  secured state and local media coverage. Feast atten-
                  dance increased by 10,000 in 1977. While docent at
                  County Historical Museum developed a four-lecture
                  series on city's founding fathers attracting largest
                  lecture audiences in museum's history. During second
                  year with Joseph Moore natural history museum took
                  "touchable" traveling exhibit to local elementary
                  schools.

Education   B.A. Earlham College, Richmond, Indiana, 1970.
                  Major: history Minor: biology
                  Graduate Study, State University of New York, 1971-72.
                  Courses in researching, cataloging, mounting exhibits,
                  and photography.

References available upon request

A GLOSSARY
OF GRAMMATICAL
TERMS

50

This glossary provides brief definitions of the grammatical terms used in this text. Cross references refer you to pertinent sections of the text. For further text references to terms defined, as well as for references to terms not included in the glossary, consult the index.

absolute phrase   Absolute constructions modify the entire remainder of the sentence in which they stand. They differ from other modifying word groups in that (1) they lack any connective joining them to the rest of the sentence and (2) they do not modify any individual word or word group in the sentence. Compare *Seeing the bears, we stopped the car,* in which the participial phrase modifies *we,* with *The rain having stopped, we saw the bears,* in which the construction *the rain having stopped* is an absolute modifying the rest of the sentence. The basic pattern of the absolute phrase is a noun or pronoun and a participle. *(She having arrived, we all went to the movies. We left about ten o'clock, the movie being over.)* Such phrases are sometimes called **nominative absolutes,** since pronouns in them require the nominative case.

Absolute phrases may also be prepositional phrases *(In fact, we had expected rain)* or verbal phrases (It often rains in April, *to tell the truth. Generally speaking,* July is hot.)

For the punctuation of absolute phrases see **20e.**

abstract noun   See *noun.*

active voice   See *voice.*

adjectival   Any word or word group used to modify a noun. Some modern grammars limit the meaning of **adjective** strictly to words that can be compared by adding *-er* and *-est (new, newer, newest; high, higher, highest).* Such grammars apply the term **adjectival** to other words that ordinarily modify nouns, and to any other word or word group when it is used as an adjective. In such grammars the italicized words below may be called **adjectivals.**

LIMITING ADJECTIVES	*my* suit, *a* picture, *one* day
NOUNS MODIFYING NOUNS	*school* building, *home* plate, *government* policy
PHRASES MODIFYING NOUNS	man *of the hour*
CLAUSES MODIFYING NOUNS	girl *whom I know*

adjective   A word used to describe or limit the meaning of a noun or its equivalent. According to their position, adjectives may be (1) **attributive,** i.e., placed next to their nouns *(vivid* example; *a* boy, *strong* and *vigorous),* or (2) **predicative,** i.e., placed in the predicate after a linking verb (She was *vigorous*).

According to their meaning, adjectives may be (1) **descriptive,** naming some quality (*white* house, *small* child, *leaking* faucet); (2) **proper,** derived from proper nouns (*Roman* fountain, *French* custom); or (3) **limiting.** Limiting adjectives may indicate possession (*my, his*), may point out (*this, former*), may number (*three, second*), or may be articles (*a, the*).

See **1b(1)** and Section **3.**

adjective clause A subordinate, or dependent, clause used as an adjective.

> The man *who lives here* is a biologist. [The adjective clause modifies the noun *man.*]
>
> Dogs *that chase cars* seldom grow old. [The adjective clause modifies the noun *dogs.*]

See also **1d.**

adjective phrase See *phrase.*

adverb A word used to describe or limit the meaning of a verb, an adjective, another verb, or a whole sentence.

According to function, adverbs may (1) modify single words (went *quickly, quite* shy, *nearly* all men); (2) modify whole sentences (*Maybe* he will go); (3) ask questions (*When* did he go? *Where* is the book?); or (4) connect clauses and modify their meaning (see *conjunctive adverb*).

According to meaning, adverbs may indicate (1) manner (*secretly* envious); (2) time (*never* healthy); (3) place (*outside* the house); or (4) degree (*quite* easily angered).

See **1b(1)** and Section **3.**

adverb clause A subordinate, or dependent, clause used as an adverb.

> *When you leave,* please close the door. [The adverb clause, indicating time, modifies the verb *close.*]
>
> The sheep grazed *where the grass was greenest.* [The adverb clause, indicating place, modifies the verb *grazed.*]

Adverb clauses also indicate manner, purpose, cause, result, condition, concession, and comparison.

See **1d.**

adverb phrase See *phrase.*

adverbial A term used to describe any word or word group used as an adverb. Common adverbials are nouns in certain constructions (She went *home*), phrases (She went *in a great hurry*), or clauses (She went *when she wanted to go*). Compare *adjectival.*

adverbial objective Sometimes applied to nouns used as adverbials. (They slept *mornings.* He ran a *mile.*)

agreement A correspondence or matching in the form of one word and that of another. Verbs agree with their subjects in number and person (in

She runs, both *she* and *runs* are singular and third person). Pronouns agree with their antecedents in person, number, and gender (in *He wanted his way, he* and *his* are both third person singular, and masculine). Demonstrative adjectives match the nouns they modify in number *(this kind, these kinds).* See Section **8.**

antecedent   A word or group of words to which a pronoun refers.

> She is a *woman who* seldom writes letters. [*Woman* is the antecedent of the pronoun *who.*]
> *Uncle Henry* came for a brief visit, but *he* stayed all winter. [*Uncle Henry* is the antecedent of the pronoun *he.*]

appositive   A word or phrase set beside a noun, a pronoun, or a group of words used as a noun, that identifies or explains it by renaming it.

> John, my *brother*   Albany, that is, *New York's state capital*
> His hobby, *playing handball*   modifiers, *words that describe or limit*

The appositives illustrated above are **nonrestrictive:** they explain the nouns they follow but are not necessary to identify them. When appositives restrict the meaning of the nouns they follow to a specific individual or object, they are **restrictive:** *my sister Ilene* (that is, *Ilene,* not *Dorothy* or *Helen*); *Huxley the novelist* (not *Huxley the scientist*). See **20c(2).**

article   The words *a, an,* and *the* are articles. *A* and *an* are **indefinite** articles; *the* is a **definite** article. Articles are traditionally classed as limiting adjectives, but since they always signal that a noun will follow, some modern grammars call them **determiners.**

auxiliary   A verb form used with a main verb to form a verb phrase. Auxiliaries are commonly divided into two groups. The first group is used to indicate tense and voice. This group includes *shall, will,* and the forms of *be, have,* and *do (shall* give, *will* give, *has* given, *had* given, *does* give, *is* giving, *was* given).

The second group, called **modal auxiliaries,** includes *can, could, may, might, must, ought, should,* and *would.* These are used to indicate ability, obligation, permission, possibility, etc., and they do not take inflectional endings such as *-s, -ed,* and *-ing.* See Section **4.**

cardinal numbers   Numbers such as *one, three, twenty,* used in counting. Compare *ordinal numbers.*

case   The inflectional form of pronouns or the possessive form of nouns to indicate their function in a group of words. Pronouns have three cases: (1) **nominative or subjective** *(we, she, they),* used for the subject of a verb, or a subjective complement; (2) the **possessive,** used as an adjective *(their dog, anybody's guess);* and (3) the **objective** *(us, her, them),* used for objects of verbs, verbals, and prepositions. Possessive pronouns may also stand alone (The car is *his*). Nouns have only two cases: (1) a **common** case (*woman, leopard*) and (2) a **possessive** case (*woman's, leopard's*). See Section **2.**

clause A group of words containing a subject and a predicate. Clauses are of two kinds: main, or independent; and subordinate, or dependent. **Main clauses** make independent assertions and can stand alone as sentences. **Subordinate clauses** depend on some other element within a sentence; they function as nouns, adjectives, or adverbs, and cannot stand alone.

MAIN	*The moon shone,* and *the dog barked.*[Two main clauses, either of which could be a sentence]
SUBORDINATE	*When the moon shone,* the dog barked. [Adverb clause] *That he would survive* is doubtful. [Noun clause]

See **1d.**

collective noun A noun naming a collection or aggregate of individuals by a singular form (*assembly, army, jury*). Collective nouns are followed by a singular verb when the group is thought of as a unit and a plural verb when the component individuals are in mind (the majority *decides;* the majority *were* slaves). See **8a(6)** and **8b.**

comma splice A sentence error in which two independent clauses are joined only by a comma without a coordinating conjunction. See Section **7.**

common noun See *noun.*

comparison Change in the form of adjectives and adverbs to show degree. English has three degrees: (1) **positive,** the form listed in dictionaries (*loud, bad, slowly*); (2) **comparative** (*louder, worse, more slowly*); and **superlative** (*loudest, worst, most slowly*). See **3e.**

complement In its broadest sense, a term for any word, excluding modifiers, that completes the meaning of a verb (direct and indirect objects), a subject (subject complements), or an object (object complements).

VERB COMPLEMENTS	Give *me* the *money.* [*Money* and *me* are direct and indirect objects, respectively.]
SUBJECT COMPLEMENTS	Helen is a *singer.* She is *excellent.* [The noun *singer* and the adjective *excellent* refer to the subject.]
OBJECT COMPLEMENTS	We elected Jane *secretary.* That made Bill *angry.* [*Secretary* and *angry* refer to the direct objects *Jane* and *Bill.*]

complete predicate See *predicate.*

complete subject See *subject.*

complex sentence See *sentence.*

compound Made up of more than one word but used as a unit, as in compound noun (*redhead, football*), compound adjective (*downcast, matter-of-fact*), or compound subject (Both *patience* and *practice* are necessary).
See also *sentence.*

compound-complex See *sentence.*

concrete noun See *noun.*

conjugation A list of inflected forms for a verb, displaying the forms for first, second, and third person singular and plural for each tense, voice, and mood. A synopsis of the third person singular (*he, she, it,* and singular nouns) forms for a regular and an irregular verb is shown below.

	Simple Form	*Progressive Form*
Active Voice		
PRESENT	*he/she* asks/drives	*he/she* is asking/ driving
PAST	*he/she* asked/drove	*he/she* was asking/ driving
FUTURE	*he/she* will ask/drive	*he/she* will be asking/ driving
PRESENT PERFECT	*he/she* has asked/ driven	*he/she* has been asking/driving
PAST PERFECT	*he/she* had asked/ driven	*he/she* had been asking/driving
FUTURE PERFECT	*he/she* will have asked/driven	*he/she* will have been asking/driving
Passive Voice		
PRESENT	*he/she* is asked/ driven	*he/she* is being asked/driven
PAST	*he/she* was asked/ driven	*he/she* was being asked/driven
FUTURE	*he/she* will be asked/ driven	*he/she* will be being asked/driven
PRESENT PERFECT	*he/she* has been asked/driven	*he/she* has been being asked/driven
PAST PERFECT	*he/she* had been asked/driven	*he/she* had been being asked/driven
FUTURE PERFECT	*he/she* will have been asked/driven	*he/she* will have been being asked/driven

Forms for first and second person singular and all plural forms may be described briefly as follows:
The present tense forms for other persons are *I/you/we/they* ask/drive.
The past and future tense forms for all persons are the same as those shown for the third person.

All perfect tense and passive voice forms that use *has* as an auxiliary in the third person use *have* in all other persons.

All perfect tense and passive voice forms that use *is/was* in the third person use *am/was* for the first person *(I)* and *were* in all other persons.

conjunction A part of speech used to join and relate words, phrases, and clauses. Conjunctions may be either coordinating or subordinating.

Coordinating conjunctions connect words, phrases, and clauses of equal grammatical rank: *and, but, or, nor, for.*

Subordinating conjunctions join dependent clauses to main clauses: *after, although, as if, because, since, when.*

See **1b(2).**

conjunctive adverb An adverb used to relate and connect main clauses in a sentence. Common conjunctive adverbs are *also, consequently, furthermore, hence, however, indeed, instead, likewise, moreover, nevertheless, otherwise, still, then, therefore, thus.* **Conjunctive adverbs,** unlike **coordinating** and **subordinating conjunctions,** are movable and can thus occupy different positions within the main clause in which they stand. See **21b.**

connective A general term for any word or phrase that links words, phrases, clauses, or sentences. **Connective** thus includes conjunctions, prepositions, and conjunctive adverbs. See **1b(2).**

construction A general term describing any related groups of words such as a phrase, a clause, or a sentence.

coordinate Having equal rank, as two main clauses in a compound sentence. See Section **34.**

coordinating conjunction See *conjunction.*

correlatives Coordinating conjunctions used in pairs to join sentence elements of equal rank. Common correlatives are *either . . . or; neither . . . nor; not only . . . but also; whether . . . or; both . . . and.* See **1b(2).**

dangling construction A subordinate construction that cannot easily and unambiguously be linked to another word or group of words it modifies. See Section **12.**

declension See *inflection* and *case.*

degree See *comparison.*

demonstratives *This, that, these,* and *those* are called **demonstratives** when used as pointing words. (*This* dinner is cold. *That* is the man.)

dependent clause See *clause.*

derivational suffix See *suffix.*

determiner   A word such as *a, an, the, his, our, your,* which indicates that one of the words following it is a noun.

direct address   A noun or pronoun used parenthetically to point out the person addressed, sometimes called **nominative of address** or **vocative.** (*George,* where are you going? I suppose, *gentlemen,* that you enjoyed the lecture.)

direct and indirect quotation   A direct quotation is an exact quotation of a speaker's or writer's words (sometimes called **direct discourse**). In **indirect discourse** the speaker's or writer's thought is summarized without direct quotation.

> DIRECT   He said, "I must leave on the eight o'clock shuttle."
>
> INDIRECT   He said that he had to leave on the eight o'clock shuttle.

direct object   See *object* and *complement.*

double negative   The use of two negative words within the same construction. In certain forms, two negatives are used in the same statement in English to give a particular emphasis to a positive idea. (He was *not* entirely *un*prejudiced). In most instances, the double negative is nonstandard. (He *didn't* do *no* work. We *didn't* see *no*body.) See **42b.**

elliptical construction   An omission of words necessary to the grammatical completeness of an expression but assumed in the context. The omitted words in elliptical expressions are understood (*He is older than I* [am]. *Our house is small, his* [house is] *large*).

expletive   The word *it* or *there* used to introduce a sentence in which the subject follows the verb.

> *It* is doubtful that he will arrive today. [The clause *that he will arrive today* is the subject of the verb *is.*]
>
> *There* are two ways of solving the problem. [The noun *ways* is the subject of *are.*]

faulty predication   A grammatical fault that results when a subject and its verb or a subject and its complement in a subject/linking verb/complement construction are mismatched in meaning. See Section **14.**

finite verb   A verb form that makes an assertion about its subject. Verbals (infinitives, participles, gerunds) are not finite forms. All finite verbs can add *-s* in the third person singular of the present tense to show agreement with their subject. Nonfinite verb forms cannot make this inflectional change. See Section **4.**

function words   A term used to describe the words, such as articles, auxiliaries, conjunctions, and prepositions, that are more important for their part in the structure of the sentence than for their meaning. They indicate the function of other words in a sentence and the grammatical relations between those words.

gender   The classification of nouns and pronouns as masculine *(man, he)*, feminine *(woman, she)*, and neuter *(desk, it)*. A few English nouns have special forms to indicate gender *(salesman, saleswoman; hero, heroine)*.

genitive case   The possessive case. See Section **2.**

gerund   A verbal that ends in *-ing* and is used as a noun. Gerunds may take complements, objects, and modifiers. See **1c(3).**

idiom   An expression established by usage and peculiar to a particular language. Many idioms have unusual grammatical construction and make little sense if taken literally. Examples of English idioms are *by and large, catch a cold, lay hold of, look up an old friend.* See **40f.**

imperative   See *mood.*

indefinite pronoun   A pronoun, such as *anybody, anyone, someone,* that does not refer to a specific person or thing.

independent clause   See *clause.*

independent element   An expression that has no grammatical relation to other parts of the sentence. See *absolute.*

indicative   See *mood.*

indirect object   See *object.*

infinitive   A verbal usually consisting of *to* followed by the present form of the verb. With a few verbs *to* may be omitted (heard her *tell;* made it *work*). Infinitives can serve as nouns (*To swim* is to relax), as adjectives (I have nothing *to say*), or as adverbs (We were ready *to begin*). See **1b(3).**

inflection   Variation in the form of words to indicate case *(he, him)*, gender *(he, she, it)*, number *(mouse, mice)*, tense *(walk, walked)*, etc. **Declension** is the inflection of nouns and pronouns; **conjugation** the inflection of verbs; and **comparison** is the inflection of adjectives and adverbs.

inflectional suffix   See *suffix.*

intensifier   A term applied to such modifiers as *much, so, too,* and *very,* which merely add emphasis to the words they modify. Words such as *actually, mighty, pretty,* and *really* often occur as vague intensifiers in colloquial English.

intensive pronoun   Any compound personal pronoun ending with *-self* used for emphasis. (I did it *myself.* The Dean *himself* wrote the letter.)

interjection   A word or group of words that is grammatically independent and used to show mild, strong, or sudden emotion. (*Ych.* I hate caterpillars. *Say!* Let's rob a bank.)

intransitive verb   See *verb.*

inversion   A reversal of normal word order. *(Dejected, he left the witness stand. The verdict he clearly foresaw.)*

irregular verb   A verb that forms its past tense and past participle by a change in an internal vowel, or by some other individualized change, as opposed to the usual addition of *-d* or *-ed* to the basic form of so-called **regular verbs,** as in *walk, walked, walked (begin, began, begun; do, did, done; fall, fell, fallen).* See Section **4.**

kernel sentence   A term used in some contemporary grammars to describe one of a limited number of basic sentence patterns from which all grammatical structures can be derived. See **1a.**

lexical word   Nouns, verbs, adjectives, and adverbs are sometimes termed lexical words, that is, words that carry most of the meaning in English, in contrast to *function words,* which indicate relationships among lexical words. Compare *function word.*

linking verb   A verb that shows the relation between the subject of a sentence and a complement. *(He seems timid. The cake tastes sweet. He is a thief.)* The chief linking verbs are *be, become, appear, seem,* and the verbs pertaining to the senses *(look, smell, taste, sound, feel).*

mixed construction   A grammatical fault that consists of joining as a sentence two or more parts that do not fit in grammar or meaning. See Section **14.**

modal auxiliary   See *auxiliary.*

modification   Describing or limiting the meaning of a word or group of words. Adjectives and adjective phrases or clauses modify nouns; adverbs and adverb phrases or clauses modify verbs, adjectives, or adverbs. See Section **3.**

modifier   A general term given to any word or word group that is used to limit, qualify, or otherwise describe the meaning of another word or word group. Adjectives, adverbs, preposition and verbal phrases, and subordinate clauses are the usual modifiers in English. See Section **3** for adjectives and adverbs and Section **1** for various word groups as modifiers.

mood   The form of a verb used to show how the action is viewed by the speaker. English has three moods: (1) **indicative,** stating a fact or asking a question (The wheat *is* ripe. *Will* he *go?*); (2) **imperative,** expressing a command or a request (*Report* at once. Please *clear* your desk); and (3) **subjunctive,** expressing doubt, wish, or condition contrary to fact. (The grass looks as if it *were* dying. I wish he *were* more friendly.) See Section **5.**

nominal   A word or word group used as a noun. (The *blue* seems more suitable. *Eating that pie* will not be easy.) Compare *adjectival.*

nominative case   See *case.*

nonrestrictive modifier   A modifying phrase or clause that is not essential to pointing out or identifying the person or thing modified.

Smith, *who was watching the road,* saw the accident.
The Wankel engine, *new to the market,* is promising.

See Section **20c.**

noun   A word, like *man, horse, carrot, trip, theory,* or *capitalism,* that names a person, place, thing, quality, concept, or the like. Nouns usually form plurals by adding *-s,* and possessives by adding *'s,* and most frequently function as subjects and complements, although they also function in other ways. See **1a.**

Nouns are divided into various subclasses according to their meaning. The most common classes are the following:

Class	Meaning	Examples
common	general classes	*tiger, house, idea*
proper	specific names	*Chicago, Burma, Lee*
abstract	ideas, qualities	*liberty, love, emotion*
concrete	able to be sensed	*apple, smoke, perfume*
collective	groups	*herd, bunch, jury*
count	able to be counted	*chicken, slice, book*
mass	not ordinarily counted (not used with *a, an*)	*salt, gold, equality*

noun clause   A subordinate clause used as a noun. *(What I saw* was humiliating. I shall accept *whatever he offers.)* See **1d.**

number   The form of a noun, pronoun, verb, or demonstrative adjective to indicate one (singular) or more than one (plural).

object   A general term for any word or word group that is affected by or receives action of a transitive verb or verbal, or of a preposition. A **direct object** receives the action of the verb. (I followed *him.* Keep *whatever you find.*) An **indirect object** indicates to or for whom or what something is done. (Give *me* the money). The **object of a preposition** follows the preposition and is related to another part of the sentence by the preposition (We rode across the *beach*). See also *complement* and **1a** and **2c.**

object complement   See *complement.*

objective case   See *case.*

ordinal numbers   Numbers such as *first, third, twentieth,* used to indicate order. Compare *cardinal numbers.*

paradigm   An illustration of the systematic inflection of a word such as a pronoun or a verb, showing all its forms.

parenthetical expression An inserted expression that interrupts the thought of a sentence. (His failure, *I suppose,* was his own fault. I shall arrive—*this will surprise you*—on Monday.)

participial phrase See *participle* and *phrase.*

participle A verbal used as an adjective. As an adjective, a participle can modify a noun or pronoun. The present participle ends in *-ing (running, seeing, trying).* The past participle ends in *-d, -ed, -t, -n, -en,* or changes the vowel *(walked, lost, seen, rung).* Though a participle cannot make an assertion, it is derived from a verb and can take an object and be modified by an adverb *(Swimming the river, completely beaten).*

parts of speech The classes into which words may be divided on the basis of meaning, form, and function. The traditional parts of speech are: noun, pronoun, verb, adjective, adverb, preposition, conjunction, and interjection. See **1a** and **1b** and separate entries in this glossary.

passive voice See *voice.*

person The form of a pronoun and verb used to indicate the speaker (first person—*I am*); the person spoken to (second person—*you are*); or the person spoken about (third person—*she is*).

personal pronoun See *pronoun.*

phrase A group of related words lacking both subject and predicate and used as a single part of speech. Phrases may be classified as follows:

PREPOSITIONAL	We walked *across the street.*
PARTICIPIAL	The man *entering the room* is my father.
GERUND	*Washing windows* is tiresome work.
INFINITIVE	*To see the sunset* was a pleasure.
VERB	He *has been educated* in Europe.

See **1c.**

plain form A term often used for the infinitive or dictionary form of a verb, as *run, stand, pounce.* See Section **4.**

possessive See *case.*

predicate The part of a sentence or clause that makes a statement about the subject. The *complete predicate* consists of the verb and its complements and modifiers. The *simple predicate* consists of only the verb and its auxiliaries. See **1a.**

predicate adjective An adjective serving as a subject complement (He was *silent*). See *complement.*

predicate noun A noun serving as a subject complement (He was a *hero*). See *complement.*

prefix   One or more syllables, such as *a-*, *mis-*, *sub-*, or *un-*, that can be added at the beginning of a word or root to change or modify its meaning: *a* + moral = amoral; *mis* + print = misprint; *sub* + standard = substandard; *un* + zipped = unzipped.

preposition   A word used to relate a noun or pronoun to some other word in the sentence. A preposition and its object form a **prepositional phrase.** (The sheep are *in* the meadow. He dodged *through* the traffic.) See **1c.**

prepositional phrase   See *phrase* and *preposition.*

principal clause   A main or independent clause. See *clause.*

principal parts   The three forms of a verb from which the various tenses are derived; the **present infinitive** *(join, go)*, the **past tense** *(joined, went)*, and the **past participle** *(joined, gone)*. See Section **4.**

progressive   The form of the verb used to describe an action occurring, but not completed, at the time referred to. (I *am studying.* I *was studying.*) See Section **4.**

pronoun   A word used in place of a noun. The noun for which a pronoun stands is called its **antecedent.** (See **1a** and **8b.**) Pronouns are classified as follows:

PERSONAL	*I, you, he, she, it, etc.*
RELATIVE	*who, which, that*
	I am the man *who* lives here.
	We saw a barn *that* was burning.
INTERROGATIVE	*who, which, what*
	Who are you? *Which* is your book?
DEMONSTRATIVE	*this, that, these, those*
INDEFINITE	*one, any, each, anyone, somebody, all,* etc.
RECIPROCAL	*each other, one another*
INTENSIVE	*myself, yourself, himself,* etc.
	I *myself* was afraid. You *yourself* must decide.
REFLEXIVE	*myself, yourself, himself,* etc.
	I burned *myself.* You are deceiving *yourself.*

proper noun   See *noun.*

reciprocal pronoun   See *pronoun.*

regular verb   See *irregular verb.*

relative clause   A subordinate clause introduced by a relative pronoun. See *pronoun.*

relative pronoun   See *pronoun.*

restrictive modifier A modifying phrase or clause that is essential to pointing out or identifying the person or thing modified. (People *who live in glass houses* shouldn't throw stones. The horse *that won the race* is a bay mare.) See **20c.**

sentence A complete unit of thought containing a subject and a predicate. Sentences can be classified according to their form as **simple, compound, complex,** and **compound-complex.**

SIMPLE	They rested. [One main clause]
COMPOUND	They rested and we worked. [Two main clauses]
COMPLEX	They rested while we worked. [One main clause, one subordinate clause]
COMPOUND-COMPLEX	They rested while we worked, but we could not finish. [Two main clauses, one containing a subordinate clause]

sentence fragment A group of words capitalized and punctuated as a sentence but not containing both a subject and a finite verb. See Section **6.**

.subject The person or thing about which the predicate of a sentence or clause makes an assertion or asks a question. The *simple subject* is the word or word group with which the verb of the sentence agrees. The *complete subject* is the simple subject together with all its modifiers. In *The donkey that Jones keeps in the back yard brays all the time, donkey* is the simple subject, and *the donkey that Jones keeps in the back yard* is the complete subject. See Section **1.**

subject complement See *complement.*

subjunctive mood See *mood.*

subordinate clause See *clause.*

substantive A word or group of words used as a noun. Substantives include pronouns, infinitives, gerunds, and noun clauses.

substantive clause A noun clause. See *clause.*

suffix An ending that modifies the meaning of the word to which it is attached. Suffixes may be **inflectional,** such as the *-s* added to nouns to form plurals *(rug, rugs)* or the *-ed* added to verbs to indicate past tense *(call, called).* Or they may be called **derivational,** such as *-ful, -less,* or *-ize* *(hope, hopeful; home, homeless; union, unionize).* Derivational suffixes often, though not always, change the part of speech to which they are added. See *inflection* and item **1** in Section **39.**

superlative See *comparison.*

syntax The part of grammar that describes the structure and function of meaningful word groups such as phrases, clauses, and sentences, as opposed to **morphology,** the part of grammar that describes the formation, function, and classification of words.

transitive verb See *verb.*

verb A word, like *confide, raise, see,* which indicates action or asserts something. (See **1a.**) Verbs are inflected and combine with auxiliaries to form **verb phrases.** Verbs may be **transitive,** requiring an object (He *made* a report), or **intransitive,** not requiring an object (They *migrated*). Many can function both transitively and intransitively. (The wind *blew.* They *blew* the whistle.) **Linking verbs,** such as *be, become,* and *appear,* are followed by complements that refer back to the subject. See Section **4.**

verb complement See *complement.*

verb phrase See *phrase.*

verbal A word derived from a verb and able to take objects, complements, modifiers, and sometimes subjects but unable to stand as the main verb in a sentence. See *gerund, infinitive,* and *participle.* See also **1b(3)** and **1c.**

voice The form of the verb that shows whether the subject acts **(active voice)** or is acted upon **(passive voice).** Only transitive verbs can show voice. A transitive verb followed by an object is **active** (They *bought* flowers). In the **passive** the direct object is made into the subject (The flowers *were bought*). See **1a,** and Section **5.**

word order The order of words in a sentence or smaller word group. Word order is one of the principal grammatical devices in English.

INDEX

Note: Numbers in boldface refer to section designations; other numbers refer to pages. Thus, for example, the entry **40f**:363 refers to Section 40f on page 363.